A Clockwork Counterpoint

Manchester University Press

A Clockwork Counterpoint

The Music and Literature of Anthony Burgess

Paul Phillips

Manchester University Press
Manchester and New York
distributed in the United States exclusively by Palgrave Macmillan

Copyright © Paul Phillips 2010

The right of Paul Phillips to be identified as the author of this work has been asserted by him in accordance with the Copyright, Designs and Patents Act 1988.

Published by Manchester University Press
Oxford Road, Manchester M13 9NR, UK
and Room 400, 175 Fifth Avenue, New York, NY 10010, USA
www.manchesteruniversitypress.co.uk

Distributed in the United States exclusively by
Palgrave Macmillan, 175 Fifth Avenue,
New York, NY 10010, USA

Distributed in Canada exclusively by
UBC Press, University of British Columbia, 2029 West Mall,
Vancouver, BC, Canada V6T 1Z2

British Library Cataloguing-in-Publication Data is available

Library of Congress Cataloging-in-Publication Data is available

The music of Anthony Burgess is copyright of Estate of Anthony Burgess (c/o Alan Roughley, executor)

"You Have Made Me Love", "The Nose Song", "No Thank You", "I Never Loved You", from Cyrano. Words and music by Anthony Burgess and Michael Lewis. Copyright © 1972, Almo Music Corp. and Cavesson Music Entertainment Co. Copyright renewed. All rights controlled and administered by Almo Music Corp. All rights reserved. Used by permission. Reprinted by permission of Hal Leonard Corporation.

Photography by Marvin Lichtner reprinted and used by permission of Time-Life/Getty Images.

ISBN 978 0 7190 7205 5 paperback

First published by Manchester University Press in hardback 20 10

This paperback edition first published 2014

The publisher has no responsibility for the persistence or accuracy of URLs for any external or third-party internet websites referred to in this book, and does not guarantee that any content on such websites is, or will remain, accurate or appropriate.

Printed by Lightning Source

To Alanna, Joanna, and, especially, Kathryne

Musik und Sprache, insistierte er, gehörten zusammen, sie seien im Grunde eins, die Sprache Musik, die Musik eine Sprache, und getrennt berufe immer das eine sich auf das andere, ahme das andere nach, bediene sich der Mittel des anderen, gebe immer das eine sich als das Substitut des anderen zu verstehen.

Music and language, he insisted, belonged together, were fundamentally one. Language was music, music a language, and when separated each always recalled the other, imitated the other, made use of the other's means, always to be understood as the substitute for the other.

Thomas Mann, *Doktor Faustus*

CONTENTS

List of Illustrations ix
Abbreviations xii
Notes on the Text xiv
Foreword by Paul Griffiths xv
Introduction xvii

PROLOGUE 1

1 The Truly Great Artistic Moment 3

BEGINNINGS 7

2 Boyhood (1917–35) 9
3 Burgeoning Composer (1935–40) 23

EMERGENT AUTHOR 33

4 War: Britain and Gibraltar (1940–46) 35
5 Peace: Brinsford Lodge, Bamber Bridge, and Banbury (1946–54) 49
6 Malaya (1954–57) 63
7 Brunei (1958–59) 68
8 "Terminal" Year (1959–60) 74
9 Nasty Little Shockers 80
10 Eschatological Escapades 95
11 Shakespeare in Love 107
12 Pure Music 114

CELEBRITY NOVELIST 123

13 Family Affairs 125
14 Kubrick the Sinny Veck 143
15 Ancient Evenings 151
16 Bonaparte Con Brio 159

RESURGENT COMPOSER 183

17 Symphonic Shakespeare 185
18 The Old Joanna 198

19	The Love Song of F. X. Enderby	214
20	Roman Carnival	228
21	Knickerbocker Holiday	237
22	Poetic License	247
23	Grace Notes	254
24	Odes to Joyce	264
25	Nuns and Lovers	283
26	Blest Pair of Sirens	292
27	Alex in Eden	302
28	The Sad Suck-and-Blow	314
29	One-Handed Clavichord	322
30	Wind and Son	331
31	Commemorations	345
32	Manchester and Mozart United	355

ENDINGS — 363

33	Confessions and Conclusions	365

EPILOGUE — 375

34	Opus Posthumous (1993–2009)	377

Appendix 1: List of Music Compositions	385
Appendix 2: Song Texts and Poems	403
Appendix 3: Prologue to *A Clockwork Orange*	409
Bibliography	413
Discography	429
Filmography	431
Acknowledgments	433
Music Index	437
Literature Index	442
General Index	446

LIST OF ILLUSTRATIONS

1 John B. Wilson (Anthony Burgess) with sister Muriel and mother Elizabeth Burgess Wilson [Manchester, ca. 1918]   168

2 With father Joseph Wilson, 1925   168

3 With unidentified younger child, Cleveleys, 1927   168

4 Llewela Isherwood Jones (Lynne Burgess Wilson), 1939   169

5 Band members of the Jaypees (l to r): Ted Norman, Richard Nutting, Stan Williams, Harry Walkling, Bill Bryan, Anthony Burgess [ca. 1941]   169

6 The Jaypees (front row, l to r): Stan Williams (drums), Harry Walkling (tenor sax, clarinet), Ted Norman (alto sax), Bill Bryan (trumpet, vocals), Ted Wright (piano), Richard Nutting (double bass); (top row, far right) Anthony Burgess [ca. 1941]. *Courtesy of Richard Nutting*   170

7 Anthony Burgess (fifth from right) singing with the Jaypees [ca. 1941]. *Courtesy of Richard Nutting*   170

8 Program of a 1941 performance by the Jaypees. *Courtesy of Richard Nutting*   171

9 Dust jacket of *A Vision of Battlements* with Richard Ennis attached to a metronome pendulum   172

10 With students at Malay College [Kuala Kangsar, ca. 1955]   172

11 Standing before arch in Indonesia   173

12 Anthony and Lynne with their dog Haji. *Photo by Mark Gerson.*   173

13–16 *Four photos shot 4 October 1968 by Marvin Lichtner for the profile of Anthony Burgess published in the 25 October 1968 issue of* Life   173

13 Leaning on his books – a variant of the published photo that shows him looking up toward the top of the stack of twenty-one volumes   173

14 Published in the article with the following caption: *"In the London suburb of Chiswick, Burgess, with his wife Liliana, is tugged home from a shopping trip by his dog Haji. They also have a cat. 'She is called Dorian Gray,' he says. 'Sorry about that.'"* 174

15 Unpublished photo similar to one in the profile that was captioned, *"Surrounded by stacked chairs – business is heavier at night – Burgess thumps out an oldie during a noon visit to a local Chiswick pub. He once arranged dance-band music."* 174

16 Unpublished photo in which Liana appears to have had more than enough of Anthony's piano playing 174

17 Liliana Macellari [ca. 1968] 175

18 With Paolo-Andrea [ca. 1971] 175

19 John Sebastian. *Courtesy of Kim Field* 176

20 Tommy Reilly. *Courtesy of Kim Field* 176

21 Larry Adler. *Courtesy of Kim Field* 176

22 Riding the New York subway, 29 October 1972. Original caption: *"The author rides the IRT. Anthony Burgess, the British writer, holds the title of Distinguished Professor of English at City College. He is working on a novel about Napoleon."*
From the archives of The New York Times 177

23 Patricia Conolly as Jocasta and Len Cariou as Oedipus in the Guthrie Theater's production of *Oedipus the King* [Minneapolis, 1972] 177

24 Rehearsing *King Oedipus* with conductor Roland Gagnon (l.) and composer Stanley Silverman (at piano) [New York, 1973] 177

25 At the piano playing for Roland Gagnon [New York, 1973] 178

26 Dedicatees of Burgess's String Quartet: the Primavera String Quartet [1980]. Clockwise from top left: Deborah Berlin (violin), Melissa Meell (cello), Diann Jezurski (viola), and Martha Caplin (violin) 178

27 Presenting the manuscript of *A Glasgow Overture* to Lord Provost Michael Kelly in the Glasgow City Chambers next to a painting by Stanley Cursiter depicting the Scottish authors Edwin Muir, James Bridie, Neil Gunn, and Eric Linklater [March 1981]. This photograph appeared in the April 1981 issue of Glasgow City Council's newspaper *The Bulletin. Reproduced courtesy of the Glasgow City Council, Libraries Information and Learning* 179

28 Dust jacket of *The Pianoplayers* [1986] 179

29 Marathon pianist playing in a storefront. *Library of Congress Collection* 180

30 Amid the members of the Aïghetta Quartet. Left to right: François Szönyi, André-Michel Berthoux, Philippe Loli, Alexandre Del Fa 180

31 Conversing with Graham Greene, ca. September 1982 181

List of Illustrations

32 At the electronic keyboard   181
33 Dust jacket of *Mozart and the Wolf Gang*, with Mozart looking
    back [1991]   182
34 Late portrait   182

All photographs are reprinted courtesy of the International Anthony Burgess Foundation unless otherwise indicated.

ABBREVIATIONS

ANTHONY BURGESS'S WRITINGS

ACO	*A Clockwork Orange* (novel)
ACO-PM	*A Clockwork Orange: A Play with Music*
BD	*Blooms of Dublin* (Hutchinson, 1986)
BDB	*But Do Blondes Prefer Gentlemen?*
BE	*Beds in the East* (from *The Long Day Wanes*)
BRW	*Beard's Roman Women*
CT	*The Clockwork Testament* (from *The Complete Enderby*)
EB	*The Enemy in the Blanket* (from *The Long Day Wanes*)
EDL	*Enderby's Dark Lady* (from *The Complete Enderby*)
EO	*Enderby Outside* (from *The Complete Enderby*)
EP	*Earthly Powers*
EWN	*The End of the World News*
HB	*Honey for the Bears*
IME	*Inside Mr Enderby* (from *The Complete Enderby*)
JPY	"Journal of the Plague Year (1951)"
LW	*Little Wilson and Big God*
MWG	*Mozart and the Wolf Gang*
NLS	*Nothing Like the Sun*
NN	*The Novel Now*
NS	*Napoleon Symphony*
PP	*The Pianoplayers*
RJ	*Re Joyce*
T1	*Trotsky's in New York!* (first version)
T2	*Trotsky's in New York!* (second version)
TMM	*This Man and Music*
TT	*Time for a Tiger* (from *The Long Day Wanes*)
UC	*Urgent Copy*
VB	*A Vision of Battlements*
YH	*You've Had Your Time*

OTHER SOURCES

Angers	Anthony Burgess Centre, University of Angers.
CC	Brian Morton and Pamela Collins, eds., *Contemporary Composers*. Chicago & London: St. James Press, 1992. ("Anthony Burgess" entry by Brian Morton, 138–9).
Coale	Samuel Coale, *Anthony Burgess*. New York: Frederick Ungar, 1981.
Eliot	T. S. Eliot, *The Complete Poems and Plays 1909–1950*. New York: Harcourt, Brace & World, 1971.
Grove	*The New Grove Dictionary of Music and Musicians*, 2nd ed., Stanley Sadie, ed. London: Macmillan, 2001.
HRC	Harry Ransom Humanities Research Center, University of Texas.
IABF	International Anthony Burgess Foundation.
Lewis	Roger Lewis, *Anthony Burgess*. London: Faber & Faber, 2002.
Life	Jim Hicks, "Eclectic author of his own five-foot shelf". *Life* (65:17), 25 Oct 1968, 87–97.
RLAB	Andrew Biswell, *The Real Life of Anthony Burgess*. London: Picador, 2005.
Saga	Saga Music Publishing Ltd.

NOTES ON THE TEXT

An American, generally employing American usage of the English language, writing about a British author who usually – but not always – used the British form of the language, faces continual dilemmas regarding spelling, punctuation, and grammar while striving for clarity, consistency, and correctness. The text adheres mainly to American spelling while preserving British spelling wherever it occurs in titles and quotations. Punctuation, which varies between American and British usage, tends toward the latter.

Archival newspaper reviews and articles clipped from unnamed publications are identified to the fullest extent possible. When multiple quotations from a single source occur within the same paragraph or passage, that source is generally identified only once in order to minimize the number of endnotes. Obvious typographical errors in quotations have been corrected.

Time signatures, normally rendered in a musical score as one integer above another, as in $\frac{2}{4}$, are generally rendered in the text on one line as 2/4. The double and triple time signatures occasionally employed by Burgess are more awkward to notate in this fashion. In Chapter 10, for example, the notation 12/8 : 6/4 : 3/2 is used for the time signature $\frac{12}{8} \frac{6}{4} \frac{3}{2}$ of Prelude IV.

FOREWORD

Language in Anthony Burgess's books does not so much sing as blare, thunder, whistle, croon and play the piano. His prose is noise music, made by a man for whom music was fundamental: an appetite, a need, a resource and, not least, another mode of expression, for besides his copious literary output – novels, memoirs, oceans of articles and reviews – he produced symphonies and chamber music, piano pieces and even a musical show based on Joyce's *Ulysses*.

Mention of Joyce at once introduces a puzzle, because where Burgess's literary ideal was a Joycean boundlessness, careering bound by bound across normal demarcations of style, genre and tone, his musical imagination was more cautious. However, there may be an explanation for this. All writers are essentially self-taught, using a language that was theirs from infancy, babbling as they then babbled. Composers generally have to be put together piece by piece, undergoing an apprenticeship or, these days, conservatory or university training. Burgess, who was one of life's great autodidacts in all kinds of fields, avoided that. He taught himself to compose, and what he composed had to come from what he knew: the music of pub, social, church and concert hall from a childhood and youth in Manchester before World War II.

It would be easy to say, then, that Burgess was a professional writer but an amateur composer. That judgement is, however, too neat. He was a professional writer in the sense that he made his living that way, but the splurge of his writing, the music and the noise of it, was that of someone who loves language and has very little respect for respect: an amateur. At the same time, he was professional in his approach and competence as a composer.

The distinction blurs, as distinctions will with Burgess. Writing and composing were not separate activities. Many of the novels and other books are composed along musical coordinates of style and form, besides having music to the fore in their subject matter and their generous substance. Many of the musical works similarly hinge on literary themes and forefathers, Shakespeare as well as Joyce.

In exploring the interconnections Paul Phillips's study illuminates not only Burgess's little known musical output but also his literary works, many of which are freshly understood. Beyond that, we begin to have a portrait of the artist as a whole man, and to appreciate the moving figure of someone who, hugely successful, went on pursuing a course in which he was, in the world's terms, bound to fail.

Paul Griffiths

INTRODUCTION

Mention the name Anthony Burgess, and people who recognize it are most likely to say, "Didn't he write *A Clockwork Orange?*" Those more knowledgeable about his work may recall *Earthly Powers*, the Enderby novels, or his writings on Joyce and Shakespeare. A few Broadway aficionados might recollect that he wrote the lyrics for the short-lived 1973 production of *Cyrano* for which Christopher Plummer won a Tony Award. But mention that Burgess was a composer, and the usual response is a pair of raised eyebrows accompanied by a quizzical "Really? I had no idea."

My interest in Burgess's music dates from 26 November 1993, the day his obituary appeared in *The New York Times*. A quotation claiming that he would rather be considered a musician than a novelist intrigued me, as did the mention of "dozens of musical compositions, from operas, choral works and song cycles to symphonies and concertos" that he had written, including *Blooms of Dublin*, *The Brides of Enderby*, and his musical stage version of *A Clockwork Orange*.[1] Unaware of Burgess's musical achievements until then, I set out to locate the compositions cited in the notice. As music director and conductor of the Brown University Orchestra, an ensemble perennially filled with musically talented polymaths who excel in a wide range of non-musical fields, I imagined that these students might enjoy playing symphonic music composed by a famous novelist. Hoping that Burgess's publishers could direct me to his compositions, I wrote to several of them, but nothing came of these efforts, so after a few months I abandoned the pursuit of Burgess's music and considered the matter closed.

Two years later, a writer living temporarily near Newport, Rhode Island, called to ask if she could attend rehearsals of the Brown Orchestra. I readily agreed and was astonished to learn, when she first showed up, that Anthony Burgess was the reason for this woman's newfound interest in music. Tess Crebbin explained that, while working on a book about Burgess, she had encountered so many references to music in his writings that she felt obliged to learn more about it and had decided that attending orchestra rehearsals would be the best way to begin! When I revealed my interest in Burgess and his music, she asked if I was still interested in seeing Burgess's scores and offered to put me in touch with his widow, with whom she was acquainted. Shortly thereafter, in late 1996, Liana Macellari Burgess invited me to organize her late husband's musical scores and catalog his compositions, thus introducing me to the musical world of Anthony Burgess.

I flew to the French Riviera the following August, arriving in Nice where I was greeted at the airport by Liana's secretary, Mireille Deveze, and a friend of Liana's with the cheerfully pleonastic name Merrily Lustig. They drove me to Monte Carlo and ushered me into a three-room condominium at 57 Rue de Grimaldi filled with hundreds of books, including many first editions of Burgess's novels, some embellished with his penciled margin notes. I discovered numerous cassette tapes of Burgess's compositions and, most importantly, a sizable wooden cabinet containing dozens of original music manuscripts. A few hours spent examining these scores quickly revealed the astounding extent of Burgess's double life as a novelist and composer.

For days I worked in solitude, poring over the scores and listening to the tapes of those compositions that had been played and recorded. Liana was away in England at the time – her absence from Monaco that summer having delayed and nearly scuttled my trip – and neither Mireille nor Merrily could say when she might return. Then suddenly one afternoon, five days after my arrival, the door of the condominium opened and a diminutive, bright-eyed, sharp-featured woman briskly entered the room. Liana had arrived.

During the remainder of my stay in Monaco, Liana Burgess was often at my side as I perused her husband's scores and set down observations about them on my laptop. Each evening we went to dinner together, and afterward she would retire to her condominium, located in the same building several floors above the one in which I was staying. (Mireille lived across the street in the Burgess's original Monegasque residence, the grand fourth-story walk-up at 44 Rue de Grimaldi.) In our daily conversations, I expressed my growing admiration for Burgess's music to Liana, who responded enthusiastically to the idea that his compositions be published, performed, and recorded. With her approval, I spent days photocopying scores so that I could continue to study them once I returned to America.

Four months later, I conducted Burgess's Symphony No. 3 in C with the Brown University Orchestra in Providence and Cambridge – the first performances since its premiere twenty-two years earlier. The positive response to those performances from musicians and audience members encouraged me to delve further into Burgess's music, convinced that the effort would be worthwhile. Since then I have scrutinized nearly all of Burgess's extant music, performed a significant number of his works as conductor and pianist, and come to regard him as a highly talented and prolific composer. For Burgess, writing music was as essential as writing words, yet, unlike his literary labors, virtually all of his composing was done without financial recompense. Considering this, one might justifiably conclude that the drive to write music was the stronger of his twin creative passions.

Introduction

Burgess dubbed the second volume of his autobiography *You've Had Your Time*, but that title hardly applies to his musical side. Most of Burgess's scores remain difficult to obtain and many of his compositions are still unrecorded. In time, however, as his music becomes increasingly available through performances, recordings, and the Internet, there will be ever greater opportunities to appreciate his considerable achievements as a composer. By examining his oeuvre through a musical prism, this book seeks to shed light upon both sides of Burgess's art in a fresh and revealing way. And if, to paraphrase Burgess, even one door to the better appreciation of this extraordinary dual artist has been opened, then the fingers of this writer have not been abraded in vain.

Note

1 Herbert Mitgang, "Anthony Burgess, 76, Dies; Man of Letters and Music", *The New York Times,* 26 November 1993, B23.

PROLOGUE

1

THE TRULY GREAT ARTISTIC MOMENT

I wish people would think of me as a musician who writes novels, instead of a novelist who writes music on the side.[1]

The hundred and four young musicians on stage watched attentively as James Dixon prepared to give the downbeat. His right hand came down in a crisp gesture, triggering a shimmering chord, played softly by violins and piano, followed seconds later by a melody in the flutes and harp that arched upward and then, in a quirky, slightly angular fashion, began to move up and down like a leisurely wave. From his seat in the Iowa City auditorium, the composer listened to the music intently, reveling in the sounds he had heard only in his inner ear until Dixon's orchestra began rehearsing his composition a few weeks earlier. Hearing the symphony in performance, he was overwhelmed. "That was me," he thought, as enthusiastic applause greeted the end of the thirty-five-minute work. "That was me, that great web of sonorities being discoursed by those hundred handsome kids under that big man on the rostrum."

Ever since the release of the notorious film *A Clockwork Orange* four years earlier, Anthony Burgess had been celebrated as one of the English-speaking world's most successful writers. In the twenty years since publication of his first novel *Time for a Tiger*, the fifty-eight-year-old author had published over thirty additional books, written the lyrics for the Tony Award-winning Broadway musical *Cyrano*, been profiled in *Life, Playboy, Penthouse*, and a dozen other major magazines and newspapers, and amassed a considerable fortune from his books, journalism, screenplays, and public appearances. But on 22 October 1975 in the heartland of the American Midwest, listening to the University of Iowa's student orchestra play his Third Symphony, those achievements no longer seemed as important. "This", he thought to himself, "was the truly great artistic moment" of his life.[2]

Throughout the remaining eighteen years of his life, Anthony Burgess composed at a furious pace, as if making up for the last two decades in which music had taken a back seat to literature. Picking up from where he left off in 1953, when, in response to a challenge from his first wife, Llewela Jones, he essentially gave up music composition to become a novelist, Burgess rapidly produced concertos for piano, violin, oboe, English horn, solo guitar, and guitar quartet, a piano concertino, a ballet suite on the life of Shakespeare, a string quartet, and a set of twenty-four preludes and fugues. He turned Joyce's *Ulysses* into an operetta, wrote the words and music for a musical about Trotsky, and composed the score for a stage version of *A Clockwork Orange*. He penned overtures for Glasgow and his native Manchester, sinfoniettas celebrating Strasbourg and his second wife, Liana Macellari, a march honoring the bicentenary of the French revolution, and a seventieth birthday self-commemoration titled *Mr Burgess's Almanack*. He composed cantatas on texts by John Dryden and Gerard Manley Hopkins, and chamber settings of verse by T. S. Eliot, D. H. Lawrence, A. E. Housman, and his own fictional poet F. X. Enderby. He wrote a film score, music for brass band, two quartets for winds and strings, an elegy for string orchestra on the death of Princess Grace, and shorter choral works and songs to verse by Shakespeare, Nashe, Hardy, D'Annunzio, Pound, and Joyce. Additionally, he composed sonatas for recorder, studies and concert pieces for oboe and English horn, pieces for harmonica, and a series of arrangements and original compositions for guitar quartet.

A large part of the reason previous commentators on Burgess have tended to regard the latter part of his life as relatively fallow is that they have failed to take his musical activity fully into account. The grounds for this are not hard to understand. Burgess's compositions have never been frequently performed, most are unpublished, and few are available on commercial disks. It was not until the late 1990s, when Liana Macellari Burgess decided to sell a large collection of Burgess's musical and literary manuscripts to the Harry Ransom Humanities Research Center, that most of his scores could be seen for the first time.

Once one has examined the many scores by Burgess that have survived from among the more than 250 that he composed between 1932 and his death in 1993, it becomes apparent that his creative life as an composer-novelist was unique. Anyone who has ever watched as Beethoven's Ninth inspires Alex to commit appalling acts of violence in Stanley Kubrick's film of *A Clockwork Orange* is familiar with Burgess's use of music in at least one of his books. What is much less well known is the extent to which music and musical thinking constitute a major element of his writing. Unlike Paul Bowles and Bruce Montgomery, who compartmentalized writing and composing as independent activities, Burgess constantly sought ways to unite both halves of his creative personality, either by setting words of his favorite authors to music, incorporating musical characters and themes into his books, or, more radically, assigning musical structure to fiction, whether this meant writing novels in sonata form, or, as in the case of *Napoleon Symphony*, modeling the form and character of a novel on Beethoven's *Eroica*.

Burgess loved to provoke, frequently issuing disingenuous statements to amuse or shock his readers and listeners. Asked by Oscar Peterson about his most famous novel in a BBC-TV interview, he replied, with a showman's earnest expression of mock sincerity, "Today is my sixtieth birthday. I've been living a long time and writing a lot of books. And I seem to have published thirty-eight books and of all the thirty-eight, A Clockwork Orange is the one I like *least*," deliberately accenting the last syllable to prompt laughter from the studio audience. Certainly Burgess was being at least partly ironic whenever he said that he wished people would think of him as a musician who writes novels rather than as a novelist who writes music. While this remark, which he repeated to the media for at least twenty-five years right up until his final deathbed interview, should not be taken literally, neither should it be dismissed as a joke. The same is true of his description of himself as a "failed musician", for no failed musician, as he well knew, could have composed his Third Symphony, *Mr W.S.,* the three guitar quartets, or the dozens of other sophisticated scores that he produced.

One way to reconcile these comments is to recognize that Burgess desperately wanted to be acknowledged as a composer but was careful to thwart unreasonably high expectations. "Please listen to my music," he seemed to be saying, "but don't expect me to be another Beethoven." He wanted those who heard his music to be pleasantly surprised. "That's no failed composer," he might have imagined them saying. "Why that's bloody good music!" Continually wanting to be "discovered" as a composer, he accepted virtually every invitation to write a new work, enthusiastically embracing these opportunities since each one represented a fresh chance at the public acknowledgment of his compositional ability that, with a few exceptions like the Iowa City performance, he rarely received. Pride demanded that he not turn composition into a vanity project. Thus, while it would have posed little financial difficulty for him to produce concerts or recordings of his music, he refused to do so, preferring instead to let others champion his music. Manuscripts accumulated at his Monte Carlo home and Lugano villa. Most of these scores were played just once or twice, or never at all. Reacting with equanimity to the lack of musical recognition, Burgess simply went on composing.

He knew, to a greater extent than any of his readers, that an understanding of music was essential for full comprehension of his books. It pained him when musical references, like his sly inclusion of the *tierce de Picardie* in *Nothing Like the Sun*, went unnoticed, and surely disappointed him that no reviewer of *A Clockwork Orange* noticed that it was written in sonata form, though he was not about to give away that secret easily. Readers would have to discover it for themselves. He gave broad hints, however, as when, responding to Oscar Peterson's query about *A Clockwork Orange*, he declared, "People never seemed to realize what the book was about . . . It is about music."[3]

While Burgess deserves attention strictly as a composer, what makes him such a singular creative figure is how he intertwined literature and music. While there are composers, like Wagner and Menotti, who fashioned their own libretti, and novelists, like Bowles and Montgomery, who were also highly regarded composers, none of them engaged in music and literature in a manner comparable to Burgess. Unlike Wagner and Menotti, whose literary work served their compositional needs by providing texts for their operas, Burgess rarely set his own words to music, and unlike Bowles and Montgomery, who regarded composing and writing as essentially separate activities, he viewed them as complementary and genuinely interrelated. As long as Burgess's musical side has remained largely unknown, understanding of his twin accomplishments has been incomplete, concealing much of what makes Burgess so distinctive. This book's primary aim is thus to examine this heretofore disregarded aspect of his creative life and, by doing so, reveal both halves of this remarkable dual artist, like casting light on the dark side of the moon so as to illuminate the entire sphere.

Notes

1 Burgess as quoted by Walter Clemons in "Anthony Burgess: Pushing On", *The New York Times Book Review*, 29 November 1970, 2. Repeated in Burgess's obituary in *The New York Times* (26 November 1993) and erroneously cited there as having been written by Burgess in *The Economist* in 1991.
2 Anthony Burgess, "How I Wrote My Third Symphony", *The New York Times* (28 December 1975), Section 2, 19.
3 *Oscar Peterson Invites,* 8 March 1977 broadcast.

BEGINNINGS

2

BOYHOOD (1917–35)

Find middle C and you have found everything.[1]

John Burgess Wilson came by his musical talent naturally, that is to say, genetically. His mother, Elizabeth Burgess, was a music hall singer and dancer; his father, Joseph Wilson, played piano in theatres, pubs, and film palaces. They met "by way of her ankles" about a decade into the twentieth century.[2] One night while filling in for the regular pianist at the Ardwick Empire, one of Manchester's leading music halls, Joe Wilson looked up from the pit and espied the shapely legs of a comely chorus girl, a fair-haired beauty who would eventually become a featured performer known as the Beautiful Belle Burgess.[3] Later she performed at a music hall in Glasgow. Wilson also journeyed to Scotland, having fled Manchester to escape retribution from encyclopedia peddlers whom he had swindled. The Scottish sojourn was a prosperous one for Wilson, for he returned to his native city of Manchester wedded to his slim-ankled sweetheart.

That, at least, is how Anthony Burgess relates the story of his parents' meeting in *Little Wilson and Big God*, the first volume of his autobiography. The fact that in an earlier published account of his ancestry, he claimed that his mother performed at the "Gentlemen's Concert Rooms", which had been demolished by 1898 when Elizabeth Burgess would have been ten years old, leaves his veracity open to skepticism. Nonetheless, lacking certifiable facts to the contrary, Burgess's descriptions of his origins and childhood are those upon which we must largely depend, while acknowledging his caveat: "When a novelist turns to [autobiography] . . . he has some difficulty . . . in disposing language to the recounting of factual truth, as opposed to the symbolic truth of his primary art."[4]

Both parents descended from respectable small tradesmen, "old but undistinguished families of Lancashire".[5] Joe Wilson, born in 1883 to an English Catholic family with strong Celtic roots, broke with tradition when he married Elizabeth Burgess, a Protestant of mainly Scottish ancestry born in 1888, though her nuptial conversion to Catholicism lessened the stigma of intermarriage.[6] After the wedding, Joe Wilson secured a position as cashier at Swift's Beef Market in Manchester while Elizabeth exchanged her stage career for that of housewife and mother. Their first child, a daughter named Muriel Burgess Wilson, was born in 1910. When World War I erupted in 1914, Joe did not immediately enlist, but eventually he joined the service, relinquishing his position at Swift's for a comparable one as cashier with the Royal Army Pay Corps. Barracked in Preston, Wilson spent his entire war career in England, visiting his family in Manchester whenever able to procure leave from the army base.

On 25 February 1917, with the war at its worst, Elizabeth gave birth to the couple's second child, christened John Burgess Wilson. He was born at noon, "just as the Sunday pubs were opening", his mother giving birth to him at 91 Carisbrook Street, the house in Harpurhey that his father had rented in northeast Manchester after they returned from Scotland. The infant shared a birthday with the painter Pierre-Auguste Renoir, dramatist Carlo Goldoni, tenor Enrico Caruso, and pianist Myra Hess; late in life Burgess mused that it was perhaps not surprising that, being born under the sign of Pisces, he would be drawn to the arts – drawing, writing, theatre, and music – throughout his life.[7]

One of history's grimmer ironies is that more people perished from the devastating outbreak of Spanish influenza that swept across the world in 1918–19 than died in battle during World War I. In England, Burgess's sister and mother were two of its victims, eight-year-old Muriel succumbing to the pandemic on 15 November 1918 followed by her thirty-year-old mother four days later. Still in the army, his father entrusted his nineteen-month-old son to the care of his wife's sister Ann Bromley, a war widow who lived with her daughters Elsie and Betty in a terraced house on Delaunays Road in Higher Crumpsall.[8]

In 1922 Joe Wilson married the widow Margaret Dwyer (née Byrne), who, upon the death of her husband Dan Dwyer, had become landlord of the Golden Eagle, a sprawling pub in the Miles Platting district of Manchester. Maggie (as she was usually called) had raised two daughters "of exceptional beauty", Agnes and Madge, "well-shaped girls with fine Irish creamy flesh".[9] Maggie herself was a repellent woman – ill-mannered, overweight, and virtually illiterate – whom Burgess later fictionalized as F. X. Enderby's revolting stepmother.[10]

Before his father's remarriage, Burgess's life "had no religion in it. My aunt and cousins were Protestant but did not go to church. My father had probably lost his faith. All his life long he said: 'When you're dead you're finished with.' Nobody taught me how to pray."[11] But once Joe Wilson married into the Dwyer clan, the situation changed abruptly. Maggie's daughters were "pure and deeply Catholic. They took me to mass, which was boring and incomprehensible, but the Gregorian line of a priest (the mass must have been high and sung) stuck in my head: *'Per omnia saecula saeculorum'*. A queer kind of English, a sort of code, the *orum* dangerous magic."[12] Thus began Burgess's complex relationship with the Catholic Church. Although he would declare himself an apostate in his teens, Roman

Catholicism constituted a vital element of Burgess's identity and a recurrent theme in his novels.

Burgess entered school in 1923, "weak and unmuscular" but a precocious reader. He attended St. Edmund's RC Elementary, where students were indoctrinated with religious dogma "which chiefly had to do with eternal punishment for trivial offences."[13] Taught that each individual was protected by a guardian angel, some students inferred that there must be an evil angel set in perpetual opposition to the other. According to this Manichaean viewpoint, we live in a dualistic universe, or "duoverse", in which Good is opposed by Evil, and God by the Devil. One is free to choose sides. The difficulty lies in the indistinct intermingling of dark and light within our world, which makes it hard to determine which side one is really choosing. In Burgess's novels this is a fundamental theme, recurring in *Tremor of Intent*, *A Clockwork Orange*, *Earthly Powers*, and *MF*.

The Golden Eagle was a large tavern that contained three singing rooms, each with its own piano, one customarily occupied by Joe Wilson, who accompanied singers and comedians each evening. When all were in use, a boisterous Ivesian cacophony would assail his family upstairs, where there was yet another piano, one that Burgess would play in the evenings. At Christmas, Wilson and the Dwyer clan would gather for family music-making, performing popular songs like "Finnegan's Ball", "Here's Another One Off to America", "Ma, He's Making Eyes At Me", and "Yes, We Have No Bananas", as well as numbers from George M. Cohan's *Little Nellie Kelly* and selections like "Musetta's Waltz" from *La Bohème*.[14]

In 1924 the family relocated to Moss Side, a then more respectable district of Manchester. Maggie had sold the Golden Eagle and Joe had given up his longtime bookkeeping job at Swift's Beef Market so that they could establish Wilson's, a tobacco shop located at 21 Princess Road where customers bought packs of Woodbines, Player's, and Black Cat cigarettes. Joe kept track of the orders and did the bookkeeping, while Maggie oversaw the money, about which she brooded incessantly.

The family lived above the shop, where they listened to recordings of Layton and Johnstone singing "It Ain't Gonna Rain No More" and "Bye Bye, Blackbird" or Jack Hilton's Orchestra playing "Me and Jane in a Plane" and "I'm Going Back to Imazaz (Imazaz the pub next door)" on their new portable gramophone.[15] From one of his tobacco shop customers, a chain-smoking music dealer, Joe Wilson acquired *The Music Lover's Portfolio*, a serial publication of classical "middlebrow music – Boccherini's Minuet, a selection from *Madama Butterfly*, Tchaikovsky's Fifth Symphony in molecular instalments, also chatty articles by Tetrazzini, Percy Pitt and even Ernest Newman."[16] Burgess's father often played selections from it in early evening before heading out for his nightly pint at the Alec.[17] Around this time Joe Wilson even composed a march dedicated to the Royal Flying Corps, though it is doubtful that any of the Royal Flyers ever heard it.

The move to Moss Side brought Burgess the opportunity to study violin, a mark of middle-class respectability. He was enrolled in Mr Bradshaw's School of Music on Moss Lane East, but was a lax pupil who often skipped lessons. In later life he claimed to have been a "hopeless" student whose playing was so awful that it could kill a cow: "I became expert in pretence, even to the use of vibrato, but I never learned to sound a note, stopped or open, that was not, as they say, vaccicidal."[18]

As a student at Bishop Bilsborrow Memorial Elementary School in Moss Side, Burgess experienced the painful discovery that he was afflicted with daltonism, "a particularly full-blooded variety of the defect" that left him unable to distinguish between green and various reds, or blue and violet.[19] Painting a watercolor in class one day, he unwittingly tinted the leaves in his artwork orange instead of green, which set his classmates laughing as they congregated around his desk to view the oddly colored artwork. Burgess was pulled away by his teacher, who denigrated the work and then struck him. "It was", as Burgess later observed with grand understatement, "a response pedagogically unsound." In his writing, he relied on his first wife for a correct vocabulary of colors. She "also would equip me with detailed wardrobes for my fictional characters. Critics would sneer at my prose and psychology but often praise the dress-sense of my women. I was cheating, but there is no art without cheating."[20] Late in life, he joked that, as "a native of Manchester, I regard it as a gesture of local patriotism to be colour-blind, since John Dalton discovered the existence of the condition in that city."[21]

Once aware of his daltonism, Burgess eschewed painting for drawing, becoming sufficiently adept to win a competition sponsored by the *Manchester Guardian* when he was eleven. The newspaper printed his prize-winning sketch – an India ink depiction of his father dozing in his armchair – and awarded him a prize of £5, which he spent on a crystal radio.

Around this time, he became aware that he possessed synesthesia, an unusual phenomenon in which a stimulus in one sense faculty produces a reaction in another. In Burgess's case, he developed "a capacity to interpret the visual as the gustatory, and, much later, the auditory as the visual. I mean that I responded to a colour as if it were something to taste: this colour, which might not be that of a lemon, stung the tongue like a lemon; what might be black or deep purple nauseated like undercooked liver." He regarded the eventual urge to write music, especially to explore the timbral possibilities of orchestral composition, as a substitute for his defective sense of color: "The urge to write for an orchestra, which came much later, was a compensation for painting the pictures I could not paint."[22]

In 1925 Maggie Wilson returned to the liquor business by purchasing an off-license located at 261 Moss Lane East. The Wilsons moved to new lodgings above the premises, a five-minute walk from the family's tobacco shop, leaving the top floors of 21 Princess Road available for whichever of Maggie's daughters would be first to marry.

The wedding of Agnes Dwyer and Jack Tollitt, an employee of Wilson's tobacco shop, took place that year. The ceremony was a grand affair at the Church of the Holy Name on Oxford Road, a large church run by the Jesuits, and eight-year-old Anthony Burgess was thrilled by the occasion: "This was the beginning of my great love of weddings, and I regret that both mine have been functional or hole-in-a-corner affairs. There is nothing like a wedding. Let the roaring organs loudly play, cried Edmund Spenser."[23] Notably, it was one of the few occasions when he received musical instruction from his father.

> "Hear that?" my father whispered to me as we went up the aisle to Mendelssohn. "That's the only bit of music I know that doesn't begin on a common chord." True: the Wedding March for Theseus and his Amazon begins with a secondary seventh of the dominant key. It was a strange time to impart that titbit of musical education.[24]

The march actually begins with five bars of three trumpets playing a fanfare on a C major triad[25], the commonest of common chords, but Joe Wilson was at least partly correct in pointing out that the main phrase (which begins in the sixth measure) does not begin on an ordinary tonic or dominant chord.[26] Apparently he was unfamiliar with the first movement of Beethoven's Symphony No. 1 or the finale of Berlioz's *Symphonie Fantastique*.

At age eleven, Burgess received a scholarship to the Xaverian College, a Catholic secondary school located in the then fashionable Manchester district of Rusholme, and it was there that music literacy became an urgent matter. As a producer and editor of *The Alpha*, the school's literary magazine, he wanted to include a particular tune, in musical notation, in one of the issues. Not knowing how to write it, he sought help from his father, who either provided it or not, according to which version of the story one believes. In *Little Wilson and Big God*, Burgess credits his father with having pointed out middle C to him, but in *This Man and Music*, maintains that he offered no help at all.

> He would not even indicate the double location of middle C – the note on the keyboard, the sign on the stave. Besides, he was beginning to give less of his spare time to his family, devoted to draught Bass and his boozing friends. But I found that middle C without his help on the untuned upright in the long cold sitting room above the liquor store.[27]

From his abortive violin studies, Burgess had already learned the names of the spaces (FACE) and lines ("Every Good Boy Deserves Fivepence") of the treble clef; by adding the mnemonics for the spaces (ACE – Gee!) and lines (Go Bring Dad Five Apples) of the bass clef, he garnered sufficient knowledge to read piano music and write out melodies on manuscript paper. Rhythmic notation remained something of a puzzle until a broadcast of a Tchaikovsky symphony helped elucidate this mystery.

> I did not know how to interpret crotchets and quavers. I could understand the vertical element in music but not yet the horizontal. But I listened to a performance of Tchaikovsky's Fifth Symphony on the radio, and I followed it with the reduced version in *The Music Lover's Portfolio*. At the end of fifty minutes of close attention, the notes began to yield their temporal secrets.[28]

As his mastery of musical notation increased, Burgess appreciated its purely visual appearance. He "admired the look of the music on the printed page. It was a kind of drawing. I wanted to be able to draw like that."[29]

One evening in early 1929, Joe Wilson dragged his son out to hear the Hallé Orchestra play music of Richard Wagner. In later years, Burgess recalled that the concert "bored" him, "except for the glockenspiel in the Apprentices' Dance from *Die Meistersinger*", yet found that afterward he could not get one of the tunes – the main theme from the Overture to *Rienzi* – out of his head. Gifted with a powerful memory, he recalled not just the melody but the harmonies as well and soon found himself falling under music's spell: "There was, I had grudgingly to admit, something in what the lowbrows called classical music."[30] Fiddling with his crystal radio set a week or two later, Burgess experienced the moment that he always described as the great musical epiphany of his youth:

> I heard a sinuous flute. I listened and went on listening. At the end of an eight-minute tissage of impressionistic colour I was told that I had been listening to Debussy's *Prélude à l'Après-Midi d'un Faune*. The fact that I knew enough French by now to understand the title was a kind of confirmation that music too could be intelligible. And, of course, a truth that still astonishes when we care to remind ourselves of it, music transcended language. My impaired colour sense was already finding, in the quiet impact of Debussy's orchestra, an auditory compensation.[31]

By 1929 music had supplanted drawing as Burgess's principal creative art. Playing the drawing-room piano for hours each day changed his life's daily pattern, interfering with his homework and causing him to feel that "there is something wrong with an education system that takes no account of passion."[32] This preoccupation with the piano cost him the favored status with Brother Martin, head of the Xaverian College, that he had previously enjoyed, but did not deter him from the pursuit of a musical education.[33] His passion increased as his knowledge grew, and within a year he made up his mind to devote his life to music. "I wanted to write my own music. At the age of thirteen I decided that I was to be a great composer, and I trained myself, pursuing an indulged hobby, to that end."[34]

Burgess's autodidactic musical education consisted chiefly of listening to the radio, practicing piano, and studying scores. To learn the traditional rules of harmony, counterpoint, fugue, and orchestration, he studied the musical treatises of the day, dutifully absorbing the contents of Novello primers, Stainer on harmony, Higgs on fugue, and Prout on orchestration. Journals like "the excellent old *Radio Times*" provided him with a broad if haphazard overview of music history: "I learned that Debussy himself had welcomed Sousa's band to Paris and described in the musical press the great Philip Sousa catching butterflies fluttering from the bass tuba. I learned a lot of things, mostly perhaps useless."[35] Burgess paid little attention to keyboard or chamber music, or even to orchestral music before Wagner, for it was the sound of the full orchestra that thrilled him most. He was also enthralled by modern compositions such as *Le Sacre du Printemps* and *Pierrot Lunaire*, eagerly examining these scores at the Manchester Central Library. "Modernity began for me with *L'Après-midi d'un Faune*, whose miniature score I bought with a fifteenth-birthday gift of five shillings – a lot of money in those days for twenty-eight pages of bad Durand & Cie engraving."[36]

As his musical knowledge increased, Burgess concerned himself with the question of musical style. If he was indeed to become a great composer, what style should his own music embrace?

> At thirteen I had a vague idea of the music I wanted to write. It was to be "modern", like Stravinsky or Schoenberg. I was finding my way about music through the simple tonalities of Handel and early Beethoven and the children's pieces by Robert Schumann (God bless his shade: he was a huge help). But I rather despised these diatonic harmonies and cadences all too easy to anticipate. Those composers were saying nothing about the modern world. Debussy, though dead in 1918, had said plenty about it: indeed, it seemed to me that he was the primal force that charged all musical innovation.[37]

Burgess's first compositions, written at age fourteen, were self-described failed attempts at modernism and pieces in the style of "diluted Debussy". The only one of his very early works to be performed was a setting of the shanty "Let the Bulgine Run" for chorus and piano: "I got my name in the programme just above that of Ralph Vaughan Williams, who had done an arrangement of 'The Golden Vanity'."[38] Since all of these early compositions are lost, it is impossible to know just how Burgess's early compositions sounded, yet one piece provides a clue, offering a unique window into the style of music that he composed in the early 1930s. Nocturne (Example 02.01) is a short, tuneful composition by Burgess for oboe and piano bearing the inscription: "Composed when I was 15 years old and suddenly remembered at the age of 70. Christmas 1987." Debussy's influence is apparent in the use of ninth chords and parallelism, while the lowered seventh scale degree (D♮ in the key of E minor) lends the work a modal quality typical of music by Vaughan Williams and the English pastoral school.

Without benefit of lessons, Burgess made steady progress on the piano while harboring no illusions about becoming a concert artist:

> By my fifteenth birthday I was able to make an attempt at any keyboard piece that did not have rapid runs in it. I never attempted the dull Parnassian climb of agile major and minor scales, as decreed by Czerny. Big chords were and still are my line. I taught myself to play the piano but not to become a pianist. I wanted to become a composer, like Debussy. My family was unsympathetic. There was no money in it.[39]

Example 02.01 Nocturne for oboe and piano (bs. 1–8)

Instead of practicing Beethoven sonatas, he learned popular "standards" and honed the art of improvisation, where "wrong notes could be interpreted as 'blue' notes" and "rhythms seemed to reconcile speech and physical movements in a way that Beethoven did not."[40] As a boy, he found the piano a useful compositional aid but ceased using it for this purpose while still in his teens.

Burgess's voracious appetite for symphonic music exceeded the meager nourishment he received from the Hallé Orchestra, whose concerts he occasionally attended. Manchester's orchestra played solid, unadventurous repertoire, "like the cuisine of the city chophouses. We were always being promised *Le Sacre du Printemps*, but we never got it." When the Hallé Orchestra attempted newer works, things sometimes went seriously wrong, as when Ernest Ansermet had to stop a performance of Debussy's *Ibéria* after three measures and begin again. To hear the twentieth-century repertoire he craved, Burgess relied mainly upon the BBC Symphony Orchestra, whose conductor, Sir Adrian Boult, dared to program "Stravinsky, Schoenberg, Hindemith and Honegger, who made horns leap and trumpets coruscate and me drunk with discords." Performances of Hindemith's *Philharmonic Concerto* and Ravel's *Bolero* made a lasting impression on Burgess, as did the sight of females playing in the orchestra: "I fell in love with the first harpist, Sidonie Goossens."[41]

Burgess's musical interests were not limited to works at the "serious" end of the spectrum. Jazz and the popular music of the early thirties held great appeal as well: "I played it on the piano, and it did me good with the girls ... And even the *Musical Times* had to admit the successful absorption of jazz tricks by Ravel and Stravinsky."[42] The British composer-conductor Constant Lambert, who "proclaimed his harmonic roots in Frederick Delius (who in his turn had taken them from Debussy)" and incorporated jazz rhythms and harmonies into his concert music in a manner akin to Gershwin, was a particular favorite.

> I felt guilty about enjoying Carroll Gibbons and his Orchestra, and Jack Payne and Ambrose and Geraldo and Harry Roy, when I had neglected to tune in to a Beethoven sonata. The guilt was resolved on November 12, 1929 (the date is in Grove's *Dictionary of Music and Musicians*), when Constant Lambert conducted at a Hallé concert the first performance of his *Rio Grande* ... I was present at that first performance, and so was my father.[43]

Eventually, Burgess's musical knowledge proved to be splendidly beneficial to the Xaverian College. In the course of an assessment by His Majesty's Inspectorate, the history specialist asked if any of the students could tell him about Elizabethan music. Burgess, then in Upper Five Alpha, was the only one able to answer, and he had plenty to tell. "I threw Byrd and Weelkes and Orlando Gibbons at him ... and informed him about the technique of the virginals. John Bull, Morley, Dowland: he got the lot."[44] Thanks to his impressive display of Elizabethan erudition, Burgess's class triumphed in the review, causing Br. Martin to proudly exclaim, "Upper Five Alpha covered itself with glory."

But meanwhile a crisis of faith had arisen. The twin raptures of music and sex (which, according to his autobiography, he had begun experiencing at age nine with a series of libidinous housemaids) had led to a weakening of Burgess's religious belief.[45] By the age of fifteen, his allegiance to the doctrines of Roman Catholicism was being replaced by passion for music and the naked bliss he had enjoyed with a promiscuous fourteen-year-old Protestant.

> If this was not the ecstasy promised in heaven on condition that one forwent ecstasy on earth, what on earth was it? Surely this smooth tawny girl's body delivered spiritual transports to the caressing fingers? Surely the gratitude for her beauty and generosity was of a higher moral import than the belch (*eructavit cor meum*) of repletion? I could feel the promise of my becoming tougher within and being willing to answer the Church back. This might have had something to do with my having become an acolyte of a new spiritual complex, which did not merely promise heaven but actually gave it with nothing asked in return: I mean music. Heaven's harps, even if Sidonie Goossens was at the first desk, would be thin compared with Richard Strauss.[46]

A sermon by an intellectual Jesuit on "the immorality of Liszt and Wagner and the incapacity of the glory of their music to redeem their habitual sinfulness" served only to undermine his faith still further.[47]

Beyond the sheer accumulation of knowledge about composers and their works, Burgess's self-directed musical education yielded important side benefits. It accorded him an introductory acquaintance with foreign languages – French, German, Italian, Russian – and, especially through opera, a growing knowledge of literature and culture: "Nobody except me could translate *noisette*; I could assert that *tanner* meant to bore."[48] From Gounod and Berlioz, he acquired not just basic knowledge of French, but differing outlooks on the Faust legend to be compared with Marlowe's *Doctor Faustus*, which was required reading at the Xaverian College. "*Carmen* led me to Merimée and *La Bohème* to Mürger."[49] From the attempt to translate *Pierrot Lunaire* into English, he learned German, while the mysterious Cyrillic script on the title page of *Le Sacre* brought him into contact with Russian for the first time.

At age sixteen, Burgess gained his School Certificate in English Language and Literature, Latin, French, History, Art, Architecture, and Mathematics. Despite curiosity about acoustics and sufficient interest in science to construct his own crystal radio, he failed Physics, attributing this a certain Brother Sebastian's incompetent teaching: "he left much of it to one of our classmates, Dowd, who grinned maniacally in the uniform of the British Fascist Party."[50] To Burgess's parents, their son's graduation from Upper Five Alpha meant that it was time for him to find a job, but his stepmother's cousin George Patrick Dwyer, who would later become Archbishop of Birmingham, convinced them to let the boy continue his schooling. His Latin, the priest argued, "would be wasted unless it got beyond the *Gallic Wars*."[51]

Returning to the Xaverian College for another year of study, Burgess passed his examinations for the Higher School Certificate in English Literature, History, and Latin with such high scores that he was urged to return for an additional year. He had earned three passes. If he were to earn three distinctions the following year, he would win a State Scholarship for university study, so it was agreed that he would return to the Xaverian College for one more year. It was assumed that Burgess would choose the same fields for examination, but he refused. To the consternation of the headmaster and prefect of studies, he insisted on music as one of his three subjects:

> I wanted to rebel, and the only subversive act I could think of was an insistence that I take Music at the advanced level and not History ... There was immense doubt about my proposal in the high echelons – they knew nothing of my musical attainments; there was nobody to instruct me – but I had my way. As public proof of my ability, I composed a Prelude and Fugue in D minor in the style of Bach.[52]

In his final year of secondary school, Burgess became more musically active, composing "an orchestral dead march, a discordant trio for flute, oboe and bassoon, a prelude and fugue for the Holy Name organist".[53] *This Man and Music* also lists "*Albumblatt* for small orchestra" from 1934. On visits back to the Xaverian College, Bernard Dunne, a former student who had become a policeman, would shock his old classmates with accounts of bigamy, incest, buggery, and other forms of socially aberrant behavior that he had witnessed in uniform. Inspired by Dunne's tales of deviance, Burgess composed "In pious times, ere priestcraft did begin", a duet for two male voices about polygamy – a setting of the first twelve lines of Dryden's *Absalom and Achitophel* – which he sang with his constabulary comrade.[54]

At the conclusion of the year, Burgess passed his music examination with flying colors. The test was an arduous affair covering harmony, counterpoint, score reduction, aural skill, and general musical knowledge. One three-hour portion of the exam required him to write an essay discussing Haydn's *Creation*, Schubert's "Trout" Quintet, and Brahms's Second Symphony. Another three hours were spent writing a piano reduction of an orchestral passage in full score, composing a setting of a sonnet by Felicia Dorothea Hemans, and writing a four-part harmonization of a given theme. Burgess found the viva voce (oral examination) much harder, and had difficulty notating pieces played by the examiner on the piano: a highly chromatic melody, a passage of four-part harmony, and a sample of two-part counterpoint. He redeemed himself with solid answers to questions about variation form and string harmonics. Asked what percussion instruments Brahms had used in his four symphonies, Burgess answered with confidence: "Timpani only, I replied, except in the third movement of the Fourth, where he introduces a triangle. I got through. I gained a distinction in music, and the school was proud of me, meaning proud of letting me have my own way."[55]

With high marks in English Literature and Music, Burgess earned esteem for himself and his school, propitiating the heads of the college who had yielded so reluctantly to his determination to study music. He passed the examination – the only student from his school to do so – but received a lower rating in Latin. Lacking the third distinction, he failed to win a university scholarship. At eighteen, having just graduated from the Xaverian College yet lacking the means to attend a university, Burgess faced the dilemma of deciding what to do next.

Notes

1 *This Man and Music*, 18.
2 *Little Wilson and Big God*, 14.
3 Ibid., 14. Burgess describes his mother as a "soubrette", meaning an attractive, light-voiced soprano who typically performed roles – often a savvy chambermaid or confidante of the ingénue – characterized by pertness, coquetry and a fondness for intrigue.
4 "You've Had Your Time: Being the Beginning of an Autobiography." *Malahat Review*, No. 44/October 1977, 10. On page 11, Burgess writes: "My mother . . . became a singer and dancer, chiefly in such Manchester music halls as the

Gentlemen's Concert Rooms (popularly known as the Snotty Parlour)." Yet according to John J. Parkinson-Bailey in *Manchester: An Architectural History* (63, 133), Lane's Gentlemen's Concert Hall was sold in 1897 and demolished to make room for the Midland Hotel, which was built between 1898 and 1903. Cf. Andrew Biswell, *The Real Life of Anthony Burgess*, 9–10.
5 *Malahat Review*, 11.
6 "My mother's family was Scotticized Irish and had a Jacobite martyr to match the Elizabethan martyr of which my father's family sometimes boasted." TMM, 12. Biswell casts doubt upon her conversion; see RLAB, 11.
7 LW, 17. He received the name Anthony (after the Paduan saint) at confirmation. For convenience, John Burgess Wilson will be referred to generally as Anthony Burgess throughout this book even though he was known principally as John or Jack Wilson until past the age of forty. Legally, he remained John Burgess Wilson his entire life and continued to be called John into his later years by some friends and relatives.
8 One of Burgess's earliest memories was of Elsie playing the piano in the front room of the house. Two-thirds of a century later, he still recalled a volume of popular songs on the piano with a star on the cover and the picture of a couple dancing. LW, 18–20.
9 LW, 22, 25.
10 Ibid., 22.
11 Ibid., 20.
12 Ibid., 25.
13 Ibid., 28.
14 Ibid., 27.
15 Ibid., 38.
16 Ibid., 44.
17 Ibid. In *This Man and Music* (13), Burgess relates the story differently, inferring that his father did not play from these volumes: "It was only when (I will come to this later) I had myself learned to make sense of the keyboard that these 'classics' were heard in our sitting room, causing the customers below to complain. They were considered by my stepmother and her family to be far above our station."
18 TMM, 14. For an explanation of "vaccicidal", see Chapter 26.
19 LW, 41. Despite this impediment, Burgess was commissioned to write introductions to more than one art catalog: "How far the ocular deficiency impairs my capacity to appreciate paintings I am not able to judge. We must all accept our limitations and love as much as we can within them. Love, even of art, is hard to quantify." "The Thyssen-Bornemisza Collection of Modern Masters: A Personal View", 13.
20 LW, 41–2.
21 "The Thyssen-Bornemisza Collection of Modern Masters: A Personal View", 13.
22 LW, 42.
23 Ibid., 51.
24 Ibid., 52.
25 Burgess invokes a related image in the final line of his Preface to *You've Had Your Time* (xi): "But to survive at all as a writer excuses the raising of the bells of three unison trumpets in C."

26 While Burgess is technically correct, it would be more accurate to describe the first inversion F#^{ø7} chord that he calls the "secondary seventh of the dominant key" as a pre-dominant seventh chord leading to the dominant of the mediant key (i.e., ii$^{ø^6_5}$ leading to V^7 [B^7] in E minor, the mediant key of C major).
27 TMM, 17. According to the milder version of the incident: "I sang the song to my father as, bowlered and ready for an evening's heavy boozing, he came out of the lavatory. He nodded and led me the few steps to the drawing-room. On top of the piano were the four volumes of *The Music Lover's Portfolio*. Beethoven's Fifth Symphony, in a simple piano reduction, was distributed throughout Volume One. He found the slow movement and pointed to the mock-martial secondary theme. 'That's the tune,' he said, and bowlered, he played it with a fag in his mouth. 'All you have to do is copy it out. That, by the way,' pointing with nicotined index, 'is middle C. Under the treble stave or over the bass stave, it's still middle C. And here it is on the joanna.' He prodded and it sounded. 'Just to the right of the lock,' meaning the ward. And then, fresh fag glowing, he went off to the Alec. He had given me a music lesson of exemplary brevity, the only one he ever gave, the only one I needed." LW, 108.
28 LW, 109.
29 Ibid.
30 Ibid., 106–7.
31 Ibid., 107.
32 Ibid., 108.
33 Ibid., 97. "I wish I had three hundred John Wilsons," Br. Martin had written on one of Burgess's earlier report cards.
34 Ibid., 109. "I did not wish to be anything but a great composer and cartoonist on the side, and I knew that this was not a practical ambition." LW, 120.
35 TMM, 19.
36 Ibid., 18. As the American composer David Diamond pointed out to Burgess in a letter dated 10 September 1983, the publisher of *Prélude à "l'après-midi d'un faune"* was Jobert, not Durand, which only published Debussy's later works beginning with *La Mer*.
37 LW, 110.
38 Ibid., 115.
39 TMM, 18.
40 LW, 111.
41 Ibid., 114–15. Ravel's *Bolero* was composed in 1928, Hindemith's *Philharmonic Concerto* in 1932.
42 TMM, 20.
43 LW, 110. According to *Grove*, Burgess's date is off by a month. The "Manchester" entry (Vol. 11, 596, of the first edition, repeated in Vol. 15, 724, of the 2nd ed.) states that the first public concert performance of *The Rio Grande* took place on 12 December 1929.
44 LW, 124.
45 Burgess's sexual good fortune ended when the family hired Nelly: "Bespectacled, leering, and deformed . . . she had a back that jutted out at opposed angles, like the outer notes of the chord of the augmented sixth." LW, 68.
46 LW, 118.
47 Ibid., 138.

48 TMM, 19. "The advantages of knowing something about music were minimal – knowing that *tanner* meant to bore, since, after the first Paris performance of *Tannhäuser*, Parisians said '*Wagner me tanne aux airs*' – and the main disadvantage was a kind of social ostracism." LW, 116.
49 TMM, 19.
50 LW, 98.
51 Ibid., 136.
52 LW, 151.
53 TMM, 22.
54 Described by Burgess as "highly literate", Dunne eventually abandoned police work to become a priest (LW, 146–7). Burgess included excerpts of the poem in his *English Literature: A Survey for Students* (Harlow: Longman, 1974), 121–2.
55 TMM, 21.

3
BURGEONING COMPOSER (1935–40)

I determined now to comfort my sad heart with the writing of a symphony.[1]

For years, Maggie Wilson had complained of overwork and vowed that it was time to move. To her stepson's surprise, in 1934 she finally sold the house on Moss Lane and moved the family to a semi-detached redbrick rental in Fallowfield, a "horribly clean and quiet" neighborhood.[2] After graduating from the Xaverian College in 1935, Burgess lived in his family's new suburban residence, spending much of the next two years in his stepmother's company. Having sold the off-license, she now spent most of her time at home, unknowingly providing her stepson with the model for Enderby's stepmother as she "picked her teeth with old tram tickets, brought up the wind without inhibition, braised beef and boiled spuds, invoked her childhood, railed at my father."[3]

Burgess's half-hearted efforts at finding employment met with little success. After being rejected for several newspaper jobs, he briefly delivered packages for the family business before enrolling, at his father's insistence, in a correspondence course ostensibly designed to prepare candidates for the Department of Customs and Excise examination. Repelled by the idea of becoming a customs officer, Burgess suffered through the prescribed syllabus of instruction in geography, chemistry, mathematics, English literature, and Latin, then failed the exam in 1936 ("Number 1,579 in order of merit").[4]

His real education was the one he pursued on his own, reading Robert Burton's *The Anatomy of Melancholy*, Doughty's *Arabia Deserta*, and volumes of the Everyman Library, as well as studying Greek and Anglo-Saxon. The fascination with Joyce that had begun with his discovery of *A Portrait of the Artist as a Young Man* at the Xaverian College progressed to the reading of *Ulysses* and installments of *Work in Progress*. Having committed all of Hopkins's poetry to memory in secondary school, Burgess devoured the modernist poetry of Pound and Eliot while producing verse of his own, original poetry as well as translations of Greek odes. He composed a choral setting of "Complaint, complaint I heard upon a day" from Pound's *Cantos*, and, returning home one day from a trip to London with his father, set Eliot to music by sketching "settings of the songs in *Sweeney Agonistes*" before the train reached Manchester.[5]

With time on his hands, Burgess set out to compose a symphony. By 1934 his infatuation with Debussy, Stravinsky, and the avant-garde had waned. He found himself drawn instead to Holst, Elgar, and Delius, all of whom died that year. Gravitating back toward traditional tonality, he felt an increasing devotion to English music and pored over the orchestral music of his homeland's finest composers.

> I found myself stuck in the British idiom of the 1930s and I have never really become unstuck. The scores I studied were of Holst's *Planets* and Elgar's First Symphony, whose first performance my father claimed to have heard at a Hallé concert in 1908. Elgar would teach me symphonic structure, Holst the use of a large orchestra.[6]

Setting his symphony in E major, Burgess sought to invent "pregnant themes", using Beethoven as a model. In search of inspiration, he started to listen more intently to Beethoven's music and tried "to play his damnable sonatas... There was no doubt about it: old Ludwig knew how to make much of nothing." But Beethoven's orchestration was too austere compared to the irresistibly lush instrumentation of Elgar, Vaughan Williams, Walton (particularly his recent First Symphony), and, especially, Holst: "from *The Planets* I stole a bass flute, six horns and four trumpets."[7] Reasoning that cost was irrelevant since the symphony would probably never be played, Burgess saw no reason to scale back its dimensions, indulging himself with a gargantuan orchestra even though "megalophonia was, as I should have realised, already out of date. The big orchestra was an Edwardian folly. Stravinsky's *Le Sacre du Printemps* was the last of the sonic supersplurges, and it was as much a parody of pretension as an act of self-indulgence – the Russian primitive in Straussian plush."

> Actually, a large orchestra was easier to score for than a small one: with four of each woodwind you could keep a four-note chord within the one family and did not need the laborious ingenuity of distributing it among tone colours that were not quite homogeneous. Eight horns in unison would ride over the ensemble more authoritatively than four, and could spread themselves across the diapason in a three-octave chord very rich and hair-raising. And then there was all the percussion – two men on kettledrums, three or four on xylophone, glockenspiel, celesta, big drum, cymbals, tambourine, whip and tubular bells. And two harps – the least audible instruments of the sonic army and the most fiddling to write for.[8]

In 1982 Burgess described the symphony as "two hundred pages of full score, as thick as the manuscript of an 80,000-word novel... Diatonic, swift to modulate, inclined to the modal, Vaughan Williams harmonies, occasional tearing dissonances like someone farting at a teaparty, bland, meditative, with patches of vulgar triumph. Totally English music, hardly able to jump twenty-two miles into Europe."[9] By 1986 it had evolved into "a three-hundred-page musical work... more laborious [to write] than the merely literary person is able to appreciate."[10] In his late sixties, he recalled with mixed emotions the strenuous youthful effort required to write it:

> I look back upon the period of composing my first symphony (in E major; the labour of copying those four sharps over and over was very exhausting) with shame rather than pride. This was no life for a young man: fatiguing study of repulsive subjects for an examination I had no hope of passing; relief through musical composition and intensive self-education in literature and philosophy; an eschewal of all youthful vice – no sex, no smoking, no drinking. No wonder I suffered from migraine.[11]

Burgess claimed that the manuscript was obliterated in a German bombing raid in 1941, having left it, when he joined the army, with a pub pianist for safekeeping. Whether or not this is true, there exists another score that provides hints of how that lost composition might have sounded. Before commencing work on his Third Symphony in December 1974, Burgess, then living in Rome, wrote out several scores in a manuscript book labeled "Sinfonie [piano reductions]". The first of these is a four-movement score, "Sinfonia (No. 1 – 1935)", preceded by the note: "This piano reduction reproduced from memory of the lost score – 1974". Perplexingly, the score differs from later descriptions of his First Symphony in several crucial respects: its primary key is C instead of E, its harmonies are quite unlike those of Vaughan Williams, and its finale's main theme is not the one identified as such in *This Man and Music*; that theme (Example 03.01) does not appear in "Sinfonia (No. 1 – 1935)" at all. Hence these are decidedly two different works, yet, since the Sinfonia purports to represent Burgess's early compositional style, for this reason it bears examination.

The opening sonata-form movement is in an angular style closer to the music of Hindemith than any of the English composers cited as models. Its slow introduction begins with a repeated, quintal/quartal six-note figure (Example 03.02) that transforms into the exposition's principal theme, its C minorish quality establishing the movement's main tonality. Quartal sonorities are equally prevalent in the eerie second movement, an Andante whose opening theme – a string of alternating, descending P4s and m2s accompanied by three-note whole-tone clusters – recalls the "Elegia" from Bartók's Concerto for Orchestra. The Scherzo, like those of Beethoven, is driving and spirited, but with passages of Stravinskian polytonality added for contrast. The work ends with a C major rondo that begins with an

Example 03.01 Symphony No. 1, Finale: "mixolydian melody" quoted in TMM

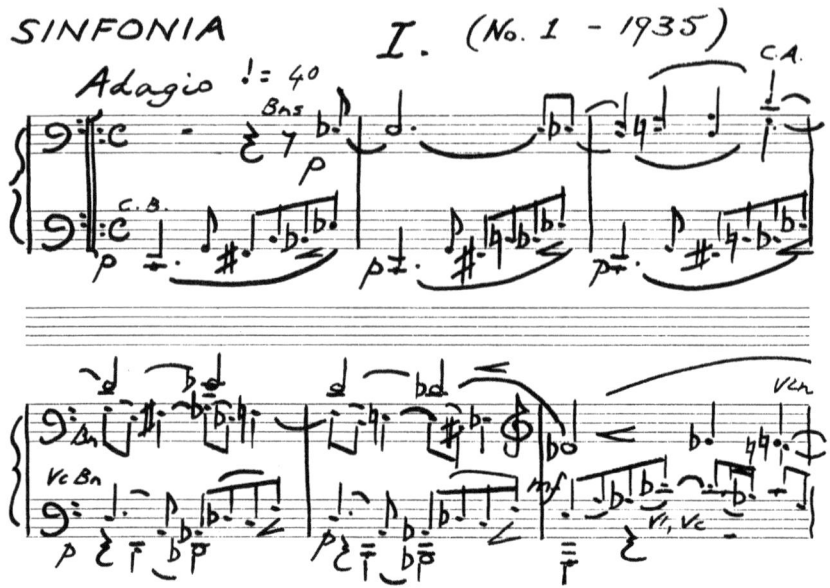

Example 03.02 Sinfonia (No. 1 – 1935), I. Adagio–Allegro moderato (bs. 1–6)

Example 03.03 Sinfonia (No. 1 – 1935), IV. Molto moderato–Allegro: Introduction (bs. 1–7)

introduction based on a theme (Example 03.03) that recurs in the piano concertino *Rome in the Rain*, among other works; the "Flower of the Mountain" melody from *Blooms of Dublin* is one of the themes presented later in the movement.

The frustration of expending so much energy on a composition that was never played helped impel Burgess toward writing literature instead of music, since words do not require a symphony orchestra in order to be presented to the public. As he once explained, when composers of symphonies turn to writing prose, they are inevitably drawn toward the novel, the symphony's lone literary equivalent:

> The lyric poem is not enough: it is an étude or prelude or entr'acte. The short story stops as soon as it starts – a symphonic exposition with no development section, no recapitulation, no coda. An expository prose work is not an expression of the imagination. The epic poem no longer exists. We are left with the novel, the only literary genre for failed symphonists.[12]

At twenty, Burgess enrolled in the University of Manchester to resume his formal education. He wished to study music but majored in English instead, offering the dubious explanation later in life that he was rejected as a music student for having failed Brother Sebastian's course in physics at the Xaverian College: "If I had passed . . . I would probably have become a professional musician, instead of the doubtful amateur I still am."[13] As a journalist and editor for *The Serpent*, the university magazine, he produced news articles, theatre notices, and book reviews. He received recognition and money for writing when his short story "Grief" won an undergraduate prize worth five guineas, yet "still wanted to be a great composer" and composed numerous works while a university student, including a string quartet, twelve-tone studies for piano, "Caedmon's Hymn" for male voices, "Ic eom of Irelonde" for soprano and flageolet, a piano sonatina, a chamber setting of Eliot's "Lines for an Old Man", and a song to a poem by Lance Godwin, a fellow student and contributor to *The Serpent*. During his freshman year, Burgess collaborated with another student on an opera about Copernicus that he later described – tongue-in-cheek, one hopes – as "a kind of *Singspiel*, parachronic in that Copernicus preached the noumenon of a heliocentric universe to a modern world satisfied with mere phenomena."[14] He composed several numbers for it in piano score, including a tango, but did not finish the opera ("There was not the time for labouring at orchestral scores").[15] Three years later he wrote a draft of Marlowe's *Doctor Faustus*, the subject of his dissertation, with the intention of turning it into a one-act opera, but did not complete it either.

Burgess found the Department of Music "childish" and blighted by "corky choirmaster quips, public humiliation over wrong notes, shouting and hockey-mistress cajolery, facetiousness about chippy-choppy rhythms"; overall, he considered himself better off making music on his own.[16] He enjoyed performing and writing lighthearted songs, and was generally regarded as a popular songwriter and pianist rather than a "classical" composer: "If university society wanted 'serious' music it went to the music department for it; from me it wanted Harold Arlen and Hoagy Carmichael."[17] The summer before he entered the university, Burgess sold an original song to a Manchester comedian for thirty shillings. It was called "Cabbage Face", the conceit being that the melody of the refrain consisted of the notes C-A-B-B-A-G-E F-A-C-E. Burgess always enjoyed transcribing words, names, and numbers into musical themes, and did so throughout his compositional career.

Theatre became another of Burgess's passions at the University of Manchester. He joined the committee of the Stage Society and participated in shows as a composer, producer, and actor, specializing in "middle-aged parts, considered appropriate since I was older than the others; either henpecked husbands ... or lecherous Ruritanian colonels."[18] He took part in readings and stagings of *The Ascent of F6* (in shortened form), *Murder in the Cathedral* (second part), *Fumed Oak*, *The Monkey's Paw*, *The House with the Twisty Windows*, and *Dr Allen G.P.*, sometimes composing the incidental music. In 1938 he wrote the music for a planned staging of James Elroy Flecker's *Hassan*, but "the production came to nothing". A more successful undertaking was a dramatization of *The Waste Land* for which Burgess composed and performed a jazz-inflected score for solo piano that included quotations from *Le Sacre du Printemps*, *Tristan und Isolde*, *Parsifal*, and *Der Ring des Nibelungen*. He considered it a "major achievement" – better, he thought, than a radio version done previously by "D. G. Bridson, the brilliant North Regional drama producer".[19] Forty years later he recreated the score, basing it upon this collegiate production.

On 18 April 1938, near the end of Burgess's second term, his father died of heart failure. Although just fifty-five, he had looked much older. Despite the fact that they did not enjoy a close bond, Joe Wilson's death brought about a surge of "morbid and excessive" guilt in his son, who claims he was subsequently oppressed, like Hamlet, by ghostly visits from his deceased parent. An apparition of Joe Wilson at a performance of the Hallé Orchestra confirmed the importance of music in their relationship: "He reappeared months afterwards in the flesh at a Hallé concert, during the final movement of Beethoven's *Eroica*. He wore his bowler hat. He nodded at me as to show satisfaction that I was still listening to music, then he vanished."[20]

After his father passed away, financial need forced Burgess and his stepmother to sell the Fallowfield house and return to 47 Princess Road in Moss Side, sharing crowded premises with Maggie's daughter Agnes Tollitt and her family. Privacy became a problem. He slept in the room where Jack Tollitt played billiards and darts in the evenings; even worse, he had to share it with his eleven-year-old nephew Dan. To make ends meet, Burgess turned to part-time piano-playing in Manchester pubs. He earned "ten shillings to play regularly at the Black Horse on Friday and Saturday evenings" until the night four of his university friends caused too much of a ruckus with drunken recitations of *Beowulf*, which sent Burgess packing. Recalling his father's warnings about the hazards of being a pub pianist ("The pianist was usually despised, especially by the casual pub-singers he had to accompany"), Burgess stoically accepted his fate and did no more pub playing until after the war, when financial necessity again demanded the extra income.[21]

If Joe Wilson actually first laid smitten eyes upon Elizabeth Burgess while she graced a Manchester stage as a chorus girl, then the way his son met his future wife Llewela Jones was uncannily alike. According to Burgess, Llewela was in the chorus of women of Canterbury in a Manchester University production of *Murder in the Cathedral* when he first spotted her.[22] He was taken with the "tall athletic girl, blonde and blue-eyed, with a superbly developed body."[23] Like her future husband's mother, Llewela was a Protestant with strong roots outside of England; Elizabeth Burgess's family hailed from Scotland while Llewela, the daughter of a Welsh mother and English father, was raised in Wales. Elizabeth was known within her family as Belle; Llewela went by the name of Lynne. Elizabeth was the younger of two sisters, as was Lynne. Both women would die at tragically young ages – Elizabeth at thirty, Lynne at forty-seven.

The beginning of the relationship between Anthony Burgess and Lynne Jones dates to when she and her friend Margaret Williams invited him and his friend Douglas Mason (the Copernicus opera librettist) to escort them to a dance. The young men failed to reply and when next they encountered Lynne, she assailed them for their rudeness. To make up for it, the youths invited Lynne and Margaret to see *The Lady Vanishes* and *Le Roman d'un tricheur*. The back-row fondling that took place at the cinema that evening between Anthony and Lynne quickly led to urgent, reckless lovemaking. Frequent sexual relations followed that, if discovered, could easily have gotten them dismissed from the university, but they escaped detection and remained safely matriculated.

During the summer of 1939, accompanied by Margaret Williams, the couple toured Belgium, France, the Netherlands, and Luxembourg. Burgess would sometimes play in hostels and nightclubs, once using the piano to illustrate the stupidity of Nazi anti-Semitism. One evening in a Luxembourgian nightclub, a group of Germans began disparaging Jews after a woman at a nearby table called Burgess one because of his "Celto-Lancastrian" nose. "There was such a thing as Jewishness," the Germans declared. "Take the music of Mendelssohn: you can hear Jewishness in every note."

> The night club trio was taking a break, so I went to the piano and played part of the second movement of Elgar's Symphony No. 2 in E flat. "That," I then said, "is from the Reformation Symphony by Mendelssohn. Where is the Jewishness?" It stuck out a mile, they shuddered; there was a certain unteutonic oleaginousness or *Schmierigkeit*. I then told them who the composer was, and they said that he must be a Jew and that they did not like this English Jewish cheating, especially when Jewish England was *das Land ohne Musik*.[24]

On 2 September 1939, days after their return to the UK, compulsory military service was declared for all able-bodied British men between the ages of eighteen and forty-one; the following day, England declared war on Germany. Frequent power outages inspired Burgess to write his "Black-out Blues". Emulating Brecht and Weill, he also penned cabaret songs in the "Weimar chic" style of *Der Dreigroschenoper*, writing the music and lyrics, which a pair of German graduate students translated from English into their native tongue.

Burgess spent much of the 1939–40 academic year writing a dissertation on *Doctor Faustus* in which he contended that the drama was a form of "symbolic autobiography". His succinct summation of his thesis – "Marlowe wanted to be a Renaissance man but Catholicism held him back" – applies as much to himself as to his subject, serving as an implicit defense of his rationale for turning his back on the Church. The simultaneous activity in literature, theatre, music, drawing, and language, plus a wide range of academic study, provides ample evidence of Burgess's ambition to become a modern-day Renaissance man. In order to achieve that ambition, he found it necessary to reject Catholicism, yet he never dismissed the notion of pure evil or discounted the eschatological possibility of hell, which led him into heated disputes with Jewish refugees in Manchester who argued that, while Hitler was "bad", he was not a manifestation of "theological evil". Of these young German immigrants, Burgess would later sigh, "They were innocent, but we were all innocent then."[25]

The summer after receiving his Bachelor of Arts degree with honors – top second (IIi), representing a good but not superior rank – the twenty-three-year-old Burgess proposed to Lynne, three years his junior, who accepted without letting their newly formalized status impinge upon her sexual freedom. Becoming Burgess's fiancée did not deter Lynne, whose carnal adventures had begun at fourteen, from regarding herself as "a free body ready and willing for the enjoyment of hearty sexual exercise with all comers" and viewing the concept of engagement as "a kind of sexual passacaglia. That is, there was to be a strong ground bass of unassailable love and free variations of philandering above it. She did not understand the image: she was not musical."[26]

When Maggie Dwyer Wilson died that fall, in autumn 1940, it left Burgess truly on his own for the first time. He rented a room near the university from a hospitable landlady who approved of his cohabitation with Lynne. A profitable stint as tutor to an eleven-year-old boy from an affluent Manchester family provided Burgess with enough money to enjoy this taste of independence, but, with a war on, it was all too brief. His induction papers arrived that fall, and, on 17 October 1940, toting volumes of Joyce and Hopkins "but little else, not even a change of shirt", he headed off to Scotland, mentally improvising a rhapsody on the "catchy little theme" B-E-C-C-rest-D-A (the melodic equivalent of his serial number 7388026) as the train chugged northward to Eskbank.[27]

Notes

1 TMM, 22.
2 LW, 147.
3 Ibid., 160.
4 Ibid., 155, 163.
5 Ibid., 157. Burgess claimed to have recorded these settings in Milan in 1981 in conjunction with the Eliot Memorial Lectures that he delivered the previous year; see YH, 359.
6 LW, 158.
7 TMM, 22–3.
8 LW, 158–9.
9 TMM, 23.
10 LW, 159.
11 Ibid., 160.
12 Ibid., 159.
13 Ibid., 125.
14 Ibid., 187.
15 Ibid. "The piano score of that tango is still around. I was told of a performance of it on BBC Radio Three in October 1985." This is highly doubtful. Tango for Pianoforte performed by Yvar Mikhashoff is almost certainly the work that was broadcast. See Chapter 18.
16 Ibid.
17 TMM, 26.
18 LW, 177–8.
19 Ibid., 179.
20 Ibid., 194.
21 Ibid., 199–200.
22 Biswell states that Anthony and Lynne met in autumn 1938; she "first set eyes on him when he was performing in a play for the Stage Society." RLAB, 72.
23 LW, 179, 206.
24 Ibid., 218–19.
25 Ibid., 228.
26 Ibid., 211.
27 Ibid., 239–40.

EMERGENT AUTHOR

4
WAR: BRITAIN AND GIBRALTAR (1940–46)

I had always wanted to be the composer of Debussy's Prélude à L'Après-Midi d'un Faune: *now was my chance.*[1]

Anthony Burgess's wartime service in the British army was unquestionably one of the defining experiences of his life. On the negative side it subjected him to physical deprivation and intimidation, developed in him a deep antipathy toward authority figures whose intelligence he disdained yet was forced to obey, and helped cause a rift in his marriage that was never fully overcome. Yet on the positive side, it helped him develop into a successful writer by providing the material for *A Vision of Battlements*, his first novel, which is essentially a fictionalized account of his Gibraltar sojourn. A number of later novels – *The Wanting Seed, Napoleon Symphony, 1985, Earthly Powers*, and *Any Old Iron* – as well as non-fiction works like *Ernest Hemingway and his world* and *Little Wilson and Big God* also draw heavily upon his military past. Further, military service gave Burgess his first sustained professional experience as a musician, establishing a degree of confidence in his abilities that had been absent before, thus bolstering his belief that he could achieve a successful civilian career as a composer-arranger once the war ended.

As an inductee into the Royal Army Medical Corps, Burgess underwent six weeks of basic training at Newbattle Abbey in Eskbank, a district of Dalkeith in southeast Scotland near Edinburgh. Conditions were grim, with the trainees barracked for weeks in cold, dimly lit huts without hot water, sleeping on kapok mattress sections instead of beds, and relieving themselves in outdoor field latrines. For the first month, the new recruits marched in their civvies, their worn-out shoes dropping off their feet, until regulation khakis and boots finally arrived.

Observing the difficulty that many soldiers experienced as they struggled to sing simple marching tunes in rhythm, Burgess determined "that most of the world was unmusical."[2] This belief in a musical schism dividing the population only exacerbated a stubborn sense of superiority that caused Burgess to have trouble fitting in with his fellow troops or behaving deferentially enough toward his superior officers. Confronted by illiterates and bullies, he adopted a confrontational attitude and an "unprecedentedly posh" accent that marked him for extra duties. Having bragged of being able to play the piano, when ancient uprights had to be moved into place for concerts presented by ENSA (Entertainments' National Service Association, the British equivalent of the United Service Organizations, or USO), he was assigned to the task. At first this was as close as he came to making music, but soon he took up the bagpipes and bugle. Playing the latter one murky morning led to an epiphany about tonality's basis in the physical world.

> I suppose it was a kind of military devotion that turned me into a bugler and a piper. I knew how a bugle worked: you evoked a segment of the harmonic series by varying lip-pressure on the metal embouchure. I was permitted occasionally to blow lights out and reveille. Blowing the latter one morning over the deep and unrousable dark, I reflected that the harmonic series was a fact of nature, and that the atonalists had tried to separate music from nature, which was a grave sin.[3]

Eventually Burgess graduated from hauling pianos to playing them. He "bashed the joanna in the NAAFI" (Navy, Army and Air Force Institute, one of a series of canteens and recreational establishments created by the British Government for its Armed Forces) and accompanied singers in modest recitals performed in the homes of a few of Eskbank's more bourgeois citizens. One night he became a temporary hero when he stood in at the piano for a band that, owing to heavy snow, failed to arrive for a village dance in Northumberland.

In early 1941, Burgess was reassigned to the 189 Field Ambulance of B Company, in Morpeth. He tried to get along with the rest of the unit, but remained an outsider.

> A bugler was needed to sound over the camp, and I volunteered. I did more: I composed company calls but, as the harmonic series is limited, it was not easy to tell them apart. I did more again: fifes were indented for and I formed a fife band. I tried to please, but I could not. I was not one of the boys.[4]

When the Entertainments Section of the 54th Division sought a soldier capable of writing musical arrangements for an Army dance band, the Regimental Sergeant Major (RSM) was only too glad to nominate his would-be fife bandmaster. To the relief of Burgess and his unit, he was accepted for the new post, and, in the spring of 1941, was assigned to Moreton-in-Marsh in Gloucestershire, where he was finally able to put his musical skills to proper use.

The Jaypees, a company of ten stage performers plus an orchestra of six musicians with an arranger, took its name from the initials of John Priestland, the general commanding officer of the 54th Division. This entertainment unit was commanded by Lieut. William T. Elliott of the First Berkshires, who had taken a reduction in rank from Captain for the assignment. The group of singer-dancers and comedians comprised Elliott himself; his wife, Mrs. Sybil Elliott; Pte. Douglas L. Close (chief comedian); Pte. Paul A. Anderson (light comedian, monologuist); Dvr. Jack Varney (tenor); L/Cpl. Pat Glover (eccentric dancer, comedian, drag artist); Pte. N. Clafton (dancer); Pte. V. J. Willis (officer's batman, "casual" comedian, electrician); and Dvr. K. F. "Bob" Morgan (violinist billed as the Great Romano). Miss Babs Evelyn (dancer), a civilian, was hired through a theatrical agency.[5] The band, which existed for the purpose of accompanying this troupe of entertainers in performance and playing on its own for dances, consisted of Sgt. Harry Walkling (tenor saxophone), Pte. William Brian (trumpet), Dvr. Stanley L. Williams (drums, xylophone), Pte. Edward Norman (alto saxophone, band leader), Gnr. Richard Nutting (double bass, accordion), and Dvr. F. Edward Wright (piano). "Pte. J. B. Wilson", as the name appears on a 1941 Jaypees program, was the "Musical Arranger and Orchestrator". He also assisted Ted Willis with the lighting (once setting Guildford Town Hall on fire), took part on stage in comedic skits, and often stood in for the band's regular pianist. Initially assembled in November 1940 in Morpeth, the Jaypees traveled widely, performing in Northumberland, Gloucestershire, Buckinghamshire, and Suffolk.[6]

Burgess's predecessor was Tommy Smith, the band's original pianist and leader. Smith had been very well liked and respected by the bandsmen, who viewed him as their mentor. When the Jaypees were reassigned from Morpeth to Moreton-in-Marsh and Smith did not come along, it created a void that took three men to fill. Ted Wright took over as pianist, Ted Norman as leader, and Burgess as arranger. Having to fill the shoes of the popular Smith placed the new arranger under stress from the start. Burgess lacked prior experience arranging for this kind of group, and when his first assignment – scoring a new opening chorus – fell flat, he felt great pressure to prove his ability not just to his bandmates but to himself. Fortunately, Bill Brian's desire for an arrangement of a particular Louis Armstrong song gave Burgess a second chance. He swiftly produced an arrangement of "If We Never Meet Again" that pleased the musicians and thereby secured his acceptance by the band.

Burgess proceeded to write arrangements of "The Folks Who Live on the Hill" (from a Bing Crosby recording), "Stardust" (written in the Glenn Miller style), "Thanks for the Memory", "I Know Why", "Let's Have Another One", "On the Track", and other big band hits of the day. He wrote music of his own – *Sinfonietta* (for jazz combo) and "a blues in waltz time" – and created "a pseudo-symphonic arrangement of 'Darktown Strutters' Ball'."[7] The Jaypees sometimes played exotic numbers like *Ballet Egyptien*, which had been performed by solo piano until Burgess arranged it for the band, and Rimsky-Korsakov's *Chanson Hindoue*, which they called "Song of India". Burgess arranged Bach's Fugue in C minor from Book I of *The Well-Tempered Clavier* for two saxophones and trumpet plus drum and double bass, but the band never performed it, though it did perform his

Example 04.01 Excerpt from "An Afternoon on the Phone" (Debussy/Burgess)

orchestration of the Celtic song "Macushla" for tenor Jack Varney. Being a better improviser than Ted Wright, Burgess would often play for dances, accompanying Bill Brian and Ted Norman on jazz renditions of tunes like "Blue Skies". When afforded the opportunity to practice piano, he concentrated on the *Warsaw Concerto*, a new work written by the British composer Richard Addinsell for the 1941 film *Dangerous Moonlight*.

Adding an arrangement of Debussy's *Prélude à L'après-midi d'un faune* to the sextet's repertoire brought Burgess particular pleasure. He retained the original key of E major even though it required Bill Brian, playing his B♭ instrument, to read a key signature of six sharps as he negotiated the chromatic opening flute solo, rewritten for muted trumpet. By fitting the music into a steady meter and adding a drumbeat, Burgess's simplified version, called "An Afternoon on the Phone" (Example 04.01), succeeded as a dance number: "It was good to see soldiers clodhopping round with local girls in flowery dresses to the strains of that refined impressionism. Number 100 proved as acceptable as any other quickstep. It was the beat that counted."[8]

To Richard Nutting, the "short and disciplined 18 months" that he played with the Jaypees under the leadership of "band leader Tommy Smith and the enthusiastic influence of John Wilson" helped greatly to prepare him for a semiprofessional playing career that lasted well over half a century until he ceased performing in 1998 at age seventy-nine. Nutting considered John Wilson to be not just a talented arranger, but also a friend with a marvelous sense of humor.

> John Wilson joined us after about 6 months. Although he was not the regular band pianist, he often deputised for the band leader. He advised Lt. Elliott, the officer in charge, on the necessary musical tips to improve our shows, and although we had all of the current arrangements for the band from the publishers, John would often write his own version time and time again. This was very refreshing because other bands were playing the usual arrangements but we were playing different versions. It made us unique. Of course, the big bands – Glenn Miller, Artie Shaw, Benny Goodman, Count Basie, etc. – were the rage at the time, but to slip in the odd special arrangement by our John was great.
>
> John had an extremely, in my opinion, good risqué sense of humour. The band went out on gigs in a large army lorry. After what might have been 4 or 5 hours of playing in the heat, we would load our gear on board and travel

sometimes 2 or 3 hours in the cold lorry. Unfortunately I developed a sweat rash on parts I do not have to mention and I suffered for over 4 weeks. When it finally cleared, John produced a new arrangement dedicated to Dick Nutting! To everyone's amusement he called it "Ball Tic Bass", an arrangement in the Count Basie style and featuring string bass, the instrument I played in the band. For John to write this for me was very flattering and was accepted as a personal gift from one friend to another.[9]

During Burgess's first year of military service, Lynne Jones worked on her dissertation, a thesis on French policy in Morocco from 1912–14. In February 1941, while stationed with the 189 Field Ambulance unit, he visited her in Manchester, extending the leave to more than a month and returning to Morpeth just in time to avoid arrest by the military police for desertion. To celebrate her graduation from Manchester University, Lynne visited Burgess that summer in Moreton-in-Marsh for a month. That autumn, she took a position as assistant principal of the Board of Trade in Bournemouth, the city where she and John B. Wilson were married on 22 January 1942.

In response to Lynne's insistence that he demonstrate more ambition and attain a higher military rank, in early 1942 Burgess applied successfully for transfer to the Army Educational Corps. Beyond simply accommodating Lynne, he had become weary of his work with the Jaypees, although he "should have been grateful for the chance to play with harmony and counterpoint at an elementary level, toughen my fingers at the keyboard, and practise Mendelssohn's Violin Concerto with the Great Romano."

> The musicians had grown sick of my providing atonal surprises in my impoverished solo passages: they were far from ready for progressive jazz. Historically speaking, it was something to have jazz at all in a country whose popular music had been maudlin waltzes and novelty numbers like "Never Be Cruel to a Vegitubel".[10]

Promoted to the rank of sergeant, Burgess was dispatched to the town of Eye in Suffolk for training as an AEC instructor. He spent most of the next twenty-two months not far from Manchester in nearby Warrington, where he worked as a speech therapist at a lunatic asylum in Winwick, amusing himself by organizing and playing piano in a small dance band and producing a show called *Hospital Blues* in which he performed the *Warsaw Concerto*.[11] Lynne secured a post as assistant principal of the Board of Trade office in Manchester, which meant that the newly wedded couple was able to live semi-connubially, with Burgess sneaking off to her rooms in Rusholme for "blissful but furtive" evenings and weekends. As the year drew to a close, they wedded anew, this time in a Catholic ceremony in Manchester, just before Burgess received a new posting, to the Infantry Training Centre in Warrington, on New Year's Day 1943.[12] There he refined his oratorical abilities by extolling the British Way and Purpose to companies of troops lodged in the vast Peninsular Barracks;

more mundane duties included frustrating work attempting to teach illiterates to read. Musical activity was reduced to occasional keyboard playing in the canteen.

In the autumn of 1943, Burgess was posted to a hospital in Walton, near Liverpool, where his service included warning "good-hearted" Liverpudlian girls against the physical attentions of "gonorrhoeal louts". Obtaining leave became a matter of importance following Lynne's transfer that summer to London, where she worked first for the Board of Trade, then the Ministry of War Transport. To gain precious furloughs, Burgess curried favor with the Military Registrar through music: writing out the melodies of popular tunes, forming a trio with other officers, organizing a dance. The London visits involved drinking in the Wheatsheaf and other Fitzrovian pubs with the likes of Julian Maclaren-Ross and George Orwell. Lynne began drinking heavily during this period and was very sexually active while they were apart; she "technically committed adultery" with Dylan Thomas several times, but, in Burgess's words, "to go to bed with Dylan was to offer little more than maternal comfort" owing to Thomas's chronic drunkenness.[13] Attempting to fit into this artistic coterie, Burgess sought out pubcrawling composers to whom he could show off his compositions, but found only writers instead.

> There were not many musicians around on that Soho circuit: such composers as had work would be busy scoring the background slush for a film; the players would be playing. I took around my recently completed piano sonata, looking for some fellow-musician who would offer an opinion, but I found none... Dylan could play a Scriabin study in F sharp major on the piano of somebody's flat after closing-time, but he had learnt it by being shown where to put his fingers; my score appealed in its calligraphy to both Dylan and Maclaren-Ross, but it was Arabic to them.[14]

This sonata was probably the one in E major listed by Burgess among the works he composed during his years of military service in Britain. These include *Ipswich* (prelude and fugue) for organ, *Hispanics* for violin and piano (evidently for the Great Romano), *Song of a Northern City* for piano (or piano and orchestra), *Nelson*: suite for piano (one eye, one arm, one arse), and a setting of Sassoon's "Everyone suddenly burst out singing" for voices and piano.

In late 1943, Burgess was posted overseas to Gibraltar with four other AEC officers from his unit. Before the transport set sail, he impressed the Officer Commanding Troops with his pianistic ability: "When the OC Troops discovered my pianist skills he wanted me to be posted to the ship. He was a musician himself and impressed by my musical memory."[15] Lacking sheet music, Burgess improvised on themes from *Tristan und Isolde* to underscore a theatrical presentation of the dungeon scene from Flecker's *Hassan*, and then "was sick on the keyboard" as turbulent seas made everyone ill. Upon their arrival on Christmas Eve, the five AEC officers were split up into two groups. Burgess paired off with Harry Stevens, a Welsh sociologist "with the eyes of a mystic", to join the First Hertfordshires stationed at Moorish Castle; the others – Ben Thomas, Norman Parker, and Jimmy Wilkinson – joined the Engineers.[16] Distressed to learn that he had been classified as a specialist in German, a language he did not know well, Burgess protested, but to no avail. He followed orders, teaching German as well as Spanish, French, and Russian; additionally, he provided instruction in piano-playing, four-part harmony, and orchestration.

In Gibraltar, Burgess composed a setting of the Lorca poem *La niña del bello rostro* for a singer named Merita who had been contracted to perform at the Universal Café. One day he cut short the lecture he was supposed to give to a group of particularly raucous dockworkers by exclaiming, "You don't need me. What you need is a drink."[17] As they all headed for the café, Merita spotted Burgess and began singing his song, but was howled down by the men, who called out for popular favorites like "Yours" and "Johnny Pedlar". He went mad and began flailing, a melee ensued, and military police arrived to subdue the dockers. Burgess escaped and went unpunished for his role in the donnybrook, but was rebuked severely for abandoning the lecture.

Another Universal Café singer, a beautiful older woman named Conchita whom he tutored in English, provided Burgess with "friendly sexual relief".[18] After her contract in Gibraltar ended and she had returned to her home in Granada, he once heard her on Spanish radio singing his song "*Muchísimas Gracias*".

There was a great deal of music on the Rock with "real, as opposed to army, musicians", and old friends from the Jaypees like Bill Brian and Harry Walkling, the latter now drum major of the 1st Herts regimental band. Before long, Burgess was composing marches for this military band and supplying arrangements for the dance band – actually a full-fledged big band that included three trumpets, trombone, and four saxophones. "I was back into music again. One hundred quires of thirty-stave manuscript paper were found gathering dust in a quartermaster's store on Line Wall Road. These had to be filled with dots."[19] Burgess "became a free agent of the arts", organizing musical appreciation sessions, rejuvenating the Gibraltar Musical Society, building up large audiences for weekly gramophone concerts at the YMCA, and even painting a mural representing the story of organic life on the walls of the AEC physics laboratory. His industriousness helped secure his promotion from Sergeant Major to Warrant Officer. Meanwhile he continued filling quires of scoring paper with new compositions.

> I set up a table for myself in the Command library and began to compose a symphony in A minor. A petty officer appeared with a cello in a ship's carpenter's coffin. I dropped the symphony and started to write a cello concerto. I wrote an orchestral overture called *Gibraltar*. I wrote a choral setting of Wilfred Owen's "Anthem for Doomed Youth".[20]

Besides the Owen setting, works from this period – all lost – include compositions for full orchestra, dance orchestra, military band, organ, and piano; incidental music for *Tobias and the Angel* and *Winterset*; and an arrangement of the Bing Crosby hit "An Apple for the Teacher" as a regimental victory march to celebrate the end of the war. Whether Burgess composed a cello concerto or sonata in Gibraltar remains unclear. Richard Ennis, the quasi-autobiographical protagonist of *A Vision of Battlements*, composes a cello sonata, not a concerto. In a 1968 *Life* Magazine profile, Burgess mentioned having composed a cello sonata, and, in the list of compositions in *This Man and Music*, included a "Sonata for cello and piano in G minor" (1944) but not a cello concerto; on the other hand, a cello concerto is included in the list of works published in *Contemporary Composers* and is mentioned in his autobiography: "I had brought home with me the score of a violoncello concerto which eventually I would convert into a violin concerto for Yehudi Menuhin".[21]

A devastating incident that occurred far from the front lines had the most damaging effect on the lives of Burgess and his wife during the war. Leaving her London office at the Ministry of War Transport late one night in April 1944, Lynne was brutally attacked by four men in civilian dress who spoke with American southern accents and "were evidently GI deserters".[22] They grabbed her handbag and attempted to pull off her gold wedding ring, threatening to break or cut the finger in order to get it. Pregnant at the time of the attack, Lynne was beaten until she lost consciousness; the blows and kicks resulted in a miscarriage and a condition of constant uterine bleeding that left her unable to bear children.[23] With Lynne too ill to write, her friend Sonia Brownwell (the future wife of George Orwell) sent Burgess a letter describing what had occurred. Anxious to join his wife in London, Burgess pleaded with William P. Meldrum, his commanding officer, for "compassionate leave", but the request was denied.

That decision by Meldrum, a Captain who later advanced to Major, engendered lasting bitterness in Burgess and an antiestablishment attitude that deepened his sense of identification with the enlisted men. Norman Crump, Warrant Officer Class One, was Burgess's immediate superior and the man who determined which AEC officers would teach what subjects. Burgess scorned both officers, describing Meldrum in *Little Wilson and Big God* as an ambitious, uncompassionate overseer and Crump as "hatchet-faced and saturnine".[24] Out of spite, he later used their names for several interchangeable minor characters in his early novels, bitterly converting them into a derisive simulacrum of Rosenkrantz and Guildenstern.

Infuriated after his furlough was denied, Burgess began drinking and brawling, especially with Americans, until an American captain named Baroja helped him overcome his rage by explaining how the war demonstrated the existence of theological evil. According to Baroja, to deny the existence of evil was to deny reality; the assault on Lynne was a manifestation of "evil for its own sake", to be regarded as part of "the human endowment" and not characteristic of any particular nationality. "Your wife's a war casualty, but the whole of life is war."[25] Baroja's philosophy brought Burgess some measure of relief while implanting an idea that would become a central issue in *A Clockwork Orange* and the basis of the *Clockwork Orange* song "What Gets Into You?"[26]

Following her assault, Lynne wrote to her husband describing how she was imbibing large quantities of liquid – preferably pints of beer – to compensate for the loss of body fluid through her continual hemorrhaging. Laced with obscenities, Burgess's replies arrived full of holes where razor-wielding British censors had carefully excised each "fuck" and "goddamn". In late 1945, he wangled a month's leave, arriving in South Wales in November for an encounter that was painfully awkward. During his absence, Lynne had become involved with Major Herbert Williams, Deputy District Education Officer in the AEC and soon-to-be Chief Instructor of the AEC Depot in Blackheath. Williams was older than her husband, balding, bespectacled, and beset by facial tics, but Burgess found him likable – a well-educated man who understood his Latin quotations of Catullus and Seneca. "He had a voice of great charm. After six halves of bitter he told me he was in love with my wife. I replied in the manner of Coco in *The Mikado*."[27] Unable to resolve the tangled mess, Burgess left England in time to spend his third Christmas on the Rock.

Contrary to the pitiful state of Burgess's personal affairs, his literary activity bloomed. He wrote film reviews for the *Gibraltar Chronicle* and won the Governor's Poetry Prize for a poem that he later attributed to F. X. Enderby and set to music as the final movement of *The Brides of Enderby*.[28] He kept up with the latest fiction, reading *Animal Farm*, *Brideshead Revisited*, *The Aerodrome*, Eliot's *Four Quartets*, Cyril Connolly's *The Unquiet Grave*, and Auden's *New Year Letter* while continuing to decipher *Finnegans Wake*.[29] Although Joyce never set foot in Gibraltar, Burgess's stay at Moorish Castle furnished him with first-hand knowledge of the land of Major Brian Tweedy and his daughter Molly.

Above all, these years provided the content of Burgess's earliest novel, *A Vision of Battlements*. Emulating Joyce's technique of basing *Ulysses* on *The Odyssey*, Burgess used *The Aeneid* as a model, though largely as veneer masking a quasi-autobiographical *roman à clef*. Written (probably) around December 1951-January 1952 and first published in 1965, *A Vision of Battlements* is based so closely upon Burgess's experiences in Gibraltar that the names of several characters – Merita, Mr. Withers, Fazacherley, and Frank (El Burro) – are left unaltered from their real-life models.[30] Except for Barasi (Iarbas) and Turner (Turnus), all of the novel's main characters can be traced to a corresponding individual mentioned or described in Burgess's autobiographical writings.

The reader is alerted to the musical nature of *A Vision of Battlements* before even opening the book. The dust jacket depicts the protagonist,

Sergeant Richard Ennis, affixed to the clicking pendulum of an old-fashioned metronome as his mistress Concepción coyly peeks out from the sounding box. Ennis, the first of Burgess's fictional alter egos, is a guitar-playing composer-pianist serving in the Army Vocational and Cultural Corps (the fictional equivalent of the Army Educational Corps).[31] Concepción, his ill-fated Andalusian lover, represents Dido to Ennis's Aeneas in Burgess's mock-Virgilian tale.

The presence of the doppelgänger is one of several recurrent Burgessian themes introduced in *A Vision of Battlements*. Burgess invents a pair of women to represent his first wife: Laurel, Ennis's English wife, who remains in Britain, and Lavinia Grantham, a Wren (member of the Women's Royal Naval Service) named for Aeneas's intended wife, whom Ennis repeatedly regards as Laurel's double. Ever the facile phonetician, Burgess chose names closely matching his wife's dual designations: Laurel for Llewela and Lavinia for Lynne. The lack of warmth in both women is symbolized by a poem, attributed to Lavinia, that begins, "She was all / Brittle crystal. / Her hands / Silver silk over steel". Burgess wrote this poem, first published as "Girl" in *The Serpent*, in 1939 shortly after he began dating Lynne; in 1977, credited to F. X. Enderby, it reappeared in *The Brides of Enderby*.[32]

Ennis's artistic comrades Julian Agate and Mr. Withers are the first of a profusion of homosexual characters in Burgess's fiction. Agate, with an appellative nod to Virgil's Achates, is modeled upon AEC Sergeant Reg Hanson, a "very Nordic ballet dancer" whom Burgess met on his 1945 pre-Christmas return voyage to Gibraltar. Withers, the epicene director of the British Council-like "Commonwealth Council for the Development of the Appreciation of the Arts in Colonial Territories", is one of the characters whose name is borrowed unaltered from the actual person.

Aversion to music pedagogues is another recurring Burgessian motif introduced in this novel, with disdainful references to professors of composition alternating between disparagement as stuffy academics on the one hand and resentful admiration stemming from implied self-doubt on the other. Ennis fumes upon learning that Lavinia, without his permission, has shown his compositions to an officer who had been Professor of Harmony at the Royal College of Music, sneering, "Coneybeare doesn't know the first thing about any kind of music after 1883", i.e. after the death of Wagner. Lavinia reports Coneybeare's low opinion of Ennis's talent: "he could see what you were getting at, but it was rather pathetic the way your effects just didn't come off. He said it's nothing to do with knowledge or experience. It's just something you don't happen to be born with." When she points out that, unlike Ennis, Corporal Coneybeare has had his compositions broadcast, Ennis sputters impotently, "Influence . . . He knows the right people. It's a conspiracy, it's a –", then mutters, "His stuff's harmless stuff, the sort of stuff you'd expect from a professor of Harmony. It's dead, correct and dead. Dead, dead, dead."[33] Burgess expresses the same combination of disdain and self-doubt in his *"Biographica Musicalis"*:

> There was a real lance-corporal professor of harmony and a private former Director of Music for the county of Kent. These academics had to be shunned; I was not of their world. I was self-taught, could not play a scale without fumbling, did not know the Köchel numbers, was ignorant of some of the later quartets of Beethoven. I was a faker, a patcher, something of a showman... I composed, but I did not let the professor of harmony see my compositions. He would point out elementary errors, the kind of thing a student of the Royal College of Music had pandybatted out of him in his first term... When the academics had been posted away from the Rock I felt freer and was more assertive.[34]

The novel's dramatic climax concerns an aborted performance combining music and dance that was to have comprised "a comedy overture that had, in fact, been suggested by *The Importance of Being Earnest* – witty, but short and easy, full of open-string work; his 'cello sonata...; a group of Spanish songs, mostly Lorca, which Merita, the café singer, already knew well; a suite of strings; a piano sonata he could play himself; the newly finished *Passacaglia*."[35] In addition to these works, compositions by Ennis cited in the novel include *"La niña del bello rostro"*, a minuet in E minor for guitar, a wedding or "funeral-wedding" march for organ, a fugato, a short piece for flute and strings, and a string quartet. Given the similarity between Ennis and his author, one can reasonably assume that Burgess actually composed these or comparable works while stationed in Gibraltar.

As Aeneas had founded the city of Rome, Ennis "was building a city of sound, a universe of ultimate meaning," deriving ecstatic pleasure from a rehearsal of his *Passacaglia*:

> As, bound by the strong eight-bar theme, the variations – romantic, malicious or martial – were spun in brief life on the warm night air, tears came to Ennis's eyes. "My God," he thought, "this will show them. I'm bigger than the lot of them, blast their eyes. I'm bigger than the Rock, I'm bigger than Muir, this is the only power I want." Now, after a welter of dissonance, the theme was twisted, underwent an agony of mutation, and then came the final threnody – the plaintive citrous oboe theme, the quiet divided bass chords, the fading to silence – *niente*, the end.[36]

Thrilled by the enterprise, Ennis devotes every available moment to it, neglecting his military duties while hubristically gloating over his superior officer until, shortly before the concert is to start, Major Muir crushes Ennis by preventing it from taking place.

Although Burgess's memoirs never mention an actual orchestral concert like the one planned by Ennis, a letter from Norman Parker, written to Burgess shortly after publication of *Little Wilson and Big God* in 1987, does:

> Your main interest was in the field of music and I remember you composed a symphony. I went along to listen to its première, which was held in the Engineers' Hall. It was played by a scratch orchestra made up of the soldiers,

sailors and airmen on the Rock ... I could not understand it, it simply seemed to me a cacophony of discords, but it didn't seem to bother you, although I felt so sorry for you when the reception was very mixed, very low-key in fact.[37]

Taking the chronology in the novel literally, this performance would have occurred around 14 September 1945. Given Parker's detailed recollection of the concert, and its dramatic importance in *A Vision of Battlements*, it is strange that Burgess omits it from his autobiography unless his memory of it was so troubling that he could only refer to it obliquely, within a fictional context.

Toward the end of Burgess's service in Gibraltar, one of the Royal Engineers constructed a record player of superlative power. Using it for one of his weekly YMCA gramophone concerts, Burgess amplified Beethoven's Ninth Symphony to such a thunderous level that "eardrums were shattered ... Part of the Rock came down." It was a way to end his tour of duty "if not gloriously, then loudly."[38] As he sailed away in May 1946 on the ship that would bring him back to England, Burgess recalled the profoundly calm sonorities of Debussy's sunken cathedral as he watched Gibraltar slowly fade into the sea: "The Rock sank, englutted to the fading of slow chords, raising not a bubble."[39]

Notes

1 LW, 259.
2 TMM, 27.
3 LW, 246.
4 Ibid., 255.
5 The surnames are taken from a program of a 1941 performance by the Jaypees. In LW (257–8) and TMM (28–9), Burgess refers to N. Clafton as Bill Clufton and to Babs Evelyn as Babs Farrell. "There was snarling for the body of Babs, but she kept that to herself." TMM, 30.
6 Richard Nutting, letter to author, 2 September 2002.
7 TMM, 30. The CC catalog of works lists "Sinfonietta (jazz combo)" for the year 1941; it is possible that this is the same work as his "pseudo-symphonic" version of "The Darktown Strutters' Ball".
8 LW, 259. "Number 100", part of a coded vocabulary used by the bandsmen, stood for a telephone, and thus, by extension, to "An Afternoon on the Phone".
9 Nutting, letter to author.
10 LW, 264–5.
11 Ibid., 273–4.
12 Ibid., 279–80. Burgess states that the wedding took place on the last Sunday of Advent, i.e. 20 December 1942. They married a third time – a full-scale affair in Wales for the benefit of Lynne's family – in the summer of 1943.
13 Ibid., 289.
14 Ibid., 291.
15 Ibid., 295–6.

16 Ibid., 295. In LW, Parker is misidentified as Albert instead of Norman, and Stevens is misspelled as Stephens. See Norman Parker's letter to Burgess, published in Lewis, 130–8.
17 LW, 307.
18 Ibid., 328.
19 TMM, 32.
20 LW, 326–7.
21 Ibid., 330–1.
22 Ibid., 301. Burgess's published accounts of the incident vary. For one alternative, see Chapter 9. See also RLAB, 108.
23 Burgess describes the condition as dysmenorrhoea, a term used for painful or difficult menstruation, but technically not for perpetual bleeding.
24 LW, 297. Norman Parker regards Burgess's judgment of Meldrum as unfair, "bordering on the scurrilous", insisting that Meldrum, as a captain, did not possess the authority to grant the leave. "No matter what Meldrum would have done or said, it would have been wrong in your eyes, for the simple reason that he was unable to send you home on leave, and I think you were assuming that he had powers he did not possess." Parker considered Burgess unduly harsh on Crump ("a loner, suffering from 'Rockitis' "), regarding him more with pity than anger. Lewis, 130.
25 LW, 302.
26 See Example 27.07.
27 LW, 323. The reference is to the comic character Ko-Ko, the "cheap tailor" and Lord High Executioner of Titipu who is engaged to Yum-Yum, his beautiful young ward, but has been condemned to death by the Mikado for flirting. Upon hearing of Ko-Ko's death sentence, Nanki-Poo, the Mikado's son and Yum-Yum's true love, returns to Titipu to woo her. In Act II, at the conclusion of the Madrigal quartet, Ko-Ko enters to discover Nanki-Poo embracing Yum-Yum, at which point he forces himself to become accustomed to the lovers' physical affection for each other:

> KO-KO. Go on – don't mind me. / NANKI-POO. I'm afraid we're distressing you. / KO-KO. Never mind, I must get used to it. Only please do it by degrees. Begin by putting your arm round her waist. (NANKI-POO does so.) There; let me get used to that first. / YUM-YUM. Oh, wouldn't you like to retire? It must pain you to see us so affectionate together! / KO-KO. No, I must learn to bear it! (*Martyn Green's Treasury of Gilbert & Sullivan*, 430)

28 The poem, "Useless to hope to hold off / The unavoidable happening," appears in LW, 321.
29 In *A Vision of Battlements* (140), Sergeant Ennis examines the first four of these titles in a Gibraltar bookshop.
30 RLAB, 101. Heinemann received and rejected the manuscript in 1952. In his introduction to the novel, Burgess states that he wrote it around Easter 1949, then contradicts himself in LW (362) by asserting that he wrote the novel during the winter of 1953, which is self-evidently erroneous.
31 Thomas Stumpf's observation that R. Ennis backwards spells "sinner" led Burgess to wonder if this choice of name was a message from his subconscious. YH, 206.
32 See *Revolutionary Sonnets*, 12; RLAB, 73n. An altered version of "Girl" appears in *Inside Mr Enderby*, 38.

33 VB, 174–5.
34 TMM, 32–3.
35 VB, 106.
36 Ibid., 109–10.
37 Lewis, 137–8.
38 LW, 329.
39 VB, 241: the final line of the novel. The line recurs, slightly varied, in LW, 330.

5

PEACE: BRINSFORD LODGE, BAMBER BRIDGE, AND BANBURY (1946–54)

> *The writing of a three-hundred-page musical work is more laborious than the merely literary person is able to appreciate . . . A desire to avoid the labour to an end unrealisable in performance led me eventually to prose composition, which I have always seen as an analogue to symphonic writing.*[1]

Upon returning to England after his army discharge in 1946, Burgess discovered that Lynne's infidelities had become even more tortuous than they had been during his furlough late in the previous year. Not only was she still involved with Major Herbert Williams, but in the intervening months she had taken up with Williams's brother Eddie, the well-to-do manager of a large bank in Calcutta. Burgess found himself relegated to the sidelines as the Williams brothers quarreled over his wife. Herbert, "perhaps to ease his own conscience," helped secure Burgess an appointment as an instructor at an army training institute near Birmingham. He also arranged a job for Lynne on the staff of a new educational magazine. After Eddie Williams returned to India and his post at Grindlays Bank, Lynne determined that it would be "less trouble to be a more or less faithful wife to me than to be a shuttlecock between the Williams brothers", so Burgess and his spouse gamely elected to uphold their marriage as he reentered civilian society.[2]

Burgess's first job after his discharge from the army was as a teacher at the Mid-West School of Education at Brinsford Lodge, located near Coven and Wolverhampton just northwest of Birmingham. Here future sergeants in the Army Educational Corps took two-week courses in Politics, International Affairs, European History, Musical Appreciation, and Drama. Burgess and his fellow instructors taught whichever courses they were assigned by the head of the school. "There was the assumption of the ignorant that the educated were educated in everything: back to the army again."[3] Although no longer in the service, Burgess was surrounded by men and women in uniform and generally saw Lynne, who remained in London, only on weekends. During the icy months of early 1947, he fell in love with a member of the Auxiliary Territorial Service, the organization for women serving in the British army that later became the Women's Royal Army

Corps. Burgess would later write that he "should have married this girl", a Jewish sergeant from London with whom he carried on an "erotically mad" affair throughout most of the year, but, "clinging to Catholic scruples" that ruled out divorce, he passively let the relationship come to an end.[4]

In his autobiographical writings, Burgess cites no musical activity at Brinsford Lodge apart from an unfinished *Sanctus* (LW, 343), presumably from the abandoned Mass in G listed in *This Man and Music*. The other works from 1946–47 listed in TMM are an abandoned Sinfonietta, *Spring Songs* for soprano and orchestra, "I sing of a maiden" for voice and string quartet, a group of stage songs titled "This was real", "These things shall be" (a celebration for Bedwellty Grammar School), a setting of Hopkins's "Inversnaid" for SATB unaccompanied, and *Three Shakespeare Songs* for voice and piano. Although all of these manuscripts are lost, later extant works bear evident similarities to some of these missing works. The choral work *Spring Rondel* shares two texts with the missing *Spring Songs* of 1946, while an undated holograph of *Three Shakespeare Songs*, probably written in the 1980s, comprises settings of the same three texts ("Apemantus's Song", "Under the Greenwood Tree", and "Come thou monarch of the vine") as the lost Shakespeare songs of 1947.

In 1948 Burgess accepted a new post at the Emergency Teacher Training College in Bamber Bridge, where he and Lynne set up home together for the first time in their six years of marriage. To accommodate the large classes expected to result from a postwar baby boom, this Lancaster school located near Preston had been established principally to train former servicemen to become primary school teachers. As Lecturer in Speech and Drama, Burgess taught courses in speech, drama production, and the history of European drama, supplementing his meager teacher's salary by playing the piano at a local pub on weekends. He directed stagings of *Doctor Faustus, Sweeney Agonistes, Hamlet,* and his own adaptation of Nigel Balchin's 1947 novel *Lord, I Was Afraid*, sometimes composing incidental music as well. "1948–49 had been, musically, a busy time for me," according to the introduction to *A Vision of Battlements*. "I had written various things for use – a piano sonata and a piano sonatina, a little concerto for piano duet and percussion, some realizations of Purcell songs, a polytonal suite for recorders, orchestral incidental music for *Murder in the Cathedral, The Ascent of F6,* and *The Adding Machine*."[5] Seeking advanced training, he applied for admission to the composition program at the Royal College of Music and the drama program at the Royal Academy of Music, but failed both entrance exams, "less through incompetence", he claimed, "than through truculence."[6] In the music examination, Herbert Howells faulted him for not recognizing a Neapolitan sixth chord. In the drama assessment, Burgess lost his temper, and thus his chance for admission, in a bungled attempt to direct a group of unruly actresses.

In 1950 he became the new English master at Banbury Grammar School, where he taught phonetics and English for the next three years. Inspired by

The Waste Land and Eliot's penchant for musical titles like "Five-finger exercises" and "Preludes", Burgess and his Sixth Form students responded to the development of the hydrogen bomb by writing a poem they called *Sonata in H,* punning on that letter's meaning as both the chemical symbol for hydrogen and German term for the note B♮.[7] In the nearby village of Adderbury, Anthony and Lynne resided in a cottage they called "Little Gidding" after the last of Eliot's *Four Quartets.*

The musical abilities of the Banbury faculty and their families engendered a series of compositions designed to showcase their particular talents. For Valerie Tryon, daughter of the German and French teacher, Burgess composed a piano sonata and bagatelle; for Alfred Batts, the music master and organist-choirmaster of St Mary's, the parish church, he wrote several organ pieces; and for the local string orchestra, founded by the school's headmaster Douglas Rose, he composed a *Partita* for strings that was performed in Banbury's Town Hall.[8] Prompted by the presence of two skilled flutists, druggist Maurice Draper and English master Kenneth Carrdus, Burgess composed Carol Settings for Flute and Strings in 1950.

As in Bamber Bridge, Burgess was active in dramatics, producing and directing plays at Banbury Grammar School and for the Adderbury Drama Group, a community theatre company that he founded. Productions included *A Midsummer Night's Dream* (December 1950) and *Sweeney Agonistes* (summer 1951), both featuring Burgess's music, and *Juno and the Paycock* (March 1952), which he directed. The music for *Sweeney Agonistes* probably drew upon the "Songs for voices and piano from T. S. Eliot's *Sweeney Agonistes*" listed in *This Man and Music* for 1935.

Imitating Defoe, Burgess kept a diary in Adderbury titled "Journal of the Plague Year (1951)".[9] The entry dated 2 January lists Piano Sonata in G, Piano Sonatina in D, Music to *The Adding Machine*, Music to *A Midsummer Night's Dream*, *Partita de Noël* for String Orchestra, and String and Flute Carol Settings as "Music written by me in 1950". Three unfinished works – Piano Quintet, Orchestral Overture, and "Zodiac" Variations – are also named. The unsuccessful attempt to compose a symphony mentioned in his autobiography (LW, 357) may refer to the "Zodiac" Variations or the abandoned Sinfonietta listed (perhaps erroneously) under 1946 in TMM.

Of the more than twenty works that Burgess composed between 1948 and 1953, all are lost except two short piano pieces from the Banbury years, Sonatina in G Major and *Wiegenlied*, the only extant manuscripts signed "John Burgess Wilson". Sonatina in G Major is a short, two-movement piano piece, dated "Christmas, 1952", written for Anne Field, a Banbury Grammar School student. The opening Allegretto movement (Example 05.01) offers a fine example of Burgess's early style, combining lyricism and traditional harmonic practice with the modernist's avoidance of predictability. The curious alternation of G♯ and D major chords in bars 14–18 recalls a similar alternation of chords with roots a tritone apart (C and F♯) in "Saturn" from *The Planets*. The perfect authentic cadence in bars 21–2,

Example 05.01 Sonatina in G Major, I. Allegretto (bs. 1–22)

replete with 4–3 suspension, is Burgess's way of tidily wrapping up in traditional fashion a passage that – through the use of irregular phrase lengths, unusual harmonic progressions, and an atypical approach to modulation – is less ordinary than its apparent simplicity suggests.

Wiegenlied, inscribed "Leicester, August 30th, 1952" and dedicated to "C. Looker", is a lullaby for Burgess's niece Ceridwen, who was born in March 1952 to Lynne's sister Hazel and her husband William Looker. Sharing the same meter (6/8) and key (E minor), and with analogous use of sicilienne rhythm, Dorian inflection, and the *tierce de Picardie*, *Wiegenlied* (Example 05.02) is evidently modeled upon the "Slow Dance" (Example 05.03) from Vaughan Williams's Suite of Six Short Pieces for Piano (1920), the main difference being the imaginative use of seventh chords and cross relations that add a pleasing spiciness to the cradlesong's harmonies.

Burgess's berceuse ends with a shocking postscript from Rimbaud's *"Le coeur supplicié"* ("The Tortured Heart") that reads, *"Ithyphalliques et pioupiesques, / Leurs insultes l'ont dépravé"* (Standing phallic and soldier-like, / Their insults have depraved him).[10] What could Burgess have meant by appending this couplet, from a poem generally interpreted as Rimbaud's response to having been raped by drunken Communard soldiers during the 1871 Paris Commune, to a lullaby dedicated to a five-month-old baby girl? Perhaps it was a cryptic gibe directed at Hazel, whom Burgess regarded

Peace: Brinsford Lodge, Bamber Bridge, and Banbury

Example 05.02 *Wiegenlied* (bs. 1–12)

Example 05.03 II. Slow Dance (bs. 1–9) from Suite of Six Short Pieces for Piano by Ralph Vaughan Williams

disdainfully as a prosaic, prudish woman who "had maintained her virginity for a time after marriage" and whimpered to her mother about "her husband's lawful but brutish advances".[11]

Whether or not Hazel appreciated Burgess's music, her sister certainly did not. Lynne's unmusicality and intolerance of his music is a recurring leitmotif in Burgess's memoirs. From the beginning of their relationship, she adamantly opposed his composing, refusing to let him "work at string quartets or piano sonatas, since music meant nothing to her."[12] Even while at Manchester University, sudden coughing eruptions habitually kept Lynne from hearing any of Burgess's music "beyond the first few measures."[13] In later years, she experienced similar fits whenever his music was played in public.

While living in Banbury, Burgess submitted his *Passacaglia for Orchestra* to the BBC. When the score was turned down, Lynne seized upon the rejection as a chance to force her husband to give up music once and for all.[14] Declaring that a long-term decision had to be made, she issued an ultimatum. Burgess would make one final attempt to write a great musical opus. If it succeeded, then he could continue as a composer, but if it did not, he would give up composing and write books instead. He accepted the challenge, determining that it demanded the composition of an opera for which he would write his own libretto. Desiring a story that would mix myth and comedy, Burgess recalled a tale by Florilegus, recounted in *The Anatomy of Melancholy*, about a young Roman gentleman about to be married who, after placing his wedding ring on the finger of a statue of Venus in his father's garden, marries the goddess instead. In Burgess's version, set in the English countryside, Ambrose is the decent young man about to marry his sweetheart Diana. He rehearses placing the ring on his bride's finger by practicing on the finger of a statue of Venus in his prospective father-in-law's garden. The statue comes to life, curls her finger around the ring, and demands a night of love with the frightened bridegroom, but subsequently she lets him go and generously blesses the wedding.

Burgess titled his opera *The Eve of Saint Venus* after the Loeb edition of the English translation of *Pervigilium Veneris* ("Pervigil of Saint Venus"), an anonymous second- or third-century Latin poem, notable for its lighthearted tone and unusual poetic meter, which describes a three-day celebration of the spring festival in honor of the Roman goddess of love and beauty.[15] He planned a cast spanning the vocal ranges: Sir Benjamin Drayton, bass; Jack Crowther-Mason, baritone; Ambrose Rutterkin, tenor; Lady Drayton, contralto; Julia Webb, coloratura; and Diana Drayton, soprano. No matter that Kurt Weill and Ogden Nash had already turned the story into *One Touch of Venus,* starring Mary Martin as the goddess.[16] Burgess, who professed to have been unaware of Weill's 1943 Broadway musical at the time, planned a more serious version of the tale, blending the comedic element with a sober storyline about exorcism and a Church of England vicar whose tussle with Roman Catholicism ritual leads him to renounce his faith through the symbolic act of tearing off his clerical collar.

In view of his life's future path, Burgess's response to his wife's challenge is revealing. He became utterly engrossed in the text, overwriting it so extravagantly that it became completely unsuitable for use as an opera libretto. Set to music, "it would have been responsible," he claimed, "for the longest three-act opera ever written."[17] After setting a few pages of his text to music, Burgess abandoned the opera, and, true to his word, focused on writing instead. He converted the libretto into a novella that remained unpublished for over a decade until Sidgwick and Jackson printed the first edition, illustrated by Edward Pagram, in 1964.[18]

Vestiges of the abandoned opera are discernable in the novella. The most prominent is the magical climactic scene in which the six main characters declaim stanzas from *Pervigilium Veneris* one after another, beginning with the Vicar who recites the first verse, which opens with the line, "Tomorrow will be love for the loveless, and for the lover love," the English translation of the novella's epigraph, "*Cras amet qui nunquam amavit quique amavit cras amet*". As Venus rises, people dance in the streets, long-married couples babble with newfound enthusiasm, cats wail in melodious counterpoint, and all of the animals in the zoo, from the tortoise to the panther, frolic in "amorous pandemonium".[19] Speech changes from prose into verse as strange and wonderful Debussyan sounds are heard: "a wilder music than the four-square dirges of Ancient and Modern, a faun-like music, full of flutes and unsubmissive to textbook harmony, full of the dreadful primal innocence."[20] Brimming with musical promise, this innately operatic scene surely would have been a highpoint of the opera that Burgess had hoped but failed to compose.

Defeated, Burgess acceded to his wife's demand: "In 1953 I deafened myself to the vocal and orchestral possibilities latent in Florilegus and, accepting Lynne's ultimatum, gave up music."[21] Although this situation would not last forever, it brought about one crucial and permanent change in Burgess's attitude toward composing. From then on, he ceased to regard composition as a means of making a living. Instead he began to pursue writing as a profession, but soon recognized a psychological need to keep composing music whether it made any money or not, or, indeed, even if no one were to listen to it:

> One thing I discovered when I had completed my third novel was that it was a temperamental necessity for me to cleanse my mind of verbal preoccupation by composing music. It no longer mattered whether the music would ever be heard: music was a kind of therapy.[22]

He found the physical act of writing down notes "a manual and visual relief from the long days at the typewriter." The "pure form" of music provided relief from the "struggle with words, their syntax and rhythms and referents". Although Burgess went on to write a great deal of music, none of it bore any significant effect on his finances. Most of his compositions were written without monetary compensation. When he was paid, the amounts were negligible compared to the fees and royalties he received for writing. As he would later explain, he composed for the pleasure it gave him: " I am writing to please myself. This often turns out to be the best way of pleasing others."

Spring Rondel, a well crafted, four-minute composition for SATB chorus and piano on the theme of winter passing into spring, illustrates the recurring pattern in Burgess's career of related literary and musical creations springing from the same fount of inspiration. *Pervigilium Veneri*s, the basis of *The Eve of Saint Venus*, is set to music in *Spring Rondel*. "*Quando ver venit meum? / Quando fiam uti chelidon ut tacere desinam?*" (transcribed by Burgess as "When will my spring come? / When shall I be like a swallow and cease to be silent?"), the choral work's central text, is declaimed in the novella by the lesbian journalist Julia Webb just after the other characters have finished reciting their stanzas from *Pervigilium Veneris*. Bitterly, she asks the assemblage when her moment of love shall arrive. "I got those lines," she explains to the silenced sextet, "from the notes to Mr Eliot's *The Waste Land*", which is where Burgess may have discovered them.[23]

The outer texts of *Spring Rondel* are the ones shared with the 1946 *Spring Songs*: "O western wind", an anonymous medieval English song with a celebrated history as the cantus firmus of masses by Taverner, Tye, and Sheppard; and "The earth has cast her winter skin," Burgess's translation (at age sixteen) of "*Le temps a laissé son manteau*", a fifteenth-century rondel by Charles d'Orléans.[24] In the first section (Adagio) of *Spring Rondel*, "O western wind" is sung by the men and "*Quando ver venit meum*" by the women, each text to its own musical theme. The choral writing is primarily in two-part texture, homophonic at first, then increasingly contrapuntal as the men reenter with a variant of their "O western wind" theme after the women have sung. The second section (Vivo) is a lively setting of the rondel, its cheerful character contrasting with the muted dynamics and mood of the Adagio. Paired men's and women's voices sing simultaneously in different meters – men in 2/4 and women in 6/8, then vice versa, switching back and forth several times. Imitative counterpoint is used to good effect at the beginning of the second quatrain, with vivid text painting on such phrases as "The floods vast, the streams thin" and "the wild and waking din". Just as the chorus is about to conclude the rondel's final line, the music breaks off abruptly at the word "winter" whereupon the tempo suddenly switches back to adagio and two solo tenors softly intone the line, "O western wind, when wilt thou blow?" As they sustain their final note, the rest of the singers burst in with "skin", their *ff* outburst completing the line in a boisterous manner practically guaranteed to prompt laughter from the audience (Example 05.04).

During his term as Writer-in-Residence at the University of North Carolina in 1970, Burgess was asked, for a newspaper article about the release of

Peace: Brinsford Lodge, Bamber Bridge, and Banbury

Example 05.04 Spring Rondel (bs. 88–98)

the first US edition of *The Eve of Saint Venus*, whether he had originally conceived the novel as a play. He replied,

> No, not a play first, actually, but an opera libretto. It was done originally for BBC with Gian-Carlo Menotti in mind as the composer, and then Edmund Crispin was to be involved in the project. But nothing came of it. A disappointment, of course, but now I think I'll do the music myself.[25]

It is striking that Burgess named two successful writer-composers as possible collaborators, yet highly doubtful that he ever would have considered not writing the music himself.

Sometime after moving to Monaco in 1975, Burgess revisited the idea of writing an opera based on *The Eve of Saint Venus*, but, after composing a few dozen pages, he abandoned the project. The undated 27-page vocal score to Act One breaks off just after the entrance of Jack Crowther-Mason, corresponding to page 7 in the Hesperus edition of the novella. The music, somewhat similar in style to Britten's operas, quotes Burgess's Third Symphony (the Trio theme from the second movement) shortly before he stopped composing, indicating, perhaps, that fresh ideas were not forthcoming.

It was in Banbury that Burgess completed *A Vision of Battlements*, partly in fulfillment of his vow to Lynne, but also to satisfy his creative need to conjoin literature and music:

> I had already foreseen, from my work on the impossible opera libretto, that writing a novel would be easier labour than composing a symphony. In a symphony many strands conjoined, in the same instant, to make a statement; in a novel all you had was a single line of monody. The ease with which dialogue could be written seemed grossly unfair. This was not art as I had known it. It seemed cheating not to be able to give the reader chords and counterpoint. It was like pretending that there could be such a thing as a concerto for unaccompanied flute. My notion of giving the reader his money's worth was to throw difficult words and neologisms at him, to make the syntax involuted. Anything, in fact, to give the impression of a musicalisation of prose.[26]

He submitted the manuscript to Heinemann largely because that firm published Graham Greene, whose writing he greatly admired at the time. It was rejected, according to Burgess, for having "too much the quality of a second novel."[27] Publisher Roland Gant of Heinemann suggested that he "go home and write a genuine first novel". Burgess agreed and went straight to work.

Having constructed one novel out of an opera libretto and another out of autobiography melded with a mythic substructure, Burgess was ready to mix all of these ingredients together in his third book, *The Worm and the Ring*, a clever satire on Wagner's *Der Ring des Nibelungen* applied to a fictionalized version of Banbury Grammar School. "The hierarchy of gods, heroes and dwarfs found a parallel in a grammar school. The gods had their specialisations, just like teachers. If Loge was the god of fire, Lodge could be the name of a chemistry master. A Miss Fry could be a sort of Freia, her golden apples her pert little breasts thrusting at her gold-weave jumper . . . The possibilities were interesting."[28] Wotan becomes Woolton the headmaster, his wife Frederica, Fricka. Froh translates as Gay, the physical training master. Richard Ennis, the protagonist of *A Vision of Battlements*, turns up in *The Worm and the Ring* as the school's music master, representing Donner. Gardner, the villainous French teacher and deputy headmaster, stands for Fafner, the giant who becomes a dragon. The first four letters of Gardner's name spell out the connection backwards, with the name of his favorite bar, the Dragon, extending the symbolism still further.

Alberich becomes a malicious student named Albert Rich, with a pal called Mimms. The Rheinmaidens are three fourth-form girls – Linda, Thelma and Flossie – whose names share obvious phonetic similarities with their Wagnerian counterparts Woglinde, Wellgunde, and Flosshilde. When this giggling trio taunts Albert and rejects his advances so scornfully that he loses all sexual interest in them, he manages to grab hold of a book from Linda's schoolbag, a diary, he soon realizes, containing vivid descriptions of sexual encounters between her and the headmaster. By her frenzied reaction ("Please, please, anything! I'll go out with you, anything!"), Albert realizes that he possesses a thing of great value. For this ugly dwarfish boy, the diary is as good as gold.

George Bernard Shaw devotes a chapter of *The Perfect Wagnerite*, his guide to the *Ring*, to an essay on "Siegfried as Protestant"; Burgess, taking the opposed position, presents Christopher Howarth, the Siegfried character, as a lapsed Catholic, like himself, unable to fully cut his ties to the Church of Rome.[29] Howarth, the school's German specialist, finds his Brünnhilde in Hilda Connor, the mathematics teacher. As fellow members of the school's faculty, they are like siblings protected by their benevolent headmaster Woolton. Christopher and Hilda acknowledge their attraction to each other, but resist the urge to act upon it until fatefully thrown together by Woolton when he orders Hilda to join Howarth on a school trip to Paris.

Howarth's wife Veronica is far more like Lynne than Gutrune, the Gibichung woman whom the spellbound Siegfried marries at the end of Act II of *Götterdämmerung* after having pledged himself to Brünnhilde. Like Lynne, Veronica suffers from dysmenorrhoea, avoids marital sex, and lavishes attention on her adored Siamese cat. The Howarths' son Peter was conceived as a fictional counterpart of the Burgess's unborn child: "They have a son who may be regarded as the imaginary fulfilment of Lynne's own thwarted pregnancy."[30]

Unlike Siegfried, Howarth prevails and prospers. Each member of his family survives a trial – Veronica, a hysterectomy; Peter, a near-fatal impalement; Howarth, guilt for his sins as an adulterer and neglectful parent. With a revitalized marriage and thriving son, Howarth leaves the wretched school behind and relocates in Italy, where a potentially lucrative new position awaits him. Prophetically, *The Worm and the Ring* foreshadowed its author's move to the Mediterranean, where he relocated with a new wife and son fifteen years later.

Like Wotan, Woolton dolefully endures the decline of the society that he has constructed and governed. Before submitting his resignation to the Governors of the School, Woolton rails at them for their lack of interest in the arts, mouthing sentiments that must echo the frustrations Burgess endured in Banbury:

You never appear at local concerts, you never assist at production of plays above the intellectual level of *Charley's Aunt*, some of you actively opposed the establishment of a repertory theatre in the town, your Watch Committee banned a film of Jean Cocteau because it was French, your Library Committee proscribed several monuments of European literature because they were insufficiently mealy-mouthed about certain natural functions... Need I go on?[31]

Soon his luck changes and Woolton learns that he is to receive a large inheritance, whereupon he contentedly hums the Freemason hymn *Integer vitae, scelerisque purus* (blameless in one's life) to the tune of *Adeste fideles*:

Despite its operatic underpinnings, the novel contains relatively few musical references aside from a few citations of Stravinsky and Elgar, and Woolton's allusion to Siegmund's aria *"Winterstürme"* from *Die Walkyre* ("And winter is near its end. There is a faint doggy smell of the hounds of spring...", 25). The only other specific reference to Wagnerian opera occurs when Hilda and Christopher meet for the last time, just before both depart for the Mediterranean, she bound for Gibraltar and he for Italy. Recalling their earlier erotic adventures, Hilda proposes one last fling before they part ways.

"Shall we," she said, "meet again before you go? As we used to?" She smiled up at him, with a sort of craning eagerness. He thought of Kundry and Amfortas.[32]

As in *A Vision of Battlements*, many of the characters are based upon actual persons. Several months after the novel's publication in mid-1961, Gwen Bustin, secretary of Banbury Grammar School and one-time Mayor of Banbury, sued Burgess and Heinemann for libel, claiming that the character of Alice Withers, the maliciously manipulative headmaster's secretary, was a slanderous caricature of herself. Heinemann settled out of court with Bustin, paying damages and agreeing to pulp all unsold copies. The few volumes that survived destruction are rare collectors' items that command premium prices in the used book market. Heinemann issued a revised edition of *The Worm and the Ring* in 1973 (dated 1970 on the title page). Although not as costly as the suppressed 1961 edition, these volumes also remain scarce.

While working in Banbury, Burgess repeatedly applied for college teaching positions. In January 1954, he was invited to an interview at the Colonial Office in London where he was informed that he had applied for a job in Malaya. Burgess insisted that he had applied for a position in Sark, but, upon being shown his neatly typed letter of application, concluded that he must have written and sent it off in a drunken stupor. He accepted the offer of a lectureship at the Malay College in Kuala Kangsar. In the summer of 1954, he and Lynne prepared to relocate by giving away their collie Suky to a local farming family. British P&O ships would not transport pets but Dutch ones would, so, accompanied by Lynne's beloved Siamese cat Lalage, they traveled on the *Willem Ruys*, a ship registered in Holland, and in late August 1954 arrived in Persekutan Tanah Melayu, the Federation of Malaya.

Notes

1 LW, 159.
2 Ibid., 335, 341.
3 Ibid., 342.
4 Ibid., 333, 343–4.
5 VB, 7.
6 LW, 350.
7 Ibid., 355.
8 RLAB, 180; see LW, 354; "Local Man's Music Played", *Banbury Guardian*, 22 March 1951: "An interesting item played by the Banbury String Players at their orchestral concert at the Town Hall on Wednesday was the work of local composer, Mr John Burgess Wilson, of Adderbury ... entitled 'Three Movements from Partita'."
9 He later wrote the introduction to the 1966 Penguin edition of Defoe's book.
10 Translation by Holly Tannen, assisted by Lydia Rand. The poem exists in three slightly different versions, called sequentially "*Le coeur supplicié*" ("The Tortured Heart"), "*Le coeur volé*" ("The Stolen Heart"), and "*Coeur de pitre*" ("Heart of a Clown"). Arthur Rimbaud wrote it in or prior to May 1871, when he sent it to his teacher George Izambard. Lee Hoiby composed a song setting of "*Le coeur volé*" as one of his *Trois Poèmes de Rimbaud*. Burgess uses the word "ithyphallus", meaning an erect phallus, in *The Clockwork Testament* (394): "He noted also with rueful pride that ... he was bearing before him ... a sizable horizontal ithyphallus lazily swinging towards the vertical." The adjectival form occurs near the end of *Byrne* (148): "An ithyphallic thrust is not a key".
11 LW, 207. Hazel Looker, a teacher, was the dedicatee of the original version of *The Worm and the Ring*.
12 Ibid., 213.
13 Ibid., 215.
14 Ibid., 355. This rejection is recounted in the final chapter of *A Vision of Battlements* (238): "He tore open the letter from the B.B.C. They thanked him for the score of the *Passacaglia*; they doubted if they could find a place for it in their programmes; it was being returned to him by surface mail."
15 It deviates from the long/short syllabification of Classical Latin poetry by relying instead upon the accents of a regular stress pattern.
16 The book of the musical was based on *The Tinted Venus*, F. J. Anstey's version of the story.

17 "Preface to the 1984 Edition", *The Eve of St Venus* (London: Hesperus/Modern Voices, 2006), vii.
18 The novella's chronology remains rather foggy. In the "Foreword to the American Edition" of *The Eve of Saint Venus*, Burgess states that he wrote it in 1950, yet in the "Preface to the 1984 Edition", he dates it from 1952.
19 *The Eve of Saint Venus* (Hesperus edition), 75.
20 Ibid., 76.
21 LW, 360.
22 TMM, 34–5.
23 T. S. Eliot, *The Complete Poems and Plays 1909–1950* (New York: Harcourt, Brace & World, 1971), 50. Eliot cites *Pervigilium Veneris* in his note to line 429, "*Quando fiam uti chelidon* – O swallow swallow", from *The Waste Land's* plaintive final stanza.
24 Saint-Saëns, Debussy, and van Dieren set this rondel in its original French text; Elgar and Warlock also set rondeaux by Charles d'Orléans, though not this one.
25 Bruce Cook, "Here's Mr. Burgess, Full of Swagger and Guilt", *National Observer*, 27 April 1970. LW, 360: "Bruce Montgomery, the film composer who wrote detective stories as Edmund Crispin, wanted to make an opera of it, but he was losing hope and energy."
26 LW, 362.
27 Ibid., 367.
28 Ibid., 368.
29 Burgess admired Shaw as a knowledgeable and prophetic writer about music. See "Shaw's Music" in *But Do Blondes Prefer Gentlemen?* (539–41) and a similar essay, "Shaw as Musician", in *One Man's Chorus* (176–9).
30 LW, 369. In an early unpublished version of the novel, Peter "falls on the spiked railings (like the Alec Mitchell of my youth) and dies in agony. The father's guilt is so extreme as to be near-comic." In the published version, Peter survives and flourishes.
31 *The Worm and the Ring*, 249–50.
32 Ibid., 261. In *Parsifal*, Kundry provides the tormented king Amfortas with a phial of balsam to salve his unhealing wound.

6

MALAYA (1954–57)

'Some day Malaya might be proud to have a major composer.'
'Oh, I see.' He giggled. 'I don't think that will happen.'[1]

The voyage to Asia began in style. Aboard the ocean liner *Willem Ruys*, dressed in a white tuxedo with Lynne in a backless evening gown, Burgess listened to the ship's small orchestra perform his composition *Middeloceann*, which he had composed according to his custom of writing music for all such maritime ensembles that he encountered.[2] He would add few additional pieces during his Asian sojourn, for this was not a time for music. Rather it was a chance to immerse himself in the exotic culture of Malaya, a federation of nine states at the southern end of the Malay Peninsula bordered by Thailand and Singapore, during the waning days of British colonialism. In the searing heat of the tropics, Burgess would become acquainted with the Islamic world, learn Malay and some Persian and Chinese, and become, for the first time, a published novelist.

In Malaya, Burgess was employed as an English teacher, first at Malay College in Kuala Kangsar in the state of Perak, then in Kelantan as head of the English Department at the Federal Training College in Kota Bharu. At the latter he wrote about the former, turning his experiences in Kuala Kangsar into *Time for a Tiger*, his first book in print. As an official of the Colonial Office, it was deemed inappropriate for John Burgess Wilson to publish fiction under his own name, so, at the suggestion of Roland Gant, he dropped his outer names, and, preceding the middle one with his confirmation name, became "Anthony Burgess", the pseudo-pseudonym by which he would be known during the second half of his seventy-six years.[3]

Time for a Tiger (1956) was followed by *The Enemy in the Blanket* (1958) and *Beds in the East* (1959), with all three novels published collectively as *The Malayan Trilogy* in the UK in 1964 and as *The Long Day Wanes* in the US the following year. Classical music is a presence throughout the trilogy – a symbol of the Western culture that British expatriates in Indonesia left behind. It represents the potential for future productive contact as well as the failure of then current communication between Western and Eastern cultures, especially in the important subplot involving

Robert Loo, an eighteen-year-old Chinese-Malayan composer whom the central character, Victor Crabbe, takes under his wing.

Samuel Coale regards the trilogy's form as "symphonic", with Loo's symphony mirroring the overall structure of *The Malayan Trilogy* in microcosm.[4]

> The first movement had seemed to suggest a programme, each instrument presenting in turn a national style – a gurgling Indian cantilena on the 'cello, a kampong tune on the viola, a pentatonic song on the second violin and some pure Western atonality on the first. And then a scherzo working all these out stridently, ending with no resolution. A slow movement suggesting a sort of tropical afternoon atmosphere. A brief finale, ironic variations on a somewhat vapid 'brotherhood of man' motif.[5]

Crabbe, a British teacher and education officer modeled on Burgess, assiduously promotes the young composer's career, partly owing to an excessively inflated opinion of Loo's talent and partly to assuage his guilt over the accidental death of another musician – his beloved but adulterous wife, a talented pianist who specialized in Shostakovich and other modernists. Loo displays admirable talent, composing a symphony and string quartet while dreaming of writing a violin concerto that will transcend both these somewhat derivative works, but Crabbe, his sense of proportion distorted by having lived too long in the tropics, vastly overestimates the youth's potential, irrationally considering him a genius comparable to Mozart, Beethoven, or Brahms. Expressing anachronistic idealism, Crabbe tries to convince Loo that the best composers have all been patriotic and that he should compose works that would be a source of pride or even political importance to his country, a viewpoint the young composer ridicules:

> 'Elgar is not one of the best composers,' said Robert Loo, with a boy's smug dogmatism. 'His music makes me feel sick.'
> 'But look what Sibelius has done for Finland,' said Crabbe. 'And de Falla for Spain. And Bartok and Kodaly . . .'
> 'The people of Malaya only want American jazz, and ronggeng music. I am not composing for Malaya. I am composing because I want to compose.'[6]

Crabbe's efforts to encourage Loo's compositional growth and career advancement fail on every level. An attempt to interest State Information Officer Nik Hassan in a performance of Loo's symphony on artistic grounds sparks only Hassan's political interest instead. The symphony could be played at the upcoming celebration of Malayan independence, the officer suggests, if Loo were to adopt a Malayan pseudonym and add a chorus singing patriotic Malay slogans.

> 'There's no singing. But,' said Crabbe, 'yes. Yes. It's an idea. A choral finale. Beethoven did it; why not Loo? It might sell the work to the public.'
> 'And if you could get the orchestra to stand up at intervals and shout "*Merdeka!*" Now that really would sell it.'[7]

Crabbe's failure recalls Richard Ennis's aborted concert in *A Vision of Battlements*, a connection underscored by the revelation that it was Ennis who first introduced Loo to Western art music. With inept mentors like Ennis and Crabbe, Loo's talent fizzles out as he abandons serious composition for kitsch. Renouncing his previous works as "immature", Loo destroys the scores, vowing to devote himself instead to writing shallow "music from the heart".[8]

Music serves as the catalyst for the trilogy's climax in a wildly improbable scene involving Crabbe and George Costard, the manager of a remote Malayan rubber plantation. Having trekked deep into the jungle to investigate a headmaster's murder, Crabbe meets Costard, the kind of condescending, upper-class British patrician whom he abhors. As Costard prates on about himself to the accompaniment of 78-rpm recordings, his Tamil serving boy obediently places these on the gramophone in random order, anticipating the "shuffle" mode of contemporary CD and MP3 players by more than a quarter century. Various popular classics are heard:

> And then the record changed, a piano pinking high a Poulenc-like theme. Crabbe heard absently, then listened incredulously. And Costard also was listening in a kind of stupid horrified wonder. 'No,' he said. 'No. That was lost. That was lost in Negri.' The piano slid in grotesque arpeggio to the bass register: a comic fugato, the left hand occasionally leaping up to pink a discord in the high treble ... The music tinkled on, a gay brief satire on Scarlatti or Galuppi.[9]

Through this event – the playing of a recording by Crabbe's deceased wife, of which but a single copy was pressed – each man is revealed to the other: Costard as the adulterer, Crabbe as the cuckolded husband. The plot device is audacious, yet Burgess claimed it was "the only part of the novel which is a direct transcription from life."[10]

In the 1955 composition *Kalau Tuan Mudek Ka-Ulu* (Five Malay Pantuns for soprano and native instruments), Burgess set to music the quatrain Crabbe utters at the end of *The Enemy in the Blanket*:

> *Kalau tuan mudek ka-hulu,* If you, my lover, go up the river,
> *Charikan saya bunga kemoja.* Pluck me a frangipani flower.
> *Kalau tuan mati dahulu,* If you, my lover, die before I do,
> *Nantikan saya di-pintu shurga.* Wait for me at the door of heaven.[11]

Like "Ode: celebration for the Malay College for boys' voices and piano" (1954), another of the few works that Burgess composed in Kuala Kangsar and Kota Bharu, the score of *Kalau Tuan Mudek Ka-Ulu* is lost. The "Suite for small orchestra of Indians, Chinese and Malays" (1956), another missing work, was presumably an attempt (like Victor Crabbe's ill-fated "bridge" party in *Beds in the East*) to span the cultural and racial divide in colonial Malaya. Years later, Burgess composed a Malay pantun for Cathy Berberian, whom he met in 1971 at the Third International James Joyce Symposium in Trieste.[12]

A diary entry, dated 14 December 1956 in one of Burgess's Malayan notebooks, provides the approximate completion date of what must have been his grandest composition from this period: "I completed a few weeks ago a 'Malayan Symphony' to celebrate Malayan independence next year. This I sent to the Federal Information Dept, but wonder what they'll do with it." Burgess's description of this work in the program note for his Third Symphony bears a conspicuous resemblance to the suggestion made by Nik Hassan in *Beds in the East* for a politically charged composition:

> The second [symphony] was composed in Malaya in 1957 and was intended to form part of the celebrations of Malayan independence. In the last movement, as an infinitely extensible coda, the timpanist rolled indefinitely on C and the crowd was encouraged to shout *"Merdeka!"* which means freedom, liberty, the yoke of the tyrannical white man has dropped from us, etc. The crowd could not be dissuaded from turning this shout into a free fight, so the timpanist stopped rolling and the whole orchestra went home in disgust. Thus, the symphony never really ended. It is still, in a kind of Platonic sense, waiting for its final chord.[13]

But in his autobiography, he asserts that no performance of this symphony ever took place! Recalling his prepseudonymous self:

> John Burgess Wilson . . . composed a farewell gift for the Federation of Malaya – *Sinfoni Melayu*, a three-movement symphony which tried to combine the musical elements of the country into a synthetic language which called on native drums and xylophones as well as the instruments of the full Western orchestra. The last movement ended with a noble processional theme, rather Elgarian, representing independence . . . The work was never to be played . . . Kuala Lumpur has American hotels whose electric supply fails and leaves guests suffocating in the elevators; it has Mercedes for the Chinese and Lambrettas for the Malays; it has *Dallas* and *Dynasty*. But it does not have a symphony orchestra.[14]

Deciding whether or not the performance and ensuing Malayan melee took place depends on which version of the story one believes. Although the second, soberer account is more likely to be true, as a storyteller Burgess knew that the first version makes for a more entertaining tale.

After three years in Malaya, Burgess and his wife returned to Europe in the summer of 1957. He was on terminal leave from August to Christmas, and, for the first time in his adult life, felt wealthy: "Malayan pay went far in Europe."[15] In London, Burgess first met Graham Greene, presenting him with a signed copy of *Time for a Tiger*. Anthony and Lynne stayed in the Leicester suburb of Eyestone to be near Lynne's widowed father and her sister Hazel's family. Burgess applied for teaching jobs in the UK, but was made to understand that he "could not relate to the youth that was being fed on rock 'n' roll and skiffle."[16] As it became increasingly apparent that he would have to seek another position abroad, Burgess turned once more to the British Council, which informed him about positions for a phonetics instructor at a college in Peshawar and an English Language specialist at a college in Brunei. Feeling better suited for the latter, which would require him to teach courses in Malayan phonetics and the history of the British Empire, Burgess, now forty, applied and was accepted, and in early 1958, embarked with Lynne on the long sea journey back to the East Indies.

Notes

1 *Beds in the East*, 435.
2 LW, 371.
3 YH, 111. By mid-1957, "The pseudonym Anthony Burgess was taking on a certain solidity", wrote Burgess in LW (416), although when interviewed by Samuel Coale in 1978 (unabridged transcript, 10), he had expressed a different attitude regarding his *nom de plume*: "I mean they are genuine names I answer to – they're not pseudonyms, just part of the social name."
4 Samuel Coale, *Anthony Burgess* (New York: Frederick Ungar, 1981), 29.
5 BE, 431.
6 Ibid., 435.
7 Ibid., 457.
8 Ibid., 614–15.
9 Ibid., 590.
10 Letter to Mr. M. T. Wignesan, Monaco, 31 October 1976. See Chapter 33.
11 EB, 403. A pantun or pantoum is a Malay verse form consisting of an indefinite number of quatrains with the second and fourth lines of each quatrain repeated as the first and third lines of the following one.
12 "I had written a setting of a Malay *pantun* for her, with alto flute and xylophone accompaniment." YH, 235.
13 "Symphony in C", program note for the University Symphony Orchestra concert at the University of Iowa on 22 October 1975.
14 LW, 416. There is also a dismissive reference to the work in Burgess, "How I Wrote My Third Symphony", *The New York Times*, 28 December 1975, Sect. 2, 1: "The second had been called 'Sinfoni Merdeka' and had been intended as a celebration of Malaya's independence in 1957, and the less said about that the better."
15 LW, 417.
16 Ibid., 419. Skiffle was an English phenomenon of the 1950s: a style of popular music deriving from hillbilly music and rock 'n' roll, played on a heterogeneous group of instruments such as guitar, washboard, ceramic jug, washtub, and kazoo.

7

BRUNEI (1958–59)

In the distance a skull xylophone began to play, over and over, a scale of six notes – D, C sharp, B flat, A, G, E – over and over and over. He thought of the mad scene of Lucia di Lammermoor.[1]

In January 1958, Anthony and Lynne set off for Brunei aboard a British P&O ocean liner; having given away their Siamese cat Lalage to visitors from Bangkok who promised to return the feline to its ancestral homeland, they did not have to book passage on a Dutch vessel for their return to Indonesia. At sea Burgess worked on *Beds in the East* and composed a piece – evidently the lost 1958 composition listed in TMM as "*Pando*: march for a P&O orchestra" – for "the drunken violinist, pianist and drummer" who provided music aboard "the *Carthage* or the *Canton* or the *Corfu*: they were all the same."[2]

Burgess's duties in Brunei consisted of teaching history and linguistics at the Sultan Omar Ali Saifuddin College, named for the ruler of this tiny, oil-rich British protectorate in northwestern Borneo. The population, as in Kuala Kangsar and Kota Bharu, comprised a turbulent mix of cultures, including Chinese, Tamil, Iban, Land Dyak, Australian, and British. The indigenous people in this primarily Islamic society were Malayan, who did no work and considered themselves a chosen people, their economic needs fully met by the "lordly welfare handouts" provided from "the miraculous gush of petroleum".[3]

Burgess spent his mornings teaching from dawn until one o'clock, devoting the afternoons to writing. He composed little music in Brunei but played piano in a jazz trio he formed with two Sarawak natives, a drummer named Joe (whose father had been a head-shrinker) and cornetist named Paul (a "giant" of Hawaiian ancestry). They entertained at social functions, always including "Sarawaki", their signature tune, among their selections. Joe and Paul believed it to be a native folk melody of ancient origin, whereas Burgess knew that it had been "written in the thirties by the band leader Harry Roy on the occasion of his marriage to Princess Pearl, youngest and most flighty daughter of the White Rajah of Sarawak."[4]

Teaching English in Malaya had taught Burgess that the literature of his homeland lacked universal comprehensibility. Never having experienced snow, natives of the Asian tropics had trouble imagining the wintry environment of *A Christmas Carol*. Some Western moral dilemmas, which they considered comic or nonsensical, required alternative explanations. For example, the crisis suffered by Scobie, the police officer in Greene's *The Heart of the Matter*, whose love for two women causes him to commit suicide, made little sense to Malayans; in their view, a man who loves two women should simply take both as wives. If the literature of England were to be made intelligible to colonial subjects living in Asia and Africa, a book had to be written that could explain it to them, and so Burgess set out to write one that "looked at the history of our literature from an angle of tropical heat, with the ceiling fan spinning and the *bilal* calling the last *waktu* of the day and flying beetles bumbling on the verandah."[5]

English Literature: A Survey for Students was written in 1957 in Kelantan, one of the northeastern states of Malaya, and published the following year. It was Burgess's second published book, the only one ever published under the name John Burgess Wilson (replaced by "Anthony Burgess" in the 1966 and 1974 editions), and brought its author a modest income and a reputation for being able to write about literature in a clear, accessible manner. The commonality between literature and its sister arts, including music, is addressed early in the volume.

> Our concern is with literature, but the student of literature must always maintain a live interest also in music and painting, sculpture, architecture, film, and theatre. All the arts try to perform the same sort of task, differing only in their methods. Methods are dictated by the sort of material used. There are spatial materials – paint, stone, clay – and there are temporal materials – words, sounds, dance-steps, stage movements. In other words, some arts work in terms of space, others in terms of time. You can take in a painting or building or piece of sculpture almost immediately, but to listen to a symphony or read a poem takes time – often a lot of time. Thus music and literature have a great deal in common: they both use the temporal material of sounds. Music uses meaningless sounds as raw material; literature uses those meaningful sounds we call words.[6]

Predictably, Burgess found those authors most appealing who possessed musical as well as literary ability. One example is the poet John Milton, whose "father was a composer of music (his works are sometimes played today)" and "who was blessed with a musical ear".

> In fact, he was destined by physical endowment and eventual physical loss to be a poet of the ear rather than the eye. After a lifetime of overworking already weak sight, he went blind, and his greatest work was written after this calamity struck him. But even in his early works it is the music of the language that strikes us first – a music like nothing ever heard before, suggesting the deep and grave tones of the instrument which Milton himself played – the organ.[7]

Of all Burgess's novels, *Devil of a State* is closest in spirit to opera, filled with farcical characters like the buffo roles in *Il Barbiere di Siviglia* or

L'Elisir d'Amore. Operatic allusions abound from the outset, with an upscale neighborhood dubbed a "Valhalla of mansions up the hill," a Czech artist named Smetana who habitually hums Siegfried's horn-call and other "aggressive and Slavonic" tunes, and a dog who thumps its tail "like the Anvil Chorus".[8] Bellowing like an enraged Don Pasquale, Nando Tasca evokes the madcap world of opera buffa; lampooning tragic opera, his much-abused son Paolo parodies Donizetti's distraught Lucia. The sound of Nando bickering with Paolo is like "rapid operatic recitative with orchestral punctuations of fist on table," while the farcical scene in which they sing Rodolfo's Act I aria from *La Bohème* – father and son vying with one another to woo the lovely Lydia Lydgate – recalls the Marx Brothers in *A Night at the Opera* and *The Cocoanuts*.[9] Based on actual Italian artisans employed in Brunei, Burgess inserted the Tascas into *Devil of a State* without even troubling to change their real names.

The novel's musical references are not confined to opera. Unlike his fellow Australian road workers, Forbes of Marmion remains awake each afternoon, and so, "like an enharmonic chord, bridged the gap between noon and evening."[10] The clownish Paolo, imagining himself as a circus strong man, "marched about as to 'The Entry of the Gladiators'," flexing his biceps "as the orchestra orchestrated the effect with cymbals and Chinese blocks."[11] The rain that drowns out the opening ceremony for the new mosque in the book's final scene is described in terms of ever-quickening musical tempi:

> When the British representative stood to six bars of his national galliard, a drop or two struck like thin notes of a glockenspiel... The anthems speeded their tempi... As the rain played its preludial largo, *staccato ma non troppo*, the black Caliph came on in shining robes... The rain attacked its allegro movement, reserving its drums for the climax... Then the rain played *presto furioso* with kettle-drums.[12]

Burgess's stated intent in writing *Devil of a State* was to offer a relatively realistic portrayal of Brunei: "what virtue the original novel had resided, as with the Malayan books, in its fairly truthful representation of a British colonial reality."[13] In 1958, the year that Burgess completed the novel, an English expatriate named Gilbert Christie successfully sued Heinemann for damages in Singapore's High Court, claiming he had been libelously caricatured by the Rupert Hardman character in *The Enemy in the Blanket*.[14] Although the ruling was reversed on appeal, Heinemann, fearing further lawsuits, refused to publish *Devil of a State* in its original form, demanding that all questionable references to actual places or people be removed. Burgess, "locked in Heinemann's cellars for two days," replaced Naraka (the Hindu word for "hell" in Sanskrit), the name he had used for his fictional version of oil-rich Brunei, with Dunia (Arabic for "world"), a made-up, uranium-rich caliphate located in East Africa "somewhere around Zanzibar".[15] Other alterations were also required:

Malay and Iban had to go and invented languages took over ... The British Adviser had to become a functionary of the United Nations, a very implausible fiction, and I had to take a paint brush to the browns and make them black.[16]

Burgess was unhappy about the changes ("The satirical bite was blunted in the fairy tale ambience") but sufficiently pragmatic to recognize their necessity if the book was to be published, which it was in 1961.

In early 1959, Burgess and his wife returned to England for the annual six-week paid leave granted by the Bruneian government to expatriates. In London, addressed as "Mr Burgess" while discussing *Beds in the East* in his first appearance on a BBC radio book programme, John Wilson began getting used to his new identity. At the same time, he felt increasingly like an outsider looking in on his native land, and incorporated this growing sense of alienation into his next novel, *The Right to an Answer*.

Begun in Brunei and completed in the UK, *The Right to an Answer* illustrates the clash between East and West, examining the issue of decadence in contemporary England and "an overriding theme that seemed to me important enough – the trouble that Britain was going to have with its new Asian immigrants." Set in the late 1950s in "an unnamed Midlands town like Leicester", *The Right to an Answer* is a story of wife-swapping and its tragic consequences. Though inspired by a true story, Burgess maintained that *The Right to an Answer* was almost entirely made up, unlike his earlier, more autobiographical novels.

Music's role in *The Right to an Answer* is primarily metaphorical, describing synesthetic perceptions of sight, smell, taste, and feel. In one example, the vision of houselights being switched on one by one is likened to the sound of individual tones combining to form a triad: "There was another light, and then another, making a full common chord of suburban light." In another instance, the narrator is served a particularly distasteful meal: "trifle made with a resinous wine, so jimmy that all my teeth lit up at once – a ghastly discord on two organ manuals". Characters' voices are also described musically, their pipes likened to orchestral instruments: a publican pleads "in a breaking E-string voice" for her customers to refrain from discussing politics; a simple-minded dishwasher speaks limply, "like a slack bass string", but when amused, laughs "like a distant ship's hooter or an empty beer bottle that is blown like a flute". The only real music-making in the book is that of a West Indian singer who plays guitar and sings in the shadows of the Hippogriff Club.[17]

In the summer of 1959, after the Burgesses had returned to the sweltering sultanate, an encounter took place that probably hastened their departure from Brunei. The Duke of Edinburgh, touring Southeast Asia, paid a visit to the protectorate, where he met with the commonwealth expatriates living there. All expressed the utmost courtesy to the Duke except Lynne, who railed at him in language befitting an enraged seaman. The British Resident and his staff blanched, though the Duke, "used to the strong language of the navy, seemed to like this intrusion of truculence into the blandness."[18] Burgess suspected that this exchange stiffened the authorities' resolve to be rid of him and his wife as soon as possible.

Not long thereafter, a fateful incident ensured their imminent departure. One September morning, Burgess passed out on a classroom floor and was transported to the local hospital, whose doctors determined that he should return to England immediately for medical treatment. He and Lynne were promptly flown to London, where he was examined at the Hospital for Tropical Diseases and the Neurological Institute in Bloomsbury, remaining hospitalized for about eight weeks. One of the physicians who treated him was Roger Bannister, famed for having run the first four-minute mile five years earlier.[19] During this period of confinement, Burgess wrote poetry and composed an "endless passacaglia" – probably the lost "Passacaglia and Bagatelle for piano" from 1959 listed in TMM – for a concert pianist hospitalized on account of a tapeworm he had contracted in Brazil; the pianist died before seeing the piece.[20] "Interlude for Small Organ", composed in late 1958 (RLAB, 203), and "Suite for miniature organ", listed under 1959 in TMM – the only other compositions cited from this period – may or may not be same keyboard work identified by slightly different titles and dates. Either way, neither still exists.

A spinal tap revealed an excess of protein in the cerebrospinal fluid. Burgess was told only that he had been suffering from psychological distress and was released from the hospital. That Christmas, Lynne tearfully disclosed the actual diagnosis: an inoperable brain tumor that would give him, at most, a year to live. Refusing to believe this dire prognosis, Burgess interpreted it to mean that he had a year to do whatever he wanted. It meant not returning to teaching, yet if he set out to enter another line of work, what could he possibly say to an interviewer? Concluding that he should spend the year as a novelist, Burgess committed himself to writing as many books as possible in the coming twelve months. The moment to become a full-time author had arrived.

Notes

1 *Devil of a State*, 57.
2 LW, 420. Cf. RLAB, 201.
3 Ibid., 422–3.
4 Ibid., 427.
5 Ibid., 403.
6 *English Literature: A Survey for Students*, 6.
7 Ibid., 113.
8 *Devil of a State*, 4, 102–3, 112.
9 Ibid., 22–3. One wonders if Burgess, a Marx Brothers fan, named Edwin Driftwood, the protagonist of *The Doctor is Sick*, after Otis B. Driftwood, Groucho's character in *A Night at the Opera*.

10 Ibid., 45.
11 Ibid., 53.
12 Ibid., 280–1. The scene is based on an actual incident recounted in *Little Wilson and Big God* (440): "For the opening of the mosque, at which bandsmen fainted in the heat while they tried to play 'God Save the Queen' in fast galliard tempo, the drought broke and Allah rained bountifully on to the ceremony."
13 YH, 55.
14 See RLAB, 192–3.
15 In the revision, Naraka is reassigned as the name of a briefly mentioned, undeveloped country of unspecified location. Burgess defines Naraka as "Malayo-Arabic for hell" (LW, 431) or simply "Arabic for hell" (YH, 55). For his further use of the term, see Chapter 25.
16 YH, 55.
17 *The Right to an Answer*, 20, 28, 31, 39, 48, 55.
18 LW, 439.
19 Not the "one-minute mile" cited in LW, 444.
20 LW, 445.

8
"TERMINAL" YEAR (1959–60)

> *I had a whole year, a long time. In that year I had to earn for my prospective widow. No one would give me a job ("How long do you propose staying with us?" – "A year. You see, I'm going to die at the end of it." – "No future in it, old boy").*[1]

December 1959 found Anthony and Lynne living in a furnished two-room apartment in Hove, a coastal town at the western end of East Sussex. It was there, where they had moved that autumn upon his release from the hospital, that Burgess completed *The Right to an Answer* and wrote "The Great Christmas Train Mystery", a short story published in the literary magazine *Argosy*. During his hospitalization, Lynne had frequented an illegal drinking club run by Jewish identical twins named Ralph and Leo, one of whom also worked as a dining-car steward for British Railways. Burgess's yuletide tale, written in the twins' Cockney dialect, was based on a scam experienced and related by one of the "interchangeable" brothers: after a fine dinner served aboard a British Railways dining car one Christmas day, a deceitful Harold Hill-like traveler exhorts his fellow passengers to dig into their pockets to amass a particularly generous gratuity for the cook and stewards, then secretly disembarks at the next stop with the loot.[2]

Although Burgess composed little during this period, Hove's proximity to the South Downs suggests that *Song of the South Downs*, an incomplete work for solo piano and orchestra, was probably written around the time he lived there.[3] After beginning in a modernist vein, the work shifts into the kind of late Romantic schmaltz exemplified by the *Warsaw Concerto*, with chromatic descending harmonies (Example 08.01) in the style of Rachmaninoff. A passage in Burgess's autobiography describes a similar piece that Burgess performed in a talent contest around 1962:

> I attended an audition organised by Southern Television in Hastings, which proposed putting out a series of amateur talent programmes. I played one of my own works, a Rachmaninoffian rhapsody whose title varied according to the place where I played it: if it was in Leeds, it was "Song of a Northern City"; if, as now, on the Channel coast, it became "Song of the Autumn Tide".[4]

Example 08.01 *Song of the South Downs*: piano part (bs. 55–61)

Owing to its title, and Burgess's penchant for orchestrating his keyboard and chamber music compositions, *Song of the South Downs* may well be an unfinished orchestration of the solo piano work described above.

Burgess wrote prodigiously in 1959–60. He had calculated that by writing two thousand words of fair copy each day, including weekends, he could produce 730,000 words in a year, ratcheting the total up to a million by marginally increasing his rate of productivity. At an average of 100,000 words per novel, that would produce ten novels in a year, which he set as his goal. Best of all, Burgess figured that if he began early enough each day, he "could complete the day's stint before the pubs opened." Despite his planning and self-discipline, he came up short owing to "hangovers, marital quarrels, creative deadness induced by the weather, shopping trips, summonses to meet state officials, and sheer torpid gloom."[5] Nonetheless, during the year that began in Hove he wrote three new novels (*The Doctor is Sick*, *Inside Mr Enderby*, *One Hand Clapping*), rewrote another (*The Worm and the Ring*), converted a verse play into a novella (*The Eve of Saint Venus*), and completed half of a novel that he would revise and finish two years later (*A Clockwork Orange*), not to mention two additional novels that he abandoned after a month's work – an extraordinary amount of writing by any standard.

The first book Burgess completed was *The Doctor is Sick*, a black comedy about his medical ordeal. Dashed off in six weeks, it relates the story of Edwin Cyril Spindrift, Ph.D., a philologist and phonetics instructor who collapses while teaching at a college in Burma, is sent to London for treatment, and there experiences bizarre adventures that turn out to be mere fantasy. Like Burgess, Spindrift enters London's National Hospital for

Nervous Diseases and is diagnosed with a brain tumor, then suffers the indignity of a promiscuous alcoholic wife who rarely bothers to visit. He is treated by Dr. Eddie Railton (a play on the name of Burgess's actual neurologist Roger Bannister), who, like his real-life model, is a coldly clinical neurologist renowned for his non-medical skills – in Railton's case, playing trumpet on a popular television show.

Continuing in the buffo mode of *Devil of a State*, *The Doctor is Sick* contains further allusions to opera as well as lighter theatrical entertainment. Years spent backstage at Covent Garden cause Les, a moustached giant on the stage crew, to belch Siegfried's horn call and other Wagnerian leitmotifs, and to sing the sailor's song from *Tristan und Isolde* "in a strange and apocryphal translation: 'The wind's fresh airs / Blow landward now. / Get up them stairs, / You Irish cow.'"[6] As sung by Les, Carmen's *Habañera* becomes: "I'm a bastard, and you're a whore. / If you were mine I'd have you on the floor."[7] Burgess's stint in the Jaypees is reflected in a vaudevillian revue featuring the identical twins Harry and Leo Stone, shady drinking club proprietors modeled on Lynne's acquaintances Ralph and Leo.

Following a common pattern in Burgess's novels, a story that begins with the protagonist paralleling the author's circumstances concludes with an entirely fictional outcome. Unlike his author, Spindrift undergoes brain surgery. After the operation, he finds himself, like Dorothy in *The Wizard of Oz*, waking in bed surrounded by the real-life models for the characters in the dream. Standing next to a cheerful Dr. Railton, Spindrift's wife announces that she is leaving him to rejoin her lover in Burma. Cured and now free of his unruly spouse, Spindrift spins and drifts his way back into society, unsure where to draw the line between fantasy and reality but ready for "piquant adventures" that will transcend the dreary web of words from which he is finally ready to emerge.

F. X. Enderby, another character caught in a web of words, also originated during the "terminal" year. Burgess's most autobiographical fictional character, this acutely introverted yet gifted poet, whose family includes a father who played piano in pubs and a repugnant belching stepmother, first appeared to his creator as an apparition in Brunei Town during a gastrointestinal attack:

> I spent too much fruitless time in the toilet. Entering it one day I saw a middle-aged man on the seat, writing poetry. It was a brief hallucination but it led me to the creation of a character named Enderby.[8]

Living in "the identical furnished rooms Lynne and I were renting" in Hove, Burgess's distorted yet recognizable alter ego confines himself mainly to the privy, writing as well as storing his poems there.[9]

Many a "posterior riposte" erupts from *Inside Mr Enderby*, which opens with one of his anal explosions: "Pfffrrrummmp".[10] Enderby's blasts echo Leopold Bloom's "Pprrpffrrppffff" from the end of the "Sirens" episode of *Ulysses* – a rank case of flatulence as flattery. Intimidated by the outside world, Enderby rarely ventures into society except to eat the greasy concoctions that produce his incessant intestinal rumblings and farts. When he dares to engage with society, the results are as comical as they are disastrous.

Burgess sprinkles musical references throughout the text, as in the early scene in which Enderby enters a saloon filled with aged men and women. A bald old man is "an ancient with the humpty-dumpty head of Sibelius." An old woman "confessed coyly to ninety. As if somehow to prove this, she performed a few waltz-twirls, humming from *The Merry Widow*."[11] As middle age advances, Enderby finds his stepmother "entering slyly into him more and more" as his body produces ophicleidean outbursts:

> He had tried to be careful about laundry and cleaning the saucepans, but poetry got in the way, raising him above worry about squalor. Yet dyspepsia would cut disconcertingly in, more and more, blasting like a tuba through the solo string traceries of his little creations.[12]

Music plays a minimal role in the novel and matters little to Enderby except as a means of achieving new methods of verbal composition. Enraged that his rival Rawcliffe has stolen the theme of his epic poem *The Pet Beast* and turned it into the plot of an Italian B-movie called *L'Animal Binato*, a furious Enderby imagines arranging a dozen obscenities into a kind of verbal twelve-tone row, to be varied and repeated as if it were the series in one of Schoenberg's dodecaphonic compositions.

In the midst of writing *Inside Mr Enderby*, Burgess and his wife left Hove to move to a semidetached house in Etchingham, a village in East Sussex in the rural southeastern region of England where Rudyard Kipling, Henry James, and Ford Madox Ford had all once resided. In "Applegarth", as the Etchingham house was called, Burgess finished *Inside Mr Enderby* in late June, rewrote *The Worm and the Ring* "in a summer month" and converted *The Eve of Saint Venus* from a verse play into a novella.[13] Following a month was wasted on two abandoned novels, *I Trust and Love You* (based on Book 4 of *The Aeneid*) and *Sealed With a Loving Kiss* (a retelling of *'Tis Pity She's a Whore*), more fruitful labor produced half of the original version of *A Clockwork Orange*.

One Hand Clapping, the last novel completed during the "terminal" year, is a grim comedy, set in postwar England, about how one's philosophical outlook determines one's reality. After using his photographic memory to amass a fortune, Howard Shirley becomes increasingly despondent while his wife Janet, the novel's irrepressible narrator, takes a shrewdly pragmatic approach to enjoying their newfound wealth, whatever it takes. Concluding that no amount of knowledge or money can make life bearable, the suicidal young protagonist moans:

> It's too late now. There are certain things I know I could never have had, like being able to understand people like Einstein and Bertrand Russell and so on. Like having an education at Oxford or Cambridge. Like being able to really appreciate the great composers, Beethoven and Bach and so on.[14]

To help dispel criticism that he was too prolific, Burgess allowed *One Hand Clapping* and *Inside Mr Enderby* to be published under the pseudonym Joseph Kell. By early 1963, when Heinemann published the first edition of *Inside Mr Enderby*, Burgess had been supplementing his income for over two years by writing book reviews for the *Yorkshire Post*. Upon receiving the Enderby novel to review, he complied, assuming that the editor, displaying a cheeky sense of humor, had sent it to him deliberately:

> This is, in many ways, a dirty book. It is full of bowel-blasts and flatulent borborygms, emetic meals ("thin but over-savoury stews" Enderby calls them) and halitosis. It may well make some people sick, and those of my readers with tender stomachs are advised to let it alone. It turns sex, religion, the State into a series of laughing-stocks. The book itself is a laughing stock.[15]

Although Burgess's critique consisted largely of self-mockery, a scandal ensued when it became known that he had reviewed his own novel. He was promptly fired from the newspaper, yet profited indirectly from the incident, which enhanced his career by helping to establish his reputation as a brash iconoclast.

Burgess's behavior as an opera critic around this time was even more roguish. In order to avoid attending the performances he was paid to review, he used to give his tickets to Terry Sutton, a London taxi driver who was one of Burgess's closest friends during this period. "He knew the operas off by heart, who was in them and where they used to stand, almost," according to Sutton. "As he used to know them, he used to say to me, 'You can go in my place and I can stay at home and write. All you've got to do is let us know if anything happens – if someone falls off the stage or something catches fire.' It was great! I saw Tito Gobbi and Maria Callas – all the operas down there, all free in Covent Garden thanks to John Burgess."[16]

Notes

1 LW, 448.
2 Ibid., 446–7. See RLAB, 216.
3 In 1966, the Washington University Library in Saint Louis purchased the manuscript with other items dating from the 1960s.
4 YH, 65–6.
5 Ibid., 5.
6 *The Doctor is Sick*, 105–6.
7 Ibid., 168.
8 LW, 431.
9 YH, 13.

10 *Inside Mr Enderby*, 1.
11 Ibid., 22–3.
12 Ibid., 27.
13 YH, 21, 24.
14 *One Hand Clapping*, 165.
15 Burgess, "Poetry for a Tiny Room", *Yorkshire Post*, 16 May 1963, 4.
16 *Great Writers: Anthony Burgess*. Kultur Video (2001, released on DVD 2006), Chapter 11: "Television, Opera and Theater Reviews".

9

NASTY LITTLE SHOCKERS

> *If the theological motto of* A Clockwork Orange *is "We must be free to make moral choices," that of* The Wanting Seed *is "Everyone has a right to be born."*[1]

Having survived the supposed year of his demise, Burgess entered 1961 as a full-fledged author with five novels and a survey of English literature in print plus five more novels and a novella completed but not yet published. Inspired by Swift and Orwell, he wrote *The Wanting Seed*, a provocative novel depicting a dismal future beset by the twin scourges of overpopulation and food shortage. In this grim dystopia, homosexuals and castrati govern a society in which families are forbidden from having more than one child and "superfluous" offspring are converted into food or fertilizer. Enspun, Ruspun, and Chinspun (English, Russian, and Chinese Speaking Unions), the main political powers, control population growth with spurious wars, planned "extermination sessions", and cannibalism. Tristram Foxe, a history teacher whose struggle to survive and reunite with his wife Beatrice-Joanna shapes the plot, articulates Burgess's theory that society is locked into eternal alternation between Pelagian and Augustinian epochs separated by violent transitional periods. The Augustinian era (Gusphase), marked by harsh governmental controls, is based on acceptance of original sin, with low expectations of people's behavior. As behavior improves and these rigid controls are relaxed, belief in mankind's fundamental goodness becomes ascendant as the Augustinian yields to the Pelagian phase (Pelphase). In time, mankind's sinfulness reasserts itself, inevitably disappointing liberal believers in Pelagianism. In the Interphase, harsh rule is reimposed, leading to a return of Gusphase and continuation of the cycle. "This playful theory of mine, perhaps not so playful, was meant to be an answer to Orwell."[2] It is summed up in a quatrain recalled by Tristram late in the novel:

> The northern winds send icy peace,
>   The southern gales blow balmy.
> Pelagius is fond of police;
>   Augustine loves an army.[3]

Singing occurs at key points throughout the story. At the start of the novel, Beatrice-Joanna relinquishes the corpse of her baby, who has died at the hands of the government so that he can be converted into phosphorus pentoxide; the state's oppressive nature during Pelphase is symbolized by the macabre song chanted by the Ministry of Agriculture worker who collects the tiny cadaver: "My adorable Fred: / He's so, so sweet, / From the crown of his head / To the soles of his feet. / He's my meat."[4] During the orgiastic Interphase, bawdy songs are sung in "an endless *da capo*" by copulating couples in farmland furrows who have decided en masse to ignore the government and celebrate their humanity with pagan abandon.[5]

Repeating a trick from *Beds in the East* (anachronistically, it would turn out, for a tale set well into the future), Burgess uses a phonograph record as a crucial plot device. During Tristram's period of army service, as troops are told to prepare for a lethal battle with an approaching enemy, a sergeant notices that the "dada *rump*, dada *rump*" noise of the purportedly advancing militia is too regular to be real.

> "Good God," said Tristram, freshly shocked. "A cracked gramophone record. Would that be possible?"
> "Very much possible. Loud amplifiers. Magnesium flashes. Electronic war, gramophony war. And the enemy, poor devils, are seeing and hearing it too."[6]

Thanks to the sergeant's insight and his own quick thinking, Tristram survives the deadly charade and safely reaches Beatrice-Joanna in Brighton, lending a certain degree of optimism to this otherwise bleak vision of the future.

On their trips back to England in 1957 and 1958, Burgess and his wife observed the phenomenon of "teddy boys" – dashingly coifed young men dressed in neo-Edwardian suits and thick-soled boots. By 1960 this fad had begun giving way to the era of "mods" and "rockers" – gangs of dandies and leather-jacketed bikers. As the growing violence of these youths created genuine fear and the possibility of significant social disruption, Burgess conceived a story about the choice between good and evil as a fundamental human right. In the latter half of 1960, he began work on this "novel of ideas" (as David Lodge would later describe it[7]), titling it after a Cockney expression for someone odd or crazy that had caught his attention years before. "In 1945, back in the army, I heard an 80-year-old Cockney in a London pub say that somebody was 'as queer as a clockwork orange.' The 'queer' did not mean homosexual: it meant mad. The phrase intrigued me with its unlikely fusion of demotic and surrealistic."[8] He set out to ponder philosophically, in the form of a short novel, whether governmental imposition of Pavlovian conditioning to prevent even the most depraved citizen from choosing to commit evil acts is ethically justifiable. "I posit the notion that one act of evil may be greater than another, and that perhaps the ultimate act of evil is dehumanisation, the killing of the soul – which is as much as to say the capacity to choose between good and evil acts ... it is preferable to have a world of violence undertaken in full awareness – violence chosen as an act of will – than a world conditioned to be good or harmless."[9] Building upon the tradition of the British dystopian novel exemplified by *Brave New World* and *Nineteen Eighty-Four*, he wrote a parable cautioning against the loss of human autonomy: "If *Orange*, like *1984*, takes its place as one of the salutary literary warnings ... against flabbiness, sloppy thinking, and overmuch trust in the state, then it will have done something of value."[10]

The story is narrated in the first person by Alex, a young gang leader who is fifteen years old as the tale begins and speaks in a bizarre teen dialect. Realizing that the contemporary slang of his first draft would need to be altered to avoid being out of date by the time the book was published, Burgess resolved to invent an artificial dialect instead. Not knowing how to accomplish this, he set the incomplete manuscript aside until the solution revealed itself the following year as he and Lynne were about to leave for a summer holiday cruise to Leningrad. In preparation for the trip, Burgess set about improving his Russian. While slogging away at word lists, he realized he had found the answer: "The vocabulary of my space-age hooligans could be a mixture of Russian and demotic English, seasoned with rhyming slang and the gipsy's bolo. The Russian equivalent for -teen was *nadsat*, and that would be the name of the teenage dialect."[11] Burgess created a vocabulary of about two hundred words, relishing the irony of equipping his apolitical hoodlums with a dialect created as an amalgam of the languages of the two chief political powers of the day. This invented dialect mitigates the story's brutality, shielding the reader from its shocking level of violence through a linguistic veil. The reader is tricked into learning some basic Russian, with meanings gradually revealed through context (although a glossary was included, against Burgess's wishes, in early editions): Nadsat "was meant to turn *A Clockwork Orange* into, among other things, a brainwashing primer. You read the book ... and at the end you should find yourself in possession of a minimal Russian vocabulary – without effort, with surprise. This is the way brainwashing works."[12] The linguistic allure of this synthetic teen lingo (Nadsat having successfully retained its appeal as "cool" slang that has never gone stale) has been a key factor in the enduring popularity of *A Clockwork Orange*, which consistently turns up on lists of the top one hundred twentieth-century English-language novels.[13]

On a personal level, the novella offered Burgess the opportunity to convert the pain of Lynne's wartime assault into fiction. His outrage at later being considered a proponent of violence (especially after the release of Stanley Kubrick's film) often led to protestations that invoked the memory of that tragic incident:

> What hurts me ... is the allegation ... that there is a gratuitous indulgence in violence which turns an intended homiletic work into a pornographic one. It was certainly no pleasure to me to describe acts of violence when writing the novel ... For my own part, the depiction of violence was intended as both an act of catharsis and an act of charity, since my own wife was the subject of vicious and mindless violence in blacked-out London in 1942 (*sic*), when she was robbed and beaten by three GI deserters. Readers of my book may remember that the author whose wife is raped is the author of a work called *A Clockwork Orange*.[14]

The fundamental idea that man's humanity is determined through freedom of choice is reinforced in *A Clockwork Orange* by the novel's thematic emphasis on Beethoven's Ninth and its setting of Friedrich von Schiller's "Ode to Joy", which Burgess believed, erroneously, to have been originally an ode to freedom. Roughly a decade after Burgess wrote *A Clockwork Orange*, Basil Deane debunked the legend that Schiller first conceived his ode as *An die Freiheit*: "Attractive though it is, the story repeated by several writers that Schiller originally wrote his ode to Freedom ('Freiheit') instead of Joy ('Freude') is not supported by any historical evidence."[15] Even Leonard Bernstein, who famously substituted *Freiheit* for *Freude* in his celebrated Berlin performance of the Ninth on Christmas Day 1989 shortly after the collapse of the Wall, acknowledged that the story was fabricated:

> There seems to have been a conjecture that Schiller had written an alternate draft for the Ode "An die Freude" entitled "An die Freiheit." Most scholars now say that this was probably no more than a hoax perpetrated by a 19th-century political figure named Friedrich Ludwig Jahn.[16]

In an essay on the Ninth written in 1990 (and also in *Mozart and the Wolf Gang*, published the following year), Burgess avows his belief in the discredited myth, claiming that *Freiheit* – a word, like *Freude*, whose meaning was gruesomely distorted by the Nazis – was the original subject of Schiller's Ode:

> The words ... by Friedrich von Schiller, who died in 1805, between the third and fourth symphonies ... belong to his "Ode to Joy" – *An die Freude*. Originally this had been *An die Freiheit* – to freedom. But joy is a less controversial and subversive subject than freedom. Strength through joy. *Arbeit macht frei*. Neither term meant very much in the Nazi vocabulary ... One is, or should be, doubtful about addressing joy in this manner. Joy can come from anything – even, to the Nazis, from liquidating Jews. The joy of a punch-up. The joy of gang-rape. Give me *Freiheit* or give me death. We can all do without Joy, unless we have a wife or sweetheart of that name.[17]

In the same essay, the relationship between the Ninth and the novel's musical structure is buttressed by the comment, "We tend to bow down before the work as the final testimony of what can be done with sonata form on a large scale."[18]

A Clockwork Orange overturns the proposition that great music possesses intrinsic "goodness". Listening to Western civilization's most admired and beloved classical masterpieces inflames the novel's "Humble Narrator" to commit acts ranging from masturbation to physical assault, rape, and murder. His broad knowledge of opera, sacred vocal music, symphonic works, concertos, and chamber music distinguishes him as a singularly bright young man, setting him apart him from nearly all of the novel's other characters, be they adults or teenage droogs, while showing that his zest for evil has nothing to do with lack of intelligence. Indeed, Alex's appeal as a character is largely attributable to his passion for serious music, which subconsciously dissuades the reader from concluding that he is "all bad", for how can anyone who loves Beethoven's Ninth, for however pernicious a purpose, be wholly evil?

Musical allusion in *A Clockwork Orange* is comparable to Nadsat in its combination of fact and fabrication. Actual musical works cited in the novel include the "Jupiter" Symphony and Brandenburg Concerto No. 6 (33–4); sacred music by Bach and Handel (79), with specific mention of Cantata No. 140, *Wachet auf, ruft uns die Stimme* (83); and the "Prague" (No. 38) and G minor (No. 40) symphonies of Mozart (138–9). The association of clockwork with counterpoint is articulated through mention of the Brandenburg Concerto, as Alex reflects upon his assault of F. Alexander earlier that evening, the title of writer's manuscript, and the polyphonic music of "the starry German master": "The name was about a clockwork orange. Listening to the J. S. Bach, I began to pony better what that meant now" (34). Claude Debussy's Quartet in G minor, op. 10, is encoded as "a very nice malenky string quartet, my brothers, by Claudius Birdman" (41), a reference to the Dutch biologist Louis Philibert le Cosquino de Bussy (1879–1943), a noted "birdman" who, after many years spent in Sumatra, donated a large collection of avian creatures to the University of Amsterdam's Zoological Museum.

An international array of fictitious composers, compositions, and performers depict Alex's musical tastes as unusually sophisticated. *Das Bettzeug* ("The Bedding" or "The Bedclothes") by Friedrich Gitterfenster ("Barred-Window") exemplifies obscure German opera, while Otto Skadelig, whose surname means "harmful" in Danish, represents Scandinavian culture.[19] Alex orders a recording of Beethoven's Ninth "by the Esh Sham Sinfonia under L. Muhaiwir", which utilizes Arabic geographic terms: *Esh Sham*, meaning "Syria" (literally, "the left"), and *Muhaiwir*, an archaeological site in Iraq (42). The recording of the American concerto that Alex plays on his stereo to cap off an evening of mayhem invokes the names of two writers of antiquity – the Greek poet Choerilos of Samos (fl. 5th century B.C.) and Roman dramatist Plautus (ca. 254-ca. 184 B.C.):

> Now what I fancied first tonight was this new violin concerto by the American Geoffrey Plautus, played by Odysseus Choerilos with the Macon (Georgia) Philharmonic, so I slid it from where it was neatly filed and switched on and waited.[20]

The name Adrian Schweigselber, whose Symphony No. 2 is chosen and played by Alex as a recessional in the prison chapel, evokes another, better known fictional composer: Adrian Leverkühn, the protagonist of *Doktor Faustus*, a book whose narrative use of music and emphasis on the theme of good versus evil resonate powerfully with the themes of *A Clockwork Orange*. Burgess greatly admired *Doktor Faustus*, calling it, in *The Novel Now*, "the finest novel ever written about a creative artist".[21] His use of the syllable "schweig" (from the verb *schweigen*, meaning "to be silent") in the name Schweigselber echoes Thomas Mann's obsessive repetition of that word throughout the critical central chapter (XXV) of *Doktor Faustus*, which recounts the Faustian bargain between Leverkühn and the Devil; moreover, "schweig" alludes to the Schweigestill family in Pfeiffering, where Leverkühn eventually settles. Pronouncements such as "Freedom is the freedom to sin" and "Evil contributed to the perfect wholeness of the universe, and without the former the latter would never have been whole, which was why God permitted evil"[22] by Leverkühn's one-time theology instructor Eberhard Schleppfuss are virtually interchangeable with lines in *A Clockwork Orange* and Burgess's explanations of its philosophical basis.

The fictional compositions of Gitterfenster and Plautus arouse Alex physically and sexually. Hearing the "devotchka" in the Korova Milkbar sing a short passage from *Das Bettzeug*, Alex feels "all the little malenky hairs on my plott standing endwise and the shivers crawling up like slow malenky lizards and then down again" (27). The Violin Concerto sends him into synesthetic rapture, the description of Alex's reaction to Plautus's music recalling Burgess's account of the bliss he felt upon discovering Debussy's *Prelude to "The Afternoon of a Faun"*.

> The trombones crunched redgold under my bed, and behind my gulliver the trumpets three-wise silverflamed, and there by the door the timps rolling through my guts and out again crunched like candy thunder. Oh, it was wonder of wonders.[23]

Through musical and sexual use of language, Burgess accelerates the "tempo" of his writing by progressively shortening phrases, increasing the "speed" of the prose until it reaches verbal "orgasm". Emulating Bloom's experience on Sandymount Beach as fireworks erupt in the sky, Alex ejaculates at the moment that Plautus's Violin Concerto reaches its climax:

> ...there were devotchkas ripped and creeching against walls and I plunging like a shlaga into them, and indeed when the music, which was one movement only, rose to the top of its big highest tower, then, lying there on my bed with glazzies tight shut and rookers behind my gulliver, I broke and spattered and cried aaaaaaah with the bliss of it. And so the lovely music glided to its glowing close.[24]

But it is the music of Ludwig van Beethoven that animates Alex above all, providing the mental "soundtrack" of well-known works that becomes one of the book's most disturbing features. By associating Beethoven with Alex's heinous acts of violence, Burgess implicitly poses the question of whether great art contains intrinsic moral value, implying that there is no equivalence between the two. Whereas most other compositions cited in the novel lead Alex only to imagine assault and rape, Beethoven's possess the power to impel him to actually carry out acts of violence. In the record shop, Alex picks up two "ten-year-young devotchkas" whom he brings home, plies with Scotch, and rapes to the accompaniment of his new recording of the Ninth. Hearing the finale of Beethoven's Violin Concerto on a passing car's radio impels Alex to whip out his knife and slash Georgie and Dim to assert his authority. Alex assaults the cat-loving "starry ptitsa" in full view of her bust of Beethoven, whose stone face "witnesses" the attack. After his arrest and incarceration in a crowded prison cell, Alex experiences a hallucinatory dream of Debussy's faun meshing surreally with Beethoven and a distorted version of the "Ode to Joy":

> Boy, thou uproarious shark of heaven,
> Slaughter of Elysium,
> Hearts on fire, aroused, enraptured,
> We will tolchock you on the rot and kick your grahzny vonny bum.[25]

With the Ode still replaying in his mind, Alex is awakened by the police, who inform him that the old woman has died of her injuries, meaning that he is now a murderer.

After Alex's incarceration, Beethoven continues to influence both his subconscious and conscious existence. His murder of a fellow prisoner spawns a grotesque autoerotic-musical fantasy in which he imagines himself a musician in a giant orchestra led by a conductor ("a like mixture of Ludwig van and G. F. Handel") who can neither hear nor see.[26] Playing the phallic "white pinky bassoon" protruding from his abdomen, Alex laughs so hard from the tickling sensation that his guffaws disturb even the deaf-blind maestro. That killing leads to Alex's selection for the notorious Ludovico Technique, a form of pharmaceutically enhanced aversion therapy that eliminates the recipient's free will and ability to choose between good and evil. Since Ludovico is the Italian form of Ludwig, Burgess surreptitiously implies Beethoven's connection to the treatment, especially when the Fifth Symphony is played during the drugged, forced viewing of films depicting acts of extreme physical and sexual brutality. The unintended consequence of the procedure – that Alex sickens upon hearing Beethoven's music – is of no concern to Dr Brodsky, the Ludovico Technique's chief proponent and practitioner. Alex's protestations ("Using Ludwig van like that. He did no harm to anyone. Beethoven just wrote music.") fall on the tone-deaf ears of the doctor, who regards the matter as immaterial: "So you're keen on music. I know nothing about it myself. It's a useful emotional heightener, that's all I know."[27] Ironically, Brodsky is right. Music *is* an emotional heightener for Alex – at least for most of the novel's first twenty chapters. Alex is fully aware of the myth that appreciation of great art is supposed to calm down youths like him, but knows it to be false, since he is acutely aware of how much it excites him instead:

> Music always sort of sharpened me up, O my brothers, and made me like feel like old Bog himself, ready to make with the old donner and blitzen and have vecks and ptitsas creeching away in my ha ha power.[28]

Once released back into society, Alex discovers that listening to any classical music, not just Beethoven's Fifth, produces the same sickened reaction. He returns to the shop where he had bought his recording of Beethoven's Ninth and asks for a recording of Mozart's Symphony No. 40 in G minor. The clerk puts on the "Prague" Symphony instead, but it makes no difference. As soon as the music comes on, Alex becomes nauseous, flees the listening booth, and inadvertently winds up in the custody of F. Alexander. Alex's former victim tortures him by forcing him to listen to the "harmful" music of Otto Skadelig, but the plan backfires when Alex's suicide attempt and subsequent medical treatment reverse the effect of the Ludovico Technique, as he discovers in his hospital bed.

Back to his old self, it is only a matter of time before Alex's broken bones heal and he returns to his former ways. To exploit him for political purposes, the Minister of the Interior pays him a visit and bribes him with music in the form of a new stereo and a collection of shiny new records. Asked what he'd like to hear – "'Mozart? Beethoven? Schoenberg? Carl Orff?'" – Alex responds, "'The Ninth . . . The glorious Ninth.'"

> Oh, it was gorgeosity and yumyumyum. When it came to the Scherzo I could viddy myself very clear running and running on like very light and mysterious nogas, carving the whole litso of the creeching world with my cut-throat britva. And there was the slow movement and the lovely last singing movement still to come. I was cured all right.[29]

Alex's maturity and newfound identity in the twenty-first chapter as a responsible member of society is reflected in his altered relationship to music, which has become the basis of his profession. Indicating that he has grown up, Alex develops a preference for "malenky romantic songs, what they call *Lieder*" over the bombastic music of "bolshy orchestras".[30] As an employee of the National Gramodisc Archives, he comprehends music more intellectually, appreciating the remarkable achievements of Mozart, Mendelssohn, and Benjamin Britten, whose early works include *Les Illuminations*, a nine-movement setting of poems by Arthur Rimbaud for soprano or tenor and string orchestra, composed in 1939 at the age of 26.

> Eighteen was not a young age. At eighteen old Wolfgang Amadeus had written concertos and symphonies and operas and oratorios and all that cal, no, not cal, heavenly music . . . And there was this like French poet set by old Benjy Britt, who had done all his best poetry by the age of fifteen, O my brothers. Arthur, his first name. Eighteen was not all that young an age, then.[31]

The novel ends with its protagonist determined to retain his job, save his earnings, marry, and have a family: "Alex like groweth up, oh yes."

When speaking with musicians, as when interviewed by Oscar Peterson on BBC television in 1977, Burgess emphasized the novel's musical nature:

> It is about music, because the hero of the book is a young thug called Alex who adores music... He becomes violent, joyously violent, when he hears the scherzo of the Ninth Symphony or the finale. But when he is cured, when the State takes him over and gives him the special injections which make him feel sick when he contemplates violence, he feels sick also when he contemplates music... The important thing was that the State, modern science, with all these techniques, could take over a boy's brain and so change it that whenever he listened to music in the future it wasn't heaven, it was hell, and that's what it was about.[32]

The idea that musical structure could be applied successfully to fiction had intrigued Burgess from his earliest years as an author. In an essay published the same month as the first edition of *A Clockwork Orange*, he proposed the application of specific musical forms to fiction:

> I still think that the novelist has much to learn from musical form: novels in sonata-form, rondo-form, fugue-form are perfectly feasible. There is much to be learnt also from mood-contrasts, tempo-contrasts in music: the novelist can have his slow movements and his scherzi. Music can also teach him how to modulate, how to recapitulate; the time for formal presentation of his themes, the time for the free fantasia.[33]

The tripartite structure of *A Clockwork Orange* represents a literary version of sonata form, a structure in which principal themes are presented in the *exposition*, freely manipulated in the *development*, and reestablished in the *recapitulation*, with a *coda* reinforcing the final sense of stability. The three parts of the novel correspond to exposition, development, and recapitulation, respectively, with the last chapter of Part Three forming the coda. The novel opens with the recurring motif "What's it going to be then, eh?", consistently identified with Alex, followed by the presentation of a series of principal "themes" in the "exposition". Most of these return, in various degrees of transformation, in the "development" and virtually all recur in the "recapitulation", often in inverted relation to the original appearance. The book's "themes" include violence; sexual acts; dreams; establishing dominance through physical confrontation; protest against the subversion of free choice, as represented by F. Alexander and the text of book; societal authority; and music, principally (though not exclusively) Beethoven's. The final chapter of Part One, in which Alex is removed from his gang and taken into police custody, corresponds to the *closing section* of the exposition, in which the presentation of new themes comes to an end in preparation for inventive manipulation of some (but often not all) of these themes in the development.

In sonata form, the development frequently begins in the minor mode of the tonic when tonic is a major key. Alex's announcement at the start of II/1, just after restatement of the main motif, that "this is the real weepy and like tragic part of the story" represents a literary version of mode change from major to minor.[34] The murder of the new inmate in II/2 takes up the theme of violence introduced in the opening chapters of Part One, while the sexual acts in I/2–4 are transmuted into the phallic imagery of the "white pinky bassoon" in Alex's dream in II/2 and the public demonstration of the "cure" of his sexual desire in II/7. Alex's nightmare in II/5 mirrors his dream about "droog Georgie" in I/4. The theme of protest against the loss of free will passes from F. Alexander in Part One to the prison chaplain in Part Two, while the theme of societal authority, represented by the truant officer P. R. Deltoid and the police in the "exposition", is taken over by various officials (Dr Brodsky, the Prison Warden, the Governor, and the Minister of the Interior) in the "development". The final part of a musical development section is the "retransition", in which the return of the tonic key in the recapitulation is signaled by the arrival of that key's dominant chord. In *A Clockwork Orange*, the last chapter of Part Two serves this function, demonstrating Alex's post-Ludovican readiness to retransition back into society.

Part Three comprises transformation and inversion of the themes presented in Part One consistent with the musical procedure of modulation and restatement typical of sonata-form recapitulation. Whereas in I/1 Alex drank moloko, consorted with his three pals, and prowled city streets by foot, in III/1 he drinks chai, rides the autobus through the city, and attempts (unsuccessfully) to reunite with his family, now consisting of three – dad, mum, and Joe, who has become "like a son to them" – to equal the number of droogs in the opening chapter. Victims of Alex's violence in the "exposition" become his victimizers in the "recapitulation" – the "starry schoolmaster" (I/1, III/2), Billyboy and Dim (I/1–2, III/3), and F. Alexander (I/2, III/5). As Burgess once summed it up, "The place where Alex and his mirror-image F. Alexander are most guilty of hate and violence is called HOME, and it is here, we are told, that charity ought to begin."[35] Following a series of analogous correspondences throughout the rest of the "recapitulation" comes the "closing section" (III/6), which finds Alex in a position parallel to those at the conclusion of the "exposition" and "development": at the culmination of one structural period in his life and ready to enter another.

The final chapter (III/7) comprises the "coda", bringing what Burgess considered a sense of resolution to the novel, although many (most notably Stanley Kubrick, who left it out of the film) have found it disappointingly anticlimactic.[36] The common musical practice of restating the opening of the exposition in the coda is imitated here through literary parody, with Alex back in the Korova Milkbar with a new trio of droogs. The mock-equivalence of this scene to the opening brings closure to the literary structure, allowing Alex to choose a mature, constructive path of responsible behavior over the destructive, evil acts of his youth.

The motif "What's it going to be then, eh?" demarcates the novel's sonata form in a manner comparable to the repetitions of the familiar four-note motif from the start of Beethoven's Fifth Symphony at structurally significant points throughout the first movement. This line occurs twelve times in the novel – four times in the exposition (I/1), three in the development (II/1), three in the recapitulation (III/1), and two in the coda (III/7) – set apart each time as a separate, complete paragraph.[37] Its final appearances in III/7 provide compelling evidence that Burgess considered the twenty-first chapter as essential to the novel's structure as a coda in sonata form. With his fondness for applying what he termed "arithmology" to the structure of his novels, he carefully constructed *A Clockwork Orange* in three parts of seven chapters each to produce a total of twenty-one chapters, symbolizing the traditional age of maturity:

> 21 is the symbol of human maturity, or used to be, since at 21 you got the vote and assumed adult responsibility... The number of chapters is never entirely arbitrary. Just as a musical composer starts off with a vague image of bulk and duration, so a novelist begins with an image of length, and this image is expressed in the number of sections and the number of chapters into which the work will be disposed. Those twenty-one chapters were important to me.[38]

(Why Alex matures at eighteen instead of twenty-one is one of the novel's chief inconsistencies.)

The twelve appearances of "What's it going to be then, eh?" are as obligatory as the novel's twenty-one chapters, and it is hardly a coincidence that 12 is the retrograde of 21. Without the "coda", there would be just ten occurrences of the motif, a number irreconcilable with the novel's arithmological structure.[39] The number 12 equals the number of different musical pitches, points in the circle of fifths, and markers on a clock, all potent symbols in a book "about music" with "clock" in its title. Like hands spinning about a clock face or themes returning in a sonata form recapitulation, the principal themes and characters return in Part Three of *A Clockwork Orange* to bring the story full circle.

Burgess's commitment to the novel's musical structure may offer the strongest explanation for the marked change of tone in Chapter 21. In sonata form, the coda's function is to bring the composition to rest, achieving resolution by offsetting the drama built up in earlier sections, especially the development. In a Beethovenian coda, such as the unprecedentedly long one that concludes the *Eroica* Symphony's first movement, resolution is achieved by repeating motifs, previously used in highly dramatic ways, within a new context that eliminates the prior sense of urgency. This is exactly what Burgess does in Chapter 21, turning the bellicose fifteen-year-old Alex of the exposition into the pacific eighteen-year-old of the coda while converting the Korova Milkbar from a location of incipient violence into a scene of quasi-autumnal calm.

In the 1961 typescript, Burgess expressed indecision about where to end the novel. Writing "Should we end here? An optional 'Epilogue' follows" after the twentieth chapter, he apparently delayed writing the twenty-first.[40] The first British edition, published by Heinemann in May 1962, included the twenty-first chapter, whereas the first US edition, published by Norton the following year, did not, ending instead with Alex's ironic pronouncement at the end of III/6, "I was cured all right." Years later, Burgess claimed that his Norton editor Eric Swenson insisted on cutting the twenty-first chapter as a condition for publishing the book, an accusation Swenson adamantly denied, calling it "merely a suggestion made for conceptual reasons".[41] Swenson claimed to have admired the novel on sight, but was unconvinced by the last chapter in which Alex, after a lifetime "of alienation, rape, torture, random brutality and rebellion from society as total as Mr. Burgess' unsurpassed imagination could project, is quickly brainwashed into morality and a sense of membership in the social order."[42] In Swenson's words, when he suggested dropping the final chapter in the original Norton edition, Burgess "responded to my comments by telling me that I was right, that he had added the 21st, upbeat chapter because his British publisher wanted a happy ending."[43] This version of events could account for Burgess's apparent pause before writing the twenty-first chapter while offering a reasonable explanation for the different actions taken by Heinemann and Norton. Burgess could well have written "Should we end here?" *after* writing the last chapter to express his doubts about its appropriateness.

Assuming Swenson's version to be true, the apparent inconsistency in Burgess's attitude toward the "truncated" version can be explained as the divergence that can occur between formulating a plan and carrying it out. Having conceived *A Clockwork Orange* as a novel in sonata form, Burgess may have recognized, upon reaching the end of the twentieth chapter, that it might be better to end his "sonata" without a coda, even if it meant departing from his original design, but feeling the need to complete the book's musical form and arithmological totals of 21 chapters and 12 presentations of the "What's it going to be then, eh?" motif, he would have felt compelled to write the final chapter even if less than fully convinced that it was best way to end the book from a literary standpoint. One can easily imagine Burgess, uncertain of which ending he preferred, leaving the final choice to his publishers, who happened to reach opposite conclusions.

Early critical reaction to the novel was divided. An anonymous reviewer in *Time* viewed the book as "a serious and successful moral essay ... It may look like a nasty little shocker, but Burgess has written that rare thing in English letters – a philosophical novel."[44] In the *Kenyon Review*, a critic who had evidently gotten hold of the British edition with the twenty-first chapter reacted angrily to its inclusion:

> There is some sort of cheat involved in making the reader suffer all those painful pages of terrible violence, only to have the perpetrators put away their

chains and knives and knuckles as childish things, and live as solid citizens ever after. So false a note is struck by this ending that the whole book in retrospect seems false – a clockwork orange put together with mild ingenuity but to no purpose and with no real vitamins.[45]

Whatever indecision Burgess may have felt in the early 1960s about the appropriateness of the final chapter had disappeared by the late 1980s. In "A Clockwork Orange Resucked", his introduction to the 1987 Norton edition (which includes the twenty-first chapter), he belittles the first US edition as a "fable" as opposed to the "British or world" edition, which merits the term "novel", failing to mention his previous characterization of the final chapter as an "optional 'Epilogue' ". Yet even this hard-line essay leaves room for doubt:

> Readers of the twenty-first chapter must decide for themselves whether it enhances the book they presumably know or is really a discardable limb. I meant the book to end in this way, but my aesthetic judgement may have been faulty. Writers are rarely their own best critics, nor are critics.[46]

Notes

1 *Future Imperfect*, "A Foreword", ix.
2 YH, 33.
3 *The Wanting Seed*, 187.
4 Ibid., 3.
5 Ibid., 174.
6 Ibid., 195–6.
7 David Lodge, *The Art of Fiction* (New York: Viking, 1992), 198–200.
8 "Clockwork Marmalade", *The Listener* (87:2238), 17 February 1972, 197.
9 Ibid., 198.
10 Ibid., 199.
11 YH, 37–8.
12 "Clockwork Marmalade", 199.
13 In 1998, *A Clockwork Orange* was ranked 65th on the list selected by the editorial board of the Modern Library and 49th by students of the Radcliffe Publishing Course. Dierdre Donahue, "100-best-novels list draws reader fury", *USA Today*, 23 July 1998, 6D.
14 "Clockwork Marmalade", 198. Since Burgess first arrived in Gibraltar in late December 1943, and had been there for some time before Lynne was attacked, the incident must have occurred in 1944 as asserted in LW (301), where it is described as having been carried out by *four* GI deserters. See Chapter 4.
15 Basil Deane, "The Symphonies and Overtures" in Denis Arnold and Nigel Fortune (eds.), *The Beethoven Reader* (New York: Norton, 1971), 312. As Nicholas Cook explains in *Beethoven: Symphony No. 9* (Cambridge: Cambridge University Press, 1993) on page 94, Edgar Quinet's claim in the mid-nineteenth century that the real subject of Schiller's Ode was *Freiheit*, not *Freude*, "is one of the most abiding myths to have become attached to the Ninth Symphony. It seems to go back to a novel, *Das Musikfest*, which was published in 1838 by

Wolfgang Griepenkerl. In this novel, one of the characters refers to the true meaning of Schiller's Ode, and an author's footnote reads: 'It was freedom.' The idea that Schiller originally wrote an Ode to Freedom, but changed it to Joy for reasons of prudence or censorship, was popularized in France during the 1880s by Victor Wilder; and from there it got into Thayer's biography of Beethoven and Grove's book on the symphonies, so enjoying wide circulation." The assertion "that it was the early form of the poem, when it was still an 'Ode to Freedom' (not 'to Joy'), which first aroused enthusiastic admiration for it in Beethoven's mind", is found in *Thayer's Life of Beethoven* (Princeton, NJ: Princeton University Press, 1973) on page 895 of Elliot Forbes's 1967 revision and in all earlier editions. See also George Grove, *Beethoven and his Nine Symphonies* (New York: Dover, 1962), 325. For discussion of Burgess's use of Beethoven's Ninth in ACO and a plot summary of *Das Musikfest*, see David Benjamin Levy, *Beethoven: The Ninth Symphony* (New York: Schirmer Books, 1995), 15–16 and 162–4.

16 Leonard Bernstein, "Aesthetic News Bulletin" from the liner notes to *Ode to Freedom: Bernstein in Berlin, Beethoven • Symphony No. 9* (compact disk by Deutsche Grammophon 429 861-2), © 1990. Levy calls Bernstein's implication of Jahn as the perpetrator of the *An die Freiheit* myth "unsubstantiated" (*Beethoven: The Ninth Symphony*), 214.

17 "The Ninth". Typescript for BBC Radio Three, to be read on air prior to a broadcast on 14 December 1990 of a performance of Beethoven's Ninth by the BBC Scottish Symphony Orchestra, 4–5. Cf. *Mozart and the Wolf Gang*, 13.

18 "The Ninth", 1.

19 *A Clockwork Orange*, 27, 80, 167.

20 Ibid., 32. Although the name of the orchestra is also fictitious, a Macon Symphony Orchestra has existed in the state of Georgia since 1976.

21 *The Novel Now*, 35.

22 Thomas Mann, *Doctor Faustus*, trans. by John E. Woods (New York: Vintage International, 1999), 111–12. See also "From Mann to modernity: Anthony Burgess and the intersection of music and literature" by Christine Lee Gengaro in *Anthony Burgess and Modernity* (Manchester and New York: Manchester University Press, 2008), 95–108.

23 ACO, 33.

24 Ibid.

25 Ibid., 73.

26 Ibid., 89.

27 Ibid., 113.

28 Ibid., 48–9.

29 Ibid., 179.

30 Ibid., 186.

31 Ibid., 189–90.

32 *Oscar Peterson Invites*, 8 March 1977 broadcast.

33 "The Writer and Music", *The Listener* (67:1727), 3 May 1962, 761–2.

34 ACO, 75.

35 "Clockwork Marmalade", 198.

36 To Edward Forman, the final chapter is "as much a betrayal as a maturing: a betrayal of creativity and above all a betrayal of Beethoven, whose angel trumpets and devil trombones have been silenced by Alex's new taste for 'very

quiet and like yearny' music." Forman, "Violence, Sex and Music – Equivalent Addictions? Music in *A Clockwork Orange*" in *Portraits of the Artist in* A Clockwork Orange (Angers: Presses de l'Université d'Angers, 2003), 139.

37 The appearances of the motif within a paragraph in II/1 (83) and in variant form ("That's what it's going to be then, brothers") near the end of III/7 (191) are structurally insignificant.

38 ACO, vi.

39 For Burgess on the arithmological significance of the number 81 in *Earthly Powers*, see YH, 356.

40 Biswell, "Editing and Publishing *A Clockwork Orange*", in *Portraits of the Artist in* A Clockwork Orange, 22. See also RLAB, 246–62. Biswell cites the altered spelling of "droogie" as "droogy" in the twenty-first chapter as orthographic evidence that a significant amount of time must have elapsed between the writing of the last two chapters.

41 ACO, "Publisher's Note", xiii.

42 Eric Swenson as quoted in Edwin McDowell, "Publishing: 'Clockwork Orange' Regains Chapter 21", *The New York Times*, 31 December 1986, C16.

43 McDowell, C16.

44 "The Ultimate Beatnik", *Time* (81:7), 15 February 1963, 103, as quoted in Boytinck (102), 14.

45 Diana Josselson, "Shorter Reviews", *Kenyon Review* (25:3), Summer 1963, 559–60, as quoted in Boytinck (105), 14.

46 ACO, x. The essay is reprinted in *One Man's Chorus*, 226–30.

10

ESCHATOLOGICAL ESCAPADES

"I shall meet the eternal soon enough. I shall get my chamber music without the trouble of having to attend to profundities squeezed sweating from sheepgut."[1]

In July 1961, Anthony and Lynne boarded the ocean liner *Alexander Radishchev* for a holiday in Leningrad. Burgess's interest in Russia's language, literature, and culture, and the knowledge he hoped to gain about the USSR for use in future writings, probably provided the primary motivation for the trip, a decidedly unconventional vacation choice for a middle-class British couple during the Khrushchev era. Confident that he would make good creative use of the experience, Heinemann granted him an advance for the trip based on future royalties. Burgess, mordantly acknowledging his wife's chronic alcoholism in his autobiography, offered a sardonic explanation for the journey: "The Russians were known to be good drinkers, and Lynne knew she would feel at home among them."[2]

The ensuing publication of *Honey for the Bears* in 1962 and *Tremor of Intent* in 1965 (Burgess's thirteenth and fifteenth novels, respectively) validated Heinemann's trust. In its depiction of nonconforming sexual identities (bisexuality, male homosexuality, lesbianism, androgyny, transvestism), *Honey for the Bears*, a black comedy parodying Soviet society, was boldly unconventional for a book published the year that, as Philip Larkin famously put it, "Sexual intercourse began . . . Between the end of the Chatterley ban / And the Beatles' first LP." *Tremor of Intent*, on its surface a story about a top British spy's attempt to repatriate a former schoolmate who became an English rocket fuel scientist and defected to the Soviet Union, is, on a deeper level, a meditation on the nature of good and evil, and the schism between Catholicism and Protestantism. Both novels are set in Manichean worlds that raise moral questions about the nature of freedom, with the reader led to conclude, as in *A Clockwork Orange*, that freedom of choice is the most important freedom of all.

How that freedom was denied to Soviet composers constitutes a vital plot element in *Honey for the Bears*, a riotous fictionalization of the Leningrad trip. Burgess parodies the USSR music delegation that toured the USA in

1959 as part of a high-profile cultural exchange program sponsored by the US Department of State, recounting the tribulations suffered by leading Soviet composers while lampooning the platitudinous pronouncements of Soviet apologists. As the novel opens, Paul Hussey, on board the ship carrying him and his wife Belinda to Leningrad, struggles to converse above the din of a garish orchestral composition by Stepan Korovkin reeking of "Soviet triumph, marching and kissing in Red Square".[3] Once the music is over, Korovkin, a caricature of Aram Khachaturian, offers an abject apology to the crowd that has gathered: "Aware of my formalistic errors and grateful for the fresh enlightenment brought about by a compulsory course of self-criticism..." Khachaturian had been forced to make a similar public statement in 1948 after being officially censured, along with Sergei Prokofiev and Dmitri Shostakovich, for musical "formalism". Korovkin, a "plumber-like man" who speaks in "a genial harangue like his own music" and writes "circus music" (a reference to Khachaturian's famous "Sabre Dance" from *Gayane*), elicits a mixture of disdain and pity from Hussey, who recognizes that "buried deep beneath the cheap brash crashes was an ineffable Slavonic sadness."[4]

Stirred by Korovkin's public humiliation, Hussey suddenly cries out, demanding to know what has happened to Opiskin, a fictional conflation of Shostakovich and Osip Mandelstam, who perished in a Siberian gulag in 1938 on government orders and whose couplet "We shall meet again in Petersburg, as though there we had buried the sun" serves as the novel's epigraph. This outburst elicits an inarticulate bellow of rage from Comrade Yefimovich, an apparatchik representing Tikhon Khrennikov, the Soviet Salieri who served as Secretary-General of the Composers Union under Stalin and Khrushchev for over twenty years. The delegation's interpreter responds with meaningless party claptrap: "Formalistic deviationist. Defector to Viennese serialism. Traitor to Soviet art. Misrepresenter of the Revolution. Polytonal lackey."[5] The confrontation continues in the ship's bar, where, in an allusion to *Katerina Ismaylova* (Shostakovich's revision of *Lady Macbeth of the Mtsensk District*, the opera that prompted his first public denunciation in 1936), a Mancunian musicologist lectures Hussey on Opiskin's "perverse and wilful" decision to create such an "abomination":

> "*Akulina Panfilovna*," said Miss Travers in clear Manchester monophthongs, "is an opera. If, of course, you can call such a reactionary hotchpotch an opera. The heroine is a Leningrad prostitute. There are, of course, no prostitutes in Leningrad, Moscow, Kiev or any other Russian town or city."[6]

Disregarding this *Pravda*-like censure of Opiskin's music, Hussey questions her about another work:

> "A piece, as I remember," said Paul, "that was all jangly. All pianos and harpsichords and bells and xylophones. Would there be such a piece?" He frowned, trying to hear it in his head.

She identifies it as *Kolokol*, Opus 64, a fictitious work that seems to represent a fusion of Shostakovich's Symphony No. 8 in C minor, composed in 1943 during the Siege of Leningrad and reviled by Soviet critics as too contemplative and uninspiring, and *Novorossiyshiye kurantï* (Novorossisk Chimes), an orchestral work without opus number composed in 1960. Miss Travers dismisses Opiskin's *Kolokol* as a work written by him "when his native Leningrad was fighting for its life against the German Fascists. He gave the people nothing to inspire them. The seeds of that final treachery were already germinating."[7]

Musical imagery abounds in *Honey for the Bears*, with metaphorical descriptions of the cathedral at St Isaac's Square with "its gold dome like, in the sun, an army of Mussorgskian brass" and "the savage bell-clang of Kiev's great gate, dead Anna Karenina under the wheels, the manic crashing barbaric march of the Pathetic Symphony, hopeless homosexual dead Tchaikovsky." After being whacked on the head, Hussey's "ear played loud electronic *musique concrète*."[8] His failed seduction of a friend's sexy girlfriend leads him to acknowledge his latent homosexuality: "Suddenly the life went out of what he was trying to do; the big proud chord (chordee?) on the electric organ faded to *niente* with the coming of a power-cut, though the player's hands still stayed in position."[9]

The novel's farcical ending owes a debt to Pushkin's *The Little House at Colonna*, the comic tale Stravinsky turned into *Mavra*, in which a Cossack ineptly disguises himself as a chambermaid. A series of calamitous events forces the desperate protagonist into agreeing to smuggle a man identified as Opiskin's son out of the USSR. Camouflaged as Hussey's wife Belinda, the burly fellow attempts to flee to Finland aboard the *Alexander Radishchev* – sharing the same cabin with Hussey that Anthony and Lynne had occupied on their sea voyage to Saint Petersburg – but is apprehended by Soviet police upon landing in Helsinki.[10]

In perfect symmetry with the opening, the novel ends with symphonic music playing in the background. The KGB spies Zverkov and Karamzin, who have been trailing Paul since his arrival in Leningrad, reveal that "Alexei Opiskin" is actually Stepan V. Obnoskin, a brutal felon. As Zverkov argues that small countries are insignificant in an age dominated by the American and Soviet superpowers, Hussey recognizes that they are listening to the last movement of Sibelius's Fifth Symphony.[11] Hearing the music of Finland's greatest composer awakens in him the realization that small nations like England and Monaco ("this gambling country where a film actress is queen") remain vital repositories of civilization's past greatness.[12] With newfound pride in his British heritage, Hussey joins Zverkov and Karamzin in a toast to freedom as the symphony's final chords resound.

Thanks to receiving a £3,000 commission for writing the "history of a great metropolitan real property corporation" that was never published and an inheritance upon the death of Lynne's father, Anthony and Lynne began feeling relatively well off in early 1963. They took a spring holiday trip to the Mediterranean, though Lynne's fragile health often left her bedridden, as in Tangiers, where William Burroughs, in "lugubrious American tones", read Jane Austen to her in her hotel room while Burgess pined after "kohl-eyed houris in a yashmak".[13] Back in the UK, increasingly depressed, she swallowed a handful of barbiturates in a failed suicide attempt. It was imperative to make a change, so in late 1963, seeking closer proximity to central London, Anthony and Lynne purchased a second home at 24 Glebe Street in Chiswick and for the next several years divided their time between there and Etchingham.

Pubs were plentiful in Chiswick as were convivial writers who spent evenings together reciting verse to one another while imbibing sufficient quantities of liquor to cause irreparable cirrhotic damage. One such writer was Martin Bell, a poet whose bibulosity, humor, gregariousness, and fondness for French poetry reminded Burgess of a medieval jester. For Bell's seriocomic end-of-the-world scenario in free verse titled "Senilio's Broadcast Script: Riposte to Peter Porter", Burgess composed a quasi-dodecaphonic keyboard piece that Bell incorporated into the poem.[14] This brief Presto comprises a pair of disjunct contrapuntal sections surrounding a soft mock-chorale, with discordant progressions of dense, dissonant sonorities serving as introduction and coda, the latter (Example 10.01) foreshadowing the opening of Burgess's piano concerto. In June 1965,

Example 10.01 *Presto* from "Senilio's Broadcast Script" (bars 65–71)

Burgess wrote Bell: "I've been playing the Senilio music I wrote for you and, by Christ, it's difficult. But I persevere."[15] Two years later, he wrote an implausibly effusive review of the *Collected Poems 1937–1966* of Martin Bell for the *Spectator*, calling it "as important a literary event as any not merely this year but this decade." Mirroring his *Enderby* prank four years earlier in the *Yorkshire Post*, Burgess disparaged his contribution to "Senilio's Broadcast Script" as "a page or so of pretentiously avant-garde music" without identifying himself as the composer.[16]

Burgess composed little else in the early 1960s: a Christmas carol for Diana Gillon and her family (1961) and two lost works, Fantasia for two recorders and piano (1960) and Twelve-tone polyrhythmics for piano (1961), listed in *This Man and Music*.[17] Another missing piece is the one he wrote for the maritime musicians of the *Baltika* while sailing back to Tilbury from Leningrad in the summer of 1961:

> Lying in the bed, not bunk, of Nikita Khrushchev's cabin companion, I composed for the ship's orchestra a jazzy little piece called *Chaika*, full of seagull riffs on the alto *saksofon*. I did not rise to hear it performed. The bandleader came in without knocking to say that we were the only passengers not up and dancing.[18]

Preludes, Burgess's most significant extant music composition from the 1960s, is a set of six short piano pieces from 1964–65 that later provided the main thematic material for his Piano Concerto. They are mentioned in a letter to Bell ("I've been writing a series of piano preludes in thick Japanese inkpencil") dated 7 July 1965, but, surprisingly, are not listed in TMM or CC.[19]

Prelude I is a rhapsodic piece that opens with a flamboyant gesture – a sweeping monophonic ascent encompassing nearly the entire keyboard balanced asymmetrically by a slower, longer descent comprised entirely of chords (Example 10.02). The ostensibly atonal harmonic language contains tonal implications through repeated assertions of A, especially in the final descending line that concludes on the piano keyboard's lowest note. The opening phrase of Prelude II (Example 10.03) resembles an inversion of the melody of "... *La fille aux cheveux de lin*". Like Debussy's prelude, Burgess's is in the key of G♭ major, though he sets the lower stave in G♮, producing bitonality that is a remarkably consonant due to deft counterpoint emphasizing the notes common to both keys, G♭ (F♯) and C♭ (B♮). Prelude III displays two hallmarks of Burgess's musical style: emphasis of the fourth and metrical ambiguity. Quartal sonorities are played nearly throughout this lively piece, with changing accentuation producing an ongoing tension between 6/8 and 3/4 meter (Example 10.04). Metrical ambiguity increases in Prelude IV, which features the tripartite time signature of 12/8 : 6/4 : 3/2; at bar 16, all three meters are expressed musically at once: 12/8 in the "alto", 6/4 in the "tenor", and 3/2 in the "bass" and "soprano" lines (Example 10.05). Prelude V, the most lyrical of the set, is

Example 10.02 Prelude I (bars 1–5)

Example 10.03 Prelude II (bars 1–4)

a gentle Ravelian piece harmonized almost exclusively in thirds and sixths (Example 10.06). Loud accented chains of parallel fifths and octaves convey a primitivistic sense of energy and strength in Prelude VI (Example 10.07), with unequal rhythmic groupings of 4+5 and 5+4 eighth notes ultimately settling into a pattern of 3+3+3. Although slashes across the second page of this piece indicate Burgess's dissatisfaction with it, this vigorous prelude in D minor serves as an effective conclusion to the set.

Over the course of his career, Burgess wrote scripts, which he often narrated, for television films on a variety of people and places, including Joyce,

Eschatological Escapades

Example 10.04 Prelude III (bars 1–9)

Example 10.05 Prelude IV (bars 16–20)

Example 10.06 Prelude V (bars 1–6)

Example 10.07 Prelude VI (bars 1–6)

Hemingway, Lawrence, Michelangelo, Rome, and Manchester. Among the earliest of these was *The Music of Exile*, a 1967 BBC documentary about Bohuslav Martinů, the Czech composer whom Burgess called "perhaps the Dvorak of our age. He went into exile quietly, and he died in a quiet place. But he left behind a music of revolt."[20] The script relates Martinů's compelling story, from his strange childhood in Policka, where he spent most of his first six years sequestered with his family atop a tower, to his student years in Prague, to the long years of exile in Paris, New York, and Switzerland, where he died in 1959 at sixty-eight. Like Martinů, Burgess was a prolific composer whose music is characterized by energetic rhythms, frequently dissonant harmony, and occasional use of jazz. Burgess was not yet an exile himself when he wrote the script, but, with his self-imposed departure from Britain just a year away, *The Music of Exile* presages the path his own life soon would take.

Tremor of Intent, a deceptively serious spoof of Ian Fleming, is Burgess's contribution to the genre of the espionage novel. Before retiring from a career in espionage, Denis Hillier is sent on a final assignment – a secret mission to locate a boyhood friend, the rocket fuel scientist Edwin Roper, now working for the Soviet Union, and bring him back to England. Beneath its James Bond veneer, the novel addresses religious issues from Burgess's Manichaean perspective:

> I called the book an eschatological spy story, meaning that it tried to present the Cold War between Russia and the West as a figure of an ultimate conflict – between X and Y or *yin* and *yang* – which paradoxically sustained a universe which was really a duoverse.[21]

Like *A Clockwork Orange*, *Tremor of Intent* is structured in sonata form, as James Bly has demonstrated.[22] In his analysis, Bly explains how the three main parts of *Tremor of Intent* correspond to the main divisions of sonata form, with the short fourth part functioning as coda, and how Burgess treated Hillier as the "first theme" and Roper as the "second", introducing them separately in the exposition, combining them in diverse ways in the development, and bringing them back, enriched by the experiences of the previous sections, in the recapitulation. (In *Re Joyce*, Burgess describes Joyce's analogous use of sonata form in his treatment of Leopold Bloom as the "first theme" and Stephen Dedalus as the "second" in *Ulysses*.)

A major opportunity for Burgess to combine his musical and literary talents came along in 1966, when he was asked to write a singable English translation for a Christmas production of Berlioz's *L'Enfance du Christ* on BBC-2. Burgess considered himself "pretty well qualified" for the enterprise: "I could read music and I could write words: twin skills became Siamese." Colin Davis, who was to conduct, wanted the performance to be sung in the original French, but the BBC insisted on English:

So, though he grumbled at every line I wrote, he allowed me to turn the work into *The Childhood of Christ*. Not even a novel could be harder work. Berlioz devised words of no great poetic resonance and found melodic lines to fit them. I had to wander the streets, gloom in the pubs, toss in my single bed coaxing English rhythms out of a French conception... W. H. Auden had been asked to make the translation, but it had to be a rapid, or journalistic, job demeaning to a major poet. Anyway, Auden found it too difficult. I, the universal mug, was all too persuasible.[23]

To Davis's annoyance, Burgess found it necessary to alter notes and rhythms in order to accommodate the accents of English. The difficulty lay in the difference between French and English accentuation. French words are accented typically on the final syllable – am-i-ti-*é*, en-*fant*, sex-u-*el* – whereas English words are commonly accented on the first syllable – *a*-mi-ty, *in*-fant, *sex*-u-al. Names are even more vexing, since they cannot be replaced by synonyms; Jé-*sus* in French is always *Je*-sus in English. The shorter the phrase, the more limited the options.

In 1967 Burgess resumed the story of his fictional alter ego in the novel *Enderby Outside*, picking up where *Inside Mr Enderby* had left off. Transformed at the end of the first book into the drudge Piggy Hogg,[24] the protagonist undergoes transformative inner and outer journeys that eventually lead him back to his original identity. A pivotal scene involves a rock band, modeled on the Beatles, called Crewsy and the Fixers, its sacrilegious name reflecting Burgess's view of rock and roll as blasphemous music. Yod Crewsy, a John Lennon parody, publicly recites poems he claims are his but are actually Enderby's, enraging the plagiarized poet, who is present. Moments later, a former band member (replaced, like the Beatles' Pete Best, before the band hit it big) shoots Yod with a revolver that he hands off to Enderby while it is still, literally, a smoking gun. Fearing that he will be charged with the shooting, Hogg flees to Morocco via Seville ("the air-cruise that Lynne and I had taken in 1963"). In a swift reversal of fortune, Enderby, like his quasi-namesake Endymion, receives the love and protection of the Moon Goddess, who grants him safety and the return of his poetic gift. Safely settled in Tangier, he is visited by a golden young beauty, both Muse and Sun Goddess, who offers herself to him. Terrified that sexual fulfillment would cause the loss of his poetic gift, Enderby spurns her, prompting the divine visitor to depart, though not before bidding him farewell with "*The final kiss and final... Tight pressure of hands*", actions that are converted into the ending of a poem whose ending had eluded Enderby throughout the novel.[25] Imitating art with art, Burgess would later convert this poem into the ending of *The Brides of Enderby*.

Notes

1 *Enderby Outside*, 327.
2 YH, 37.

3 *Honey for the Bears*, 8. The real-life basis of this scene is described in YH (39), where Burgess writes, "A brassy song of Soviet triumph rang from the ship's loudspeakers as we boarded.".
4 HB, 8–9.
5 Ibid., 10.
6 Ibid., 29.
7 Ibid., 32.
8 Ibid., 56–7, 75, 182.
9 Ibid., 146. The pun on chord and chordee (OED: a painful inflammatory downward curving of the penis) is as clever as it is obscure. Foreshadowing the central premise of *The Pianoplayers* is the association of piano technique with the use of fingers for sexual stimulation in this and other passages, as when Belinda, revealing her lesbianism in a letter to Paul, describes her friend Sandra and the "special physical things she knew, and my God did she know them," as being "like someone who can play pieces on the piano only through having been shown where to put her fingers." HB, 202.
10 Burgess claimed that he and Lynne, on their return from Leningrad aboard the *Baltika*, traveled in the same cabin that Khrushchev had once slept in. YH, 51–2.
11 Unlike the British and American editions, the French edition of *Honey for the Bears* (*Du Miel Pour les Ours*) includes an excerpt from this movement in musical notation handwritten by Burgess.
12 HB, 255. The reference to Monaco foreshadows Burgess's emigration there in 1975. Burgess believed that a great Canadian nationalist composer would lend that country a sense of unity that would transcend the divisiveness of the Quebec separatist movement: "What Canada needed was a great poet who, like Whitman, would celebrate the totality of the land. It already had a considerable novelist in Robertson Davies. Perhaps a great composer, a Canadian Sibelius or Kodály, would better bridge the blood-gap." YH, 198.
13 YH, 70.
14 Martin Bell, *Collected Poems 1937–1966* (London: Macmillan / New York: St Martin's, 1967), 81–5. "Senilio's Broadcast Script: Riposte to Peter Porter", was written in response Porter's poem, "Your Attention Please". "Pets", a poem "For Anthony and Lyn (*sic*) Burgess" published in the same collection, is notable for its use of repeated phrases like "Fattened for slaughter ... Fattened for slaughter" and "Provided meat, provided meat" (lines 10–13), a stylistic oddity that Burgess would later incorporate into his verse novel *Moses*.
15 Letter to Martin Bell from Etchingham, signed "John" and dated 22 June 1965.
16 "Summoned by bell", *Spectator*, 11 May 1967.
17 The listings in CC appear to be erroneous, attributing works to the 1960s that are cited in LW and/or TMM under the previous decade. "*Concerto* (flute, strings) 1960" in CC is probably the same work listed in TMM as "Concerto for flute and strings" under 1951. The "*Passacaglia* (orchestra) 1961" listed in CC and *Passacaglia for Orchestra* cited in LW and TMM, dating from around 1952, are probably the same composition.
18 YH, 52–3.
19 The title page, "Preludes – Anthony Burgess, Etchingham, 1964", identifies where and when they were begun.
20 "The Music of Exile", typescript, 1.
21 YH, 109.

22 James I. Bly, "Sonata Form in *Tremor of Intent*", *Modern Fiction Studies* (27:3), 1981, 489–504. Reprinted in Geoffrey Aggeler, ed., *Critical Essays on Anthony Burgess* (Boston: G.K. Hall & Co., 1986), 158–72.
23 YH, 122.
24 Following Burgess's example, F. X. Enderby assumes his mother's maiden name as his new surname.
25 EO, 370.

11

SHAKESPEARE IN LOVE

> *To go back to the world of Shakespeare, in which the distinct but germane functions of literature and music were instinctively but perfectly known, is to encounter the life of a lost Eden, the air healthy, the food wholesome, no walls up anywhere.*[1]

The 400th anniversary of William Shakespeare's birth prompted a series of projects celebrating his life and work. The first was a fictional biography based upon clues about Shakespeare's life culled from the plays and poems. Deriving its title from Sonnet 130, *Nothing Like the Sun* is presented as a farewell lecture delivered by Burgess to his Indonesian students "who complained that Shakespeare had nothing to give to the East."[2] As it progresses, the author-lecturer grows ever more inebriated until, in conjunction with Shakespeare's death, he collapses in a drunken stupor. The "lecture" is divided into two parts, each consisting of 10 chapters, those in the second part exactly twice as long as the analogous ones in the first part, like a set of musical variations with repeats. A brief epilogue serves as a coda. As Samuel Coale once pointed out, the book's bipartite form is reflected in its protagonist, who is portrayed with two distinct personas.[3] WS represents Shakespeare's thoughtful, spiritual dimension, while Will exemplifies his emotional essence, each regarding the other almost as if observing a separate individual:

> Had he not himself watched WS and WS watched Will? Where was truth, where did a man's true nature lie? There was, as it were, an essence and there was also an existence. It was, this essence, at the bottom of a well, of a Will.[4]

The novel's faux Elizabethan text elicited strong critical reaction, from disparagement of its "bogus archaic style"[5] to praise as "writing of the highest order"[6] that even its author considered excessive: "Not quite so, really. I had taught myself the trick of contriving a satisfactory coda by what, in music, is termed aleatory means: I flicked through a dictionary and took whatever words leaped from the page. I did this again at the end of my Napoleon novel: the effect is surrealist, oceanic, and easily achieved."[7] He considered the musical allusions important and was disappointed that so few critics noticed them: "What hurt me most, I think, about the reception of the Shakespeare novel was that nobody seemed to spot the musical references. For example, a barber tells Shakespeare of the massing of troops in Picardy, and the barbershop lutenist accompanies his statement with a final tierce. I was referring to the tierce da Picardie, a major triad at the end of a piece in a minor key."[8] References to lute playing (17, 97, 187–8), madrigals like "The Silver Swan" (156), and consorts of viols, recorders, and brass (98, 112–13, 183) provide a musical backdrop reinforced by quotations displaying Shakespeare's use of musical metaphor, as in Sonnet 8 ("Music to hear, why hear'st thou music sadly?"), which compares a family's happiness to the concord of well-tuned lute strings. *Nothing Like the Sun* also includes references to *Love's Labour's Lost*, which Burgess would later set to music in his Third Symphony.

Shakespeare in Music, a book-length collection of essays examining music in Elizabethan drama, song settings of Shakespeare's verse, Shakespeare and opera, and orchestral music inspired by Shakespeare, including an extensive catalog of Shakespeare-inspired compositions, is the subject of a 1964 Burgess review in *The Musical Times* in which he mourns the dissolution of the Elizabethan Age, in which all the arts were connected as a kind of "continent", into separate "islands" of music, literature, and painting. This "lost Eden" is glimpsed through Shakespeare's plays as well as those of Marlowe, whose *Doctor Faustus* "must strike many a musician as a ready-made libretto." The Bard's universal appeal is reflected in the wide range of composers who have set his words to music, from Schubert, Quilter, and Warlock to Ellington and Dankworth. Through "a miracle of transference", the "Queen Mab" Scherzo by Berlioz "is an exact musical equivalent of Mercutio's speech, not an ideal accompaniment for it", yet no musicalization of *Romeo and Juliet* surpasses "the greatest Shakespearean orchestral work of them all: Elgar's *Falstaff*. This astonishing symphonic poem achieves the ultimate penetration . . . Music is an international art, but only an Englishman could have composed *Falstaff*."[9]

Three Shakespeare Songs for voice and piano, undated but bearing a dedication suggesting they might have been written in 1986, are settings of the same texts mentioned in the TMM listing of an identically named lost work from 1947: "Under the Greenwood Tree" from *As You Like It*, "Apemantus's Grace" from *Timon of Athens*, and "Come, thou Monarch of the Vine" from *Antony and Cleopatra*.[10] "Under the Greenwood Tree" (Example 11.01), the finest of the three, is a lilting ballad in 6/8 meter best suited for low voice in its original D major key. "Apemantus's Grace", whose vocal part, though written in treble clef, lies in the baritone range, is set in an angular atonal style with thick piano accompaniment, while "Come, thou Monarch of the Vine" is a short, simple piece for male chorus.

Shakespeare in Love

Example 11.01 "Under the Greenwood Tree" (bars 1–15)

Burgess's text for two oversized coffee-table books about the post-Elizabethan period – *Coaching Days of England* (1966) and *The Age of the Grand Tour* (1967) – does not overlook the musical aspects of that era:

> It was the guard who... blew the yard-long horn that warned inns that the coach was coming. He burst into a momentary glamour when he sounded his

brass, hovering on the margin of musicianship. He often showed himself to be a genuine musician on the long empty stretches between stages, for he carried, as well as a straight horn, a curved one. The straight horn could, by varying lip-pressure, be made to yield the harmonic series of a bugle; but the curved horn had three keys, like the brass instruments of the modern orchestra, and the guard could beguile the tedium of the journey by playing tunes – popular songs, operatic arias – and encouraging the passengers to join in.[11]

In the final week of 1967, a summons from Hollywood lured Burgess back to Shakespeare. The success of recent British period pictures like *Lawrence of Arabia* and *Camelot* had led Warner Brothers to consider producing a film musical about Shakespeare in love. The studio began calling it *The Bawdy Bard* and placed the actor-director William Conrad in charge of the project. Having decided to base it on *Nothing Like the Sun*, Conrad arranged to fly Burgess to California, where they spent several days discussing the film capped by a lavish farewell party that Conrad threw for his guest before his return to England. As Burgess later recalled, he paid closer attention at this gathering to his host's instrument collection than to the houseful of "dithering shelved bit-players" and former beauty queens:

> Bill was one of those music-lovers who seemed to believe that surrounding himself with musical instruments would osmotically also make him a musician. There was a piano in his office, and in his house a three-manual organ and an Erard harp, though with nobody to play them. I had always wanted to try out the glissandi at the beginning of *L'Après-Midi d'un Faune*, and I spent too much time unsociably learning how to tune the harp pedals.[12]

Back in Chiswick, Burgess worked on the script, which included song lyrics. As he wrote these, he decided to set them to music and wound up composing twenty songs, writing them in short score with indications of instrumentation in Elizabethan style, which entailed using "shawms, sackbuts, a chest of recorders, tabors".

> The Queen's Men arrived in Stratford with Dick Tarleton and Will Kemp and sang who they were . . . Shakespeare's father sang a song about loving life, and the Mayers chorused about bringing the maypole home . . . Anne Hathaway warned Will against ambition . . . Will sang to little Hamnet in the Stratford snow, with a counterpointed Christmas carol.[13]

As Burgess busied himself with the film treatment, Lynne's final decline set in. On his birthday, she downed large amounts of gin as they watched a television production about Byron, Shelley, and Wollstonecraft for which he had written the script. A few days later, she suffered a massive portal hemorrhage and was taken to a hospital in Ealing where she lingered for several weeks. Llewela Wilson succumbed to heart and liver failure shortly before 6:00 a.m. on 20 March 1968, a bleak rainy morning. Taxied home from the hospital later that day by a surly cabman who refused to switch off his radio, Burgess was forced to endure the macabre irony of listening to the Grateful Dead during the drive back to Chiswick.

Lynne had requested that she be cremated to allay her fear that she might, as in *The Fall of the House of Usher*, awaken underground in her coffin, so Burgess arranged for her cremation. A week later, Bill Conrad rang up with condolences and an invitation to fly back to Hollywood to meet Joseph Mankiewicz, who had been engaged to direct the Shakespeare film, which was now to be called *Will!* In California they discussed the script and recorded the film music Burgess had composed, which was done in first-class Hollywood style, "fully orchestrated and with mixed chorus".[14] He kept composing, but with diminishing faith in the project: "The truth was that only Shakespeare could write the lyrics and John Dowland the music... Plenty of singing in rural Stratford but not much occasion for it when Essex was executed or Will, if the Hays Office or the Catholic League of Decency allowed, handled his hard chancre. You could hardly enclose the man Shakespeare in grand opera even." Burgess came to believe that, if the story of Shakespeare were to be presented in a film, it needed to be a "non-musical... that told as much of the truth as we knew... This would never be made."[15] Thirty years later, he was posthumously proven wrong when *Shakespeare in Love*, with a screenplay by Marc Norman and Tom Stoppard, won seven Academy Awards, including Best Picture.

In autumn 1969, the installation of a new head of the Warner Brothers–Seven Arts corporation led to the cancellation of all unlaunched projects. *Will* (having, at Mankiewicz's insistence, lost its exclamation point) was dead. The script had been too long and the story unconducive to musical treatment. To Burgess, the cancellation "was something of a relief, nor was it really a waste: some day I could write a novel [*Enderby's Dark Lady*] about the making of a Shakespeare musical."[16] Neither the songs written for the film nor the historical research went to waste. He converted the music into the ballet suite *Mr W.S.* and utilized the research for a biography that "being highly visual, would be a substitute for the film."[17]

Published in 1970, Burgess's *Shakespeare* provides a multifaceted portrait of the man and his milieu incorporating the few known facts of Shakespeare's life. In the chapter titled "London", Burgess summons the sounds, smells, and physical feel of the city, and, naturally, its music:

> People sang readily, perhaps because of their malted euphoria. You bought ballads in the streets, and there was a large public repertoire of popular songs. The gap between music as pastime and music as uplift, a distressing feature of our own times, did not then exist, and doctors of music, like Byrd and Weelkes and Wilbye and the saturnine genius called John Bull, were ready to compose fantasias on "The Carman's Whistle" or "John Come Kiss Me Now". As for the educated classes, it was assumed that an ability to bear a part in a madrigal was one of the unremarkable marks of a lady or gentleman. Sight-reading (for which British musicians even today are famous among continental conductors) was no rarer a gift in music than in the field of words, and some of the madrigals they sang are, for us, not easy to read at sight. There were plenty of skilled players on the lute (or guitar) and the recorder. The keyboard instrument of

the day was the virginals – perhaps so-called because it was considered fitting for young girls: the name became very appropriate when the Virgin Queen herself was known to excel at it, or them. (The Elizabethan term was plural – a pair of virginals.) Among the louder instruments were cornetts (trumpet-sounding cylinders of ivory or wood, holed like recorders) and sackbuts – our own trombones. The Elizabethans were mad for sweet and strong concords.[18]

Like every biography of the great playwright, Burgess's relies upon conjecture, but in this case speculation is so abundant as to exceed the common boundaries of the genre. His concern with the Bard's level of musical understanding also distinguishes this book from other Shakespeare biographies. Burgess imagines Will listening to drunken singers in taverns and lute-playing minstrels in barbershops, vocalizing over the "scraping and clipping": "In this musical London he would have to learn how to write lyrics not just good enough for a play, but good enough for remembering when the play was over. He would have to be Lorenz Hart as well as William Shakespeare." Pointing out musical references in *Macbeth* and *Romeo and Juliet*, Burgess argues that Shakespeare's musical knowledge must have been considerable, for, if not, he would not have used the image of tuning a lute in Lady Macbeth's memorable rebuke to her hesitant husband: "Screw your courage to the sticking-place".[19]

The book received a warmer response from American critics than British ones, such as the anonymous reviewer for *The Economist* who wrote, "The work ... is plainly another one of Burgess' fictions. His Shakespeare is very much an Anthony Burgess character – lusty, hard-headed in money matters, and a word-reveller ... The literary opinions are wilfully odd and coarse; they suggest that Burgess is carelessly writing down for an ignorant public."[20] Burgess accepted such criticism philosophically, candidly admitting his mercenary motive: "I ought to be ashamed, but I am doing it for the money ... The book will look very lovely when it comes out, full of colored pictures of Mary Fitton and the Earl of Pembroke, and it will stand, unread although regularly dusted, on several thousand coffee tables."[21] It also provided an opportunity to make creative use of the labor he had expended on the film script: "The critics could denigrate the Shakespeare biography as much as they wished: it was only a portable version of the film that would never be made, a means of clearing a preoccupation out of my system."[22]

But Shakespeare was far too deep a preoccupation to be purged with this one book. In the years to come, Burgess would write not only *Mr W.S.*, but also several short stories about the dramatist and a novel in which the identities of Shakespeare, Enderby, and Burgess become entangled in a kind of Joycean web. During the 1960s, Burgess became ensnared by another Joycean web, one that would not release him until he had thoroughly engaged with Joyce's art as an essayist, editor, scholar, screenwriter, and composer, devoting himself as much to the daedal Dubliner as the bawdy Bard.

Notes

1 "Shakespeare in Music", *The Musical Times* (105), December 1964, 901.
2 *Nothing Like the Sun*, epigraph.
3 Coale, 158.
4 NLS, 51.
5 Elizabeth Jennings, "New Novels", *Listener* (71:1830), 23 April 1964, 693.
6 Anon., Review of *Nothing Like the Sun, Choice* (1:11), January 1965, 477.
7 YH, 95.
8 Ibid. Cf. NLS, 187–8.
9 "Shakespeare in Music", 901–2.
10 The inscription "Happy birthday to Micaela from Anthony Burgess" on the third song implies a connection to *Carmen*, for which he wrote a new libretto in 1986. Yet why Burgess would have given this set, comprising two songs for male voices and a third for low voice, to a soprano remains a mystery.
11 *Coaching Days of England*, 19–20.
12 YH, 146.
13 Ibid., 146–7.
14 Ibid.,157.
15 Ibid.,147.
16 Ibid.,185.
17 Ibid.,190.
18 *Shakespeare*, 72.
19 Ibid.
20 Anonymous, "A Novel Picture", *Economist* (237:6634), 17 October 1970, 60–1 [Boytinck (773), 126].
21 Burgess, quoted in Boytinck (769.2), 126. Ironically, color plates were lavished on neither Mary Fitton nor William Herbert, 3rd Earl of Pembroke. She appears only in a black-and-white illustration; he, in none.
22 YH, 231.

12

PURE MUSIC

> *The men of letters who were also men of sound – how many were there? I was drawn to the few I find and still am.*[1]

Shakespeare's quatercentenary was also the year Burgess began work on a series of projects honoring the other author he venerated most:

> I start this book on January 13th, 1964 – the twenty-third anniversary of the death of James Joyce. I can think of no other writer who would bewitch me into making the beginning of a spell of hard work into a kind of joyful ritual, but the solemnisation of dates came naturally to Joyce and it infects his admirers.[2]

Burgess's devotion to Joyce was infused with an intense awareness of the parallels in their lives: Catholic upbringing and education, subsequent renunciation of the faith, self-imposed exile, even the same birth month. Burgess took great pride in his Gaelic ancestry and shared with Joyce a passion for words that embraced neologism and all manner of linguistic games and riddles.

But what links the two most, and sets them apart from most other authors, is the fundamental importance of music and sound in their work. Like Burgess, Joyce inherited musical talent from his father, a singer once hailed as "the best tenor in Ireland".[3]

> John Joyce was not just a tenor but a fine tenor, and his eldest son was almost a great tenor. The importance of song in his books cannot be exaggerated. *Ulysses* sings all the way or, when it does not sing, it declaims or intones. It has been turned into a stage-play – *Bloomsday*; it could also be turned into an opera.... The Dublin of his youth nourished his auditory gift. It was very much his father's city, keen on rhetoric and Italian opera; it found its colours and shapes in sounds.[4]

As young men, both authors considered professional careers in music. While Joyce pursued music neither as long nor as earnestly as Burgess, initially he attained greater success.[5] On 16 May 1904 (exactly one month prior to Bloomsday), he won the bronze medal in the *Feis Ceoil* (Festival of Music), a Dublin vocal competition for tenors, greatly impressing the judge, Luigi Denza, with his rendition of "No Chastening" from Sullivan's *The*

Prodigal Son and the Irish air "A Long Farewell".[6] The apex of Joyce's musical career occurred three months later when he shared a program with the winner of the previous year's *Feis Ceoil*, John McCormack, then near the start of his illustrious career. Although chronic stage fright, a limited range (to A♭) and an aversion to formal musical study deterred Joyce from a singing career, his wife Nora was known to declare, "Jim should have stuck to music instead of bothering with writing," an opinion she shared with his father.[7]

Silence, Exile and Cunning, a 1965 BBC-TV documentary that takes its title from Stephen Dedalus's declaration of his emergence as an artist, features Burgess narrating his own highly personal text stressing the similarities between himself and his subject. Visually, the film provides a literary tour of Dublin, with images of Martello Tower, Sandymount, Ringsend, Glasnevin Cemetery, 7 Eccles Street, and other Joycean landmarks.[8] *Here Comes Everybody*, Burgess's first book-length literary study of Joyce, was published the same year as the film and dedicated to Christopher Burstall, its director. Retitled *Re Joyce* for the US edition, the book is structured in three parts, the first ("The Stones") covering the poems and early writings; the second ("The Labyrinth"), devoted to *Ulysses*; and the third ("The Man-Made Mountain"), an analysis of *Finnegans Wake*. Borrowing freely from Henry Morton Robinson, Harry Levin, Richard Ellmann, and, particularly, Stuart Gilbert, Burgess highlights the aural, musical quality of Joyce's writing: "My own best claim to an appreciation of his work, apart from application to it, is a Lancashire Catholic upbringing, a superstitious grandmother called Finnegan, and a strong auditory bias."[9] Joyce expressed a similar attitude toward his work, declaring that the technique and form of *Finnegans Wake* were based on sound and rhythm. Asked once whether the book was a blending of literature and music, Joyce responded wryly, "No, it's pure music."[10] After her husband's death, Nora Joyce recalled that her dominant memories of him were his turbulence and the keen pleasure he derived from sounds.[11]

Much of *Re Joyce* was recycled into *Joysprick: An Introduction to the Language of James Joyce*, which Burgess wrote in Bracciano in 1971. (After the manuscript was stolen from him in Rome as he was about to send it to his publisher, he retyped it from memory, explaining that his "brain had already photocopied it."[12]) In it, Burgess extends his discussion from *Re Joyce* on the use of language in "Sirens" through musical illustration, analogizing Joyce's vowel-less words to chords from which the thirds and sevenths have been removed.

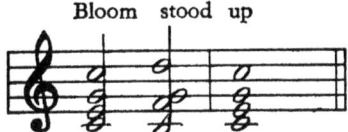 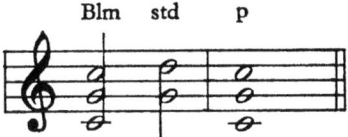

Burgess's penchant for inserting musical notation into his books *(The Worm and the Ring, Honey for the Bears, The Pianoplayers, MF, Beard's Roman Women,* and others) was inspired by Joyce, who pioneered the practice. In "Scylla and Charybdis", the ninth episode of *Ulysses*, Joyce inserts *"Gloria in excelsis Deo"*, the opening phrase of the Angelic Hymn.

This line of Gregorian chant from the *Liber Usualis* follows the blasphemous parody of the Apostles' Creed that interrupts Stephen Dedalus's discourse at the National Library on the meaning of *Hamlet*, in which he argues that it is not Shakespeare but his son Hamnet who should be identified with the Prince of Denmark, an interpretation that Burgess would later insert into *Mr W.S.* (Scene 6). "Little Harry Hughes", an anti-Semitic ballad sung by Stephen as he and Bloom trudge along in the early hours, appears in Episode 17, "Ithaca". In *Re Joyce* (171), Burgess notes that the baritonal setting, notated in bass clef, is too low for Stephen's tenor voice, and in *Joysprick*, proffers the explanation that the deeper pitch may represent "the fusion of Stephen and Bloom".[13]

Stressing the musical quality of *Finnegans Wake*'s pun-laden prose, Burgess reinforces Joyce's belief that the book "would come clear to the reader if the reader listened to its music."

> Joyce demonstrated how potent this music is when he made a recording of part of the end of Book I, the *Anna Livia Plurabelle* section . . . the appeal is ultimately to the auditory imagination, which is what Joyce probably meant, and the book is music perhaps in the sense that the orchestral score one reads in bed is music. A bad score-reader tackling, say, Wagner's *Ring* (which *Finnegans Wake* in some ways resembles) may not be able to hear much with his inner ear, but he may be able to recognise the recurrence of the *Leitmotive* by their configurations on the stave.[14]

This verbal music is full of songs and allusions to songs, mostly confined to words and verses for which no actual music is provided with the exception of "The Ballad of Persse O'Reilly", though only the first of its fourteen verses fits the given melody (Example 12.01). The notation disturbed Burgess, who observed, "there is something subtly wrong, or subtly symbolic, about it. Perhaps . . . the impending burial of HCE is suggested by most of the notes of the hymn of hate being thrust below the stave." If intended to be sung by a tenor, then the melody should have been written an octave higher, and if meant for a baritone, it should have been notated in bass clef. Burgess decided to renotate the tune in alto clef "as it might be performed on the viola d'amore, with singer in unison," adjusting the melody, in the example he provided, to accommodate the expanded form of the ninth verse (Example 12.02).[15] (In the late 1980s, Burgess arranged the song for guitar quartet as the first of his *Trois Morceaux Irlandais*.)

In 1966 Faber & Faber published *A Shorter Finnegans Wake*, an abridged version preserving about a third of the original text. Since this version relied on the original typesetting, Burgess's linking commentary had to be crafted to fit precisely into the spaces left by the textual cuts. Although some criticized Burgess for relying too heavily on *A Skeleton Key To Finnegans Wake*, a similar previous effort by Joseph Campbell and Henry Morton Robinson, Campbell himself lauded Burgess for providing "a sensible and sound contribution to what I suppose should now be called the 'hermeneutics' of Joycean theology."[16]

On the 28 November 1966 broadcast of *Desert Island Discs*, a weekly BBC radio program that asks each guest to name the eight recordings, one book, and one "luxury" he or she deems most indispensible, Burgess demonstrated his love of English music by compiling a list dominated by British composers:

Purcell, 'Rejoice in the Lord Alway' (Alfred Deller / Deller Consort / Oriana Concert Orchestra / Deller)
Bach, Goldberg Variations No. 13 (George Malcolm *harpsichord*)
Elgar, Symphony No. 1 in A flat major (Philharmonia Orchestra / Barbirolli)
Wagner, 'Walter's Trial Song' (from *Die Meistersinger*) (Sandor Konya / Berlin Philharmonic / Kraus)
Debussy, '*Fêtes*' (Orchestre de la Suisse Romande / Ansermet)
Lambert, *The Rio Grande* (Philharmonia Orchestra / Lambert)
Walton, Symphony No. 1 in B flat minor (Philharmonia Orchestra / Walton)
Vaughan Williams, *On Wenlock Edge* (Alexander Young / Sebastian String Quartet)

His "luxury" was a set of items needed to compose – "Music manuscript paper, pencils and an india-rubber" – and his book, *Finnegans Wake*, which, in real life, he had kept with him throughout his years of army service.[17]

Beyond his prolific production of novels and his writings on Shakespeare and Joyce during the 1960s, Burgess published three books on language and literature plus a volume of collected journalism. *Language Made Plain*, published in 1963, was designed to elucidate "the structure of speech, the nature of meaning, the volatility of both."[18] Comparing speech to music, he notes the former's utility versus the latter's direct effect on the emotions:

Example 12.01 "The Ballad of Persse O'Reilly" from *Finnegans Wake* (44)

Example 12.02 "The Ballad of Persse O'Reilly" renotated by Burgess (*Joysprick*, 154)

> We are moved by music in ways that words cannot describe, and such emotion can drive us to action – war, murder, love, religion. There is obviously a sort of communication in music which digs down to unconscious levels of the mind, hardly as yet understood, and this special communication of art is one of man's most incredible activities. We cannot deny the width of appeal that music possesses: the man in Stoke-on-Trent may not be able to read Pushkin, but Tchaikovsky can move him to tears; Benjamin Britten speaks louder than W. H. Auden.[19]

Extending the concepts of conventional and iconic communication to music, he posits that musical language is almost exclusively conventional, its meaning recognizable perhaps only on the subconscious level. A few composers, like Strauss in *Don Quixote* and Vaughan Williams in *Sinfonia Antartica*, did introduce iconic elements into their works: "This kind of iconic composing is rare and it is frequently condemned for its alleged crudity, but no composer faced with setting the words 'He ascended into Heaven' is likely to make his vocal line move downwards."[20]

One of Burgess's aims in writing *Language Made Plain* was to help convert "men of letters" into "men of sound": "We forget that language is primarily sounds, and that sounds existed long before visual signs were invented."[21] He bemoans the fact that, except for a few keen-eared novelists like Vladimir Nabokov and Kingsley Amis, most writers are little concerned with the art of language and even less with music:

> There was a nearly total lack of interest among literary people in language and, for that matter, the sister discipline of music. Shakespeare scholars responded dully when I told them of the two solmised themes which were the poet's singing to us out of the past – the CDGAEF intoned by Holofernes in *Love's Labour's Lost*, the CDE low B insolently chanted by Edmund in *King Lear* (from this Richard Addinsell had made his main theme in the *Warsaw Concerto* pastiche). Literary people just did not care about sound.[22]

Apart from occasional analogies to literary style and the role of jazz in Kingsley Amis's *Take a Girl Like You* and John Wain's *Strike the Father Dead*, music is mentioned little in *The Novel To-day*, a thin volume published the same year and the first of Burgess's published surveys of the genre. *Harris's Requiem* by Stanley Middleton is lauded as "one of the very few novels that show a literate attitude to music."[23] Malcolm Lowry is praised for his Joycean "use of the musical *leitmotif*" and Anthony Powell for pauses in the text of *The Kindly Ones* that produce "the feeling of a midway double-bar," although *A Dance to the Music of Time* is faulted for the "stately rhythm of the prose [that] never lets up . . . the tempo remains pretty constant."[24]

The Novel Now: A Student's Guide to Contemporary Literature, completed in 1966, is a much fuller examination of the subject.[25] Among discussion of hundreds of twentieth-century novels (including several of his own), Burgess sounds his dominant themes: boundless admiration for Joyce, fascination with Lawrence and Hemingway, and myriad connections between music and literature. Aldous Huxley employs polyphonic technique in *Point Counter Point* resembling a Bach fugue – "many plots proceeding at the same time, very nearly independent of each other, on the analogy of the melodic strands of a complex piece of counterpoint" – while Flann O'Brien displays "a means of counterpointing myth, fiction and actuality."[26] Samuel Beckett's books "have a shape that suggests music" whereas temporal freedom in *A Dance to the Music of Time* is comparable to melodic inventiveness: "Time can only provide the music if the narrator's hands can move freely up and down on its keyboard ... if we view time mechanically (as most of us do), then we are merely playing a dull chromatic scale starting at bottom A and ending at top A; if we view time creatively (as Powell does), then time is capable of a great number of melodies." Extending the keyboard metaphor to the social strata, the lower register represents the lower class: "The character-interest of *The Music of Time* is very considerable, though all the personages are drawn from, as it were, the tenor register; there are large areas of the keyboard which are never struck."[27] Popular contemporary novelists are exempted from consideration because, according to Burgess's musical metaphor, "We recognize the time for the Strauss waltz and the time for the Strauss symphonic poem, but, while we write a long essay on *Till Eulenspiegel* or *Also Sprach Zarathustra*, we bring to *The Blue Danube* the tribute of unanalytical enjoyment."[28] Trilogies and tetralogies are analogous to multi-movement compositions, their volumes so organized that "each novel has a fixed and foreseen relationship with every other novel in the little sequence" like a concerto or symphony as opposed to the riverine flow of the *roman fleuve*:

> When I myself began to write my *Malayan Trilogy* ... I saw very clearly how a symphonic scheme (the second movement is a scherzo) would enable me to record, each as a very nearly complete entity, the different stages of an expatriate Englishman's love affair with Malaya, as well as the stages of the process which brought Malaya from British protection to independence. A single long novel would not do: there had to be the feel of a very substantial pause between movements which could, at a pinch, be taken as separate and isolated compositions.[29]

Alternatively, Doris Lessing's *The Golden Notebook* emulates "a one-movement symphony like Sibelius's Seventh, in which contrasting sections take the place of separable movements."[30]

The book's authoritativeness is undermined by Burgess's occasionally capricious selection of novels and novelists, which lists Ronald Firbank among the "giants" yet omits J. R. R. Tolkien from the chapter on "History and Myth", Agatha Christie and Arthur C. Clarke from the summary of detective and science fiction writers, and Harper Lee from the survey of writers who produced a single great novel. Finding "most Scandinavian novels unsympathetic", he barely mentions the Icelandic Nobel Prize winner

Halldor Laxness and completely ignores Italo Calvino, Henry Miller, Anaïs Nin, and Gabriel Garcia Marquez, all of whom had written major novels by 1966.[31] Yet this guide to hundreds of contemporary novels by nearly two hundred authors remains an impressive achievement, one most writers would have required years to complete, but that Burgess tossed off while writing *Tremor of Intent*.[32]

Burgess's wit, range of knowledge, linguistic virtuosity, and unfailing ability to meet every deadline placed him among the busiest and best paid English freelance writers of his time, but, despite abundant journalistic success, he habitually underplayed this activity: "The title of journalist is probably very noble, but I lay no real claim to it. I am really, I think, a novelist and a musical composer *manqué:* I make no other pretensions."[33] Hundreds of his reviews and essays were anthologized in hardbound collections, the first being *Urgent Copy*, published in 1968. Although none of its fifty-five essays are about music, musical analogies were never far from Burgess's thoughts: "Some fine nervous prose can be jerked out by deadlines. Fine nervous music also: think of Mozart composing the Overture to *Don Giovanni* while the audience was coming in."[34] More non-fiction was yet to come, but not right away. Recognizing that the Joyce centenary in 1982 would occasion new projects and commemorations, Burgess returned to fiction with a renewed focus while exploring new challenges as a writer. It was time to set scholarship aside and become a celebrity in his own right.

Notes

1 YH, 83.
2 *Re Joyce*, 17.
3 Richard Ellmann, *James Joyce* (Oxford: Oxford University Press, 1982), 15–16.
4 RJ, 28–9.
5 In a letter to Nora Barnacle dated 29 August 1904, Joyce wrote, "I started to study medicine three times, law once, music once." Ellmann, 169.
6 Denza, a professor at the London Academy of Music, is chiefly remembered for his composition "Funiculi-Funicula".
7 Ellmann, 169, 611.
8 "I will not serve that in which I no longer believe whether it call itself my home, my fatherland or my church: and I will try to express myself in some mode of life or art as freely as I can and as wholly as I can, using for my defence the only arms I allow myself to use, silence, exile and cunning." Joyce, *A Portrait of the Artist as a Young Man*, edited by Hans Walter Gabler with Walter Hettche (New York & London: Garland, 1993), 275.
9 RJ, 34.
10 Ellmann, 702–3.
11 Ibid., 743.
12 YH, 290. See also 243.

13 Alternatively, "It may be that Joyce was looking ahead to one of the musical keys for Anna Livia Plurabelle in *Finnegans Wake*, or, and more likely, it may indicate that Stephen has symbolically replaced his father." Jack W. Weaver, *Joyce's Music and Noise: Theme and Variation in his Writings* (Gainesville: University Press of Florida, 1998), 89.
14 RJ, 268.
15 *Joysprick*, 153–4.
16 Quoted on the dust jacket of *A Shorter Finnegans Wake*.
17 BBC listing of *Desert Island Disc* broadcasts, 139–40. Programme 837: "Anthony Burgess, Writer".
18 YH, 82.
19 *Language Made Plain*, 10.
20 Ibid., 11.
21 Ibid., 8.
22 YH, 82.
23 *The Novel To-Day*, 44.
24 Ibid., 16, 27.
25 The book was issued in 1967 in London as *The Novel Now: A Student's Guide to Contemporary Literature* and in New York as *The Novel Now: A Guide to Contemporary Fiction*. A new US edition of *The Novel Now* was published in 1971 by Folcroft Library Editions as *The Novel Today*, which, despite its similar title, is not the same as *The Novel To-day*, the pamphlet published in 1963 by the British Council.
26 *The Novel Now*, 40, 78.
27 Ibid., 76, 82, 84.
28 Ibid., 207.
29 Ibid., 94.
30 Ibid., 100.
31 Ibid., 9.
32 "The writing of this little book has been proceeding *pari passu* with the writing of my novel *Tremor of Intent*." NN, 210.
33 *Urgent Copy*, 10. "His Contessa took on the duties of a subsidiary agent, and negotiated the highest fees in British freelance journalism for him, often as much as a pound a word." Anon., "Anthony Burgess" (obituary), *The Times*, 26 November 1993, 23.
34 UC, 9.

CELEBRITY NOVELIST

13

FAMILY AFFAIRS

It is in the nature of a structure to be as inexplicable as a passage of music.[1]

By 1968, Burgess had attained a level of fame few living authors ever achieve. Beside a photo of him peering up at a stack of twenty-one of his books, a flattering profile in an October 1968 issue of *Life* begins, "Some people call Anthony Burgess the most prolific writer of quality in the English language today."[2] One picture shows him sitting casually at a pub piano with a cigarette dangling from his lips; in another, clutching a musical score, "he describes one of his symphonies" with evident intensity: "Music is really my first love. I regret that no one ever refers to me as a composer. I am always called a writer who happens to compose music, never a composer who happens to write words ... My work is modern, but in the British tradition ... I still write music ... I can't help it." According to *Life*, "some minor works, including incidental music for the theatre, have been publicly performed" (which was true) as well as two symphonies (which was not, since the first and possibly the second were never played and the third had not yet been written). The article also mentions "a flute concerto, a concerto for piano and percussion, two piano sonatas and a cello sonata. Now he is in the middle of a bassoon concerto and is composing an underscore for the *Enderby* movie, although the producers have not commissioned him to do it."[3]

Meanwhile Burgess's personal life was changing dramatically. Shortly after Lynne's death, he revealed that he was romantically involved with Liliana Macellari, an attractive, Italian thirty-eight-year-old translator and language teacher affiliated with Cambridge University. He had met Liana (as she was usually called) in late 1963 when she sought to interview him for an article on contemporary English literature. They had lunch together in December and then made love in the Chiswick house at 24 Glebe Street that he had recently purchased. Eight months later, on 9 August 1964 in Bethnal Green Hospital, Liana gave birth to a son she named Paolo-Andrea.

In *You've Had Your Time*, Burgess maintains that he knew nothing of Paolo-Andrea's birth and did not see Liana again from the day they met until her surprise arrival at his doorstep in spring 1968, when she announced "almost incidentally" that the three-year-old boy at her side was his.[4] But in a July 1978 interview with Samuel Coale, he offered a more plausible account of his relationship with Liana:

> we had been consorting together since 1963 ... I had to have some sexual outlet, because I was having none with my wife. It was all guilt. This was kept absolutely quiet. The liaison was not a regular one. It was very very clandestine and we didn't feel free to get away ... We were living together openly from about April on, caused a scandal, wife hardly cold in the grave, etc. And then we were married.[5]

Seeking residence in a sunny low-tax region, Anthony and Liana decided on Malta, a Mediterranean country in the sterling zone. They traveled there in summer 1968 and purchased a marble-floored manor in Lija undeterred by the knowledge that its former owner had committed suicide on the premises. They returned to England and were married on 9 September in a civil ceremony at the Hounslow Register Office. Since the house in Malta was not yet ready for occupancy, they bought a Bedford Dormobile and in October set out in their mobile home on an automotive peregrination through France and Italy. Burgess never learned to operate motor vehicles, so Liana did all the driving while he spent weeks "hammering away" at his typewriter on manuscripts that "carried the breath of the open road."[6]

Disenchantment set in almost as soon as they arrived at their Maltese mansion in December. Electrical and telephone service were undependable, unwelcome strangers expecting employment as gardeners or maids showed up on their doorstep, and strict censorship laws obstructed the delivery of books and periodicals. Worst of all, when the government learned that Burgess was a working professional and not a pensioner, it denied his request for immigrant status and ordered him to leave after the standard three-month stay permitted to ordinary tourists. Although this crisis was resolved, the purchase of the house in Malta proved a reckless decision that Burgess soon came to regret.

Intentionally or not, in the wake of his new marriage and sudden immersion into fatherhood, he labored on writings sharing ill-fated familial relationships as a common theme. For the Tyrone Guthrie Theatre in Minneapolis, he wrote translations of *Oedipus the King* and *Cyrano de Bergerac*, but, first, Burgess developed Oedipal themes of riddles, incest, and hidden identity in *MF*, his major opus from this period and the novel he considered his best: "the toughest I ever had to write and, of all those I have written ... the one that displeases me least."[7]

Burgess wrote *MF* under the influence of Claude Lévi-Strauss, whose writings exerted a profound influence upon him beginning in 1967, when he first read and reviewed *The Scope of Anthropology*, which details the connection between incest and riddles in the cultures of ancient Greece and certain Native American tribes, two entirely separate civilizations.[8] According to a tale told by the Iroquois and Algonquin tribes, incest is the fate of the individual who possesses the rare gift of being able to solve the riddles posed by magical half-human creatures, a striking parallel with Oedipus. Lévi-Strauss's examination of the relationship between incest and riddles, which Burgess considered "one of the three major revelations of my later life", cast fresh light upon familiar works of literature.[9] Under the spell of the French structuralist, he identified examples of the incest-riddle nexus in *Finnegans Wake* and even his own *Tremor of Intent*, seizing upon the theories emanating from Paris to provide the foundation for a new kind of fiction based upon structural systems that could be "fulfilled without the uninstructed reader's needing to know or care."[10]

> Why a riddle put by a being half-animal half-human should be associated with the act of incest, we cannot say ... Questions about these structural relations are as meaningless as attempts to find out the meaning of a fugue or a sonata ... I do believe ... that it is possible to juggle with the free will of fictional characters and the predestination of an imposed structure. This is, after all, the manner of music, in which the component strands seem to go their own way but are locked in a preconceived pattern.[11]

The novel's title, a homage to William Conrad's facetious notion of making an Oedipus movie called *Mother-Fucker*, represents the initials of Miles Faber, whose name in Latin unites the opposed concepts of "soldier" (destroyer) and "maker" (creator).[12] Miles, a twenty-year-old New York college student with a gift for solving riddles, decides to travel to the Caribbean island of Castita (*chastity* in Italian) to view firsthand the works of the native poet-painter Sib Legeru (*incest* in Anglo-Saxon) upon being introduced to them by Professor Keteki (*riddle* in Sanskrit). During the course of the journey, the protagonist encounters "disguised talking animals" who pose riddles: Loewe (*lion* in German), the family lawyer; Pardaleos (*leopard* in Greek), another lawyer; Dr. Gonzi, a man "with the lion-face of a leper", who dines at a restaurant named Pepeghelju (*parrot* in Arumanian); and Dr. Zoon Fonanta (*talking animal* in Greek), a mysterious character ultimately revealed to be Miles's grandfather. Upon arriving in Castita, Miles meets and murders his twin Llew (*lion* in Welsh), is drawn inexorably into marriage with his sister Catherine, and is nearly killed by his mother Aderyn (*bird* in Welsh) and her magic owls. Ultimately the "soldier" is victorious, overcoming the incestuous curse that has plagued his ancestors for generations, and becomes the "maker" of a healthy family of his own.

MF thoroughly combines musical and literary elements, featuring text embedded with structuralist and musical symbolism, and a literary version of Wagnerian thematic technique. In tribute to Lévi-Strauss, the opening scene takes place in New York City's Algonquin Hotel, where Miles watches televised images of athletes "dreamily levitating to waltz-music – *Artist's Life, Morning Papers, Vienna Blood*, one of those" – by Johann Strauss. The song "You will be my summer queen" (Example 13.01), included as a footnote, is an auditory emblem of incest used as a leitmotif to link Miles

Example 13.01 "You will be my summer queen" (*MF*, 40)

Example 13.02 "Sengwi d'Iijsuw, Leve mij, leve mij" (*MF*, 120)

with his sister Catherine, its appearances and transformations providing the novel's "soundtrack" underscoring the inevitability of their incestuous union. References to Miss Emmett, Miles's childhood nanny who becomes his sister's scissor-wielding caretaker, and Castita, the Caribbean nation where Catherine has been raised in order to distance her from Miles, are repeatedly accompanied by this theme. Dozing aboard a flight from New York to Miami, Miles dreams that he is a schoolboy at home listening to Miss Emmett sing "her one song" as she tidies the house. Upon arriving in Castita, Miles hears it sung as a hymn by women who have gathered around a statue of the baby Jesus in the capital's main square to witness the *mij-regulu* or miracle of blood discharging from its penis, the tune a variant of the one in the dream, its mode changed from major to minor, and the English words replaced by Castitan lyrics (Example 13.02). Moments later, it is revealed to be the Castitan national anthem (Example 13.03); fully harmonized, it is blared by a police band to announce the arrival of the island's President. When Miles, pretending to be Llew, places the ring on Catherine's finger at their marriage ceremony, it undergoes a final transformation into their wedding march (Example 13.04).

Zoon Fonanta discloses essential truths to Miles through musical metaphor. The doctor condones the disappearance of Miles's twin brother with a casual allusion to *Rigoletto* and compares the difference between absurdity and freedom of expression to the logical impossibility of exceeding the limits of musical meter or instrumental range: "You can't have five crotchets in a bar when the time signature is three-four. A lot of nonsense. Look— that bassoon part goes down to F sharp below the stave. Impossible."[13] As in *Beds in the East*, a crucial hidden relationship is revealed through music, as Dr. Fonanta reveals his true identity to Miles through a riddle:

—And what sort of a conundrum would you write on *your* name?
—It would go best in music, he smiled. Then he sang to *lah* four notes, in intervals which I have since learned to designate as a major third, a whole tone, a fourth, adding: The last letter of the name can't be sphynxified, but R in Tudor notation stood for a rest.

Maestoso

Example 13.03 Castitan National Anthem (*MF*, 121)

Example 13.04 Wedding March (*MF*, 202)

> –And your relationship to me, if any?
> –Grandfather.
> I stared at him for five seconds, long enough to sing F A B E with a rest after, and nearly fool enough to ask jauntily: *maternal or paternal?*[14]

The doctor reveals that Sib Legeru never existed and that (like Burgess) he is a composer unrecognized for his musical talent, explaining that he and his patients, who are all victims of incest, actually created the artworks attributed to the fictitious mystic. Inspired by the discovery of "an orchestral score headed *Sinfonietta* with parts for such instruments as chimburu blocks and Tibetan nosehorn", Miles learns to read music "very thoroughly" so that he can fully appreciate all of his grandfather's compositions, and goes on to marry a Chinese woman and establish a splendidly unincestuous, multiracial household (for Miles is black, as the reader ultimately discovers) full of adopted children "of varying colors and nationalities."[15]

For his inaugural season as Artistic Director of the Tyrone Guthrie Theatre, Michael Langham commissioned a new translation of *Cyrano de Bergerac* from Burgess, granting him unconstrained artistic license to impart greater believability to the poignant tale of Cyrano's unrequited love for his beautiful cousin. Starting work on the adaptation in early 1970 while finishing *MF*, Burgess compressed five acts into three, merged minor characters, converted Roxane's name to Roxana, and cut nonessential scenes like the one in which she sneaks through enemy lines implausibly transporting a feast and fine cutlery for the starving Gascony cadets. Burgess substituted rhyme for blank verse, and, for variety, used different poetic styles and occasional bits of prose, "seeing in *Cyrano* something of the quality of an opera, with set pieces like arias that require the prosy dryness of recitative before and behind them."[16]

By the final weeks of rehearsal in summer 1971, Burgess had composed incidental music for the play and was eager to try it out. In Minneapolis he befriended Stanley Silverman, a New York composer-guitarist who had written music for several previous Langham stagings. Silverman helped convince Langham to use Burgess's music, offering "a professional verdict on my score, which was playable enough for me to be paid $500 for the theatre's sempiternal right to perform it. This was the first money I had ever earned for composing music, and it thrilled me far more than the far more substantial earnings that would accrue from the play."[17]

Starring Paul Hecht as Cyrano and Len Cariou as Christian, the production was a financial and artistic success. After it opened on 22 July 1971, *The New York Times* ran a rave review by Clive Barnes that even lauded the score:

> The 'Cyrano' deserves many bouquets, but the first and most important must go to Mr. Burgess, who, in his translation and adaptation of the original, has taken daring liberties and yet emerged triumphant with a romantic comedy for our time. Mr. Burgess has given the play a positive blood transfusion of wit, imagination, and Cyrano, the perfect embodiment of gallant folly, that conspicuous expenditure of the heart, becomes a strangely contemporary hero . . . I was fascinated to note that Mr. Burgess, in addition to everything else, composed his own attractively flamboyant music.[18]

The score comprises thirteen pieces encompassing an eclectic array of styles ranging from the Renaissance to the twentieth century. In the Prelude to Act I, an archaic-sounding tune over open fifths anachronistically evokes the sound of Tylman Susato (ca. 1500–64), a sixteenth-century Flemish composer who anteceded the historical Cyrano de Bergerac (1619–55) by a century; elsewhere in the score, modal harmonies, especially Dorian, Aeolian, and Mixolydian, with their lowered seventh scale degrees, provide an air of antiquity, as in Cyrano's tender Act II love ballad ("Cyrano's Song"), reminiscent of Renaissance lute music with its flute and guitar accompaniment. The song of the Officers of Gascony, which concludes Act I, is a parody of the children's chorus from Act I of *Carmen*, while in Act II, modern harmony is applied to Purcellian form in a chromatic "Chaconne

Example 13.05 *Cyrano de Bergerac:* Chaconne for Small Organ (bs. 1–16)

for Small Organ" (Example 13.05), the "defunctive music" that underscores Cyrano's final speech in III:ii. The score's most imaginative number is "Music for Ragueneau" (I:ii), which augments an ensemble of flute, clarinet, trumpet, and cello with a battery of whisks, spatulas, and other baker's tools. Burgess was fascinated by the exotic sounds the percussionist was able to produce with metal kitchen utensils and techniques applied to a cymbal, "striking it on the head of a kettledrum pedalled in a rising glissando, so that the tones became attached to a toneless instrument; lifting a cymbal rolled with kettledrum sticks from a tub of water, with the consequent rise in pitch. I became more interested in these inarticulate noises than in those being made on the stage."[19]

Delighted by the prospect of returning to Lévi-Strauss and the theories that had inspired *MF*, Burgess readily accepted a new commission from Langham to adapt *Oedipus Tyrannus* for the Guthrie. Silverman was engaged as composer. Writing to Langham from Rome on 11 April 1972, Burgess proposed that there be singing throughout much of the play, even though "in English-speaking tradition, so far as the Greek tragedies are concerned, sung choruses have always been taboo." For the Chorale toward the end of Part One he envisioned "a real Bach-type chorale, recalling one of the *Passions*", but Langham steered him toward more primitive styles, explaining that he and Silverman were drawn to the sounds of "Tibetan chants, the Pygmies, Hebraic influences, the Greek Orthodox Church, and Coptic chants."[20] After meeting with Silverman, Burgess embraced the director's concept, as reported by Silverman in a letter to Langham from Rome dated 24 May 1972: "He *loves* the primitive music (Pygmy, etc.) and would like to write an Indo-European chant to accompany the sacrifice you planned for the beginning, which would set the tone for the primitivism."[21]

Anticipating the caveman language he would later devise for *Quest for Fire*, Burgess invented a pseudo-prehistoric tongue chanted ritualistically by the Chorus at key points in *Oedipus*. Emulating *The Waste Land*, he used alliteration and triple word repetition in the "Opening Ritual", which begins with the Chorus chanting "Aghes Aghes Aghes: / Bhlaghme(n), Bhle / Aghes Aghes Aghes" in Silverman's atmospheric score, an exotic blend of Buddhist bowls, Chinese "plate" cymbals, and conventional instruments.

After *Oedipus the King* opened at the Guthrie on 24 October 1972, Burgess and Silverman adapted the script and music for concert performance as *King Oedipus, for Speaker, Chorus, and Orchestra*. The cantata was presented on 16 May 1973 at the Whitney Museum in New York, performed by Speculum Musicae and Speculum Voci conducted by Roland Gagnon with Burgess narrating. *The Midsummer Night's Dream Show: A Madrigal Comedy Celebration in E major*, an earlier Burgess-Silverman collaboration, was performed on the same Composers' Showcase concert, which was devoted to Silverman's music. Called *The MND Show* for short, this work had been commissioned by the Fromm Music Foundation and the Creative Artists Public Service Program and premiered in Boston in 1971 at New England Conservatory conducted by Lorna Cooke deVaron. Scored for chamber singers, large choir, and instrumental ensemble, it ranges in style from early Romantic to gospel, incorporating excerpts from Mendelssohn's incidental music sung in the classical scat style of the Swingle Singers.[22]

One of the more intriguing unfulfilled projects in Burgess's career was a proposed collaboration with Orson Welles on a musical. In the summer of 1972, Burgess's New York agent Robby Lantz informed him that Welles wanted him to write the words for a musical about Houdini that Welles would direct. Responding eagerly, Burgess wrote: "As a long admirer of yours (but of course everybody is, so there's no point in saying, but I leave it said nevertheless) I foresee a great artistic and conceivably financial achievement... Shall I start writing a draft script complete with draft lyrics?"[23] Although the Houdini project went nowhere, Burgess was already busy writing another musical that eventually made it to Broadway.

Convinced that a musical based on the Guthrie production of *Cyrano de Bergerac* could be as popular as *Man of La Mancha*, Richard Gregson set out in late 1971 to produce *Cyrano*. He assembled the creative team of Michael Langham to direct, Burgess to write the book and lyrics, and Michael J. Lewis to compose the music for a production that would feature Christopher Plummer in the title role. Prior to becoming a producer, Gregson had been a talent agent whose client list included Lewis, winner of the Ivor Novello Award three years earlier for *The Madwoman of Chaillot*. Although Lewis's career had been limited to jingles and film scores hitherto, Gregson expected him to make a smooth transition to writing music for the Broadway stage.

Gregson flew Lewis to Rome to meet Burgess where, after lounging for hours in a Trastevere restaurant, the two men set off for musical adventure. According to Lewis,

> I think he permanently had the keys to the Church of Santa Cecilia, which was across the road from the apartment he had. And so we trundled down the street ... and had an organ extemporization contest in the church [taking] turns to see who could outdo the other.[24]

It was bitterly cold in Minneapolis when Gregson, Langham, Lewis, and Burgess convened there in January 1972 to begin creating the show. Unfortunately, inner warmth was lacking as well. From the start, Burgess recoiled against what he perceived as Gregson's "imperious" attitude and a contractual obligation that required far more time than he had anticipated. He had naively assumed he could speedily deliver the musical's book and lyrics, then promptly resume his other commitments, which included teaching at the City College of New York, numerous lecture engagements, and writing *Napoleon Symphony*. Once Burgess recognized how much his freedom would be compromised until *Cyrano* opened on Broadway, he fretted continually over how to fulfill all his obligations.

Burgess and Lewis created songs at a rapid pace – "nearly ninety" by the end of the run – but few satisfied the producer or director.[25] The more they wrote, the worse things became owing to the fundamental stylistic incompatibility between composer and lyricist that undermined their work together. Burgess was an intellectual writer, adroit at sophisticated wordplay and double meanings while invariably preferring cleverness to simplicity and polyphony to monody, whereas Lewis was a tunesmith disinclined toward counterpoint or harmonic complexity, at least in his show music. Lewis's preference for straightforward melodies is borne out by the published score of *Cyrano*, with its preponderance of solo numbers; even in those numbers for multiple voices, characters generally alternate lines rather than sing together.

One could easily imagine Burgess's temptation to compose his own settings, yet, according to John Covelli, a young pianist-conductor from New York City Opera who was brought in as *Cyrano*'s rehearsal pianist and assistant conductor, he never interfered with the composer's role: "Anthony couldn't help but expose his musical gifts, but he never made any changes or suggestions to Michael Lewis's music."[26] Lewis, agreeing that Burgess always remained extremely professional, recognized his desire to compose: "He wanted to be doing what I was doing."[27] Thrilled to be working with a writer of Burgess's stature, Lewis felt connected to him by a musical bond; any concerns Burgess may have had about his colleague went unspoken at the time. Lewis always composed at the piano and did not bother much with things like C clefs and transposition, habits that led Burgess to doubt Lewis's mastery of the craft of composition, as expressed years later in the parodic character of Mike Silversmith (a composite of

Michael Lewis and Stanley Silverman) in *Enderby's Dark Lady* and his autobiography:

> Lewis had the Celtic gift of being able to knock out a tune, so long as he had a piano for the knocking. This was not composition as I understood it: in my own amateur writing of music I had seen the whole process as a cerebral one, with the keyboard kept at a distance. Only thus can one inwardly hear vocal or orchestral sounds. Lewis ... preferred his singers to have the gift of absolute pitch, which is a rare one, except in the novels of D. H. Lawrence. There was lordliness in his professionalism, which I presumed to be that of the cinema and the recording studio. What, as *Cyrano* was to prove, was quite beyond him was the crass kind of inspiration which would produce a popular song.[28]

Covelli found much to admire in both men. He regarded Lewis as "a wonderful natural musician and a natural melodist ... A magnificent songwriter [with] a gift for melody that just never ends." But "Anthony was the focus":

> Burgess would just constantly keep writing new lyrics and we were up to 2, 3 o'clock in the morning every night in various bars or in our hotel rooms and they would be "nursing" ... a drink or two with a piano, without a piano, just talking about the lyrics that they had to redo or they found that just weren't working that day ... [This] went on for literally 9, 10 weeks ... Song after song was either changed or thrown out and new ones would come along – as far as I was concerned, better than ever.[29]

Doubts as to whether *Cyrano de Bergerac* should be turned into a Broadway musical at all nagged Burgess from the start. Once the show opened at the Guthrie in the early spring of 1972, his misgivings only increased. He expresses them so often and emphatically in his account of the genesis of *Cyrano* that one can only surmise that immutable resolve to honor the terms of the contract and not let anyone down, stoic grit to complete what he had started, and/or sheer determination to fulfill the ambition of writing a Broadway show kept him from abandoning the project.[30]

The Minneapolis premiere did not slow down the rewriting. To the contrary, it became even more desperate, with Burgess increasingly convinced that music was diminishing rather than enhancing the story. As the weeks dragged on, the stress grew, especially once Burgess took up residence in New York. Gregson expected his lyricist to remain wherever the show was playing so that he could keep rewriting until opening night, whereas Burgess was anxious to attend to other matters. Inevitably, hard feelings arose. Burgess attempted to preserve as much of the spirit of the original play as possible while Gregson sought middlebrow entertainment, leaving Lewis caught uncomfortably in the middle. According to Burgess, Lewis agreed with him that the musical would have been best served by a small instrumental ensemble like the one used in Minneapolis for Burgess's incidental music, but was forced to write for a standard Broadway pit orchestra of nearly three dozen musicians.

The artistic style shifted dramatically when Gregson dismissed Langham as director, replacing him with Michael Kidd, who was, in Covelli's words, "very Hollywood":

> He was going to start changing some of the more sophisticated songs into more toe-tappers. A little dancing. They had to raise their legs in the Rockettes style. A little buffoonery, if it was possible, because you had to get a couple of chuckles from the audience. It didn't start out that way. That wasn't Anthony Burgess and it wasn't Michael Lewis.[31]

Once Kidd took over in Minneapolis and began rewriting the script, Burgess had his name removed from the book credit, amending the attribution to "Book based upon Anthony Burgess's adaptation of *Cyrano de Bergerac* by Edmond Rostand".[32]

In Toronto came more rewrites, complicated by the fact that Burgess, as the holder of a British passport, was subjected to maddening cross-examinations each time he crossed the border from the United States into Canada and vice versa. While Burgess juggled the continued production of lyrics for Gregson with his duties at City College, Lewis went on writing new songs at the piano installed in his hotel room. In Burgess's estimation, the show was received "moderately well in Toronto," Christopher Plummer's birthplace, which hailed the star "as a distinguished native son."[33] *Cyrano* had offered Plummer his first major musical role since Captain von Trapp in the 1965 film *The Sound of Music* and he relished the chance to play the eloquent Gascon on Broadway. Covelli regarded Plummer as "a great actor" and "wonderful colleague" who played Cyrano "magnificently, every night through the changes and the fight scenes that were changed and choreographed every day. It was a part made for him."[34]

After the Ontario engagement, *Cyrano* enjoyed a very successful run in Massachusetts in the spring of 1973; "Boston took very kindly to *Cyrano*, and it had to be retained at the Colonial Theatre for a further two weeks."[35] In John Covelli's view, a summer of fine-tuning in Los Angeles would have primed the production for a triumphant Broadway opening in August or September and an extended New York run, but Gregson was in a hurry to bring *Cyrano*, his first Broadway-bound show, to New York and rushed it there straight from Boston before it was ready.

Cyrano opened in New York on 13 May 1973 to mixed reviews that generally extolled Plummer's acting, panned Lewis's music, and offered Burgess's words reserved praise. Clive Barnes's review in *The New York Times* was more positive than most:

> The musical "Cyrano", in which Christopher Plummer triumphed at the Palace Theatre last night, is altogether very good and partly excellent. Why the qualification? Well, simply because the music is the weakest part of this particular musical. Indeed, there are times when one wished the music would simply go away, and others when one could easily imagine that it had.

> The adaptation of the Edmond Rostand play has been undertaken by Anthony Burgess, who has done an excellent and appropriately flamboyant job. His lyrics tend toward the flashy rather than the fluent, but even here the work has been well done. Mr. Burgess has taken the opportunity of subtly updating Rostand – always the privilege of a translator – and yet still maintaining that heady mixture of rhetoric, rodomontade and romanticism that is the old play's stock-in-trade.[36]

Four days later, the Senate Watergate Committee convened. As New Yorkers, along with rest of the US population, sat transfixed before their television sets watching the Watergate hearings, Broadway ticket sales plummeted. *Cyrano* closed after just forty-nine performances, yet despite the brevity of its six-week run, it earned Christopher Plummer the 1974 Tony Award for Best Actor in a Musical. *Cyrano* also received a Grammy nomination for the original cast recording, a double album recorded on 17 June 1973 for A&M Records.

Burgess's view notwithstanding, a Broadway musical based on *Cyrano de Bergerac* could have produced a great show. The triumph of *Les Misérables*, which opened a dozen years after *Cyrano*, amply demonstrated that a successful musical can be based on a nineteenth-century French literary masterpiece. *Cyrano*'s most striking weakness is the absence of ensemble numbers to strengthen its characters' relationships. A duet when Cyrano agrees to combine his eloquence with Christian's good looks to woo Roxana would fortify the two men's bond and could have served as a rousing Act I finale along the lines of "A Little Priest" in *Sweeney Todd*. The absence of a duet for Cyrano and Roxana in the final scene is an even more regrettable omission. The most grievous missed opportunity is the lack of a trio in the Act II balcony scene, a moment so perfectly suited for musical treatment that its absence is shocking. Liner notes for the reissued cast recording provide the explanation:

> Plummer, armed with a star's right of song approval, kept suggesting potential showstoppers to the beleaguered Burgess, who was doing his best to write a commercial show, although he felt that when Langham started calling *Cyrano* "a play with music" rather than a musical, they were in trouble ... One of the few songs to excite Burgess's enthusiasm was written in Boston, a trio for Cyrano, Christian, and Roxana to be sung under her balcony. Plummer declined to learn it, however; seven songs, two duels, one dance, and a death scene – he had enough to do already.[37]

The impasse over this number helps to explain Burgess's frustration with the show and his disparagement of its star's "petulance" and "madness": "with Plummer I met self-consciousness about stellar rank and large pride in hard-won techniques."[38]

The score of *Cyrano* possesses charm and some fine tunes in the style of such shows as *Camelot*, *Oliver*, and, especially, *Man of La Mancha*. What it lacks is variety, for it is made up almost exclusively of solo songs or ensemble numbers consisting mainly of single vocal lines. Duets are generally the kind in which one singer alternates phrases with another, avoiding harmony or counterpoint, and company numbers are mostly sung in unison. The declamatory "Nose Song" is a strong opener, but the succession of similar numbers – "Tell Her", "Till Forever", "No Thank You", "It's She and It's Me", "Panooshe", "The Paris Cuisine" – becomes tiresome. Lewis's strength lies in the ballads, several of which, like "Bergerac", "You Have Made Me Love", and "Love Is Not Love", are lovely.

"Cyrano's Nose", one of the show's strongest numbers, afforded Burgess the perfect opportunity to showcase his linguistic virtuosity. In this catalog of Cyrano's self-directed proboscidean insults, Burgess's witty lyrics are skillfully matched by the music, practically a miniature tone poem, with Lewis providing aural equivalents of a Parisian perfume shop and the Red Sea. The lyrics exhibit Burgess's command of such rhetorical tropes as antanaclasis (repetition of identical words having separate definitions) and alliteration:

> There are fifty score varieties of insult you could find –
> the lyrical, satirical, commercial, controversial,
> and quite frequently the kind kind –
> if you possessed a minimal amount of mind.

Burgess indulges his fondness for polysyllables while producing clever internal rhymes:

> Should my nose ever burgeon to that hypertrophic state,
> I wouldn't wait – I'd urge a surgeon to amputate.

Imaginative rhyme schemes produce some delightful surprises, such as the succession of rhymes on "-ess" and "-ude" culminating brilliantly in the line "an attitude less crude":

> Not everyone, I must confess
> is opprobrious or rude.
> A genuine goodheartedness
> leads quite a number to express
> an attitude less crude.

A splendid internal rhyme follows a torrent of metaphor in the final verse, where use of the possessive creates an identity between the gloomy Gascon's name and his most striking attribute:

> This monumental edifice, this fortress, this peninsula,
> this promontory, obelisk, this portable Gibraltar,
> most uncommon of phenomena that goes
> by the name of Cyrano's nose.

Indignant refusal to bow down to the nobles and clergy is expressed in the fiery number "No Thank You", each of whose verses culminates in Cyrano's fierce rejection of a sequence of sarcastic rhetorical questions:

> Shall I crawl on my knees
> until I wear out the skin?
> Commit the ultimate sin
> of trying madly to please?
> Shall I be one of the fleas
> on the flesh of the great?
> A lousy louse of the state?
> No thank you![39]

The song's lyrics and musical style recall the character of the Frank Sinatra hit "I've Gotta Be Me" while its stepwise ascending chromatic modulations, first from E♭ to E♮, then from E to F, emphasize its pop origins. Lewis keeps a handwritten parody of this song, written for him by Burgess, framed and hung on a wall of his California home:

> *Burgess is sitting on the toilet writing:*
> Shall I sit costive and grim in my poetical nook
> and spend my life on one book
> that's penitentially slim?
> Would it be better to dim
> all this fire in my head
> and be a critic instead?
> No thank you!

The individual contributions of Lewis and Burgess are least compatible in "You Have Made Me Love" (Example 13.06), a problematic number that exemplifies the score's strengths and weaknesses. Thrilled by the fervent proclamation of love extemporized by Cyrano posing as Christian, Roxana expresses in this song the newfound love that such eloquence has aroused. Where the vocal line contains a series of soaring fifths and sevenths that skillfully convey the intensity of Roxana's response to Cyrano's wooing, the lyrics are rambling, with awkward ill-placed rhymes that distract by failing to match the accents and contours of the melodic line.

One of the show's most beautiful songs is "Love Is Not Love", in which Roxana confesses to Christian that, because of the passion and eloquence of his letters, she would love him even if he were ugly. In this attractive ballad, tastefully alliterative lyrics based on Shakespeare's Sonnet 116 ("Let me not to the marriage of true minds / Admit impediments") are wedded to an elegant melody, gracefully expressing the sentiment that true love transcends appearances.

> Love is not love that looks for grandeur or grace,
> Haunted by handsomeness of form or of face.
> That is no love but just a shell on the shore.
> Tides will engulf it and you'll see it no more.

The lack of a duet in the final scene subverts the show's emotional climax, denying Roxana the opportunity to musically express her belated recogni-

Family Affairs

Example 13.06 Cyrano: "You Have Made Me Love" (bs. 1–42)

tion of the love she has misconstrued for so long while preventing Cyrano from finally giving voice to his long concealed feelings. Instead, it ends with Cyrano's "I Never Loved You", an anticlimactic number that Burgess dubbed a "reluctant and perverse revelation".[40]

Example 13.06 *Continued*

I never loved you. I may not lie
And say I love you – not I.
I never loved you – that word must fly
And die like smoke in the sky.

Be thankful for all the love that lives on,
But sometimes let fall just one gentle tear upon
The memory of this truth or this lie:
I never loved you, my dear love, not I.

After *Cyrano*, Michael Lewis wrote again for film and television, but never composed again for the stage. John Covelli became a successful orchestra conductor. Michael Langham went on to direct numerous films and plays, while Michael Kidd staged three more Broadway musicals. As for Burgess, his life had changed drastically between the Guthrie production of *Cyrano de Bergerac* and *Cyrano*'s short-lived Broadway run. Thanks to Stanley Kubrick, he had become not just one of the world's most famous living novelists, but its most notorious.

Notes

1 TMM, 164.
2 Jim Hicks, "Eclectic author of his own five-foot shelf", *Life* (65:17), 25 October 1968, 87–97. This issue, which headlined "Schirra and Apollo 7" on the cover and included an editorial endorsement of Richard Nixon in the upcoming US presidential election, also included articles about James Earl Jones starring on Broadway in *The Great White Hope*, how soldiers in Vietnam viewed the 1968 presidential candidates, and the fortieth anniversary of Mickey Mouse.
3 No known music exists related to the proposed Enderby film, for which he had just completed the script. Other projects then in progress and mentioned in *Life* include the script for *Will*, completion of *MF*, and the imminent publication of *Urgent Copy*. For the description of a bassoon concerto that may be the one cited in the article, see Chapter 30.
4 YH, 160.
5 Samuel Coale, "An Interview with Anthony Burgess", *Modern Fiction Studies* (27:3), Autumn 1981, 436.
6 "The World Doesn't Like Gipsies", *One Man's Chorus: The Uncollected Writings*, ed. by Ben Forkner (New York: Carroll & Graf, 1998), 140.
7 YH, 210. At the "Avatars of *A Clockwork Orange*" conference in Angers in December 2001, Liana Burgess publicly confirmed that *MF* was her husband's favorite of all his novels.
8 "If Oedipus had read his Lévi-Strauss", *Washington Post Book World*, 26 November 1967, 6 (reprinted in *Urgent Copy*, 258–61). *The Scope of Anthropology* is the transcript of the inaugural lecture that Lévi-Strauss delivered upon becoming Chair of Social Anthropology at the Collège de France in 1960.
9 YH, 208.
10 Ibid., 209.
11 TMM, 178–9.
12 YH, 208. Burgess referred to the title alternately as *M.F.* or *M/F*, stating that it could also stand for *male/female* and *mother/father*.
13 MF, 229.
14 Ibid., 229–30. The convention of allowing a rest to represent the letter R is one that Burgess would later use similarly in *Beard's Roman Women*.
15 Ibid., 228, 239.
16 Preface to *Cyrano de Bergerac* (New York: Vintage Classics), viii.
17 YH, 237.
18 Clive Barnes, "Langham Revitalizes the Guthrie Theatre", *The New York Times*, 20 September 1971, 31.

19 YH, 237.
20 Sophocles, *Oedipus the King*, trans. and adapted by Anthony Burgess (Minneapolis: University of Minnesota Press in Association with the Guthrie Theater, 1972), 83–4, 86.
21 *Oedipus the King*, 88–9.
22 As confirmed by Ward Swingle, the actual Swingle Singers never performed the piece.
23 Letter to Welles, 13 July 1972, sent from 16a Piazza Santa Cecilia, Rome.
24 Michael J. Lewis, interview with author, 21 February 2000.
25 YH, 252.
26 John Covelli, interview with author, 19 August 1998.
27 Lewis interview.
28 YH, 240–1.
29 Covelli interview.
30 See Chapter 21. Cf. *New York*, 117.
31 Covelli interview.
32 Laurence Maslon, "The Winner By a Nose", program note for the compact disk reissue of *Cyrano* (Decca Broadway B0004083-02 © 2005), 13.
33 YH, 284.
34 Covelli interview.
35 YH, 284.
36 Clive Barnes, "Plummer Triumphs in Musical 'Cyrano'", *The New York Times*, 14 May 1973, 37.
37 Maslon, "The Winner By a Nose", 13.
38 YH, 263, 284.
39 *Cyrano*, Libretto Vocal Book (New York: Music Theatre International), 1-2-42.
40 Burgess, program note for *Cyrano*, original cast album (A & M Records). Reprinted in the booklet (7–8) of the compact disk reissue.

14

KUBRICK THE SINNY VECK

Righty right. And real horrorshow. And lashings of deng for the carmans of Zubrick. And for your malenky droog not none no more. So gromky shooms of lip-music brrrrrr to thee and thine. And all that cal.[1]

Shortly after its publication in 1962, *A Clockwork Orange* began attracting the interest of filmmakers in Britain and the US. A BBC dramatization (now lost) of the book's first three chapters for the program *Tonight* in the early 1960s was followed in 1965 by *Vinyl*, a low-budget film adaptation produced by Andy Warhol. The novelist and screenwriter Terry Southern subsequently purchased a six-month option for about $1000, adapted the novel into a screenplay, and pitched it to several film producers without success.[2] Southern, who had collaborated with Stanley Kubrick on the screenplay of *Dr. Strangelove*, tried to interest him in *A Clockwork Orange* during the filming of *2001: A Space Odyssey* by giving him a copy of the novel, but Kubrick, preoccupied with his next project, a Napoleon film starring Jack Nicholson, paid little attention. Lacking the money to renew the option, Southern let it expire, but his enthusiasm for the project led his attorney Si Litvinoff to purchase the film rights together with Litvinoff's business partner Max L. Raab. At one point, Litvinoff and Raab intended to produce a film, using Southern's script and directed by John Boorman, starring David Hemmings as Alex; later they commissioned Burgess to write the screenplay himself.[3] There had also been talk of filming *A Clockwork Orange* with Mick Jagger and the Rolling Stones cast as Alex and his three droogs, but none of these plans were carried out.[4]

Just before Kubrick's Napoleon epic was about to start filming, Dino De Laurentiis produced a Napoleon film of his own: *Waterloo*, a lavish Soviet-Italian production starring Rod Steiger as the Corsican conqueror and Christopher Plummer as the Duke of Wellington. When *Waterloo* failed miserably at the box office, Kubrick's investors abruptly withdrew their backing, which left him suddenly casting about for a new project. At this juncture, in the summer of 1969, Kubrick finally picked up the copy of *A Clockwork Orange* that Southern had given him two and a half years earlier, read it in one sitting, and immediately became strongly attracted to the idea of filming it. As he told one reporter, "One could almost say that it's the kind of book that you have to look hard to find a reason not to do."[5] To another, he enthused: "The narrative invention was magical, the characters were bizarre and exciting, the ideas were brilliantly developed, and, equally important, the story was of a size and density that could be adapted to film without simplifying it or stripping it to the bone."[6] In January 1970 he contacted Malcolm McDowell, whom he pictured right away as Alex, despite the fact that, at twenty-eight years of age, the actor was nearly twice as old as the character in the novel. McDowell read the novel, agreed with Kubrick that the book would make a brilliant film, and, upon being offered the principal role, accepted at once. Kubrick's eagerness to have this actor play Alex was so great that he later declared, "If McDowell hadn't been available, I probably wouldn't have made the film."[7]

Busy writing *MF* and his adaptation of *Cyrano de Bergerac* at the time, Burgess's reaction was decidedly muted when he learned that Kubrick planned to direct *A Clockwork Orange*. He worried that the film might make the acts of "ultra-violence", veiled in the novel through the use of Nadsat, all too explicit and that his book might be misrepresented on-screen, as Nabokov's *Lolita* had been by the same director. Moreover, he anticipated scant earnings since his agent had sold the film rights long before for a paltry sum, though he had already received a handsome fee of $50,000 for the film treatment he wrote for Litvinoff and Raab. Recognizing that profits from Kubrick's film could dwarf that figure, Burgess now feared he might be excluded from the potential windfall.[8]

Indeed, Kubrick excluded Burgess almost entirely from the production. The director wrote the screenplay alone and filmed *A Clockwork Orange* without consulting the novelist about the script or music save for one detail. In the spring of 1970, during a trip to Australia for the Adelaide Arts Festival, Burgess received a series of telegrams from Kubrick requesting a meeting in London, later learning that the director had only wanted to know whether the lines sung by the old man in I:2 were under separate copyright. Once assured that Burgess had written them, Kubrick avoided further contact until production on the film was completed.

To score the film, Kubrick engaged composer Wendy Carlos and her associate Rachel Elkind, electronic music pioneers whose 1968 Grammy-winning debut album *Switched-On Bach* popularized the Moog synthesizer and became the first ever Platinum classical recording. Burgess and Beethoven were the links that brought Kubrick and Carlos together, both of whom discovered *A Clockwork Orange* at roughly the same time. Carlos began reading it while composing an electronic piece called *Timesteps* and was so struck by what she perceived as parallels between the mood of the book and her new work – regarding it, in her words, as "an autonomous composition with an uncanny affinity for *Clockwork*" – that she completed *Timesteps* as an intentional musical counterpart to Burgess's novel.[9] Eager to produce the soundtrack for Kubrick's film, Carlos and Elkind sent him a tape of *Timesteps* and their new rendition of the finale of Beethoven's

Ninth Symphony, which synthesized the sound of the human voice using their new Vocoder technology. Their creation of an electronic version of Beethoven's Ninth, begun before they knew of its prominence in the novel, had been especially fortuitous, as they realized by the time they contacted the director. Kubrick responded quickly, inviting Carlos and Elkind to his home for a meeting, and they were promptly hired to produce the soundtrack.

In England, Carlos and Elkind discovered that Kubrick had already incorporated into his current edit sections of *Timesteps* and some of the other pieces they had sent. They also learned that he had already decided on Purcell's *Music for the Funeral of Queen Mary* and Rossini's *William Tell* Overture for the soundtrack, and was depending on them to convert these into futuristic electronic timbres:

> The Purcell struck him as the right mood – very formal, to counter the violence to come – but the LP track seemed a bit "wimpy". I came up with the "nasty-ization" via cleverly processed electronic and concrete percussion, *sfz* thuds, whams, hits, and bap sounds, trying many ideas, finding out what sounded really good. We sent him a few versions of our new Purcell, and the first one, our favorite too, is the one he selected for the final soundtrack . . . I suggested how much more effective it might be for the orgy sequence to create a special "souped-up" version of the William Tell. He was skeptical, but . . . thanked us for "a big improvement!" He really preferred it, including the way I tried to grind it into a long ritardando, then let it die off into thin air at the end, as Malcolm descends the staircase "all worn out".[10]

Having successfully pioneered the technique of scoring films with preexisting works in *2001: A Space Odyssey*, Kubrick relied again on his musical instincts in *A Clockwork Orange*, though now in conjunction with compositions mentioned in Burgess's novel, emphasizing Beethoven's Ninth while excluding other Beethoven compositions cited in the book, such as the Violin Concerto and Fifth Symphony.

Though not mentioned in the novel, Purcell and Rossini were apt, even inspired choices for the film.[11] Purcell was a Burgess favorite – the first name on his list of *Desert Island Discs*.[12] Selections by Rimsky-Korsakov and Elgar (another *Desert Island* composer) also suited the tone of the novel. "Singin' in the Rain", which wound up in the film by happenstance, is another matter.[13] Since Alex loves only classical music and disdains pop, having him sing this during the assault of F. Alexander and his wife violates the consistency of his character. Burgess, disapproving the choice on these grounds, nevertheless enjoyed demonstrating to Kubrick how it could be played contrapuntally with Beethoven's Ninth.

> I showed him, on his piano, that the Ode to Joy and "Singin' in the Rain" (which Alex sings while thumping the husband of the woman he proposes to ravish) go in acceptable counterpoint. I could see the gleam in his eye of a commercial exploitation, but he let it go.[14]

In his 1986 stage version of *A Clockwork Orange*, Burgess set both tunes together polyphonically in a satirical scene poking fun at Kubrick.

Burgess first viewed the motion picture in the fall of 1971 at a private screening in Soho. As he had feared, the brutality depicted in the novel came sickeningly to life in Technicolor.[15] Ten minutes into the film, Burgess's agent Deborah Rogers got up to leave followed moments later by Liana. In order not to insult Kubrick, who was standing at the back of the screening room, Burgess implored them to stay, which they did, but their reaction vividly illustrated to the author the degree to which his philosophical novella about good and evil had become a profoundly disturbing display of graphic violence. Kubrick's decision to base the film on the truncated American edition of the novel set Burgess raging in interviews, articles, and his autobiography about the publisher's decision to issue the book without the final chapter:

> A vindication of free will had become an exaltation of the urge to sin. I was worried. The British version of the book shows Alex growing up and putting violence by as a childish toy; Kubrick confessed that he did not know this version: an American, though settled in England, he had followed the only version that Americans were permitted to know. I cursed Eric Swenson of W. W. Norton.[16]

Yet, unbeknownst to Kubrick or the public, Burgess had ended his screenplay for Litvinoff and Raab at exactly the same point – an inconvenient fact that supports Kubrick's aesthetic judgment while exposing Burgess's more disingenuous side.[17]

A Clockwork Orange opened in New York City on 20 December 1971 to some of the most impassioned and sharply divided reviews in cinematic history, from Judith Crist's rave ("a stunningly original work which does full justice to Burgess's novel"[18]) to Pauline Kael's fiery condemnation ("an abhorrent viewing experience" by a "martinet" director "with an arctic spirit"[19]). Burgess's reaction to the film was staunchly positive. In an interview published in *Penthouse* in June 1972, he was quoted as saying, "I think on the whole Kubrick has got it right. I think the final sequence sums it all up; it's a very ambiguous sequence, and a very cynical sequence, in some ways, but I think he's got the main message across. He's followed it very closely."[20]

Despite its X rating, the film was an enormous hit in the US, achieving the second-highest gross ticket sales (after *My Fair Lady*) of any Warner Brothers film up to that time, but in Britain, it provoked controversy that soon spun out of control. Within weeks of its British release on 13 January 1972, newspapers and politicians were calling for a ban on the film before it spawned copycat crimes. Throughout the year it was repeatedly blamed for assaults, triggering warnings in the press that it would "lead to a clockwork cult which will magnify teen violence."[21] In early 1973, worn down by the constant media attacks and intimidated by death threats to him and his family if the picture were not withdrawn, Kubrick took the extreme step of forbidding the film to be shown in Britain. Films had been banned before, but for a director to prohibit the showing of his own film was without precedent. Taking legal action when necessary, Kubrick strictly enforced and never lifted the ban, which remained in effect until 2000, a year after his death.

While Burgess gave frequent press interviews and appeared continually on television, radio, and college speaking tours, defending the film and his novella with arguments espousing the imperative of allowing free choice, "the fulfilled artist Kubrick," in a Joycean metaphor, "pared his nails in his house at Borehamwood".[22] With remarkable equanimity, Burgess had accepted not only the director's insistence on billing the film as "Stanley Kubrick's *A Clockwork Orange*", but also the fact that Kubrick had received the lion's share of the profits: forty per cent according to his contract with Warner Brothers.[23] What Burgess could not accept was the director's decision to issue a *book* titled *Stanley Kubrick's A Clockwork Orange*, which he viewed as an unforgivable transgression. This publication – a collection of still photographs from the film – prompted an indignant Burgess to attack Kubrick in a *Library Journal* review written in Nadsat, punning on the rhyme between the director's name and *zubrick*, a rather colorful Arabic vulgarism for penis:

> Our starry droog Kubrick the sinny veck has, my brothers, like brought forth from his like bounty and all that cal this kniggiwig ... you can like viddy as well that the Great Purpose in his jeezny which this veck Kubrick or Zubrick, that being the Arab eemya for a grahzny veshch is like now at last being made flesh and all that cal, was to have a Book. And now he has a Book. A Book he doth have, O my malenky brothers, verily he doth. A Book. Righty right.[24]

Shortly thereafter, on 9 May 1973, Burgess filed suit in London against Warner Brothers and the executive producers Litvinoff and Raab (though not Kubrick) for conspiracy to defraud him of the film rights to his novel. The court decided in Burgess's favor, granting him ten per cent of the profits. Although Burgess liked to downplay the financial value of this settlement, it brought him a great deal of money; one royalty statement alone from Warner Brothers, dated June 1985, shows a payment of $713,081.[25] Moreover, Kubrick's film increased Burgess's international fame enormously, and, by helping turn his novella into a worldwide bestseller, laid the foundation for the considerable wealth he amassed during his lifetime.[26]

Burgess transmuted the bedlam surrounding *A Clockwork Orange* into *The Clockwork Testament*, a wickedly funny book resuming the tale of F. X. Enderby, now resembling the author much more closely than in the previous two novels. Written in Italy in July 1973 in just ten days, the story takes place during a single day climaxing, literally, in sexual intercourse and death. Employed as a Visiting Professor at the University of Manhattan, the protagonist is vilified as a rabid promoter of violence after one of his screenplays, a chaste film treatment of Hopkins's *The Wreck of the Deutschland*, is produced as a controversial sex- and violence-laden disaster flick set in the Third Reich. Enderby endures an endless stream of confrontations with belligerent students, dangerous thugs, a Pelagian professor, a fatuous talk show host, and, finally, a fanatical gun-toting messenger of death whom he seduces – *"Enderbius triumphans, exultans"* – just before dying of a heart attack.[27]

Enderby, expressing Burgess's aesthetic attitudes, regards Beethoven as the pinnacle of musical art and imagines the afterlife as "a kind of infinite Ninth Symphony."[28] Strolling the dangerous streets near Times Square, Enderby accepts the risk of potential violence, justifying it as the price one must pay to stay fully engaged in the world: "Die with Beethoven's Ninth howling and crashing away or live in a safe world of silly clockwork music?"[29] Dismissing rock and roll as musical trash, Enderby sneers that, under the permissive educational philosophy then in vogue, college students may study anything they like, including courses in "petromusicology, that being teenage garbage now treated as an art."[30]

This *roman à clef* contains a number of thinly veiled celebrity portraits. Enderby receives a visit from "a Hollywood producer-director, not unlike Kubrick", who wangles a film script from him for a negligible fee.[31] He sublets the apartment of "a rabid ideological man-hater" modeled on Adrienne Rich, the "famous feminist and man-hater" whose flat Burgess rented during his Manhattan sojourn.[32] On a New York television talk show, Enderby pits his wits against Professor Man Balaglas, whose arguments in favor of behaviorism are lifted verbatim from B. F. Skinner's *Beyond Freedom and Dignity*, which was published in 1971, the same year that Kubrick's film was released.

Despite the satire and court case over film rights, relations between Burgess and Kubrick remained cordial and extended to the discussion of future potential collaborations. Aware of Burgess's interest in combining music with literature, and still lacking a screenplay for the Napoleon film he still hoped to make, Kubrick shrewdly proposed a project that would channel Burgess's twin passions into producing the script he needed: "Annnthony, if you're gonna write a [novel] why don't you write about Napoleon, cause yunno, you've already got a symphony to work with: Beethoven's *Eroica*, which was of course, dedicated to Napoleon."[33] Burgess seized upon the idea enthusiastically even though he knew that the film might never be made, as turned out to be the case.

The other potential film subject was *Traumnovelle* ("Dream Novel") by Arthur Schnitzler, which, like the Napoleon film, was a subject that Kubrick had first considered long before he filmed *A Clockwork Orange*. In October 1976, a year after the release of *Barry Lyndon*, Kubrick sent a photostat of the book to Burgess in Monaco, asking him for his opinion about adapting it to a contemporary setting. Responding swiftly, Burgess recommended that the original milieu be retained: "I think the setting should be Schnitzler's own Vienna . . . with the music drawn from Strauss's *Metamorphosen*, which I'm sure you know. The question is – do you want me to do anything about it? If so, how and when and for how much."[34] Kubrick's conviction that the story required updating led him to collaborate instead with the screenwriter-novelist Frederic Raphael on what became his last film, *Eyes Wide Shut*.

For Burgess, the consequences of the film *A Clockwork Orange* were enormous. He emerged from the frenzy not only with one new novel completed and another on the way, but also with new opportunities in the television and film industry – opportunities that now led him away from the futuristic dystopia of *A Clockwork Orange* back in time to ancient Egypt and the prophet who led the Jewish people from slavery to freedom.[35]

Notes

1 "Burgess on Kubrick on 'Clockwork'", *Library Journal* (98:9), 1 May 1973, 1506 [Boytinck (121), 16].
2 Gene D. Phillips and Rodney Hill, *The Encyclopedia of Stanley Kubrick* (New York: Checkmark Books, 2002), 51.
3 The film was to have been shot independently in England in February 1968, according to *The Encyclopedia of Stanley Kubrick*, 208.
4 Of Mick Jagger's suitability to play Alex, Burgess wrote: "I admired the intelligence, if not the art, of this young man and considered that he looked the quintessence of delinquency." YH, 142.
5 Andrew Bailey of *Rolling Stone*, as quoted by Vincent LoBrutto in *Stanley Kubrick: A Biography* (New York: Donald I. Fine Books, 1997), 338.
6 Judith Crist, "A Feast, and About Time", *New York* (4:5), 20/27 December 1971, 90 [Boytinck (132), 18].
7 David Hughes, *The Complete Kubrick* (London: Virgin, 2000), 163.
8 See RLAB, 337-8.
9 Wendy Carlos as quoted in Chris Nelson's liner notes to the compact disk *Wendy Carlos's Complete Original Score: A Clockwork Orange*, East Side Digital ESD 81362.
10 Wendy Carlos, email to author, 3 February 2005.
11 The view that "the Germanophilic Alex would probably have only contempt" for Rossini contradicts the protagonist's fondness for music by composers neither German nor Austrian. Since Alex enjoys music from America (Plautus), Denmark (Skadelig), and France (Birdman, representing Debussy), there is no reason to assume that he would dislike the music of Italy in general or Rossini in particular. See Peter J. Rabinowitz, "A Bird of Like Rarest Heavenmetal", in Stuart Y. McDougal (ed.), *Stanley Kubrick's* A Clockwork Orange (Cambridge: Cambridge University Press, 2003), 123.
12 See Chapter 12.
13 Unhappy with the way rehearsals had been going for the scene in which the droogs assault F. Alexander and his wife, Kubrick decided to try a new approach. As McDowell tells the story, "When we got to the scene where the writer is

beaten and his wife raped, Stanley suddenly called, 'Hey, Malcolm, can you sing and dance?' 'I can't do either,' I said, and just sort of started dancing, then kicking the writer. And I began 'Singin' in the Rain,' as it's the only song I know. Within three hours, Stanley had bought the rights to it." Tom Burke, "Malcolm McDowell: The Liberals, They Hate 'Clockwork'", *The New York Times*, 30 January 1972, D13.
14 YH, 246.
15 As Christopher Ricks, Susan Caruthers, and others have pointed out, the brutality inflicted by Alex in the film is muted in comparison to the nastier and more sustained violence depicted in the novel. See Christopher Ricks, "Horror Show", *New York Review of Books* (18:6), 6 April 1972, 28–9 [Boytinck (152), 22].
16 YH, 245.
17 See RLAB, 338.
18 Crist, "A Feast, and About Time".
19 Pauline Kael, "*A Clockwork Orange*: Stanley Strangelove", *New Yorker* (47:46), 1 January 1972, 50–3 (reprinted in *Stanley Kubrick's* A Clockwork Orange, 134–139).
20 George Malko, "Anthony Burgess", *Penthouse* (3:10), June 1972, 84.
21 Hughes, *The Complete Kubrick*, 170.
22 YH, 245, an allusion to *A Portrait of the Artist as a Young Man* (483): "The artist, like the God of the creation, remains within or behind or beyond or above his handiwork, invisible, refined out of existence, indifferent, paring his fingernails.".
23 Hughes, *The Complete Kubrick*, 172.
24 "Burgess on Kubrick on 'Clockwork'", 1506.
25 See YH, 248; RLAB, 353.
26 By 1993, the Burgesses owned three condominiums in Monte Carlo plus homes in Switzerland, Italy, France, and England.
27 *The Clockwork Testament*, 469.
28 Ibid., 403–4.
29 Ibid., 453.
30 Ibid., 414. Burgess's disdain for rock did not deter rock stars from admiring his work. Pete Townshend of The Who, whose seminal 1969 rock opera *Tommy* has probably been studied in every "petromusicology" course ever offered, wrote Burgess a glowing fan letter on 26 March 1981: "I have just, unfortunately, finished reading Earthly Powers. I am staggered by it, and will read it again after brief respite ... Yours is truly a great book ... the devastating, explosive wrangling of the English language ... is simply exhilarating page after page ... I look forward, desperately, to your future work, stay alive forever.".
31 YH, 285.
32 CT, 394; YH, 269.
33 Kubrick, as quoted by Burgess, as quoted by Sheila Weller in 1972 in the *Village Voice*, as quoted in LoBrutto, 331. Knowing of Burgess's intention to write a novel in the form of a Mozart symphony, Kubrick was suggesting that he merely switch the model to Beethoven instead. The bracketed word *novel* replaces *symphony*, an apparent error that must have crept in during the successive quotations.
34 Letter to Kubrick, 20 October 1976.
35 YH, 260.

15

ANCIENT EVENINGS

The Italians would listen to Aaron, but not to Moses.[1]

Life in Malta soon became intolerable for Burgess. He delivered a lecture on censorship and obscenity at the University of Malta that greatly offended the local clergy, and shortly afterward, the government attempted to confiscate his house. Although the Burgesses successfully retained their property in Lija, they decided to move to Italy. From the American sculptor Milton Hebald they purchased a small fifteenth-century house in Bracciano, a picturesque town 35 km northwest of Rome, and moved there in 1970.

One of the first major projects to come Burgess's way after the move to Italy was an invitation from Vincenzo Labella, a professor-turned-producer specializing in Biblical subjects, to write the film script for a television miniseries about Moses to be co-produced by Radiotelevisione Italiana and Sir Lew Grade. Burt Lancaster would star as Moses, with Anthony Quayle portraying Aaron. Burgess began work in autumn 1972 on a verse novel, later published as *Moses: A Narrative*, from which he fashioned scripts for the six hourlong episodes of *Moses the Lawgiver*, finishing them in Rome the following summer. To denote Moses's halting speech, Burgess used interruptive punctuation to create a linguistic equivalent of irregular musical rhythm: "'But they will. Not believe me. They will / Say: the Lord has. Not appeared unto you.'"[2] Filming took place in 1973 in Italy and Israel, with Burgess remaining behind in Rome to work on the editing and extensive lip-synchronization required by the polyglot production. In lieu of money, he agreed to accept renovations to his Bracciano home as remuneration.

Upon completing the script, Burgess composed a score for *Moses the Lawgiver* consisting mainly of chants, prayers, songs, and dances – eighteen numbers in all.[3] "Title Music", composed in the grandiose style of Korngold and Rósza, is the only orchestrated number. Written out in full orchestral score, this majestic piece comprises an introduction followed by two contrasting themes – a robust, Phrygian martial theme in F with a Middle Eastern character and a merry dance tune in E♭ major. After both themes are presented individually, they return together in counterpoint. Most are of the other numbers are simply words set to a melody, with a rudimentary drum rhythm or chordal accompaniment added in several cases. In 1974

Example 15.01 "Moses's Song" from *Moses: A Narrative* (188)

Burgess incorporated the "Egyptian March" into his Third Symphony as the first movement's second theme (see Example 17.02). "Moses's Song", a stately A major tune in 7/4, is the *Moses* score's final number. In Burgess's handwritten notation, a C major version of the melody, without words or time signature, appears in *Moses: A Narrative* (Example 15.01).[4] This melody also turns up in the Third Symphony, serving as the first movement's third theme (see Example 17.03).

The *Moses* score was unsolicited and unexpected by the producer, who turned down Burgess's request to compose the music for the entire miniseries. The prominent Italian film composer Ennio Morricone was hired instead, which Burgess resented: "Lew Grade tried to soothe me by commissioning words for the main theme, these to be sung by Barbra Streisand. It was decided finally that she had better not sing them."[5] Nearly a decade later, Burgess remained sufficiently rankled to cite the score, in his list of works in *This Man and Music*, thus: "Music for television series *Moses* (unacceptable to Sir Lew Grade)".[6]

Around the time of the *Moses* project Burgess composed an Ezra Pound setting titled *Bethlehem Palmtrees*.[7] In 1969 or 1970, Burgess had paid a visit to Pound in Venice during which the aged poet said nothing, upholding the "mysterious silence" that he maintained during his final years.[8] *Bethlehem Palmtrees*, probably composed as a memorial shortly after Pound's death on 1 November 1972, is a setting for unaccompanied SATB chorus of the second strophe of "A Song of the Virgin Mother", Pound's translation of a stanza from the play *Los Pastores de Belen* by Lope de Vega.[9]

> O Bethlehem palm-trees
> That move to the anger
> Of winds in their fury,
> Tempestuous voices,
> Make ye no clamour,
> Run ye less swiftly,
> Sith sleepeth the child here
> Still ye your branches.[10]

Set in C minor, this short, chromatic composition ventures harmonically from tonic to G♭ major and back, ending on a C major chord owing to a Picardy third. A wordless descant penned in different ink from the rest of the manuscript – a sort of contrapuntal doodle abandoned after twelve bars – was evidently not meant to be performed, as is true of the keyboard reduction of the vocal parts, which is tagged for "Rehearsal Only".

Moses had made money, so Lew Grade laid plans for additional Biblical projects, declaring: "Lads, we're going to do Jesus."[11] *Jesus of Nazareth* was the result, another British-Italian joint venture financed by Lew Grade and RAI, with Labella again the executive producer. Robert Powell, as Jesus, headed a dazzling cast that included Olivia Hussey, Laurence Olivier, Ralph Richardson, Rod Steiger, Peter Ustinov, Christopher Plummer, Anne Bancroft, James Earl Jones, and James Mason. Franco Zeffirelli directed. Burgess shared scriptwriting credit with Zeffirelli and Suso Cecchi d'Amico, but maintained that he wrote the script himself, completing it in sixteen days and delivering it to Zeffirelli in May 1974. The television version, which premiered in Europe on 3 April 1977 and was broadcast the following year in the US, was nearly six and half hours long, requiring a lengthy musical score that Maurice Jarre composed. Although Burgess wrote no music for this project, he expressed passionate feelings about how the film should be scored in a letter to Labella after shooting and initial editing had been completed.

> May I say a word about the proposed music for *Jesus Christ*? I know this is not my province, but I think I am the only one in the "team" who can lay any claim to technical musical knowledge. I am deeply disturbed by the possibility of a fine film being ruined by a merely competent score – which is what you will get at most from Jarre. I am obviously not offering myself for the job of composer, but I have one very serious suggestion to make. The entire score should be in the form of a passacaglia – that is, a bass of eight measures over which the upper part weaves diverse patterns but are always unified by the bass theme. There are two good examples of passacaglie to listen to, and these will show what I mean. The first is in Bach's Passacaglia and Fugue in C minor (do minore) for Organ; the second is the last movement of Brahms's Fourth Symphony in Mi Minore (E Minor). You need something much more modern of course, but the advantage of having a musical unity between, say, the Nativity and the Crucifixion should be evident. What the film needs is a musical structure and not impressionistic burblings. I feel strongly about this; can anybody else be made to feel as strongly?[12]

Following his usual practice, Burgess wrote a full-length novel from which he adapted the script. Naturally, he wanted the book, *Man of Nazareth*, to be published in conjunction with the television broadcast, but that honor went to *Jesus of Nazareth*, a collection of still photographs from the film with text by William Barclay. *Man of Nazareth* first appeared in print in French, as *L'Homme de Nazareth* (1976), translated by Georges Belmont and Hortense Chabrier, and then as *L'Uomo di Nazareth* (1978), rendered into Italian by Liana Burgess. The English original, first published in 1979, pointedly contains no reference to the film.

In 1976–77, Burgess wrote the script for another Labella venture – "a mammoth *Cyrus* for the Iranians" that was never produced.[13] Subsequent films that were made include *Anthony Burgess's Rome*, an hourlong program for Canadian television produced in 1978, and *Celebration*, a 1980 broadcast for Granada Television featuring Burgess revisiting his native city. Burgess wrote and narrated the scripts for both, and would have composed the score for the Manchester film had his offer to do so not been declined by the producers.

For the 1981 film *Quest for Fire*, a French motion picture depicting human life 80,000 years ago, Burgess was engaged by the director Jean-Jacques Annaud to invent the language of the prehistoric characters. Having already pondered in *Language Made Plain* the sounds our distant ancestors might have uttered as they began to develop speech, Burgess devised an artificial Ur-Indo-European tongue praised by some as lending veracity to the picture, but generally regarded less favorably than the Stone Age body language devised by Desmond Morris for the film.

How to write music is one of the topics amusingly addressed in *On Going to Bed*, a slender, handsomely illustrated book intended for the nightstand:

> Musical composition is possible in bed, unless one has reached the monumental phase of the orchestral score, which requires a lectern and an upright posture . . .
> I heard of a composer whose wife suffered from dermatographia – a condition of the skin which enables fingers to draw or write on it in the expectation that the imprint will not disappear for an hour or more. One night a theme came to him. He lacked pencil and paper. I need not go on.[14]

The publication of *On Going to Bed* was a minor credit among Burgess's many accomplishments in 1982, a year that included publication of *The End of the World News* and *This Man and Music*; the broadcast premiere of *Blooms of Dublin*; and composition of *In memoriam Princess Grace*, *The Wreck of the Deutschland*, and the Joyce songs "Strings" and "Ecce puer". Further achievements included an Honorary Doctorate from the University of Manchester, publication of a story adaptation of *Der Rosenkavalier* for The Metropolitan Opera Classics Library, articles on Delius, Elgar, Wagner, Sir Walter Scott, Lewis Carroll, James Joyce, and Flann O'Brien, and essays on *The Aerodrome*, air travel, Bamber Bridge, 20th-century British literature, the making of a writer, Malaysia, the relationship of food and music, and *The Planets*.

An essay titled "Artist's Life", a summary of the following year's accomplishments as of 21 March 1983, lists additional projects beginning with the script for *A.D.* (*Anno Domini*), the last of the Burgess–Labella Biblical collaborations:

> I write these words on the first day of spring, and I look back to less than a third of a year in which I have written a ten-hour television script about the agonies and triumphs of the early Christians, a six-hour television script on Attila the Hun, about ten book reviews and half a dozen newspaper articles. I try to write at least one thousand words every day, including weekends, and I have not been able to survive by writing less.[15]

For *A.D.*, a five-part miniseries chronicling the birth of Christianity amid the political intrigue and religious factionalism that arose in the aftermath of Jesus's crucifixion, Burgess composed approximately forty minutes of music in a substantial musical score comprising fourteen numbers. Half of these are brief, sparsely scored items: "Organ in Amphitheatre" (for solo organ), two songs for voice and lyre ("Roman Lullaby" and "Nero's Song"), three slow pieces for strings or small orchestra ("Chaconne", "Meditation", and "Lamentation"), and "Roman March" for brass and percussion. The rest are scored for full orchestra with SATB chorus added in the "Pentecostal Chorus", which is inscribed "Monaco / July 12, 1983" (the only movement bearing a date).

The main theme of the "Prelude", a vigorous composition intended as title music, is a G major melody containing a melodic Phrygian twist in the second bar (Example 15.02); this theme turns up again in the *A.D.* score as the ground bass of the "Chaconne" and principal theme of the "Meditation" and "Pentecostal Chorus". As a musical pun on the title of the series, the "Prelude" opens with repetitions of the notes A and D played by violins, flutes, and clarinets. The movement ends with similar repetitions in the timpani (Example 15.03); here, Burgess spells out the letters "A D" beneath the timpani part to hammer home the point.

The score of *A.D.* abound with echoes of Burgess's favorite composers. One hears the vigor and harmonic style of Walton in the "Prelude",

Example 15.02 Music for *A.D.*: "Prelude" (main theme, bs. 8–11)

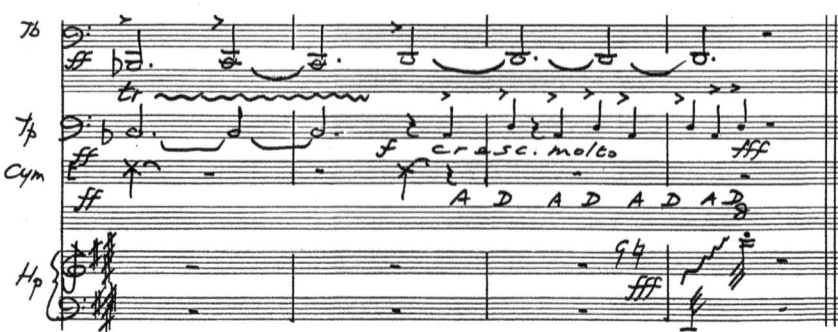

Example 15.03 Music for *A.D.*: "Prelude" (bs. 88–91, excerpt of full score)

Example 15.04 Music for *A.D.*: "Nero's Song"

especially the Allegro vivo section toward the end of the piece, while Holst's influence is evident in the "Storm", whose primary rhythmic figure is borrowed from "Mercury". The sound of Debussy's *La Mer* is evoked unmistakably in the undulating texture, alternating whole-tone harmonies, harp glissandi, and delicate use of glockenspiel in "Sea Pictures", while the nobility of Elgar's *Pomp and Circumstance* marches is mirrored in the robust piece called "Civic Splendour". Burgess also borrows from his own music, especially the Piano Concerto. "Nero's Song" (Example 15.04) quotes the theme the solo piano plays toward the end of the last movement; this subject reappears in "Fire of Rome" along with other themes borrowed from the concerto. Transposed down a fifth and transcribed into neumes on an archaic four-line stave, the same tune appears in the associated novel *The Kingdom of the Wicked* (Example 15.05).[16] In 1987 Burgess utilized this theme once again, employing it as the principal subject of *Mr Burgess's Almanack*.

Labella thought highly of Burgess's music for *A.D.* and wanted to use it for the soundtrack, but was opposed by music producer Gilbert Marouani, who instead hired Lalo Schifrin to score the series. In a letter to Schifrin requesting the return of Burgess's score, Labella lauds it as "a musical

Example 15.05 *The Kingdom of the Wicked*: "Nero's Song" (253)

contribution that I consider not only beautiful but in unison with the spirit, the inner structure of a complex work which has resulted from a long, painstaking collaboration." Labella explains that Marouani had originally found Burgess's score suitable, then changed his mind, calling it "too elaborate, too expensive to be performed and therefore unfit for 'A.D.'" An obviously frustrated Labella describes himself as "trapped by actions and decisions made without my timely knowledge" and forced into "a very difficult position, a totally impossible quandary".[17] While it is possible that Burgess's music was used in the original series, the abridged nine-hour videotape edition of *A.D.* includes none of his music despite Burgess's listing in the credits as composer (along with Schifrin) as well as screenwriter.

What little Burgess wrote about *A.D.* plainly expressed his frustration with the project:

> Earlier this year my name was attached as chief scenarist to a television biblical epic called *A.D.* The *Observer*'s anonymous TV prospectist dismissed the dialogue as vapid, and an *Observer* reader gleefully picked on this to demolish my pretensions to literary competence. But the text so disparaged was not mine: it was what had been made out of mine by producer, director, actors and, for all I know, somebody in the cutting room with a gift for mimicry.[18]

As in the case of *Jesus of Nazareth*, the producers arranged for a like-named book, based on Burgess's screenplay but written by a different author, to be released in conjunction with the television broadcast. This time it was *A.D. Anno Domini* by Kirk Mitchell, which credits Burgess and Labella for the screenplay but leaves Burgess's name off the book jacket. Unsurprisingly, *The Kingdom of the Wicked* includes no mention of its connection to *A.D.*

Notes

1 YH, 290–1.
2 *Man of Nazareth*, 37. The stylized use of repetition – "Through green mazes, reaching cool stone, effigies, / Effigies, the palace of the princess. The princess" (18) – recalls a similar technique found in the poetry of Martin Bell.
3 Roman numerals in the score indicate which piece of music belongs with which of the six episodes ("*puntate*"), not eight as stated in YH (289).
4 *Man of Nazareth*, 188.
5 YH, 300.
6 TMM, 39. Although the composition is listed under 1972, Burgess probably composed it in 1973 after completing the script.

7 Burgess's only previous Pound setting is a lost composition from 1936 listed in TMM: 'Complaint, complaint I heard upon a day' (from Ezra Pound's *Cantos*) for SATB unaccompanied.
8 John Tytell, *Ezra Pound: The Solitary Volcano* (New York: Anchor Press, 1987), 337.
9 First published in *Exultations* in 1909, "A Song of the Virgin Mother" was also included in *Provença* (1910) and *Personae & Exultations* (1913).
10 That this strophe alone is quoted in *The Life of Ezra Pound* by Noel Stock (New York: Pantheon, 1970) suggests that this biography (73) was Burgess's source for the text.
11 YH, 301.
12 Letter to Labella, 2 November 1976.
13 Letter to Norman Swallow, 11 January 1977.
14 *On Going to Bed*, 59.
15 *One Man's Chorus*, 211.
16 *The Kingdom of the Wicked* was published in 1985 by Arbor House and in a signed, private printing issued by the Franklin Press.
17 Vincenzo Labella, letter to Lalo Schifrin, 20 November 1984.
18 "Not Only Carmen", *Observer*, 28 December 1986.

16

BONAPARTE CON BRIO

The symphonisation of fiction is shown to be an implausible undertaking, but things have occasionally to be done to show that they cannot be done.[1]

As an experiment in literary form, Burgess had long considered writing a novel based on a musical work, its plot determined by symphonic form instead of psychological probability. A Jane Austen parody, he surmised, might follow the pattern of a Mozart opus, with large-scale sections of the novel corresponding to the four movements of a typical Classical symphony: Allegro, Andante, Minuet and Trio, and Finale. Elements of a musical structure like sonata form could be reflected in the actions of characters who would be introduced in the exposition, undergo dramatic experiences in the development, and resume their prior relationship in the recapitulation. The presentation of the male protagonist would correspond to the first theme in a sonata-form movement; the appearance of the leading female character, to the traditionally "feminine" second theme. The problem of literature's unsuitability for the kind of exact repetition found in sonata form would be addressed through the use of "inexact repetition – characters recapitulating their actions in a changed prose-style, or doing new things in a style which recalled, in rhythm and imagery, what had already been stated."[2]

Such a revolutionary approach to writing must have seemed daunting even to Burgess until Kubrick suggested he write a novel about Napoleon based on the *Eroica*, inverting Beethoven's act of composing a symphony to honor the French general.[3] Spurred by the challenge, Burgess decided to incorporate the myth of Prometheus into the novel, mirroring Beethoven's use of a theme from *The Creatures of Prometheus* in the *Eroica's* finale. The movements of the symphony, each with its own distinct quality, would be transformed into their literary equivalents:

> The first movement was clearly about struggle and victory, the second about a great public funeral, and in the third and fourth the hero was raised to the level of myth – a specific myth, that of Prometheus, which Beethoven spelt out by drawing on his own *Prometheus* ballet music.[4]

The book had to be called *Napoleon Symphony* ("the only possible title") and consist "of not much more than 100,000 words" on roughly 365 pages, its plot sufficiently compressed so as to be easily convertible into a screenplay. Burgess set for himself the Joycean challenge of formulating correspondences between the novel and the symphony that would take into account not just character and form but also tempo and duration.[5] The novel's overall structure would closely follow the form of the *Eroica*, its four main parts corresponding to the symphony's four movements: I. Allegro con brio; II. *Marcia funebre*. Adagio assai; III. Scherzo. Allegro vivace; and IV. Finale. Allegro molto. The novel could be calculated to match the proportions of the *Eroica* by correlating the lengths of the book's four sections to the symphony's four movements as determined by the number of pages, the number of measures, or the duration of each movement. Burgess suggests that he followed the second approach:

> What I have in front of me when I'm working is the score of the *Eroica*. I will make the various sections of the novel correspond to the various sections of the symphony, so that if I take, say eight bars of Beethoven, it's roughly equivalent to three pages of my own work.[6]

Yet when one compares the novel to the score of the *Eroica* (in this case the old Breitkopf & Härtel edition, although any other edition would be equivalent), one finds that he did not follow either of the first two approaches, which show no consistent ratio between the number of pages of each section of the novel and either the number of pages or measures of each movement of the symphony.

Pages (novel)	Pages (symphony)	Measures (symphony)
I. 120	I. 33	695 (without repeat)
II. 128	II. 19	247
III. 34	III. 18	452 (without repeats)
IV. 115	IV. 26	475 (without repeat)

Rather, he followed the third approach, correlating the number of pages of each section of the novel to the duration of the corresponding movement. For instance, the timings of the *Eroica*'s four movements on Toscanini's 1953 recording with the NBC Symphony are 14:05, 15:20, 5:21, and 11:10. Taking the ratio of the duration of the first movement (14:05) to the number of pages of Part I (120) as a constant, i.e. just over seven seconds of music per page of text, the durations of the second, third, and fourth movements work out to 15:01, 3:59, and 13:30, which are reasonably close approximations to the timings on the recording.[7]

Musical gestures and structures are mirrored explicitly in the text. The two explosive chords that begin the symphony are represented by a pair of painful tugs on the ear:

> He strode in. "Wake up. Get your leg out of the fire." He gave her two excruciating love-pinches, one on each lobe, and cried:
> "Begin!"[8]

The horizontal bars in the text represent partitions equivalent to the music's structural boundaries. In Part I, the bars located on pages 3, 30, 70, and 97 indicate the start of passages corresponding, respectively, to the first movement's exposition, development, recapitulation, and coda. The sections of text beginning with the phrases "Germinal in the Year Four" (3) and "Germinal in the Year Seven" (70) are analogous to the exposition and recapitulation, the verbal repetition emulating that of the music.

The rise and fall of Napoleon (abbreviated throughout the novel as N) is signified through textual and musical references to the symbolic themes of earth, fire, air, and water. N is associated principally with earth, denoting safety and strength, and fire, symbolizing his identity as a Promethean hero. At the height of his power, N fully commands the element of air. Despite his short stature, N is a broad-chested man with immense lung capacity; his remarkable ability to project his voice bestows upon "that huge tank of air he bore above his ribs some extraneous property of myth".[9] During his ascendancy, N proclaims "I am sun and wind", but as his dominance wanes, his control of air degrades into empty "windiness".[10] "Your breath is bad", he is told. "It's a bad breath that is blowing over Europe."[11] Water represents constant danger to Napoleon. England's naval superiority prevents him from conquering the British Isles, indirectly causing him to undertake his ill-starred offensive against Russia. The fear of water proves to be well founded, as borne out by N's defeat at *Water*loo and exile to the remote island of St. Helena, where he is imprisoned by the sea.

Earth is associated with the *Eroica's* tonic key of E♭ major. The passage in *Napoleon Symphony* (3) representing the start of the exposition establishes the tonic key through images and symbols of earth: topography, maps, the coastline, the valley. Because the note E♭ is called Es in German, Burgess uses the letter S as another means of signifying the tonic, drawing attention to this letter through inclusion and omission – for instance, misspelling the name Balcombe as Bascombe, and writing *Der Volk* instead of the correct form, *Das Volk*.[12] Water and blood, representing danger, are associated with D♭, a note (in its enharmonic spelling C♯) contained in the main theme as well as a key briefly visited toward the start of the recapitulation and coda. Corresponding to the music's sudden shift to D♭ major at bar 561 as the coda begins is the text's stark pronouncement, "Water was the enemy."[13]

Part II, modeled on the symphony's great C minor *Marcia funebre*, begins with a contrasting pair of water-related dreams corresponding to the opening section (bs. 1–68) of the funeral march. In the first section (123–40), N, in Moscow, experiences a nightmare in which he is roped onto a rough board like a corpse upon a bier, then cast by British sailors into the icy depths of the English Channel. Fearing he is about to drown, N awakens, surprised to find that his pulse is normal: "His heart was not pounding, as it should from nightmare, but kept calm time to the beat of the funeral march that had been in the dream".[14] Meanwhile, in Malmaison,

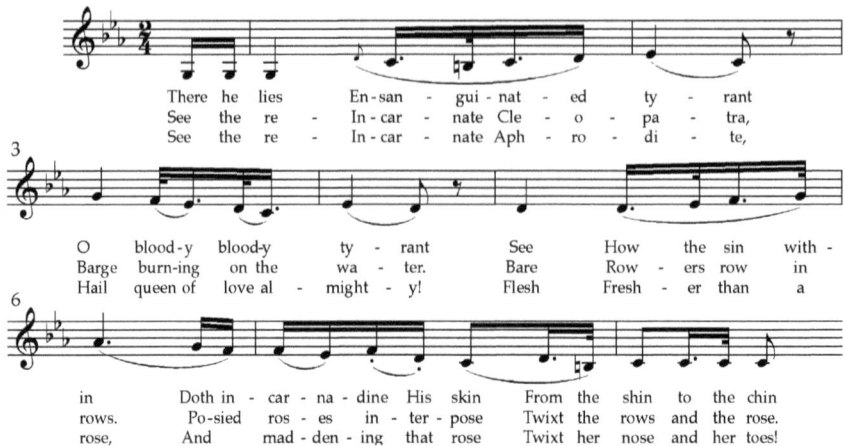

Example 16.01 Verses from Part II of *Napoleon Symphony* (123, 140, 143) set to Theme 1 (bs. 1–8) of the *Eroica*'s second movement

slumbering Josephine, who regards water as a female principle and ally, enjoys a rapturous dream in which she imagines herself as "the reincarnate Cleopatra" languorously floating down the Nile on an elaborate barge.[15] Playfully thrust into the river by her attendant nymphs, she is suddenly transformed into Aphrodite, the Goddess of Love and Beauty. Rising out of the water, she is "poised on the surface of delicious iced champagne foam", exemplifying the literal meaning of Aphrodite: "foam-risen".[16] Italicized stanzas in the text summarizing these three visions represent "appropriate but ridiculous dream choruses" carefully crafted to fit the rhythm and contour of the movement's principal theme (Example 16.01).[17]

These dreams, described as occurring simultaneously, pertain to events three years apart – Josephine's divorce from N in 1809 and N's Russian campaign in 1812. Burgess considered this non-linear approach to chronology a key aspect of the novel's style:

> The point about following the structure of the "Eroica" was less the looking for verbal parallels to musical effects than accepting the non-linear presentation of the hero's life that seems to lie under, or over, Beethoven's score. The hero dies in the second movement, is resurrected in the third and fourth and, at the end of the finale, is seen on horseback leading his troops once more into battle.[18]

The emergence of German nationalism, signaled anachronistically by quotations from *Die Meistersinger*, poses a looming threat to Napoleon. Germany's ascendancy is proclaimed by the words "O Deutschland arise / Light is rising in the / Deutschlander skies", which are associated with the funeral march's second theme, as illustrated in the first line of Example 16.02.[19] When this theme returns in the recapitulation, the addition of the

Example 16.02 Verses from Part II of *Napoleon Symphony* (128, 211) set to Theme 2 of the *Eroica*'s second movement

Example 16.03 Verses from Part II of *Napoleon Symphony* (171, 173) set to the C major theme (bs. 90–104) of the *Eroica*'s second movement

B♭ appoggiatura in the third bar is matched by the added word *echt* (German for *genuine*), as shown in the second line of that example.

N's euphoric recollection of the height of his power, epitomized by his 1807 meeting with Czar Alexander at Tilsit, corresponds to the movement's C major section, music that "brings comfort and hope on its wings, like a sudden ray of sunlight in a dark sky", as Sir George Grove once poetically described it.[20] But joyful memories of the past yield to the harsh reality of the present as N faces the brutal Russian winter with his army trudging toward Warsaw: "See a fif / ty mile long column shuffle / through / Borovsk and Vereya" (171). The stark quatrain "What is left / is left of the Great Army / through / Borovsk and Vereya" (173) continues the image of Napoleon's tattered forces in retreat. Together, these verses fit the music comprising the close of the C major section (bars 90–104), with a musical elision occurring exactly at the point where the two stanzas overlap.

Burgess puns on the word *fuga*, which means both "fugue" and "escape", by converting the funeral march's great double fugue into a passage about building a pair of bridges to enable Napoleon's army to cross the Berezina and flee Russia. To match the double fugue linguistically, two different types of language ("an alternation of officialese and demotic"[21]) are employed to describe the construction of the twin spans:

> The primary need, General Eblé said, is to obtain the requisite structural materials and this will certainly entail the demolition of civilian housing in the adjacent township. *Now the first job, Sergeant Rebour said, is to get planking, and the only way to get it is to pull down all those fucking houses.*[22] (italics added)

Part III unfolds as a rapid summary of N's life, ending with his defeat at Waterloo and the collapse of his empire. Mirroring the fast, lively tempo and impetuous character of the *Eroica*'s Scherzo, key episodes from N's career are depicted in Part III at a comically whirlwind pace. The opening sentence, "From bivouac to bivouac to bivouac to bivouac to bivouac and all the way it was torches held aloft . . .", which depicts Emperor N's trek through a military encampment on his way to an anniversary celebration of his coronation, matches the animated staccato style and rhythm of the Scherzo's opening theme (Example 16.04). Dactylic prose-poetry imitates the waltz rhythms heard at the ball: "Glance at the France that he taught how to dance. And advance. Assuming a stance leaving little to chance. La France."[23] N praises opera, a complex undertaking involving the precise coordination of large numbers of highly trained participants, by comparing it to battle: "Opera. Nothing like opera. The only art that comes close to the art of war".[24]

Example 16.04 The first line of Part III of *Napoleon Symphony* (251) set to the opening of the *Eroica*'s third movement (bs. 1–6)

Part IV finds Napoleon defeated and exiled on the island of St. Helena, where he is likened sacrilegiously to Christ through parody of the motto INRI, *Iesus Nazarenus Rex Iudaeorum* (Jesus of Nazareth, King of the Jews), into *Interfecimus Napoleonem Regem Imperatorem* (We have killed the Emperor King Napoleon) and related constructions. Earlier, in Part II, Bonaparte rebukes his soldiers for their disloyalty during the army's retreat from Moscow; suspecting them of murmuring "Let us kill the Emperor King Napoleon" among themselves, N lashes out:

> "Faith," he breathed, "you talk of faith, all ye of little faith. INRI. Imperatorem Napoleonem Regem Interfaciamus. I know what's in the collective mind of the whole collection of you, traitors."[25]

The identification of Bonaparte with Prometheus, which began in Part III, continues throughout the rest of the novel until both figures eventually merge into Promethapoleon (367):

> I heard the first four notes of Beethoven's bass – E flat B flat B flat E flat – as singing INRI – *Interfaciamus Napoleonem Regem Imperatorem* – and made a blasphemous identification of Christ and Prometheus, Prometheus being Napoleon removed from history and transferred to mythology. INRI pounds away like four nails being hammered in (the cross is appropriate to St Helena, since St Helena found the cross).[26]

In a 1974 letter to the American scholar and novelist Geoffrey Aggeler, Burgess illustrated the opening notes of the *Prometheus* theme in the form of a cross (Example 16.05).[27]

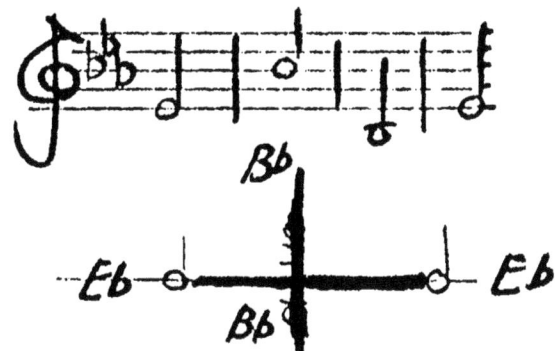

Example 16.05 The first four notes of the *Prometheus* theme (bs. 12–15) from the *Eroica*'s fourth movement in the form of a cross

A fragmentary version of the INRI parody, interspersed with N's botched attempts to speak English, accords with the full thirty-two bars of the complete *Prometheus* theme (Example 16.06).

This presentation of the *Prometheus* theme in the *Eroica* is followed by a set of variations capped by a presto coda. In Part IV, the literary equivalent of these musical variations is a pastiche of the prose styles of Jane Austen, Thomas Hardy, Sir Walter Scott, Charles Dickens, William Wordsworth, Alfred Lord Tennyson, T. S. Eliot, Edward Bulwer-Lytton, and Henry James "shot through with tropes from Gerard Manley Hopkins in a last desperate attempt at counterpoint," the Hopkins quotations drawn mainly from "The Windhover" and *The Wreck of the Deutschland*.[28]

Napoleon Symphony, Burgess's boldest experiment to that time in combining the arts of music and literature, marked a turning point in his artistic career. For the twenty years up to its creation, he had largely suppressed the ambition to compose, writing music infrequently and almost exclusively in short forms involving few instruments. After writing this novel, his

Example 16.06 Text from Part IV of *Napoleon Symphony* (288) set to the *Prometheus* theme (bs. 12–15) of the *Eroica*'s fourth movement

twenty-first, Burgess's compositional activity increased dramatically and remained prolific throughout the rest of his life. Musical themes and characters are a major presence in his later novels and stories, with *Earthly Powers*, *Enderby's Dark Lady*, *The Pianoplayers*, *Any Old Iron*, *The Devil's Mode*, and *Byrne* all featuring musicians as main characters. *This Man and Music* and *Mozart and the Wolf Gang* are fundamentally about music, while the musical nature of Burgess's libretti for *Oberon* and *Carmen*, and his dramatization of *A Clockwork Orange* as "a play with music", is self-evident. During his last two decades, along with thirty published books, Burgess composed over eighty music compositions beginning with the crucial one spawned by his book about Napoleon. Having turned Beethoven into a novel, it was time to turn Shakespeare into a symphony.

Notes

1 *Mozart and the Wolf Gang*, 146.
2 YH, 247.
3 Burgess dedicated the novel to Kubrick along with Liana, writing, "*To my dear wife, a Buonapartista, who, in her extreme youth, could never understand why the British had named a great railway terminus after a military defeat. Also to Stanley J. Kubrick*, maestro di color..."
4 YH, 247.
5 TMM, 180.
6 Charles T. Bunting, "An Interview in New York with Anthony Burgess", *Studies in the Novel* (1973), 505.

7 Other recordings, such as the slower 1973 Philips recording by the Leipzig Gewandhaus under Kurt Masur, produce comparable results.
8 *Napoleon Symphony*, xiii.
9 Ibid., 93.
10 Ibid., 120.
11 Ibid., 138.
12 The German method of transcribing musical notes into letters is used internationally. For example, Dmitri Shostakovich turned the first four letters of the German spelling of his name, *D. Sch*ostakowitsch, into his musical signature D–E♭–C–B♮.
13 NS, 97.
14 Ibid., 126.
15 Ibid., 140.
16 Ibid., 143.
17 TMM, 185.
18 YH, 294.
19 NS, 128.
20 George Grove, *Beethoven and his Nine Symphonies* (New York: Dover, 1962), 72.
21 TMM, 186. In YH (292), the passage is described as written "alternately in soldier's low language and the chaste prose of a military chronicle."
22 NS, 176.
23 Ibid., 253.
24 Ibid., 256.
25 Ibid., 206.
26 YH, 294.
27 Geoffrey Aggeler, *Anthony Burgess: The Artist as Novelist* (Tuscaloosa: University of Alabama Press, 1979), 226.
28 YH, 294.

1 John B. Wilson (Anthony Burgess) with sister Muriel and mother Elizabeth Burgess Wilson [Manchester, ca. 1918]

2 With father Joseph Wilson, 1925

3 With unidentified younger child, Cleveleys, 1927

4 Llewela Isherwood Jones (Lynne Burgess Wilson), 1939

5 Band members of the Jaypees (left to right): Ted Norman, Richard Nutting, Stan Williams, Harry Walkling, Bill Bryan, Anthony Burgess [ca 1941]

6 The Jaypees (front row, left to right): Stan Williams (drums), Harry Walkling (tenor sax, clarinet), Ted Norman (alto sax), Bill Bryan (trumpet, vocals), Ted Wright (piano), Richard Nutting (double bass); (top row, far right) Anthony Burgess [ca. 1941]

7 Anthony Burgess (fifth from right) singing with the Jaypees [ca 1941]

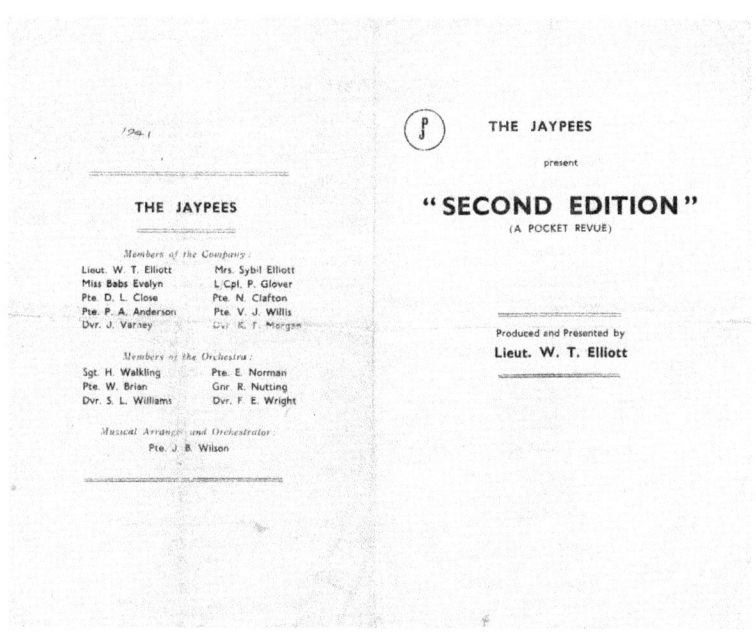

8 Program of a 1941 performance by the Jaypees

9 Dust jacket of *A Vision of Battlements* with Richard Ennis attached to a metronome pendulum

10 With students at Malay College [Kuala Kangsar, ca. 1955]

173

11 Standing before arch in Indonesia

12 Anthony and Lynne with their dog Haji

13–16 *Four photos shot October 4, 1968 by Marvin Lichtner for the profile of Anthony Burgess published in the 25 October 1968 issue of* Life

13 Leaning on his books – a variant of the published photo that shows Burgess looking up toward the top of the stack of twenty-one volumes

14 Published in the article with the following caption: *"In the London suburb of Chiswick, Burgess, with his wife Liliana, is tugged home from a shopping trip by his dog Haji. They also have a cat. 'She is called Dorian Gray,' he says. 'Sorry about that.'"*

15 Unpublished photo similar to one in the profile that was captioned, *"Surrounded by stacked chairs – business is heavier at night – Burgess thumps out an oldie during a noon visit to a local Chiswick pub. He once arranged dance-band music."*

16 Unpublished photo in which Liana appears to have had more than enough of Anthony's piano playing

17 Liliana Macellari [ca. 1968]

18 With Paolo-Andrea [ca. 1971]

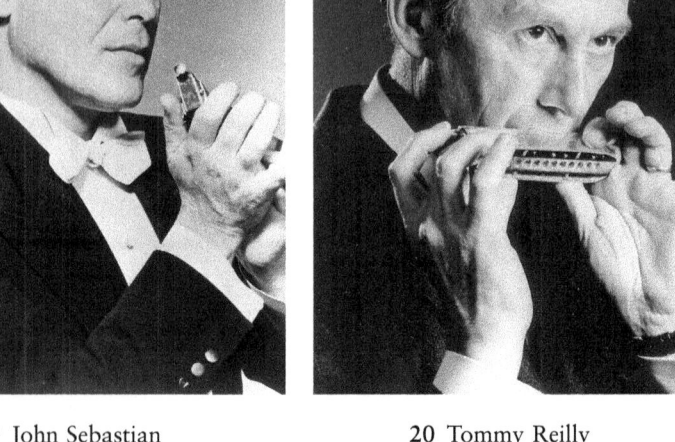

19 John Sebastian 20 Tommy Reilly

21 Larry Adler

22 Riding the New York subway, October 29, 1972. Original caption: *"The author rides the IRT. Anthony Burgess, the British writer, holds the title of Distinguished Professor of English at City College. He is working on a novel about Napoleon."*

23 Patricia Conolly as Jocasta and Len Cariou as Oedipus in the Guthrie Theater's production of *Oedipus the King* [Minneapolis, 1972]

24 Rehearsing *King Oedipus* with conductor Roland Gagnon (left) and composer Stanley Silverman (at piano) [New York, 1973]

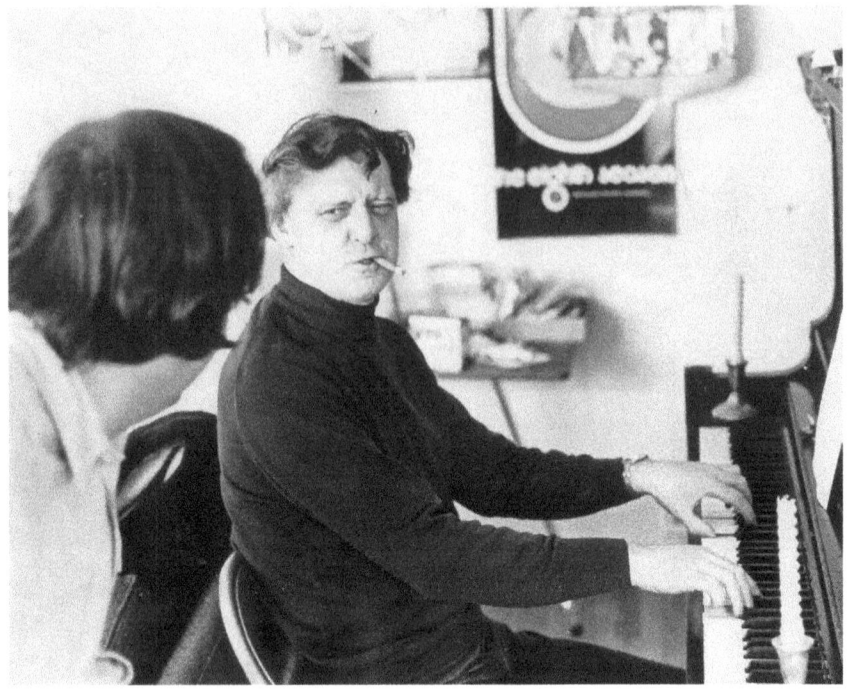

25 At the piano playing for Roland Gagnon [New York, 1973]

26 Dedicatees of Burgess's String Quartet: the Primavera String Quartet [1980]. Clockwise from top left: Deborah Berlin (violin), Melissa Meell (cello), Diann Jezurski (viola), and Martha Caplin (violin)

27 Presenting the manuscript of *A Glasgow Overture* to Lord Provost Michael Kelly in the Glasgow City Chambers next to a painting by Stanley Cursiter depicting the Scottish authors Edwin Muir, James Bridie, Neil Gunn, and Eric Linklater [March 1981]. This photograph appeared in the April 1981 issue of Glasgow City Council's newspaper *The Bulletin*

28 Dust jacket of *The Pianoplayers* [1986]

29 Marathon pianist playing in a storefront

30 Amid the members of the Aïghetta Quartet. Left to right: François Szönyi, André-Michel Berthoux, Philippe Loli, Alexandre Del Fa

31 Conversing with Graham Greene, ca. September 1982

32 At the electronic keyboard

33 Dust jacket of *Mozart and the Wolf Gang*, with Mozart looking back [1991]

34 Late portrait

RESURGENT COMPOSER

17

SYMPHONIC SHAKESPEARE

> *He had, in* Love's Labour's Lost, *composed a musical theme of six notes and given it to Holofernes. Curiously, no musician has ever taken that theme up and developed it.*[1]

Without *Napoleon Symphony*, there might never have been a Third Symphony by Anthony Burgess. In an addendum to the novel titled "An Epistle to the Reader", Burgess described his ambitious dream of devising a style of "narrative prose made to behave like music":

> I was brought up on music and compose
> Bad music still, but ever since I chose
> The novelist's métier one mad idea
> Has haunted me, and I fulfill it here
> Or try to – it is this: somehow to give
> Symphonic shape to verbal narrative,
> Impose on life, though nerves scream and resist,
> The abstract patterns of the symphonist.[2]

These lines caught the attention of James Dixon, music director of the University Symphony Orchestra of the University of Iowa, who wondered what sort of music such an audacious writer might produce. Eager to find out, the conductor wrote to Burgess with a request that he send one or two scores. Although Dixon could not furnish a monetary commission, he offered to perform either an existing orchestral work or a new one. Burgess promptly accepted the invitation, declaring that he would compose a symphony for Dixon and his orchestra. And thus, through its literary manifestation as *Napoleon Symphony*, Beethoven's Third Symphony led Burgess to compose a Third Symphony of his own.

The work represented a fresh start, "an attempt to see if – after 20 years spent on the strenuous manipulation of words – I could compose something for large forces on a largish scale that should not be total musical nonsense."[3] In December 1974, Burgess bought himself a half-hundredweight of scoring paper and began composing, first in Rome, then in Siena. He completed the first movement in January, and, after embarking on a North American lecture tour in late February, continued composing in Florida,

California, British Columbia, and other locations throughout the US and Canada. He wrote in hotel rooms and airport waiting areas, dividing his attention between the symphony and a script commissioned for (though not used in) the James Bond film *The Spy Who Loved Me*. Having composed "a good half of the work" on tour, Burgess completed the symphony in early April 1975 "in a Holiday Inn bedroom in a small town in Georgia (U.S.A.)." He sent the finished score to Dixon from Oshkosh, Wisconsin, without "having checked a note of it aurally (Holiday Inns have muzak but no pianos)."[4]

Burgess's Symphony No. 3 in C is a four-movement work in a vigorous, dynamic style. Compared with much of the concert music composed in the 1970s, this generally tonal work is stylistically conservative. It is thirty-five minutes long and scored for woodwinds in pairs, full brass, timpani, percussion, piano, celesta, harp, mandolin, and strings.[5] In the last movement, tenor and baritone soloists sing texts from *Love's Labour's Lost*.

While rooted in sonata form, the first movement (Andantino–Allegro) possesses a rhapsodic character reminiscent of Sibelius, whose symphonies, particularly the Seventh, Burgess viewed as works "in which the aim was gradual transformation of themes, the development not being an incidental fantasy between two near-identical statements of a dual reality, but the essence of the work."[6] Composing this symphony, Burgess felt he may "have unconsciously been following Sibelius's example, organizing thematic wisps into a new totality."[7] This developmental quality is also attributable to Burgess's method of writing musical works from start to finish without revision. "Professional composers compose in pencil, erasing as much as they write. I am foolhardy enough to set everything down in ink, evading errors as though I were performing a surgical operation."[8] He wrote books similarly, producing a quota of finished pages each day and always proceeding without amending what had come before. This uncommon creative process helps to explain Burgess's astonishing prolificacy as a writer and composer.

Theme groups in C minor, D minor, and F major enter sequentially in the exposition. First played slowly in the introduction, Theme 1 (Example 17.01) recurs in a jaunty skipping rhythm at the start of the Allegro. The double time signature, 3/4 : 6/8, does not signify that the two meters alternate strictly, but rather that each measure is in one meter or the other. Seconds and fourths occur prominently throughout the first theme, an extended melody in three sections (1a, 1b, and 1c), as well as in the descending cadential figure occurring at the end of the introduction, exposition, development, and coda. Further transformations of Theme 1 lead to the entrance of the second theme group (Example 17.02), a flowing, Vaughan Williamsian theme in D Aeolian played by violins and harp interwoven with a spiccato countermelody in the low strings and a soulful tune in woodwind octaves described by Burgess as "a rather 'jazzy' theme (viz., it uses minor intervals where major ones would have done as well)."[9] By way of a modu-

Symphonic Shakespeare

Example 17.01 Third Symphony: I. Andantino–Allegro, Theme 1 (bs. 1–12)

Example 17.02 Third Symphony: I. Andantino–Allegro, Theme 2 (bs. 88–95)

latory sequence in descending minor thirds derived from Theme 1a, the second theme group transitions to the third, where Theme 3, described by Burgess as "a very 'English' pendent theme which suggests a jig gone wrong", is set in counterpoint to Theme 1a in rhythmic augmentation (Example 17.03).[10] Motivic similarities, like the neighbor note figures that open Themes 1b and 2a, and the F-D-C motif at the start of Themes 2b and 3, impart a strong sense of thematic unity to the movement. This is particularly evident in the polyphonic tour de force that concludes the exposition, where Themes 1a, 2b, and 3 are all played in counterpoint. Theme 4 (Example 17.04), an E♭ minor figure consisting almost entirely of

Example 17.03 Third Symphony: I. Andantino–Allegro, Theme 3, with Theme 1a in the bass (bs. 135–46)

Example 17.04 Third Symphony: I. Andantino–Allegro, Theme 4 (bs. 239–46)

pairs of perfect fourths, is introduced by the brass at the end of the development. Burgess described it as "a codetta or pendant [to Theme 2a] which emphasizes that the melody has a right to a full close on the tonic."[11] In the recapitulation, all themes return except 2a and 4, which are withheld until the coda, when the key of C minor is reestablished. A pair of reminiscences of Theme 1 – first a ghostly *ppp* one played by the violins in an unusual mixture of *col legno* and *naturale* bowing, then a *ff* version in the brass – precede the movement's quiet ending. "Part of the first movement was evidently composed drunk, probably on Christmas Day," Burgess explained in *The New York Times*, "since there are obscenities written in Arabic script between the harp part and the first violins, though the music seems sober enough."[12] The inscriptions are indeed present: the first (at bar 215 in the development section), a transliteration of "And fuck you too", and the second (at bar 293 in the recapitulation), of "schlock".

Emulating Beethoven's Ninth and Walton's First Symphony, Burgess followed the first movement of his symphony with a scherzo (albeit one mainly in 2/4) rather than a traditional slow movement: "Since the first movement has ended in a slow tempo – the coda, indeed, being a virtual slow movement in itself – it seems reasonable to place the scherzo next."[13] Structured ABABA, the movement opens with a series of sharply accented, irregularly placed pairs of chords that lead into an animated tune played by flutes and oboe (Example 17.05). The second theme (Example 17.06), played in

Symphonic Shakespeare

Example 17.05 Third Symphony: II. Allegro molto giocoso, Theme 1 (bs. 7–12)

Example 17.06 Third Symphony: II. Allegro molto giocoso, Theme 2a (bs. 60–6)

Example 17.07 Third Symphony: II. Allegro molto giocoso, Theme 3a (bs. 96–104)

canon, is succeeded by a lovely pastoral melody in E♭ Dorian played by flutes (Example 17.07). Repeated by English horn, this Dorian theme is joined by two new countermelodies: a flowing tune in the cellos and, in the first violins, a variant of the first theme. The shimmering background of glissandi, running scales, and oscillating chords creates a brilliant Stravinskian texture evocative of passages in *Petrouchka* and *The Rite of Spring*. Later, muted trumpets and trombones play acerbic, accompanimental tone clusters marked *pernacchiando*, viz. "sounding like a Bronx cheer"! Burgess enlivens the rest of the movement with rhythmic diminution, uneven meters, and amusing orchestration, such as reassigning the first theme to solo tuba. The scherzo concludes with a rousing final statement of the first theme ending with a *fff* flourish led by brass and percussion.

The third movement, an elegy dedicated to the memory of Shostakovich, begins as a solemn processional in F♯ Dorian. An important thematic element in the movement is the falling perfect fifth, a motif imbued with wartime associations for Burgess. In his analysis of the symphony, he explains that the figure represents bugles signaling "Retreat or Last Post" and that he borrowed it subconsciously from his 1944 setting of Owen's "Anthem for Doomed Youth", in which the word "bugles" is sung to a descending fifth (Example 17.08).[14] Beginning with the same motif is a related theme (Example 17.09), first played by solo violin at bar 38, which dominates the rest of the movement and recurs in the finale.[15] In his

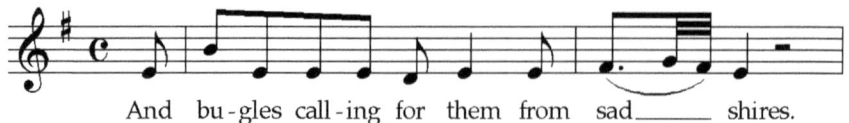

Example 17.08 Setting of line 8 of "Anthem for Doomed Youth"

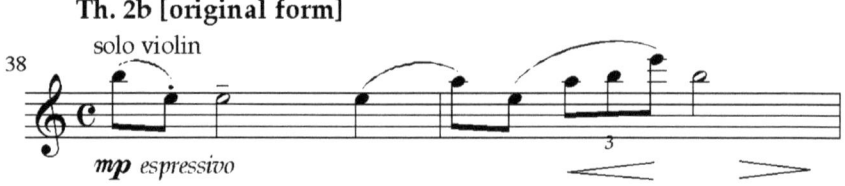

Example 17.09 Third Symphony: III. Andante lugubre, Theme 2b (bs. 38–9)

autobiography, Burgess links the third movement's genesis to gastronomic misfortune:

> At Christmas 1974 I had nearly finished the first movement. But on Christmas Day I was ready to die of food poisoning... Being the sole true northerner of the family, I ate [spoiled Brussels sprouts] with the Christmas turkey while the others ate fresh spinach. Then death seemed to announce itself. Recovered, I composed the slow movement, which was a funeral march. The last, Shakespearean, movement celebrated, with winter and spring, my, or man's resurrection. The scherzo was merely fast and noisy.[16]

"My intention," wrote Burgess in 1982, "was to express regret at the death of Dmitri Shostakovich" despite the inconvenient fact that he completed the symphony four months before the Soviet composer's death on 9 August 1975.[17] In contradictory comments, Burgess wrote in his Iowa program note that Shostakovich's stylistic influence "may occasionally be heard here as a foil to the Englishry", but, seven years later, asserted "there is nothing of Shostakovich" in the movement, which "has more to do with the slaughter of two world wars than with the death of a solitary composer."[18]

Burgess had long been fascinated by the string of six solfège syllables in *Love's Labour's Lost* – the only such "tune" in Shakespeare's plays except for a similar four-note phrase in *King Lear* – and wondered why no one had ever used it in a musical composition: "C D G A E F – it is suitable for a ground bass; it can be extended into a fugal subject. If we repeat it a tritone higher or lower, we have a perfect twelve-tone *Grundstimmung* for a serial composition."[19] Burgess took on this challenge in the finale, a symphonic setting of the Bard's words and music. This double homage to Shakespeare consists of two roughly equal halves, the first purely instrumental and the second incorporating the two vocal soloists.

Example 17.10 Third Symphony: IV. Allegro con spirito, Theme 1 (bs. 61–65)

Example 17.11 Third Symphony: IV. Allegro con spirito, Theme 2 (*Venezia* melody; bs. 119–24)

The first part begins with the first three notes of Shakespeare's theme, transposed down a fourth to G-A-D and played as a timpani solo. Burgess then manipulates fragments of the theme before presenting, in the flute, the original six pitches (Example 17.10). The second theme, a bittersweet melody marked "*nel modo di canto popolare*" (in the style of popular song) is later revealed as a setting of lines about Venice. Burgess described it as "an appropriate Adriatic- or Neapolitan-type melody, corny, full of schmalz, and with a mandoline tinkling away in the background."[20] In its initial appearance, this *Venezia* melody, which alternates between major and minor modes, is played instrumentally (Example 17.11). Further treatment of the Shakespeare and *Venezia* themes occupies most of the rest of this half of the movement. The second half comprises two vocal episodes, an orchestral interlude and a coda, the first vocal episode ushered in by a piano "arpeggio of the major thirteenth, in the manner of the late Lord Britten, many of whose themes were made out of that arpeggio."[21] After the baritone sings a few lines from *Love's Labour's Lost* as recitative, the tenor enters with the *Venezia* tune, singing the Italian text that inspired the melody. The baritone reenters and concludes this episode with the six solfège syllables sung on their true pitches. A brief tripartite orchestral interlude follows. Led boisterously by the brass, "The orchestra now rejoices in [the Shakespeare theme] and its variants. The notes blur in a trumpet bell-chime. The horns blur the inversion, the trombones the reversion, and then the whole ensemble blurs, chimes and clashes." With a nod to Gabrieli, Burgess deftly evokes the Italian Renaissance, admitting us "to a kind of princely court, where [the *Venezia* theme] is converted into the music of a processional."[22] The climactic third part contrapuntally combines variants of the Shakespeare theme and *Venezia* melody plus part of the first theme (1b) from the previous movement. The second vocal episode begins with the tenor and baritone vocalizing on "Ah" in bitonal counterpoint to harp accompaniment until they are overwhelmed by a swelling timpani roll. "The baritone stills the timpanist with a gesture", according to the composer's instruction, then invites his listeners to hear the "dialogue... in praise of the owl and the cuckoo" compiled by "we two learnèd men", whereupon the tenor and baritone sing the "Spring" and "Winter" songs from the end of the play. The movement's last forty bars, which Burgess called "damnably and insouciantly dissonant", form a "riotous coda" based on the Shakespeare theme.[23] Two measures from the end, the orchestra breaks off abruptly, leaving the baritone to declaim the play's final lines during a grand pause. As he finishes, the orchestra reenters with a single, short, very loud chord to end the symphony with the musical equivalent of an exclamation point.

Paradoxically, and despite multiple allusions to it in *Nothing Like the Sun*, *Love's Labour's Lost* was one of Burgess's least favorite Shakespearean plays. In his biography of the playwright, he disparages it as "full of witty quibbles, big words, and allusions to foreign travel," finding it "almost painfully aristocratic."[24] While Adrian Leverkühn's operatic version of the play in *Doktor Faustus* may have piqued Burgess's interest in setting portions of it to music, ultimately what attracted him to *Love's Labour's Lost* above all was the presence of Shakespeare's longest musical "theme". Ironically this set of solfège syllables was not a composed theme at all, but rather a simple scale sung incorrectly for comic effect. Burgess probably knew this as well as anyone, but chose to use the theme all the same, since, no matter how it came to exist, as a musical motif it suited his purposes to a tee.

The lines sung in the first vocal episode are delivered by the foolish schoolteacher Holofernes, whose drollery stems largely from his pretentious malapropisms. In this speech from Act IV, Scene ii, the pompous pedant mangles quotations in Latin, Italian, and solfeggio in a hapless attempt to demonstrate his supposed erudition:

Fauste, precor gelida quando pecus omne sub umbra ruminat, and so forth.
Ah, good old Mantuan! I may speak of thee as the traveller doth of Venice:
  Venezia, Venezia,
   Chi non ti vede non ti prezia.
Old Mantuan, old Mantuan! Who understandeth thee not, loves thee not.
Ut, re, sol, la, mi, fa.   (IV.ii, 89–95)

The initial line, the opening of the first eclogue of Mantuan (Baptista Spagnuoli), whose verses served as primers throughout Europe for approximately two centuries beginning around 1500, would have been one of the first Latin phrases memorized by Shakespeare or any other well-educated Englishman of his day.[25] George Turbervile's standard translation of 1567 rendered it into English as "Friend Faustus, pray thee, since our flock in shade and pleasaunt vale doth chewe the cudde". In the most accurate versions of the play, Shakespeare intentionally misquotes the line for comic effect as "*Facile precor gelida quando pecas omnia sub umbra ruminat*", meaning roughly "Easily, I pray, since you are getting everything wrong under the cool shade, it ruminates."[26] Editions of *Love's Labour's Lost*, such as the one used by Burgess, which restore Mantuan's proper text effectively nullify the line's admittedly esoteric humor.

The next four lines, a florid apostrophe to Mantuan, incorporate John Florio's saying, "*Venezia, Venezia, chi non ti vede non ti prezia*", meaning "Venice, Venice, who loves you not, sees you not."[27] The line "Old Mantuan, old Mantuan! Who understandeth thee not, loves thee not" ironically references Holofernes's misunderstanding not only of Mantuan but also Florio, whose maxim he mispronounces as "*Venechia, Venechia, que non te vede, que non te prechia.*" Again missing the point, some editions, such as Burgess's source, restore the uncorrupted version of the quoted text.

The last line of the passage represents Holofernes's botched attempt to sing a simple C major scale in solfeggio. Beginning with "ut", the original solfège syllable for C (still used in France but generally replaced elsewhere by "do"), he gets the next tone right ("re" for D) but confuses the rest, erroneously singing "sol" on E, "la" on F, "mi" on G, and "fa" on A instead of "mi, fa, sol, la" on E, F, G, A. Thus this Shakespearean "melody" is actually nothing more than the disordered solmization of the first six notes of a C major scale.

The text of the second vocal episode comes from the end of Act V, Scene ii, during a masque staged by the "fantastical Spaniard" Don Adriano de Armado to amuse King Ferdinand of Navarre, the Princess of France, and the lords and ladies assembled at Ferdinand's court. When Armado's entertainment is interrupted, he proposes to the king that they skip to the songs that were to have come at the end of the masque: "Will you hear instead", he asks, "the dialogue that the two learnèd men have compiled in praise of the owl and the cuckoo?"[28] The king agrees, and so, to the accompaniment of strings evoking the icy sounds of winter with a series of *col legno* glissandi followed by warm Vaughan Williamsian harmonies suggestive of spring, Armado announces the presenters: "This side is Hiems, Winter; this Ver, the Spring: the one maintained by the owl, the other by the cuckoo. Ver, begin!"

Vivid orchestration and musical text painting reinforce the colorful imagery and pun-laden wit of Shakespeare's song texts. The pleasing sound of the owl, represented by "oboe twits", alternates with the familiar call of the cuckoo – descending thirds played by the clarinet. Spring, a colorful profusion of "daisies pied", "violets blue", "lady-smocks all silver-white", and "cuckoo buds of yellow hue" that "paint the meadows with delight", is a lively season of shepherds who "pipe on oaten straws", farmers who rise each day at dawn with the larks, and maidens, who, to clean their warm weather clothing, "bleach their summer smocks". Yet spring is also a menacing time of unconstrained sexual activity that "mocks married men" who shudder when they hear the ominous cuckoo "on every tree" sounding its "word of fear". Winter, a time of cold, discomfort, and illness, is also a season of cheerfulness, wisdom, and holiday feasts. Though "all aloud the wind doth blow" and "birds sit brooding in the snow", at the blazing hearth, "greasy Joan doth keel the pot" to keep the cauldron filled with steaming soup from boiling over. The "staring owl" presides over wintry nights, hooting "a merry note" that, to an Elizabethan ear, contained sexual puns on "Tu-who" (To who?) and "Tu-whit" (To it!). Burgess summarized this section of the symphony thus:

> Cold (superposed fourths) and heat (tritonal fourths) are complementary aspects of the cycle of life. The orchestra leaves enunciating abstract musical patterns and blatantly illustrates the words of the conjoined songs. There is a riot of birdsong while the tenor tells of spring. The cuckoo which mocks married men blares major and minor on brass. Icicles hang by the wall (xylophones), Dick the shepherd blows his nail (breathy flute), Tom bears logs into the hall (deep clumsy brass: he drops some of them), milk is frozen (glockenspiel), coughing drowns the parson's saw or sermon (rim shot on side drum), roasted crabs hiss in the bowl (sizzle cymbal). In springtime the birds tread (woodwind), merry larks are ploughmen's clocks (aspiring solo violin out of Vaughan Williams), maidens bleach their summer smocks (the only dominant-seventh–tonic progression in the whole work). And then, unaccompanied, the vocal cadenzas which celebrate synchronically the owl and the cuckoo.[29]

The first stanza of "Spring" is sung to the Shakespeare theme by the tenor, with the second stanza sung by the baritone to the *Venezia* melody; in "Winter", the pattern is reversed. Defying the logic that would prevent spring and winter from occurring at the same time, the tenor and baritone sing their respective final lines together in a vocal cadenza with the calls of the cuckoo (baritone) and owl (tenor) sounding simultaneously. As Burgess described this in his program note:

> They deliver the two songs that end *Love's Labour's Lost*, using the two main chunks of musical material already presented, and allow winter and spring, the owl and the cuckoo, to become mixed together, to appear – to use a Holofernian kind of pedanticism – synchronically instead of, what nature decrees, diachronically. Which is absurd. But the singers do not mind.

The songs are followed by an instrumental coda interrupted, just before it is about to end, by the play's final lines.

Having sung, they wish to finish the proceedings as quickly as possible, so the movement ends as *Love's Labour's Lost* ends – with these spoken words: "The words of Mercury are harsh after the songs of Apollo." The orchestra plays a single fortissimo chord of C major, and everybody goes off for a drink.[30]

The symphony earned Burgess an entry in *Baker's Biographical Dictionary of Musicians*. When Nicolas Slonimsky, the dictionary's editor, lectured at the University of Iowa in 1976, he examined the score, which, according to one music professor there, "made a very positive impression on him (and Nicolas is not easily impressed)."[31] For Burgess's entry, which first appeared in the sixth edition in 1978, Slonimsky wrote, "Despite his great success as a novelist, he continued to write music, and developed a style of composition that, were it not for his literary fame, would have earned him a respectable niche among composers. His music is refreshingly rhythmical and entirely tonal, but not without quirky quartal harmonies and crypto-atonal melodic flights."[32]

Proud of his role in bringing about Burgess's increased musical recognition ("I cannot escape the feeling that you are my discovery"), James Dixon hoped to record the Third Symphony and other Burgess compositions in London, since "union problems" prevented him from doing so with his university orchestra.[33] Dixon invited Burgess to compose additional works for the University of Iowa Orchestra and his other orchestra, the Tri-City Symphony in Davenport, but nothing came of these proposals.

Burgess was well aware that his symphony's conservative style placed him distinctly out of step with most contemporary composers. During a six-week residency at SUNY-Buffalo in the spring of 1976, he was disheartened by students in the English Department who regarded most great literature of the past as irrelevant: "I was made to feel very old-fashioned, like Shakespeare." In the Department of Music, where Morton Feldman was head of composition, things were still worse:

> I was made to feel even more old-fashioned when I took a tape of my Iowa symphony to the music department. The head of the composition section was a Bronx man who spoke of dis and dat and de woiks of Beethoven (the mention of the name provoked a delicate sneer among the students, one of whom was a transvestite). My first movement would be okay for a battle scene in a B movie: as serious music it did not begin to exist.[34]

Burgess's Third Symphony represents a dynamic, original example of late twentieth-century symphonic composition, presaging the "New Romanticism" that sent many composers stampeding back to tonality in the early 1980s. The composition of this work, more than any other, gave Burgess greater confidence in his musical ability than ever before and marked the moment when he genuinely began to fulfill his long-delayed ambition of being a composer. Having savored "the truly great artistic moment" of its performance, Burgess wrote music prolifically for the rest of his life. Indeed, from that point on, he never really stopped composing again.

Notes

1 *Shakespeare*, 252.
2 *Napoleon Symphony*, 364.
3 "How I Wrote My Third Symphony", 1.
4 "Symphony in C", program note for the University Symphony Orchestra concert at the University of Iowa on 22 October 1975.
5 The mandolin part, written for one player, requires two instruments and players in order for the parallel thirds and four-part chords to be played as written.
6 TMM, 51.
7 Ibid., 60.
8 Ibid., 55.
9 Iowa program note.
10 Ibid.
11 TMM, 60.
12 "How I Wrote My Third Symphony", 1, 19. The inscriptions appear on pages 30 and 38 of the manuscript.
13 TMM, 62.
14 Ibid., 65.
15 In his Iowa program note, Burgess describes this variant of the motif as "a kind of deformed bugle call".
16 YH, 311.
17 TMM, 64.
18 Ibid., 64, 66.
19 *Shakespeare*, 252. In *King Lear*, Edmund utters the phrase "Fa, sol, la, mi" in Act I, Scene ii (line 133).
20 Iowa program note.
21 TMM, 70.
22 Ibid.
23 Ibid., 71.
24 *Shakespeare*, 130.
25 Baptista Spagnuoli, *The Eclogues of Mantuan*, transl. George Turbervile (New York: Scholars' Facsimiles & Reprints, 1937), 1.
26 William Shakespeare, *Love's Labor's Lost*, ed. Peter Holland, *The Pelican Shakespeare* (New York: Penguin Books, 2000), 52.
27 John Florio (ca. 1553–1625), the son of an Italian emigrant to London, achieved distinction as the author of an Italian-English dictionary, translator of Montaigne's *Essais* into English, secretary to the Earl of Southampton, and tutor to Prince Henry, the son of James I. The eighteenth-century literary scholar William Warburton and others have suggested that Holofernes is a caricature of Florio, who may have been an acquaintance of Shakespeare. Florio's proverb about Venice appeared in *Firste Fruites* (1578) and *Second Frutes* (1591), bilingual pedagogical publications that incorporated common phrases into dialogues about everyday activities and were regarded as manuals of polite conversation, handbooks for self-improvement, and digests of popular journalism combined into one.
28 Although the phrase "the two learnèd men" refers to Holofernes and the curate Sir Nathaniel, some editions, including the one used by Burgess, substitute *we* for *the*.

29 TMM, 71.
30 Iowa program note.
31 Letter from University of Iowa music professor Lowell Cross to Burgess, 22 July 1976.
32 Nicolas Slonimsky (editor), *Baker's Biographical Dictionary of Musicians* (New York: Schirmer Books, 8th ed., 1992), 268.
33 James Dixon, letter to Burgess, 14 September 1976.
34 YH, 335.

18

THE OLD JOANNA

If the harpsichord is the Alexander Pope of music, the piano is its Lord Byron.[1]

The piano was the musical cornerstone of Burgess's life. He learned to play it as a child, performed on it during and after the war, and composed concert works for it throughout his life. It was of prime importance to him especially from 1976 to 1986, the decade in which he composed his greatest keyboard works, which include a concerto, concertino, and set of twenty-four preludes and fugues modeled on Bach's *Well-Tempered Clavier*. As an essayist and novelist, he also wrote extensively about the piano and those who play it.

"The Well-Tempered Revolution: A Consideration of the Piano's Social and Intellectual History" is the first and longest of the eight chapters in *The Lives of the Piano*, a 1981 book written "by men and women who have carried on a nearly lifelong love affair with the piano".[2] In this essay, Burgess traces the piano's development from the harpsichord to electronic keyboards equipped with "ready-made chords and bongo drums activable at the touch of a switch."[3] Ending with a "final meditation...on the metaphysical significance of the piano or pianoforte or fortepiano or *Hammerklavier*", he reflects on its varied roles as a "medium for German *Innigkeit*" in lieder, "reflection in miniature of the Wagnerian orchestra" in the post-Napoleonic era, and symbol of alienation in Bernstein's musicalization of Auden's *Age of Anxiety*.[4] With his background in popular music, Burgess writes just as knowledgeably about the piano as a jazz instrument:

> Early jazz kept to hymn-tune harmonies, but it was not long before impressionistic chords came in. Melodically its rhythms were closer to those of speech than to the formalized patterns of traditional song. Certainly jazz piano insists on a new way of using the instrument. Its music defies traditional notation. It is far from easy to learn. And if it is harmonically impressionistic, it can also favor the dry, pecking sound of the baroque. Some jazz keyboard players have even gone back to the harpsichord. The sustaining pedal is not loved. The soft pedal might as well not have been invented. The pianoforte is, in jazz, a forte.[5]

In his introduction to *Pianoforte: A Social History of the Piano*, Burgess hailed the instrument as the ideal means of expressing the Romantic spirit during the age of Napoleon: "the piano concerto . . . exhibited magisterially the heroic implications of a single man fighting, and being reconciled with, an orchestra of a hundred." For musical valor, other instruments just cannot compare: "Berlioz represented Childe Harold, who is really his author Byron, in a solo viola poeticising against an orchestra, but he should properly have chosen a piano."[6]

What little Burgess wrote about his piano concerto appears in *The Lives of the Piano*:

> A few years ago I composed a concerto (in a kind of E-flat) for piano and orchestra. It is dedicated to the memory of my father, whose craft brought him little money and a measure of hard work and suffering. It is too difficult for me to play, and it would have been difficult for him, who was always impatient with written notes. It was written for a pianist; both he and I have been merely piano players.[7]

The pianist for whom it was written was probably the British virtuosa Moura Lympany (1916–2005), who resided near Burgess in Monte Carlo. Knowing that she had championed the music of such British composers as Frederick Delius, Benjamin Britten, Cyril Scott, John Ireland, Richard Arnell, Alan Rawsthorne, and Malcolm Williamson throughout her career, Burgess sent her the score of his concerto soon after he completed it. By her own account, she would have played it had the Orchestra of Monte Carlo agreed to program the work, but the orchestra would not commit to a performance, so she never learned it.[8]

Concerto for Pianoforte and Orchestra in E♭ was Burgess's first major composition following his Symphony No. 3 in C. Completed in Monaco on 1 July 1976, it consists of three movements lasting thirty-three minutes and is scored for full orchestra with a large percussion battery requiring four players. The music is, in a word, ebullient. The soloist doesn't just play the piano but practically attacks it. Cascading arpeggios, rapid scalar runs, and two-handed trills abound, powerful glissandos sweep from one end of the keyboard to the other, and great Ivesian polytonal chords erupt from the solo piano as well as the orchestra.

As previously noted, most of the concerto's main themes come from the *Preludes* of 1964–65. The first three preludes provide most of the first movement's principal thematic material. The molto moderato slow introduction (Example 18.01) is based largely on Prelude I. Following a two-bar orchestral fanfare, the piano enters with the prelude's initial ascending figure (see Example 10.02), with the rest of the introduction closely matching its source. The allegro giocoso exposition presents three principal subjects. Theme 1 (from Prelude III) is jaunty and sometimes jazzy while Theme 2 (from Prelude II) is contrapuntal and strongly pentatonic. Both are notated in 6/8 : 3/4, with Theme 1 felt primarily in 6/8 and Theme 2, entirely in 3/4. Theme 3 (Example 18.02), an angular staccato figure in 5/4, bears a

Example 18.01 Piano Concerto, mvt. 1: Introduction (bs. 1–9)

superficial resemblance to Prelude VI, but is less closely related than in the other cases. Only Themes 3 and 1, in that order, appear in the development of this sonata-form movement. All three themes, plus material from the introduction, are reprised in the recapitulation, with a lengthy solo cadenza comprising the latter half of this section; the first two themes alone return in the coda.

The andantino semplicissimo second movement opens with a flowing piano solo in 3/4 akin to the opening of the slow movement of Ravel's G major Concerto and closely based on Prelude V (see Example 10.06). Toward the end, a loud outburst in the brass and timpani interrupts the tranquil atmosphere, but calm is soon restored with the return of the

The Old Joanna 201

Example 18.02 Piano Concerto, mvt. 1: Theme 3 (bs. 164–66)

opening theme in the solo piano, now embellished by a counterpoint of running sixteenth notes.

The presto con fuoco finale begins with a series of dance forms (jig, Viennese waltz, *polacca*), then switches to eclectic music incorporating twelve-tone rows and the blues. The opening jig tune (foreshadowed in the final bars of the previous movement) comes from Prelude IV, its melody transposed from C major to E♭ (see Example 10.05). Like its source, this movement features metrical ambiguity, rhythmic intricacy, and polyrhythms. Immediately following a lengthy cadenza for the soloist comes a passage in 15/16 that is particularly complex, with measures organized in nine different rhythmic groupings: 2+2+2+3+3+3, 4+4+4+3, 6+1.5+6+1.5, and so on. Although the harmonic language is mainly tonal, at one point the tone row of Berg's Violin Concerto is quoted – literally – within quotation marks (Example 18.03). The movement reaches its astonishing zenith of stylistic diversity directly after the Berg episode when the solo piano launches into eight bars of Burgessian blues.

When Burgess composed the work, this type of eclecticism was unusual. Although his music was too little known to have influenced postmodern musical trends, his style and ideas were remarkably prescient. William Bolcom's Violin Concerto in D (1983), a modern amalgam inspired by ragtime, rhythm-and-blues, and the playing of jazz violinist Joe Venuti, and Christopher Rouse's Flute Concerto (1993), with its jig-like scherzo and incorporation of Celtic influences, are among many later works bearing stylistic affinities to Burgess's pre-postmodern style.

Samuel Coale, an English professor at Wheaton College, interviewed Burgess in the summer of 1978 for a monograph on his novels. Upon arriving in Monaco on 7 July, Coale was surprised that the first thing Burgess wished to discuss was his Third Symphony, which he played in its entirety at their first session before discussing any of his books.[9] Attempting to find

*The quotation is from Alban Berg's Violin Concerto.

Example 18.03 Piano Concerto, mvt. III: Theme 3 (bs. 269–83)

musical common ground, Coale mentioned having taken piano lessons as a boy. Upon hearing this, Burgess pledged to compose a piece for him. For the next three days, the two men conversed convivially, laying the foundation for the book that the Frederick Ungar Publishing Company issued three years later as part of its Modern Literature Series. On 11 July, Coale's final day in Monaco, Burgess presented him with a four-movement suite titled *Master Coale's Pieces*.

"Master Coale's Maggotte", a chromatic, quasi-atonal Adagio ending in E minor, derives its unusual title from an archaic term for a dance-tune; as Oliver Sacks explains in *Musicophilia*, the term "earworm" (German *Ohrwurm*) or "maggot" refers to a tune that sticks annoyingly in one's brain like a maggot in a rotting piece of fruit.[10] "Allegro vivo", a short Hindemithian piece also in E minor, begins as a two-part canon in which the voices are, remarkably, an augmented octave apart. "Lento", a chaconne based on a six-bar twelve-tone ground, ends on a traditional F major chord following eight statements of the basso ostinato. "Rhapsody", the most tuneful of the pieces, shifts repeatedly between slow and fast tempi before ending squarely in E major.[11]

A Scottish Rhapsody for the 17th birthday of Andrew, a four-minute-long piano work dated 9 August 1981, is a tribute to Burgess's son's ardor for his paternal grandmother's ancestral homeland. This medley of five original tunes in Scottish style, preceded by an andante introduction, bears the inscription "Love and lang may your lum reek / frae your auld faither" (Love and long may your chimney smoke / from your old father). On the reverse side of the last page, Burgess composed a keyboard fugue on "Ye Banks and Braes".

Tango for Pianoforte owes its creation to Yvar Mikhashoff (1941–93), an American pianist on the music faculty of SUNY-Buffalo whom Burgess most likely met in spring 1976 during his residency there. On 8 October 1984, Burgess sent him a copy of his new choral work *In Time of Plague*, which probably prompted Mikhashoff to invite Burgess to compose a piece for his International Tango Collection, an initiative that Mikhashoff, a former competitive ballroom dancer, had conceived the previous year. Burgess completed his tango on 24 November 1984, and on 14 April 1985 it was one of eighty-eight tangos premiered by Mikhashoff at the North American New Music Festival in Buffalo.[12] Mikhashoff subsequently performed many of these tangos, including Burgess's, on international tours, reporting in a 1986 letter to Burgess that he had played his more than fifteen times "from New York to Seoul to Stockholm – it's always a great success!"[13] Burgess's tango follows the standard two-part form with each section presented twice, the melody first played unadorned, then embellished. The piece modulates from D minor in the first section to G major in the second, then ends abruptly on an unexpected altered dominant seventh chord, a surprise ending sure to evoke a smile from any listener.

The Bad-Tempered Electronic Keyboard is Burgess's most extensive keyboard work: a set of twenty-four preludes and fugues in all the major and minor keys plus a fugal finale.[14] Despite the jocular Bachian title and its reference to the middling electric piano in Burgess's Monaco condominium, the music is serious, composed is a wide variety of tempi, meters, and styles ranging from mock-Baroque to late-Romantic chromaticism, the latter used especially in the pieces in slower tempi. Composed in 1985 as a tribute to Johann Sebastian Bach on the 300th anniversary of his birth, this homage is made explicit in the B♭ major fugue and B♭ minor prelude, both of which are based on the B-A-C-H motif.

The D minor prelude and fugue illustrate a mix of Bachian style with late-Romantic harmony and greater dissonance than employed in the

Example 18.04 Preludio No. 3 in D minor

The Old Joanna

Example 18.04 *Continued*

Example 18.05 Fuga in D minor

Example 18.05 *Continued*

Baroque era. The prelude shows that Burgess's passion for counterpoint was not limited to fugue. Opening as a canon at the octave in the first half, the prelude becomes contrapuntally freer and more chromatic in the second half, its last ten bars incorporating several short canonic phrases and repeating motivic material from the first half, like the sixteenth-note run in the left hand in bar 8. The final chord contains the Picardy third typical of Burgess's minor-key preludes and fugues. The fugue adheres to traditional fugal practice, with a four-bar subject entering in the tonic key followed by entries of the other voices in bars 5 (dominant) and 10 (tonic). Upon completion of the exposition, a two-bar episode ensues in bar 14, leading to a subdominant fugal entry in bar 16. After another two-bar episode, the subject (inverted) enters in the tonic in bar 22. Three measures later, the final entrance of the subject, back in tonic and in its original form, leads to the final cadence and another Picardy third.

Composing a cycle of preludes and fugues in all the major and minor keys is an achievement that has been carried out by few composers apart from Bach and Dmitri Shostakovich.[15] What makes Burgess's feat especially remarkable is the speed with which he accomplished it. With just five weeks of the tercentennial year remaining, he started work on 23 November, composing the C major prelude and fugue that day. Four movements followed on the 24th, two on the 25th, four on the 26th, and five on the 27th, his most prolific day. He continued with two pieces on the 28th, two on the 29th, three on the 30th, and three on 1 December. Fifteen pieces were written between the 3rd and 7th, with two more finished by the 12th.[16] On 13 December, Burgess composed the B minor prelude (the only piece in the set based on an earlier Burgess theme, in this case the one from bar 263 of the Piano Concerto's third movement) and a bonus Christmas finale, a fugue on "Good King Wenceslas" with "The First Noel" and "God Rest Ye Merry Gentlemen" woven in, bringing the total duration to about ninety minutes.

Another homage to Bach is an untitled set of keyboard pieces, all in A major, that could aptly be called Brief Suite in A. Over the course of its six movements – Prelude, Sarabande, Gigue, Air, Fuga, Gavotte – the suite's harmonic language becomes progressively simpler, from highly chromatic to diatonic, ending in charming neo-Baroque pastiche. Six short pieces – four in A major and two in A minor – form another untitled set comprising three fugues, an air, a passacaglia, and a hornpipe on a theme from the first movement of *Mr W.S.* A pair of twelve-tone pieces ("****1." and "****2.") are written for keyboard, although the second, an unfinished sketch with indications of instrumentation, may have been a sketch for a chamber or orchestral piece. Judging by their appearance, all of these undated manuscripts were written around the late 1980s.

From roughly the same period comes a quirky, untitled group of parodic short pieces combining Satie's wit, Stravinsky's irony, Bach's purity,

Example 18.06 3. Rhumba

Debussy's impressionism, and Webern's brevity. These Nine Miniatures, as they might be called, begin with "Prelude", a wisp of a piece in which middle C is softly and almost continuously sounded while other pitches, mostly from within the whole-tone array, are quietly played against it. "Fughetta" is a brief contrapuntal exercise, mainly in two voices, based on a quartal subject that begins with ascending fourths on the notes C–F–B♭. "Rhumba" (Example 18.06), conceptually based on Satie's *Vexations*, consists of a single measure of whole-tone music marked "repeat indefinitely in *pp* < *ff* > *ppp*". "Alla marcia" resembles the "March" from Stravinsky's Three Easy Pieces for piano duet. "Waltz" pairs a mainly whole-tone melody in the left-hand with an accompaniment of mostly whole-step dyads in the right. Recalling Bach's "Air on the G string", "Arietta" couples a legato melody with a quarter-note staccato bass line. "*Feux d'artifice*" revisits the texture and sonority of Debussy's eponymous prelude. "National Anthem", a brief chromaticization of "God Save the Queen", is followed by "Envoi", the quasi-atonal, dream-like piece that concludes this untitled and undated suite of miniatures.

Flurrying downward runs, pointillistic clusters, and delicate dynamics create a miniature musical portrait of a Swiss snowfall in ШНЕГ В САВОСЕ or *Schnee in Savosa*, as Burgess called his only extant piano duet. This brief atonal piece, lasting just over a minute, requires the two pianists to play in different meters simultaneously and deal with other rhythmic complexities. As the title suggests, Burgess composed it in the house he and Liana purchased in 1985 in Crocifisso di Savosa, near Lugano, which served them as a retreat from the din of motorbikes along Rue Grimaldi.

Feuerwerk is a colorful, two-minute piano showpiece full of white- and black-note glissandi, whole-tone runs, and quartal sonorities; judging by the stylistic similarity to the Presto for Martin Bell and notational resemblance to the *Preludes* manuscript, this undated piece may have been composed in the mid-1960s. Around 1973 during their work together on *Cyrano*, Burgess composed for John Covelli a bagatelle that is "a little atonal – not Bergian or Schoenbergian – no tone row" and a short piece jestingly described by Covelli as "the unfinished phone number" – the opening of a fugue based on a subject containing the notes G–C–D–C, a transcription of the numbers 5-8-2-1, which formed part of Burgess's phone number in Rome.[17] These are but a few of dozens of less significant keyboard works, including numerous fugues and fugal expositions, that Burgess drafted in music notebooks and on loose sheets of manuscript paper. Including lost pieces mentioned in *This Man and Music*, *Contemporary Composers*, autobiographical writings, and other sources, the tally of his keyboard compositions amounts to roughly fifty works, including eight for organ of which only an arrangement of *In Dulci Jubilo* (written Christmas Day 1981) and a prelude and fugue based upon it still exist. The most important of the more than twenty extant works are the ones already cited plus the concertino *Rome in the Rain* and several large-scale chamber works with keyboard discussed later in this volume.

Music and sex conjoin in *The Pianoplayers*, a salaciously entertaining novel published in 1986 that traces the careers of Billy Henshaw, a piano player based on Joseph Wilson, and his daughter Ellen, the narrator, whose personal history mirrors Burgess's, both having grown up in the same neighborhood, attended the same schools, known the same people, owned homes in the same French village of Callian de Var, had soubrette mothers and a sibling who died in the influenza pandemic, and been born on the same day.[18] Like *The End of the World News*, *The Pianoplayers* is assembled from diverse pre-existing sources, principally a novella about his father that Burgess completed by April 1977 and mentioned to Samuel Coale the following year.[19] Reviving his penchant for mixing elements of opera into his novels, Burgess grafts the plot of *I Pagliacci* onto an episode about Billy Henshaw playing "the old joanna" for a troupe of entertainers modeled on the Jaypees. Franz Kafka's "A Hunger Artist" and Horace McCoy's 1935 novel *They Shoot Horses, Don't They?* (or Sydney Pollack's Oscar-winning 1969 film adaptation) may have helped inspire the story of the fatal piano marathon that represents the artistic summit of Billy's tragic life. The fact that Pollack was the guest of honor at the University of Iowa film festival at which Burgess played the piano for a screening of Fritz Lang's silent masterpiece *Metropolis* (an incident fictionalized in *The Pianoplayers*) lends credence to this supposition.[20]

The novel's ending is drawn from the macabre tale "An American Organ", one of three stories written by Burgess in the mid-1960s, during the years leading up to Lynne's death, that share the theme of a husband murdering his wife.[21] In keeping with the erotic spirit of *The Pianoplayers*, the story's grisly ending is converted into a scene of carnal delight, as Ellen's son Robert, intending to murder his frigid wife Edna in the bath, becomes aroused instead. "It was the first time they'd either of them got anything out of Sex". From then on, "Edna, as you might expect, couldn't get enough of it now, and they were the cleanest couple in Hammersmith."[22]

Example 18.07 "Fingers Off" from *The Pianoplayers* (206–8)

Ellen's memoir concludes with "The One-armed Fiddler's Waltz" or "Fingers Off" (Example 18.07), a piece for violin and piano composed by her father as a teaching tool. Convinced that anyone could learn to play the violin with proper instruction, Billy wrote this beginner's etude on the

The Old Joanna

Example 18.07 *Continued*

open strings, which he taught Ellen. Naturally by Burgess himself, this slightly jazzy piece, the completion of a sketch found in *This Man and Music*, was composed in 1947 for what he called *The Young Fiddler's Tunebook*, which J. Curwen & Sons rejected for publication. In the novel,

Burgess turns it into a hit by having it published in the Suzuki-like Sukiyaki Violin Method and eventually broadcast worldwide by the BBC Overseas Service.

Notes

1. Introduction to *Pianoforte: A Social History of the Piano* by Dieter Hildebrant (New York: George Braziller, 1988), v.
2. *The Lives of the Piano*, ed. by James R. Gaines (New York: Holt, Rinehart & Winston, 1981), vii. Other chapters include Ned Rorem's "Beyond Playing: A Composer's Life with the Piano", William Bolcom's "Song and Dance: The American Way of Pianism", and Samuel Lipman's "The Ordeal of Growth: Confessions of a Former Prodigy".
3. *The Lives of the Piano*, 30.
4. Ibid., 36.
5. Ibid., 25.
6. Introduction to *Pianoforte: A Social History of the Piano*, v-vii.
7. *The Lives of the Piano*, 3–4.
8. "As I did not wish to spend hours learning it if I did not have a concert date for it, I asked the Monaco Orchestra whether they would play it. They told me to send it to the librarian, which I did, and never heard any more." (Moura Lympany, fax to author, 9 June 2001.) Although no dedication appears on the manuscript, on one document in the HRC archives, Lympany's name is listed as the dedicatee but crossed out, suggesting that Burgess considered dedicating the concerto to her but changed his mind.
9. Interview with Samuel Coale, 23 September 1997.
10. Oliver Sacks, *Musicophilia: Tales of Music and the Brain*, revised and expanded edition (New York: Vintage Books, 2008), 46n.
11. This sequence provides the strongest ending and most satisfying tonal progression of the movements, whose order Burgess did not specify. An edition published by Saga Music in 1994 reverses the outer movements while allowing the option of switching the middle ones.
12. Eventually the collection grew to 127 tangos for piano, which are listed at http://ublib.buffalo.edu/libraries/units/music/spcoll/mikhashoff/tangos/tangopublications.html. Burgess's tango was published in 1995 by Saga Music (SAGA 95041).
13. Yvar Mikhashoff, letter to Burgess, 26 September 1986.
14. On the cover of the manuscript, Burgess wrote "Vol. 1", implying that he intended to compose, like Bach, a second volume.
15. Shostakovich composed his set of 24 preludes and fugues (Opus 87) in 1950.
16. In his Preface (vi, dated 7 December 1985) to David W. Barber's amusing book *Bach, Beethoven and the Boys: Music History As It Ought To Be Taught*, Burgess describes the circumstances under which he composed the A minor fugue: "By a curious chance (I do not joke, any more than Barber does) I got up at five this morning because my cough was keeping my sleeping partner awake (my wife, if you must know). As any musician will tell you, there is only one thing to do when you wake at five, and that is to compose a fugue. I composed a fugue, and then the mail came, with Barber's typescript. It is a fugue

for four voices, in A minor. It is the twenty-second fugue I have written in little over a week. God knows why I am writing fugues. It is certainly not to awaken the sleeping soul of Bach. Fugue is something that gets into you and, when one has composed forty-eight of the bastards, flies, or fugues, out again."
17 John Covelli, interview with author, 19 August 1998.
18 *The Pianoplayers*, 14, 19; LW, 35; RLAB, 9. *The Pianoplayers* contains so much material drawn from the lives of Burgess and his father that John J. Stinson grouped it with the autobiographical writings in Chapter One, "Biographical Sketch, the First Volume of the Memoirs, and One Highly Autobiographical Novel", of *Anthony Burgess Revisited* (Boston: Twayne, 1991).
19 "My father was a cinema pianist. I've written a little novel about him called *Piano Players*, which I've not published yet." Samuel Coale, "An Interview with Anthony Burgess", *Modern Fiction Studies* 27:3 (Autumn 1981), 431. See also RLAB, 324.
20 See YH, 325–6.
21 For descriptions of "A Pair of Gloves" and "I Wish My Wife Was Dead", see RLAB, 322–324.
22 PP, 205.

19

THE LOVE SONG OF F. X. ENDERBY

> *To find in the opening lines about April being the cruellest month a verbal analogy to the opening of Stravinsky's* Sacre du Printemps *may seem over-arbitrary, but those of us who, in Manchester in 1937, presented* The Waste Land *as melodrama, could not evade that opening on a high solo bassoon . . .*[1]

The Brides of Enderby and its companion piece *The Waste Land*, settings of verse by F. X. Enderby and T. S. Eliot, are two of Burgess's finest chamber works. Composed in the late 1970s, they were the first of a series of pieces Burgess composed for similar instrumental combinations. Yet in stark contrast to the joyful debut of his Third Symphony three years earlier, the events leading up to their premieres constitute one of the unhappiest episodes in his musical career. This ill-fated enterprise is well-documented thanks to papers preserved by Michael Rudiakov, who initiated the project by writing to Burgess in March 1977:

> Dear Mr. Burgess,
> I am director of the Chamber Music Series whose flyer is enclosed. Several years ago you visited Sarah Lawrence College as a musician, and I would like to invite you to visit us as one again. We have a flexible ensemble of 5 (The Laurentians), to which a moderate number of players can be added. Should you have a piece for our combination we would like to perform it, if you don't, would you consider writing one?[2]

The Laurentian Chamber Players (soprano Catherine Rowe, keyboardist Joel Spiegelman, flutist Gerardo Levy, oboist Ronald Roseman, and Rudiakov on cello) had played as a group since 1969 and were known for their stylistic versatility, performing repertoire ranging from Baroque arias to the latest contemporary works. Burgess replied enthusiastically, recalling his visit to Sarah Lawrence in January 1971 to deliver a lecture there and having played the piano as "a sort of sideshow to my main job, which was talking about my books . . . your suggestion that I write something for the Laurentians fills me with great pride and, indeed, resolution." Mentioning that he had recently scored the film *The Eyes of New York* for a quintet of winds, strings, and piano, he continued, "I have the sound of that kind of combination in my mind and I'd be delighted to write something. I'll start soon... my thanks for your kindness and encouragement."[3]

Rudiakov initially planned the premiere for 9 April 1978, but, upon learning that the fiftieth anniversary of the college's founding would take place the following fall, he and Sarah Lawrence College President Charles DeCarlo decided to postpone Burgess's appearance until then. The delay did not deter Burgess, who informed DeCarlo in September 1977 that his new work was almost complete: "I have indeed nearly finished a song cycle called 'The Brides of Enderby' ... and propose to send it off within the next month."[4] He completed the score in November and sent the original manuscript to Rudiakov, who expressed thanks for such a "very attractive and playable" work, though "the high notes for the Soprano may be a bit taxing here and there."[5] The cellist informed Burgess that he had secured a performance at the Library of Congress, "obtained in no small measure due to your piece", and outlined plans for additional concert and television appearances. Burgess then surprised Rudiakov with the news that he planned to compose a work to perform himself with the Laurentians:

> I'm glad the score got there safely, and I'm sorry about the high soprano C's, though these could be dropped an octave in some instances... October 1978 it will be then. I suggest the following as my part of the act – A reading of T. S. Eliot's THE WASTE LAND as melodrama, with an accompaniment (not of course going on all the time) that I'll write for your combination (there'll be bits of Stravinsky, Wagner, jazz etc in it, and the female voice will be a necessity). Alternatively, or additionally, I could just read some of my own work – novels, that is, of course – without accompaniment. But I know that THE WASTE LAND would be a great riot. I've done it before in America, but never yet with live music. Tell me what you think.[6]

Greatly encouraged by this unexpected and welcome news, Rudiakov eagerly proceeded to arrange events featuring Burgess as composer and performer. For several months the two men exchanged cordial letters expressing growing excitement about the enterprise until Rudiakov made the critical mistake of casting himself as Burgess's booking agent. This ill-advised insistence on a contract stipulating a ten per cent commission on Burgess's fees for all concerts with the Laurentian Chamber Players and related media engagements led to increasing distrust and suspicion on both sides, and, ultimately, the heartbreaking collapse of Rudiakov's ambitious plans.

Burgess's steadfast refusal to sign Rudiakov's contract, or even acknowledge that he had received it, was accompanied by an immediate change to a cooler, more cautious tone in his letters. Once he completed *The Waste Land*, Burgess sent Rudiakov a copy of the score rather than the original manuscript, as he had done with *The Brides of Enderby*. Four weeks passed without a response from Rudiakov after Burgess sent him *The Waste Land* on 19 April 1978, leading the composer to send this note of concern:

> I am worried. I have not heard from you about the score of THE WASTE LAND that I sent with all the devices available for ensuring safe delivery. Could you let me know? How are things going?[7]

In reply, Rudiakov reiterated his determination to obtain the agreement that Burgess had been deliberately ignoring: "Very happy with score to Wasteland. Am extracting parts for both works. Must have signed agreement before proceeding..."[8]

But the dispute over the contractual agreement had to be set aside when a grim new complication arose – the Eliot estate's refusal to permit *The Waste Land* to be played. Burgess "assured me along the way that there wouldn't be any problem," recalled Rudiakov, but when the cellist contacted Faber & Faber in June 1978 to formally secure the rights, "they said 'Absolutely not. Nothing doing. We won't allow it.' Well, I had a tremendous shock. You can imagine."[9] A representative of the Rights Department explained that while a reading of the poem interspersed with musical interludes might be permissible, she doubted that consent would be given for a recitation with musical accompaniment. Blindsided by this turn of events, Rudiakov turned to Burgess, who, in his attempt to secure the all-important permission, downplayed his composition's musical scope while citing Eliot's approval of a similar setting forty years earlier:

> The "musical setting" of THE WASTE LAND is actually no more than a recital of the poem itself with musical insertions, to be played by piano, flute, oboe and cello, which illustrate Eliot's own musical references. Thus, he had Stravinsky's *Le Sacre du Printemps* in mind (the opening bassoon solo) for the preludial opening, and he quotes Wagner, jazz, popular song throughout. The aim of my arrangement is to show what the musical references are – *Tristan*, *Parsifal* etc. There is no singing, only recitation...
>
> I have to go back a long way, to 1938, in fact... when Eliot gave permission to Geoffrey Bridson to present the poem on BBC North Regional (Manchester) and then transferred the same permission to myself, who presented a modified version of Bridson's arrangement at the University of Manchester. I had assumed that Eliot's lack of objection to such a presentation had not been modified over the years.
>
> So that is the position. In good faith, an attempt to make the poem clearer through the means of the music quoted by implication in it – the juxtaposition of "The moon shone bright on Mrs Porter" and the "amen" in *Parsifal* ("O et ces voix d'enfants..."), for instance.
>
> I do hope that I shall be allowed to go ahead with what is not a musicalisation but a recitation with musical punctuation.[10]

While Rudiakov further planned a busy October 1978 schedule of concerts and media events, his communications with Faber & Faber continued to go nowhere, so Burgess intervened again, writing to the Subsidiary Rights office to reiterate his earlier comments while adding this appeal:

> What I am requesting is permission to give two performances of my arrangement – for my solo voice and five instruments – in New York. These are more

or less private, being respectively in a college and a Young Men's Jewish Association auditorium. The work itself, the poem I mean, is not harmed. I have been too strong an advocate of its importance for nearly 45 years, have taught the poem, and am one of the few who know it by heart. I do not wish to tread in delicate preserves controlled by Mrs Eliot, but I do not see what she can really have against it.[11]

On 31 August, Faber & Faber reported that Valerie Eliot remained opposed to Burgess's unauthorized setting and categorically denied permission for its use on television. Regarding the 1938 Manchester presentation, the publisher explained that Eliot, after allowing several early experimental settings, had adopted a longstanding policy of denying all requests to set his poetry to music in order to keep his poems from being used for musical inspiration and to prevent any other artist's images, musical or visual, from coming between his words and the reader. Four frantic weeks of negotiation ensued, climaxing in a last-minute recording session and overnight delivery to London of a tape of *The Waste Land* for Valerie Eliot's approval. Finally she relented, and, just two weeks before the scheduled premiere, granted the Laurentian Chamber Players permission to give two performances of *The Waste Land* in connection with Sarah Lawrence College's fiftieth anniversary celebration. Although this decision precluded additional performances, it allowed the most critical ones to take place.

Yet Rudiakov's troubles were far from over. Having steadfastly refused to respond to Rudiakov's persistent reminders about the agent fee and contract, Burgess expressed mounting concern throughout the summer about the schedule, doubting that he could fulfill his many writing obligations on top of the busy itinerary that Rudiakov had arranged for him that fall. A pending compromise regarding the length of his stay broke down when Burgess stopped replying to Rudiakov's phone and cable messages throughout September. Finally, on 29 September, a telegram arrived from London with the devastating news that Burgess would not be coming at all.

LONDON DOCTORS FORBID ABSOLUTELY USA VISIT OCTOBER STOP DEEP REGRETS STOP WILL WRITE STOP KINDLY INFORM ALL CONCERNED
REGARDS
LIANA BURGESS

Rudiakov desperately attempted to salvage the situation, cabling to suggest a curtailed visit from 12 to 19 October, but to no avail. Burgess never arrived. With Chester Biscardi conducting and Brendan Gill, who had narrated the taped reading sent to Valerie Eliot, filling in again for Burgess, Rudiakov and the Laurentians gamely premiered *The Waste Land* on October 14 at Sarah Lawrence College and gave the first performance of *The Brides of Enderby* there the following day. In Burgess's absence, Rudiakov and the others proceeded as best they could: "we did the performance but, of course, it was nothing like we were hoping... the gala part of it was gone and finished."[12]

On 30 September 1982 the Laurentian Chamber Players gave the second performance of *The Waste Land*, this time in Manhattan with Raffael Adler conducting and Charles DeCarlo narrating. Rudiakov's failure to inform Burgess about it beforehand, and Burgess's icy response upon learning about it afterward, only increased the mutual distrust. In 1988 the Poetry Center in New York contacted Faber & Faber to request permission to present *The Waste Land* in honor of Eliot's centenary, but Valerie Eliot refused to grant any performances beyond the two she had previously allowed. Burgess's agent Gabriele Pantucci protested, disputing the inequity of this prohibition while performances of *Cats*, then in its sixth season on the West End, went on by the thousands, but Faber & Faber did not relent. Resignedly, Burgess wrote the publisher, "I merely wished this year to honour Eliot's centenary in the only way I could... Most of those now seeking to protect Eliot's work from musical contamination are probably too young (this includes, certainly, Mrs Eliot) to know of the musico-dramatic presentation of *The Waste Land* on BBC North Region in 1937... Eliot goes unhonoured by at least one admirer this year."[13] In *You've Had Your Time*, he carped:

> Mrs Eliot was not impressed by me. I had set some of Enderby's poems for a soprano accompanied by flute, oboe, violoncello and keyboard... and I followed this with a version of *The Waste Land* for the same combination with a narrator. Mrs Eliot permitted only two performances, but she was prepared to see *Cats* run for ever. God preserve us from literary widows.[14]

The Brides of Enderby is a setting of six gloomy texts (see Appendix 2) about love and sex. This melancholy reflection on F. X. Enderby and his failed relationships draws its title from "The High Tide on the Coast of Lincolnshire (1571)", a tragic poem by Jean Ingelow in which a young husband loses his wife to a devastating tidal wave.[15] As this "mighty eygre" threatens to engulf an East Midlands village, church bells ring out the tune "The Brides of Enderby" to warn the populace:

> "Play uppe, play uppe, O Boston bells!
> Ply all your changes, all your swells,
> Play uppe 'The Brides of Enderby.'"[16]   (lines 5–7)

Burgess's song cycle contains little of the poem's drama, only its lugubrious spirit of doomed love. Except for the first text, an original poem not otherwise found in any of Burgess's writings, all are verses attributed to the fictional poet Enderby. Notated drily, with few expression marks or tempo indications apart from metronome numbers, *The Brides of Enderby* is one of Burgess's more self-consciously modern compositions, especially the first song, which sounds like a demonstration of his ability to compose in the dissonant atonal style of the 1960s and '70s. As the cycle progresses, its style becomes increasingly tonal and sentimental.

The first song, a rumination on love and how unfortunate its consequences can be, finds the poet perplexed by ancient mysteries. The textual key is the rhyme of "hyacinth" with "labyrinth", associating Eliot's *Waste Land* and its references to the myth of Hyacinthus with Enderby's *Pet Beast*, an allegory on the legend of the Minotaur. The opening line refers to Zephyr, the jealous West Wind equally capable of causing a gale or gentle breeze, which blows Apollo's discus off course killing Hyacinthus, the beautiful Greek god of fertility. Love's tangled path is symbolized by the Labyrinth, constructed by Daedalus to imprison the Minotaur, the monstrous offspring of Pasiphaë and the bull (Poseidon's gift to King Minos) with which she falls in love. The song consists of an instrumental introduction followed by three vocal sections corresponding to the poem's three couplets, proceeding in a brisk steady tempo with the intricate twists of the maze symbolized by crooked sixteenth-note figurations.

The text of the second and shortest song of the cycle, a bleak poem that Enderby rejects while rummaging for verses to help Arry woo Thelma in a Cyrano-like arrangement, finds the poet so obsessed with his subject ("But that you were there really was all I knew") that everything else becomes irrelevant.[17] The song opens in A minor while retaining vestiges of the previous movement's atonality. As the poem's intensity heightens, text painting on phrases like "passionless frenzy" and "mad wings of motion" produces swooping glissandi and great melodic leaps in the demanding vocal part (Example 19.01).

References to the Virgin Mary, the Holy Family, and Enderby's detested stepmother intertwine in the next song, its text a jumble of profane images with stubborn elements of religious faith that Enderby, like Burgess, cannot evade despite having formally abandoned his Catholic faith. In its spare counterpoint and refined instrumental detail, the musical setting is reminiscent of Mahler's *Kindertotenlieder*. Pitched in G minor, the song begins and ends with cello solos that convey feelings of sentimentality and loneliness. The tone is subdued, with soft dynamics and subtle accompanimental effects that include flute tremolos, both *naturale* and flutter-tongue, *Firebird*-like cello glissandi on natural harmonics, and cello tremolos played *col legno*.

The fourth song is a parody of Henry Purcell's "Nymphs and Shepherds", its text a mélange of sexual imagery, Spenglerian *Weltschmerz*, erotic encounters in darkened movie theaters, and porcine allusions to Piggy Hogg, Enderby's dreary alter ego.[18] It starts out sounding like a Baroque trio sonata gone mad, with Purcell's melody, quoted in the introduction, played on a harpsichord to emphasize its Baroque lineage (Example 19.02). Burgess's extreme text painting style requires the soprano to sing sustained high Cs on the words "tautest then!", then descend two and a half octaves to sing "down again", quasi parlando, on a low G♭, resulting in the highest and lowest singing contained within the cycle.

Example 19.01 The Brides of Enderby, mvt. 2 (bs. 16–22)

The poem set in the fifth song, about a cold beauty who cruelly uses her attractiveness for heartless manipulation, was written by Burgess around 1939 shortly after meeting Lynne, its apparent inspiration.[19] Like the third song, this one begins with an instrumental solo – here, an unaccompanied oboe melody – and ends with a return of this introductory material. Once

Example 19.02 The Brides of Enderby, mvt. 4 (bs. 1–8)

the soprano enters, the oboe continues, producing a delicate two-part counterpoint. The unhurried 6/8 tempo and protracted nature of the setting make this slow, reflective song in C minor the longest of the cycle.

The text of the final song, which affirms that it is futile to resist that which cannot be avoided, is the poem associated with the return of the Muse as Enderby begins to recover his true personality following his disastrous "rehabilitation" into Piggy Hogg.[20] Set "in the style of a drawing room ballad", it is the most Romantic and harmonically rich song of the set, with an unabashedly sentimental vocal line supported by a Schumannesque accompaniment in D major.

Like *The Brides of Enderby*, *The Waste Land* is a chamber work in six parts scored for flute, oboe, cello, piano, and soprano, in this case with narrator added. Its eclectic assortment of compositional styles and techniques corresponds to the poem's vivid imagery and varied linguistic sources, resulting in a work that musically illuminates and intensifies Eliot's text. The many musical references embedded in the text are manifested in Burgess's thirty-seven-minute-long composition through excerpts from Stravinsky, Wagner, wartime popular songs, and music hall ditties. Portions of the text are declaimed above soft sustained sonorities, with cues indicating where key words and chords coincide, while other lines are spoken above melodic passages, the pacing of the words indicated only approximately in relation to the music. Aleatoric techniques are used for special effects, as when imitating the noise in a pub; for particular emphasis, certain phrases are spoken in silence.

The Prelude is a brief setting of the Epigraph, composed in a spare Modernist style akin to such late Stravinsky compositions as *Movements* or *Variations: Aldous Huxley in memoriam*. The first of countless instances of text painting in the work has flute, oboe, and cello plummeting precipitously as the narrator intones the word *pendere*, meaning "to drop" (Example 19.03).

"The Burial of the Dead" opens with a quotation of the initial bars of *The Rite of Spring*, illustrating Burgess's contention that Eliot had this work in mind while writing the lines that begin "April is the cruellest month." A pair of mock-Viennese waltzes – a lively Schoenbergian example followed by a slower sentimental one marked *schmalzvoll* and *wienerisch* – provide apt accompaniment to the lines based on the memoirs of Marie Larisch, an Austrian countess with strong family ties to Wagner's patron, King Ludwig II of Bavaria.[21] Eliot's borrowing from *Tristan und Isolde* ("*Frisch weht der Wind...*") is set to Wagner's melody, sung by soprano instead of tenor. *Tristan* quotations continue as the flute plays the cello melody from the beginning of Act I and the ensemble plays bits of the Prelude, which leads to the soprano singing "*Oed' und leer das Meer*". (In the opera, this line is sung by the Shepherd near the beginning of Act III, not by Isolde toward the end of that act, as asserted in *This Man and Music*.) This phrase leads to a continuation of the *Tristan* Prelude played in salon style (*stile di salone*).

Lively sardonic music in the style of Stravinsky's *Ragtime* underscores the passage about "Madame Sosostris, famous clairvoyante". Instances of text painting and "arithmology" include a repeating, spinning phrase in the oboe representing the turning of "the Wheel"; a three-part canon illustrating the line "I see crowds of people, walking round in a ring"; and nine

The Love Song of F. X. Enderby

Example 19.03 The Waste Land: Prelude (bs. 1–11)

bars of agitato music ending in silence on the final word of the line "With a dead sound on the final stroke of nine." Framing this section musically, the opening solo from *Le Sacre* returns after recitation of the final line, "You! hypocrite lecteur! – mon semblable, – mon frère!"

The grandiose piano solo that opens "A Game of Chess" quotes *Tannhäuser*, reinforcing Eliot's allusion to *Antony and Cleopatra* by linking

Example 19.04 The Waste Land: 2. A Game of Chess (bs. 140–50)

Shakespeare's Egyptian queen to Wagner's Venus (Example 19.04). The cakewalk-style accompaniment of "that Shakespeherian Rag", Eliot's parody of the 1912 hit "That Shakespearian Rag", offers comic relief, with the narrator speaking or singing the lines in the precise rhythm of the original rag music that Burgess meticulously crafted to the cadence of the text.

The Love Song of F. X. Enderby

The tavern scene relating the domestic troubles of Albert and Lil is underscored by "Let the Great Big World Keep Turning" notated as it might have been played by a pub pianist back in 1917 when it was written.

"The Fire Sermon" begins with a melancholy instrumental introduction that leads into faux-Elizabethan accompaniment to "Sweet Thames, run softly, till I end my song." Instead of quoting "The Pauper's Funeral", the 1845 song echoed in the line "The rattle of the bones, and chuckle spread from ear to ear", Burgess mimics osseous clatter and gleeful laughter with brittle arpeggios and trills in the piano.[22] Quotations of the song "Red Wing" and the Dresden Amen from Wagner's *Parsifal* underscore Eliot's ribald pairing of references to a vulgar army ballad ("O the moon shone bright on Mrs. Porter") and Paul Verlaine's genteel sonnet *"Parsifal"* (*"Et O ces voix d'enfants, chantant dans la coupole!"*), the allusion to Mrs. Porter's whorish daughter starkly juxtaposed to the rarified image of gently babbling daughters whose charms fail to sway the virgin youth Parsifal from his destiny of becoming the priestly king entrusted with the Holy Grail.[23] Varied instances of text painting – a twittering flute for Philomel, jazzy accompaniment for the one-eyed seller of currants, a strummed cello emulating the "pleasant whining of a mandoline", a chant-like melody for "Magnus Martyr" – precede another Wagner reference (Example 19.05). Here the soprano sings a "jazzed or ragged version" of

Example 19.05 The Waste Land: 3. The Fire Sermon (bs. 307–12)

the Rhinemaidens' melody that was Eliot's inspiration for "The Song of the (three) Thames-daughters."[24]

In the spare musical setting of "Death by Water", which takes up just one score page, the image of dead Phlebas floating inertly in the sea's whirlpool is reflected in the music by a poignant muted melody in the cello and swirling arpeggios in the flute. (Burgess also composed an alternative setting of "Death by Water" consisting even more simply of narration above a flute solo.[25])

Burgess's setting of the nine strophes comprising "What the Thunder Said" is almost entirely original, with distinct, evocative sections of music underscoring each of the first seven strophes, from declamatory piano chords intermixed with rumbling cello tremolandos for the first strophe to tranquil undulating sonorities for the seventh. Most of the climactic eighth strophe is recited in silence save for thunderous instrumental chords on the syllable DA preceding each of the Sanskrit commands – *Datta* (give), *Dayadhvam* (sympathize), *Damyata* (control) – that the soprano intones in sprechstimme. The hollow mood of the final strophe is echoed by streams of open fifths and quiet fragments of "London Bridge is falling down", gradually building up to the climax that immediately precedes the final repetition of "Datta Dayadhvam Damyata" spoken in silence. *The Waste Land* ends with the insightful and moving juxtaposition of the "Dresden Amen" with the final threefold utterance of "Shantih" (meaning "The Peace which passeth understanding"), symbolizing the confluence of Christianity and Hinduism, or put more broadly, the "collocation of East and West."[26]

Notes

1 TMM, 100.
2 Michael Rudiakov, letter to Burgess c/o Robert Lantz Agency, New York, 30 March 1977.
3 Letter to Rudiakov, 23 May 1977.
4 Letter to Charles DeCarlo, 3 September 1977.
5 Rudiakov, letter to Burgess, 19 November 1977.
6 Letter to Rudiakov, 26 November 1977.
7 Letter to Rudiakov, 16 May 1978.
8 Rudiakov, telex to Burgess, 21 May 1978.
9 Interview with Rudiakov, 21 January 1998.
10 Letter to Judith Fiennes, 10 July 1978.
11 Letter to Mavis Pindard, 19 August 1978.
12 Interview with Rudiakov, 24 May 2000.
13 Letter to Mavis Pindard, 23 April 1988.
14 YH, 360.
15 First published in 1883, it was anthologized in 1935 by W. H. Auden and John Garrett in *The Poet's Tongue*, where Burgess may have first read it.
16 Jean Ingelow, *The Poetical Works of Jean Ingelow* (New York: Thomas Y. Crowell & Co., 1887), 111.

17 *Inside Mr Enderby*, 38.
18 Purcell's setting of Thomas Shadwell's text is from his incidental music to *The Libertine* (1691). In 1929, the Manchester School Children's Choir sang "Nymphs and Shepherds" with the Hallé Orchestra under the direction of Sir Hamilton Harty, and twelve-year-old John Wilson may have heard it, or even sung in the chorus, on that occasion. Burgess wrote the poem "Nymphs and Satyrs" in early 1942 in Eye, the Suffolk town where he trained to become an AEC instructor.
19 Titled "Girl", it was originally published in *The Serpent* (vol. 24, 1939–40, 26), as cited in RLAB, 73n. See also *Revolutionary Sonnets*, 12. In *A Vision of Battlements* (143), it is one of the verses that Lavinia Grantham shows to Richard Ennis, and in an incomplete and altered state, is one of the verses that Enderby considers for his *Arry to Thelma* cycle (IME, 38).
20 See LW, 321. This is the poem for which Burgess received the Governor's Poetry Prize in Gibraltar in 1945.
21 Marie Larisch's family castle was on the Starnbergersee, the lake in which her uncle King Ludwig drowned at the age of 41. For a full account of her memoir *My Past* and its influence on *The Waste Land*, see George L. K. Morris, "Marie, Marie, Hold on Tight" in C. B. Cox and Arnold P. Hinchliffe (eds), *T. S. Eliot The Waste Land: A Casebook* (London: MacMillan Press, 1968), 165-7. See also Robert L. Schwarz, *Broken Images: A Study of* The Waste Land (Lewisburg: Bucknell University Press, 1988), a comprehensive study of the poem's source material.
22 "Rattle his bones over the stones; He's only a pauper who nobody owns!" (refrain from "The Pauper's Funeral", words by Thomas Noel and music by Judson Joseph Hutchinson). Joyce borrows from the same song in *Ulysses* in his description of Paddy Dignam's funeral procession: "The carriage climbed more slowly the hill of Rutland square. Rattle his bones. Over the stones. Only a pauper. Nobody owns." (Schwarz, *Broken Images*, 160.)
23 During World War I, Australian troops set bawdy lyrics to the melody of the popular song "Red Wing: an Indian fable", written in 1907 by Thurland Chattaway (words) and Kerry Mills (music), thereby immortalizing Mrs. Porter, the madam of a Cairo brothel, and her daughter, who worked there as a prostitute: "O the moon shone bright on Mrs. Porter / And on the daughter / of Mrs. Porter. / They wash their cunts in soda water / and so they oughter / To keep them clean." The quotation in *The Waste Land* derives from a less obscene variant of the song.
24 See Eliot's note to line 266 of *The Waste Land*.
25 Preceding the alternative version of "Death by Water" is a shorter ending of "The Fire Sermon", in which all music ceases before the narration of lines 307–11.
26 TMM, 102.

20

ROMAN CARNIVAL

"Italian is nothing but a Neapolitan tenor."[1]

Giuseppe Gioacchino Belli (1791–1863) had been a writer of undistinguished Italian verse in his youth until, at age twenty-five, he began writing sonnets in the Trastevere dialect of Romanesco. In so doing, he discovered his true artistic voice, achieving distinction as "the only writer of genius that Rome ever gave birth and education to."[2] In his earthy style, Belli told fourteen-line stories that are like miniature dramas or ballads imbued with deep feeling for the underprivileged citizens of Trastevere. Living in Rome, Burgess became fascinated by Belli, whom he celebrated in the novels *Beard's Roman Women* and *ABBA ABBA*. The former originated with a series of dreamlike images of Rome photographed by David Robinson; the latter, with Burgess's translations of Belli's sonnets and the fantasy of an imagined meeting between Belli and Keats.[3]

Belli and music link the main characters of *Beard's Roman Women*. Ronald Beard, a screenwriter with a passion for Belli's verse, is a widower haunted by his deceased wife's spirit; Paola Lucrezia Belli, a photographer, is a direct descendant of the poet. When they meet, Paola establishes her social superiority to Beard by casually mentioning that she has spent the day "photographing Frank Sinatra at his rehearsals."[4] On a drive back to their hotel, they listen to Debussy's *Danses sacrée et profane* on the car radio. Wondering whether or not to take her hand in his, the would-be Don Juan "contented himself with humming *La ci darem la mano*, despite the Debussy, and she responded, also humming, with *Vorrei e non vorrei*."[5] When the seduction occurs a few hours later, it is on Zerlina's terms, not Don Giovanni's, as Paula shows up unannounced at Beard's hotel room, disrobes, and hops into his bed.

Like Robinson's distorted reflections, Beard provides a hazy looking-glass image of Burgess. Both are British writers who worked as education officers in Brunei and scriptwriters in Hollywood, and who became involved with youthful, dark-haired Italian beauties soon after their Welsh wives succumbed to cirrhosis on the same day. Correspondingly, Paola Belli mirrors Liana's Italian heritage, good looks, and impulsive temperament as well as her address. Echoing Burgess's scornful view of composers who write at the keyboard, the fictional Alfred Trenchmore is dismissed as a hack who "could not compose film music out of his head; he had to bang about on his Steinway grand, looking for themes and discords."[6] As Burgess acknowledged in a 1976 interview the year the book was published, "I must have been lacking in inventiveness at the time, so I fell back more than ever I would normally on the facts of my own life."[7]

Poetry and music converge in the scene in which a "thick-haired and brutal looking" British guitarist recites Belli above strummed chords. As Beard reflects Burgess's literary side, the guitarist reflects his musical one, parroting the novelist's disdain for Italian music and musicians: "Verdi and his rum-tum-tum accompaniments. Fault of the language, of course. They always say how musical it is, meaning unmusical, meaning lacking in rhythmical variety, meaning too many rhymes, too few vowel-sounds."[8] Explaining that rendering Belli's sonnets into English is his "real job", the guitarist recites one of his translations, bracketing it with the chords "E B E G sharp B E" and "A E A C sharp E" before admitting, "Needs going over a bit". "Needs going over a lot, excuse me," Beard retorts, his remark followed by "B E A crotchet rest D", a device symbolizing the two characters' shared identity.[9] The guitarist bears no name and does not know Beard's, yet spells out the musical signature B E A (R) D with the R representing a quarter (crotchet) rest, as readers of *MF* already will have learned.[10] Moreover, the pitches B E A – D represent a stacking of perfect fourths, that favorite Burgessian sonority, which may even have been the source of this particularly autobiographical character's name.[11] It is fitting that these notes are associated with the guitar, since tuning (mainly) by perfect fourths rather than fifths is typical only of guitars (and contrabasses) among the common stringed instruments.

Unlike Burgess, Beard lacked the courage to embrace life on the Mediterranean and rejected Paola to marry another Welsh woman instead. Realizing his mistake, Beard writes Paola a letter begging forgiveness and confessing his love, planning to deliver it by hand and continue suicidally dashing up and down the steps to her apartment until intentionally felled by a heart attack. At the threshold of Paola's apartment on the Piazza Santa Cecilia, he hears a recording of John Dryden's 1687 ode to St. Cecilia as he slips the letter under the door. Twice more he lurches up and down the long staircase, with correspondingly later sections of the cantata emanating from Paola's flat. On his third and final ascent, he hears its final bars: "*The dead shall live, the living die, / And music shall untune the sky.*" Taking this as a sign that he will survive, Beard, "as happy as he had ever been in his life", emerges rejuvenated, bearing witness to the power of music and its patron saint.[12]

Vincenzo Labella's plan to turn *Beard's Roman Women* into a motion picture prompted Burgess to compose a score for the proposed film. Although never produced, it spawned two compositions: *Rome in the Rain*, a melodious piano concertino, and the cantata *Song for Saint Cecilia's Day*.

Since *Rome in the Rain,* Burgess's preferred title for the novel, had been overruled by the publisher, he applied it to the concertino, a short rondo whose dreamy tunefulness and jaunty jazz rhythms are reminiscent of Constant Lambert's *Rio Grande*.[13] It opens with a wistful C major melody (Example 20.01) from the earlier Sinfonia (No. 1 – 1935) score (Example 03.03), a tune that would recur in the second movements of the *Concerto Grosso pour Quatuor de Guitares* and Sonatina for Harmonica and Guitar. Following the introduction of a pair of faster themes in the B section of this seven-part rondo (ABACABA) – the second theme based on the "Flower of the Mountain" tune from *Blooms of Dublin* (and used in the sinfonia cited above) – and a brief return of A, the C section introduces two new themes: an energetic sixteenth-note melody played by the soloist that soon shifts into 3+3+2 "Charleston" rhythm (Example 20.02) and a

Example 20.01 *Rome in the Rain*: Theme 1 (bs. 1–12)

Example 20.02 *Rome in the Rain*: Theme 4 (bs. 90–102)

fughetto in F♯ minor. The work climaxes at the start of the third A section at the modulation back to C major, then finishes with various combinations of themes and keys (primarily C and G♭ major) introduced earlier. There being no musical figure designated as "Roman", the sudden Neapolitan modulation to D♭ major near the end of the piece, preceding the final return to the tonic key of C major, could perhaps be a pun symbolizing the work's Italian roots.

The undated manuscript was probably composed not long after *Beard's Roman Women*, which Burgess wrote "fairly rapidly in the summer of 1975, mostly in the Bedford Dormobile," starting in Montalbuccio and finishing in Monte Carlo.[14] Since *Rome in the Rain* does not appear on the TMM list, it probably corresponds to the "Concertino for piano and orchestra" listed for 1978, and since the Piano Concerto, also listed for 1978, was composed in 1976, it seems likely that *Rome in the Rain* was composed in 1976 as well.[15]

Song for Saint Cecilia's Day is Burgess's "piquant modernish setting" of the fictitious cantata from *Beard's Roman Women;* completed on 3 July 1978 in Monaco, it is scored for SATB chorus and soloists with orchestra and organ, and is structured in eight movements, each corresponding to one of the stanzas of *A Song for St. Cecilia's Day, 1687* by John Dryden in their original order.[16] The first stanza, a paean to music and its power, opens with streams of parallel seventh chords and extended sonorities of ninth and eleventh chords representing "Heav'nly harmony" (Example 20.03). Invoking the memory of Jubal, "the ancestor of all those who play the lyre and pipe", the merry second movement celebrates music's "celestial sound" with bouncing rhythm and extensive imitative counterpoint in the vocal parts. A martial spirit animates the third movement, with full orchestra led by trumpets and drums providing a faithful sound-image of the text. The cantata's only minor key movement is the melancholy fourth, a dirge with musical forces limited to men's voices, a pair of flutes, and pizzicato violas and cellos. The fifth stanza begins with the clamor of violins divided into four parts, with divided altos in perfect fifths imitating the sound of the violin's open strings. Solo organ is emphasized in the sixth movement, with harp, representing Orpheus's lyre, prominently featured in the seventh. A lengthy instrumental introduction, fast and energetic, opens the last and longest movement. The chorus enters in an extended a cappella passage, is joined gradually by full orchestra, then builds to a great climax on the closing lines "The dead shall live, the living die, / And music shall untune the sky." The high tessitura of the soprano part, which includes sustained high Cs, poses the work's greatest performance challenge, along with sections of two- and three-part divisi in soprano, alto, and tenor, and basses divided into as many as four parts. Soloists, required only for the brief tenor solo in the first movement and an eight-bar-long passage for solo quartet in the second, might also be used in the lightly scored fourth movement.

Example 20.03 *Song for Saint Cecilia's Day*: I. Allegro moderato (bs. 1–9)

During the filming of *Anthony Burgess' Rome*, a television documentary shot in autumn 1977, a thunderstorm suddenly erupted from a cloudless sky as Burgess recited John Keats's last sonnet, "When I have fears that I may cease to be", outside the poet's residence.[17] Interpreting this as a sign of "fierce creative energy" in the vicinity, he decided to incorporate Keats and his house into a novel set in the Italian capital.[18] Belli wrote the first of his 2,279 Romanesco sonnets during Keats's brief sojourn in Rome, a concurrence that lays the basis for the plot of *ABBA ABBA*, which portrays

Keats as the person who convinces Belli to begin writings sonnets in Roman dialect. *ABBA ABBA*, whose title signifies the octave's rhyme scheme, is structured like a sonnet in two unequal parts: a longer novella followed by shorter collection of Burgess's translations of seventy-one Belli sonnets.

In accordance with historical fact, the painter Joseph Severn accompanies Keats to Rome as the novel begins. Portrayed as a Haydn enthusiast, Severn plays a movement from a keyboard sonata by the composer of the "Surprise" Symphony, prompting a gleeful Keats to proclaim, "He's like a child. You never know what he will do next."[19] Referring to the "Clock" Symphony, Keats imagines his head moving back and forth in steady rhythm, going "into the clickclock of the Haydn slow movement Severn had once played."[20]

The character who introduces Belli to Keats's sonnets and arranges for the poets to meet is an anachronistically self-referential figure whose name, Giovanni Gulielmi, is Italian for John Wilson. Gulielmi is described as a "man of letters and citizen of Rome", lover of poetry who knows Keats's *Endymion* well, linguist and translator who brings Keats and Belli together, and owner of a house in Trastevere facing the Basilica of Santa Cecilia, all of which were true of Burgess in the late 1970s.[21] As a private joke, paintings by "Labella, Macellari and Zappone, minor painters of respectively the Umbrian, Florentine and Venetian schools," hang on his walls.[22] In the book's mock-historical epilogue, the life story of Gulielmi and his descendants is traced along a path that leads almost to the birth of John Burgess Wilson in 1917. At his English mother's request, Gulielmi transports her from Rome to Manchester in 1832 so she can die in her native land. Once there, he meets and marries Sara Higginbotham, who in 1840 gives birth to Joseph Joachim Gulielmi, who studies voice at the Manchester Royal College of Music and becomes a notable oratorio singer and bass soloist at the Church of the Holy Name in Manchester. Joseph Joachim Gulielmi's youngest son, Joseph John Gulielmi, anglicizes his name to Joseph John Wilson and fathers Joseph Joachim Wilson, who is born in Moss Side in 1916 and eventually develops Burgessian passions for Gerard Manley Hopkins, Petrarchan verse forms, and Belli's sonnets, which he translates into English.

Quartet Giovanni Guglielmi (1917–45), *ABBA ABBA*'s musical counterpart, is a five-movement work for flute, oboe, cello, piano, and soprano, the same combination used in *The Brides of Enderby*. Burgess wrote down the quartet directly after *The Waste Land* in the same notebook, meaning that he probably composed this undated work in mid-1978 (no earlier than April), approximately a year after *ABBA ABBA* was written and published. The first movement is an energetic Allegretto in C, primarily in 7/8 with a contrasting lyrical 3/8 middle section, written in Burgess's quartal Hindemithian style. The influence of Bach and Shostakovich can be heard in the Lento, a melancholy D minor movement containing contrapuntal and polytonal passages. The gigue-like third movement, a lively Allegro con anima

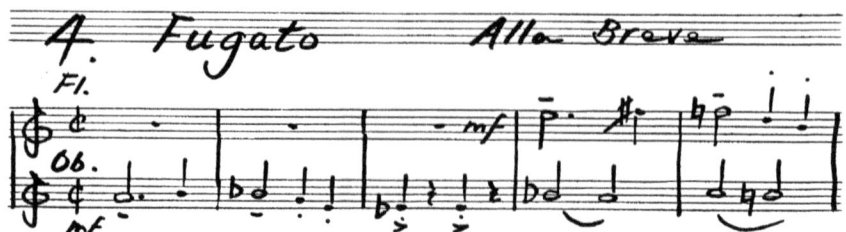

Example 20.04 *Quartet Giovanni Guglielmi (1917–45)*: 4. Fugato (bs. 1–5)

Example 20.05 *Quartet Giovanni Guglielmi (1917–45)*: 4. Fugato (bs. 90–5)

in 9/8 that begins with imitative counterpoint, shifts back and forth between faster and slower (meno mosso) tempi before ending in an exuberant presto stringendo. The fourth movement is a fugato that links Burgess's name with Bach's, with A–H–B–G–E–S–S, Burgess's musical signature, forming the subject, and B-A-C-H, the countersubject (Example 20.04). To ensure his intentions would be clear, Burgess took the trouble to write his and Bach's names into the score at the final fugal entry (Example 20.05). The soprano sings only the last movement, a solemn setting of A. E. Housman's "Epitaph on an Army of Mercenaries", which lies on the cusp of tonality, maintaining a generally atonal character yet tending toward D as tonic, where it ultimately comes to rest.

Around 1971, the year of the Guthrie production of *Cyrano de Bergerac*, Burgess composed four pieces for voice and keyboard for an Italian production of John Osborne's *The Entertainer*. "Archie's Theme" is in the English music hall style of songs like "Any Old Iron", which it closely resembles.

"Old Country", a mock-patriotic song in march style, quotes "Hail Britannia" and "God Save the Queen". *"E chi ci pensa?"* (And who thinks about it?) and *"Se c'e uno di quelli"* (If there is one of those) are written in the same 1940s swing style as "You blister my paint" and "There's got to be someone in charge" from the singspiel version of *A Clockwork Orange;* the middle section of *"Se c'e uno di quelli"* is a keyboard transcription of the trio of Elgar's *Pomp and Circumstance* March No. 1, to be played beneath spoken dialogue.

Two of Burgess's most whimsical books are *A Long Trip to Teatime* (1976) and *The Land Where the Ice Cream Grows* (1979), both illustrated by Fulvio Testa. Evidently inspired by *Through the Looking-Glass*, *A Long Trip to Teatime* is a fable about a schoolboy named Edgar who slips through a tiny hole in his desktop, undergoes a series of fantastic adventures – many associated with "E" and derived by Burgess from encyclopedia entries beginning with that letter – and manages to return home in time for tea. Although Burgess described the book as a "free fantasy" for children, its greater appeal is surely to adult aficionados of puns and wordplay. "E and D and G and A", the fifth of the book's eight chapters, relates the story of a lottery in which musical notes determine the "winner" (whose dubious "prize" is to be made a prisoner in a castle presided over by a monster). The townspeople of Edenborough (all evidently possessing absolute pitch) listen as a military band plays a series of notes; as soon as one is played that is not in one's name, that person must exit. E, D, and G are played, leaving only Edgar and men named Edgbaston and Edgeware still standing in the square. When "A" is played next, the others depart as Edgar is declared the winner to the strains of "See, the Conquering Hero Comes" from Handel's *Judas Maccabaeus*. As he is carried off, Edgar cries out asking, "Where?", but the only reply is a fanfare from the band made up of the first four letters of his name, which Burgess urges the reader to play for himself.[23]

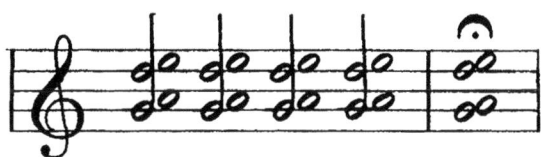

Unlike *A Long Trip to Teatime*, *The Land Where the Ice Cream Grows* is a sugary confection truly suitable for children. Testa conceived and illustrated this picture book about a visit to a fantastic region inhabited by a giant ice-cream-eating monster that understands only one word: *gelato*. Burgess provided the clever text for this weeklong adventure, which is related in chapters with the Joycean titles "Munchday", "Chewsday", "Wethersday", "Thawsday", "Fryday", "Shatterday", "Sundae Morning", and "Sundae Night".

Notes

1. *Beard's Roman Women*, 126.
2. Miller Williams in his introduction to *Sonnets of Giuseppe Belli* (Baton Rouge and London: Louisiana State University Press, 1981), xvi.
3. Although the title of the Keats-Belli novella is sometimes spelled *Abba Abba*, as in the Vintage edition published posthumously in 2000, Burgess consistently spelled the title with all capital letters.
4. BRW, 22.
5. Ibid., 23–4.
6. Ibid., 34.
7. Robert Robinson, "On Being a Lancashire Catholic", *Listener* (96), 30 September 1976, 399, as quoted in John J. Stinson, *Anthony Burgess Revisited* (Boston: Twayne, 1991), 132.
8. BRW, 126.
9. Ibid. A related scene occurs in *The Doctor is Sick* (174) as a young guitarist in a club sings a ballad that concludes with the word "Cage", then plays those letters as notes: "(And CAGE went the guitar-chord.)"
10. See Chapter 13 and *MF*, 229–30.
11. The similarity of the surnames Belli and Beard, both of which comprise five letters beginning with B and E, is self-evident.
12. BRW, 155.
13. The phrase is introduced in Beard's "seemingly pointless dream about Rome in the rain (Grail, Waste Land, pope, redemption?)" just before he is awakened by a call informing him that his wife Leonora is on the verge of death (BRW, 14). The German edition uses the original title, translated as *Rom in Regen*.
14. YH, 319.
15. The similarity between the passage for solo piano and percussion in *Rome and the Rain* (Theme 4, b. 90, Example 20.02) and a comparable one in the first movement of the Piano Concerto (b. 115) makes it likely that both works were composed around the same time.
16. YH, 323. In TMM, this work is erroneously listed under 1975, perhaps because Burgess wrote *Beard's Roman Women* and possibly his score for the proposed film that year.
17. Burgess wrote and narrated the script of this fifty-minute video portrait of the Italian capital, which was co-produced for Canadian television by John McGreevy Productions and Nielson-Ferns International, and later distributed in the US by Learning Corporation of America.
18. YH, 327–8.
19. *ABBA ABBA*, 14.
20. Ibid., 53.
21. Ibid., 10.
22. The last name of Bernardino Zappone, one of the scriptwriters of *Moses*, is misspelled as "Zampone" in YH, 260.
23. *A Long Trip to Teatime*, 76.

21

KNICKERBOCKER HOLIDAY

"Music," said Dr Adams, *"we* must *have music."*[1]

Burgess spent part of the early 1970s living in and around New York, teaching creative writing in 1970–71 at Princeton and Columbia, and serving as Visiting Distinguished Professor of English at the City College of New York in 1972–73. This was a period of intense activity and pressure for Burgess, who wrote, "I had energy in 1972, and I needed energy. New York exacts every ounce – physical, intellectual, creative – but it feeds the nerves while trying to exhaust them."[2] Out of this experience came, inevitably, a book. Burgess's *New York* is an encomium in nine chapters, including one, "The Great White Way", in which he reflects on the glamour of *Cyrano* running on Broadway: "My name was not up in lights but it was printed large on the posters outside the Palace Theater. I had achieved a mythical ambition."[3]

After *A Clockwork Orange*, Burgess was frequently hired to write scripts for proposed film and television projects. These included *The Crystal Cave* (based on Mary Stewart's novel), *Cyrus* (an Iranian venture sanctioned by the Shah, then terminated by the Ayatollah), and television series on the lives of Aristotle Onassis and General "Vinegar Joe" Stilwell, none of which were ever produced. One that was made was a Labella production on the life of Michelangelo, which Burgess scripted but never saw.

Gli Occhi di New York was an Italian film project intended for the emerging home videocassette market. Having acquired a large quantity of film shot in New York, Mondadori engaged Burgess to write a script that would put this material to profitable use. Though the publishing house paid only for his services as scriptwriter, it also contracted Burgess to score the film, which made the project especially attractive to him. Upon receiving in late September 1976 a continuity breakdown, scene descriptions, and suggestions for musical placement, he worked quickly, composing a score for flute, clarinet, violin, cello, and piano. Michael Billingsley, the film's editor, sounded quite happy with Burgess's score in the upbeat report he sent him on 21 November, a day after the recording sessions wrapped up in Rome:

I am pleased ... with your music. The chaconne for the last part of the murals is lovely, and the piece accompanying the photos of the immigrants is very moving (I told the musicians to think of themselves as Hungarian gypsies of Jewish extraction leaving a Polish *shtetl*.) And I am going to try and find space for that Fuga.[4]

But the public never laid eyes on *The Eyes of New York*. Mondadori decided not to release it and subsequently all traces of the video, score, and recording disappeared.

Burgess's birth occurred within days of the February Revolution, a coincidence that may have helped inspire him to compose *Trotsky's in New York!*, a musical celebrating the curious fact that the Bolshevik leader was living in Manhattan when the Russian Revolution erupted on 23 February 1917.[5] Working to a concept for an off-Broadway musical by Stanley Silverman, who intended to write the music, Burgess crafted a fable in which socialism collides with capitalism, political principles confront family priorities, and love (almost) conquers Lev (Davidovich Bronstein, that is).

The action takes place on the streets of New York and in the office of the Russian-language newspaper *Novij Mir* ("New World" or "New Peace"), where the socialists Bokharin, Volodarsky, and Chudnorsky (nicknamed Bok, Vol, and Chud, like a Russian equivalent of Puccini's Ping, Pang, and Pong) work as journalists. Trotsky arrives at the peak of the political debate over whether the US should enter World War I or remain isolationist. His devotion to hardline Communist principles wavers when he falls in love with Olga, a young widow who espouses socialist evolution over revolution. Meanwhile, Trotsky's wife Natalia, a dancer and ballet producer, is seduced by American amenities and a certain Doctor Goldstein from New Jersey. Sasha, the young man who cleans the *Novij Mir* office, reveals himself to be a Russian prince and orders Trotsky arrested by Russian Imperialists, but, moments later, news arrives of the revolt in St. Petersburg, leaving the Bolshevik leader a free man. A false crisis ensues when Trotsky's son Seryozha appears to have been kidnapped, forcing Trotsky to realize that family can matter more than politics, but the scientifically-minded boy was simply investigating the logic of New York City street names. Trotsky nearly acknowledges his love for Olga, but ultimately resists and boards a Russian-bound ship to join the revolution while American servicemen depart to fight in the Great War that the US has just entered.

When Silverman withdrew from the project, Burgess composed the score himself. In *You've Had Your Time*, he casually mentions the feat: "I wrote the music myself for the Trotsky project and put it in a drawer, though I performed one of the songs on BBC radio."[6] In fact he wrote the music twice, generating 350 pages of handwritten manuscript in all. One has to marvel at the sheer industry of the man, able to toss off a musical between novels and film scripts, yet Burgess must have struggled with *Trotsky*, for it is one of the rare musical works he felt compelled to rewrite. He produced two versions of the libretto, which differ little from each other; the two musical scores, however, diverge to a much greater extent. He completed the first draft of the libretto and lyrics by March 1977; this is the unpublished typescript bearing a copyright date of 1979. By April 1979, he had nearly finished the piano-vocal score of Act One and probably completed the rest within the next few months. This earlier score (henceforth T1) is a setting of the 1979 typescript. The later one (T2), a setting of the revised libretto published in *The End of the World News*, is nearly a third longer – 199 pages versus 151 – and generally more operatic. While there is much melodic similarity between the two versions, harmonies are generally more complex and chromatic in T2, with several choral numbers, including "We're Having a Socialist Party" and "Trotsky's in New York!", changed from (mostly) unison singing to four-part writing. Some songs are transposed into different keys, reharmonized, and provided with more complex accompaniments while others are completely rewritten. T1 consists of an overture plus twenty-four musical numbers, lacking the finale of T2 but containing one song, "Thesis, Antithesis", omitted in the later version. Instead of division into distinct musical numbers, T2 consists of two acts comprising three scenes each.

Both versions of *Trotsky* were influenced by show music dating back to the 1930s. The opening scene, "1917", recalls the hard-edged quality of *The Cradle Will Rock,* while the lively tongue-twisting trio "Bokharin, Volodarsky, Chudnorsky" is a throwback to the Danny Kaye showstopper "Tchaikovsky" from *Lady in the Dark. Trotsky* draws upon folk and classical sources, quoting from Tchaikovsky's Sixth, Shostakovich's Seventh, and "Song of the Volga Boatmen" in "Bokharin, Volodarsky, Chudnorsky", while quotes from *Night on Bald Mountain* and the *1812 Overture* appear in "Amenities" and "Change", respectively. "All Through History", which Trotsky sings whenever he struggles to understand love, refers back to *Tristan und Isolde, Madama Butterfly,* and Tchaikovsky's *Romeo and Juliet.* "Ya vas lyubil", a simple folk-like setting for solo voice and balalaika of the Pushkin verse discussed in *Language Made Plain* (163) and *A Mouthful of Air* (166–7), is sung in Russian, the words transliterated into English exactly as they appear in both books.

In T2, "Driven by the Wind" and "Trotsky's in New York!" – the show's two "big" tunes – form the basis of the prelude. The opening motif from "Trotsky's in New York!" doubles as the opening theme of "1917", relating these two songs in a way not found in T1. Olga's T2 songs ("New World", "The Fields of France") are written in a higher register for a more operatic soprano instead of the belt voice required by T1. T2 eliminates some of the musical cleverness found in the earlier version, including all the quotes in "All Through History" and some from "Bokharin, Volodarsky, Chudnorsky", yet much musical wit remains. The "Bokharin, Volodarsky, Chudnorsky" trio retains the "Volga Boatmen" quote, and, in the dance interlude, substitutes a tune from Dvorak's "New World" Symphony (a natural choice considering the plot) for T1's Shostakovich Seventh theme (the one Bartók parodied in his Concerto for Orchestra). Further Broadway influences are heard in the songs of Act Two, most of which are only moderately altered from T1. After the opening music (a reprise of "1917" followed by "Driven") comes "That is No Way", a bluesy trio for Bokharin, Volodarsky, and Chudnorsky that recalls the jazz-inflected idioms of *Lady in the Dark* and *West Side Story*. "I Don't Like It", an insouciant quartet about the attraction of American society, and "People Speak Dance", the choral number that sets up the ballet to follow, are reminiscent of *Chicago*'s "All That Jazz". The ballet music is found only in the later version; apparently Burgess was not entirely satisfied with it, for underneath it he wrote, "The above is a rough draft only."[7]

"Driven by the Wind" (Example 21.01), which Burgess sang for the BBC in 1982, was apparently a late addition to T1 since the 1979 typescript originally did not contain the lyric.[8] This mellow melody accompanied by a progression of seventh chords typical of 1940s pop ballads is one of the best songs in the show and a prime example of Burgess's show music style. Unorthodox seven-bar phrases keep the song from being too predictable, but otherwise it falls within the conventional style of composers like Kurt Weill and Frank Loesser, whose song "Joey" from *The Most Happy Fella* is echoed by the descending third motif at the start of the vocal line.

The optimal way to present *Trotsky's in New York!*, which has never been performed with Burgess's music, would be from an edition combining the best numbers from each version, since not all of the changes in T2 are for the better.[9] The melodic, harmonic, and registral changes in the T2 version of the quintet "You Can't Make an Omelette" are improvements, and the enriched harmonization of "God Save the Workers" in T2 also improves on the earlier version. On the other hand, "Amenities", "Yanovska", and the amusing waltz-like number "We're Having a Socialist Party" (a parody of "We're Having a Real Nice Clambake" from *Carousel*) are not helped by the harmonic and metrical complications introduced in T2. Most of the Act Two songs are only moderately altered from T1 to T2 and are generally improved in the later version. One difficulty in either version is that Trotsky's portrayal as an intellectual is conveyed by an abstruse vocabulary that can be virtually unintelligible, as in this lyric from "All Through History" in T1 (Act One, No. 10), which recurs as "Monologue – Trotsky" in T2 (Act One, Scene 2):

> The shape of a girl's face,
> The thought of an embrace –
> Irrelevant nugacities, totally absolutely supererogatory –
> So say Engels, Marx *et al.*,
> No *die Liebe* in *Das Kapital*.[10]

With no prospects for a production on the horizon, Burgess decided to convert the *Trotsky* libretto, along with two other unproduced scripts, into a novel:

Knickerbocker Holiday

Example 21.01 "Driven by the Wind" from *Trotsky's in New York!* (T2)

All three sat in the same folder in instalments of varying length, and when all three were finished I saw that they were aspects of the same story. They were the story of the twentieth century, in which the major discoveries have been of the human unconscious, the possibility of extra-terrestrial colonisation, and of the salvation of human society through world socialism. Writing respectively a television series, the libretto of a musical, and a science fiction novella, I had really written a tripartite novel in a form appropriate to the television age.[11]

Example 21.01 *Continued*

The result was *The End of the World News* (a pun on the sign-off of a popular BBC newscast), published in the UK in 1982 followed by the US edition a year later. Mimicking *Pale Fire* and *Lolita*, Burgess begins the book with a Nabokovian foreword by the fictitious literary executor "John

Knickerbocker Holiday

Example 21.01 *Continued*

B. Wilson, BA". Foreshadowing the real-life accumulation of manuscripts and possessions itemized in the epilogue of *You've Had Your Time*, the foreword offers this comically self-deprecating description of the allegedly dead author's atelier and its fanciful contents:

Example 21.01 *Continued*

I discovered a large number of manuscripts, some in a finished state and in fair copy, others, in the foulest of foul copy, clearly unfinished or, indeed, hardly begun. Some of the manuscripts were musical. One consisted of three hundred pages of full orchestral score with vocal and choral lines – an incomplete opera in mock-Puccinian style, its provisional title *The Hamlet of Roaring Gulch* and its libretto a version of Shakespeare's tragedy with a Wild West setting (Claudius the owner of a saloon formerly the property of his dead brother, Hamlet the grieving son back from a law college in the East, Polonius the old doc with nubile daughter, Laertes and Hamlet confronting each other with guns at high noon, and so on). There was a set of twelve stories with the collective title *The Bad-Tempered Clavicle*, seemingly attempts at assimilating fugal to narrative form, or it may be the other way about. Our author, to neither critical nor financial profit, was much concerned with the musicalization of fiction. I distinctly remember his muttering, and occasionally shouting, on more than one occasion the word 'Counterpoint!'[12]

Setting aside the tongue-in-cheek references to *La Fanciulla del West* and *The Bad-Tempered Electronic Keyboard*, not to mention Shakespeare and Bach, the comment about the "musicalization of fiction" reflects a serious aim, for the interweaving of three stories is a form of literary counterpoint. By changing the length of the excerpts, Burgess varies the tempo. For example, the exposition (pages 3–75) moves slowly, with the beginnings of each story told in largish chunks of eight to twenty pages each. Contrast this with pages 178–85, in which short extracts of the Freud and Trotsky stories, less than a page each, are rapidly alternated, and one perceives the difference between adagio and presto.

Music is a background presence in the Freud tale, an account of the psychoanalyst's departure from Vienna in 1938 and death in London the following year, with flashbacks to earlier stages of his life and career. Citations of Mozart's *Eine kleine Nachtmusik* and waltzes by Johann Strauss help to establish the Viennese atmosphere, while references to Wagner invoke the presence of the Nazis. ("Adolf as Parsifal gloomed mystically from the wall near customs and immigration."[13]) Seeking to rescue prominent artists and scientists from the Third Reich is the historical figure W. C. Bullitt, the US ambassador to France who secured exit visas for Freud and his family:

> 'We try to think of certain acts of your government as – well, internal matters. Even the sudden silence of – well, certain world-respected Jewish musicians and writers. But there's a scale of values. Some men don't belong to the Third Reich at all. Schoenberg. Einstein. Dissident Gentiles too. Thomas Mann, Paul Hindemith.'[14]

In *Lynx*, written on commission from Universal as the screenplay for a futuristic remake of the 1950s science fiction thriller *When Worlds Collide*, the most poetic and musical character, and surely the most autobiographical, is the aging Falstaffian actor Courtland Willett.[15] As the gravitational pull of the rogue planet Lynx triggers worldwide flooding, Willett recalls *A Sea Symphony*: "'All intrepid captains and mates,' he trolled, 'and those who went down doing their duty.' He la-la-lahed a few measures of presumable orchestral fill-in, blowing strenuously a fiddle of air, and said: 'Walt Whitman's words. Vaughan Williams's music. That sounds like a regular sea symphony outside. Jesus. Cacophony rather.'"[16] Later, as the final devastation approaches, he cries out, "'Well, I say balls to a universe that can afford to waste a Keats or a Shakespeare or a Charles Ives or a Vaughan Williams. Balls, balls, balls.'"[17]

Music and literature are banished from the spaceship *America* to force the crew to focus on the future instead of the past, but, as it hurtles away from Earth moments before the planet is annihilated by Lynx, the spacecraft's doctor convinces the captain to play her contraband cassette of Mozart's last symphony:

> From the four corners of the ceiling music poured – the essence of human divinity or divine humanity made manifest through the gross accidents of bowed catgut and blown reeds.[18]

Citing this passage in an essay written in honor of Burgess and Claude Lévi-Strauss, the ethnomusicologist Bruno Nettl described it as "The 'Jupiter' ... presented literally as the final climax of the world's music. To Burgess, as to many, Beethoven represents worldly achievement, and Mozart the gift of the otherworldly."[19] At the climax of Burgess's cataclysmic tale, the awesome finale of the "Jupiter" reminds the planet's survivors of their humanity, imparting to them, through the magic of Mozart's art, the divine essence of mankind.

Notes

1 *The End of the World News*, 385.
2 YH, 285.
3 *New York*, 117
4 Billingsley, letter to Burgess, 21 November 1976.
5 According to the old Russian calendar. The date was 8 March in the New Style calendar in use throughout Europe and America at the time.
6 YH, 327. In a BBC radio broadcast aired on 4 November 1982, Burgess performed "Driven by the Wind" during an interview by Waldemar Januszczak in which he discussed *The End of the World News* and described literature as music to which words have been added.
7 T2, 159.
8 Burgess added a handwritten note in the typescript to mark the insertion of the song after the lyrics to the reprise of "1917", which opens Act Two. The note says, "Trotsky enters alone. He sings 'Driven'".
9 In 1992, Ronald Senator received permission from Burgess to set the *Trotsky* libretto to his own music. In November 1997 three staged readings of Senator's version, directed by Roger Hendricks Simon, were presented in Manhattan by the AMAS Six O'Clock Musical Theatre Lab. A recording of the production was later broadcast by the New York radio station WBAI.
10 T2, 85–6; EWN, 128.
11 YH, 326–7.
12 EWN, vii.
13 Ibid., 3. Had he seen Ruth Berghaus's 1983 Oper Frankfurt production of *Parsifal*, in which Titurel's wounded son hung from the wall, Burgess might have written "Adolf as Amfortas".
14 Ibid., 10–11.
15 Among Burgess's sketches are two songs, both based on songs from *Blooms of Dublin*, related to *Lynx* (which he had originally titled *Puma*): "Willett's Song", a "Quick Waltz" modeled on "Full-Blooded Life", and "Pounce on Me, Puma", set to the tune of "Flower of the Mountain".
16 EWN, 166. The actual Whitman lines are "Token of all brave captains and all intrepid sailors and mates. / And all that went down doing their duty." Ralph Vaughan Williams, *A Sea Symphony* (London: Stainer & Bell, 1918), 64–75.
17 EWN, 309.
18 Ibid., 386.
19 Bruno Nettl, "Mozart and the Ethnomusicological Study of Western Culture: An Essay in Four Movements" (149) in *Disciplining Music: Musicology and Its Canons,* ed. by Katherine Bergeron and Philip V. Bohlman (Chicago and London: University of Chicago Press, 1992).

22

POETIC LICENSE

"You can rhyme anything in a song. In Massachusetts ah took the pledge. Each glass ah chew sets mah teeth on edge."[1]

Always one to salvage whatever he could from aborted projects, Burgess made sure that work on *Will* did not go to waste. He incorporated the script into *Enderby's Dark Lady*, the last of the four Enderby novels, and recycled the music into other compositions. In 1974, when he was engaged to write the script for *Shakespeare da Noi* (Shakespeare Among Us), another Labella project financed by Lew Grade, he augmented the script with a musical score based on the music for *Will*. This ambitious RAI production was intended to present Shakespeare's life from an Italian perspective, showing him discussing cosmology with Giordano Bruno and visiting Padua, Verona, Venice, and Rome with the Earl of Southampton, but the end product was a watered-down version that used neither Burgess's script nor his score. Subsequently Burgess converted the music into the ballet suite *Mr W.S.*, writing it in Rome in a friend's apartment on the Piazza Santa Cecilia: "I wrote it without the aid of a keyboard to check the harmonies, putting myself entirely in the situation of the deaf Beethoven (whose harmonies were simpler than mine and did not have to be checked)."[2] With attractive themes, imaginative and well-balanced instrumentation, and a variety of descriptive movements well suited to dance, *Mr W.S.* is one of Burgess's strongest compositions. It effectively evokes the Shakespearean era through a combination of original music and genuine Elizabethan melodies, and, within an otherwise conventional orchestra, the optional use of period instruments like the tabor and shawm.

The scenario of *Mr W.S.* is a choreographic adaptation in nine scenes of *Nothing Like the Sun*. The ballet begins with the Prelude *nel modo di una toccata* (Scene 1), a lively movement that opens with strings playing an energetic C major theme representing the bustle of Elizabethan London. Young Will's entrance is followed by a martial theme (Example 22.01) that became a Burgess favorite, recurring in *Petite Symphonie Pour Strasbourg, Meditations and Fugues*, and *A Manchester Overture*. A drum cadence connects the first part of the Prelude with the second ("The Theatre"), which begins with a jaunty tune played by piccolo and flute

Example 22.01 *Mr W.S.* 1. Prelude (bs. 27–30)

Example 22.02 *Mr W.S.* 1. Prelude: "Queen's Men" Theme (bs. 1–15)

(Example 22.02) as the Queen's Men perform a primitive version of *Romeo and Juliet*. When one of the actors injures his leg, Will steps forward to take his place, acting the part of a lover to a lyrical E♭ major theme, but pestilence intervenes, sending the audience scurrying. The sight of plague-stricken corpses gives rise to fearful brass discords and frightful silence before cautious actors and townspeople tentatively reenter to the subdued sound of a fugue for double reeds above hushed drumbeats. When the plague interrupts again, this time the emboldened actors stoutly continue. Imitating the sound of bagpipes, oboe and English horn (*quasi cornamusa*) herald the entrance of the Earl of Southampton, with music and dance climaxing at the return of the "Queen's Men" theme as Will's splendid dancing (representing his acting) attracts the earl's attention.

To a tender Sarabande (Scene 2) for muted strings, Southampton seduces Will into leaving the stage and becoming his personal poet. The Dark Lady appears during the Galliard (Scene 3), a courtly dance whose merry tune is tossed back and forth from strings to woodwinds before being taken up by the full orchestra. At first the Dark Lady dances alone, then is joined by Will, who is so spellbound by her mysterious seductive beauty that he neglects his wife and child when they arrive at the start of the Carol (Scene 4). Ignoring them, Will vies unsuccessfully with Southampton for the Dark Lady's favor, remaining preoccupied even as his sickly son Hamnet collapses and is borne away by a sobbing Anne Hathaway. The characters' competing interests in this scene are reflected in dualistic music that pits duple and triple rhythms against each other.

As if awakened from a trance, Will desperately forces his way through the crowd to reach his wife and son, but is unable to prevent Hamnet's death. Meanwhile, the English fleet's victory over the Spanish Armada is celebrated in the Quodlibet (Scene 5), the most animated and rhythmically complex movement, with frequently changing meters and a quotation of "Browning" (Example 22.03), an authentic Elizabethan tune.[3] A somber mood prevails in the next movement, The Deaths of Princes (Scene 6), as Will, delirious and alone, envisions Hamnet's funeral procession to a doleful march for brass and percussion. No sooner has the boy's body been lowered into the grave than a black-clad figure arises. It is Hamlet, who dances an anguished pas de seul and then expires. Will grabs his pen and begins writing furiously.

Spectators assemble during Scene 7, the Opening of the Globe ("Totus Mundus Agit Histrionem"), to attend Shakespeare's latest play and witness

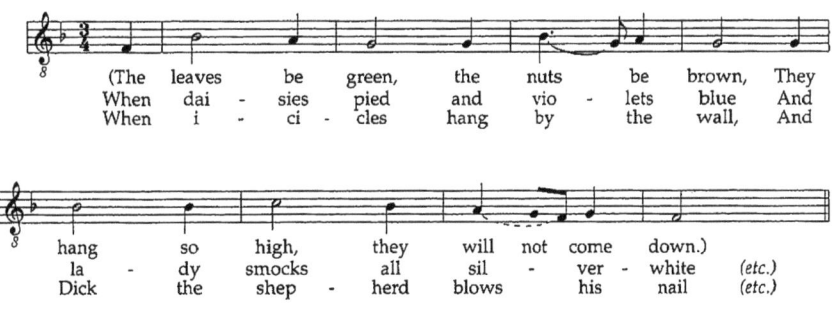

Example 22.03 "Browning" ("The leaves be green")

a pantomime of the seven ages of man featuring Romeo as lover, Henry V as soldier, Falstaff as justice, and King Lear as old man. The music, which begins energetically in D Dorian, alters accordingly, with Death represented by a string quartet and the soul's ascent to heaven by a long ascending solo violin line. Will collapses during a general dance and is led away. Lying on his deathbed, he imagines his dead son standing before him in Stratford, April, 1616 (Scene 8). A solo violin again symbolizes mortality, this time descending, *morendo*, to the open G string as Shakespeare's life expires. Before King James I and his court, characters from the plays promenade across the stage to the strains of the March "Non Sanz Droict" (Scene 9), named for the motto on the coat of arms granted to the playwright's father in 1596. The last to enter is Hamlet, who transforms into Shakespeare and dances triumphantly to the strains of a rousing march, more Edwardian than Elizabethan, whose central theme is the "mixolydian melody" (Example 03.01) allegedly from Burgess's lost first symphony.[4]

Atypically among his large-scale works, the manuscript of Burgess's Shakespeare ballet bears no date. Derived from music written earlier for *Will* and *Shakespeare da Noi, Mr W.S.* was evidently composed in 1979, the year listed in *This Man and Music* and *Contemporary Composers*, and the year the BBC recorded and broadcast the work. Although Burgess maintained that the tape of the BBC broadcast was intentionally destroyed after two airings due to "Musicians' Union regulations", he retained a recording that he played in 1980 at the conclusion of his Eliot Lectures: "I ended the series with an enquiry as to the meaning of music and, to establish belated credentials, blasted the lecture hall with a movement from my ballet suite *Mr W.S.*"[5]

The projected score for *Will* included vocal music not incorporated into *Mr W.S.* such as the rebels' song "Who'll March with Essex?"; closely related lyrics ("Who'll fight for Essex, / Our uncrowned king?") appear in *Enderby's Dark Lady*. The choral works *In Time of Plague* and *Weep You No More* may also have been intended for *Will* even though those manuscripts date from 1984. Burgess set *In Time of Plague*, a poem from Thomas Nashe's masque *A Pleasant Comedie, called Summers Last Will and Testament*, for SATB chorus a cappella, completing it "Oct. 1, 1984 / Monaco" and sending a copy to Yvar Mikhashoff in Buffalo a week later. The inevitability of death is conveyed in six strophes detailing how neither wealth, beauty, strength, nor wit can stave off mortality as the plague-stricken poet repeatedly utters his pitiable adieu: "I am sick; I must die. / Lord, have mercy on us." Expressing this doomed sentiment in a highly chromatic idiom marked by shifting harmonies, Burgess deploys the voices in various combinations and textures (polyphonic, homophonic, monodic) in music notated without time signatures in bars of varying lengths. The through-composed setting begins in D minor, modulates to A minor and C minor, and ultimately cadences in E.[6] Two days after writing *In Time of Plague*,

Burgess composed *Weep You No More* to an anonymous Elizabethan text previously set by John Dowland, Hubert Parry, Roger Quilter, and Ivor Gurney.[7] Burgess's mainly homophonic setting is considerably less chromatic than *In Time of Plague* although it features an unusual modulation, ending in C♯ major instead of the A minor key in which it opens. As in *In Time of Plague*, measure lengths vary according to the amount of text set in each musical phrase. On the back of the last page, Burgess began an unfinished setting of Ben Jonson's poem "Still to be neat".

The discredited theory that Shakespeare inserted his name into Psalm 46 in the King James Version of the Bible fascinated Burgess, who mentioned it in his Shakespeare biography. He recounted the idea in *Will and Testament: a fragment of biography*, illustrated by Joe Tilson and published in 1977 in an opulent collectors' edition limited to just eighty-six numbered, handcrafted volumes, each autographed and sheathed within its own custombuilt oak case.[8] In this story, whose title mimics Nashe's, Burgess combines the Psalm 46 legend with a fictionalized account of the Gunpowder Plot crediting Ben Jonson and Shakespeare with heroic roles in thwarting the conspiracy.

In "The Muse: A Sort of SF Story", originally published in the *Hudson Review* in 1968, a time-traveler named Paley from the year 2266 sets out to prove whether or not Shakespeare wrote the plays attributed to him.[9] In this *Twilight Zone*-like story, Paley visits a lowly Elizabethan hack, the author of such inferior dramas as "*Heliogabalus. A Word to Fright a Whoremaster. The Sad Reign of Farold First and Last. The Devil in Dulwich.*"[10] The story's wry conceit is that all of the masterpieces credited to this "Maister Shairkespeyr" come from doomed time-travelers like Paley, who bring this third-rate scribbler editions of Shakespeare's work that he copies out in his own hand, "not blotting a line."[11]

Enderby's Dark Lady, a droll fictionalized blend of Burgess's experiences on *Cyrano* and *Will*, recounts Enderby's travails as the browbeaten librettist of *Actor on His Ass*, "a ridiculous musical about Shakespeare in a fictitious theatre" located in "Terrebasse", Indiana.[12] The aforementioned stories function as a framing device, with *Will and Testament* (Chapter One) purportedly the piece of writing that brings Enderby to the attention of the Indiana producers, and "The Muse" (Chapter Twelve), his response to a suggestion by a PhD candidate moonlighting as a cab driver that he write a science fiction story about the Bard.[13]

Like *Earthly Powers* and *The End of the World News*, *Enderby's Dark Lady* incorporates lyrics, in this case ones from *Will*, into the text. By combining them with melodies from *Mr W.S.*, one can partially reconstruct the songs that Burgess composed for William Conrad's proposed film. The lyrics to "The Queen's Men", for example, perfectly match the "Queen's Men" tune (Example 22.01) from the *Mr W.S.* Prelude.[14]

> The Queen's Men,
> The Queen's Men,
> Not beer-and-bread-and-beans men
> But fine men,
> Wine men,
> Music-while-we-dine men.

Drawing on his *Cyrano* experience, Burgess caricatures Michael Lewis, John Covelli, Christopher Plummer, and Richard Gregson as, respectively, the "musically unalphabetic" composer Mike Silversmith, a répétiteur named Coppola, the overbearing film star Pete Oldfellow, and the director Gus Toplady, who has previously directed "in Minneapolis at the Tyrone Guthrie".[15] April Elgar, the dazzlingly beautiful African-American woman who plays the radiant Dark Lady in *Actor on His Ass*, is one of most appealing fictional characters ever created by Burgess. Née May Johnson, she takes her stage name from the composer: "I always liked that what I used to call when I was a kid Pompous Circus Dance of his."[16] Back home in Chapel Hill for Christmas, she passes Enderby off to her family as a British clergyman, obliging him to extemporize a sermon at her mother's Baptist church. This comical incident recalls the blundering Goodby Poetry Prize speech in *Inside Mr Enderby* and the outrageous Gervase Whitelady lecture in *The Clockwork Testament*, providing a tenuous thread between the comparably humorous but stylistically inconsistent Enderby novels.

In later years, Burgess revisited the Elizabethan era in a short story and historical novel. "A Meeting at Valladolid", published in *The Devil's Mode* in 1989, pictures what an encounter might have been like between the greatest English and Spanish authors of Elizabethan times. Rebuffed by a disdainful Cervantes while visiting Valladolid in 1605 as part of a diplomatic delegation, the offended Shakespeare, envious of the immense popularity of *Don Quixote*, combines his greatest characters in a preposterous, seven-hour play titled *The Comedy of Hamlet Prince of Denmark*. Burgess subsequently converted the story into a like-named play broadcast on BBC radio on 10 April 1991.

The year 1993 marked the publication of *A Dead Man in Deptford*, an artfully conceived explanation of Christopher Marlowe's mysterious death four hundred years earlier. This memorial to the subject of Burgess's university thesis relies heavily upon discoveries and speculations presented in Charles Nicholl's *The Reckoning*, though alternatively drawing the ambiguous conclusion that responsibility for the murder lay either with the Earl of Essex, or Sir Walter Raleigh, or both together. As the assassins are about to deal the fatal blow, they inform Marlowe, "we speak not of treachery but of its possibility. There is one reason for your being voided. There are two others, and you will never know whether it is a knight or an earl who wishes the voiding."[17] In yet another instance of Burgess inserting himself into his novels, the name of the story's narrator (not revealed until the last page) is Jacke Wilson: "Your true author speaks now, I that die these deaths, that feed this flame. I put off the ill-made disguise and, four hundred years after that death at Deptford, mourn as if it all happened yesterday."[18] Ultimately, neither Wilson nor Burgess provides a definitive solution to the mystery surrounding Marlowe's death, maintaining that "the true truth – the *verità verissima* of the Neapolitans – can never be known."[19]

Notes

1. *Enderby's Dark Lady*, 513.
2. YH, 309–10.
3. Quoted in Appendix C (John Caldwell, "A Note on the Music") of *Love's Labour's Lost*, G. R. Hibbard (ed), The Oxford Shakespeare (Oxford: Clarendon Press, 1990), 242–4. In Shakespeare's day, "Spring" and "Winter" from *Love's Labour's Lost* may have been sung to this melody.
4. TMM, 24. As played by horns in F (thus sounding a fifth lower), the theme would sound in E Mixolydian, exactly matching its first entrance in *Mr W.S.* at bar 51 (where it is played, however, by strings, not horns).
5. YH, 309, 360
6. A printed edition of *In Time of Plague*, published in 1994 by Saga Music (THA-978484), alters some of the barring and omits several words of the text.
7. As the first of Quilter's *Seven Elizabethan Lyrics*, op. 12, and second of Gurney's *Five Elizabethan Songs (The Elizas)*.
8. That same year, the same publisher, Plain Wrapper Press of Verona, brought out *A Christmas Recipe*, another limited edition by Burgess and Tilson, this one comprising an illustrated formula for preparing trifle, written in verse.
9. *Hudson Review* (21), Spring 1968, 109–26.
10. EDL, 628.
11. Ibid., 626, 631.
12. Ibid., 486, 513.
13. Ibid., 511.
14. Ibid., 523. Excerpts from these and other lyrics from *Will* appear in YH, 146–7.
15. Ibid., 570, 519.
16. Ibid., 562. April's brother Ben shares his name with both Shakespeare's contemporary and Liana Macellari's first husband: "She was married to a black Bostonian named blasphemously Ben Johnson." YH, 88.
17. *A Dead Man in Deptford*, 266.
18. Ibid., 269.
19. Ibid., 271.

23

GRACE NOTES

Perhaps the kind of humanity that can produce Hamlet, Don Giovanni, *the* Choral Symphony, *the* Theory of Relativity, Gaudí, Schoenberg *and* Picasso *must, as a necessary corollary, also be able to scare hell out of itself with nuclear weapons.*[1]

Friendship with Yehudi Menuhin, Princess Grace, and Stanley Silverman led Burgess late in life to compose three significant works for strings. Earlier works – a string quartet in G major (1936), *Hispanics* for violin and piano (1941), a cello sonata or concerto (1944), *Music for Hiroshima* for double string orchestra (1945), a partita for string orchestra (1950), and a string quartet (ca. 1972) – are mentioned in his writings, but all these are lost, leaving the violin concerto, elegy for strings, and string quartet that Burgess composed in his sixties as his major extant works featuring string instruments.

Burgess became acquainted with Menuhin when they appeared together on a BBC television program in 1964. In the cordial correspondence that ensued, Burgess expressed his opinions to Yehudi and his wife Diana on violin concertos, televised concerts, and other musical matters. Reiterating a view he had expressed two months earlier in the *Listener*,[2] Burgess wrote to Diana Menuhin in December 1964 declaring his dislike of Beethoven's Violin Concerto on the eve of the composer's birthday:

> I still can't make up my mind about the viability of my new and middle-aged attitude to the Beethoven. I've listened again and again since to my record of Menuhin (who else?) doing it, and I DON'T THINK I REALLY LIKE THE WORK, but there may be a tangle of extra-musical factors working against a pure aesthetic response. I don't think I can get over what I regard as the near-vapidity of that first subject. I mean, contrast it with the Elgar. I mean, contrast it with the Brahms. But I'm aware again that this may have nothing to do with the music. Was I once brutally assaulted as a child to a tune with the same rhythm as the Beethoven? I don't know, and I remain worried.[3]

Burgess goes on to argue that television's visual nature hinders one's ability to focus on the compositions performed in musical broadcasts:

I can't see why music isn't enhanced by the sight of the performers. But it evidently isn't. The trouble is that when I write about music-on-TV, as I have to, I have to find some gimmicky approach which doesn't get in the way of what the pure music critics are doing, and it usually ends up as one of these nexus things – viz., WHAT THE MUSIC MEANT TO ME VISUALLY. This may mean a subtle and unconscious twisting of approach which inhibits willingness to listen to the music alone. I don't know. I don't don't know. The whole thing's wrong somewhere, and I suppose I should be less lazy and try to find out.[4]

The publication of Menuhin's autobiography in early 1977 led to renewed correspondence. In a generally laudatory review of *Unfinished Journey* for the *Times Literary Supplement*, Burgess asserted that Menuhin, whose "prose is that of a Scottish engineer", commissioned a concerto from Bartók yet never performed the one by Berg.[5] In a letter to Burgess, Menuhin politely refuted these errors before publicly setting the record straight in a letter to the editor:

> Sir, – I read Anthony Burgess's review of my *Unfinished Journey* (April 8) with appreciation and hope I shall live up to the future he confidently predicts. May I be allowed a correction? I have played the Berg Concerto quite often and have recorded it with Pierre Boulez. I have deviated from the standard repertory, incidentally commissioning a new work for each of my ten Bath festivals. I would like to be able to claim Bartók's Violin Concerto, but it was on playing this marvellous work, dedicated to Zoltan Székely, that I plucked up the courage to ask him to write the Sonata for Solo Violin.
>
> It is suggestive and no doubt appropriate that my literary style should be likened to that of a 'Scottish engineer'. I have tried to build bridges all my life; alas! none as successful as those of the Scottish engineer![6]

Burgess dashed off a letter to Yehudi and Diana on 16 April, apologizing contritely:

> Many thanks for your delightful letters and mea maxima culpa about my allegation that the Berg concerto had never been played. Because there was no whisper about it in the autobiography I assumed etc... When I say that Yehudi writes like a Scottish engineer it's meant to be high praise, but many readers of the review may think otherwise. If you've seen how Scottish engineers write you'll know I mean objectivity, exactitude, tough elegance, not the kind of false artiness you get from many autobiographers who consider they have an aesthetic duty, whatever that means.[7]

He proceeds to wonder how the Menuhins tolerate British taxation ("How you manage to cope with the fiscal cauchemar of living in England I don't know") while commenting on Monaco's cultural life and his recent musical activities:

> It is a musical place, though quite unliterary. I have responded to the musical ambience by buying Josephine Baker's old piano and starting to write music again. I had a symphony performed in Iowa City by 120 young musicians,

I have written a film score, I have completed a piano concerto. Getting back to orchestral composition means, mainly, studying the technique of stringed instruments again, and I am starting, old as I am, to play the violin and am doing it by writing little pieces on a system which may work. I mean this sort of thing:[8]

Ever gracious, Yehudi Menuhin responded warmly: "When I next write, I may say something about the situation of artists generally . . . and if I may give you a few tips on the violin I shall be delighted! What is your new system all about? At least the Barcarolle is not on open strings. Is that part of the system? And it could be played fairly well in tune by using only the first and second fingers."[9] Menuhin subsequently introduced Anthony and Liana to Prince Rainier and Princess Grace while in Monaco to perform Bruch's Concerto in G minor with Rafaël Kubelik and the National Opera Orchestra of Monte-Carlo on 16 July 1978 at the Palais de Monaco. After meeting the Grimaldis, the Burgesses "were regular guests at the palace parties."[10]

The following year, Burgess composed his Concerto for Violin and Orchestra in E Minor, dedicating it to Menuhin, to whom he sent the original manuscript without retaining a copy for himself. The inscription "Gibraltar, Summer 1945 – Monaco, July 27, 1979" indicates its derivation from a lost wartime composition: "I had brought home with me the score of a violoncello concerto which eventually I would convert into a violin concerto for Yehudi Menuhin."[11] This three-movement work, stylistically akin to the Third Symphony and Piano Concerto, combines Burgess's typically spicy tonality with his predilection for quartal sonorities, angular melodies, and propulsive rhythms. The influence of Brahms's Fourth is evident in the concerto's E minor key, the three-against-two rhythms in the first two movements, and the presence of a passacaglia in both works, while the concerto's finale is more self-referential and modern, borrowing a theme from *Blooms of Dublin* and set largely in 5/4 meter.

In quick succession, the solo violin introduces the first movement's principal subjects, an expressive legato melody (Example 23.01) followed by a lighthearted *scherzoso* theme (Example 23.02) played in a faster tempo. Built principally upon this thematic material, the movement ends with a

Example 23.01 Violin Concerto, I. Allegro con spirito: Theme 1, solo violin part (bs. 6–15)

Example 23.02 Violin Concerto, I. Allegro con spirito: Theme 2, solo violin part (bs. 21–27)

Example 23.03 Violin Concerto, II. Andante con moto: ground (solo violin, bs. 3–11)

virtuosic solo cadenza followed by a rousing coda. The passacaglia is built upon a ground first presented by the solo violin (Example 23.03). During the course of the movement the ground is presented thirty-two times, first in A major, shifting to A minor at its fifth appearance, then back to major for its last ten occurrences. The rondo-like finale begins with an introduction derived from the "Flower of the Mountain" melody; the same passage, little changed apart from orchestration, returns as the opening of the last movement of Guitar Quartet No. 3 (see Example 29.04). The principal subject, initially played legato and in thirds by the soloist during the introduction, arrives at bar 32 (Example 23.04) in the spirited style characteristic of the rest of this lively movement. (Like the introduction, this music also recurs in Guitar Quartet No. 3.) The close resemblance of the final solo violin phrase (bs. 304–307 in Example 23.05) to the start of the fourth

Example 23.04 Violin Concerto, III. Allegro vivo: Theme 1 (solo violin, bs. 32–37)

Example 23.05 Violin Concerto, III. Allegro vivo (score excerpt, bs. 299–308)

movement of Concerto for Orchestra may be Burgess's way of tacitly acknowledging Menuhin's connection to Bartók.

Upon receiving the score, Menuhin wrote to Burgess with gratitude and appreciation for the work's quality:

> I was amazed to receive so excellent, professional and viable a violin concerto from you ... The concerto has flow, impetus, thematic construction, a good cadenza and an interesting slow movement in its development and its gradual acceleration of pace. When time permits, which is unfortunately not this year – or possibly even next, I should like to suggest that I should one day perform it in Monte Carlo; but please don't hold me to this too absolutely or too soon.[12]

Despite his initial interest, Menuhin never performed the work, which was found among his scores after his death in 1999 and acquired by the Royal Academy of Music four years later.

Another violin virtuoso, Pablo de Sarasate, is featured in "Murder to Music", a Sherlock Holmes story published in *The Devil's Mode*.[13] At a London recital at the St James's Hall attended by Holmes, Sarasate's accompanist is shot, surviving just long enough to play a few meaningful notes on the piano before expiring. Thanks to this melodic clue, Holmes solves the murder and saves the life of the killer's next intended victim. Cameo appearances by Gilbert and Sullivan, George Bernard Shaw, Gerard Manley Hopkins, and other famous cultural figures of the day enliven this clever musical mystery.

Burgess became acquainted with the Primavera Quartet, winner of the 1977 Naumburg Award in chamber music, through Stanley Silverman, who married Martha Caplin, the group's first violinist, in 1980. Upon hearing the ensemble, Burgess decided to compose a string quartet and on 8 March 1980 completed the work, which he dedicated to the ensemble. Much of the Allegro commodo, an angular atonal movement reminiscent of Shostakovich, is built upon the A–C–G♯ motif played by Violin I in the opening phrase (Example 23.06). Converted into a fugue subject, this motif is presented in prime form, inversion, diminution, and augmentation, ultimately returning, in a final variant played by viola, in the presto coda. The second movement is a melancholy Adagio in ABA form whose outer sections, with their arching solo melodies and heartrending harmonies, recall the sound of early Schoenberg; the central B section is an animated più mosso filled with pervasive 32nd-note motion and nervous pizzicati. The Allegro molto, the most tonal of the three movements, is firmly rooted in the key of A major, with a lyrical section beginning at the meno mosso (Example 23.07) that is particularly lovely.

In memoriam Princess Grace is a somber lament for strings composed in tribute to the Monegascan monarch shortly after her untimely death on 14 September 1982 a day after she lost control of her vehicle on a twisting mountain road. In his autobiography, Burgess mourned her passing with these lines of tribute:

> Perhaps Princess Grace and I were alone in regarding literature as a commodity not to be disdained in a territory dedicated to pleasure ... Grace, after all, had practised an art and I was practising one. There was a *rapport*, there was an occasional palace lunch, followed by a walk through Monacoville, during which the cloaked bare-headed Grace would greet and kiss the older inhabitants. Her charm was a constant property. Her death was a great loss.[14]

Example 23.06 String Quartet, I. Allegro comodo (bs. 1–4)

Example 23.07 String Quartet, III. Allegro molto (bs. 33–44)

Example 23.08 *In memoriam Princess Grace* (bs. 1–5)

This single-movement work consists of a fugal Adagio followed without pause by a passacaglia in a slightly faster tempo (Molto liscio, poco più mosso). Both are based on the same theme, a quartal fugue subject (Example 23.08) whose first nine pitches, played as equal quarter notes, become the passacaglia's ground bass. Ending with a *ppp* C major/minor chord in the high strings sustained above a delicate pizzicato rendering by cellos and basses of the fugue subject in retrograde, the moving passacaglia evokes an otherworldly state of quietude and timelessness.

The String Quartet was not performed during Burgess's lifetime, the Primavera Quartet having disbanded in 1981 before playing it. *In memo-*

riam Princess Grace also went long unperformed until becoming, in effect, an elegy for Burgess himself when it was premiered, along with the quartet, at the commemorative concert "Anthony Burgess: The Years in Monaco", which took place in Monte Carlo on 21 November 1994, a year after his death.

In the mid-1970s, Burgess accepted a commission from Little, Brown and Company to write a book commemorating *1984*. Foreshadowing *Mozart and the Wolf Gang*, he wrote *1985* in an eclectic style incorporating diverse literary styles and genres. Structured in two main parts, the first is a critical commentary on Orwell's novel addressing subjects ranging from Orwell's indebtedness to Zamyatin's *We* to the seeming paradox of Nazi commandants weeping with joy as they listened to Schubert. The second part is a bleak novella about Bev Jones, a history teacher imprisoned by the Islamic powers that have seized control of his native Britain and literary descendant of Orwell's Winston Smith and Burgess's own Tristram Foxe. After years spent behind bars lecturing on English history to his fellow inmates, Jones concludes, as his lessons approach the present day, that society can no longer be explained or understood and calmly bares his breast to the electrified fence at the compound's perimeter, taking leave of a life that has lost all meaning.

Upon its publication in 1978, *1985* received tepid reviews, yet in the post-9/11 era, Burgess's vision of a not-so-distant future in which Islamic anger at the West results in war between Muslim and non-Muslim worlds seems eerily prescient. Comparing the world of the late-1970s to that of the late-1940s, when Orwell wrote *1984*, Burgess wrote, "The literal power that drives machines sleeps in Islamic oil . . . Islam is one of the genuine super-states, with a powerful religious ideology whose mailed fist punched Christendom in the Dark Ages and may yet reimpose itself on a West drained, thanks to the Second Vatican Council, of solid and belligerent belief."[15]

They Wrote in English, published in Italy in 1979, is an expanded and updated version of *English Literature: A Survey for Students*, published two decades earlier. It was issued in English in two volumes, the first being a history of the language and its leading authors, and the second, a collection of their writings. Roguishly, Burgess included F. X. Enderby, represented by "Nymphs and satyrs", among those poets anthologized in Volume 2. In 1982, *They Wrote in English* was published in Japanese translation as *Bajesu no bungakushi* and in 1988 was reissued by Hutchinson in English; nonetheless it remains one of Burgess's rarest publications, found in few libraries and virtually unknown in the used book trade.

The many books Burgess had published through the 1970s only increased a frustrated awareness that he "wanted to write a masterpiece and did not have the courage to do it", so, adopting an attitude of "grace under pressure", Hemingway's memorable expression for courage, he concentrated on the novel that eventually became *Earthly Powers*.[16] Meanwhile he produced a short biography, *Ernest Hemingway and his world*, highlighting musical aspects of that writer's life and work. Hemingway's mother Grace was "a fine contralto" from Chicago who once sang in Madison Square Garden before abandoning her operatic aspirations.

> She wanted Ernest to become a professional violoncellist, and he did in fact play the easy 'cello parts of light operatic and musical comedy scores in his high-school orchestra. He also sang in the choir of the Third Congregational Church but, like his father, he was never able to carry a melodic line... What he probably inherited from his mother was the concern with tone and rhythm that was to make him into a major literary stylist. Joyce too had a musical background. One can read neither *Ulysses* nor *A Farewell to Arms* without being aware of a preoccupation with words as sound, as well as a structural capacity analogous to that of a musical composer.[17]

In Burgess's words, the "Hemingway tune was a new and original contribution to world literature", his spare stark prose "a new music".[18] The film *Grace Under Pressure*, which Burgess scripted and narrated for London Weekend Television, was a straightforward video adaptation of the biography embellished by clips of films adapted from the novels.

Beyond motivating the writing of *1985*, Orwell provided Burgess with cause for publishing a book listing his favorite novels published between 1939 and 1984: "This seems a good moment to look back upon what has been done in the novel over the past forty-five years. Why not wait for the round number fifty? Because it is more poetic to begin with the beginning of a world war and to end with the non-fulfilment of a nightmare."[19] *99 Novels: The Best in English Since 1939* is a collection of concise descriptions, few more than a page long and none longer than two. Most of the entries in this survey derive from *The Novel Now*, with some drawn from the still earlier publication *The Novel To-day*. Burgess deliberately excludes his own books from the survey but draws attention to them by way of omission. The list is limited to ninety-nine novels, he explains, so that the reader may add his or her own choice to round off the list to one hundred. To do so, he coyly suggests, the reader "may even choose one of my own".[20]

Notes

1 *1985*, 97.
2 "The Arts", *Listener* (72:1855), 15 October 1964, 9.
3 Letter to Diana Menuhin from Etchingham, 16 December [1964], the first of three letters from Burgess preserved by the Menuhin estate. In his autobiography, Menuhin takes the opposing view, praising the "the inevitability of the notes chosen" through motivic analysis of the concerto's first movement. Yehudi Menuhin, *Unfinished Journey* (New York: Knopf, 1977), 136–40.

4 Letter to Diana Menuhin from Etchingham, 16 December [1964].
5 'The vocation of a virtuoso', *TLS*, 8 April 1977, 419.
6 Yehudi Menuhin, letter to the editor, *TLS*, 22 April 1977, 488.
7 Letter to Diana and Yehudi Menuhin, 16 April 1977.
8 Ibid. According to the printed program, the number of musicians who played his Third Symphony was 104.
9 Yehudi Menuhin, letter to Burgess from London, 28 April 1977.
10 YH, 331.
11 LW, 330–1.
12 Yehudi Menuhin, letter to Burgess from London, 22 August 1979.
13 "Murder to Music", published in 1989, is a slightly early centennial homage to "The Adventure of the Red-Headed League" by Sir Arthur Conan Doyle, set in 1890 and first published in 1891, in which Sherlock Holmes and Dr. Watson similarly attend a recital by Sarasate at the St James's Hall. The historical Sarasate performed at the St James's Hall in 1874.
14 YH, 332.
15 *1985*, 59.
16 YH, 351.
17 *Ernest Hemingway and his world*, 13.
18 Ibid., 116, 41.
19 *99 Novels*, 11.
20 Ibid., 14.

24

ODES TO JOYCE

> *A musical of* Ulysses *clearly had to be done sometime, and I have done it... and if even one door to the better appreciation of the book has been opened, then the fingers of the composer have not been abraded in vain.*[1]

On 1 February 1982, the eve of the centenary of James Joyce's birth, the BBC and Radio Telefis Eireann broadcast a radio production of *Blooms of Dublin*, Burgess's musical adaptation of *Ulysses*. Of the hundreds of literary scholars who have written books, essays, and articles about Joyce, only Burgess transformed *Ulysses* into a musical. Given his lifelong love of Joyce's writing, the deeply musical nature and literary style of both authors, and Burgess's passion for music composition, it was a labor he seemed destined to undertake. A remark in *Re Joyce* that *Ulysses* could "be turned into an opera" indicates that by 1965 he was already considering how to do it.[2] Once he got to work writing out the piano-vocal score, he accomplished the task speedily even by his own remarkable standards, as reported in August 1971 to Geoffrey Aggeler:

> I... have just completed book, lyrics and music for a musical of ULYSSES I tentatively call BLOOMS OF DUBLIN. All done in three weeks, quite a record really, but one has to kill the Italian heat somehow.[3]

The development of *Blooms of Dublin* from its beginnings in the mid-1960s until its completion in early 1981 parallels the evolution of *Earthly Powers*, which was published in 1980 about fifteen years after Burgess started to conceptualize it. Around 1966, Burgess began conceiving an epic novel from the premise that the testimony of an elderly gay British novelist would play a crucial role in determining whether or not a controversial pope would be elevated to sainthood: "I was fascinated... by the possibility that W. Somerset Maugham... a big best-seller who was thoroughly homosexual... what would have happened if his brother-in-law had been Pope John? And out of that bizarre image came the possibility of a book."[4] *Earthly Powers* is written entirely from the point of view of Kenneth Marchal Toomey, the Maugham character, who, as the novel begins, lounges in bed in Malta on the afternoon of his eighty-first birthday with his dissolute catamite. With an ironic sense of detachment and profoundly cynical attitude toward art and life, Toomey narrates an expansive tale encompassing a panorama of pivotal events in twentieth-century cultural and political history. He spends Bloomsday in Dublin losing his virginity; rubs elbows with Joyce, Hemingway, Eliot, Wyndham Lewis, and Ford Madox Ford in Paris during the early 1920s; takes the Hindenburg to Berlin in the 1930s; and lives long enough to suffer losses from a Jonestown-like mass suicide in the Mojave Desert and terrorist murders in Africa in the 1960s. Set in perfect counterpoint to Toomey, Don Carlo Campanati, the Pope John XXIII character, believes fervently in humanity's essential goodness and perfectibility, and is genuinely convinced that he does God's work on earth. The ambiguous interplay of good and evil that results from Don Carlo's actions, however, suggests otherwise, intimating that this "man of God" may actually be an agent of the devil.

While the interplay between the Augustinian Toomey and Pelagian Don Carlo unquestionably forms the novel's central relationship, from a musical perspective, the bond between Toomey and Don Carlo's brother Domenico is of greater interest. Here, once again, are two characters jointly representing Burgess, with Domenico Campanati and Kenneth Toomey (two o' me?) comprising the musical and literary sides of his creative personality. Like Burgess, Domenico Campanati begins his career by setting out to compose an opera, pens a "partita for string orchestra", considers Italians unmusical, has trouble earning a living as a composer, plays piano in a small jazz band, and writes dance band arrangements.[5] Domenico derives musical motifs (HCE = B–C–E; SEC = E♭–E♮–C) from *Finnegans Wake* and is described as "a musician of mediocre talent who found his vocation in the composition of mediocre music for mediocre Hollywood films" which is, one imagines, how Burgess might have described himself had his repeated attempts to compose film music been more successful.[6] Toomey, like Burgess, is paid handsomely for writing unproduced screenplays ("the projected musical on Shakespeare's life called *Will!* . . . the colossal *Middlemarch*") and appears frequently on television in his later years, having yielded to the temptation of becoming a media personality – "the Writer as International Figure, meaning one who talked more than he wrote."[7] By the end of their first meeting, Domenico and Kenneth decide to write an opera together, *I Poveri Ricchi*. They write another – *Una Leggenda su San Nicola*, on the life of Saint Nicholas – and reach the pinnacle of their joint career with a successful New York production of *Blooms of Dublin*, a musical virtually identical to the one that Burgess, composer/librettist in one, had already written himself. (Lyrics to seven songs from the show are printed in the novel.) Yet, observing Domenico and his wife Hortense, Toomey's sister, at the Broadway opening, Toomey muses, "Was, I wondered, this musical remake of a, to be totally honest, totally unadaptable masterpiece of literature recalling for them the good Paris days of the avant-garde, youth and hope?" (550).

Beyond these self-referential musical allusions, Burgess filled *Earthly Powers* with musical terms and mentions of composers from Beethoven and

Rossini to Stravinsky and Antheil, their compositions providing a diverse musical backdrop to the story. Jazz and popular music by the likes of Novello, Kern, Berlin, and W. C. Handy are present, too, as is Italian verismo opera by Mascagni and Puccini, the French school of Chabrier and Debussy, and the English style represented by Elgar and Holst. Listening to his friend fume about the complexity of family relationships, Toomey observes, "That was a complicated statement for Domenico, a twelve-tone ground with a couple of *appoggiature*" (546). Emotional and physical pain, especially concerning teeth, are expressed through musical metaphor. As Toomey, a dental surgeon's son, returns from having sent away his decadent lover Geoffrey, "Halfway home the bad tooth sang a forte measure of rage" (46); in a grisly depiction of dental torture, "The drill grumbled down the scale and ceased its ghastly melody" (413). Having fled to Cagliari toward the end of World War I, Toomey mocks his ignoble survival of the conflict by turning the wartime ditty "I Wore a Tunic" upon himself, singing "'You wore a tunic, / A dirty khaki tunic, / While I wore civilian clothes" (94). Observing poorly garbed Sardinians treading past in their clunky shoes and oversized pants, he recalls a railway porter who once sang, to the tune of "Red Wing", "Oh the moon shines bright on Charlie Chaplin, / His boots are cracking / For want of blacking, / And his little baggy trousers they'll want mending / Before they send him / To the Dardanelles" (62, 94).

The year that Burgess composed *Blooms of Dublin*, the Israeli actor Topol starred as Tevye in the film version of *Fiddler on the Roof*. Burgess imagined him as the ideal lead in *Blooms of Dublin* on Broadway and inserted a Topol-like star into the fictional *Earthly Powers* production as "an act of wish fulfillment."[8] Zero Mostel, Broadway's original Tevye, had won an Obie Award in 1958 for playing Bloom in an acclaimed Off-Broadway production of *Ulysses in Nighttown* and "was ready to be signed up as the singing Leopold Bloom of the project," but in Burgess's opinion, "Mostel was in his sixties and too old for the rôle, though he himself did not think so."[9] Mostel was actually fifty-six in 1971 (albeit eighteen years older than Bloom's fictional age); ironically, he went on to win a Tony nomination for recreating Bloom in the 1974 Broadway revival of *Ulysses in Nighttown*.

By 1980, with the centenary looming and prospects dimming for a staged production of *Blooms of Dublin*, Burgess concluded that it was "important to turn the dream into a compromise reality by converting the draft stage script into one suitable for radio."[10] That fall he and the BBC's John Tydeman drafted plans for a radio production to be recorded in Dublin, and that winter he orchestrated *Blooms of Dublin* for thirty-one instruments plus chorus, taking consolation in the fact that the radio production permitted him to write for a larger orchestra than most stage productions would have allowed.

Blooms of Dublin presents *Ulysses* in a form celebrating the popular musical culture of Joyce's Dublin embedded so copiously into the novel that there are references in it to over three hundred songs, mostly popular ones of the day.¹¹ Burgess inserted multiple musical allusions into the score of *Blooms*: "Warm Fullblooded Life" includes quotations from *Martha*, *The Bohemian Girl*, *La Bohème*, and Beethoven's Fifth Symphony, while the closing cadence of "Copulation Without Population" quotes the opening bars of *Tristan und Isolde*. Apart from the "Prelude", whose polyphonic complexity "reflected Joyce's crabbed ingenuity", Burgess ensured that "the work as a whole stayed close to the tonalities of the music hall" and that it was "the kind of thing Joyce might have envisaged, or eneared, for his characters. He was the great master of the ordinary, and my music is ordinary enough."[12]

A variety of traditional musical styles are employed in the show. There are eight slow ballads (including "Mother", "Flower of the Mountain", and "Paris is a Lamp Lit for Lovers"), six character songs (including "Today", "Warm Fullblooded Life", and "Gibraltar") and four comic up-tempo numbers (notably "Copulation Without Population", a show-stopper in the Broadway style of "With a Little Bit o' Luck" from *My Fair Lady*). Several choral and orchestral pieces, the poignant duet "The Heaventree of Stars" that Stephen and Bloom sing just before Molly's *gran scena*, and other vocal numbers of a more serious nature (dealing with anti-Semitism, nationalism, and Bloom's relationship to Ireland) lend *Blooms of Dublin* a soberer quality than is typical of most musical shows, leaving the precise genre of this operetta-cum-musical difficult to define. Burgess called it simply a "musical play".

The score begins with an aleatoric "Tune-Up" (Example 24.01) consisting of "odd fragments from the classical repertory" ("e.g. 'Till Eulenspiegel' for the horn").[13] These are arguably the most "Joycean" and certainly the most Stravinskian pages of *Blooms of Dublin*, with layers of activity creating a modernist musical fabric denser than anything else in the work. As bits of many of the show's numbers are sung by eight-part chorus in counterpoint to "Love's Old Sweet Song", the orchestra plays equally intricate counterpoint, thematically independent of the chorus, leading to a climax resembling the build-up in *Le Sacre du Printemps* just prior to the return of the solo bassoon at rehearsal number 12. The conductor ends the "Tune-Up" by "bringing the noise to an end raggedly", leading directly into the "Prelude", which opens with the "Flower of the Mountain" theme, a Burgess favorite that he regarded as "the hit song of the show" (and inserted into numerous other compositions).[14] More complex textures follow as a double fugue in 5/8 is succeeded by a return of the "Flower of the Mountain" theme played in 5/4 time in polymetric counterpoint to the fugue, which continues in 5/8 meter until it collapses, "Joyceanly enough, into a cracked church bell and the voices of old crones in shawls reciting the Holy Mary."[15] The voices fade into the sounds of sea gulls and boat whistles as the clock strikes eight in the morning and the play begins.

Example 24.01 *Blooms of Dublin*: "Tune-Up" (bs. 10–12)

Act One, consisting of seven scenes and nineteen musical numbers, corresponds to Episodes 1–13 of *Ulysses*. Set atop Martello Tower, Scene One (based on *Telemachus* and *Nestor*) opens with Buck Mulligan celebrating his mock mass with a razor and bowl of lather as Stephen Dedalus yawningly approaches. Jesting on the dactylic quality of their names, Malachi Mulligan urges Stephanos Daidalos to travel with him to Athens (if he can get his aunt to pay for it) to "learn how to do something for this benighted green isle". Mulligan sings "Hellenise the Island", a lively number in Greek style, exhorting Dedalus to help him exorcise Irish "gloom and sin" by letting the Hellenic "pagan sun shine in!" After teasing Dedalus, Mulligan asks him seriously why he refused his dying mother's request that he kneel and pray for her. Mulligan walks off crooning the opening line of "Fergus's Song", triggering Stephen's memory of having sung it in his mother's house as she lay near death. In a mellifluous tenor voice, Stephen sings the ballad once again, accompanied on a piano required "to be badly out of tune", until a haunting vision of his mother provokes him to cry out, "Leave me alone and let me live!"[16] Bitter that "We Irish are plagued with mothers", he sings "Mother", a poignant ballad about a trio of oppressive maternal figures: Mother Ireland, Mother England, and the Holy Mother (sacra mater). Mulligan scandalizes Dedalus and the arrogant gun-toting Englishman Haines, another resident of Martello Tower, by singing the blasphemous "Ballad of Joking Jesus" as they eat breakfast. Leaving for the hospital where he studies medicine, Mulligan passes Mr. Garrett Deasy, the head of the school where Dedalus teaches, who has come to say there will be no classes that day owing to a field trip. Deasy asks Dedalus to deliver a letter of his to the *Freeman's Journal*, pressuring him to influence his "literary friends" at the newspaper to see that it gets printed. Outspokenly anti-Semitic, Deasy sings "England's in the Hands of the Jews", claiming they are obstructing the cure for foot-and-mouth disease (the subject of his letter) and responsible for all of Britain's ills.

Scene Two (based on *Calypso*) takes place on a Dublin street. After purchasing a pork kidney at the corner butcher shop, Leopold Bloom, a baritone, sings "Today" (Example 24.02), a ballad, performed with a relaxed swing, in which he anticipates meeting someone new on this otherwise ordinary day. Scene Three (also based on *Calypso*) takes place in the bedroom of Bloom's house on Eccles Street, beginning, like both previous scenes, at 8:00 a.m. His wife Molly, a soprano known professionally by her maiden name Marion Tweedy, is still in bed. She sings "Four O'Clock Tea", a melody set in counterpoint to the tune of "Love's Old Sweet Song", as she envisions her rendezvous that afternoon with her lover, Blazes Boylan. Bloom interrupts, entering with her breakfast on a tray. She is surprised to see him wearing black, the first time he has done so since the death of their son Rudy, and tells him that Boylan will be coming over that afternoon to bring the programme for her upcoming tour. Molly and Leopold sing a duet, "Boylan", in which she sings "Love's Old Sweet Song" while he, in

Example 24.02 *Blooms of Dublin*: "Today..." (bs. 1–12)

counterpoint, rages at her lover.[17] Molly remarks that she smells something burning in the kitchen, causing Bloom to dash off to remove a sizzling kidney from the stove. Alone once more, Molly sings "It's Your Fault" in which she blames her husband for her infidelity, lamenting the fact that they have had no sexual relations since Rudy's death eleven years before. Bloom reenters, singing the first phrase of "*La ci darem la mano*", which Molly is due to perform on her upcoming concert tour. She responds with the next phrase but sings the wrong word (*voglio* instead of *vorrei*), prompting Leopold to seek a tutor to correct her faulty Italian. He departs to attend Paddy Dignam's funeral as a "death bell rings in the distance".

Scene Four (based on *Hades*) takes place at 11:00 a.m. at Glasnevin Cemetery. Stephen's father Simon Dedalus, Jack Power, and Martin Cunningham converse at Dignam's grave. Simon weeps as he thinks of his wife, who is buried in the same cemetery, and expresses concern about his son. Overhearing Simon, Bloom wonders what Rudy would be like if he had lived, singing "My Son" as the funeral cortège of a deceased child passes by. Bloom proposes to the other men that they take up a collection for the Dignam family, suggesting that they meet that afternoon at four o'clock at Barney Kiernan's pub for that purpose. Joe Hynes arrives and asks to see the newspaper sticking out of Bloom's pocket to check on the name of a horse running in that day's Ascot Gold Cup. Bloom offers him the paper, saying that he was just about to throw it away. Regarding the comment as a tip on Throwaway, a twenty-to-one long shot, Hynes runs off to place a bet on that horse. As the other men set out to visit the tomb of Charles Stewart Parnell, Bloom turns in the direction of Rudy's grave, his thoughts wandering in stream-of-consciousness fashion from Rudy to flowers to dying and hell and finally back to living. Standing alone in the cemetery, Bloom rejects mortal gloom in the song "Warm Fullblooded Life", an ode to the pleasures of human existence. In the middle of the final stanza, as Bloom sings of men dancing with each other's wives, his thoughts return to Molly and her lover, whose voices are heard in the distance while Bloom expresses the same jealousy and outrage conveyed previously in "Boylan".

Deciding not to visit Rudy's grave ("What good will it do? I need a live son, not a dead one"), Bloom walks instead to the office of the *Freeman's Journal*, where Scene Five (based on *Aeolus*) takes place at 12:00 noon, to solicit advertisements for the newspaper. All his attempts to discuss business are rebuffed by the editor, an anti-Semite named Myles Crawford who prefers dithering away the afternoon with his cronies. Bloom leaves in frustration. Returning, he encounters Stephen Dedalus, who has come to deliver Mr. Deasy's letter. Upon hearing Stephen utter a few words in Italian, Blooms asks the young man to coach Molly with her pronunciation. Feeling like the proverbial Wandering Jew, Bloom broods about the Promised Land in "Melonfields", an aria comparable in its most dramatic moments to Menotti's style in *The Medium*. Afterward, Crawford apologizes brusquely to Bloom for his earlier behavior and shamelessly asks to borrow money, which Bloom lends him even though Crawford still owes him from the previous month. "Thanks, Bloom", says the editor. "You're a real Christian."

Scene Six (based on *The Cyclops*) takes place at 5:00 p.m. at Barney Kiernan's pub. Matt Lenehan gloomily reports that his horse lost the Ascot Gold Cup to Throwaway. Meanwhile, Bloom arrives seeking Martin Cunningham. With his mangy dog lying at his feet and his drinking buddies forming a chorus, the Citizen, a rabid nationalist and anti-Semite, sings "Song of Ireland", a ballad in five verses that escalate from patriotic rhetoric to vile bigotry. Bloom interrupts the rant to espouse love over hate, then leaves in search of Cunningham. In "Love Loves to Love Love" ("A Vapid Waltz"), the publicans mock Bloom, who returns to the pub and responds bravely to their insults. Cunningham, having arrived moments before Bloom's return, hustles him out of the pub to skirt a fight. In a parody of Polyphemus's errant rock toss at Odysseus's fleeing ship, the Citizen hurls an empty biscuit-box at Bloom and misses, then leads the men in an especially odious reprise of "Song of Ireland".

Scene Seven (based on *Nausicaa*) takes place at 8:00 p.m. at Sandymount shore. Accompanied by a banjo, two minstrels sing "Pretty Little Seaside Girls", a simple ditty. At the beach, Gerty MacDowell and her friends Cissy and Edy watch over Cissy's younger twin brothers. Nearby, men at a temperance retreat sing "Hymn to the Virgin" to organ accompaniment in the parish church. Bloom sits on the rocks and watches Gerty, who finds him handsome and mysterious, "a man to be trusted to the death". Aware that Bloom is observing her, Gerty reveals her private parts to him during the Mirus Bazaar fireworks display as the sounds of firecrackers, organ, church bells, a band, and a bat are heard in the distance. Her exhibitionism sends Bloom into orgasm just as rockets explode during the climax of the pyrotechnic display. Surprised and pleased by his ejaculation, Bloom remains on the beach as the girls leave with the twin boys, Gerty limping behind the others. Realizing that she is lame, he reflects: "Oh, poor girl ... I'm glad I didn't know it when she was on show. Hot little devil all the same." Noticing that his watch has stopped at half past four, Bloom wonders if that was when Molly and Boylan had sex, consoling himself with the observation, "Well, I had that. Not the same but." Recalling a blissful day of love years ago with Molly on the Head of Howth, Bloom sings "Flower of the Mountain" (Example 24.03), then realizes that Gerty is the Citizen's granddaughter, musing, "Well, that's funny. Queer way of getting your own back." Recalling her gratefully, he sings "Goodbye, Dear". A cuckoo clock sounds as a distant bell strikes nine, causing Bloom to exclaim, "All right, don't rub it in", but he cannot escape reminders of his cuckoldry. As a band plays the "Mirus Bazaar March", with the chorus singing "cuckoo" over and over, Bloom repeatedly cries out "No!" to end Act One.

Act Two, consisting of four scenes and fifteen musical numbers, corresponds to Episodes 14–18 of *Ulysses*. Scene Eight (based on *Oxen of the*

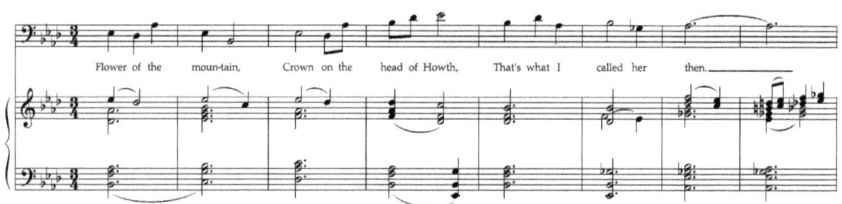

Example 24.03 *Blooms of Dublin*: "Flower of the Mountain" (bs. 51–73)

Sun) takes place at 10:00 p.m. at the National Maternity Hospital on Holles Street. The chorus sings "Invocation to Hecate", a prayer for healthy babies addressed to the Greek goddess of childbirth. Just as the considerate Bloom arrives at the hospital to inquire about Mina Purefoy, who has spent three days in labor, in storms a group of rowdy medical students and their friends, Stephen among them, singing ribald songs. Backed by male chorus, the two minstrels sing "Copulation Without Population", the show's most authentic throwback to music hall style. Bloom's attempts to subdue the young men's raucous behavior go unheeded, drowned out by peals of thunder from a torrential rainstorm and the cries of Mrs. Purefoy's newborn baby boy. Hearing Stephen declare that he fancies "a night in a whore's bed", Bloom decides, with fatherly concern, to follow him into Nighttown.

Scene Nine (based on *Circe*), which takes place at midnight, opens with "Music for Nighttown", a piquant orchestral march in the style of Prokofiev's *The Love for Three Oranges* (which, like *Ulysses*, dates from around 1921/22). Sinister glissandos set the scene for a phantasmagorical foray into Dublin's red-light district, where Bloom immediately confronts reminders of his wife's adultery: apparitions of Molly and Boylan singing "Gibraltar", a duet in Spanish style that ends with "noises of grotesque sexuality", and a repeat of the "Mirus Bazaar March" as a whore cries out, "Eh, I know you, mister. Bloom the cuckold." As the march ends, Bloom suddenly finds himself in court, accused of being "a wellknown dynamitard, forger, bigamist, bawd and cuckold and a public nuisance to the citizens of Dublin." In czardas style symbolizing his Hungarian heritage, he defends himself brilliantly, causing the crowd to cheer and praise him in "Bloom for Mayor", his detractors becoming supporters as Simon Dedalus and the Citizen insist that honors be bestowed upon him. "Carnival Waltz" fulfills Bloom's call for a celebration; it is interrupted by "Coronation Fanfare" and followed by "God Save King Leo", in which the populace hails Bloom once more. Orating in the style of the King James Bible, Bloom proclaims "the new Bloomusalem", eliciting an ecstatic response in "Let the Trumpets" as the women sing "Song of Ireland", now with laudatory lyrics, in counterpoint to "God save King Leo" sung by the men. Suddenly the people turn against Bloom, singing "Lynch Him". Martin Cunningham exhorts the crowd to set him on fire, which they attempt to the cacophonous instrumental accompaniment of "The Burning of Bloom". Awakening from this nightmare, Bloom finds himself in Bella Cohen's brothel, where the prostitutes Zoe and Florry entreat Stephen to tell them about Paris. Obliging, he sings "Paris is a Lamp Lit for Lovers", which segues from gentle ballad to lively cancan and back. The dominatrix Bella Cohen appears and excites Bloom with her sadomasochistic song "Bella, Bellicose", describing all the ways she will subjugate him. Stephen dances with Zoe to "Mother", played as a fast waltz by piano duet "in the style of a mechanical piano". He reprises the song, but as he is about to finish, a terrible crash heralds "The Apparition of Stephen's Mother" as eerie music, intoned wordlessly by a vocal double quartet accompanied by strings and percussion, is heard beneath the specter's chilling voice. Stephen lashes out at the phantom, smashing a chandelier and leaving it to Bloom to settle matters with Bella.

Outside, Stephen quarrels with Private Harry Carr and his whore Cissy while bystanders remark on the action in "Choral Comments".[18] The clash between Stephen and Carr turns political as the Citizen, in a continuation of "Choral Comments", bitterly denounces the English while espousing militant Irish nationalism. The chorus responds with a short commentary ("So God's curse on England...") to the tune of "God Save King Leo" followed by a reprise of the "Song of Ireland" melody. Increasingly agitated by the anti-English sentiment, Carr lands a blow that knocks Stephen out, triggering chaotic music consisting of repeated aleatoric phrases from the orchestra and chorus ("Give him air... He's fainted... The soldier hit the professor", etc.). The scene concludes with defiantly anti-English stanzas of "Choral Comments", first sung separately, then in counterpoint by the crowd, which departs. Bloom and Stephen are left alone, the latter still half delirious from the fight, when Rudy appears to his father. Wonderstruck, Bloom hears the apparition of his dead son chanting the *Kol Nidrei*.

Scene Ten (based on *Eumaeus*) takes place at 1:00 a.m. at the cabman's shelter just west of the Custom House. Bloom leads the semi-conscious Stephen to the shelter where an old sailor named W. B. Murphy banters with two drivers. At the tolling of the one o'clock chime, Bloom sings a reprise of "Today", with Murphy taking over midway through the song.[19] As his head clears, Stephen gratefully acknowledges the way Bloom has looked after him. The figurative union of the men as father and son is symbolized musically in the serene contrapuntal duet "The Heaventree of Stars" (Example 24.04). The men bid each other goodbye as Stephen goes off, declining Bloom's offer to stay overnight. Having had his humanity and maturity "reborn" through Bloom's paternal love, Stephen assumes his newfound identity as a writer, reciting the lines ("Mr Leopold Bloom ate with relish the inner organs of beasts and fowls...") that open Episode 4 of *Ulysses*, the novel he will write ten years hence.

Scene Eleven (based on *Penelope*) takes place in the Blooms' bedroom as the clock of St George's church strikes two. Bloom enters and boldly commands Molly to bring him breakfast in bed, reversing years of subservience, then promptly falls asleep. She recognizes the change in his behavior, noting that he has ejaculated earlier that day ("I can tell by his appetite"), and sings "Molly's Scena", a sixteen-minute-long solo number corresponding to the final episode of *Ulysses*, in which her memories and present feelings mingle in a musical blend of new material with reprises of "Boylan" ("Love's Old Sweet Song"), "It's Your Fault", "Gibraltar", and "Flower of the Mountain".[20]

Meteorological and moral dilemmas came dangerously close to derailing the radio production. The day before recording was to begin, heavy snow

Example 24.04 *Blooms of Dublin*: "The Heaventree of Stars" (bs. 1–11)

in Dublin nearly prevented the singers, actors, and orchestral musicians from reaching the studio. Eventually all managed to arrive, but new problems arose when female choristers, outraged by what they regarded as a blasphemous libretto, threatened to strike. The musicians' union's decision not to authorize a sympathy strike by the orchestra allowed the recording to proceed, though under protest by those women. At each instance of profanity in the score, the ladies left the studio while the men sang alone; English actors took the roles containing obscenities so that "Dublin morality was not seriously sinned against."[21] Recording took place 13–17 January 1982 in Dublin with editing speedily completed in London at the BBC studio to produce a finished program nearly three hours in length.

The day following the February 1982 broadcast on BBC Radio 3, Humphrey Burton sent Burgess a short handwritten note saying he enjoyed *Blooms of Dublin* "very much indeed and I hope it has a long life and a varied one; I hope somebody from the R.S.C. was listening." Producer Michael Heffernan reported,

> Immediate reactions from listeners have been uniformly enthusiastic. My father, who was a student in Dublin in the thirties, was enraptured, and his brother tells me how it brought back the atmosphere his father, my grandfather, carried with him from turn-of-the-century Dublin: as a medical student, it seems, he was a connoisseur of music hall and drawing room concerts.

Joyce biographer Richard Ellmann wasted no time sending his congratulations:

> I listened to the Blooms of Dublin last night. At first it perplexed me as I heard Joyce's words with occasional variations, but gradually I found myself caught up in it, and the second half seemed to me even better than the first. What especially pleased me was that unlike the film *Ulysses* your work met head on the difficulties of the hard chapters, and extracted from them as from the more obvious ones all the humor that is present in them though usually ignored by people who allow themselves to be bored. Anyway I congratulate you. And so musical.[22]

Burgess was praised by critics for "some delightful songs"[23] and "a remarkable job of editing the text."[24] Several reviewers shared Ellmann's view that the second half of *Blooms* was stronger than the first, with David Wade writing in the *Times* that it "gained enormously in confidence, impetus and cohesion. The second and final act seemed to me to have taken off into assured independent existence." His main criticism concerned the use of separate singers and actors for Stephen Dedalus and some of the other main characters: "It was, for instance, extremely disconcerting to hear Frank Grimes's dry-voiced Dedalus suddenly replaced by Frank Patterson's lush, light operatic tenor."[25] Others questioned whether it was wise to try to turn *Ulysses* into a musical, with the *Sunday Times* reviewer finding that "the music washed over the whole intrusively and uncomfortably, better suited to a work called Gilbert and Sullivan Take the Slow Road to Hollywood." Yet even she found merit in Burgess's effort: "he was able to make the words in 'Bloom' hum and sing, sometimes, gloriously".[26] Overall, reaction in the press was positive.

In a class by itself was the review by Hans Keller, a British critic and musicologist of Austrian birth. *Blooms of Dublin* filled this fervent advocate of the Second Viennese School with such fury that he addled his review with tortuous prose amounting to pseudo-intellectual gibberish:

> Burgess's pathetic pastiche evinced a centrifugal incompetence which pervaded its entire orbit, so that continuous listening became impossible for any naturally musical ear, professional or naive. The score teems with tuberculous attempts at updating it all, at enlivening both its harmonic progress and its rhythm with the help of unmotivated, aimless dislocations and distortions. An early 5/4-time (3 plus ill-assorted 2) makes it easy for all but the tone-deaf to

find out how the whirlwind blows: in the more modern manner but without the slightest formal justification, the number "progresses" from F major to E flat major, though a conventionally concentric tonality would at least have accorded with the structure's primitive terms of harmonic reference.[27]

Ever since Keller incurred Burgess's wrath in the 1960s for his scholarly embrace of rock music, the two men had regarded each other with animosity. Burgess loathed what he called "pop garbage" and was appalled by critics like Keller who professed to find it of intellectual interest. Although their musical preferences overlapped to some degree – both admired Elgar, Stravinsky, and Shostakovich, for example – Keller's tastes were largely antipathetical to Burgess's. He did not care for the music of Debussy, Delius, and Vaughan Williams, and championed such minor serialists as Nikos Skalkottas and Mátyás Seiber.[28] Seiber, a British composer of Hungarian origin whose music is described in *Grove* as achieving "a fine balance between Bartók and Schoenberg", was one of Keller's closest friends; Seiber's 1947 cantata *Ulysses*, a work singled out by Burgess as the antithesis of his own demotic approach, represented, to Keller, the proper way of setting Joyce to music.[29]

Burgess wrote but did not send a lengthy response in which he attacked Keller's attempt "to force shoddy grandiloquence on his readers as a substitute for aesthetic analysis and appraisal":

> I have long worried about musical critics, and for two reasons. They are, first, not forced by their craft to show their competence in the art which sustains that craft. A literary critic has at least to show literacy, and is thus drawn into the orbit of the art he evaluates. A music critic has no parallel obligation. Second, the impossibility of conveying the effect of music in words makes him indulge in verbalism which resembles music only in not possessing a separable semantic content ... I smiled secretly at Mr Keller's demand for my suppression as a mere man of letters claiming the right to initiate discussion of an art which, I now learn, is the province of musical functionaries like Mr Keller. I knew that he would leap at the chance of denigrating music of my own and that I would not have long to wait for this denigration.[30]

Instead, he wrote a brief letter to the editor of the *Listener* later that month faulting Keller's misuse of a technical term misapplied to his setting of the word "mother":

> I set that word to a semiquaver duplet in slow time. Mr Keller ought to have listened more carefully or else looked up "Scotch snap" in some musical dictionary or other. Such inaccuracy is not really tolerable in a musical journalist of, I gather, some reputation.[31]

Burgess saved the real riposte for a book, where it would sting longer. The list of compositions in *This Man and Music*, published that year, ends with "*Homage to Hans Keller* for four tubas", a sardonic joke on Keller's overblown pomposity. Burgess never wrote such a piece (see Chapter 30) – the title is what mattered – but did leave an undated, incomplete Allegro

Example 24.05 Excerpt from unfinished quartet for bass tubas (bs. 20–2)

moderato for four bass tubas, evidently a sketch for this ophicleidean Bronx cheer. An excerpt from it illustrates the kind of derisive tribute he must have had in mind: three colossal fortissimo blasts producing a flatulent fanfare worthy of F. X. Enderby (Example 24.05).[32]

Blooms of Dublin has never been staged. When Baltimore's Center Stage decided in 1983 to produce it, Burgess rescored it for a small instrumental ensemble before the production was cancelled, leaving his rewrite (now lost) of the original 438-page full score an enormous wasted effort.[33] Proposed stagings at a Swedish theatre (in Swedish) in 1984 and London's Man in the Moon Theatre in 1986 also fell through. In September 1991, when Trieste's Teatro Comunale "Giuseppe Verdi" proposed an Italian-language production of the show with a reduced instrumental ensemble, Burgess, with Liana's help, set to work translating *I Blum Di Dublino* (as he called it) into Italian, completing over one hundred pages of the vocal score by October 1992, but, in March 1993, the Trieste production of *Ulyssea* (as Teatro Comunale planned to call it) was cancelled.

Would *Blooms of Dublin* succeed on stage? Until someone mounts a production, it remains impossible to know for sure, but an audience attuned to Joyce's artistic world would probably find it highly enjoyable. The show is a finely crafted adaptation of *Ulysses* with several fine songs (especially "Today" and "Copulation Without Procreation"), potent dramatic impact, and a high degree of accessibility compared with its literary source. *Blooms of Dublin* would surely inspire audience members to turn, or return, to Joyce's original text, which, as Burgess pointed out in his essay "Musicalising *Ulysses*", was reason enough to undertake the project:

> Finally, a musical of *Ulysses* clearly had to be done sometime, and I have done it. Any other sufficiently equipped lover of Joyce is welcome to supersede my

Odes to Joyce

own effort. *Pygmalion* remains after the lucrative illiteracies of *My Fair Lady* . . . and *Ulysses* will continue to stand as a great monolith when all the incrustations of adaptation to stage and film and radio musical have been washed away by the rains. But the scholarly complainants might care to consider sometime that a popular musical version is as legitimate an act of criticism as a doctoral thesis.[34]

The show's chief shortcomings are a score with insufficient variety (too many slow ballads and too few ensemble numbers) and, most seriously, a weak ending, with Molly's lengthy aria-cum-monologue failing to build to a satisfactory climax. By repeatedly switching back and forth between music and spoken dialogue, Burgess's adaptation of the Penelope episode fails to achieve the powerful flow and momentum of Joyce's original stream-of-conscientiousness ending. Reconstruction of this scena might produce a

Example 24.06 "Strings" (bs. 1–6)

Example 24.07 "Ecce Puer" (bs. 1–6)

more dramatically effective finale, but, despite this shortcoming, *Blooms of Dublin* is a stageworthy piece of musical theatre that warrants the production that its creator not only eneared, but envisaged.

Burgess's attendance at the International Joyce Symposium in 1982 resulted in two Joyce settings for voice and piano thanks to the encouragement of Myra Teicher Russel, an expert on musical settings of Joyce's *Chamber Music*.[35] Burgess told her that, in his youth, he had set the *Chamber Music* poems and would try to recall as many as he could. On 18 June he wrote down his setting of "Strings", the first poem in *Chamber Music*, and two days later, while riding a train from Dublin to Cork, wrote out "Ecce Puer" in the same music manuscript notebook that Russel had given him. Having set down the two songs in the notebook, he graciously returned it to her without retaining copies of the songs for himself.

'Strings" (Example 24.06) is a tender, melodious song in a gently chromatic idiom, beginning in F major and ending in the relative minor. Rolled chords in the accompaniment imitate the sound of a guitar, with chromatically descending arpeggios in the final phrase deftly conveying the image of "fingers straying upon an instrument". "Ecce Puer" (Behold the boy), which Joyce wrote in 1932 to celebrate the birth of his grandson, is one of Burgess's rare twelve-tone compositions. Although serial technique is not applied throughout, the row is presented in prime and retrograde forms in the piano introduction (Example 24.07), returning in prime as the initial vocal melody and bass line of the coda.

Notes

1 "Musicalising *Ulysses*". Typescript © 1982 sent 6 February to *Corriere della Sera* and other European periodicals for publication.
2 *Re Joyce*, 28. Liana Burgess's statement that Anthony worked on *Blooms of Dublin* off and on for seventeen years confirms that he would have begun the project around 1965.

3 Letter to Aggeler, 21 August 1971. The first page of "Flower of the Mountain" (piano-vocal score, 49) is dated "9 Aug '71". Assertions in YH (290), that he "started drafting a musical version of *Ulysses*" just after writing *Joysprick*, and in BD (5), that a "draft of both the libretto and the score had been available in 1971 when I was living in New York", support this chronology.
4 Interview with Don Swaim on *Book Beat*, 19 September 1985 (http://wiredforbooks.org/anthonyburgess). See also "The Genesis of 'Earthly Powers'", *Washington Post Book World*, 23 November 1980, 1–2, 13.
5 *Earthly Powers*, 101, 118, 158, 173; TMM, 38 ("Partita for string orchestra").
6 EP, 184, 501.
7 Ibid., 453.
8 *Blooms of Dublin: A Musical Play based on James Joyce's "Ulysses"* (Hutchinson 1986), 5. The libretto, dated 1980, published in this edition differs marginally from the revised version found in the 1981 unpublished full score and sung in the 1982 BBC radio production.
9 Ibid.
10 Ibid., 6.
11 Don Gifford with Robert J. Seidman, *Ulysses Annotated*, 2nd. ed. (Berkeley, Los Angeles and London: University of California Press, 1988), 670–3.
12 YH, 371.
13 The "Tune-Up" was deleted from the radio production, probably because of its complexity, and replaced by a simple solo piano rendition of the chorus of "Love's Old Sweet Song" (words by J. Clifton Bingham and music by James L. Molloy, 1884).
14 see EP, 549–50.
15 YH, 371.
16 The Hutchinson text, unlike the score, calls for "a choir singing in Stephen's skull" (17). Joyce composed a melody to Yeats's melancholy poem, "Who Goes with Fergus?" (1893, from *The Rose*), which he sang for his youngest brother as he lay on his deathbed, and, a year later, for his dying mother. Burgess set only the beginning of the second stanza (lines 7–9).
17 This number, 6b in the Hutchinson edition, is preceded by 6a, an angry quatrain about Boylan that Bloom "sing-mutters" to himself.
18 "Choral Comments" corresponds to BD, Nos. 26–30.
19 According to William York Tindall in *A Reader's Guide to James Joyce* (New York: Octagon, 1971), 215, the figure of the returning hero is divided between Bloom and Murphy. The former personifies Odysseus as the recognized father; the latter, a maritime teller of tall tales, represents Odysseus as the disguised voyager. To signify the conflation of these two characters, Burgess divides the reprise of "Today" between them.
20 "Molly's Scena" matches BD, Nos. 33–7.
21 YH, 372.
22 Letter to Burgess ("John"), "Candlemas, 1982" (2 February). Ellmann's reference is to Joseph Strick's 1967 motion picture starring Milo O'Shea as Bloom.
23 Anne Karpf, "Singing Bloom", *Listener*, 11 February 1982, 26.
24 Paul Ferris, "Musical Blooms", *Observer*, 2 February 1982.
25 David Wade, "Bloomsday to music", *The Times*, 6 February 1982.

26 Susie Cornfield, "Shipwrecked with Ulysses", *Sunday Times*, 7 February 1982, 41.
27 Hans Keller, "Phoneydom", *Listener*, 11 February 1982, 27.
28 "All we need, then, is (*sic*) geniuses. To my knowledge, there has been one symphonic genius after Schoenberg – Nikos Skalkottas." Hans Keller, *Essays on Music* (Cambridge: Cambridge University Press, 1994), 191.
29 YH, 373. See "Mátyás Seiber 1905–1960" in Keller, *Essays on Music*, 86–8.
30 Letter addressed but not posted "To the Editor, *The Listener*", [February 1982].
31 Letter to the editor, *Listener*, 25 February 1982 (written 16 February).
32 See *MF*, 108: "... the other clowns were on to him, buffeting and kicking, leaving the noise to synchronized rimshots on side-drum and farts of tuba." See also YH, 373.
33 "The proposed production in Baltimore could not accommodate more than a couple of keyboard instruments, a clarinet or trumpet, and a percussionist." BD, 8.
34 "Musicalising *Ulysses*".
35 Burgess is one of the 141 composers listed in Russel's book *James Joyce's Chamber Music: The Lost Song Settings* (Bloomington and Indianapolis: Indiana University Press, 1993), 113.

25

NUNS AND LOVERS

Music, one might say, is Hopkinsian.[1]

Burgess was nearly seventy before he first set D. H. Lawrence to music. In June 1983 he was invited to participate in the Lawrence Centenary Festival scheduled to take place two years hence in Eastwood and Nottingham, and promised the festival director he would "compose a musical setting of at least one DHL poem" for the occasion. He proceeded to write a cycle of four songs titled *Man Who Has Come Through*, scoring it for the Laurentian instrumentation of high voice, flute, oboe, cello, and piano.[2] Carefully recording the date he finished each movement, Burgess completed the work in Monaco on 8 April 1984. With a duration of thirty-five minutes, it is his longest song cycle and the largest work he composed that year, having abandoned work on a new symphony after sixty-eight pages.

As in the case of *The Waste Land*, Burgess proceeded without first securing the right to use the texts and again had to petition the author's estate for permission after composing the work. Fortunately this time things went smoothly. A letter to the estate's agent reveals Burgess's sober assessment of the economics of classical music:

> I am interested in this question of copyright, having assumed that Lawrence's works were now in the public domain, since he died more than fifty years ago. Why are they still in copyright, and how long does this situation last? The question is purely academic, since there is no money in serious music. The songs were written as a gesture of homage and not for commercial gain. They may even not be performed.[3]

But they were, premiered in Nottingham on 22 September 1985 by tenor Stephen Williams, pianist Alla Kravchenko, and principals of the East of England Orchestra at the East Midlands Music Theatre conducted by Malcolm Nabarro.[4] Three days later, Peter Palmer, the theatre's Artistic Director, thanked Burgess for "bravely entrusting us with your DHL suite. Curious how the one self-commissioned centenary piece should be (in my opinion) the most substantial of the lot. It gave my colleagues great pleasure to prepare it; we are only sorry the composer was not there to take a bow."[5]

A repeat performance took place at Nottingham University on 23 January 1986 with Burgess again unable to attend.[6]

There are certain musical similarities between Burgess and Max Reger – emphasis on fugue and counterpoint, thick textures, frequent modulation, and the extremely chromatic harmonic style of very late Romanticism – and nowhere are these more pronounced than in this work. *Man Who Has Come Through* also harks back to composers like Strauss, Mahler, Schoenberg, and Stravinsky, whose music from around 1910 straddles the line between tonality and atonality. Perhaps Burgess had in mind Alban Berg, whose *Sieben Frühe Lieder* from 1907 epitomize this transitional moment; Berg, like Lawrence, was born in 1885 and died young, outliving him by just five years.

Framing the four Lawrence settings, whose order matches the texts' chronology, is an optional "Prelude &/or Postlude", a wistful Lento in which languid cello, flute, and oboe solos waft torpidly above soft, Debussyan harmonies in the piano. The text of "End of Another Home Holiday", one of Lawrence's early verses, from 1909, expresses the poet's awareness that it is time for him to make his own way in the world and part from his aging, loving mother: "She, so lonely, greying now! / And I leaving her, / Bent on my pursuits!" This highly chromatic setting, though it begins and ends in A minor, modulates restlessly, often on the brink of atonality. "Song of a Man Who Has Come Through" is a vigorous, optimistic ballad that Lawrence penned in 1914 after his marriage to Frieda. Here, destiny becomes "the fine, fine wind that takes its course through the chaos of the world", carrying the poet, guided by "three strange angels", to his fate. Beginning in a kind of D Mixolydian/major and ending in B major, it is the most tonal of the four songs and the briefest by far, its allegro molto vivace tempo reflecting the urgency of Lawrence's words. Disregarding all Biblical or Freudian interpretations of "Snake", written in Taormina around 1920–21, on the surface this celebrated poem describes an encounter with a serpent whose nobility awes the poet, prompting a fierce inner struggle over whether or not to slay it: "Was it cowardice that I dared not kill him? / Was it perversity, that I longed to talk to him? / Was it humility, to feel so honoured?" Burgess's languorous setting exceeds a quarter hour and is sung mainly in a relaxed, parlando style to a quiet, often sparse accompaniment. The last song is a setting of "Bavarian Gentians", a poem Lawrence wrote in Germany six months before his death in March 1930. Perhaps sensing that he had not much longer to live, Lawrence combined the image of the Bavarian gentian with the myth of Persephone, who descends annually into Pluto's deathly realm. Burgess's setting (Example 25.01), whose opening recalls the start of the final song from *The Brides of Enderby*, begins in D major and gradually modulates to B, ending with delicate cello harmonics ascending into nothingness above hollow chords without thirds in the piano – an aural fade into silence symbolizing the disappearance of Persephone and Pluto into the darkness of the underworld.

Example 25.01 *Man Who Has Come Through*: 4. Bavarian Gentians (bs. 1–5)

Flame Into Being, Burgess's centennial study of Lawrence's life and work, draws its title from the once scandalous passage on the penultimate page of *Lady Chatterley's Lover*: "We fucked a flame into being. Even the flowers are fucked into being, between sun and earth."[7] In the opening chapter Burgess reveals how his musical interests led him to Lawrence:

> I was attracted to the music of Delius and the songs of his young friend and adorer Peter Warlock. Reading about both, I learned that Peter Warlock, whose real name was Philip Heseltine, thought highly of a novelist named Lawrence but eventually became his enemy and was ridiculed in one of his novels . . . I also learned that Heseltine appeared, exalted more than libeled, in a novel by Aldous Huxley called *Antic Hay*. This novel led me to *Point Counter Point*, a promising musical title, and there I met Mark Rampion, who, I was told, was really Lawrence.[8]

Burgess repeatedly employs musical metaphor and terminology to describe Lawrence's fiction. The ending of *Women in Love* is a letdown – "an *una corda* chord, not very convincing . . . All novels are difficult to bring to a conclusion, but one has become used to the Laurentian noise and fire and expected a Mahlerian consummation."[9] Preference for the novels over the short stories is expressed through a Beethovenian analogy – "I am inclined to think that the short story is usually a waste of a good novel: by the time the setting and the characters have been set up, it is almost time to leave them. There are many who do not hold this view and, as far as Lawrence is concerned, believe that he did his best work in the form. This, to me, is like preferring Beethoven's bagatelles to his sonatas."[10] Forms of artistic expression that required technical mastery painstakingly acquired from a skilled pedagogue were antithetical to his nature – "Lawrence did not like to be taught techniques. He scorned the piano and mistrusted 'art' music: you had to learn scales to master the one and the other was full of harmonic and contrapuntal nonsense."[11] Yet even while professing to spurn serious music, Lawrence featured it prominently in such novels as *The Trespasser*, *Mr. Noon*, and *Aaron's Rod*, displaying a contradictory aesthetic attitude that Burgess closely examines.

To address the "absurd question" of whether Lawrence's death from tuberculosis at forty-four came too soon, Burgess cites music critic Ernest Newman, who in 1927 argued provocatively that Mozart, Schubert, and Purcell had already reached "the limit of their capacity" when they met their early deaths, whereas, because they were still developing their compositional ability, "the composers who died too young were Wagner, at the age of seventy, Beethoven, at fifty-seven, Brahms, at sixty-four, Puccini, at sixty-six, and Verdi, at eighty-eight."[12] Applying Newman's reasoning, Burgess concludes that Lawrence, "having written unremittingly for a quarter of a century, had probably written enough" by the time of his passing.[13] On the other hand, Mozart, according to Burgess, would have continued to evolve as a composer had he lived into his sixties or seventies:

> I personally have no difficulty in imagining a Mozart who took in his stride the spirit of the Revolution, the *Hammerklavier*, horns with valves, and the need to shout his ego through an expansion of symphonic form. But it is easier to see him as having done enough, fulfilled the needs of the eighteenth century, and after a brief life granted a fourth dimension of hard work, which is a kind of tangential prolongation, yielding to sickness or the fictitious stroke of Salieri.[14]

In *The Rage of Lawrence*, a 1985 television documentary written and narrated by Burgess as yet another centennial tribute, he beatifies Lawrence as the "patron saint" of all writers, like himself, who have not had an Oxford or Cambridge education, and plays "Love's Old Sweet Song" on an ancient pub piano in Nottingham.[15] Shorter writings, like his introduction to *D. H. Lawrence and Italy* and the essay "The Large World of Lawrence" contain assorted bons mots, like the observation that "the world Lawrence describes [in his travel books] has long disappeared—except, of course, for the unchanging human groundbass which is his main, perhaps only, concern."[16]

As one who cherished a poem's aural effect no less than its literal sense, Burgess regarded Gerard Manley Hopkins as "a superb poet, perhaps the greatest and certainly the most original of the nineteenth century".[17] He treasured the musical quality of Hopkins's writing even (or especially) when the sound of his language obscured its referential significance, maintaining that "if we take in verbal constructs primarily as sound and structure without a clearly separable meaning, then we are much in the position of listening to music."

> Language distinguishes between the autosemanteme (or word containing meaning) and the synsemanteme (the morpheme which assists in the making of meaning but has no meaning in itself), but in music all units are meaningful: there is nothing that is purely structural. Music deals in sounds without clear referents. Music is multiguous, since it is capable of many interpretations.[18]

The second of Burgess's Eliot Lectures, "Rhythm, Sprung and Unsprung", is devoted to the explication of Hopkins's verse style. The chapter in *This Man and Music* titled "Nothing is so Beautiful as Sprung", which is adapted from that lecture, concludes with a passage in Sprung Rhythm written in musical rhythmic notation that shows each Stress and Slack (Example 25.02). "It will not please literary academics," Burgess warns, "but musicians will understand."[19] Like Joyce, Hopkins was musical not just in the literary sense, but as an actual musician, which further endeared him to Burgess.

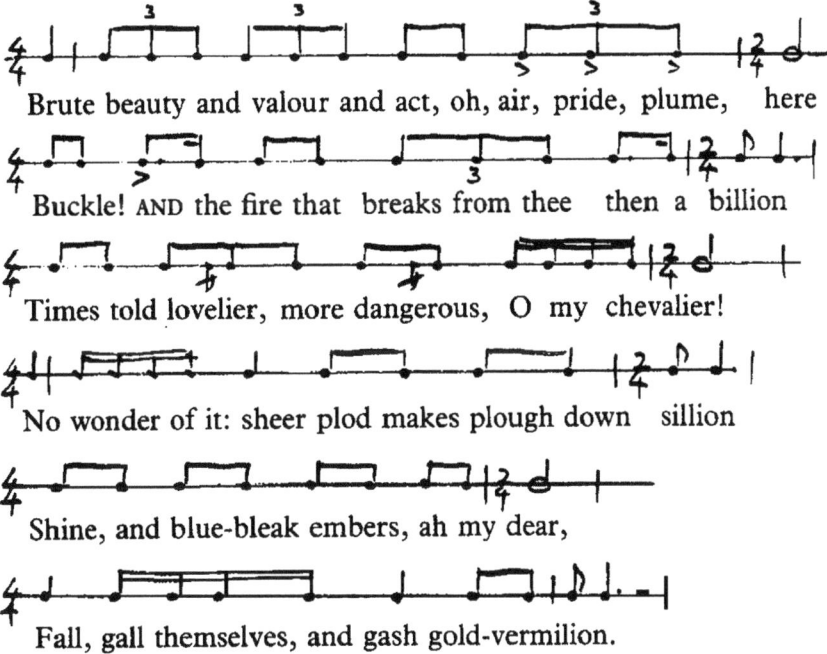

Example 25.02 Sestet from "The Windhover" by G. M. Hopkins, notated rhythmically by Anthony Burgess in *This Man and Music* (133)

> He composed music, none of it very good, though in his setting of Canon Dixon's "Fallen Rain" he demonstrated a sharpness of ear which enabled him to distinguish microtones: he anticipated Hába of the twentieth century by finding a notation for half-flats and half-sharps. The melody of "Fallen Rain" is not in itself daring enough to justify division of the semitone. Dutifully I have given the song the piano accompaniment Hopkins was not skilled enough to provide himself.[20]

In truth, Burgess exaggerates Hopkins's use of microtones, which amounts to a single instance of text painting – inserting a quarter tone into the descending minor second F to E on the word "agony" – within an entirely conventional melody.[21]

Eight years after substituting *The Wreck of the Deutschland* for *A Clockwork Orange* in *The Clockwork Testament*, Burgess began setting it to music: "I . . . fixed myself up at an outdoor café table with ballpoints and scoring paper and set Hopkins's 'The Wreck of the Deutschland' for baritone soloist, chorus, and large orchestra. It could not, of course, be done, but I had to prove this to myself."[22] Composed mainly in Callian de Var during the summer of 1981, he completed the score of this one-movement oratorio in Monaco on 8 March 1982. Lasting approximately thirty-two minutes, it is the longest single movement among all of Burgess's works and one of his most powerful compositions. Along with the role of Leopold Bloom in *Blooms of Dublin*, the solo part represents Burgess's finest writing for the baritone voice.

While the work's maritime character is reminiscent of *A Sea Symphony*, its harmonic style is closer to *A Child of Our Time*. The musical setting mirrors the poem's two-part format, with Part One, comprising the first ten stanzas, dominated by the baritone, who sings all but two of them. The chorus takes a much greater role after that, singing twenty-one of the twenty-five stanzas that make up Part Two, four of these in combination with the soloist. Except for a brief instrumental introduction and short interlude between Parts One and Two, the orchestra plays a strictly supporting role, with singing continuing almost without pause throughout. Emphasizing the highly dramatic quality of Part Two, which includes the fierce storm, soloist and chorus alternate frequently, with tempos and the disposition of vocal forces changing at nearly each new stanza. Multiple choral textures are employed, with occasional separate use of women's and men's voices, a cappella passages, and varied use of divisi. Although Burgess used the term "choral counterpoint" in reference to *The Wreck of the Deutschland*, the choral writing is predominantly homophonic, fostering textual intelligibility. Several of the stanzas for baritone solo are to be sung "freely" in a parlando, quasi-recitative style, as in the setting of the twelfth stanza (Example 25.03).

In addition to *The Wreck of the Deutschland*, Burgess composed a number of smaller Hopkins-related works. Besides adding piano accompaniment to the aforementioned "Fallen Rain", he set *Inversnaid* for

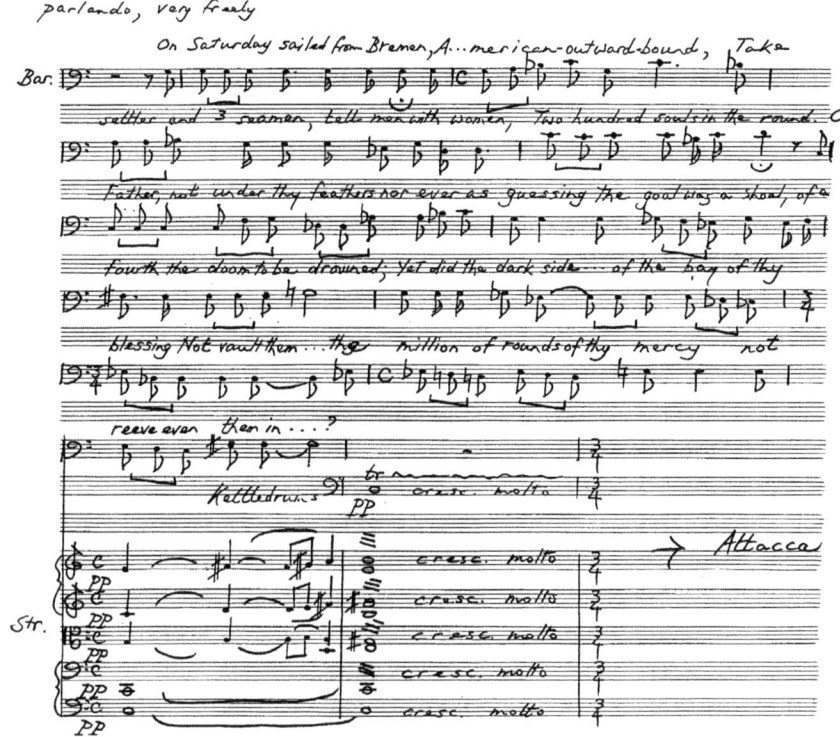

Example 25.03 *The Wreck of the Deutschland*: Stanza 12 (bars 176–88)

unaccompanied chorus in 1947 and composed *Terrible Crystal*, a setting of three sonnets for baritone, chorus, and orchestra, in 1952.[23] Shortly after the premiere of his Third Symphony, he composed *Fanfare for Three Trumpets* for a liturgical commemoration marking the centenary of the shipwreck of the *Deutschland*. This event, held at Rockhurst College in Kansas City, Missouri, on 8 December 1975, began with Burgess's fanfare and included a performance of "Fallen Rain". For the Hopkins centenary in 1989, BBC Radio commissioned Burgess to adapt *St Winefred's Well*, an unfinished dramatic poem recounting the story of Gwenvrewi, who, according to legend, was beheaded by a jilted suitor, was then miraculously healed by her uncle Beuno, a monk, and went on to become a nun, abbess, and saint. Burgess completed the text and composed the incidental music (a minimal affair consisting of just three passages for solo flute) for the broadcast, which occurred on 23 December 1989.

Given his penchant for celebrating anniversaries with music compositions, it is likely that Burgess's undated setting of Thomas Hardy's "The Oxen" was composed in 1990, seventy-five years after the poem was written, during the sesquicentennial of Hardy's birth. First published in *The*

Example 25.04 "The Oxen" (bs. 1–7)

Times on 24 December 1915, the eve of England's second Christmas during World War I, the poem reflects Hardy's sense of nostalgia and regret at the painful loss of faith and innocence caused by the war. Burgess's pastoral setting, composed in a gentle tonal style and rocking 6/8 meter, begins in C major and modulates to the relative minor, altered through the use of a Picardy third to end with a final A major cadence. The vocal range, limited to the octave above middle C, is best suited to a mezzo-soprano or baritone yet singable by higher voices without transposition. Hardy's poem recounts the legend that barnyard creatures whose ancestors were present when Jesus was born in Bethlehem kneel each Christmas Eve at midnight to commemorate Christ's birth.

Notes

1 TMM, 121.
2 Letter to Kevin West, 2 August 1983.
3 Letter to Laurence Pollinger, 2 October 1984.
4 *Man Who Has Come Through* concluded a program that included Debussy's *Syrinx*, piano works by Franck and Scriabin, and, aptly, songs by Peter Warlock.
5 Peter Palmer, letter to Burgess, 25 September 1985.
6 Eleven months after this performance, Liana Burgess wrote to Palmer on 30 December 1986: "It is a pity that Anthony could not be with you in January last. He had to be in New York and then he fell ill. He was recently in Birmingham, as you may know, to listen to some of his music for brass performed."

7 D. H. Lawrence, *Lady Chatterley's Lover*, ed. Michael Squires (Cambridge: Cambridge University Press, 1993), 301.
8 *Flame Into Being*, 2.
9 Ibid., 129–30.
10 Ibid., 87.
11 Ibid., 21.
12 Ibid., 260.
13 Ibid., 264.
14 Ibid., 260.
15 Produced and directed by Jill Freeman and edited by Melvyn Bragg, *The Rage of Lawrence* is Volume 5 in London Weekend Television's "Profile of a Writer" series.
16 Introduction to *D. H. Lawrence and Italy*, vii.
17 TMM, 132.
18 Ibid., 120–1.
19 Ibid., 133.
20 Ibid., 119. To view "Fallen Rain", with its curious use of quartertones in Hopkins's notation, visit http://www.entretemps.asso.fr/Hopkins/FallenRainAutograph.html
21 See http://www.entretemps.asso.fr/Hopkins/FallenRainAutograph.html to view the manuscript.
22 YH, 369.
23 TMM, 38.

26

BLEST PAIR OF SIRENS

> *Literature, in the form of the text to be set to music, must always be ready to help the composer; whether music can help literature is another matter.*[1]

In spring 1980 at the University of Kent, Anthony Burgess delivered the T. S. Eliot Memorial Lectures, drawing his title and theme from the opening of John Milton's *At a Solemn Music*: "Blest pair of Sirens, pledges of Heaven's joy, / Sphere-born harmonious sisters, Voice and Verse". In four lectures titled "Blest Pair of Sirens: Thoughts on Music and Literature", delivered 28 April–1 May, Burgess examined Eliot's incorporation of popular song into his verse, musical aspects of Hopkins's poetry, Joyce's writing, and the novel in general. Two years later, he adapted the lectures for publication in *This Man and Music*, the book that demonstrated, more than any of his previous writings, the depth of his musical involvement.[2] He is at his best in the four chapters based on the Eliot lectures, which convey many of his fundamental beliefs about the ties between music and literature. Elsewhere he ponders the common existence of music and literature within the temporal dimension, conveying his ardor for the *sound* of language in "A Matter of Time and Space", while in "Meaning Means Language", he explores music's limited ability to express programmatic ideas: "It was, I suppose, a doubt about the capacity of music to provide me with a language that drove me to the craft of the novel, where there are solidities of character and *récit* and corresponding semantic and syntactical solidities."[3] In "Bonaparte in E flat", he explains the method by which he applied the formal structure of Beethoven's *Eroica* to *Napoleon Symphony*, but strays off the musical path in "Oedipus Wrecks" to focus instead on the structuralist underpinnings of *MF*. He gets into trouble in "Music and Meaning", a rumination on symphonic form, when, forgetting that themes from the first two movements return in the finale of Brahms's Third Symphony, he writes, "Post-Beethoven symphonists have followed the master on the road to formal unification (not Brahms, of course) by recalling themes, as in the Fifth".[4] Ironically, in the chapter "Let's Write a Symphony" about his own Third, he includes several inaccurate musical examples, having recalled them from memory without access to the score.

The opening chapter of *This Man and Music* represents Burgess's longest autobiographical writing prior to *Little Wilson and Big God*. Despite its flaws and omissions, the list of compositions at the end of this "*Biographia Musicalis*" is an invaluable inventory of his works, since many of these titles are mentioned nowhere else. In his personal copy of the book, Burgess extended the register by appending six titles by hand: 1984 – *Man Who Has Come Through*; 1985 – Twenty-four Preludes and Fugues for Keyboard; 1986 – Festal Suite for Brass, Quartet for Guitars; 1987 – Concerto for Guitar and Orchestra, Rhapsody for Oboe.[5] In the *Guardian*, Frank Kermode appraised *This Man and Music* as "a rather serious book about the relations of literature and music, as understood by one of the few novelists who can produce both . . . Obviously he has a prodigious memory and never looks things up, or he would not be telling us that Wagner gave the line '*Oed' und leer das Meer*' to Isolde, or that Plutarch's *Parallel Lives* yoke historical figures and mythological characters."[6] Robert Craft's qualified approval did not extend to such exaggerated pronouncements as "Behind all music of an instrumental nature lies the dance", for, as Craft reasonably countered, "Mozart's concertos and serenades are well stocked with arias for instruments. And what kind of dance is behind the *Tristan* Prelude?"[7] But he foundered when criticizing the musical examples, dismissing one of "a bitonal canon" from Burgess's Third Symphony as "neither canonic nor tonal, let alone a combination of two tonalities", when the example is exactly what Burgess says it is.[8] Ironically, Craft, no mean sesquipedalian himself, chastised Burgess for his abstruse vocabulary:

> Burgess employs so many obscure words that one suspects he may experience his greatest satisfaction when introducing a term that absolutely nobody understands. "I never learned to sound a note . . . that was not, as they say, vaccicidal," he writes. Who, may we ask, says "vaccicidal"?

Those, we might answer, familiar with "Terence, this is stupid stuff" from A. E. Housman's *A Shropshire Lad*:

> The cow, the old cow, she is dead;
> It sleeps well, the horned head:
> We poor lads, 'tis our turn now
> To hear such tunes as killed the cow.

"Perhaps I don't really care for opera after all," wrote Burgess to his friend Martin Bell in 1965. Given the scope of his later operatic involvement, those reservations must have been short-lived.[9] In 1971, Universe Books published the libretti of *Idomeneo* and *Don Giovanni* with an introduction by Burgess expressing seemingly genuine enthusiasm for these masterpieces. His concept of Mozart's art representing the quintessence of musical divinity, an idea he would recapitulate in *The End of the World News* and *Mozart and the Wolf Gang*, here receives one of its earliest expressions:

> Perhaps it is worth dying young and in poverty if one can produce – among other masterpieces – an *Idomeneo* and a *Don Giovanni*... In Mozart's own works there is neither anger nor self-pity, only humour, elegance and a nobility sometimes – though always impersonally – tragic. His music contains the image of a perfectly ordered civilization which is itself an image of divine order.[10]

The Metropolitan Opera Classics Library was inaugurated in 1983 to celebrate the company's centenary with a series of books on favorite works from its repertoire. Each richly illustrated volume included a story adaptation of the libretto by a prominent writer, and Burgess was chosen for *Der Rosenkavalier*, the initial volume in the series.[11] In his retelling of Hugo von Hofmannsthal's sophisticated Viennese comedy, Burgess embellished the tale with such amusingly repulsive details as this depiction of Baron Ochs as a kind of male counterpart of Enderby's repellent stepmother:

> His nose was a maimed beacon: its red shine was marred by the lumps of good living and a wart on the left-hand slope that sported three filaments which waved in the breeze of his bark. His eyes of a sharp blue were couched in fat. A high noble forehead might have counteracted the meanness of the mouth, with a pouting lower lip that flared crimson, the vast jowls and cheeks, the potman's nose and the swinish eyes, but his brow was narrow and low. It was a face that might have been more acceptable if nature had placed it on his no-neck upside down.[12]

In March 1980, interviewing Graham Greene for the *Observer*, Burgess brought the conversation round to *My Fair Lady* and even suggested they write a show together, but Greene had no interest in collaborating with Burgess.[13] George Mikes did. The Hungarian-born British humorist contacted Burgess in late 1982 to request a song for his new play *The Virgin and the Bull*, a farce, scheduled to open in Wales the following spring, about a Welsh wife and Italian husband caught up in art world corruption.[14] Burgess's affirmative response prompted the quip, "I am absolutely delighted. I have worked with some quite distinguished composers in the past but never with one who, one day, is going to win the literary Nobel Prize as a sideline."[15]

Luigi, an indigent art collector, sings "A Poor Man Can't Be Free" after he learns that a painting he has bought for £4 may be a Caravaggio worth millions and finds his life alarmingly disrupted as a result. Burgess's song ends with a comic twist: "Yet having weighed the arguments, / I cannot fight the itch. / So give me my Mercedes Benz, / Give me dollars, even cents: / I must, I must be rich!"[16] Completed on 7 January 1983, the song, a typical show tune with straightforward rhythms and harmony, calls for a chorus to provide wordless back-up harmonies and repeat final strophic lines à la Gilbert and Sullivan.

Carl Maria von Weber's *Oberon* has long been considered a "problem opera" on account of its weak libretto, a disjointed affair in English cobbled together by James Robertson Planché, a minor British playwright, from Shakespeare's *A Midsummer Night's Dream* and William Sotheby's translation of *Oberon*, a *romantische Heldengedicht* by Christoph Martin Wieland based on medieval legends of the Fairy King Auberon and Huon of Bordeaux, a knight from Charlemagne's court. The score is a motley mix ranging from short instrumental segments to Reiza's *gran scena*, "Ocean! thou mighty monster" – "too beautiful an opera to be consigned to the reference shelf"[17] yet too uneven and dramatically weak to be staged without alteration, which led Gustav Mahler and Felix Weingartner, among others, to revise it extensively.

When John Cox, Artistic Director of Scottish Opera, decided that the time had come to reclaim *Oberon*'s English heritage, he wrote Burgess in February 1983 asking him to write a completely new libretto to go with Weber's music. Responding speedily, Burgess enthused that he would be "only too delighted to have a stab at a new *Oberon* . . . The music is ravishing and deserves something better".[18] Before starting, he wanted to know how much freedom he would be allowed:

> How far should the story-line be changed? It's tempting to do a modernisation, with a girl as a Khomeini hostage and kidnapping instead of slavery. The first scene has television in it. Would that be going too far? Would you prefer to retain what we have in improved language? Clearly, one can't wander too far from the original concept, because Oberon is needed – otherwise, no title . . . I think the opera can be done poetically, wittily, and acceptably, but I'm scared of knowingness and campiness. How free is my hand?[19]

"I hope that you will feel free to be as radical with it as your muse dictates", Cox replied.[20] "Let's retain the title but thereafter it is over to you."[21] With that issue settled, Burgess tackled the project swiftly, completing it within a week. He sent Cox a typescript of the new libretto with a note summarizing his approach:

> One couldn't travel too far away from the original, because the music so much depends on it, but I think a modernisation, a self-conscious A-Effekt (we know we're in an opera and we know it's by Weber) and a bit of humour might make it work. The lyrics fit the music exactly, and, if you agree with the concept, the next job for me is to pencil the words into the score.[22]

Writing in the aftermath of the Iranian Revolution that brought the Ayatollah Khomeini to power in 1979, Burgess drew heavily upon those events and the rise of Islamic fundamentalism. In an obvious analogy to the Iranian crisis of 1979–81, characters in the new version of *Oberon* are taken hostage even though Burgess realized this could soon cause his work to feel dated:

> I don't think a permanent version of this is possible. The opera itself is not great enough. It doesn't deal with permanence; it's an entertainment. The music is brilliant, but the concept as a whole is not one of the great Traviata or

Carmen things. I don't think this will work for more than a couple of years. Someone else must have another go. I was exploiting the topical. The fact is that the original libretto does suggest a modern version, Islam versus the West: Islam is nasty; Planché had Harun Alraschid; and now you have the equivalent in people like the Ayatollah. When I was writing it we had this very topical situation of the Iranian ransom business, with members of the American Embassy in Tehran stuck there and unable to get out. So it struck me as an obvious thing to do.[23]

Burgess replaced Planché's Baghdad with the fictional state of Naraka (representing Iran, not Iraq), the original alias for Brunei in *Devil of a State*. Caliph Harouin Alraschid became Harun, the ruler of Naraka, and acquired a Westernized brother, Lot, a new character. The realm of Charlemagne became the United States with the Franks recast as Americans and Charlemagne, the President. For Oberon's kingdom, Burgess devised a science-fiction atmosphere as a means of retaining the original libretto's supernaturalism, which was too essential to the story to be eliminated. Oberon and Titania are "guardians of the natural order" and Planché's elves, "Roblets". Sir Huon of Bordeaux and Sherasmin his Squire become Hugh and Geoffrey, two US test pilots, while Harouin's daughter Reiza and her attendant Fatima are transformed into Rezia and Selina, "former secretaries in a Western embassy". Hugh and Rezia are the noble young lovers; Geoffrey and Selina, the comic leads.

Almost all of the original score is retained and played in its original order, with nearly every musical number in the new libretto mirroring the dramatic significance of its counterpart in Planché's version.[24] For example, in the updated libretto Act III begins with Selina singing an aria about her home state of New Mexico in place of the ode that Fatima had sung to her native Araby:

Planché	Burgess
O Araby! Dear Araby!	New Mexico, New Mexico;
My own, my native land!	The state where I was born.
Methought I cross'd the dark blue sea,	Where Pluto's palace broods below
And trod again thy strand.	The miles of waving corn.
And there I saw my father's tent	I dreamed I was in Santa Fé,
Beneath the tall date trees,	Back at the old State U.
And the sound of music and merriment	Where I strove so hard to achieve an A
Came sweetly on the breeze.	But had some good times too.
And thus to the lightly touch'd guitar	I'd visit the pueblos just to hear
I heard a maiden tell	The Mexican guitars,
Of one who fled from a proud Serdar,	Or eat my tacos and sip my beer
With the youth she loved so well.	Under Albuquerque's stars.

A persistent flaw in the libretto, evident in this aria, is the tendency for certain deliberately Americanized phrases to sound unnatural to an American ear. For instance, "Back at old NMU" would sound more colloquial than "Back at the old State U." In another example, to bolster Hugh's courage as he sets out in Act III to defeat Harun, Geoffrey employs the British idiom "That's the boy" instead of the common American one, "That a boy!"

In contrast to Planché's mainly serious text, Burgess's version is, as he suggested at the start, full of puns, literary references, and Brechtian *Alienations-Effekt*, though, unfortunately, much of the humor is ham-handed. This excruciating Act II exchange between Geoffrey and Selina illustrates the problem:

> SELINA: What or who is this Oberon guy? I thought he was just someone in Shakespeare – you know, that play with Bottom in it. And you say you've met him. Were you stoned?
> GEOFFREY: I met him all right. He used to be called the fairy king. I always liked the idea of fairies – you know, real ones – not fags, like those down there in the orchestra.
> SELINA: How do you know there are fags down there?
> GEOFFREY: It says so in the score. Fag One and Fag Two.
> SELINA: You dope. Fag means fagotto. A fagotto's a bassoon.
> GEOFFREY: You're right. I forgotto.[25]

The Weber-Burgess *Oberon* opened in Glasgow on 23 October 1985 to generally poor reviews, with Hutchinson publishing *Oberon Old and New*, Burgess's new libretto coupled with Planché's original version, the following day. Burgess skipped the premiere, waiting instead to attend an Oxford performance on 10 December. Writing to John Cox afterward, he expressed great satisfaction with the production, gallantly assuming sole responsibility for any of its shortcomings. In spring 1987, La Fenice staged *Oberon* in Italian using Burgess's own translation, and in conjunction with the production, the Aïghetta Quartet performed his arrangement of the overture for guitar quartet. The Washington Opera and Metropolitan Opera expressed interest in mounting the production, but those prospects fell through as did efforts to present *Oberon* at the Edinburgh Festival.

One composer who tried to persuade Burgess to collaborate on a new opera was Bernard Rands, who envisioned a music theatre work based on the life and letters of Vincent van Gogh. In January 1975 Rands sent Burgess a detailed proposal:

> My knowledge of your work leads me to believe that we share a number of ideas and ideals, and of all English writers today, you are the one I would most like to work with. When I last spent some time with Berio (who is my former teacher and close friend) we discussed the problems of making new works for theatre and in particular the question of collaborations between writers and composers today. My statement that the only English writer with whom I felt a collaboration would be possible was yourself brought an immediate enthusiasm from Berio.[26]

After showing initial interest, Burgess decided not to proceed due to reservations about projects in "outright experimental non-narrative forms".[27] Rands was disappointed ("I still feel a twinge of sadness that the efforts to engage Burgess in the project did not come to fruition"[28]), but successfully converted the van Gogh concept into his award-winning *Le Tambourin* orchestral suites.

Nearly twenty years after translating *L'Enfance du Christ* for Colin Davis in 1966, Burgess was given a second opportunity to provide English words for that Berlioz opus. In May 1984, producer Michael Waterhouse of Thames Television proposed that Burgess "write a dramatic adaptation of the oratorio for television. The work will be sung in French, but I should like to give an English translation in bottom-of-frame subtitles. I thought you would be the best person to approach for a translation that took account of the French verse, but conveyed succinctly the import of the text."[29] Burgess accepted and essentially recycled the version he had written eighteen years earlier, defending his approach thus:

> This translation, like the one of BBC-2, followed the rhythms of the music. The critics mostly scoffed at my words, saying that they would have preferred a literal rendering of the original. But my, and the producer's aim, had been to show what the singers might have been singing had they not, because of the need to sell the programme abroad, been committed to French. An intelligent kind of synaesthesia might have persuaded the critics that they were actually hearing the words they were only scornfully reading. But the obtuseness of critics is a great sorrow to the creative.[30]

An excerpt from the Narrator's opening passage demonstrates the extent to which Burgess was able to preserve Berlioz's rhythms while retaining many of the rhymes. While the translation is certainly not literal, it conveys the sense and spirit of the original text in singable, graceful verse.

Dans la crèche, en ce temps,	On that first Christmas day,
Jésus venait de naître.	When love lay in a manger,
Mais nul prodige encor	No trumpets had proclaimed
ne l'avait fait connaître;	The coming of the stranger.
Et déjà les puissants tremblaient,	But a chill struck the kings of earth
Déjà les faibles espéraient.	While in the meek, raising their heads,
Tous attendaient...	Hope came to birth.

In early 1985, David Pountney, Director of Productions at English National Opera, wrote to request an updated version of *Carmen* for a new production slated for the following season. Burgess took months to decide whether or not to undertake the project but eventually agreed, completing the new libretto by February 1986. In Burgess's words, the question of which version or combination of versions to use "drove me mad when I attempted a new translation for the ENO. Operas are not solid like symphonies; they are overfluid, subject to daily addition, excision, key-change. They have to be tinkered with, and this is like repairing an aircraft already on its journey."³¹ He decided to base his adaptation on the original Opéra-Comique version with spoken dialogue: "For a translator, it is a relief not to have to render recitative, and I hope that my dialogue reproduces some of the flavour of the Mérimée original."³²

Relative to most other English translations, Burgess's version is unusually harsh in tone. In the opening scene, for example, the soldiers' repeated line "drôles de gens que ces gens-là" (What funny folks these people are) is translated as "Look at the fools go to and fro", with *fools* sung on the highest, loudest note each time. Don José's "Flower Song" illustrates further awkwardness:

Meilhac/Halévy original text	Burgess translation
La fleur que tu m'avais jetée,	Carelessly throwing me this token,
dans ma prison m'était restée,	You could not read, nor could I spell,
flétrie et sèche, cette fleur	The message locked within its shell.
gardait toujours sa douce odeur;	I broke the code, inside my cell.
et pendant des heures entières,	For although the petals broke and fell
sur mes yeux fermant mes paupières,	Sick and dry, like human despair,
de cette odeur je m'enivrais	A richer hue, a sweeter smell
et dans la nuit je te voyais!	That spoke of you, Carmen, rode the air.³³

This translation distorts not just the literal meaning of the French text, but, more adversely, the expression of Carmen's attitude. The opening line misrepresents the spirit motivating her action, for, when the gypsy tosses the acacia bloom at Don José, she is anything but careless. Since Bizet's musical setting emphasizes the French rhyme scheme, Burgess's failure to match it throws his libretto into conflict with Bizet's music by displacing the rhymes from the musical stresses. Strangest of all is the omission of the word *flower*, for, unlike virtually every other English translation, in Burgess's version of the aria, this key word is never sung.

Set in a Latin-American auto junkyard, Pountney's staging of Burgess's adaptation succeeded in evoking some sense of the shock that nineteenth-century Parisians must have experienced at *Carmen*'s premiere. The Scottish Opera production premiered in Glasgow in September 1986 followed by an English National Opera production that opened at the London Coliseum on 27 November. Reviews ran the gamut, from a rave in the *Sunday Times* ("compellingly streamlined and very sexy... blessed with the clarity of Anthony Burgess's agreeably racy English version"³⁴) to an acid denunciation in the *Observer* ("one of the ghastliest examples I've seen of an opera on auto-destruct... destroy the atmosphere... destroy the context... destroy the characters... Along the way, destroy the libretto by giving it to Anthony Burgess to rewrite"³⁵). Although he was in London at the time promoting sales of *The Pianoplayers*, Burgess chose not to attend the ENO premiere, shrugging off his non-appearance with world-weary ennui: "I know they are going to do things to the text that I won't approve of . . . On the stage, directors and actors always know better. It's even more true in the film world, where the director might not know English at all. You have to get used to tampering."[36] Confirming his distrust, the 1993 ENO revival, which featured Sally Burgess (no relation) as Carmen, costumed Escamillo as glam rocker Gary Glitter, a stunt that garnered a fair amount of publicity but was condemned for turning the bullfighter into a "posturing clown" instead of a "swaggering charismatic toreador."[37]

The predominantly negative critical response to Burgess's adaptations of *Oberon* and *Carmen* begs the question of what caused this reaction, especially in comparison to the theatrical triumphs that he enjoyed in Minneapolis a decade earlier. The answer lies in the fact that Burgess's skill in writing words to be sung rarely matched his ability as a novelist or adapter of spoken plays. Despite his deep-rooted belief in the relation of words and music, he often lacked the sensitivity to the melody of language that great lyricists possess – the gift of creating the perfect unexpected rhyme or deft turn of phrase that conjoins words and music with an unmistakable sense of rightness and inevitability. Although he could achieve delicacy in his music, his manner of speaking reveals his shortcomings as a lyricist, for he spoke in an aggressive, sometimes hectoring manner, with an accented staccato attack, forced from the back of the throat, that could be almost painful to listen to. No matter how much he may have admired or desired it, the light touch of the natural lyricist was a gift that Burgess simply did not possess.

Notes

1 *Mozart and the Wolf Gang*, 145.
2 Years earlier, Burgess had considered writing a book on music history, as mentioned in a letter to a television producer stating his qualifications to host a program on the history of northern England: "I was minimally trained in the discipline, in Manchester, by A. J. P. Taylor, have published a history of English and have been contemplating for years a History of Western Music." Letter to Norman Swallow, Executive Producer of Granada Television, 11 January 1977.
3 TMM, 95.
4 Ibid., 79.
5 He mistakenly listed the "Twenty-Four Preludes and Fugues for Keyboard" (i.e. *The Bad-Tempered Electronic Keyboard*) under 1983.
6 Frank Kermode, "Maggots, modesty, and Mozart", *The Guardian*, 16 September 1982.
7 TMM, 74; Robert Craft, "Burgess and Music" in *Small Craft Advisories: Critical Articles 1984–1988* (New York: Thames and Hudson, 1989), 238.
8 Example 18: the clarinet parts in bars 16–21 of the fourth movement (TMM, 68).
9 Letter to Martin Bell from Etchingham, 7 July 1965.
10 Introduction, *Don Giovanni* and *Idomeneo*, 22.
11 Volumes featuring V. S. Pritchett on *La Bohème* and Mary McCarthy on *La Traviata* were published the following year, whereupon the series was discontinued.

12 *Der Rosenkavalier*, 28. Compare to the passage in *Inside Mr Enderby* (26) that begins "Oh, she had been graceless and coarse, that one."
13 See "God and Literature and So Forth...", *Observer*, 16 March 1980, 33, 35 [reprinted in A. F. Cassis (ed.), *Graham Greene: Man of Paradox* (Chicago: Loyola University Press, 1994), 317–25]. After this interview was published, Greene famously remarked, "Burgess put words in my mouth which I had to look up in the dictionary" (YH, 358). See RLAB, 381–2.
14 Directed by George Roman, *The Virgin and the Bull* played at Clwyd Theatr Cymru in Flintshire 23 April - 14 May 1983.
15 Georges Mikes, letter to Burgess, 31 December 1982.
16 Mikes's *How to be Poor* (London: André Deutsch, 1983) quotes lines from the song (17) and refers to *The Virgin and the Bull* (11) without mentioning its title.
17 John Warrack, *Carl Maria von Weber* (Cambridge: Cambridge University Press, 1976), 338, 343.
18 Letter to Cox, 18 February 1983.
19 Letter to Cox, 22 March 1983.
20 Cox, letter to Burgess, 4 March 1983.
21 Cox, letter to Burgess, 29 March 1983.
22 Letter to Cox, 6 April 1983.
23 As quoted by Gerald Larner in "Operation Oberon", *Guardian*, 23 October 1985.
24 Only Oberon's entrance (No. 9) and the replacement aria "O, tis a glorious sight to see" are omitted from the adaptation, while the only significant reordings are having Huon's aria (No. 5) open Act II instead of coming just before the Act I finale and positioning the Preghiera (Appendix I) before Rezia's Scene and Aria (No. 13). The numbering of Nos. 16 and 17 is erroneously reversed in *Oberon Old and New* (43, 45).
25 *Oberon Old and New*, 38–9.
26 Rands, letter to Burgess, 14 January 1975. Rands's "Outline for an opera" proposed ten characters (3 male, 7 female), the use of chorus, dancers/mimes, a "normal sized Opera/theatre orchestra" and electronics, and the division of the work into three acts incorporating aspects of non-operatic musical styles and forms, including "Oratorio" and "Concerto".
27 Rands, aerogramme to Burgess from Perth, Australia, 16 February 1975.
28 Rands, email to author, 3 May 2006.
29 Waterhouse, letter to Burgess, 2 May 1984.
30 YH, 123–4.
31 "Coloratura work amid the archive" (review of Winston Dean, *Essays on Opera*), [1990].
32 *Carmen: An Opera in Four Acts*, x. This publication does not include the original French libretto.
33 Ibid., 41–2.
34 Felix Aprahamian, "Drive-in Carmen", *Sunday Times*, 30 November 1986.
35 Nicholas Kenyon, "Chaotic, crashing Carmen", *Observer*, 30 November 1986.
36 As quoted by John Gaskell, "Bizet as Burgess", *Sunday Telegraph*, 30 November 1986.
37 Arline Usden, "Opera: Carmen", *The Lady*, 26 January–1 February 1993.

27

ALEX IN EDEN

> GOD: *Good and evil.*
> ALEX: *It's me that's supposed to be in charge of the slovos.*
> GOD: *Not those two.*[1]

A quarter century after writing *A Clockwork Orange,* Burgess transformed his most famous opus into what he called "a play with music". The change in tone from the novel is startling. What had been a serious fable about good and evil becomes, in the stage version, a satirical black comedy closer to Monty Python than Harold Pinter. Burgess's justification for converting the book into a play was "to stem the flow of amateur adaptations" and "provide a definitive actable version which has auctorial authority", yet, while most previous adapters had taken an earnest approach, Burgess's version reveals a flippant attitude toward *A Clockwork Orange* that had grown ever more strident as his association with the film increasingly threatened to overshadow his reputation as a novelist.[2] When Burgess quipped to Oscar Peterson in 1977 that, of the more than three dozen books he had published by then, *A Clockwork Orange* was the one he liked least, he had not been entirely facetious. Fed up with sanctimonious attitudes toward the book that he had endured for decades from both its proponents and detractors, by 1986 Burgess could no longer resist poking fun at all those who had taken the story's philosophical themes a little too seriously. In the play, as Alex is about to undergo the dreadful Ludovico Treatment, a chorus merrily chirps, "In just a fortnight or two he knows he's going to be free"; an author's note cheekily informs the reader, "The inanity of the words is deliberate. Who the hell knows what freedom is? I don't for one."[3]

The *Clockwork* dramatization offered the bonus of a chance to pay Kubrick back for remaining safely out of sight in his Hertfordshire manor while Burgess took the heat from furious politicians and citizens enraged by what they considered the film's pernicious impact on society. Here was an opportunity for a comic yet cutting response to the director's willful decision to undermine the musical consistency of the novel's protagonist by having Alex, in the notorious rape scene, croon Nacio Herb Brown's best known Hollywood hit. Accordingly, in the play's final scene, as the cast sings "Do not be a clockwork orange, / Freedom has a lovely voice" to the "Ode to Joy" melody, Burgess's script calls for an actor "bearded like Stanley Kubrick" to enter, "playing, in exquisite counterpoint, 'Singin' in the Rain' on a trumpet". After tooting a few bars, the Kubrick look-alike is ingloriously kicked out as the assembled company exuberantly concludes the play with the final couplet of the "Ode to Joy" parody: "Choice is free but seldom easy – / That's what human freedom means!"

But, arguably, Burgess's chief motivation in creating this version of *A Clockwork Orange* was musical. Naturally, he composed his own score for the play. Throughout his career he favored artistic projects that allowed him to merge his creativity with that of his favorite authors and composers, and transforming his novella into a "play with music" was, literally, a chance for Burgess to *play with music*, Beethoven's above all: "It is appropriate that the music chosen for the setting of my harmless little lyrics should be derived from Beethoven ... the Beethoven spirit must be here – the spirit of the mature creative mind which can reconcile the creative and the destructive."[4]

From first page to last, music dominates the play, which begins and ends with song. The considerable extent to which the story has been abridged and dialogue minimized in the play accentuates the music's importance. Alex expresses himself principally through parodies of Beethoven and opera; pastiches of Baroque, English music hall, swing, and pop music are also present in the score, which consists of sixteen musical numbers, two of which are repeated. The script contains thirty-six musical cues, half of them supplied by Burgess's score. The rest are citations of excerpts from specific works (mainly Beethoven's) and general descriptions, such as "atmospheric music", to be rendered freely in each staged production. Burgess wrote a first draft of the music before composing the final version – the one published in the 1998 Methuen edition. Despite notational shortcuts – most of the lyrics are omitted or indicated in the score by just a few key words, for example – this final version matches the script precisely and is suitable for performance with minimal alteration.

The bare-bones score recalls Burgess's theatrical roots in amateur dramatic societies with limited resources: "This is not grand opera. It is a little play which any group may perform." He did not insist that his score be used in productions of the play as long as the Beethovenian element was present: "There are three numbers which call for music of my own, or somebody else's, but the Beethoven spirit must be here." Although only keyboard and voice – plus the aforementioned lone use of a trumpet – are specified in the score, Burgess authorized the discretionary use of additional instruments: "Beethoven is long out of copyright and may be freely banged around on a piano with whatever percussion suggests itself."[5]

Following an instrumental opener (1. Prelude, discussed later in the chapter), Alex and his droogs step out of the Korova Milk Bar, singing "What's it going to be then, eh?" (2. Alex and Droogs; Example 27.01) to

Example 27.01 A Clockwork Orange: 2. Alex and Droogs (bs. 1–6)

the diminished triad motif of the *Dragnet* theme before launching into their "theme song", a celebration of their teenage violence sung in Nadsat to the main theme of the Scherzo of Beethoven's Ninth.[6] As they embark on an evening of mayhem, the droogs whistle the trio of the Scherzo (3. Droogs' March), then thrash Billyboy and his gang in a fight "very exactly choreographed" to the Finale of Beethoven's Seventh (4. Fight Ballet). When the droogs question Alex's right to head their gang, he asserts his dominance in "There's got to be some one in charge" (5. Alex's Song), an original tune in 1940s swing style. Upon encountering F. Alexander, Alex ridicules the writer's manuscript, which bears the "fair gloopy title" *A Clockwork Orange*, by singing an excerpt of its pretentious prose in mock-operatic style (6. Alex's Recitative). The droogs assault F. Alexander and rape his Wife while lewdly singing "In and out, / We love the old in-out" (7. Droogs' Chorus; Example 27.02) to the slow movement of the *Pathétique* Sonata. Back in the Korova Milk Bar, Dim selects a song crooned by Johnny Zhivago (8. Jukebox Song, "You blister my paint"), a Johnny Mathis-like parody of 1950s pop containing lyrics that are a curious blend of vulgarity and polysyllabic sophistication:

Alex in Eden

Example 27.02 A Clockwork Orange: 7. Droogs' Chorus

> When I shove my saint
> Into your quaint
> Cathedral,
> I get all tetrahedral,
> Got no restraint.[7]

Ivesian cacophony ensues when a Girl in a dark corner of the bar sings the "Ode to Joy" while "You blister my paint" blares from the jukebox. As Alex applauds the Beethoven singer, the probation officer Mr Deltoid steps forward and expresses his frustration in a lament (9. What Gets Into You?). Alex responds with a facile explanation sung to the "Ode to Joy", which he whistles in counterpoint to Deltoid's melody. Deltoid and his friends leave the milk bar singing the "Ode to Joy" as does Alex as he leads the droogs out again, this time to the home of the Old Lady, whom Alex murders with her bust of Beethoven. This action lands Alex in jail as he mutters, "And me only just gone fourteen."

In the prison chapel, the inmates sing a pseudo-Lutheran chorale, "Weak tea are we" (10. Prisoners' Hymn).[8] After the sermon, Bach's chorale prelude *Wachet auf* serves as the recessional, preceding the Chaplain's emphatic attempt to dissuade Alex from volunteering for the Ludovico Technique: "When a man cannot choose, he ceases to be a man."[9] Pedofil, a new inmate, enters the prison and is promptly thrashed to death by Alex and four other prisoners as they sing an up-tempo song in English music hall style (11. Discipline). Following this bit of black comedy, Alex, who "has been comparatively unviolent" during the assault, is falsely pegged by the other inmates with the murder and consequently selected by the Governor and the Minister of the Interior for the experimental new treatment. Alex's enthusiastic response is countered by the despondent reaction of the drunken Chaplain, who tearfully sings: " 'God works in a mysterious way / His wonders to perform . . .' " Banal commentary (12. Chorus: "In just a fortnight or two he knows he's going to be free"), sung to the first theme of the first movement of Beethoven's "Pastoral" Symphony, platitudinously extols the idea that Alex will soon be free. As Dr Brodsky prepares to administer the Ludovico Technique, Act One ends with a reprise of "What's it going to be then, eh?"

Act Two opens with the Scherzo of Beethoven's Ninth "thumping away" as Alex undergoes the procedure, crying out in vain that the music be stopped. Once Alex is considered "cured", the Minister of the Interior proudly demonstrates the technique's success by singing an ode to this achievement set to the first theme of the second movement of Beethoven's Fifth Symphony (13. Minister and Chorus: "With some pride Government presents the end-result of Government's experiments"). After watching Alex remain docile and compliant while being abased by a sadistic Comedian, the guests convey their amazement (13a. Chatter Chorus: "It's an experiment that really seems to work") to the second variation of the same movement, which continues playing as the entrance of a beautiful Girl, nearly naked, proves that Alex is physically unable to react either lustfully or violently. Overjoyed, the guests sing triumphantly (13b. Chorus: "Let the heavens rejoice") to the movement's second theme.

After his release from prison Alex returns home, where his callous parents reject him. He encounters his three former comrades, now policemen, who beat him "balletically" to the Scherzo of the Ninth, then winds up at the residence of F. Alexander, who expresses his love for his late wife in the play's most lyrical song (14. She Was All Things to Me; Example 27.03), based on the Adagio of the Ninth. Once the writer's friends arrive and expose Alex's identity, they play the first movement of the Ninth on the stereo to induce his suicide attempt, but Alex survives his leap out of the window, which neutralizes the Ludovico treatment. When the Minister of the Interior pays him a visit at the hospital and presents him with a new stereo set, Alex demonstrates his recovery from Brodsky's behavioral therapy by choosing to listen to the last movement of "The Ninth. The glorious Ninth."

The final scene, which corresponds to the novel's twentieth-first chapter, ends with a blast of satirical levity instead of the moral earnestness of the novel's literary coda. Burgess's disingenuous assertion that, "unlike Kubrick's cinema adaptation", his dramatization "draws on the entirety of the book, presenting at the end a hooligan hero who is now growing up, falling in love, proposing a decent bourgeois life with a wife and family,

Example 27.03 A Clockwork Orange: 14. She Was All Things to Me (bs. 1–12)

and consoling us with the doctrine that aggression is an aspect of adolescence which maturity rejects", neglects to mention the play's slapstick ending.[10] Alex, now eighteen and sporting a moustache, is visibly bored by another reprise of "What's it going to be then, eh?", this one sung by Rick, Len, and Bully, his new droog pals, whom he quickly abandons in favor of his seventeen-year-old girlfriend Marty. When she resists Alex's proposal that they marry and start a family, he explains, to the melody of the "Ode to Joy", how he has matured (15. Finale: "Being young's a sort of sickness"), whereupon he is joined by the entire company in a second, final verse in praise of freedom of choice. At this point the Kubrick clone enters and plays "Singin' in the Rain" against the "Ode to Joy" (Example 27.04) just long enough to make the contrapuntal point before being booted off the stage.

Example 27.04 A Clockwork Orange: 15. Finale (bars 51–56)

Returning now to the play's musical opening, one recognizes it as yet another response to Kubrick's film, albeit a much subtler one than the final scene's farcical prank. The Prelude, an acerbic mock-Baroque overture full of modern discords, calls to mind the "nasty-ized" version of Purcell's *Music for the Funeral of Queen Mary* in the film's opening sequence. Whereas Wendy Carlos distorted the Purcell original through electronic sound modification, Burgess achieved an analogous effect by distorting the

Alex in Eden

Example 27.05 A Clockwork Orange: 1. Prelude (bs. 1–21)

underlying consonant harmonies through dissonance. By comparing the Prelude as written (Example 27.05) with a recomposed version (Example 27.06) that eliminates the dissonances, the underlying Handelian harmonies are revealed.

Example 27.06 A Clockwork Orange: 1. Prelude (bs. 1–16, reharmonized in Baroque style)

A stage production of *A Clockwork Orange* in German ran for six months in 1988 at the municipal theatre in Bonn; as Burgess noted in his autobiography, "My *Singspiel* version of *Uhrwerk Orange* has been performed in Bonn: this was an insolent affront to Beethoven's birthplace, since most of the songs and choruses are perversions of Beethoven."[11] The German punk rock band *Die Toten Hosen* provided its own original music for that production, and, on 31 October 1988, released an album titled *Ein kleines bisschen Horrorschau: Die Lieder aus* Clockwork Orange *und andere schmutzige Melodien* (A little bit of horrorshow: The songs from *Clockwork Orange* and other dirty melodies), which includes six songs from the Bonn production linked together by excerpts from Beethoven's Ninth. The play's title song, "*Hier kommt Alex*" (Here comes Alex) – the first track on the album – became one of the band's best known songs and is featured in *Guitar Hero III: Legends of Rock*.

In 1990, the Royal Shakespeare Company presented a revised version of the play at the Barbican Theatre in London. Titled *A Clockwork Orange 2004*, it featured music by The Edge (Dave Evans), guitarist of the rock band U2, and starred Phil Daniels as Alex. This revision, adapted by director Ron Daniels with Burgess's approval and published by Arrow in 1990, improves upon the earlier version of the play by restoring passages from the novel, altering dialogue, and deleting some of the weaker musical numbers.

Burgess's music for *A Clockwork Orange* was performed in a US production of the play presented by the Fabulous and Ridiculous Theatre in May 2000. Directed by AnnaCatherine Rutledge, this staging at the John Henry Faulk Living Theatre in Austin, Texas, featured a cross-gendered cast led by Sonya Tsuchigane as Alex. Later that year, Rutledge reprised *A Clockwork Orange* in New York City at ShowWorld.

A previously unpublished prologue by Burgess (Appendix 3) adds an entertaining mock-Biblical dimension to the play. Set in the Garden of Eden as a scene that Alex is dreaming, this comic parody of Adam and Eve tasting the forbidden fruit introduces the principal *Clockwork* themes of freedom of choice and the conflict between good and evil.[12] Alex, his girlfriend Marty, the Prison Chaplain, and the Minister of the Interior are given alternate Biblical identities. Alex as Adam and Marty as Eve are joined first by God (played by the Chaplain actor), then by a satanic character "dressed in a suit of snakeskin" (played by the Minister actor). The setting is "Early morning, delicate greenish light, a tumult of bird-song" as the prologue opens with Alex and Marty discussing – indeed, creating – language.

>   ALEX: Zavtrak.
>   MARTY: What's zavtrak?
>   ALEX: It's a word that just came. Like all words. It means the first thing you eat when you stop spatting.
>   MARTY: Spatting?
>   ALEX: This. *(He does an exaggerated and brutal mime of sleep.)*
>   MARTY: What you mean is breakfast.
>   ALEX: Zavtrak tastes better. Or will when I've had it.
>   MARTY: I'll pick you some fruit.

The naked couple confronts God, then Lucifer, as they strive to make sense of the newly created world in which they find themselves. Alex, as Adam, is curious, proud, quick-witted – not afraid to stand up to God, or, as he refers to him in Nadsat, Bog, which God, apparently unfamiliar with Russian, does not seem to understand.

>   ALEX: Bog.
>   GOD: What's that?
>   ALEX: Bog. You said I'd got to give names to everything. Ptitsa – the thing that flies. Devotchka – her. Yarblocko – the hard round thing that grows on trees and that I'm fed up of eating. Bog – you.

GOD: Beware of the yellow yarblocko.
ALEX: Now I pony. You never skaz about why beware. Why?
GOD: You must not know too much.
ALEX: Why not?
GOD: Because there's limits.
MARTY: *Are* limits.
GOD: I stand corrected.
MARTY: Sit you mean.

God, long-bearded and in spotless white, tries to explains the rules of his world to the couple. "Free will has to have limits. Your will must not be as free as mine. You see that?" Alex/Adam wants to know why God is warning him not to eat the yellow yarblocko if "it's there to eat. Reach up my rooker, pull it down, munch munch. Too easy, isn't it?" God explains: "It's a way of testing your capacity for obedience. You're free to obey and free to disobey. That's free will. That's choice." God, evidently troubled, relates how "the one I placed in charge of the light" caused problems in heaven by deciding "that he was as free as I am. Free as I am meant being me. You see that?" But God was not free to stop him: "That's not in the rules ... Once rules are made, they're not to be changed. I detest the arbitrary." He sternly warns Alex not to eat the fruit, describing in grim detail the ills that will be visited upon the world if it is tasted. "Take it away then", pleads Alex. "No," answers God. "Remember the rules."

Puzzled by God's incomprehensible rules and explanations, Alex turns to nature to ease his confusion as God departs. Hearing a birdcall, Alex whistles in imitation, creating his own cantilena. Excited by this act of composition, Alex goes on whistling as Marty enters with a basket of fruit.

ALEX: Did you hear that? *(He whistles again)*
MARTY: Nice. But what's it for?
ALEX: It needs a slovo. Mouse sick. Moose sick. I call it music.
MARTY: But what's it for?
ALEX: It just is.
MARTY: Listen – I met this man –
ALEX: Man? You can't have. I'm the only one. So far.

As Alex tries to embrace her, Marty drops several pieces of fruit. Alex's attention is caught by "the large yellow one, orange really, that he picks up from the ground. He holds it gingerly to his ear."

ALEX: There's a noise inside. Like ticking. Ticking. I just made up that slovo. We'd better see what's inside. *(He pauses)* It was only eating he said, wasn't it? No harm in looking. We viddy it every day.
MARTY: It smells all right.
Alex breaks the rind and juice spatters on to his hand. He licks it.
MARTY: Now you've eaten it.
ALEX: I don't call that eating. Taste.
She tastes.

At the exact moment that Marty samples the forbidden fruit, the Ninth Symphony bursts forth from the heavens. As the "Ode to Joy" resounds, the Minister enters, dressed in his snakeskin suit. He tells Alex and Marty that the "old thunderer" wanted them to taste the fruit:

> MINISTER: Now things are going to be interesting... Men and women exhibiting the most incredible kinds of ingenuity, the delicious fruits of disobedience. And they have to be ruled, of course. They have to be told how to be good. You too, my little friend.
> ALEX: I know all about it. I'm *not* your little friend. I don't have to be told. We have to have the two veshches [good and evil] or there wouldn't be anything to choose. It's the choosing that counts.
> MINISTER: I'll choose for you. That's my privilege.
> ALEX: I'll choose for myself. That's mine.

The Minister and Alex argue as the lights dim and the sound of wind drowns out the music. Alex tries to warm himself as the Minister exits, laughing. Suddenly cold, Alex huddles on the ground, then "wakes to the music of the Prelude. It was all a dream. Naked, he is speedily dressed by his three friends or droogs. The play begins."

Notes

1 Prologue to *A Clockwork Orange*.
2 *A Clockwork Orange: a play with music*, ix.
3 Ibid., 25.
4 Ibid., x.
5 Ibid.
6 Credited in 1947 to Walter Schumann for his theme to the original *Dragnet* radio series, Miklós Rózsa later successfully sued Schumann for having plagiarized this diminished triad motif from Rózsa's score for the 1946 film *The Killers*, where it occurs prominently near the end of the film in the restaurant scene.
7 ACO-PM, 9. The lyrics recall a passage from *The Doctor is Sick* (163) in which Edwin Spindrift is reminded by the North African woman known as Carmen of a song with similar words: "For some reason a Spanish folk song he had once heard on the Third Programme – 'Let me put my little saint in your chapel' – came into his mind, and he foolishly said the words aloud. 'Notty,' said Carmen with joy, and she swung her heavy body an instant so that the cathedrals wagged obscenely."
8 In the original manuscript of the novella, Burgess notated the words of this chorale to a different melody. See Biswell, "Editing and Publishing *A Clockwork Orange*", in *Portraits of the Artist in* A Clockwork Orange, 20.
9 ACO-PM, 19.
10 Ibid., ix.
11 YH, 390.
12 In *Earthly Powers* (167–70), Kenneth Toomey reinterprets the Garden of Eden from a homosexual perspective in his novella *A Way Back to Eden*.

28

THE SAD SUCK-AND-BLOW

> *Of all musical instruments, the harmonica and the guitar are the most difficult to write for: you have to know how they work before you can scribble notes for them.*[1]

To Burgess, the mouth organ was the "most melancholy of instruments", a sonic symbol of World War I and the grim fate of countless doughboys holed up along the Somme between 1914 and 1918.[2] Many an anxious British infantryman attempted to preserve a bit of normalcy in the trenches by playing familiar tunes on his "Tommy Atkins", a diatonic harmonica of the time similar to the Hohner "Blues Harp" commonly played by folk and rock musicians today. In *The Wanting Seed*, the mouth organ's presence conjures up the dismal atmosphere of the Great War even though the plot is set well into the future. As the restless soldiers in Tristram Foxe's platoon anxiously await battle, the mournful sound of a harmonica is heard. To this reedy suck-and-blow accompaniment, the troops sing a sad little song that transports Tristram, a historian by profession, "to a time and place he had never visited before", making him feel as if he were suddenly in World War I, experiencing firsthand the era of "Kitchener, napoo, Bottomley, heavies, archies, zeppelins, Bing Boys".[3]

The 1920s brought the development of the chromatic harmonica, which enabled a player to produce all twelve notes of the scale through the use of a small hand-controlled spring mechanism able to raise or lower the pitch in each air hole by a semitone. Thanks largely to the talent and fame of Larry Adler (1914–2001), the chromatic mouth organ (as Adler insisted on calling it) became a popular solo instrument in the 1930s. His name became virtually synonymous with the harmonica, especially once the Hohner Company named its four-octave model "The Larry Adler Professional 16" even though Adler preferred the twelve-hole model instead, which encompassed three octaves plus one note, with middle C its lowest pitch. In 1936, Cyril Scott wrote *Serenade* for Adler; Jean Berger, Darius Milhaud, Malcolm Arnold, Gordon Jacob, Arthur Benjamin, and Ralph Vaughan Williams composed works for him in the 1940s and '50s. Adler's two great contemporaries, John Sebastian (1914–80) and Tommy Reilly (1919–2000), further expanded the harmonica's repertoire by inspiring compositions from Heitor Villa-Lobos, Luciano Chailly, Alexander Tcherepnin, Frank Lewin, George Kleinsinger, Norman Dello Joio, Alan Hovhaness, and Henry Cowell (for Sebastian), and Michael Spivakowsky, Graham Whettam, Gordon Jacob, Paul Patterson, and James Moody (for Reilly).

The only composer to write music for Adler, Sebastian, and Reilly was Anthony Burgess, who once reflected, "God has put me on earth to, among other things, write for the harmonica."[4] He met Sebastian first, in Rome in the early 1970s while both were residing there. As fellow musicians and English-speaking émigrés, a warm bond soon developed between them: "To me he was a good friend, a supreme intermediary between the American and European cultures and the man who taught me to appreciate Italy."[5] Sebastian, a Philadelphia native of Italian heritage, had become the first harmonica virtuoso to perform an entirely classical repertoire, first by adapting music from the seventeenth and eighteenth centuries, then by performing works that he commissioned. Incessant piano problems on tour had convinced Sebastian that it would be much simpler and less expensive to perform with a guitarist instead; all he needed was enough music to fill up two hours of recital time with arrangements and original compositions. Upon discovering that Burgess was a composer, Sebastian commissioned him to compose two works for harmonica and guitar intended to constitute part of this new repertoire.

Burgess composed *Faunal Noon* and the Sonatina in E minor for Sebastian in the late summer of 1972.[6] Sailing with his family from Naples to New York aboard the ocean liner *Leonardo da Vinci*, Burgess wrote the compositions in his usual manner, without consulting a keyboard: "As I penned my notes, a drinking mafioso told me that you not a write a music a that a way, you use a pianoforte, so I told him to stick to his killing business and I would stick to mine."[7] Little is known about this lost music for Sebastian apart from brief comments published a decade later in a guitar magazine: "I wrote him first a little Pierné-like fantasy called *Faunal Noon*, with a cautious guitar part that proved awkward to finger but didn't have to be substantially changed by the player. More ambitious, I then produced a sonatina in three movements whose guitar part didn't have to be changed at all. I was proud of this."[8]

For steering him back to composition and teaching him how to write for the mouth organ ("John produced a very useful guide to the harmonica, showing what chords were possible and what not, and I keep this carefully in my files"), Sebastian earned Burgess's lasting gratitude. Although it was surely an exaggeration to write "I doubt if I would have returned to music at all if it had not been for John Sebastian's encouragement", the affection and admiration that Burgess expressed in his memorial essay "John Sebastian – A Personal Reminiscence" seem unusually genuine:

> I knew him as a lover of art and literature before I was aware of his skill and reputation as a musician. He was, in fact, an all-round Renaissance man –

handsome, a great reader, a great traveller, learned in painting and sculpture, a fine cook, and exquisitely well-informed in all branches of classical, romantic and modern music. As for popular music, he left that to his son [John B. Sebastian of the Lovin' Spoonful], who carried the same name as himself and had a greater reputation – though only among young American aficionados of rock ... He was without doubt the finest harmonica virtuoso of our day, and I was angry when the new Grove Dictionary of Music (1980) gave lengthy entries for both Adler and Reilly but did not mention John Sebastian at all.[9]

A guest appearance on a BBC television show led to Burgess's next harmonica convergence. Upon learning that he and Tommy Reilly would be guests on the same 8 March 1977 broadcast of *Oscar Peterson Invites* two weeks after Burgess's sixtieth birthday, he decided to celebrate the occasion by composing a piece for harmonica and piano that they could – and did – perform together on the program.

Tommy Reilly had learned to play the mouth organ in his native Ontario where his father, a Canadian bandmaster and orchestral conductor, founded and led a prize-winning harmonica band in the early 1930s. Trained as a violinist, Reilly was studying violin at the Leipzig Conservatory when he was arrested by the Nazis in September 1939 and forced to spend the next five and a half years in prison camps in Germany, Poland, and France. Allowed to retain his harmonica, Reilly used the time in captivity to master the instrument, developing unparalleled virtuosity, based on Jascha Heifetz's style of violin playing, which would redefine the limits of harmonica technique. After the war, Reilly settled in England where he performed and recorded with many leading conductors and orchestras, most notably Sir Neville Marriner and the Academy of St Martin in the Fields, which released two recordings featuring him as soloist. Classical composers wrote over thirty works for Reilly, of whom Stravinsky once said, "After hearing your interpretation of my *Chanson Russe*, I would be happy to let you play anything of mine." Equally successful playing popular music, Reilly worked with many top stars, from Bing Crosby to George Harrison, and recorded extensively for television and film, where the sound of his playing is familiar from the themes of *Gunsmoke*, *Rawhide*, *The Fugitive*, and *Midnight Cowboy*.

Burgess's piece for Tommy Reilly, completed in Monaco on 15 February 1977, is a melodious ballad called *Romanza*.[10] This three-minute piece, structured as a brief introduction followed by a pair of andante A sections surrounding a scherzando B section, employs the harmonica's full three-octave range. The introduction (Example 28.01) consists of an unhurried cantabile melody above lush eleventh-chord harmonies in the piano that drift up and down by half step in the style of cocktail lounge improvisation; the first A section, which begins in bar 8, introduces the main theme while establishing the tonic key of A♭ major. The jaunty B section begins in bar 31 (Example 28.02); four years later, this melody would reemerge as the opening theme of *A Glasgow Overture*.

Example 28.01 *Romanza* (bs. 1–11)

The performance of *Romanza* with Tommy Reilly was one of the rare televised instances of Burgess playing piano. The following month, Reilly wrote Burgess an enthusiastic letter saying that he intended to give additional performances of *Romanza* "on the radio here and on the continent" and to record it, but these plans were never carried out.[11]

Burgess met Larry Adler in 1980 at a London cocktail party during the publicity tour for *Earthly Powers*. Of the three great harmonica virtuosi with whom Burgess came into contact (all of them North Americans who wound up living in Europe), Adler, a Baltimore native, achieved the greatest stardom, performing in vaudeville, on Broadway, and in Hollywood, where he appeared in six films between 1934 and 1948. Like Benny Goodman, Adler was equally adept at playing jazz, popular, or classical music. He counted Eddie Cantor, Fred Astaire, George and Ira Gershwin, Lorenz

Example 28.02 *Romanza* (bs. 31–6)

Hart, Igor Stravinsky, and Ralph Vaughan Williams among his friends, and benefited from a provision in Maurice Ravel's will exempting him from paying royalties on *Bolero* when he performed it. Beginning with his acclaimed 1953 score for *Genevieve*, Adler also became a successful film composer despite the fact that he did not learn to read music until his mid-thirties, when, at the insistence of Ingrid Bergman, he took lessons from Ernst Toch before emigrating to England in 1949 to avoid political persecution during the McCarthy era.

Having already written music for Sebastian and Reilly, Burgess was eager to score a musical hat trick: "Now it only remained for me to compose for Larry the eagle and one of the minor patterns of my life would be fulfilled."[12] On 10 November 1980 he completed Pieces for Harmonica, a three-movement work he dedicated and sent to Adler from Monaco without retaining a copy himself.[13] Six years later he composed Sonatina for Harmonica and Guitar, his last completed work for mouth organ. (An incomplete, undated Concerto for Harmonica and String Orchestra, abandoned after the first 190 bars of the opening movement, is Burgess's only other extant work for the instrument.[14])

Description of the Pieces for Harmonica is limited by the poor quality of the sole available copy of the score, a partially illegible fax in the HRC archive able to provide only a general idea of the music. The work comprises three pieces in contrasting styles, each about two minutes long: "Rigadoon", stylistically akin to Bach's Brandenburg Concerto No. 2, with

The Sad Suck-and-Blow

Example 28.03 Sonatina for Harmonica and Guitar, 1. Allegro vivo (bs. 1–8)

a fast-moving melodic line in the harmonica; "Siciliana", a flowing air in E♭ major; and "Fantasia on the Keel Row", a lively C major number that ends with a rousing presto coda.

Sonatina for Harmonica and Guitar, a much more substantial work nearly three times as long as the other, harks back to the pieces Burgess composed for John Sebastian fourteen years earlier, although its D major key minimizes the possibility that it could be a recreation of the earlier E minor composition. Completed on 9 June 1986, its sprightly tempi, rapid passagework, extensive chromaticism, and disjunct melodies demand great technical facility from both players. It begins with a D major sonata-form movement that opens with both instruments playing in octaves (Example 28.03). The second movement is closely based on the opening theme of *Rome in the Rain* (Example 20.01), whose espressivo quality and accompanying arpeggios lend themselves perfectly to the new medium. Burgess transposed the music from C to E in the sonatina and later reused it, again in E major, in the second movement of his *Concerto Grosso pour Quatuor de Guitares et Orchestre en La mineur*. The Scherzo (Presto giocoso) relies heavily upon perfect fourths melodically and harmonically; at the trio, marked *con ironia*, the key shifts from A to a polytonal combination of F minor in the harmonica against C major in the guitar. The allegro non troppo Finale, loosely structured in sonata form, borrows two themes from *Moses the Lawgiver* that recur in the Third Symphony: "Moses's Song" (Ex. 15.01) and "Egyptian March", the former arriving in the guitar at bar 13 in D major, the latter in the harmonica at bar 62 in C♯ major.

The music Burgess composed for Adler made little impression upon its recipient. Adler, a self-described "melody man"[15], considered Burgess's compositions insufficiently tuneful and ill-suited to the mouth organ. Although Adler considered him a friend and was grateful for Burgess's glowing review of his 1984 autobiography *It Ain't Necessarily So* in the *Observer*, he never played any of the compositions Burgess wrote for him. For his part, Burgess never asked him to. Referring to the Pieces for Harmonica, he shrugged off Adler's neglect of his music philosophically: "I wrote him a dissonant baroque suite but, so far as I know, he has never played it. No matter." Of his association with Sebastian, Reilly, and Adler, Burgess mused that he was somehow fated to compose for these three maestros of the mouth organ: "The connection between that instrument and the kind of books I wrote was in doubt, but the three supreme players were somehow drawn to me as I to them. Something to do, perhaps, with my essentially vulgar psyche aspiring to high art, the sad suck-and-blow of the Somme elevated likewise."[16]

Despite being ignored by Adler, the Sonatina for Harmonica and Guitar proved to be a pivotal composition for Burgess. After writing it in 1986, he shifted his attention from the harmonica to the guitar, and that year began composing a series of works for solo guitar and guitar quartet that rank among his finest compositions.

Notes

1 "John Sebastian - A Personal Reminiscence". Typescript © 1988.
2 *The Wanting Seed*, 240.
3 Ibid., 241.
4 YH, 365.
5 "John Sebastian - A Personal Reminiscence".
6 See YH, 267–8. Both works are erroneously listed in TMM under 1973.
7 YH, 268.
8 "The Guitar and I", *Classical Guitar* (1:3), Jan/Feb 1983, 23.
9 "John Sebastian - A Personal Reminiscence".
10 TMM lists it as *"Tommy Reilly's Maggot* for harmonica and piano". According to Reilly's manager Sigmund Groven, Burgess was noncommittal about the title: "Tommy remembers Mr. Burgess saying that "you may call it 'Ballad' or 'Romanza' or whatever you like!" Groven, letter to author, 15 January 1999.
11 "I hope to put it on the harmonica & piano L.P. I am making with Richard Rodney Bennett. I don't think he will object to playing it even though you & he have (*sic*) some differences some time ago." Tommy Reilly, letter to Burgess, 6 April 1977.
12 YH, 365. Adler means eagle in German.
13 This work is listed in TMM as "*Larry Adler's Maggots* for harmonica and piano".

14 Written for a four-octave instrument, the solo part in the concerto extends down to the C an octave below middle C. Throughout the score (which Burgess playfully autographed "Antoine Bourgeois"), each of the string sections is written divisi, requiring a total of ten string staves per system. The abundance of different tempi – five within the sixteen-page fragment – suggests a piecemeal compositional approach that was ultimately unsustainable.
15 Larry Adler interview with author, London, 14 April 2000.
16 YH, 365.

29

ONE-HANDED CLAVICHORD

> *In the symphony I wrote a few years ago for performance in Iowa City I introduced a mandolin part among the second violins. But it can't touch the guitar, an instrument which has the difficult nobility of a great disease.*[1]

The guitar is a recurring presence in Burgess's novels and compositions, from Richard Ennis in *A Vision of Battlements* up to the works for the Aïghetta Quartet composed in the late 1980s. After Ennis came a series of shadowy strummers like the lanky young balladeer in *The Doctor is Sick*, the Hippogriff Club's West Indian singer in *The Right to an Answer*, the surly English expatriate in *Beard's Roman Women*, and the unshaven thrummer in *Any Old Iron*, all anonymous and none as memorable as Burgess's first protagonist. In *A Vision of Battlements*, the alluring widow Concepción plays a little minuet that Ennis had written especially for her: "It was in E minor, an easy key for the guitar." Ennis's music is the prelude to their passion, for, moments later, as a downpour erupts overhead, "The rains broke in him. A single stride in his clumsy boots, he held her . . . Then spoke the thunder."[2]

In a case of life imitating art, in 1969 Burgess encouraged his new wife to take guitar lessons and "wrote little minuets for her in E minor, a key whose three principal chords are easy on the guitar."[3] Years later, when Liana resumed lessons after a long hiatus, he began composing for the guitar anew. On 25 September 1986, Liana's fifty-seventh birthday, he presented her with a "Birthday Greeting" for guitar with piano accompaniment. Like the violin etude at the end of *The Pianoplayers* (published the same year), the guitar part is played entirely on open strings above chromatic keyboard harmonies. Three months later he composed *Pezzetto per Chitarra* for a total stranger from Sweden who had written asking about his guitar music. Burgess strummed the guitar a bit himself, learning to play his own arrangement of *Greensleeves*, his minuet in E minor, and a few other short pieces including "a Bach minuet at the speed of a sarabande."[4] Other extant guitar pieces include an undated Fugue and Impromptu (the latter closely related to the Quodlibet from *Mr W.S.*) and the 1986 Sonatina for Harmonica and Guitar, while the lost works include an "unplayable" Guitar Sonata in E composed in Banbury in 1951, the pieces for harmonica and guitar written for John Sebastian in 1972, and the 1981 composition *Preludio e Fuga per flauto, violino, chitarra e pianoforte* listed in *This Man and Music*.

The Aïghetta Quartet, an ensemble founded in Monte Carlo in 1979 by André-Michel Berthoux, Alexandre Del Fa, François Szönyi, and Philippe Loli, played a large role in rekindling Burgess's interest in the guitar. In 1986 Burgess met Loli in Monaco's Académie de Musique and engaged him to give Liana guitar lessons. Upon learning about the Aïghetta Quartet, Burgess offered to compose a work for the ensemble. Loli accepted, expecting it to take months, but, to his amazement, Burgess completed *Quatuor (N° 1) pour Guitares* just four days later on Easter Sunday (30 March 1986).[5]

Subtitled *Quatuor en hommage à Maurice Ravel*, Burgess's first guitar quartet is an appealing, well-crafted work in three movements with strong thematic and harmonic ties to his Violin Concerto and Third Symphony. The rapidity with which Burgess composed the quartet is largely attributable to his customary self-borrowing, with material from the concerto used in the middle movement and from the symphony in the outer ones. The sonata-form opening movement is based on two subjects from the symphony's second movement. The first theme (Example 29.01) enters in G major, as in the symphony (Example 17.05), with variants of this theme serving as fugal subjects in the development and coda; the second theme (marked "Plus lent, cantabile") arrives in G minor in the quartet (Example 29.02), a tone lower than in the symphony (Example 17.06). The

Example 29.01 *Quatuor N° 1 pour Guitares*, I. Très vif (bs. 1–10)

Example 29.02 *Quatuor N° 1 pour Guitares*, I. Très vif (bs. 33–42)

minor form of the ground (Example 23.03) from the Violin Concerto's second movement serves as the basis of the quartet's second movement, a wistful passacaglia (Assez lent) in F minor. Like the first movement, the lively finale (Très vivace) is in G major, contains fugal passages, and borrows themes from the symphony's second movement, including the one illustrated in Example 17.07. Despite its subtitle, the quartet's style draws less from French music than from the English fount that inspired Burgess's orchestral works of the previous dozen years: "It flirts with the polytonality of Darius Milhaud but in other respects may be regarded as very British."[6] In the 1988 essay "The Twenty-four-string Guitar", Burgess associates his first guitar quartet with Purcell, Poulenc, and that celebrated lutenist Don Quixote, who accompanies himself on the vihuela while singing an original ballad in Cervantes's great novel.[7]

> I make no great claims for my Quatuor. Though dedicated to the memory of Ravel, it is closer to Poulenc than to that half-Basque master. Written on Monegascan ground, it is aware of the vast stretch of French territory all around (except for the Mediterranean) and of the fact that you can get on the train at Monte Carlo and cross the Pyrenees in a few hours. In the last movement I had a very clear image of the lean knight and the fat squire taking the road. It is hard to expunge the Spanish, since one has so many clear memories of the illiterate flamenco masters just north of Gibraltar. The second movement

is a passacaglia. I was thinking there more of our own English tradition – not the lutenist one but the Purcellian one, since Purcell was the great master of the passacaglia.[8]

Quatuor N° 2 pour Guitares, completed in Lugano on 19 July 1988, is the most substantial of Burgess's three guitar quartets, for it possesses the greatest number of movements (four), is the longest in duration (sixteen minutes), and is the only one not based upon previous compositions.[9] The Prélude (poco lento; senza misura), comprising an unmeasured cadenza divided between the four guitars, proceeds attacca into the first movement, Fuga, which is based on an atonal, three-bar subject (Example 29.03) containing all but one of the twelve tones.[10] The Scherzo, a 6/8 presto abounding in three-against-two rhythms, repeated-note motifs, and whole-tone sonorities, includes a fughetto on a jig-like subject midway through the movement. The soothing harmonies and moderato tempo of the Chorale, the quartet's longest movement, precede the Rondo finale, which begins in D minor and, after multiple modulations, ends in F major; a melodious folkloric theme in E minor (Example 29.04) provides one the movement's longer periods of harmonic stability.

Example 29.03 *Quatuor N° 2 pour Guitares*, I. Fuga. Molto moderato (bs. 1–6)

Example 29.04 *Quatuor N° 2 pour Guitares*, IV. Rondo. Allegro (bs. 88–96)

Example 29.05 *Quatuor N° 3 pour Guitares*, I. Allegro vivace (bs. 1–9)

On 19 November 1989, Philippe Loli wrote to Burgess requesting a new quartet for the Aïghetta Quartet to premiere at a music festival in Arles the following summer. Burgess quickly obliged by composing *Quatuor No. 3 pour Guitares*, completing it on 28 December. There are no breaks between the work's three movements, the first of which begins with an inverted V-shaped, twelve-tone motif (adjoining whole-tone scales, one ascending followed by one descending), which enters imitatively in all four voices (Example 29.05).[11] In the meditative Andantino, a delicate series of cantando melodies are layered contrapuntally one above the other. The last movement, which, like the first, alternates between fast and slower tempos, borrows material from *Blooms of Dublin* and the Violin Concerto, shifting between a theme based on "Flower of the Mountain" (Example 24.03) and a variant of the concerto finale's first theme (Example 23.04).

These three attractive works represent a significant contribution to the guitar quartet repertoire and are the first Burgess compositions to have been commercially recorded. The Aïghetta Quartet recorded the first quartet in 1987, releasing it on a recording titled *Oeuvres pour Quatuor de Guitares* that also included music by J. S. Bach, Ferdinando Carulli, Antonio Ruiz-Pipó, and Robert Delanoff.[12] Two years later the Aïghetta Quartet brought out a recording of the second quartet on a CD that is also titled *Oeuvres pour Quatuor de Guitares* yet is an entirely different recording than the 1987 LP, containing music by Federico Moreno Torroba and other works by Delanoff.[13] In 1996, the Aïghetta Quartet (with Pascal Rabatti replacing André-Michel Berthoux) released all three quartets on the CD *Musique d'un écrivain anglais sur la Riviera*.[14]

Between the first two quartets, Burgess composed two large-scale works for guitar and orchestra plus two transcriptions for guitar quartet. *Concerto per Chitarra ed Orchestra en Mi minore* is a sprawling work in three movements inscribed "Monaco, 21 jan. 1987" and dedicated to Philippe Loli, the intended soloist. As in the case of the first guitar quartet, Burgess stressed the work's English character:

> Of the works for guitar and orchestra composed in our day, I note that some are Spanish and have a strong Spanish flavour, while others are progressive and atonal. In other words, some smell of Andalusia and others of

Schoenberg's Vienna. But there is in my native country a tradition of guitar-playing which dates back to the great John Dowland, whom Shakespeare admired, whose instrument was the lute, ancestor of the modern guitar. My aim was to compose a guitar concerto which should be in the English tradition – tonal, melodic, formally orthodox. It should also provide an opportunity to display the exceptional skill of Philippe Loli in extended cadenzas. Here is the work – in three movements and of thirty minutes duration. At one point, with British irony, I allow a Spanish flavour to intrude, but that is only to emphasise how fundamentally non-Spanish the work is.[15]

The opening E minor Rondo, based on an arching melody (Example 29.06) later reemployed in Sonata No. 4 for Great Bass Recorder and Pianoforte, affords the guitarist numerous solo passages, culminating in a lengthy cadenza preceding the coda. The modal harmony and mixture of pastoral and march-like styles in the Andantino, which alternates flowing music in 7/8 with a faster contrasting subject in 2/4, makes it the most English sounding movement. The Finale, a robust movement in E minor featuring bitonality, polymetric interplay, and fugal writing, opens with an energetic theme (Example 29.07) introduced by the orchestra before being taken over by the soloist; the second theme, a quirky waltz played "*con ironia*", adds a touch of mirth to this otherwise rather serious concerto.

Concerto Grosso pour Quatuor de Guitares et Orchestre en La mineur, one of Burgess's most appealing compositions and a worthy addition to the limited repertoire of works for guitar quartet and orchestra, was composed shortly thereafter. Having completed the Guitar Concerto on 21 January and *Mr Burgess's Almanack* on 24 February, Burgess finished the *Concerto Grosso* that spring sometime between 20 March (the completion date of the first movement) and 1 June 1987 (the date on the piano reduction).

Example 29.06 *Concerto per Chitarra*, I. Allegro moderato (bs. 8–11)

Example 29.07 *Concerto per Chitarra*, III. Allegro molto vivace (bs. 3–9)

It is nearly identical in instrumentation to the Guitar Concerto – both requiring pairs of woodwinds, full brass (4331), timpani, percussion, and strings – and contains some of Burgess's most imaginative instrumental writing, including a passage in the first movement in which a theme, played in chordal harmony by a trio of muted trumpets, is accompanied by the orchestral strings playing *col legno* while the four guitarists pound their instruments *sul legno*. The first performance took place on 26 February 1989 in Cannes, performed by the Aïghetta Quartet with Philippe Bender conducting the Orchestre Régional de Cannes Provence Alpes Côte d'Azur; later that year, in an interview with Jeremy Isaacs on the BBC series *Face to Face*, Burgess described this premiere as one of the most joyful experiences of his compositional career.[16]

The opening movement is an especially straightforward example of sonata form in Burgess's music, with an exposition repeat, clearly defined development and recapitulation sections, and a coda that begins with the main theme in the tonic key; a particular sequence of ascending fourths in the second theme (bs. 60–61 in Example 29.08) is a motif that recurs in

Example 29.08 *Concerto Grosso pour Quatuor de Guitares*, I. Allegro non troppo (bs. 57–64)

two later works, the Quartet for Flute, Oboe, 'Cello and Piano and the Sonatina for Recorder. The Andantino is another refacimento of *Rome in the Rain*, whose dreamy character transfers as beautifully to the tender sonority of four guitars accompanied by soft sustained strings as it did to harmonica and guitar.[17] This movement, which also features a tender passage for strings reminiscent of Vaughan Williams, carries the second *Rome in the Rain* theme over into the finale (Allegro molto vivace), which juxtaposes energetic Waltonian passages of rhythmic and polyphonic complexity (including an intricate fugato for the four guitars) with a recurring waltz of dulcet simplicity.

During this period, Burgess also penned guitar quartet transcriptions of "Mercury", from *The Planets*, and *Oberon* Overture, the former inscribed "21 janvier 1987", the same day as the Guitar Concerto. The fragmentary orchestrational style of "Mercury" lends itself surprisingly well to the new medium, although requiring several brief cuts that leave Burgess's version eighteen bars shorter than Holst's original. The contemporaneous Weber arrangement was written to celebrate the Venetian premiere of *Oberon* in early 1987 at La Fenice and was performed there by the Aïghetta Quartet, along with *Quatuor N° 1*, in conjunction with the opera production.

In late 1988 or early 1989, Burgess transcribed "The Ballad of Persse O'Reilly" (from *Finnegans Wake*), "The Lark in the Clear Air", and "The Irish Washerwoman" for a concert of his guitar quartet music at the Princess Grace Irish Library in Monaco.[18] Titled *Trois Morceaux Irlandais*, this set of three Irish pieces premiered on 18 January 1989 as an encore to "An Evening with Anthony Burgess and his Music" presented by the Aïghetta Quartet.

Burgess began publishing articles on the guitar years before he became associated with the Aïghetta Quartet and probably wrote more about this instrument than any other except the piano. He believed that when Shakespeare wrote "Screw your courage to the sticking-place" in *Macbeth*, "he was probably friendly with John Dowland and watched him when he was screwing."[19] "The physicality of the guitar", Burgess once wrote, "is matched by one's sense of its history – from the Elizabethan lutenists to the greasy-haired flamenco thugs."[20] To stress the difficulty of composing for the guitar, Burgess was fond of repeating admonitions by Hector Berlioz, who, as a guitarist, "was the first orchestral composer to warn non-guitarists away from the hexachordal hell of trying to write chords for it that can be played."[21] Reflecting his limited success in mastering the guitar, Burgess was equally prone to emphasize how hard it is to play: "To turn the instrument into a kind of one-handed clavichord requires rare skill, strength, and long application. It is perhaps the simplest instrument in the world to play badly and the most difficult to play well."[22]

Notes

1. "The Guitar and I", *Classical Guitar* (1:3), Jan/Feb 1983, 23.
2. *A Vision of Battlements*, 57–8.
3. YH, 208.
4. "The Twenty-four-string Guitar", *Classical Guitar* (6:9), May 1988, 48.
5. CC erroneously lists 1984 as the date of composition and 1985 as the year of the premiere (in Monaco).
6. Liner notes for *Oeuvres pour Quatuor de Guitares* (REM N° 11032).
7. Míguel de Cervantes, *Don Quixote*, trans. Edith Grossman (New York: Ecco, 2003), 754–5.
8. *Classical Guitar* (6:9), May 1988, 48.
9. The year of composition is listed erroneously in CC. Along with the original manuscript, Burgess sent Philippe Loli a letter on 21 July 1988 characterizing the quartet as "*tonale, mélodique, pas trop longue ni trop difficile*" while expressing the hope that the Aïghetta ensemble will play "*Mercure*" soon and wryly noting Liana's difficulties with her guitar lessons: "*Ma femme a cassé le bras droit. Tout conspire contre son envie de continuer son travail avec la guitare.*"
10. Burgess, who considered himself primarily a tonal composer, felt that to "evade triads, which is to evade tonality, is a kind of perversion." Nonetheless, he often experimented with atonality and dodecaphonic technique, and admired Berg's method of synthesizing twelve-tone music and tonality: "When Alban Berg composed his violin concerto, he almost threw into the faces of the auditors the abiding truth of the GDAE of the fiddle. His *Grundstimmung* is a wonderful compromise – G B flat D F sharp A C E G sharp B C sharp E flat F – that shows tonality sitting happily with serialism." ("The Twenty-four-string Guitar", 48.)
11. The division of the last movement into two tracks on the Aighetta Quartet recording is misleading. Track 11 begins at the start of the third movement; Track 12 begins at bar 25 where the tempo shifts from Moderato molto to Allegro. Burgess transcribed the first movement for full orchestra, completing the undated score except for the last fourteen of the movement's 134 measures.
12. REM N° 11032, issued by REM Éditions of Lyon.
13. REM N° 311111 XCD.
14. ED13049, issued on the *l'empreinte digitale* label distributed by *harmonia mundi*.
15. "A Few Words About a Guitar Concerto by Anthony Burgess".
16. Website of the Aïghetta Quartet: http://aighetta.chez-alice.fr/burgeen.htm
17. As in the second movement of the Sonatina for Harmonica and Guitar, here the *Rome in the Rain* theme has been transposed from C to E major.
18. "The Ballad of Persse O'Reilly" is discussed in *Joysprick* (153–4). The manuscript is inscribed "by Anthony Burgess (assisted by James Joyce)."
19. "The Guitar and I", 23.
20. "The Twenty-four-string Guitar", 48.
21. "The Guitar and I", 23.
22. Liner notes for *Oeuvres pour Quatuor de Guitares* (REM N° 11032).

30

WIND AND SON

To be quite honest, I can do without Paolo Andrea.[1]

From his teenage discovery of the "sinuous, exotic, erotic" flute of Debussy's faun, the timbre of wind instruments captivated Burgess throughout his life.[2] In *Beds in the East*, Burgess wrote synesthetically of "the sudden citrous tang of the oboe", the instrument for which he wrote his earliest known piece.[3] *Byrne*, his last novel, includes this artful account of brass playing:

> The trombone's a descendant of the sackbut:
> Its music, solemn, martial, crisply clear, is
> Produced by sliding forward and then back, but
> You have to lip out the harmonic series
> In something like an oscular attack, but,
> In a young boy like Byrne, the action wearies.[4]

Assorted writings and interviews refer to projected concertos and solo works for woodwinds and brass, only some of which were ever written. In a 1971–72 *Paris Review* interview, Burgess mentions having been asked to compose a clarinet concerto, but no trace of it exists.[5] An unfinished bassoon concerto in the Burgess archive at the University of Angers is probably the one mentioned in the 1968 *Life* profile. Consisting of two incomplete movements, it is notable for containing themes used in Symphony No. 3 and *Mr W.S.* The main theme of the Third Symphony's second movement (Example 17.05), which reappears in Guitar Quartet No. 1 (Example 29.01), corresponds – allowing for a change of key – to the opening theme of the bassoon concerto's first movement (Example 30.01). The similarity between the bassoon concerto's second movement and the sixth movement of *Mr W.S.* is even stronger, with both passages written in the same F minor key and scored mainly for brass.

Nocturne and Chorale for four bassoons is a pastoral miniature whose relaxed tempi, modal tonality, and piquant chromaticism are like a blend of Warlock and Stravinsky. Lydian inflections add harmonic zest to the lilting C major nocturne while the influence of *L'Histoire du Soldat* is apparent in the highly chromatic chorale. Judging by the inscription

Example 30.01 Bassoon Concerto: I. Allegro moderato (solo part, bs. 1–3)

("Kenyon Oct. 17 1980"), Burgess composed the work while at Kenyon College in Gambier, Ohio, to deliver the John Crowe Ransom Memorial Lectures, which recapitulated thoughts on music and literature presented in the Eliot lectures earlier that year. The fact that the HRC score is a photocopy suggests that Burgess gave away the manuscript, probably as a gift composed for a specific bassoonist or quartet.

Toward the end of his life, Burgess set out to compose a work for tuba and orchestra, but did not carry out the plan. Jay Rozen, the then tuba instructor at Southwest Texas State University, wrote to Burgess in October 1991 asking about *Homage to Hans Keller*, Nocturne and Chorale for four bassoons, and "any other pieces for or including tuba".[6] Later that fall, while in Washington to read from *Mozart and the Wolf Gang* at the Woodrow Wilson Institute, Burgess met with S. M. Clark, who wished to compose an opera based on Burgess's version of *Cyrano de Bergerac*, and peppered the young American composer with questions about the tuba, confiding that he planned to write something for it. In December Burgess replied to Rozen, mentioning none of the pieces cited by the Texan tubist. Instead he proposed a new composition: "At the moment I'm composing a work for you – *Rhapsody for Bass Tuba & Orchestra*. I hope to have finished it in the New Year."[7] Despite that promising message, Burgess failed to join the ranks of Ralph Vaughan Williams, Roger Steptoe, and other British composers of works for bass tuba and orchestra, for no score or sketches of the proposed tuba rhapsody are known to exist.

Once Paolo-Andrea (Andrew) began playing the oboe and English horn, Burgess composed numerous works for those instruments, often dedicating them to his son. Apart from their titles, nothing is known of the Suite for oboe and Nocturne for oboe, two lost works from 1977 listed in *This Man and Music*, but scores exist for six other solo works plus several chamber works that include oboe. Rhapsody for oboe and piano, dated 11 December 1986, features thick quartal harmonies, contrapuntal passagework, vigorous rhythmic activity, and a challenging oboe part spanning the instrument's full range. Alternately slow and fast, it progresses from atonality to music grounded in D. A brief, undated Allegretto, similarly for oboe and piano, is one of Burgess's rare twelve-tone compositions. Extremely disjunct and technically demanding despite its brevity, it is inscribed "for Andrew"; fittingly, it resembles "Ecce Puer", another dodecaphonic piece, which is also in 3/8 meter and contains comparable rhythmic and melodic figures. Study for Cor Anglais or Oboe, an unaccompanied etude on sequential scalar and disjunct patterns, whole tone scales, and varied kinds of articulation, is an undated work published in 1994 by Saga Music.

Quartet for Oboe, Violin, Viola & Violoncello, completed on 3 October 1987, represents Burgess's contribution to the limited repertoire of oboe quartets.[8] The work opens with a vigorous sonata-form Allegro moderato based on a theme from the *Mr W.S.* Prelude (Example 22.01) that recurs in *A Manchester Overture* (Example 32.03). The Presto scherzoso recalls the quick spiccato style found in some Sibelius fast movements, such as the third movement of the Second Symphony. In cyclical fashion, the closing theme of the first movement returns as the second theme of the Andante, the quartet's third and most lyrical movement. Each of the work's first three movements contains sections of imitative counterpoint, as does the Allegro giocoso Finale, a Brahmsian passacaglia comprising a series of twenty-three continuous variations on a Mixolydian ground bass, with a five-bar presto tag serving as a coda. An unusual feature is the composer's note allowing great freedom in how to perform the work: "Movements may be played in any order, or singly, or 2 or 3 or 4."

While the writing for strings poses no difficulties, the oboe part contains multiple lengthy phrases with few rests and often lies in an unduly high tessitura, as in one strenuous passage in the first movement that ascends to A6 (Example 30.02). Meant to be climactic, such excessively high parts generally sound pinched and ineffective even when played by professionals, and pose insurmountable technical challenges for most students or amateurs. The fact that Burgess rarely heard his music performed may account for such unrealistically difficult – albeit theoretically possible – oboe writing.

A few months after composing the Oboe Quartet, Burgess spent Christmas Day 1987 setting down from memory the Nocturne for oboe and piano (Example 02.01) he had composed fifty-five years earlier, adding to it a tiny Bergamasque. Then came what he called A Little Concerto for Oboe and Orchestra, completed on 29 February 1988. The oboe writing in the

Example 30.02 Quartet for Oboe, Violin, Viola & Violoncello: I. Allegro moderato (bs. 139–42)

concerto is much more confident and idiomatic than in the quartet. Generally the solo part lies in the instrument's secure midrange; when the writing ascends into the extreme high register, as it still does occasionally, it does so with greater skill and elegance.

The sprightly Allegro vivo is delicately scored, with the solo oboe consistently well balanced with such imaginative instrumental combinations as two bassoons, violas, and cellos in one case, and trombone and timpani in another. The movement ends with a cadenza that carries over into the opening of a somber passacaglia that uses as its ground bass a twelve-tone row that converges intervallically from M7 to m2 (Example 30.03). The ground is played a dozen times in a variety of instrumental combinations, ending as a brief solo cadenza. The finale (Tempo di Gavotta) comprises a Bachian succession of dances – gavotte, minuet, gigue – surrounding a contrasting molto moderato section before concluding with a brisk allegro molto coda.

Also in 1988, Burgess composed *Concertino per Corno Inglese ed Orchestra*, a one-movement work in three main parts.[9] Undaunted by the English horn's relatively soft dynamic range, Burgess scored the concerto for full orchestra, achieving effective balance through skillful orchestration while showcasing the solo instrument's entire range, from the plaintive quality of its low notes to the thin nasal sound of its high register. Following the relatively weak first part, consisting of a slow introduction followed by a longer allegro non troppo section, the work comes to life at the start of the second part with the arrival of a soulful G major theme (Example 30.04) that

Example 30.03 A Little Concerto for Oboe and Orchestra II. Passacaglia (ground bass, bs. 3–8)

Example 30.04 *Concertino per Corno Inglese ed Orchestra* (solo part, bs. 106–10)

provides the main thematic material for the rest of the piece. A few moments later the theme returns, altered into a catchy E major melody with a bluesy lowered third à la Bernstein. Lending a cyclical quality to the work, material from the first two parts returns in the third, a jaunty C major rondo. This section begins with a cheerful refrain, another variant of the G major theme, and includes a virtuosic yet lyrical cadenza. With Stella McCracken as the splendid English horn soloist and Peter Cynfryn Jones conducting the BBC Scottish Symphony Orchestra, the concertino was recorded on 28 May 1994 for broadcast in the radio program *An Airful of Burgess*.

Quartet for Flute, Oboe, 'Cello and Piano, a postmodern blend of serious and popular styles, is one of Burgess's finest chamber works. Dated "Ash Wednesday 1990" (28 February), this late composition employs the same favored instrumental combination first used in *The Brides of Enderby*. The Allegro moderato, an episodic rondo-like movement in sober Hindemithian style, alternates between time signatures of 3/4 and 5/8, the former associated mainly with the first theme, the latter with the second. A variant of the second theme serves as the principal subject of the second movement, a predominantly contrapuntal Andantino. The wildly eclectic finale, Quodlibet (Allegro giocoso), begins with imitative counterpoint on a bluesy subject (Example 30.05) until the entrance of the piano, which bursts in with a riff on that theme sounding almost like an Oscar Peterson or Earl Hines improvisation. The music continues in this jazz vein until abruptly interrupted by a lugubrious twelve-tone fugue in a suddenly slower tempo (Allegretto quasi andantino lugubre), followed by a new blues theme and then the arrival of another variant of the first movement's second subject. With all of these diverse thematic ingredients now introduced, they are combined into an energetic mix that culminates in the most high-spirited ending found in any of Burgess's chamber works.

When Andrew's interest shifted from the oboe to the recorder in the late 1980s, so did his father's. Having paid scant attention to the instrument since composing *Ludus Polytonalis* in 1948 and Fantasia for two recorders and piano twelve years later, Burgess composed extensively for recorder during the last five years of his life, completing more than a dozen works including several for the seldom heard great bass recorder. The catalog begins with "Happy Birthday!" for treble recorder and piano, composed for Andrew's twenty-fifth on 9 August 1989. This brief *pièce d'occasion* in C major consists of a short introduction followed by a fugue in three voices

Example 30.05 Quartet for Flute, Oboe, 'Cello and Piano, III. Quodlibet (bs. 1–4)

on the "Happy Birthday" melody. Then come several undated compositions. *Sonate pour flûte à bec alto*, in D minor, is an easy four-movement composition in the style of Vivaldi for unaccompanied alto recorder. Sonatina for Recorder is a three-movement composition with a partially missing middle movement.[10] The opening movement, available in facsimile through the American Recorder Society Erich Katz Contemporary Music Series, is a vigorous G major Allegro for recorder and keyboard based on one theme in common time and another in 3/4. Only the third and final page of the second movement survives, indicating a moderate or slow piece in G minor. The gigue-like finale (Allegro molto) opens with a motto formed from the violin's open strings, G-D-A-E, though written an octave higher, and takes "Moses's Song" (Example 15.01, also used in the Third Symphony) as its second theme; heavily chromatic and mainly without a strong tonal center, the movement proceeds in sonata form, ending in A major. Two little pieces "for flute or recorder & piano" – a gigue in G major and a three-part fughetto in C major – were published in 1994 by Saga Music as *Due Pezzetti*. A set called Three Little Pieces for Wind Quintet or Recorder Quintet, also published in 1994 by Saga Music, comprises Preludio (in B minor), Fugato (in C major), and Gigue (in A minor), with "Nero's Song" (Example 15.04, also found in *Mr Burgess's Almanack*) and themes from the third movement of the Piano Concerto and the "Fire of Rome" section of *A.D.* used in the third piece.

In 1990 Burgess began composing for the great bass recorder, an instrument usually limited to playing bass parts in recorder consorts. In four three-movement sonatas for great bass recorder and keyboard, he treated it instead as a solo instrument comparable to a bassoon, employing its full compass up to – and beyond – the highest notes of its range. The first of these works is the Sonata in C, completed on Good Friday (13 April) 1990 soon after he became acquainted with the instrument.[11] Sonata No. 2 for G.B.R., dated 18 September 1992, shares themes with *A.D.*, Three Little Pieces for Wind Quintet, and the finale of the Piano Concerto, the source of the tune that enters in the fifth bar of the sonata's second movement (Example 30.06). The keys of this sonata's movements – C major, G minor and E minor/major – depart from the conventional key relationships typically found in tonal multimovement works; this is characteristic of several other Burgess multimovement compositions as well.

Two different works bear the title Sonata No. 3, one published in 1994 by Saga Music and one unpublished, the latter here to be called Sonata No. 4 to distinguish it from the other. Sonata No. 3 for Great Bass Recorder or Bassoon and Piano is a diminutive composition combining classical and jazz styles, with a cheerful ABA first movement, blues middle movement, and passacaglia finale.[12] Far more substantial is Sonata No. 4 for Great Bass Recorder and Pianoforte, which is grander in style than any of Burgess's other recorder compositions. Its outer movements are closely linked, sharing the same tonal center (B) and written in a matching calligraphic style with

Example 30.06 Sonata No. 2 for G.B.R., mvt. II. Andante lugubre (bs. 1–13)

a firm hand, using identical paper and ink. The Moderato, featuring an arching solo line accompanied by thick chords in the piano (Example 30.07), is based on the first movement of the Guitar Concerto (see Example 29.07). The expressive middle movement, the heart of the sonata, is a wistful Andantino, "*Elegy: A.B.*", that Burgess composed knowing he did not have long to live. Evidently this movement was composed separately, in a fainter hand and with different ink, though the attacca link to the finale leaves no doubt that it belongs to this sonata. The theme (Example 03.01) from the final scene of *Mr W.S.*, in which Shakespeare arises from death to dance triumphantly with his most memorable characters, returns here, in the same key (B Mixolydian), as the main theme of the Maestoso finale. Perhaps it is not too fanciful to imagine Burgess, as he approached the end of his life, identifying through his music with

Example 30.07 Sonata No. 4 for Great Bass Recorder and Pianoforte, mvt. I. Moderato (bs. 1–9)

Shakespeare, the hope of resurrection, and the dream of achieving immortality through one's art.

The Sonata for Violin, Great Bass Recorder, and Piano evokes the sound of Bartók through its repeated-note themes, intervallic emphasis on the tritone, and comparable instrumentation to *Contrasts* (also scored for violin, piano, and a wind instrument). The energetic Allegro first movement, dated "Jan. 18, 1993", eventually eschews the predictability of its opening 3/4 meter for the irregular liveliness of 5/8. The contemplative "Pastorale", a C Mixolydian Andantino, consists of two main solos, one for recorder and one for violin, followed by a shorter closing solo for recorder; as in the "Intermezzo Interrotto" of Bartók's Concerto for Orchestra, boisterous interjections disrupt the ruminative atmosphere. The principal theme of the finale, a B Lydian Allegro vivace, is strongly reminiscent of the repeated-note motifs in the finales of Concerto for Orchestra and Dance Suite.

In November 1993, Burgess filled a spiral-bound notebook with his last musical writings: two recorder sonatas, the beginning of a third, and a short trio for flutes or recorders. Toward the end of Sonata 1 (St. John's), a brief three-movement composition for recorder and piano, Burgess adds the yogic marking "pure breath" to three low Fs, perhaps echoing the repetitions of "Shantih" at the end of *The Waste Land* (see Example 33.01).[13] The third movement of Sonata 2 for recorder and keyboard, a longer four-movement composition, ends with a quotation from the *Concertino per Corno Inglese ed Orchestra* (Example 30.04). The last entries are a fragment of what was to have been Sonata 3 for recorder and keyboard, and Burgess's final piece, an Andante for flute or recorder trio. Short yet complete, it builds to a fortissimo climax, then fades away in quiet counterpoint to pianissimo, arriving on a final C major triad (Example 30.08).

Compared to most of his other music, it is peculiar how many of Burgess's compositions for oboe and recorder are awkwardly written and extremely difficult to play. The excessively high tessitura of several of the oboe pieces would be more appropriate for a flute or E flat clarinet, whereas the nearly three-octave span required by Sonata 1 (St. John's) and Sonata 2 far exceeds the recorder's compass. Moreover, the frequent use of accents, staccato articulation, and loud dynamics in several recorder pieces contradicts the instrument's relatively soft, smooth sonority. Several of these pieces are better suited to woodwinds than recorders, and, depending on range and style, could be played more effectively on flute, oboe, clarinet, or bassoon. Indeed, there is no compelling reason why some of them could not be played by strings; Sonata 1 (St. John's), for example, lends itself nicely to the violin, while the rich texture of Sonata No. 4 for Great Bass Recorder and Pianoforte suits the cello very well. Given the fact that many of Burgess's works for oboe and recorder ignore practical performance considerations and are ill-suited for these instruments, one is forced to wonder what he could have meant by writing such unplayable pieces for his son.

As Burgess acknowledged, he was a neglectful parent, too preoccupied with his writing and composing to take much notice of the high-spirited urchin who often ran naked through the house and the neighborhood. "Artists (and I have to call myself an artist, not out of the pretension that critics scoff at but because I try to practise an art) do not, with the best will in the world, make good fathers. The fathering of works of arts distracts them."[14] He regarded children as fearsome creatures who could "reasonably be expected to micturate silently on a near-finished novel, carbon copy and all". His son possessed a "demented creativity: he makes sugar by mixing salt, cigarette ash and sputum and warming all this by the fire; there is also a surrealist compound made out of lemon shampoo,

Example 30.08 Andante for three flute or recorders

nail-polish remover, beer and, floating on the surface, grubby curlicues of best butter." Burgess confessed that the boy was too young to possess a sense of responsibility, "but I can't help responding to his misdemeanours – florescences of bare ego – with loud and perhaps trauma-inducing anger. I swear a good deal at him, arguing to myself that he will learn the obscenities anyway, and he might as well learn them right."[15]

Burgess's exceptional ability to focus on his work utterly frustrated the boy's attempts to gain his attention. Stanley Silverman has described how Burgess would enter an almost trance-like state as he worked amidst nearly constant household chaos: "That's why he found it hard to revise what he wrote."[16] In order to avoid interrupting his writing, Burgess would habitually accede to the boy's wishes, no matter how unnecessary or indulgent he considered them, while Liana would sometimes leave the boy with strangers for hours at a stretch.[17]

Ever since his birth in Bethnal Green Hospital, the boy's identity was subject to confusion and recurrent reinvention. Things most children take for granted – paternity, language, name – were matters of profound uncertainty to him. Burgess claimed that the child, "a boy named, though not baptised, Paolo Andrea", was his, conceived as the result of a furtive afternoon tryst with Liana in December 1963.[18] An alternative explanation is presented in Roger Lewis's biography, which cites evidence that Paolo-Andrea's biological father was Roy Halliday, the man with whom Liana had been living in London's East End at the time.[19] When Burgess began introducing Liana to friends shortly after Lynne's death, he openly referred to Paolo-Andrea as the son of a lorry driver, and, in "Thoughts of a belated father", published in the 6 September 1968 issue of *Spectator*, identified himself as the four-year-old's stepfather: "These cold summer evenings, we – mother, stepfather and Paolo Andrea – have been wandering round London looking for some place where we can all be together." In this chilling essay, which appeared just days before his marriage to Liana Macellari on 9 September, Burgess expresses disdain of his newly acquired son, and children in general, with repugnant candor:

> I have just married again and my Italian bride's dowry consists mainly of a four year old boy called Paolo Andrea. He is monoglot, meaning he speaks only modified East Anglian, so the only communication difficulties are such as might be expected to subsist between a boy of his age and a man of mine, me being fifty and never till now having had any experience of fatherhood, whether true, spiritual, step or foster . . . The duty of getting to know him is . . . proving easier than I had thought possible, but I sometimes wonder if there is anything in all this that lies beyond duty . . . It isn't that children are just naughty or, under the influence of Mr Golding, innocently evil. They're bores. They're ineffable, unutterable crashing bores . . . I want him to be at least fourteen, but he refuses to be hurried. There's a lot of boredom still to come, so I must contrive a pretence that this boredom is really interest, concern, and something that may as well be called love.[20]

Frequent travel and relocation meant that during his childhood, this only child repeatedly changed not just geographic location, but language as well. At four, he moved with Anthony and Liana to the township of Lija in Malta, where he learned to speak Maltese plus some Moghrabi Arabic.[21] Subsequently the family moved to Italian-speaking Bracciano and, still later, Rome, with its distinct Roman dialect. When he was twelve, they settled in French-speaking Monaco. Journeys in the Bedford Dormobile "to collect book royalties unpaid" led the Burgesses to Spain, where "Andrea got gently drunk for the first time in his life."[22] Caretakers of various nationalities (including "adoring Iranians" in Cambridge, England) and lengthy residencies in various regions of the United States compounded his linguistic confusion.

The boy's name changed almost as frequently as the locations. Dubbed Paolo-Andrea at birth (Anthony generally omitted the hyphen), he was called Paolo by his maternal Italian relatives but Andrea by his playmates, parents, and family friends. In Monaco, classmates ridiculed him as a foreigner, scorning him as much for being Italian as English. There his name was Gallicized to André, but not for long. In his teens, desperately seeking a permanent identity, he seized upon Anthony Burgess's maternal birthright: "There was Scottish blood in the family, thanks to my mother, and Andrew filled up his arteries with it, denying the Irish inheritance. He chose a nation to which he could be devoted. He wore the tartan of the Wilson sept of the Gunn clan, learned Gaelic, read Burns and Hugh MacDiarmid. He was to be called Andrew Burgess Wilson."[23] Musically affirming his son's decision, Burgess composed *A Scottish Rhapsody for the 17th birthday of Andrew* in 1981.

According to Burgess, *Cyrano* sparked Andrew's interest in music when he was eight years old:

> Andrea ... fell in love with *Cyrano*, which he had seen in Minneapolis, Toronto and Boston and was now to see on Broadway. It was the pretty banal little tunes he fell chiefly in love with, though the sacrificial aspect of *panache* was to have a large influence on his love-life, and he yearned to play the tunes on a wind instrument. He went back to Italy to play them on a clarinet but, later, he played more exalted melodies on an oboe. He is still playing the oboe, and the cor anglais as well.[24]

With Anthony's help, Andrew also dabbled in composition. At age nineteen, Andrew wrote a simple, strophic song for voice and guitar titled "Where?" and later composed a dissonant sonatina for piano.

By Andrew's early teenage years, Burgess had realized that the boy's lack of a single principal language was a problem: "He settled into trilinguality but was not happy about it." Anthony credited the nonverbal medium of music with maintaining Andrew's mental health ("Music, the transcendent language, kept him sane"[25]) but this, as he knew, was an overstatement. Andrew drank heavily, fell victim to muggers, was badly injured in an automobile accident and was tormented by "prick-teasing French girls". Suffering from severe depression, he attempted suicide. Seeking a vocation in the culinary arts, he toiled in restaurants in France and Britain, went back to Monaco, then returned to England permanently, taking up residence outside London. Burgess wrote of his son, "He has, if belatedly, fulfilled my own ambition to become a professional musician", but as he knew, this was hardly true.[26] Unpublished footage of Andrew's playing demonstrates musical ability well below the level required of a professional, a fact of which Burgess must have been all too well aware.

Music was one of the strongest bonds between Anthony and Andrew, yet what was the genuine nature of this connection? While a definitive answer lies beyond the scope of this inquiry, Burgess's works for oboe and recorder express deeply conflicted emotions. Some of the pieces written for Andrew, like Nocturne and Bergamasque, *Concertino per Corno Inglese*, and Sonatina for Recorder, convey a sense of warmth and caring. Such accessible, tuneful, technically modest works would have provided a positive experience for a young player studying to become an expert musician. On the other hand, how must Andrew have felt upon receiving the Quartet for Oboe, Violin, Viola and Violoncello, A Little Concerto for Oboe and Orchestra, or Sonata No. 2 for G.B.R., whose solo parts could be played only by professionals of the highest caliber? Was Burgess driven to compose such technically challenging pieces by an exorable compulsion to test the limits of virtuosity, indifferent to his son's musical shortcomings, or did he scorn the boy's limitations by dedicating works to him that he knew Andrew would never be able to play? The extreme duality of this group of compositions suggests that Burgess seesawed back and forth between feelings of love and disdain for Andrew, leaving the unfortunate youth in a debilitating emotional limbo. Andrew must have suffered from torturous doubt, as uncertain of Burgess's feelings toward him as he was of his true name, nationality, language, or paternity, longing for assurance of his love, but, as these pieces demonstrate, never sure which way the wind would be blowing.

Notes

1 "Thoughts of a belated father", *Spectator*, 6 September 1968, 322.
2 TMM, 17.
3 *Beds in the East*, 461. See Example 02.01.
4 *Byrne*, 15.
5 John Cullinan, "The Art of Fiction XLVIII: Anthony Burgess". *Paris Review (56)*, Spring 1973, 131.
6 Jay Rozen, letter to Burgess, 15 October 1991.
7 Postcard to Jay Rozen postmarked London, 23 December 1991.
8 Burgess cites Mozart's "masterly Oboe Quartet" (K. 370) in the Introduction to *Don Giovanni* and *Idomeneo* (Universe Opera Guides), 16. Besides Britten's Phantasy Quartet, oboe quartets by British composers include works by Gordon Jacob, Lennox Berkeley, and Malcolm Arnold, among others.

9 Although "Lugano 1988" is clearly inscribed on the manuscript's final page, the full score and piano reduction published in 1993 by Saga Music list 1987 as the year of composition.
10 It is misidentified as a one-movement work in Scott Paterson's article "Anthony Burgess: The Man and His Recorder Music" in *American Recorder* (41:4), September 2000, 17.
11 See note in the Saga edition (THA-978601) of Sonata No. 3 for great bass recorder.
12 A note in the published edition states: "Of the three sonatas, Andrew Burgess Wilson prefers the lightness of touch of this, the third . . . the second pushes both player and recorder to and perhaps beyond their normal limits." A performance by bassoonist Thomas Dubos and pianist Maureen Turquet at the 2001 *Avatars* conference in Angers was recorded and issued on the CD included with the book "*Portraits of the Artist in* A Clockwork Orange".
13 Eliot, 50, 55n.
14 YH, 345.
15 "Thoughts of a belated father", 322.
16 Stanley Silverman, interview with author, New York, 12 November 1998.
17 See YH, 343, and "Do I Owe You Something?" by Michael Mewshaw in *Granta* (75), Autumn 2001, 29–40.
18 YH, 160.
19 Lewis, 339.
20 "Thoughts of a belated father", 322.
21 YH, 195.
22 Ibid., 343.
23 Ibid., 344.
24 Ibid., 287.
25 Ibid., 343.
26 Ibid., 345.

31

COMMEMORATIONS

"What is a Frenchman doing in Dublin? Ah, I may know the answer. To escape from the centenary junketings in Paris perhaps."[1]

After delivering his Eliot Lectures in the spring of 1980, Burgess traveled to Malaysia to film an installment of *Writers and Places*, a BBC television series in which successful British authors explored their literary roots by revisiting the locales where their writing careers initially took hold. In recognition of his unsuccessful attempt to import Western culture to the country then called Malaya, Burgess titled the program "A Kind of Failure". The trip, his first to Indonesia since his departure in 1959, led him to reconsider the relationship of Western and Eastern culture: "Why should an Oriental state have a national theatre or a symphony orchestra or a library above the level of the Ipoh Club's cupboard of tattered bestsellers? ... I do not know whether there is an obligation to absorb Beethoven and Shakespeare along with the technology that serves them."[2]

That summer Burgess appeared at the Edinburgh Festival, suffering during his trip from intense pain in his left leg assuaged only by alcohol: "In Inverness, I drank deeply. I drank very deeply ... The deep drinking brought on a fresh remission. I was grateful to Scotland. I wrote an overture for the Scottish National Orchestra in gratitude, and this was performed. I never heard it: the Musicians' Union forbade an unpaid recording. But I keep meeting musicians who played it."[3] The work, *A Glasgow Overture*, is a robust, sonata-form piece that starts in D major and ends in C, with frequent modulation and use of modal, especially Mixolydian, inflections along the way. Scored for full orchestra, it begins with a theme from *Romanza* (see Example 28.02) featuring a Scotch snap at the end of each of its opening bars (Example 31.01). A rambling development section, overly sequential and repetitious, is followed by a brusque recapitulation and a coda that mimics the 3/4 section of Holst's "Jupiter". The score, inscribed "Monaco / Feb. 26 1981", bears a dedication "To the Lord Provost of Glasgow" dated 12 March. Once the Lord Provost received the score, he sent it to Sir Alexander Gibson, who decided to premiere it that spring with the Scottish National Orchestra on 14 June, the first night of the Glasgow Proms. In response to the SNO's request for performance

Example 31.01 *A Glasgow Overture* (woodwinds, bs. 1–3)

materials, Burgess explained that they did not exist but that he would be willing to pay to have them produced from the score. The premiere was thus postponed until the following year, when Gibson conducted it with the SNO (now called the Royal Scottish National Orchestra) in May 1982.

The ensuing years produced a succession of commemorative musical works. The year 1982 brought forth *Blooms of Dublin* to mark the Joyce centenary and *In memoriam Princess Grace* in honor of the deceased monarch. Burgess composed *Man Who Has Come Through* for the D. H. Lawrence centennial in 1985, and in 1987 wrote his first Guitar Quartet for the semicentennial of Ravel's death. Also in 1987, he commemorated himself with a work composed in response to a request from Jonathan Haskell, an American contrabassist in the Orchestre de la Suisse Romande, who, upon learning that Burgess was a composer, had asked him to write a piece for large chamber ensemble. This was *Mr Burgess's Almanack*, completed on 24 February, the eve of his seventieth birthday. After Radio Suisse Romande declined to program it, Burgess was invited to speak at Sotheby's in Geneva; to the surprise of the auction house officials, he set one condition – that *Mr Burgess's Almanack* be performed in conjunction with his lecture.[4] Sotheby's agreed and contacted Haskell, who copied out the parts, recruited the musicians (mainly OSR principals), and conducted. The premiere took place in Geneva at the Hotel Beau-Rivage on 11 April 1988 before an invited audience of about one hundred guests directly after Burgess's talk, "Under the Bam: Thoughts on Words and Music", adapted from his Eliot lectures.

Mr Burgess's Almanack is a set of twelve variations on the "Nero's Song" melody (Example 15.04) originally from the Piano Concerto (Example 18.03, bs. 278–81). Scored for woodwinds, brass, timpani, percussion, and piano,

Example 31.02 *Mr Burgess's Almanack*: Movement X (bs. 1–10)

it is a technically challenging work with particularly demanding parts for horn, trumpet, and piano. Its structure is based on the "curious fact" that the number of notes in the chromatic scale equals the number of months in the year, a correlation hinted at in the work's mock-eighteenth-century title: "As the year moves from January to December, so in my work the musical intervals I exploit harmonically run from the minor second to the octave."[5] Fixed parallel intervals occur similarly in the second movement of Bartók's Concerto for Orchestra, where two clarinets play in minor sevenths as in Movement X of *Mr Burgess's Almanack* (Example 31.02). Just as the months are grouped in seasons, the twelve numbered movements are bracketed into four groups of three in the Schema appended to the score. By counting the introductory "Exordium" and concluding "Postlude" (the latter marked "facoltativo", i.e. optional) as movements, the number of movements – fourteen – equals the number of musicians, a correlation unlikely to have been accidental in a work so purposefully organized and mathematically structured.

Schema

		Exordium	–	tritone + maj. 3rd
A	⎡	I	–	minor 2nd
	⎢	II	–	major 2nd
	⎣	III	–	minor 3rd
B	⎡	IV	–	major 3rd
	⎢	V	–	4th
	⎣	VI	–	tritone
C	⎡	VII	–	5th
	⎢	VIII	–	minor 6th
	⎣	IX	–	major 6th
D	⎡	X	–	minor 7th
	⎢	XI	–	major 7th
	⎣	XII	–	octave
		Postlude	–	tritone + maj. 3rd

To commemorate the fiftieth anniversary of the death of the Italian author and nationalist leader Gabriele D'Annunzio on 1 March 1938, Burgess set *La pioggia nel pineto* for tenor and piano. One of D'Annunzio's best known poems, it describes the narrator and his companion Ermione listening attentively to the rain in a pine grove, as the falling drops create individual quasi-musical sounds on each variety of tree and plant, like "different instruments under numberless fingers" *(stromenti diversi sotto innumerevoli dita)*. Using a highly chromatic style similar to his Lawrence settings (especially "Snake"), Burgess conveys the image of rainfall through a recurring Chopinesque motif of repeated eighth notes on a single pitch – principally E, perhaps because it is Ermione's initial (Example 31.03). An unaccompanied vocal cadenza just after the midpoint provides an effective contrast to the dense harmonies used throughout much of the song, which Burgess completed in Monaco on 4 March 1988.

Also in 1988, Burgess composed *Petite Symphonie pour Strasbourg* to celebrate the bimillennial of that city's founding in 12 BC, honoring its turbulent past, historic oath and magnificent eleventh-century Gothic cathedral. He introduced the work, completed that June, at its premiere on 25 November 1988 at the Strasbourg Conservatory, describing the programmatic significance of its three movements: Toccata reflecting Strasbourg's economic vitality and long troubled history as a war trophy because of its location near the German-French frontier; Serment paying homage to the "great Oath of Strasbourg with which, one could say, the French language truly began"; and Fugues, an impression of urban life, incorporating "stolen

Example 31.03 *La pioggia nel pineto* (bs. 1–6)

Example 31.04 *Petite Symphonie pour Strasbourg*: I. Toccata (bs. 1–5; partial score)

glances" at the Cathedral of Notre Dame, the city's most recognizable landmark.[6] As illustrated in the score (Example 31.04), the work's main theme comes from the musical letters in "Strasbourg": S-A-S-B-G, i.e. E♭-A-E♭-B♭-G. This "Strasbourg motif" contains the notes of an E♭ major triad; accordingly, the outer movements are set in E♭ (more Mixolydian than major because of the frequently lowered seventh scale degree) with the presence of the A♮ lending a Lydian inflection.

Toccata is an energetic Allegro vivo in sonata form, serious in tone and typical of Burgess's Hindemithian harmonic style emphasizing quartal and quintal sonorities. The "Strasbourg motif", prominent in the exposition and recapitulation, is altered to E♭-E♭–A–B♭-E♭ in the coda to emphasize the tonic. Recalling similar figures from the third movement of Symphony No. 3 (see Example 17.09), distant-sounding trumpet and horn calls evoke a sense of antiquity in Serment (Oath). This contemplative Adagio, which begins in B and ends in G Dorian, opens with a succession of solos for flute, oboe, and trumpet above a timpani roll, continuing in this somber vein until the entry of a theme borrowed from the *Mr W.S.* Prelude (Example 22.01).

Example 31.05 *Petite Symphonie pour Strasbourg*: III. Fugues (bs. 1–10)

Fugues (Example 31.05) is a contrapuntal Allegro non troppo comprising five fugal sections, three with subjects derived from the "Strasbourg motif", and one non-fugal yet partially contrapuntal episode; the *Mr W.S.* theme from the Adagio returns as countersubject to the "Strasbourg motif" and as the movement's final fugal subject.

In *You've Had Your Time*, Burgess describes a wretched journey to America in June 1986 during which he felt his cardiac system beginning to weaken: "my heart gave over its regular music and, like the percussion section of *Le Sacre du Printemps*, went in either for manic bashing or long stretches of doing nothing."[7] At New York's Marriott Marquis Hotel, he "scored for four horns, three trumpets, three trombones, tuba and timpani cynically festive music. Its rhythms contradicted those of my heart, and my heart sulked and gushed."[8] From New York, he was due to fly to England to receive an honorary doctorate from the University of Birmingham and attend a performance of this new composition played by the brass section of the City of Birmingham Symphony Orchestra. The work, Festal Suite for Brass, was performed at the 1986 Birmingham Festival of Music, but Burgess did not retain a copy of the score, which remains lost.[9]

Another opportunity to write for brass and percussion arose in 1989 when he was invited by D. K. Wilson of Salford College of Technology to compose something for the school's brass band.[10] In response to Burgess's request for samples of band repertoire, in July 1989 Wilson sent him a recording of Harrison Birtwistle's *Salford Toccata*, one of the school's prior commissions, and several scores, including Malcolm Arnold's Fantasy for Brass Band. On 10 August in Lugano, Burgess completed a two-movement work, *Meditations and Fugues*, with the same scoring as Arnold's Fantasy: soprano cornet, solo cornet, ripieno cornet, 2nd cornet, 3rd cornet, flugelhorn, three horns, two baritones, three trombones, euphonium, E♭ and B♭ bass tubas, and percussion.[11] Several days later he wrote to Wilson, informing him that the new work was finished, and, referring to the British brass band tradition of writing all parts (except bass trombone) in treble clef, admitting his "trauma" regarding transposition. Thanking Wilson for the scores he had sent, Burgess wrote:

> These were a revelation. As a Mancunian, I've heard enough brass band music in my time but I had no idea of what a score looked like. I, being an amateur, have always granted myself permission to compose straight into full orchestral score, but transposing instruments are few there, and one has the comforting bulk of the strings at the bottom of the page, with a couple of solid bass lines... The initial trauma of E flat instruments, especially one in the treble clef near the bottom, was considerable, but after ten or so pages I got into it. Perhaps you ought not to take "Meditations and Fugues" too seriously at first, though I'd like your serious opinion of it. I'll try again soon. I can see that the whole thing may become obsessive. I feel vaguely superior to Elgar now, since he had to get someone else to do his scoring.[12]

What Burgess failed to disclose was that *Meditations and Fugues* was not an original composition, but rather an arrangement of the last two movements of *Petite Symphonie pour Strasbourg*. Apart from the instrumentation, both works are nearly identical as can be seen by comparing the opening of the third movement of *Petite Symphonie pour Strasbourg* (Example 31.05) with the start of the second movement of *Meditations and Fugues* (Example 31.06). Burgess simply adjusted his description of the

Example 31.06 *Meditations and Fugues*: 2. Fugues (bs. 1–9, partial score)

music to apply it to Manchester instead of Strasbourg, tacitly acknowledging this fiction with a closing disclaimer:

> *Meditations and Fugues* is a twofold study. The slow section evokes the war dead, and may be taken as a stroll through Moston Cemetery, where all my people are buried. The Fugue that follows depicts the city itself – noisy, capricious, polyglot. But finally it is just music.[13]

Burgess marked the *bicentenaire* of the French revolution with music and words. On 21 April 1989 he completed *Marche pour une Révolution 1789–1989*, a work similar to the march from *Mr W.S.* Scored for full orchestra, it is in A Mixolydian with a D major trio that returns in the tonic key. The work is dedicated to Philippe Bender, who conducted the premiere in Vence on 30 September 1989 with the Orchestre Régional de Cannes Provence Alpes Côte d'Azur. Another bicentennial tribute was *1789: An Opera Libretto*, which was adapted and translated by Jean-Pierre Carasso as the libretto of a marionette opera called – with a nod to Stendhal – *Le Bleu-Blanc-Rouge et le Noir*. Lorenzo Ferrero composed the polystylistic score, heavily influenced by Mozart, Stravinsky (especially *The Rake's Progress*) and Ellington, whose "Mood Indigo" is quoted in one aria. The premiere took place at the Centre Pompidou in Paris on 15 November 1989, with subsequent productions throughout Europe. In the spirit of *Les Miserables*, the story pits a priest named Paul Deslandres, "our hero and a baritone", against the villainous rent collector Deschanel, whose tenacious efforts to crush the righteous but all-too-human cleric ultimately fail, incurring the wrath of the revolutionary forces upon himself instead. Father Paul's human frailty had led him in his youth to father an illegitimate daughter. That act, and his supposed sedition for espousing the virtues of reason and law from the pulpit, leads to his being defrocked, imprisoned, and tried for treason. A young woman named Paulette, virginal at first but soon defiled, may or may not be his daughter; Burgess leaves this issue unresolved. In the final scene, in which they are released from their ordeals and reunited, he writes in a stage direction, "Paul and Paulette embrace, though we cannot know the meaning of the embrace."

The year 1989 also marked the centennial of the Exposition Universelle, which Burgess celebrated in "1889 and the Devil's Mode", the title piece in the collection of nine stories published as *The Devil's Mode*.[14] In this work of historical fiction packed full of events and people related to Claude Debussy and the 1889 Exposition in Paris, Burgess espouses William W. Austin's hypothesis that Debussy transformed the melody "*Ah! réponds à ma tendresse*" from *Samson et Dalila* into the initial descending phrase of the *Prélude à "l'après-midi d'un faune"*.[15] As Austin points out, the idea is plausible since Debussy, according to his fellow student Paul Vidal, had known and "deeply loved" the score of Camille Saint-Saëns's opera from as early as 1883, more than a decade before he finished his *Faune*.

Example 31.07 *Sinfonietta for Liana*: Epilogo (bs. 27–30, partial score)

Burgess's reemergence as a composer in the early 1970s soon after his marriage to Liliana Macellari was no coincidence. After suffering Lynne's antipathy toward his music for so many years, once wedded to Liana, he felt free to resume composing. His last orchestral work is *Sinfonietta for Liana*, which he inscribed "From Antonio – A Birthday Gift – 25 September 1990", having completed it the previous day on her sixty-first birthday.[16] Essentially the work is an arrangement of *Quatuor No. 2 pour Guitares*, embellished with countermelodies, doublings, thickened textures and enriched harmonies made possible by orchestral scoring, with a fifth movement added. This brief, palindromic Epilogo is based on themes from prior movements presented first in prime, then in retrograde, followed by a coda that ends with a pianissimo reminiscence from the second movement (Example 31.07).

Notes

1 *The Devil's Mode*, 106.
2 YH, 363.
3 Ibid., 364.

4 Several years earlier, Sotheby's had engaged Burgess to write the introduction for the catalog of a major collection of modern paintings on exhibition at the Royale Academie. The color-blind author mused then that it must have been the first time a Daltonian had ever been asked to write the preface to an art exhibition catalog.
5 YH, 389.
6 Burgess cites the Strasbourg Oath in *The Worm and the Ring* (200) in a passage he later described as "sheer literary self-indulgence" (LW, 368).
7 YH, ix–x. He had flown to New York to cover the rededication of the Statue of Liberty on the Fourth of July.
8 Ibid., x.
9 See Chapter 25, note 6.
10 Salford College of Technology, as it was known from 1970–92, became University College Salford (1992–96), and, later, the University of Salford (since 1996).
11 Except for the bass tubas, the published score and parts (Saga Edition THA 978492) do not specify the keys of the instruments, which are: soprano cornet and horns in E♭; other cornets, flugelhorn, baritones, and euphonium in B♭; trombones 1 and 2 in B♭, notated in treble clef; and bass trombone in C, notated in bass clef. Apart from the divergence in nomenclature between Arnold's B♭ and Burgess's BB♭ bass tuba, Burgess's instrumentation matches Arnold's Fantasy exactly, right down to the misspelling of *ripieno* as *repiano*.
12 Letter to D. K. Wilson, Lugano, 15 August 1989.
13 Letter to David King quoted in the notes to the published score. King conducted the premiere with the Salford College of Technology Brass Band on 8 May 1991 and edited the work for publication by Saga Music.
14 In a *New York Times* review (10 December 1989; Sect. 7, 38), Helen Benedict cites this as "the most human and moving of the stories" in the collection. Others, such as "The Most Beautified", a variation on the Faust theme, and "The Endless Voyager", a sour bagatelle about an air traveller who learns the limits of freedom by tossing away his passport, are undistinguished examples of Burgess's fiction.
15 William W. Austin, "The History of the Poem and the Music", in *Claude Debussy: Prelude to "The Afternoon of a Faun"*, edited by Austin (New York: Norton, 1970), 8–9.
16 The last page of the score is inscribed "Lugano, Sept. 24 1990".

32

MANCHESTER AND MOZART UNITED

BEETHOVEN: Ach, mein Gott – the infant prodigy.
MENDELSSOHN: And now his father appears, presumably to turn the pages. Strange. It does not seem to be Leopold Mozart.
BEETHOVEN: Oh God.
MENDELSSOHN: Precisely.[1]

Hun, a spin-off from the 1983 script for the unproduced miniseries about the "Scourge of God", relates the tale of the Sword of Mars and how it is said to have passed, via a series of rulers all sharing the initial A, from Attila to King Arthur, who dubbed it Excalibur.[2] Burgess extends the legend to modern times in *Any Old Iron*, an elaborate saga of two families caught in the maelstrom of twentieth-century history, from the sinking of the *Titanic* to the Russian Revolution, World War II, and the founding of Israel. The novel's narrator, Harry Wolfson, is an explosives expert and shadowy government operative from a Mancunian Jewish family; his sister Zipporah plays percussion in the Hallé Orchestra. The Welsh Jones clan is traced back through four generations to Haydn Mozart Jones, a gold prospector who is "tone deaf, unlike the choirmaster who had begotten him on one of his contraltos".[3] Bonded over the years through friendship and sex, the Wolfson and Jones families are ultimately united through marriage, with a child of Zipporah and Reginald Morrow Jones (namesake of the fictitious author of *Hun*) about to be born on an Israeli kibbutz as the story ends, lending a hopeful note to this otherwise prevailingly dark novel. In Burgess's words, "I don't think there's any optimism in the book, except the scent of oranges and tangerines at the end."[4]

The whimsical name of the Jones family patriarch is the first of many musical allusions in the novel, whose title comes from a music hall favorite composed around 1911 for the Cockney comedian William Henry Crump better known as Harry Champion (Example 32.01).[5] When autographing the novel, Burgess would sometimes write out the song's first few bars (Example 32.02). Like so many Burgess novels, *Any Old Iron* features an autobiographical character, in this case a multilingual protagonist, Reg Jones, who is stationed with the British Army in Gibraltar, lacks a sense of smell (corresponding to Burgess's colorblindness), and flees England with

Example 32.01 *Any Old Iron* (chorus)

his dark-haired wife for a home on the Mediterranean; the similarity between the youthful Llewela Jones and the fictional Ludmila Jones – a fit, golden-haired beauty fluent in Welsh – is equally pronounced. The novel also reflects Burgess's memories of the orchestral scene in Manchester from the 1920s to the early 1940s, its text abounding with references to

ANY OLD IRON

ANTHONY BURGESS

Example 32.02 Bilingual autograph of *Any Old Iron* with song quotation

prominent British composers and compositions, including Kenneth Alford [*Colonel Bogey* March (127)], Benjamin Britten (265) [*The Young Person's Guide to the Orchestra* (307)], Sir Edward Elgar (11) [*Cockaigne* Overture (299)], Constant Lambert [*The Rio Grande* (74)], Hubert Parry (11) [*Jerusalem* (76), *Blest Pair of Sirens* (268)], Ralph Vaughan Williams [*A Sea Symphony* (7), *Flos Campi* (74), *Toward the Unknown Region* (268)], and Sir William Walton [*Portsmouth Point* Overture (76), *Belshazzar's Feast* (154, 300)]. Many of these references relate to Zipporah Wolfson, whom

Burgess modeled on three real-life musicians: Sidonie Goossens, the BBC harpist who was one of Britain's first professional female orchestral musicians; the "very beautiful girl who played percussion"[6] in the 1971 Guthrie Theatre production of *Cyrano de Bergerac*; and Martha Caplin, the first violinist of the Primavera String Quartet.

Any Old Iron's musical counterpart is *A Manchester Overture*, likewise dating from 1989 but evidently conceived years earlier. Completed in Lugano on 11 June 1989, it closely resembles the first movement of "Sinfonia (No. 2 – 1944)", a piano reduction from the 1974 *Sinfonie* notebook.[7] Autobiographical elements are suggested by musical clues such as the quotation of the *Mr W.S.* Prelude (Example 22.01) associated with Will's arrival in London as an inexperienced youth, which in the overture may represent Burgess as a young man in Manchester. Another involves the transformation of a lyrical theme (Examples 32.03) into a military march (Example 32.04), perhaps symbolizing Burgess's progression from student to soldier. A third clue involves the use of two harps, rare in Burgess's music and possibly a throwback to his lost first symphony; this unusual orchestrational feature may hark back to his teenage years in Manchester, symbolizing his infatuation with Sidonie Goossens, who sometimes performed dual harp parts with her sister Marie.[8] Structured in sonata form without development, *A Manchester Overture* is in A Mixolydian with frequent key shifts through sequential modulation. Two episodes of *Petrouchka*-style polytonality, with keys paired at the tritone (D and A♭, then B and F), are followed by a typically Burgessian fughetto. In a nod to Walton's First Symphony, and through that work to Sibelius's Fifth, the overture ends with thunderous chords separated by great voids of silence.

Mozart and the Wolf Gang, an eccentric medley of musical musings published in 1991, celebrates that year's Mozart bicentennial. This eclectic collection, described in the US edition (*On Mozart: A Paean for Wolfgang*) as "a celestial colloquy, an opera libretto, a film script, a schizophrenic dialogue, a bewildered rumination, a Stendhalian transcription, and a

Example 32.03 *A Manchester Overture* (oboe 1, bs. 131–6)

Example 32.04 *A Manchester Overture* (clarinet 1, bs. 235–9, transposed)

heartfelt homage upon the bicentenary of the death of Wolfgang Amadeus Mozart", is one of Burgess's most idiosyncratic amalgamations of music and literature. Having ended *The End of the World News* with the crewmembers of the spaceship *America* commencing their lonely journey into space to the sounds of the "Jupiter" Symphony, here Burgess shifts the heavenly setting from the physical to the metaphysical realm as celestial composers from Gluck to Gershwin dispute one another, universally agreeing only that "Mozart is supposed to be the being closest to God."[9] In order for Wolfgang to teach him to play the harpsichord, the Almighty has even grown hands!

Written during the first Gulf War, Burgess's fictional fantasia is framed by that conflict, opening with Beethoven (his hearing restored) remarking on the gunfire disturbing the peace of heaven and ending with the celestial arrival of four Israeli string players killed by an Iraqi scud missile while rehearsing Mozart's K. 458 quartet, "The Hunt", for a bicentennial concert. Mendelssohn, the organizer of the celestial bicentennial celebration, is confronted by Wagner, as fervently anti-Semitic in the afterlife as on earth. Rossini, Berlioz, and Stendhal compare the relative virtues of music and literature, while Henry James and Lorenzo Da Ponte argue over the meaning of life and libretti. The centenaries of Bliss and Prokofiev, eclipsed by Mozart's commemoration, provoke discussion of English and Soviet music, as Gershwin and Schoenberg debate the merits of tonality versus dodecaphonism over martinis. In witty repartee, "Anthony" and "Burgess" consider Mozart's place in musical history, echoing a comparable dialogue on religion and art published nearly a quarter of a century earlier.[10] Mozart himself is observed obliquely, in an opera libretto on his loves and labors, and in a film treatment that examines his relationship with his father, his unobsequious manner toward the nobility, and his frustration regarding his contemporaries' limited understanding of his music.

The "Stendhalian transcription" of Symphony No. 40 in G minor, composed in 1788, portrays France on the eve of revolution. Matching Mozart's initial theme, Burgess's "First movement" begins by describing an anxious aristocrat pondering the future of the current political and social order; the description of a noblewoman in her luxurious surroundings, corresponding to the second theme, follows. Now and then, phrases tailored to Mozart's rhythms emerge from the verbiage, like one, near the start of the development section, describing the nervous nobleman: "He himself, he himself, he himself trod in the chill wind that sang through the walls" (Example 32.05).

Example 32.05 Mozart's Symphony No. 40, I. Allegro molto (vln. I, bs. 103–107) with text added from *Mozart and the Wolf Gang* (83)

In accordance with the movement's sonata form, the arrival in the recapitulation of the feminine second theme in the masculine tonic of G minor is represented by sexual intercourse:

> She is his, he hers, they theirs, two are one. Lips sadly greet, sadly join. Wallmirror sees, indifferent as time's running. Her own hair, silk most lustrous, falls, silk, lustrous, odorous. Bare skin on bare skin slides, glides. Burn, lips. Loins conjoin.[11]

The first paragraph of the "Second movement", signaling the advent of the coming revolution, is carefully fashioned to fit the opening phrase of Mozart's music (Example 32.06). In the "Third movement", the nobility attend the last ball before the revolution, dancing with trepidation to music too fast and too sad. The trio offers a remembrance of happier times – a

Example 32.06 Mozart's Symphony No. 40, II. Andante (bs. 1–8) with text from *Mozart and the Wolf Gang* (85)

Venetian gondola ride when there was nothing to fear – but soon the minuet returns, portending "shadows of the future" that intensify in the "Fourth movement", as the populace is about to rise up in revolt: "Well, the tumbrils are coming."[12] But none of this is to be taken too seriously, as the ensuing "schizophrenic dialogue" cautions:

ANTHONY: Gibberish.
BURGESS: Yes, a good deal of it. There's a musical structure underneath, filched from Mozart, but one art cannot do the work of another. Music is all verbs... That gibberish is part of my programme of evasion.[13]

Concluding this postmodern potpourri, Burgess confesses ambivalence, readily acknowledging Mozart's "greatness" and "superiority" while confessing, "as a young man, I found it difficult to fit Mozart into my sonic universe... A boy born into the age of Schoenberg's *Pierrot Lunaire* and Stravinsky's *Le Sacre du Printemps* (I was born five years after the first, four years after the other) found it hard to be tolerant of the Mozartian blandness."[14] Mozart exemplifies Burgess's ideal of prolific production, yet induces "a bitterness that the cultural conditions which made Mozart possible have long since passed away. The division between the music of the street and that of the salon and opera house was not so blatant as it now is."[15] Ultimately Burgess finds Mozart almost *too* perfect, *too* gentlemanly, and *too* representative of the "static tranquillity of the Austro-Hungarian Empire". If only the genius from Salzburg had been a little clumsier or had occasionally, like Shakespeare, "put a foot wrong", he would have been more pleasing, evoking love instead of the quasi-religious awe that results from the "perfection" and "prickly elegance" of his irreproachable music.[16]

Notes

1 *Mozart and the Wolf Gang*, 138.
2 "The novella *Hun* may, by readers of my novel *Any Old Iron*, be attributed to the fictitious author Reginald Morrow if they so desire." ("Author's Note" to *The Devil's Mode*).
3 *Any Old Iron*, 6.
4 As quoted by Susan Fromberg Schaeffer, "Beware of Justice, Truth and Beauty", *The New York Times Book Review*, 26 February 1989, 12.
5 *Any Old Iron*, music by Charles Collins and words by Fred Terry & A. E. Sheppard, © 1911 by Herman Darewski Music Publishing Company.
6 YH, 237.
7 Additionally, an undated incomplete "Allegro Risoluto" amounts to a draft of the first forty bars of *A Manchester Overture*.
8 See LW, 115 and 118. *Marche pour une Révolution 1789–1989* is Burgess's only other work requiring two harps.
9 MWG, 9.
10 *The God I Want* (New York: Bobbs-Merrill, 1967), a collection of reflections on God and religion by nine British authors, editors and clergymen, includes a

dialogue between "Anthony" and "Burgess" on the relation between God and art. This excerpt (66) echoes sentiments later expressed in *The Clockwork Testament* (403–4):

Burgess: When I think of God I think of a work of art which is the ultimate paradigm of all works of art.
Anthony: A symphony playing to itself? A canvas with nobody to look at it?
Burgess: No. Here's where God differs from a sublunary symphony or picture. He's a work of art that appreciates itself. Infinitely beautiful and infinitely appreciative of His own beauty.

11 MWG, 84.
12 Ibid., 89–90.
13 Ibid., 92.
14 Ibid., 139.
15 Ibid., 146.
16 Ibid., 143–4.

ENDINGS

33

CONFESSIONS AND CONCLUSIONS

The work ends when the work ends,
Not before, and rarely after.
And that explains, my foes and friends,
This spiteful burst of ribald laughter.[1]

Of all Burgess's talents, perhaps his greatest was as an essayist. He could write a thousand words of informative, stylish prose about virtually anything, and did so abundantly. *Urgent Copy*, published in 1968, is a compilation of more than fifty essays, all on literary themes. *Homage to Qwert Yuiop: Selected Journalism 1978–1985*, issued in 1986, contains 190 essays representing approximately one third of Burgess's journalistic output during that period.[2] The last seventeen are all on topics related to music, including Beethoven, Shaw, Sullivan, Wagner, Weill, Elgar, Monteverdi, the hurdy-gurdy, countertenors, *The New Grove Dictionary of Music and Musicians*, opera, percussion, conductors, and Harriet Smithson, the actress who inspired Berlioz's *Symphonie Fantastique*. The most indispensable of these is "The Maestro Heresy", an impassioned polemic against "the cult of the interpreter". Written in 1982, the Stravinsky centenary, Burgess's eloquent essay includes recollections of performances by Manchester's Hallé Orchestra, "the finest in Europe", and of "a student from the Manchester Royal College of Music [who] played, to a near-empty house, the little-known piano concerto of Frederick Delius. That, to me, was worth all the visits of Schnabel and Horowitz and Rubinstein put together." He rails against personality cults surrounding opera divas and superstar conductors, denouncing the practice of honoring musical interpreters over creators with one great exception: "If I approach reverence to any conductor who ever lived, that conductor can only be Arturo Toscanini... When you hear Toscanini's Wagner or Beethoven you are, you believe, as close to what the composer intended as it is possible to conceive." Excluding one or two other special cases (like Hans Richter, whose flawless, spur-of-the-moment ability to play a supposedly "unplayable" Wagner brass part once silenced, it is said, a hostile Hallé hornist), Burgess adamantly condemns the "philistine" worship of *chefs d'orchestre* and *prime donne*, concluding, "It's time to view the maestri as what they really are – schmucks with batons and voices."[3]

Robert Craft lauded *Homage to Qwert Yuiop*, asserting that the scope and quality of these essays, written at an average of two per week during a seven-year timespan, "sets a standard few can match" while gushing, "the mind reels . . . Burgess's prolificacy – a flood in a time of drought – his virtuosity and polymathy are among the wonders of the deutero-Elizabethan age." Examining the musical essays with particular care, Craft concludes that although they are "no less competent than the pieces on fiction, they do not come from inside the subject in quite the same way, and their primary importance seems to lie in disparaging bad writing on music." Burgess's references to his own music stimulate Craft's curiosity: "Though some of his music has been performed, it remains an all but unknown quantity. Perhaps an enterprising recording firm could be induced to release the soundtrack of his musical *Will!* (Shakespeare)." Similarly, autobiographical fragments scattered throughout these critical writings foster Craft's desire to read Burgess's life's story: "*Homage to Qwert Yuiop* contains so many tidbits of autobiography that the reader, this one anyway, looks forward to the full repast that Burgess says he is not quite ready to prepare."[4]

On 21 September 1985, seated in the vestibule of New York's Plaza Hotel, Burgess began preparing that flavorsome feast, calling it, after Saint Augustine and Rousseau, his "Confessions". He had written about himself before – the 1964 entry in *Who's Who* in which he listed "wife" under "Hobbies" ("It was true enough, except that Lynne was really a full-time occupation"[5]), the "Biographia Musicalis" in *This Man and Music* – and been interviewed in *Penthouse* (June 1972), *The Paris Review* (Spring 1973), *Playboy* (September 1974), *Modern Fiction Studies* (Autumn 1981), and elsewhere. His life and work had been the subject of countless books, theses, bibliographies, monographs, and articles, the postscript to Martin Amis's 1980 piece in the *Observer* providing one of the more amusing commentaries on Burgess's prodigious capacity for work and drink:

> A few more words about that lunch. We began with gin-and-tonics (two each), followed by a tremendous amount of cheap red wine. I did my best to keep pace with Burgess, who, by five o'clock, was drinking double brandies as if against time: three swallows, and then the glass held up for more. At six, he ordered a *gin-and-tonic*. This ended the session, though it seemed for a moment that we were about to repeat it, or relive it. I would go on to endure an authentically frightening hangover which lasted for half a week. At eight in the evening on the day after the day after, I was still sitting in an armchair with a hand on my brow and saying, 'Dear oh dear. Dear oh dear oh dear . . .' Whereas Burgess (I am sure) went home, did the kitchen, spring-cleaned the flat, wrote two book reviews, a flute concerto and a film treatment, knocked off his gardening column for *Pravda*, phoned in his surfing page to the *Sydney Morning Herald*, and then test-drove a kidney-machine for *El Pais* – before settling down to some serious work.[6]

Distinguishing fact from fiction in *Little Wilson and Big God* and *You've Had Your Time* is no easy matter knowing that Burgess's aim as a writer was, above all, to spin a good yarn.[7] He had previously begun and discontinued writing his memoirs by 1976, when he replied to a would-be biographer that he had "nothing at all against the idea of your writing about me, though I wonder if you would find very much to write about. A good deal of my life is contained in my novels and I recently started an autobiography which, however, I have abandoned temporarily: I find it a difficult form, since lying is so much more pleasant than telling the truth."[8] Does the passage below – Burgess's response to a request for information about *The Long Day Wanes* and his experiences in Indonesia – represent the novelist at play or could it possibly be true?

> The characters are mostly based on real people . . . Crabbe's experiences were roughly mine. I'm sorry the plot comes unstuck for you in the Costard-Crabbe episode – but this is the only part of the novel which is a direct transcription from life. I except naturally the drowning that follows.[9]

The two volumes of "confessions" can be read as an arch that takes its subject from a life immersed in music to literature and back over the course of roughly sixty years. The first volume begins with an elusive epigraph: "Time, in fact, is rather vulgarly dramatic; it is the sentimentalist of the dimensions."[10] In its original context, this line from Constant Lambert's *Music Ho!: A Study of Music in Decline*, a contentious treatise arguing that music in the early 1930s has fallen into a disheartening stasis, appears in a passage contending that music, because it must exist – unlike visual art – within a timespan, is inherently dramatic. According to Lambert, visual art is devoid of drama because the viewer determines the order in which images are perceived: "The repetitions of a certain underlying curve in an abstract or representational picture have no dramatic content because they occur in the same moment of time – one's eye can choose which it looks at first, or take in the various statements of the same form simultaneously." Music, on the other hand, cannot avoid being dramatic: "the return of the first subject after the development in a symphonic movement has an inevitable touch of the dramatic, merely through the passage of time that has elapsed since its first statement. Time, in fact, is rather vulgarly dramatic; it is the sentimentalist of the dimensions, and small wonder that *visuels*, like Wyndham Lewis, feel that it is occupying too much space in our lives."[11] The epigraph signifies that Burgess analogized his life to sonata form, regarding his actual existence as the exposition and his autobiography as the recapitulation, with the mere passage of time adding sentimentality and drama.

No review of *Little Wilson and Big God* matches Burgess's wit and humor more brilliantly than the one written by Gore Vidal for *The New York Review of Books* in May 1987. Vidal begins by recounting his first encounter with Anthony and Lynne Burgess at a London literary cocktail party in 1964. Lynne abuses him for being more successful than her husband at too young an age, to which Vidal blithely responds, "I have written more books than Mr. Burgess ... And over a greater length of time," which sends both authors into frenzied calculation, each reckoning how many books he and the other has written.

> he was certain that he was well ahead in units of production. I was not. But before I could begin the long count, he said, "Anyway, I'm actually a composer." This was superb, and I ceded the high ground to him. Lynne did not. She rounded on him: You are *not* a composer. Pussy-whipped, he winced...[12]

Calling him "easily the most interesting English writer of the last half century", Vidal extols Burgess's literary genius, considering it likely that his musical talent is also of a high order. All too aware that "it is an article of faith (bad) in our dull categorizing time that no one may practice more than a single art", Vidal inveighs against this small-minded prejudice:

> even worse, within the house of literature itself, the writer must keep to only one, preferably humble, room; yet a gift for any art is almost always accompanied by at least the ability to master one or more of the other arts. This is a secret of genius's lodge that is kept from every faculty room lest there be nervous breakdowns and losses of faith and transfers from English studies to physics. But where Goethe, say, was allowed his universality, today's artist is expected to remain cooped up in mediocrity's vast columbarium. The reputation of our best short-story writer, Paul Bowles, has suffered because he is, equally, a fine composer: For musicians, he is a writer; for writers, a composer.

To a self-described "born-again atheist like myself, it is clear", Vidal explains, "that each of us has multiple selves, talents, perceptions." But to a Roman Catholic like Burgess, "unity is all ... One god for each; one muse for each", which puts him in a predicament. Vidal ventures no opinion as to whether his fellow novelist is a good composer or not, but deems him perplexed by the lack of enthusiasm for his compositional efforts.

> He set poems, wrote symphonies, attempted operas. He still does, he tells us, somewhat defensively because, parallel to his successful literary career, he has been a not-so-successful composer. Plainly, he is puzzled. Are they right? Is he any good?... I suspect that Burgess has been severely shaken by those music critics who have put him in his place, high in the gallery of Albert Hall; as a result, he believes that they are probably right because one person cannot be more than one thing.

Did Burgess really believe this? Gore Vidal's comments invite further consideration of Paul Bowles (1910–99) and Bruce Montgomery (1921–78), whose careers proved that writer-composers could excel in both areas. Bowles, an American from Queens, New York, traveled to Paris at the age of twenty, where he befriended Gertrude Stein, Aaron Copland, Stephen Spender, and Christopher Isherwood, participating in elite musical and literary circles while still quite young. Upon returning to New York, he enjoyed a successful career as a composer, working concurrently as a music critic for the *New York Herald Tribune* from 1935 to 1946. While in New York, Bowles did little writing apart from music reviews, but things changed dramatically when he moved to Morocco in 1947. He abruptly shifted his main creative energy from music to writing, producing novels, short stories, poems, travel books and autobiography. Composing became a sideline, especially after the success of his first novel, *The Sheltering Sky*, in 1949. Unlike Burgess, who created complementary musical and literary works throughout much of his life, Bowles regarded the two pursuits as entirely separate and incompatible: "I always put it that they're in two different rooms. And I go out of one, shut the door, and go into the other. And in there it's different."[13] Bruce Montgomery established a solid reputation as a composer of vocal and choral music, writing in a Romantic style influenced by the music of William Walton, before becoming a leading composer of scores for British films, especially comedies, in the 1950s. Under the pseudonym Edmund Crispin, he wrote popular crime mysteries and short story collections, editing science fiction anthologies as well. Before his dual career was cut short by the alcoholism that caused his early death at age fifty-six, he managed during his most productive years to combine music and writing to a greater degree than Bowles. In 1961 Montgomery wrote both the screenplay and the score for the film *Raising the Wind*, an achievement that Burgess must have envied given his repeated, unsuccessful attempts to accomplish a similar feat. Although as a writer Burgess was more widely renowned, and certainly more prolific, than either Bowles or Montgomery, he never achieved the level of success as a composer that both did during their lifetimes. One suspects that, given the choice, he might well have traded away some of his literary reputation for greater musical recognition.

Having selected a serious epigraph by a composer for *Little Wilson and Big God*, Burgess chose a facetious one by a novelist (Joseph Conrad, from *Chance*) for "the second part of his confessions": ". . . as I waited I thought that there's nothing like a confession to make one look mad; and that of all confessions a written one is the most detrimental of all. Never confess! Never, never!"[14] In *You've Had Your Time* it is evident that music has become, in the late 1980s as it was in the 1930s and 1940s, a central activity in Burgess's life. He mentions performances of recent compositions like *La pioggia nel pineto*, *Mr Burgess's Almanack*, and his musical dramatization of *A Clockwork Orange*, and reports that he has begun an opera on the life of Sigmund Freud.[15] In the midst of this discussion of his musical activities, he issues a pronouncement as polemical as any in *Music Ho!*:

> Music, which we think to be an international language, is profoundly national, even profoundly regional: you can even pin Schoenberg and his pupils down to a capital city. I sometimes feel that the growth of my musical sensibility came to a full stop in 1934, when Elgar, Holst and Delius died. These three composers move me inexpressibly because they are English. What the English quality is I do not know; it is over-fanciful to suppose that they are presenting

Turner landscapes in sound or conveying the taste of ale in a country inn. The mystery of music cannot be probed. If a love of England, whatever England is, can be aroused in me, Elgar above all will do the arousing.[16]

This declaration of allegiance to his native land's musical heritage echoes Constant Lambert, connecting the beginning and end of Burgess's autobiography to 1934, the year *Music Ho!* was published. In Burgess's "confession", one hears reverberations of Lambert's belief in the ineluctably national character of English music.

> The theory that music is an international language may be compared to the statement that blood is thicker than water. They are both so obviously untrue that no one worries about them any longer or is likely to protest at their frequent occurrences in public speeches ... Music, far from being an abstract art, is as naturally emotional as painting is naturally representational ... Elgar and Delius have, in their widely different ways, written music that is essentially English in feeling without having to dress itself up in rustic clothes or adopt pseudo-archaic modes of speech.[17]

A Mouthful of Air: Language and languages, especially English is Burgess's last volume of non-fiction, its title derived from the concluding lines of W. B. Yeats's poem "Aedh thinks of those who have spoken Evil of his Beloved":

> But weigh this song with the great and their pride;
> I made it out of a mouthful of air,
> Their children's children shall say they have lied.

Completed in 1991 and published the following year, it borrows and expands upon linguistic concepts introduced almost thirty years earlier in *Language Made Plain*, with close attention to the music of language and sound, as in this sample rumination:

> Whistling, like riding a bicycle, is best not enquired into too curiously. Think about it, and you cannot do it. If you are homosexual, according to the late Ian Fleming, you cannot whistle. It is conceivably a medium of communication older than speech, and it relates man to birds, otters and guinea pigs. Taboos are attached to it. "A whistling woman, a crowing hen / Whistled the devil out of his den." Witches whistle (thrice), also whores. Yet *siffleuses* have achieved as acceptable a music-hall art as *siffleurs*. Elizabeth Mann shocked me into awe by whistling a florid Bach top line with fine tone and expression. The violinist in her father Thomas's novel *Doktor Faustus* has the same gift. Whistling enables a man to be his own ensemble. I was once able to hum "Swanee River" and whistle Dvorak's *Humoresque* at the same time but have lost the knack.[18]

A Dead Man in Deptford, published in the UK in early 1993 (though not until 1995 in the US) was Burgess's last novel to appear in print during his lifetime. As the end of his life drew near, he continued to write essays and reviews for major newspapers and periodicals on both sides of the Atlantic.

Confessions and Conclusions

In late 1992, he translated ГОРЕ ОТ УМА (*Gore ot uma*, or *Woe from Wit*) by the playwright and diplomat Aleksandr Sergeyevich Griboyedov (1795–1829), who, like Burgess, composed both music and verse. *Chatsky*, as Burgess's translation of the Russian comedy was called, opened on 11 March 1993 at the Almeida Theatre in a production directed by Jonathan Kent starring Colin Firth as Chatsky and Minnie Driver as Liza. As mentioned earlier, Burgess labored for eighteen months on an Italian version of *Blooms of Dublin* until plans for that Trieste production were cancelled in early 1993, which was around the time that he completed *Byrne*, his final novel. After composing *Sinfonietta for Liana* in 1990, Burgess completed no more orchestral works, focusing instead on recorder music in his last years.

Example 33.01 Sonata 1 (St. John's): III. Allegro molto (bs. 46–56)

In late 1993, surgery on Burgess's glottis left him unable to speak. Interviewed for the last time on 4 November, he responded to questions from the literary editor of Madrid's *El Mundo* with handwritten faxed replies. In this laconic colloquy, published posthumously in the *Guardian* on 26 November, he maintained his passion for music to the very end.

> **Writers do not usually have a sense of music in their stories. What are your examples to the contrary?**
> All my work. I can't help it.
> **Has music brought you more satisfaction and benefits than literature?**
> Generally, yes.[19]

Perhaps Burgess was referring to Saint John the Silent, a medieval monk known for his vow of silence and gifts as a healer, rather than John the Baptist in the title of his deathbed opus Sonata 1 (St. John's). On 12 November, ten days before his death, he signed and dated the last page of that composition, adding the inscription *"post operationem glottalem"* beneath his autograph, the last one ever to grace a sheet of his music (Example 33.01).

Anthony Burgess died of throat cancer in a private London hospital on Monday, 22 November 1993. At Liana's insistence, public announcement of his death was delayed for three days, causing newspapers worldwide, including *The New York Times*, to report on 26 November that he had died the previous day, with the result that numerous sources still persist in erroneously listing 25 November as his death date. His remains were interred in the Cimetière de Monte Carlo, also the final resting place of Cécile Chaminade and Josephine Baker, whose piano Burgess had acquired when he moved to Monaco around the time of her death eighteen years before.

Notes

1 *The Clockwork Testament*, 479.
2 In the US, it was published as *But Do Blondes Prefer Gentlemen?*, taking its title from an essay on the death of Anita Loos, author of *Gentlemen Prefer Blondes*.
3 BDB, 578–84.
4 Robert Craft, "A Flood in a Time of Drought" from *Small Craft Advisories*, 232–6.
5 YH, 97–8.
6 As reprinted in Martin Amis, *Visiting Mrs. Nabokov and Other Excursions* (New York: Harmony, 1993), 245.
7 In a friendly letter dated 26 March 1992, sent after publication of *You've Had Your Time*, Eric Swenson jokes that his "country mansion outside Hartford" (YH, 127) was "so unmansionlike that you had to spend a freezing night in a child's playhouse on the tiny island in our pond", and describes himself as distressed, not "enraged" (YH, 162), when he flew to the UK to try to convince

Burgess not to leave Norton. (They did not even meet, since by the time Swenson arrived in London, Burgess had flown to Malta.) Geoffrey Aggeler denies thinking Burgess's call (YH, 351) was a hoax; he recognized him immediately, invited him to stay overnight and lent him a coat to take to Idaho. (Burgess wears it in the final scene of *Grace Under Pressure*.) And so on.
8 Letter to Jonathan Fryer, Monaco, 27 November 1976.
9 Letter to Mr. M. T. Wignesan, Monaco, 31 October 1976.
10 LW, v.
11 Lambert, *Music Ho!* (London: Faber & Faber, 1937), 115.
12 Gore Vidal, "Why I Am Eight Years Younger than Anthony Burgess" in *At Home: Essays 1982–1988* (New York: Random House, 1988), 231–40. Orig. pub. in *The New York Review of Books* (34:8), 7 May 1987.
13 Paul Bowles, *Paul Bowles on Music*, edited by Timothy Mangan and Irene Herrmann (Berkeley, Los Angeles, London: University of California Press, 2003), viii.
14 YH, v.
15 No musical sketches for the projected Freud opera are known to exist.
16 YH, 389–90. Otto Karolyi begins his book *Modern British Music: The Second British Musical Renaissance – From Elgar to P. Maxwell Davies* with a quotation from Burgess's essay "All Too English?": "I know that Elgar is not manic enough to be Russian, not witty or *pointilliste* enough to be French, not harmonically simple enough to be Italian and stodgy enough to be German. We arrive at his Englishry by pure elimination." BDB, 567.
17 Lambert, *Music Ho!*, 116, 141, 173.
18 *A Mouthful of Air*, 69.
19 Elvira Huelbes, "Appreciation: Anthony Burgess – The last words", *Guardian*, 26 November 1993.

EPILOGUE

34

OPUS POSTHUMOUS (1993–2009)

> 'But what happens when you die?'
> 'You're finished with,' Enderby said promptly. 'Done for ... You wander around and then you come into contact with a sort of big thing ... God, if you like ... like a big symphony, the page of the score of infinite length, the number of instruments infinite but all bound into one big unity. This big symphony plays itself for ever and ever. And who listens to it? It listens to itself. Enjoys itself for ever and ever and ever. It doesn't give a bugger whether you hear it or not.'[1]

Linguistically inventive to the end, Burgess stipulated that his tombstone be engraved with a succinct epitaph uniting his name with the Biblical term for God the Father, and, obliquely, his twin creative passions, literature and music:

ANTHONY BURGESS
1917–1993
A B B A
A B B A

ABBA represents Anthony Burgess's initials, forward and backward, and is the transliteration of the Aramaic and Hebrew words for *father*; compounded to ABBA ABBA, it echoes Christ's invocation to God. This double tetragram also signifies the rhyme scheme of the octave of a Petrarchan sonnet (as in the title of his novel about Keats and Belli) and the note names of a little melody based on his initials – an elaboration of the two-note ideogram he sometimes wrote beneath his name, as printed on the title page of *This Man and Music*:

A backlog of unpublished material, including two reviews for the *Observer*, meant that new writings by Burgess continued to appear for some time after his passing.[2] *Joyce Images*, a volume of photographs and drawings designed by Bob Cato and edited by Greg Vitiello, was published in 1994 with an introduction by Burgess written in August 1993. *Byrne*, the most substantial work left unpublished at his death, was issued in the UK in 1995.

On Bloomsday 1994, "A Memorial Celebration for the Life and Work of Anthony Burgess" was held in St Paul's Church in Covent Garden. Fittingly, the program began with "Today is the Sixteenth of June" from *Blooms of Dublin*. Auberon Waugh and William Boyd spoke, recordings were played of Burgess reading from *Little Wilson and Big God* and *Nothing Like the Sun*, and Michael Ratcliffe, John Tydeman, Antony Sher, and John Walsh read excerpts from *Homage to Qwert Yuiop* ("Ulysses, my favourite novel"), *Mozart and the Wolf Gang*, *Inside Mr Enderby*, and *A Dead Man in Deptford*, respectively. After I Fagiolini sang *In Time of Plague*, the Barbican Virtuosi played the second movement of Burgess's String Quartet. William Boyd recalls "a wonderful Burgessian moment" that occurred during the Prayer and Blessing at the end of the service.

> The memorial service was taking place at the Actors' Church, which backs on to the Piazza where, at all times of the day, street theatre troupes perform. As I recall, it was just as the service was ending and people were beginning to file out when one of these troupes burst into song, quite coincidentally and innocently. And we left the church with "Roll out the Barrel" ringing in our ears, counterpoint to whatever bit of organ music was being played... I could imagine Anthony's shade delighting in its aptness.[3]

After Anthony's death, Liana turned to Boyd to ask how Burgess's music might be recorded. From this request, "one thing led to another" and soon Boyd had written *Homage to AB*, a radio play for BBC Radio Scotland.[4] Boyd's "masque", a warm and witty tribute to Burgess combining biography with excerpts from his writings and music, was performed before a studio audience and broadcast live on 21 August 1994 as part of a program called *An Airful of Burgess*. Leading a strong cast of actors, John Sessions gave a virtuoso performance in the double role of Anthony Burgess / F. X. Enderby. Music was performed live by baritone Alan Watt, singing "Warm Fullblooded Life", "Copulation Without Population", "Mother", and "Love Loves to Love Love" from *Blooms of Dublin*, and "Song of a Man Who has Come Through" and "Bavarian Gentians" from *Man Who Has Come Through*, accompanied by Penny Smith; Cappella Nova, singing *In Time of Plague* under the direction of Alan Tavener; and musicians of the BBC Scottish Symphony Orchestra, conducted by Peter Cynfryn Jones, performing excerpts from *Mr Burgess's Almanack*. Recordings of *A Glasgow Overture*, *Concertino for Cor Anglais*, and *Mr W.S.*, prerecorded on 28 May 1994 by Jones and the SSO, were also broadcast.[5]

On 21 November 1994, the eve of the first anniversary of his death, the Princess Grace Irish Library presented a Burgess retrospective at the Salle des Variétés in Monaco. Between a panel discussion and the viewing of a filmed interview conducted by Jeremy Isaacs, six of Burgess's music compositions were played: String Quartet, *Master Coale's Pieces*, Prelude to *Trotsky's in New York!*, Tango for Pianoforte, Rhapsody for Oboe and Piano, and *In memoriam Princess Grace*. On 10 December 1996, the Aïghetta Quartet released the compact disk *Burgess: Musique d'un écrivain anglais sur la Riviera*, the first commercial recording devoted entirely to Burgess's music.

In 1998 the Harry Ransom Humanities Research Center at the University of Texas in Austin acquired a large collection of Burgess's manuscripts, papers, first editions, and correspondence. Stored in 154 boxes and three folders, this archive documents Burgess's life and work from 1956 to 1997, with most of the material dating from the 1970s and 1980s. The collection contains all but a few of Burgess's extant musical works – approximately 130 scores, mostly original handwritten manuscripts, dating from 1970 to 1993.

Also in 1998, the Anthony Burgess Centre was established in France at the University of Angers. Funded by Liana Burgess and organized by Professor Ben Forkner, its founding director, the Centre comprises an archive of Burgess's manuscripts, books, and personal items, including his typewriter, writing desk, and "bad-tempered electronic keyboard". The Centre began publishing the *Anthony Burgess Newsletter* in 1999 and has hosted three international symposia: "The Avatars of *A Clockwork Orange*" in December 2001, "The Lives of Anthony Burgess: Auto(biography) and Burgess" in December 2004, and "Anthony Burgess: Music in Literature and Literature in Music" in December 2006. Collections of selected papers delivered at these conferences were published as *Portraits of the Artist in A Clockwork Orange* (2003), *Anthony Burgess, Autobiographer* (2006), and *Anthony Burgess: Music in Literature and Literature in Music* (2009), with a compact disk of Burgess's music included in each of the first two of these volumes. The Anthony Burgess Society (*Les Amis d'Anthony Burgess*) was established in 2000 near Angers in the town of Saumur with support from the winery Bouvet-Ladubay, which produced a vintage called *Le Trésor d'Anthony Burgess* in honor of its namesake.

One Man's Chorus, a collection of sixty-eight essays selected and edited by Forkner, was published in 1998. Its six essays on musical subjects include a centennial tribute to Wagner from 1982, a bicentennial commemoration of Gluck from 1987, and, from the same year, an homage to Ravel on the fiftieth anniversary of his death.[6]

The Burgess Variations: *Theme and Thirty Variations on the Life and Works of Anthony Burgess*, a two-hour television documentary written and narrated by Kevin Jackson, and produced and directed by David Thompson, was first broadcast on BBC2 on 26 and 27 December 1999. It is based on the premise that "language, music, and the conflict of good and evil" were "the three obsessions" to which Burgess returned repeatedly in his work.[7] Combining extensive footage of Burgess and his family, excerpts from interviews with over two dozen individuals associated with Burgess or his work, and performances of several of his compositions, it provided an illuminating biographical profile while shedding new light on his musical achievements.

In 2003 the International Anthony Burgess Foundation was established in the Manchester suburb of Withington as a research center and depository for Burgess's personal possessions. Founded by Liana Burgess in cooperation with Dr. Alan Roughley, the IABF formally opened on 25 June 2004 with performances of several of Burgess's piano pieces and songs. The book *Anthony Burgess and Modernity*, edited by Roughley and published in 2008, is a collection of papers from the first IABF symposium, which took place in Manchester in July 2005. A second symposium, "Anthony Burgess: Selves & Others", was held in Liverpool in July 2007; a third, "Conflict, Dialogue and Resolution", took place in Kuala Lumpur in July 2009.

Having bemoaned the omission of entries for John Sebastian and Stanley Silverman (and, implicitly, himself) in *The New Grove Dictionary of Music and Musicians* when he reviewed it for the *Times Literary Supplement* in early 1981 ("Is it I who put the kiss of documentary neglect on musicians with whom I have associated?"[8]), Burgess gained posthumous recognition in the second edition (2001), prior biographical entries having already appeared in *The New Everyman Dictionary of Music* (1988), *Contemporary Composers* (1992), and *The New Grove Dictionary of Opera* (1992). *Revolutionary Sonnets and other poems*, a collection that includes juvenilia from his college years, was published in 2002, as was *Will's Son and Jake's Peer*, a study by Ákos I. Farkas on the influence of Hopkins, Eliot, and, especially, Joyce in Burgess's writings.

The year 2002 also produced a self-indulgent psycho-biography by Roger Lewis, whose caustic sarcasm, deceit (on the Harry Ransom Center: "They haven't got any correspondence"), and rationalization of his book's "irony" ("It was all language and cleverness") severely undermine its merit and appeal.[9] Regarding Burgess's music, Lewis displays an utter lack of familiarity or research, offering only disdain and information repeated from *This Man and Music*, whether accurate or not, as illustrated by this typical comment:

> In 1976, he wrote a song cycle for soprano, flute, oboe, cello and keyboard entitled *The Brides of Enderby*. I wonder what that is like? I'd have thought the subject required tubular bells, hand bells, gongs, musical glasses and a Hammond organ.[10]

Conversely, *The Real Life of Anthony Burgess* by Andrew Biswell, published in 2005, provides a wealth of carefully researched biographical information, especially about the period of Burgess's life preceding his marriage to Liana.

From her base in southern France, pianist Maureen Turquet has long championed Burgess's music with performances of his piano and chamber works, some of them available on the compact disks included with *Anthony Burgess, Autobiographer* and *Portraits of the Artist in* A Clockwork Orange. In 1997, a musical adaptation of *Mozart and the Wolf Gang* was produced at the Université de Bourgogne as *Mozart et son Wolf Gang: opéra en trois actes*. Since becoming acquainted with Burgess's music the same year, I have performed much of his music, conducting the premieres of Concerto for Pianoforte and Orchestra (with pianist Gary Steigerwalt), *Song for Saint Cecilia's Day*, and *A Manchester Overture*, and the US premieres of *In memoriam Princess Grace, Mr W.S.*, and *Mr Burgess's Almanack*. Other performances include Symphony No. 3 in C, *The Brides of Enderby, The Waste Land, A Clockwork Orange: A Play with Music*, plus a number of his songs (with soprano Kathryne Jennings), chamber works, and keyboard pieces. S. M. Clark's *ABBA ABBA In Memoriam Anthony Burgess* (1994–95), for piano sextet, is one of the compositions written in tribute to Burgess or based upon his works. Others include my *Three Burgess Lyrics* (1999), for violin, piano, and SATB chorus, and *A/B: A 90th Birthday Celebration of Anthony Burgess in Words and Music* (2007), for actor and chamber ensemble.

Residing in a Twickenham townhouse, Andrew Burgess Wilson led a quiet private existence. Between 1993 and 1995, he was associated with Saga Music Publishing, a small press that issued printed editions of nine Anthony Burgess compositions plus a short piano sonatina by Andrew himself. Apart from rare interviews, including one for *The Burgess Variations*, he declined all similar requests, and, unlike his mother, shunned all Burgess conferences and symposia. On 15 June 2002, Andrew's life came to a tragically premature end when he died suddenly, at age thirty-seven, of causes attributed to epilepsy. Thirteen days later, he was laid to rest in Twickenham Cemetery not far from his home in Saint Margarets village.

Andrew's death dealt a severe blow to Liana Burgess, who was so grief-stricken that she could not bring herself to attend his funeral. Increasingly frail and weak, she eventually left Monaco for nearby Bordeghera to spend her final months in her native Italy. Weakened by stroke and a cirrhotic liver, she ultimately succumbed to heart failure, passing away on 3 December 2007. Two weeks later she was buried, not alongside her beloved Anthony, but beside her son in Twickenham Cemetery, nine hundred miles from Burgess's solitary gravesite in Monte Carlo.

Having used the metaphor of sonata form in his autobiography, Burgess turned to the circular structure of *Finnegans Wake* as a model in his final years, with themes from the past returning in his autumnal writings. *A Dead Man in Deptford* returns to Marlowe, the subject of his Manchester

University thesis, while mirroring the mock-Elizabethan prose style of *Nothing Like the Sun*. *A Mouthful of Air* expands upon ideas first presented in *Language Made Plain*. *A Manchester Overture* harks back to *Song of a Northern City* from 1942, while *Marche pour une Révolution 1789–1989* echoes the *Dead March* for orchestra from 1934, the first title in the list of compositions published in *This Man and Music*.

Nowhere is this sense of circularity stronger than in *Byrne*, in which poems written in his youth and subsequently published in the early novels *A Vision of Battlements, The Worm and the Ring*, and *Inside Mr Enderby* return once more, embedded into the text of this exuberant, picaresque tale told in verse. As in his first novel, Burgess's final protagonist is a "failed" composer – a hack whose career consisted of writing sappy scores for third-rate films – and, like Richard Ennis, Michael Byrne is better at copulation than counterpoint. The protagonist's sexual prowess is underscored by Burgess's use of *ottava rima*, the rhyming pattern of *Don Juan* (the similarity of the names Byrne and Byron surely no coincidence). The ABABABCC rhyme scheme, which poets and professors call Byronic, gave Burgess one last chance to jest and blaspheme in a metered style both comic and ironic.

To compare *Byrne* with *A Vision of Battlements* is apt but insufficient, for this valedictory work abounds with references to earlier writings, compositions, and autobiographical themes. There are evident parallels with *Earthly Powers*, especially the sequence in which Byrne, like Kenneth Toomey, winds up in Nazi Germany in the company of Hitler's inner circle. One finds allusions to "The Most Beautified" and *1789: An Opera Libretto* (6), *Enderby Outside* (41), *Faunal Noon* (115), and *Summer's Last Will and Testament* (137), along with mentions of authors and places that resonate with Burgess's life story. Dana Gioia has cited further autobiographical elements in the novel, whose two main characters represent disparaging semi-self-portraits. Michael Byrne, the Anglo-Irish son of two musicians, is a lapsed Catholic who spends his life laboring at two arts, one of them music composition. As the novel ends, he lies on his deathbed, evidently fondest of the "musician son who called me back / To hear by ear what I hear in my head" (146). One of Michael's compositions, *The Zodiac* (19), employs a technique ("Twelve movements rising by a semitone / To come full circle") comparable to that of *Mr Burgess's Almanack*, its title recalling the unfinished "Zodiac" Variations listed in Burgess's "Journal of the Plague Year (1951)". Byrne leaves an uncertain legacy – paintings, a few poems, music heard on late-night television on the soundtrack of mediocre motion pictures – wondering whether "life pays too much for art" (148). Michael's son Tim, a faithless Catholic priest, considers a new vocation as scriptwriter of religious documentaries for television. Chillingly, he begins coughing up blood, discovering, like his author, that he has terminal cancer: "As a medieval monk might place a skull on his writing desk as a *memento mori*, Burgess put his own dying body into his final book."[11] Like so many works before it, *Byrne* was completed on a personal anniversary:

24 February, "Ash Wednesday 1993", the eve of Burgess's seventy-sixth birthday, which he knew by then would be his last.

Byrne teems with musical wordplay, with dozens of clever strophes invoking the names of composers, performers, and works both fictional and historical, like this one about Michael Byrne's parents, mezzo Sybil and tenor John Byrne:

> One Christmas he sang solo in *Messiah* –
> With "Comfort ye, my pee-eople" etcetera.
> She was a dark-haired mezzo in the choir,
> And a few days after he'd properly met her a
> Fleshly affection in them both took fire.
> They kissed and colled in parks and fields and, better, a
> Warm bed, her own. There's danger, I suppose,
> In singing sacred oratorios.[12]

The question of Burgess's musical legacy is one that only time can clarify. He was unquestionably talented and prolific, so why is he not better known as a composer? The answer begins with the observation that, in our time, very few composers of serious art music become well known to the general public. Beyond possessing talent for writing music, the rare composer who achieves widespread celebrity historically has done so through some combination of a sudden public breakthrough (as Stravinsky experienced after *Firebird*), having powerful champions of one's music (as did Aaron Copland in Serge Koussevitzky and the Boston Symphony Orchestra), holding an important academic affiliation, being published by a major music publisher and recorded by a major recording company, possessing great determination to bring one's music to the public's attention, and plain luck. Other than talent, when it came to music, Burgess had none of these, and lacked the training that might have cultivated his musical talent to a higher level. Had he heard his music played more often, his skill would certainly have improved, allowing him to compose more music at or above the level of his best works – compositions like the Third Symphony, *Mr W.S.*, the three guitar quartets, and the Quartet for Flute, Oboe, 'Cello and Piano.

In years to come, as more of Burgess's music is made available through printed editions and recordings, the public will have a chance to decide whether he deserves a place in the pantheon of English composers whose music he so deeply loved. In *Byrne*, he penned this strophe on the names of British composers:

> Strange that the names of English-born composers
> Should often sound (Delius, van Dieren) foreign:
> Holst, Rubbra, Finzi, Elgar – names like those, as
> Though the native stock skulked in a warren
> Shivering at Calliope's bulldozers.
> McCunn, true, rather overdid the sporran.
> That Handel was staunch British to the end'll
> Still be denied by Huns who call him Haendel.[13]

John Burgess Wilson clearly does not belong in this stanza, for his is unquestionably the name of an English-born composer who sounds English-born. But if some future poet, fancying Anthony Burgess's music, found reason in a line of verse to include his name next to Holst, Rubbra, Finzi, and Elgar, his shade would surely beam with heavenly pride, knowing truly then he'd had his time.

Notes

1. *The Clockwork Testament*, 403.
2. Gore Vidal, Michael Ratcliffe, et al., "Not so poor Burgess", *Observer*, 28 November 1993.
3. Boyd, email to author, 11 January 2005. Boyd recounts the same story in *The Burgess Variations*.
4. Ibid.
5. Movements 1–3 and 5 of *Mr W.S.* and the "Exordium" plus movements I-VI and X of *Mr Burgess's Almanack* were played in the broadcast.
6. Writings on Shaw, Elgar, *Symphonie Fantastique*, and the Joyce centenary essentially replicate essays previously published in *Homage to Qwert Yuiop*.
7. *The Burgess Variations: Theme and Thirty Variations on the Life and Works of Anthony Burgess*, text by Kevin Jackson. BBC Television, 1989.
8. "A mystery and its monument", TLS, 20 February 1981, 183, reprinted as "Wandering Through the Grove", BDB, 531–9. In the anthologized revision, Cathy Berberian's name was added to the list of musicians snubbed by *Grove*, while George Perle and Paul Lansky were fused into the fictitious George Perle Lansky (535).
9. http://www.classicsnetwork.com/essays/An_Interview_with_Roger_Lewis/837 (9 October 2002).
10. Lewis, 315.
11. Dana Gioia, "Deathbed Confessions", *The New York Times*, 30 November 1997, 79.
12. *Byrne*, 11.
13. Ibid., 19.

APPENDIX 1
LIST OF MUSIC COMPOSITIONS

1. DATED WORKS, IN CHRONOLOGICAL ORDER
1917–37   JUVENILIA

ca 1931   "Let the Bulgine Run". Shanty for chorus and piano [LW/115]

ca 1932   Nocturne. Andantino for oboe and piano. Insc "Composed when I was 15 years old and suddenly remembered at the age of 70. Christmas 1987". ms HRC / also listed as **1987 (25 Dec) Nocturne**

Dead March for full orchestra [1934 TMM/22]

"In pious times, ere priestcraft did begin" (Dryden's *Absalom and Achitophel*) for two male voices [1934 TMM 22; LW/146]

Trio for flute, oboe and bassoon [1934 TMM/22]

Albumblatt for small orchestra [1934 TMM]

ca 1934   Prelude and Fugue (for the Holy Name organist) [in D minor] [TMM/22; LW/151]

Songs from T. S. Eliot's *Sweeney Agonistes* for voices and piano [1935 TMM/22; LW/157] / cf. 1951 (summer) *Sweeney Agonistes* (Eliot) for voices and piano

ca 1935   Symphony (no. 1) in E major [1935 TMM/22–4; LW/158–9] / *Symphony* [1937 CC] / **cf. 1974 *Sinfonie:*** Sinfonia (No. 1 – 1935)

"Complaint, complaint I heard upon a day" (from Ezra Pound's *Cantos*) for SATB unaccompanied [1936 TMM] / cf. **Bethlehem Palmtrees** (est 1972)

String Quartet in G major [1936 TMM]

1937   "Cabbage Face". Song for vaudevillian [LW/163–4]

1937–41   MANCHESTER UNIVERSITY

Five twelve-tone studies for piano [1937 TMM]

"Nu we sculan herian" (Caedmon's Hymn) for male voices [1937 TMM]

"Ic eom of Irelonde" for soprano and flageolet [1937 TMM]

ca 1937   *The Waste Land* (T. S. Eliot). Dramatization for reciter and piano [LW/179–80; 1937 TMM/100] / cf. **1978 (ca 19 Apr) *The Waste Land***

ca 1937–38   "The rattle basket dry". Song to text by Lance Godwin [LW/184–85]

ca 1937–38   Opera about Copernicus (Douglas Mason, librettist). Incomplete p-v. Includes tango "One kind of love" [LW/187]

Sonatina in E flat for piano [1938 TMM]

Music for James Elroy Flecker's *Hassan* [1938 TMM/26; LW/179]

Ich weiss es ist aus. Group of cabaret songs with words and music by AB, lyrics translated into German by Klaus Pickard and Oskar Bünemann [1939 TMM/26; LW/213]

"Black-out Blues". Group of cabaret songs in English [1939 TMM; LW/224]

"Lines for an Old Man" (T. S. Eliot). For old man and four instruments [1939 TMM]

§ *Dr Faustus.* Draft of a one-act opera [1940 TMM]

1941–43   THE JAYPEES / ARMY EDUCATIONAL CORPS, ENGLAND

1941   "War, work and worry may shake you". Chorus for the Jaypees [TMM/29]
Prelude and Fugue for organ: *Ipswich* [1941 TMM]
Hispanics: for violin and piano [1941 TMM]
ca 1941   Arrangements for the Jaypees:
  "If We Never Meet Again" (Louis Armstrong song) [TMM/29; LW/258; Nutting]
  J. S. Bach, Fugue in C minor from *The Well-Tempered Clavier*, Book I. np [TMM/32]
  Debussy, *Prélude à "l'après-midi d'un faune"*, titled *An Afternoon on the Phone* (arr for six-piece dance orchestra) [1941 TMM/32; LW/259]
  Rimsky-Korsakov, *Chanson Hindoue* (called "Song of India") [LW/258]
  Ballet Egyptien [LW/260]
  "Macushla" (Celtic song, for Jack Varney) [TMM/30; LW/258]
  "The Folks Who Live on the Hill" (from Bing Crosby recording) [TMM/29]
  "Stardust" (written in Glen Miller style) [Nutting]
  "Thanks for the Memory" [LW/259]
  "I Know Why" [LW/259]
  "Let's Have Another One" [LW/259]
  "On the Track" [LW/260; TMM/30]
"blues in waltz time" [TMM/30]
Sinfonietta (jazz combo) [1941 CC] / cf. "pseudo-symphonic arrangement" below
"pseudo-symphonic arrangement" of 'Darktown Strutters' Ball'" [TMM/30; possibly cognate with Sinfonietta listed above]
"Ball Tic Bass" (in Count Basie style, featuring string bass, for Richard Nutting) [Nutting 1941]
"Everyone suddenly burst out singing" (Siegfried Sassoon) for voices and piano [1942 TMM]
Nelson: suite for piano (one eye, one arm, one arse) [1942 TMM]
Sonata for piano in E major [1943 TMM, LW/291] / Sonata (piano) [1946 CC] / one of "two piano sonatas"? [*Life*/94]

1943–46   ARMY EDUCATIONAL CORPS, GIBRALTAR

Reveille Stomp for large dance orchestra [1943 TMM]
Purple and Gold: march for military band [1943 TMM]
Retreat music for flutes and drums [1943 TMM]

§ Symphony in A minor (abandoned) [1943 TMM; LW/327]
Prelude and Fugue for organ: *Calpe* [1943 TMM]
Sonata for cello and piano in G minor [1944 TMM/33; VB/16, 106] / "cello sonata" [*Life*/94] / Cello Concerto [1944 CC; LW/327, 330–1] / cf. **1979 (27 July) Concerto for Violin and Orchestra in E minor**, § **Concerto for Violoncello and Orchestra** (nd)
Nocturne for piano [1944 TMM]
"Anthem for Doomed Youth" (Wilfred Owen) for chorus and orchestra [1944 TMM; LW/327]
"*La niña del bello rostro*" (Lorca) for Spanish singer Merita [LW/307, VB/2–3]
*"a group of Spanish songs, mostly Lorca" [VB/106]
"*Muchísimas Gracias*" for Spanish singer Conchita (sung on "Franco's radio") [LW/329]
*"little minuet... in E minor" for guitar [VB/57] / cf. ca 1969 "little minuets for [Liana] in E minor"
*"wedding march", also "funeral-wedding march" for organ [VB/63, 73]
ca 1945 (Aug) "An Apple for the Teacher" (song popularized by Bing Crosby), arranged as regimental victory march [LW/319]
Music for Hiroshima for double string orchestra [1945 TMM]
*"short piece for flute and strings" [VB/106]
*"suite for strings", rescored for brass [VB/106–7]
Sonata for piano in E minor [1945 TMM; VB/106] / Sonata (piano) [1946 CC] / one of "two piano sonatas"? [*Life*/94]
**Passacaglia*, with parts for brass band to left and right of the orchestra [VB/86, 104–7] / cf. ca 1952 *Passacaglia for Orchestra*
Overture for large orchestra: *Gibraltar* [1945 TMM; LW/327] / *Gibraltar* (symphonic poem) [1944 CC]
*"comedy overture... suggested by *The Importance of Being Earnest*" [VB/106, 109]
Tobias and the Angel (incidental music) [TMM/33]
Winterset (incidental music) [TMM/33]

1946–48   MID-WEST SCHOOL OF EDUCATION AT BRINSFORD LODGE

§ Sinfonietta (abandoned) [1946 TMM]
§ Mass in G for chorus and orchestra (abandoned) [1946 TMM] / § *Sanctus* [LW/343]
Spring Songs for soprano and orchestra: "O western wind"; "The earth has cast her winter skin" (Charles d'Orléans, trans. A.B.); "Spring the sweet spring" (Thomas Nashe) [1946 TMM] / cf. **est 1972 *Spring Rondel***
"I sing of a maiden" (anon.) for voice and string quartet [1946 TMM]
"This was real": a group of stage songs [1947 TMM]
"These things shall be": a celebration for Bedwellty Grammar School [1947 TMM]
"Inversnaid" (Gerard Manley Hopkins) for SATB unaccompanied [1947 TMM]
Three Shakespeare Songs for voice and piano: "Apemantus's Song"; "Under the Greenwood Tree"; "Come thou monarch of the vine" [1947 TMM] / cf. **Three Shakespeare Songs** (est 1986)

1948–54 EMERGENCY TEACHER TRAINING COLLEGE, BAMBER BRIDGE (1948–50) – BANBURY GRAMMAR SCHOOL (1950–54)

ca 1948 *Murder in the Cathedral* (Eliot) [LW/347]: incidental music for small orchestra [1948 TMM/34] / orchestral incidental music [1948–49 VB/7]

ca 1948 *The Ascent of F6* (Auden) [LW/347]: incidental music for small dance orchestra [1948 TMM/34] / orchestral incidental music [1948–49 VB/7] / dance band [1947, prem Bamber Bridge, Lancashire 1949 CC]

Moto Perpetuo, for large orchestra [1948 TMM]

"polytonal suite for recorders" [1948–49 VB/7] /*Ludus Polytonalis* for chest of recorders [1948 TMM] / *Ludus Multitonalis* (recorder consort) [1951 CC]

Six Purcell Realizations [1948 TMM] / "some realisations of Purcell songs" [1948–49 VB/7]

"little concerto for piano duet and percussion" [1948–49 VB/7] / "concerto for piano and percussion" [*Life*/94] / Sinfonietta for two pianos, whistlers, and percussion band [1949 TMM] / Concertino (piano, percussion) [1951 CC] / for flutist-percussionist Kenneth Carrdus? [LW/354]

1950 Piano Sonata in G [1950 JPY] / sonata for Valerie Tryon [LW/354] / "piano sonata" [1948–49 VB/7] / Sonata (piano) [1951 CC] / Sonata in C for piano [1949 TMM] / one of "two piano sonatas"? [*Life*/94]

1950 Piano Sonatina in D [1950 JPY] / bagatelle for Valerie Tryon? [LW/354] / "piano sonatina" [1948–49 VB/7] / Sonatina in G for piano [1949 TMM] / one of "two piano sonatas"? [*Life*/94]

1950 *The Adding Machine* (Elmer Rice) [1950 JPY]: orchestral incidental music [1948–49 VB/7] / dance band [1949; prem Bamber Bridge, Lancashire 1950 CC]

1950 *A Midsummer Night's Dream* (Shakespeare): prem 7 Dec 1950, Banbury Grammar School [BG] / [1950 JPY] / incidental music for small orchestra [1950 TMM] / orchestral incidental music [1948–49 VB/7] / [LW/347]

1950 *Partita de Noël* for String Orchestra [1950 JPY] / Partita for string orchestra [1950 TMM/34 "performed in Banbury Town Hall"] / *Partita* for Dr Rose's string orchestra [LW/354] / *Partita* (string orchestra) [1951 CC]

1950 Carol Settings for Flute and Strings [1950 JPY] / for flutist Maurice Draper and/or flutist-percussionist Kenneth Carrdus? [LW/354]

§ 1950 Orchestral Overture [1950 JPY]

§ 1950 Piano Quintet [1950 JPY]

§ 1950 *"Zodiac" Variations* [1950 JPY] / Variations for double symphony orchestra (abandoned) [1951 TMM]

Two wedding marches for organ [1950 TMM] / {"wedding march", also "funeral-wedding march" for organ [VB/63, 73]}

1951 (summer) *Sweeney Agonistes* (Eliot) for voices and piano [1951 BG] / cf. Songs from T. S. Eliot's *Sweeney Agonistes* (1935)

Guitar Sonata in E (unplayable) [1951 TMM]

Concerto for flute and strings [1951 TMM] / "flute concerto" [*Life*/94] / for flutist Maurice Draper and/or flutist-percussionist Kenneth Carrdus and Dr Rose's string orchestra? [LW/354] / Concerto (flute, strings) [1960 CC]

Terrible Crystal: three Hopkins sonnets for baritone, chorus and orchestra [1952 TMM]

List of Music Compositions 389

1952 (30 Aug)   *Wiegenlied* (Berceuse/Cradlesong). Piano. 2 pp, 3:00 (w/rpt). Ded "to C. Looker". Loc Leicester. Insc "John Burgess Wilson". Epigraph from Rimbaud's *Le coeur supplicié* (The Tortured Heart). Fdp Paul Phillips, 26 Feb 1999, Brown Univ. ms McMaster Univ

1952 (12/25)   **Sonatina in G Major.** Piano. Folio: 6 pp. Ded Anne Field. Insc "John Burgess Wilson / Christmas, 1952". ms priv

ca 1952   *Passacaglia for Orchestra* ["rejected by the BBC" LW/355, TMM/34, VB/238] / *Passacaglia* (orchestra) [1961 CC] / cf. {*Passacaglia,* with parts for brass band} 1943≈6.

Toccata and Fugue for cathedral organ [1953 TMM]

§ 1953   *The Eve of Saint Venus.* Opera, libretto and music by AB [LW/357–60] / cf. nd **The Eve of Saint Venus,** 1975≈93

1954–59   MALAYA

1954   *Middeloceann.* Composed for the small orchestra aboard the ocean liner *Willem Ruys* [LW/371]

Ode: celebration for the Malay College for boys' voices and piano [1954 TMM] / *Cantata for Malay College* [1954 CC]

Kalau Tuan Mudek Ka-Ulu: five Malay pantuns for soprano and native instruments [1955 TMM; LW/413–4]

Suite for small orchestra of Indians, Chinese and Malays [1956 TMM]

1956 (ca Nov)   Symphony No. 2: *"Malayan Symphony"* [Malayan notebook entry, 14 Dec 1956] / *Symphony – Sinfoni Melayu* [1956 CC] / *Sinfoni Malaya* for orchestra and brass band and shouts of "Merdeka" ("Independence") from the audience [1957 TMM; LW/416; "How I Wrote My Third Symphony", Sec 2, 1; "Symphony in C", program note for Iowa prem]

1958 (Jan)   *Pando*: march for a P&O orchestra [1958 TMM] / "piece of music for . . . violinist, pianist and drummer" aboard a British P&O ocean liner ("the *Carthage* or the *Canton* or the *Corfu*") [LW/420]

1959–68   HOVE – ETCHINGHAM – CHISWICK

Passacaglia and Bagatelle for piano [1959 TMM, LW/445]

Suite for miniature organ [1959 TMM] / cf. "Interlude for Small Organ" [1958 RLAB/203]

§ est 1960   *Song of the South Downs.* Unfinished concert-piece for solo piano and orchestra. 16 pp. Inst 2 2 2(A) 2 – 4 3 3 1 tp 1pc(sd, sus cym, gong) str solo-pf. Insc "to Jake". ms Washington Univ. Perhaps cognate with "Song of a Northern City" or "Song of the Autumn Tide" [YH/65–6, played ca 1962] and thus also with *Song of a Northern City* (piano, orchestra) [1947 CC] and *Song of a Northern City* for piano [1942 TMM]

Fantasia for two recorders and piano [1960 TMM]

Twelve-tone polyrhythmics for piano [1961 TMM]

1961 (summer)   *Chaika*, for ship's orchestra (including alto saxophone), composed aboard the *Baltika* [summer 1961 YH/52–3]

1961 (Dec)   "Christmas carol for Diana Gillon". ms priv

1964–65 *Preludes.* Piano. 6 mvts, 10 pp, 10:00. Insc "Etchingham, 1964", yet letter to Martin Bell indicates that AB was still composing this work in July 1965. Fdp Gary Steigerwalt, 26 Feb 1999, Brown Univ. ms McMaster Univ.

1965 (June) Presto in "Senilio's Broadcast Script: Riposte to Peter Porter" by Martin Bell. Piano. 71 bs, ca 2:00. Pub in *Collected Pomes 1937–1966* by Martin Bell (London: Macmillan/New York: St Martin's, 1967), pp 81–5.

est late 1960s *Feuerwerk.* 3 pp, 66 bs, 2:00. *Molto Vivo,* 2/4, atonal. nd, ms Angers

§ est 1968 Bassoon Concerto. 2 mvts, 16 pp. Inst 2 2 2 2 – 4 3 3 1 tp pc hp str solo-bn. ms Angers / [*Life*/94]

1968 (early) Songs for *Will* (a film about Shakespeare projected but unrealized by Warner Bros; music recorded) [1968 TMM; YH 146–7, 157] / cf. ca 1974 *Shakespeare da Noi,* **1979 Mr W.S.**

ca 1968 "Who'll March with Essex?" kbd. 1 pg, 1:00. Insc "Ebauche d'après une musique traditionnelle" (rough draft based upon a piece of traditional music); probably intended for use in *Will.* The related lyric **"Who'll fight for Essex, / Our uncrowned king?"** appears in *Enderby's Dark Lady* [EDL/574]

1968 "an underscore for the *Enderby* movie" [*Life*/94]

1968–76   MALTA – BRACCIANO – ROME

ca 1969 "little minuets for [guitar] in E minor". Ded Liana [YH/208] / cf. *"little minuet... in E minor" for guitar [VB/57] 1943≈46

1971 *Cyrano de Bergerac* (Rostand, trans. AB): incidental music for voices and chamber ensemble [fl, cl, tpt, gtr, kbds (small org and hpsd), vc, pc(tamb, sd, kitchen implements)]. 13 sections, 20 pp. Prem 22 July 1971 at Tyrone Guthrie Theatre, Minneapolis, MN. ms Stratford Festival, Canada [TMM/35; YH/237–40]

ca 1971 *The Entertainer* (John Osborne): incidental music, 10 pp, 4 mvts. **"Archie – Tema"** (Archie's Theme), kbd; **"Vecchio Paese"** (Old Country), voice and kbd; **"E chi ci pensa?"**, voice and kbd; **"Se c"e uno di quelli"**, voice and kbd. nd, ms HRC [1971 TMM]

Southern City: overture for large orchestra [1971 TMM]

Roman Wall: march for orchestra [1971 TMM] / possible reference to *Roman Wall Blues* (Oct 1937), Song XI from W. H. Auden's "Twelve Songs" (Auden, *Collected Poems,* 143)

ca 1971 "setting of a Malay *pantun*" for voice, alto flute and xylophone, composed for Cathy Berberian [YH/235]

Suite for piano duet [1972 TMM]

1972 (ca Aug) *Faunal Noon* for harmonica and guitar. Ded John Sebastian. Composed on board ocean liner *Leonardo da Vinci* traveling from Naples to New York [YH/267–8; TMM]

1972 (ca Aug) Sonatina in E minor for harmonica and guitar. Ded John Sebastian. Composed on board ocean liner *Leonardo da Vinci* traveling from Naples to New York [YH/267–8; TMM] / cf. **1986 Sonatina for Harmonica and Guitar**

ca 1972 String Quartet (based on CDGAEF, Shakespeare theme in *Love's Labour's Lost*) [*Paris Review* 56/150, interview 1971–72] est 1972   *Spring Rondel:* "O western wind"; *Pervigilium Veneris* (Quando ver venit meum?); "The earth has cast her winter skin" (Charles d'Orléans, trans. AB). SATB chorus and piano. One mvt in 2 main parts, 10 pp, 4:00. nd, ms-c HRC / cf. *Spring Songs* [1946 TMM]

est 1972 (1 Nov)   **Bethlehem Palmtrees** (Lope de Vega, trans. Ezra Pound) SATB chorus a cappella (piano for rehearsal only). 3 pp, 1:15. Fdp 24 Sept 2003, Louisiana State Univ Chamber Choir, cond Randall Hooper, Baton Rouge, Louisiana. nd, probably composed as memorial to Pound after his death on 1 Nov 1972 ms HRC [1972 TMM] / cf. "Complaint, complaint I heard upon a day" [1936 TMM]

est 1973   *Moses the Lawgiver.* Score intended for 6-part television miniseries. "Title music" (full score, 18 pp, 3:00). Inst 3(3rd db picc) 2 2 2 – 4 3 3 1 tp 2pc(sd, bd, cym, gong, jingles, tamb, glock) hp org str; rest of score (26 pp, p-v) provides music for 18 sections. nd, ms HRC [YH, 297–303] / "unacceptable to Sir Lew Grade" [TMM/39]

ca 1973   **Bagatelle.** Piano. Short piece, "a little atonal". Ded John Covelli. Composed during their work together on *Cyrano.* ms priv

§ ca 1973   **"the unfinished phone number".** Opening of a fugal exposition based on 5-8-2-1 , part of Burgess's telephone number in Rome. Ded John Covelli. ms priv

1974   **Sinfonie.** Piano reductions of three orchestral works contained in one manuscript book. ms HRC

   Sinfonia (No. 1 – 1935). 4 mvts, 29 pp, 25:00. C major. Insc "This piano reduction reproduced from memory of the lost score – 1974" / cf. ca 1936 Symphony (no. 1) in E major

   Chaconne (1943). 2 pp, 2:00.

   § **Sinfonia (No. 2 – 1944).** 2 mvts only. 1st mvt, 10 pp, complete: basis of *A Manchester Overture* (and **Allegro Risoluto,** an incomplete sketch for that work). 2nd mvt, 4 pp, incomplete: sketch for 3rd mvt of **Symphony No. 3 in C**

ca 1974   **Shakespeare da Noi.** Music for an unproduced film for RAI, later incorporated into *Mr W.S.* ms unknown [YH/309–10] / cf. 1968 (early) Songs for *Will,* **1979 Mr W.S.**

1975 (Apr)   **Symphony No. 3 in C.** 4 mvts, 169 pp, 35:00. Inst 2(both db picc) 1+1 2 2 – 4 3(1 db cornet) 3 1 tp 3pc(sd, bd, tabor, cym, tamb, xyl) hp cel pf mandolin(2) str TB soloists. Ded "To Jim Dixon – with fond regards – *con molto affetto*". Composed Dec 1974–early Apr 1975. Prem 22 Oct 1975, Univ Sym Orch, cond James Dixon, Univ of Iowa School of Music, Iowa City, IA. ms Univ of Iowa Libraries [LW/160; TMM/35, 50–72, 80–3; YH/310–13, 324, 335; CC] / cf. **1974 Sinfonie:** § Sinfonia (No. 2 – 1944)

est 1975 (Nov)   "Fallen Rain (Silent fell the rain)", music by G. M. Hopkins, words by Canon Dixon; arrangement for voice and piano by AB. Prem 8 Dec 1975, Rockhurst College, Kansas City, Missouri (USA); liturgical commemoration marking the centenary of the wreck of the *Deutschland* (6–7 Dec 1875). ms unknown [TMM/119]

1975 (ca Nov)   **Fanfare for Three Trumpets.** Composed after prem of Symphony No. 3. Prem Dec 8, 1975, Rockhurst College, Kansas City, Missouri (USA); liturgical commemoration marking the centenary of the wreck of the *Deutschland* (6–7 Dec 1875). ms priv

1976–93 MONTE CARLO – LUGANO

est 1976   *Rome in the Rain.* 18 pp, 6:00. 2 2 2 2 – 4 2 3 1 tp 4pc(glock, tri, cym, sd, bd, Chinese blocks) hp solo-pf str. nd, np, ms HRC [TMM as "Concertino for piano and orchestra"]

1976 (1 July)   Concerto for Pianoforte and Orchestra in E♭. 3 mvts, 69 pp, 33:00. Inst 2+1 2+1 2 2 – 4 3 3 1 tp 4pc(sd, b.d, crash and sus cym, tamb, xyl, Chinese blocks) solo-pf str. Prem 13 Feb 1999, Gary Steigerwalt (pf), Pioneer Valley Sym, cond Paul Phillips, Greenfield, MA. ms-c HRC [1976 CC; TMM as "Concerto for piano and orchestra"]

§ est 1976   Concerto for Harmonica and String Orchestra. 16 pp, 190 bs. Inst solo-harm, divisi strings (4 vln, 2 vla, 2 vc, 2 cb). For a four-octave instrument with range to C3. Insc "Antoine Bourgeois' (suggesting that it was composed after moving to Monaco). nd 1975≈1993; est 1976 because written on the same kind of manuscript paper as *Rome in the Rain.* ms HRC

1976 (Sept–Nov)   *The Eyes of New York (Gli Occhi di New York).* Music for sixty-minute film for Mondadori. Inst fl cl vln vc pf. Rec Nov 1976 in C.A.M. studios (Rome) under direction of Michael Billingsley. ms unknown [YH/339–40; TMM]

1977 (15 Feb)   *Romanza.* Harmonica and piano. 5 pp, 3:00. Ded Tommy Reilly. Loc Monaco. Prem 8 March 1977, Tommy Reilly (harm), Anthony Burgess (pf) on the Oscar Peterson BBC-TV show. US prem 13 Oct 2007, Chris Turner (harm), Gary Steigerwalt (pf), FirstWorksProv Festival, Providence, RI. ms priv [1977 YH/365; TMM as "*Tommy Reilly's Maggot* for harmonica and piano"]

Suite for oboe [1977 TMM]

Nocturne for oboe [1977 TMM]

1977 (ca early Nov)   *The Brides of Enderby* (AB). Song cycle for soprano and chamber ensemble. 6 mvts, 23 pp, 15:30. Inst S fl ob vc pf/hpsd. Prem 11 Oct 1978 (radio, WQXR), 15 Oct 1978 (concert), Laurentian Chamber Players, cond Chester Biscardi, Sarah Lawrence College, Bronxville, NY. Rec 1 Dec 1978, Coolidge Auditorium, Library of Congress, Wash, DC (concert). nd, ms priv [YH/360; TMM; CC]

1978 (ca 19 Apr)   *The Waste Land* (Eliot). Melodrama for speaker, soprano and chamber ensemble. Prelude + 5 mvts, 46 pp, 37:00. Inst speaker S fl ob vc pf. Prem ("closed reading") 14 Oct 1978, Laurentian Chamber Players, narr. Brendan Gill, cond Chester Biscardi, Sarah Lawrence College, Bronxville, NY. nd, ms HRC [YH/360; TMM] / cf. ca 1938 *The Waste Land*

est 1978 (after 19 Apr)   *Quartet Giovanni Guglielmi (1917–45).* Chamber work with setting of A. E. Housman's "Epitaph on an Army of Mercenaries". 5 mvts, 27 pp, 15:00. Inst fl ob vc pf, plus S in 5th mvt only. nd, np, ms HRC

1978 (3 July)   *Song for Saint Cecilia's Day* (John Dryden). Cantata in 8 mvts for SATB soloists, chorus, organ and orchestra. 66 pp, 25:00. Inst 2(2nd db picc) 2 2 2 – 4 3 3 1 tp 4pc(sd, bd, crash and sus cym, tamb, xyl, bells, gong) hp cel org str. Loc Monaco. Prem 16 Nov 2002, McGill Chamber Singers and Opera Chorus, Brown Univ Orch, cond Paul Phillips, McGill Univ, Montreal. ms unknown, ms-c HRC [YH/323; TMM]

1978 (11 July)   *Master Coale's Pieces.* Piano. 4 mvts, 6 pp, 9:00. Ded Samuel Coale. Fdp 21 Nov 1994, Yüseyin Sermet, "AB: The Years in Monaco", Monte Carlo. Pub 1994, Saga THA 978536. ms priv

est 1979   **Mr W.S.** Ballet suite for orchestra. 9 mvts, 121 pp, 36:00. Inst 2(2nd db picc) 2(1 db shawm *ad lib.*)+1 2(A, B♭) 2 – 4 3 3 1 tp 3pc(sd, bd, tabor, tamb, cym, gong, bells, castanets, xyl) hp str. Based upon 1968 Songs for *Will* and 1974 *Shakespeare da Noi*. Prem 1979, BBC Orch, recorded and broadcast. Rec 28 May 1994, BBC Scottish Sym Orch, cond Peter Cynfryn Jones; broadcast 21 Aug 1994 in *An Airful of Burgess* (4th and 6th mvts omitted; 9th played with cut). US prem (complete) 23 Oct 1999, Pioneer Valley Sym, cond Paul Phillips, Greenfield, MA. ms Angers [1979 TMM; 1979 CC; YH/309–10 1974]

1979 (ca June)   ***Trotsky's in New York!*** Broadway-style musical, libretto and music by AB. 2 versions of p-v: earlier (T1) = 151 pp, later (T2) = 199 pp. T1: Overture, Act I (16 nos.), Act II (8 nos.); T2: Overture, Act I (3 scenes), Act II (3 scenes). Perf "Driven by the Wind", 1982, played and sung by AB on BBC radio [YH/327]; "Prelude", Nov 21, 1994, Yüseyin Sermet (pf), "AB: The Years in Monaco", Monte Carlo. AB's musical setting np; prem of libretto set to music by Ronald Senator, Nov 11, 1997, AMAS Musical Theatre, NY. Libretto pub in EWN, ms HRC [YH 326–7; TMM]

1979 (27 July)   **Concerto for Violin and Orchestra in E minor.** 3 mvts, 90 pp, 35:00. Full orchestra. Ded Yehudi Menuhin. Insc "Gibraltar, Summer 1945 – Monaco, July 27, 1979". np, ms Royal College of Music Library, London [YH/331; 1979 TMM] / cf. Cello Concerto [1944 LW/330–1]

1980 (8 March)   **String Quartet.** 3 mvts, 24 pp, 17:30. Ded "For the Primavera 4tet". Loc Monaco. Fdp 2nd mvt only, 16 June 1994, Barbican Virtuosi, Memorial Celebration, St. Paul's Church, London; mvts 1–3 (w/cuts), 21 Nov 1994, Ronald Patterson (vln), Marius Mocanu (vln), Jean-Pierre Pigerre (vla), Lane Anderson (vc), "AB: The Years in Monaco", Monte Carlo. US prem (complete) Oct 14, 2007, Katherine Winterstein (vln), Charles Sherba (vln), Consuelo Sherba (vla), Jing Li (vc), FirstWorksProv Festival, Providence, RI. ms HRC

1980 (17 Oct)   **Nocturne and Chorale for Four Bassoons.** Nocturne (Andantino), 4 pp, 2:15. Insc "Kenyon Oct. 17 1980"; Chorale (Lento), 1 pg, 1:30. ms-c HRC [YH/364–5; 1980 TMM]

1980 (10 Nov)   **Pieces for Harmonica.** Harmonica and piano. 3 mvts, 8 pp, 6:00. Loc Monaco. Ded "To Larry Adler". np, ms priv, ms-c (poor condition) HRC [YH/365; 1980 TMM as "*Larry Adler's Maggots* for harmonica and piano"]

1981 (ca early Feb)   ***Blooms of Dublin***. Light opera in two acts based on *Ulysses*, libretto and music by AB. Prelude, Act I (19 nos.), Act II (15 nos.), ca 150:00. Orig. version completed 1971 (ca 21 Aug). Scores: p-v, 125 pp; orch, 438 pp. Inst 1 1 2 1 – 1 1 1 0 tp pc(xyl, glock) hp pf str SSAATTBB chorus, plus principals. Rec 13–17 Jan 1982, Dublin; broadcast prem 1 Feb 1982, Radio Telefís Éireann and BBC. Parts of libretto pub in EP. np on stage, ms HRC [YH/290, 370–4; TMM as "*The Blooms of Dublin*"]

1981 (26 Feb)   ***A Glasgow Overture***. Orchestral overture. 48 pp, 10:00. Ded "To the Lord Provost of Glasgow, March 12 1981". Loc Monaco. Inst 2+1 2+1 2+1 2+1 – 4 3 3 1 tp 3pc(sd, bd, crash and sus cym, xyl, tamb, tam-tam) str. Prem May 1982, Scottish National Orch, cond Alexander Gibson, Glasgow. Rec 28 May 1994, BBC Scottish Sym Orch, cond Peter Cynfryn Jones; broadcast 21 Aug 1994 in *An Airful of Burgess*. ms Library of the Royal Scottish National Orch [YH/364; 1981 TMM; CC]

Preludio e Fuga per flauto, violin, chitarra e pianoforte [1981 TMM]
1981 (9 Aug) *A Scottish Rhapsody for the 17th birthday of Andrew.* kbd. 3 pp, 4:00. Ded Andrew. Fdp Gary Steigerwalt (pf), 26 Feb 1999, Brown Univ, Providence, RI. ms HRC
1981 (25 Dec) *In Dulci Jubilo.* Kbd. 1 pg. Insc "Natale 1981". ms-c HRC
est 1981 (ca 25 Dec) *Preludio e Fuga su* In Dulci Jubilo. Organ. 3 pp, 3:00. Allegro giocoso. nd, ms HRC
est 1982 (Feb) *Homage to Hans Keller* for four tubas [1982 TMM]. § **Allegro moderato,** 5 pp, for four bass tubas, evidently an incomplete draft of *Homage to Hans Keller.* nd, ms HRC. Title is retaliation for Keller's review of *Blooms of Dublin*; complete work unlikely to exist.
1982 (8 Mar) *The Wreck of the Deutschland* (G. M. Hopkins). Oratorio in one mvt. 138 pp, 32:00. Inst 3 2+1 2 2+1 – 4 3 3 1 tp 3pc(sd, bd, crash and sus cym, glock, gong) hp str solo-B SATB chorus. Loc Monaco. np, ms HRC [YH/369; 1982 TMM]
1982 (18 June) "Strings" (James Joyce). Song for voice and piano. 2.5 pp, 1:40. Loc Dublin. Prem Kathryne Jennings (S), Paul Phillips (pf), 22 Jan 1999, Longmeadow Chamber Music Society, MA. ms HRC
1982 (20 June) "Ecce Puer" (James Joyce). Song for voice and piano. 3.5 pp, 1:35. Insc "In the train – Dublin-Cork". Prem Kathryne Jennings (S), Paul Phillips (pf), 22 Jan 1999, Longmeadow Chamber Music Society, MA. ms HRC
1982 (on or after 13 Sept) *In memoriam Princess Grace.* Elegy for string orchestra. 3 pp, 6:00. Prem (string quintet) 21 Nov 1994, Ronald Patterson (vln), Marius Mocanu (vln), Jean-Pierre Pigerre (vla), Lane Anderson (vc), Libero Lanzilotta (cb), "AB: The Years in Monaco", Monte Carlo. Perf (orch, US prem) 4 Dec 1998, Brown Univ Orch, cond Paul Phillips, Providence, RI. ms HRC
1983 (7 Jan) "A Poor Man Can't Be Free" (George Mikes). Song for the play *The Virgin and the Bull* by Mikes. 8 pp, 4:00. Inst voice, chorus, pf, wind instrument ("Preferably a Flute"). Perf 23 Apr-14 May 1983 at Clwyd Theatr Cymru, Wales. ms-c HRC, ms priv
1983 (12 July) *A.D. (Anno Domini).* Score intended for 12-hour, 5-part television miniseries. 14 sections, 111 pp, ca 40:00. Inst 2 2 2 2 – 4 3 3 1 tp pc hp org str; chorus, solo voices. ms HRC
1984 (8 Apr) *Man Who Has Come Through* (D. H. Lawrence). Song cycle for tenor and chamber ensemble. Prelude/postlude + 4 mvts, 48 pp, 35:00. Inst T fl ob vc pf. Loc Monaco. Prem 22 Sept 1985, Stephen Williams (T), principals from the East of England Orch, cond Malcolm Nabarro, D. H. Lawrence Centenary Festival, East Midlands Music Theatre, Nottingham. ms HRC [1984 CC]
§ **1984 (est summer)** Symphony [1984]. Unfinished one-mvt symphony in 8 sections. 68 pp, 408 bs. Inst 3(3rd db picc) 2+1 2+1 2+1 – 4 3 3 1 tp 3pc(bd, cym, glock, xyl) cel str. ms HRC
1984 (1 Oct) *In Time of Plague* (Thomas Nashe). Choral work. 8 pp, 6:00. SATB a cappella. Loc Monaco. Fdp 16 June 1994, I Fagiolini, Burgess Memorial Celebration, London. Pub 1994, Saga THA 978484. ms HRC
1984 (3 Oct) *Weep you no more* (anon. Elizabethan text). Choral work. 3 pp, 4:00. SATB a cappella. Fdp 24 Sept 2003, Louisiana State Univ Chamber Choir, cond Randall Hooper, Baton Rouge, Louisiana. ms HRC

§ 1984 (ca 3 Oct)   *Still to be neat* (Ben Jonson). Unfinished choral work. 2 pp (19 bs), 2:00. SATB a cappella. ms HRC

1984 (24 Nov)   **Tango for Pianoforte.** 6 pp, 3:00. Prem 14 Apr 1985, Yvar Mikhashoff (pf), North American New Music Festival, Buffalo, NY. Pub 1995, Saga THA 95041. ms HRC

est 1984 (Dec)   **Allegro Moderato.** Kbd piece sent as Christmas greeting. 1 pg, 2:00. Quodlibet of Christmas carols. ms-c HRC

1985 (29 June)   **Andantino.** Contrapuntal piece for 3 unspecified instruments. 1 pg, 1:00. ms HRC

§ 1985 (Nov)   **Fugues.** 25 pp of kbd fugues, complete and incomplete, most in 4 voices. One dated 12 Nov 1985, another dated 18 Nov 1985, the rest undated. ms HRC

1985 (13 Dec)   *The Bad-Tempered Electronic Keyboard,* **Vol. I: 24 Preludes and Fugues.** 12 preludes and fugues in all the major keys, 12 preludes and fugues in all the minor keys, and *Finale: Natale 1985.* 83 pp; 90:00. Composed 23 Nov–13 Dev 1985. Fdp Maureen Turquet, various mvts. ms HRC

1985 (20 Dec)   *Fuga a 4 voci.* Kbd, E♭ major. 2 pp, 42 bs, 3:00. ms HRC

1986 (30 Mar)   *Quatuor pour Guitares* (also called *"Quatuor No. 1 pour Guitares"* and *"Quatuor en Hommage à Maurice Ravel"*). Guitar quartet. 3 mvts, 24 pp, 12:30. Insc "Paque 1986". Prem Jan 1987, Aïghetta Quartet, Académie Rainier III de Monaco. Rec 1987 by Aïghetta Quartet on *Oeuvres pour Quatuor de Guitares* (1987 LP, REM 11032) and 1995 by Aïghetta Quartet on *Musique d'un écrivain anglais sur la Riviera* for *l'empreinte digitale* (1996 CD, ED13049). ms HRC [CC]

1986 (9 June)   **Sonatina for Harmonica and Guitar.** 4 mvts, 18 pp, 16:45. D major. Copy probably sent to Larry Adler. np, ms HRC / cf. 1972 (ca Aug). Prem 14 Oct 2007, Chris Turner (harm), Mark Davis (gtr), FirstWorksProv Festival, Providence, RI. ms HRC

1986 (July)   **Festal Suite for Brass.** Prem July or August 1986, Birmingham Festival of Music. ms unknown [1986 YH/x]

ca 1986 (July)   *A Clockwork Orange: a play with music* (words and music by AB). Incidental music for voices and kbd (plus tpt in last number). Prelude, Act I (12 nos.), Act II (5 nos.). 39 pp, ca 90:00, pub in Methuen edition, 1998. Intro to Hutchinson edition of the play insc "Lugano, July 1986". Perf: Schauspielhaus Bonn, 1988 (in German); Royal Shakespeare Company, London, 1990 (previews began 26 Jan; opened 6 Feb) – revised version titled *A Clockwork Orange 2004*; Fabulous and Ridiculous Theatre, Austin, TX, May 2000. ms (and earlier draft version of the score) HRC

1986   **"Fingers Off".** Piece for "Fiddles" and "Joanna or Orch." pub in *The Pianoplayers* (206–8). 25 bs, in F major. Easy violin part (all open strings) with piano part of moderate difficulty, similar to **"Birthday Greeting"** (below)

1986 (25 Sept)   **"Birthday Greeting".** Piece for guitar and piano in E minor. 1 pg, 24 bs, 2:40 (w/rpt). Ded Liana. Easy guitar part (all open strings) with piano part of moderate difficulty, similar to **"Fingers Off"** (above). ms HRC

est 1986   **Three Shakespeare Songs.** Voice(s) and piano. "Under the Greenwood Tree" (voice, pf; 2 pp), "Apemantus's Grace" (B, pf; 2 pp), "Come thou monarch of the vine" (TTBB chorus, pf; 2 pp. Insc "Happy birthday to Micaela from Anthony Burgess"). ca 8:00. Fdp "Under the Greenwood Tree", Kathryne Jennings (S), Paul Phillips (pf), 22 Jan 1999, Longmeadow Chamber Music Society, MA. nd, ms HRC / cf. *Three Shakespeare Songs* [1947 TMM]

1986 (11 Dec)   Rhapsody. Andantino for oboe and piano. 8 pp, 4:00. Ded Andrew. Fdp 21 Nov 1994, Jean-Paul Barrellon (ob), Yüseyin Sermet (pf), "AB: The Years in Monaco", Monte Carlo. ms HRC

est 1986   Allegretto. Oboe and piano. 1 pg, 1:00. Twelve-tone. Ded Andrew. nd, ms HRC. verso: **Andantino** (below)

est 1986   Andantino. Piano. 1 pg, 1:00. nd, ms HRC. verso: **Allegretto** (above)

1986 (21 Dec)   *Pezzetto per Chitarra*. Little piece for guitar and piano. 2 pp, 25 bs, 2:00. E minor Loc "44 rue Grimaldi, Monaco". Ded Roger Nyström of Norrköping, Sweden. ms HRC

1987 (21 Jan)   *Concerto per Chitarra ed Orchestra en Mi minore*. Concerto for guitar and orchestra. 3 mvts, 30:30. Loc Monaco. Ded Philippe Loli. Scores: orch (79 pp; dated Jan 21, 1987), piano reduction (59 pp; dated Jan 28, 1987). Inst 2 2 2 2 – 4 3 3 1 tp 1pc(tamb, glock, crash and sus cym) str solo-gtr. np, ms HRC

1987 (21 Jan)   "Mercury" from *The Planets* (Gustav Holst). Arrangement for guitar quartet. 18 pp, 278 bs, 4:00. Prem Aïghetta Quartet, ca 1987. Fdp 18 Jan 1989, Aïghetta Quartet, Monaco. ms HRC

1987 (ca Jan-Feb)   Overture to *Oberon* (Carl Maria von Weber). Arrangement for guitar quartet. 23 pp, 9:00. Prem Aïghetta Quartet, Venice, spring 1987. Fdp 18 Jan 1989, Aïghetta Quartet, Monaco. ms HRC

1987 (24 Feb)   *Mr Burgess's Almanack*. Work for large chamber ensemble (14 players). 53 pp, 12 mvts plus "Exordium" and "Postlude", 26:00. Inst 2 2 2 2 – 1 1 0 0 tp 2pc(xyl, glock, vibraphone) pf. Prem (w/optional Postlude omitted) 11 Apr 1988, musicians from l'Orchestre de la Suisse Romande, cond Jonathan Haskell, Hotel Beau-Rivage, Geneva. Broadcast (mvts I-VI and X only) 21 Aug 1994 in *An Airful of Burgess*, musicians of the BBC Scottish Sym Orch, cond Peter Cynfryn Jones. Perf (US prem, complete) 29 Apr 2005, musicians of the Brown Univ Orch, cond Paul Phillips, Providence, RI. ms HRC [YH/389; CC]

1987 (ca May)   *Concerto Grosso pour Quatuor de Guitares et Orchestre en La mineur*. Concerto grosso for guitar quartet and orchestra. 3 mvts, 63 pp, 23:00. End of 1st mvt insc "Milan, 20 mars 1987". Scores: orch (63 pp), piano reduction (18 pp, dated "1 June 1987"). Inst 2(1st db picc) 2 2 2 – 4 3 3 1 tp 1pc(sd, bd, tri, tamb, crash cym) str solo-gtr quartet. Prem 6 Feb1989, Aïghetta Quartet, Orch Régional de Cannes/Provence-Alpes-Côte d'Azur, cond Philippe Bender, Cannes. ms HRC [CC]

est 1987   Impromptu for Guitar. 1 pg, 18 bs, 1:30 (w/rpt). Allegretto Grazioso, B minor. Ded Liana. nd 1976≈93 ms HRC. verso: **Fugue for Guitar** (below)

est 1987   Fugue for Guitar. 1 pg, 12 bs, 2:00 (w/rpt). Moderato, E minor. Ded Liana. nd 1976≈93 ms HRC. verso: **Impromptu for Guitar** (above)

1987 (3 Oct)   Quartet for Oboe, Violin, Viola & Violoncello. 4 mvts, 35 pp, 17:00. Ded "For Andrew". Insc "NOTE: Movements may be played in any order, or singly, or 2 or 3 or 4". Prem 13 Oct 2007 (1st mvt only). Aurea Ensemble, FirstWorksProv Festival, Providence, RI. ms unknown, ms-c HRC

1987 (25 Dec)   Nocturne. Andantino for oboe and piano. 5 pp, 3:00. Ded "for Andrew". ms HRC / also listed as 1932 **Nocturne /** verso (p. 5): **Bergamasque** (below)

1987 (ca 25 Dec)   Bergamasque. Oboe and piano. 1 pg, 1:00. ms HRC. verso: **Nocturne** (above)

1988 (29 Feb)   A Little Concerto for Oboe and Orchestra. 3 mvts, 45 pp, 13:00. Ded "For Andrew". Inst 2 0 2 2 – 4 3 3 1 tp pc(xyl, sd) hp str solo-ob. np, ms-c HRC

List of Music Compositions 397

1988 (4 Mar) *La pioggia nel pineto* (Gabriele d'Annunzio). Song for tenor and piano. 14 pp, 12:00. Loc Monaco. Prem spring 1988, Gian Paolo Fagotto (T), Mauro Castellano (pf), Amsterdam, repeated by the same performers 2 July 1988, Spotorno, Italy. ms HRC [YH/380, 390; CC]

est 1988 Study for Cor Anglais or Oboe. Unaccompanied. ca 3 pp, 4:00. Pub 1994, Saga THA 978478. nd, ms unknown.

1988 *Concertino per Corno Inglese ed Orchestra.* One-mvt concertino in 3 sections. 42 pp, 14:00. Ded "For Andrew". Inst 3 2 2+1 2 – 4 3 3 1 tp hp str solo-EH. Loc Lugano. Rec May 28, 1994, Stella McCracken (EH), BBC Scottish Sym Orch, cond Peter Cynfryn Jones; broadcast 21 Aug 1994 in *An Airful of Burgess*. ms-c HRC

1988 (June) *Petite Symphonie pour Strasbourg.* Sinfonietta for chamber orchestra. 3 mvts, 38 pp, 17:00. Inst 1 1 1 1 – 1 1 0 0 tp pf str (66442 or 66433). Prem 25 Nov 1988, l'Orchestre de Chambre du Conservatoire National de Région de Strasbourg, cond Étienne Bardon. ms HRC [CC] / cf. **1989 (10 Aug)** *Meditations and Fugues for Brass Band*

1988 (19 July) *Quatuor N° 2 pour Guitares.* Guitar quartet. Prelude + 4 mvts, 26 pp, 17:00. Loc Lugano. Prem Jan 1989, Aïghetta Quartet, Théâtre Princesse Grace de Monaco. Rec 1989 by Aïghetta Quartet on *Oeuvres pour Quatuor de Guitares* (CD, REM 311111) and 1995 by Aïghetta Quartet on *Musique d'un écrivain anglais sur la Riviera* for *l'empreinte digitale* (1996 CD, ED13049). ms HRC [CC] / cf. **1990 (09/24)** *Sinfonietta for Liana*

ca 1988 (Dec) *Trois Morceaux Irlandais.* Arrangement for guitar quartet of 3 Irish songs: "The Ballad of Persse O"Reilly" (from *Finnegans Wake*), "The Lark in the Clear Air", and "The Irish Washerwoman". 4 pp, 5:00. Prem 18 Jan 1989, Aïghetta Quartet, Monaco. ms HRC

1989 (21 Apr) *Marche pour une Révolution 1789–1989.* Orchestral march. 33 pp, 245 bs, 6:00. Inst 3(3rd db picc) 2 2 2+1 – 4 3 3 1 tp 3pc(cym, bd, sd, tamb, glock) 2hp str. Ded "Pour Philippe Bender avec mes amitiés et mon admiration". Prem 30 Sept 1989, l'Orchestre Regional de Cannes Provence Alpes Cote d'Azur, cond Philippe Bender, Vence. ms HRC [1989 CC]

§ **est 1989 (May)** Allegro Risoluto. Unfinished orchestral piece; evidentally a sketch for *A Manchester Overture*. 10 pp, 40 bs, nd, ms HRC / cf. **1974** *Sinfonie*: § Sinfonia (No. 2 – 1944) and **1989 (11 June)** *A Manchester Overture* (below)

1989 (11 June) *A Manchester Overture.* Orchestral overture. 43 pp, 12:00. Inst 3(3rd db picc) 2+1 2+1 2+1 – 4 3 3 1 tp 3pc(glock, xyl, sd, bd, cym) 2hp str. Prem 28 Oct 2005, Brown Univ Orch, cond Paul Phillips, Providence, RI. ms HRC / cf. **1974** *Sinfonie*: § Sinfonia (No. 2 – 1944) and § **est 1989 (May)** Allegro Risoluto (above)

1989 (ca 23 June) Minuet. Kbd. 1 pg, 1:30. nd; according to note attached to ms, a copy was mailed on 23 June 1989. ms HRC

1989 (4 Aug) "Happy Birthday!" Fugue in 3 voices on "Happy Birthday" for rcdr (F) and pf. 1 pg, 48 bars, C major. 1:00. Ded Andrew for his 25th birthday on 9 Aug1989. ms HRC

1989 (10 Aug) *Meditations and Fugues for Brass Band.* Arrangement of the last 2 mvts of *Petite Symphonie pour Strasbourg*. 12:00. Loc Lugano. Prem 8 May 1991, Salford College of Technology Brass Band, cond David King, Peel Hall, Univ of Salford. Broadcast Dec 10, 1995, BBC Radio 3. Pub 1994, Saga THA 978492, 27 pp. ms HRC

1989 (ca Aug)   *St. Winefred's Well* (G. M. Hopkins): incidental music for play (adapted and completed by AB). Inst solo-fl (3 passages). Broadcast prem 23 Dec 1989, BBC. ms unknown.

1989 (28 Dec)   *Quatuor N° 3 pour Guitares.* Guitar quartet. 3 mvts, 13 pp, 12:30. Prem Aug 1990, Aïghetta Quartet, Théâtre Antique d'Arles. Rec 1995 by Aïghetta Quartet on *Musique d'un écrivain anglais sur la Riviera* for *l'empreinte digitale* (1996 CD, ED13049). ms HRC / cf. § est 1990 (early) Allegro Vivace (below)

§ est 1990 (early)   Allegro Vivace. Unfinished orchestral transcription of 1st mvt of *Quatuor N° 3 pour Guitares.* 19 pp, 121 bs. Inst 2 2+1 2+1 2+1 – 4 3 3 1 tp pc(cym, bd, sd, xyl) pf str. ms HRC / cf. 1989 (28 Dec) *Quatuor N° 3 pour Guitares* (above)

est 1990   *Sonate pour flûte à bec alto* (treble rcdr). Sonata for unaccompanied rcdr (F) in the style of Vivaldi. 4 mvts, 5 pp, 10:00. nd, ms HRC

§ est 1990   Sonatina for Recorder. Rcdr (F) and kbd. 3 mvts, 18 pp, 9:00. Outer mvts complete; first 2 pp of 3-page middle mvt missing. Facsimile of 1st mvt pub 2000, American Recorder Society Erich Katz Contemporary Music Series. nd, ms HRC

est 1990   *Due Pezzetti:* Two little pieces for flute (or recorder) and piano. 2 mvts, 2:15. Pub 1994, Saga THA 978471. nd, ms unknown.

1990 (28 Feb)   Quartet for Flute, Oboe, 'Cello and Piano. 3 mvts, 19 pp, 14:00. Insc "Ash Wednesday 1990". Prem 23 Apr 2000, Boston Conservatory Chamber Players, Boston. ms HRC

1990 (13 Apr)   Sonata in C, or Sonata [No. 1] for Great Bass Recorder and Keyboard. 3 mvts, 15 pp, 8:00. Insc "Good Friday, April 13 1990". ms HRC

1990 (ca July)   *Quatre Préludes.* Orchestral arrangements of four piano preludes by Claude Debussy. 4 mvts, 48 pp, 12:00. Insc "June 21 1990" at end of 1st mvt; other mvts undated. I. *Lent et mélancolique... Feuilles mortes;* II. *Grave... Hommage à S. Pickwick Esq. P. P. M. P. C.;* III. *Lent... La terrasse des audiences du clair de lune;* IV. *Dans le style et le mouvement d'un cake-walk... "General Lavine" – eccentric.* Inst 3 2+1 2+1 2+1 – 4 3 3 1 tp pc(glock, tamb, sd, bd, Chinese block, tri, xyl, cym) 2hp cel str. Originally called *Cinq Préludes;* using tape, AB changed title by covering *Cinq* with *Quatre.* ms HRC

§ 1990 (ca July)   *Feux d'artifice.* Unfinished orchestral arrangement of piano prelude by Claude Debussy. 11 pp, ca 3:00. Evidently intended as the 5th of the *Cinq Préludes.* Inst 3 2+1 2+1 2+1 – 4 3 3 1 tp pc 2hp str. nd, ms HRC

1990 (24 Sept)   *Sinfonietta for Liana.* Orchestral arrangement of *Quatuor No. 2 pour Guitares.* Insc "From Antonio – A Birthday Gift – 25 September 1990". 5 mvts, 88 pp, 16:00. Inst 3(3rd db picc) 2+1 2+1 2+1 – 4 3 3 1 tp 4pc(sd, glock, crash and sus cym, xyl, bd, bells, gong) cel str. Loc Lugano. np, ms HRC

est 1990 (24 Dec)   "The Oxen" (Thomas Hardy). Song for voice and piano. 2 pp, 3:00. Fdp 22 Jan 1999. Kathryne Jennings (S), Paul Phillips (pf). Longmeadow Chamber Music Society, MA. nd; possibly composed 1990 for 150th anniversary of Hardy's birth and 75th of poem's publication on Dec 24, 1915. ms HRC

est 1991   Three Little Pieces for Wind Quintet or Recorder Quintet. Inst fl ob cl hn bn or 5 rcdrs – sopranino, descant (soprano), treble (alto), tenor, bass (or great bass). 3 mvts, 5:00. Ded "for Andrew". Pub 1994, Saga THA 978537; parts for both combinations of instruments included. nd, ms unknown.

List of Music Compositions 399

1992 (18 Sept)   Sonata No. 2 for G. B. R. Great bass rcdr (C) and kbd. 3 mvts, 18 pp, 8:00. ms HRC

§ 1992 (31 Oct)   *I Blum Di Dublino* (Italian p-v of *Blooms of Dublin*). Act I only. 114 pp, np, ms HRC

1993 (18 Jan)   Sonata [for Violin, Gt. B. Recorder & Piano]. 3 mvts, 20 pp, 9:30. ms-c (mvts I-II, poor condition), ms (mvt III, excellent condition) HRC

1993 (early)   Sonata No. 3 for Great Bass Recorder or Bassoon, and Piano. 3 mvts, 4:30. Pub 1994, Saga THA 978601. "written early in 1993" according to Saga edition. ms unknown.

est 1993   Sonata No. 4 for Great Bass Recorder and Pianoforte. Although "Sonata No. 3" is written on the ms, here it is called "Sonata No. 4" to distinguish it from the different work listed above. 3 mvts, 19 pp, 11:30. nd, ms HRC

1993 (12 Nov)   Sonata 1 (St. John's). Rcdr (F) and pf. 3 mvts, 8 pp, 4:00. Insc *"post operationem glottalem"*. Prem 13 Oct 2007, Charles Sherba (vln), Paul Phillips (pf), FirstWorksProv Festival, Providence, RI. ms-c HRC

1993 (after Sonata 1, 12≈23 Nov)   Sonata 2. Rcdr (F) and kbd. 4 mvts, 9 pp, 7:00. ms-c HRC

§ 1993 (after Sonata 2, 12≈23 Nov)   Sonata 3. Rcdr (F) and kbd. Fragment: 1 pg, 6 bs, ms-c HRC

1993 (after Sonata 3, 12≈23 Nov)   Andante, for Flutes or Recorders. 3 fl or 3 rcdr (F or C, C, F or C). 1 pg, 14 bs, 1:00. ms-c HRC

2. UNDATED WORKS, BY GENRE, IN ALPHABETICAL ORDER
KEYBOARD

Berceuse pour un nouveau né. Kbd. 1 pg, 15 bs. *Doucement*, 6/8, E minor. nd, ms-c HRC

Birthday Music. 1. Fanfare (Presto), 2. Passacaglia (Grave), 3. Fugue (Allegro Vivo). Kbd. 3 pp, based on "Happy Birthday". nd, ms Angers

[Brief Suite in A]. 6 mvts, 9:00. Fdp Dana Muller, 26 Feb 1999, Brown Univ. nd, ms HRC

[Fughetta]. Kbd. 2 pp, 38 bs. 6/8, F major. nd, untitled, ms HRC

"Happy Birthday to my Dear Wife". Kbd. 2 pp, 73 bs, C major to G major. Ded Liana. Insc "Antonio". nd, 1968≈1993, ms HRC

[Nine Miniatures]. Kbd. 6 pp, 9 mvts, 6:00. Fdp Paul Phillips, 25 June 2004, IABF, Withington. nd, untitled, ms HRC

Preludio. Kbd. 1 pg, 16 bs, A minor. ms-c HRC

Preludio e Fuga. Kbd. 4 pp, C major. Includes a bitonal Moderato non troppo (E♭ minor l.h. vs. C major r.h.) between the Preludio (Andantino) and Fuga (Allegramente). nd HRC

Schnee in Savosa. Piano, 4 hands. 2 pp, 1:10. Fdp Gary Steigerwalt and Dana Muller, 26 Feb 1999, Brown Univ. nd 1986≈1993 (after moving to Savosa). ms HRC

[Eight short pieces]. Kbd. 13 pp, 8 mvts: Fuga (2 pp), Fuga 2 – Allegro (2), Fuga 3 – Moderato (2), Air 2 – Lento (2), Hornpipe – Allegro (1), 1. In tempo commodo (1), 2 (1), Passacaglia – Moderato (2). nd, ms HRC

INSTRUMENTAL

Air (Lentamente, 1 pg.) and § **Gigue** (Molto Animato, 1 pg). For low treble instrument and kbd. ms HRC

III. Allegro Vivo. Probably for soprano rcdr or ob and kbd. 4 pp, 102 bs, 2:30. Mvts I-II missing.

ORCHESTRAL

§ **Concerto for Violoncello and Orchestra.** Unfinished 1st mvt, Allegro deciso. 12 pp. Inst 3 2+1 2+1 2+1 – 4 3 3 1 tp pc str solo-vc. nd, ms HRC / cf. *Cello Concerto* [1944 CC, LW/327, 330–1]

§ **Overture:** *The Cotton Masters.* For orch, unfinished. 14 pp. Inst 3+1 2+1 2+1 2+1 – 4 3 3 1 tp pc(cym, glock, bd, sd) 2hp str. nd, ms HRC

§ **2. Presto.** Unfinished sketch of a concerto mvt; unspecified solo part probably for vln.

VOCAL

§ *The Eve of Saint Venus,* nd 1976≈1993. Score written in French music notebook, suggesting it was composed after move to Monaco. 27 pp, p-v. ms HRC / cf. § 1953 *The Eve of Saint Venus*

"I thank you for your kindness". Fuga (Andantino gratitudinosamente) for SATB a cappella. 3 pp, 45 bs, G minor to A major. Ends with coda that musically spells out the names "AntHony BurGESS" and "BACH". nd, ms HRC

Songs: 1. "**Willett's Song**" (Quick Waltz), 2. "**Flower of the Mountain**" (Slow), 3. "**Pounce on Me, Puma**". Three short, unaccompanied melodies in treble clef, evidently connected with characters from EWN. nd, ms HRC

"**Women Swallow Anything**". Song for unaccompanied voice (treble clef). 1 pg, 39 bs, A minor. nd, ms HRC

In addition to the works cited above, there are numerous sketches and short pieces, mostly incomplete.

3. PROJECTED, UNWRITTEN COMPOSITIONS

Clarinet Concerto [*Paris Review* 56/131, interview 1971–72]

Musical play based on *The Transposed Heads* by Thomas Mann [*Paris Review* 56/158]

Sigmund Freud opera [YH/390 1990]

Rhapsody for Bass Tuba & Orchestra [AB postcard to Jay Rozen, Dec 1991]

4. ARRANGEMENTS OF COMPOSITIONS BY ANTHONY BURGESS

Prelude and Fugue 11 in B♭ major from *The Bad-Tempered Electronic Keyboard.* Arr. for string quartet by Paul Phillips. Prem 14 Oct 2007, Charles Sherba (vln), Katherine Winterstein (vln), Consuelo Sherba (vla), Jing Li (vc), FirstWorksProv Festival, Providence, RI.

KEY

Dates and titles of extant works are in bold type; lost works are in regular type.

§ = unfinished or incomplete work; * = work attributed to fictional composer Richard Ennis that may or may not indicate a work actually composed by Burgess.

Information source is cited in brackets, i.e. [TMM] signifying *This Man and Music*; in cases of conflicting references to the same composition, the source considered most reliable is listed first.

Number after slash indicates page number of citation in that source, i.e. [*Life*/94].

Year specifically cited in a source is listed before the source, i.e. [1961 TMM]; references to the TMM and CC work lists do not list page numbers.

Year implied but not specifically stated in a source is listed after the source, i.e. [LW/361 1960].

A date precedes the title when
  a) it is inscribed on the holograph, i.e. 1979 (07/27) for "July 27, 1979".
  b) it can be reliably determined through correspondence, contemporaneous press accounts or other sources; such cases are often preceded by "ca".
  c) it can be reasonably deduced on the basis of an anniversary, style of paper or handwriting, or comparable grounds; such cases are usually preceded by "est".
  d) it is given in a note in the printed score, as in some works published by Saga Music.

A date does not precede the title when
  a) it occurs only in the TMM and/or CC work list without additional corroboration.
  b) different sources list dissimilar dates without clear evidence of which is correct; in cases where precise dates cannot be determined, the one considered likeliest is listed first.

The symbol "≈" indicates the time span when an undated work could have been written, i.e. ***Schnee in Savosa,*** nd 1986≈1993.

For any extant work whose title or date is listed incorrectly in a work list or other published source, the source alone is listed, without date, i.e. [CC].

All clarinet parts are in B♭, horn parts in F, and trumpet parts in C unless otherwise indicated.

ABBREVIATIONS USED IN THE LIST OF WORKS

A	alto	cl	clarinet
AB	Anthony Burgess	cond	conductor, conducted by
arr	arrangement, arranged by	cym	cymbals
B	bass	db	doubling
bd	bass drum	Ded	dedicated to or written for
BG	*Banbury Guardian*	EH	English horn
bn	bassoon	est	estimated as
bs	bars	Fdp	first documented performance
ca	circa		
cb	contrabass	fl	flute
cel	celesta	glock	glockenspiel

gtr	guitar	pc	percussion
harm	harmonica	Perf	performed
hn	French horn	pf	piano (pianoforte)
hp	harp	picc	piccolo
hpsd	harpsichord	prem	premiere
Insc	inscribed	priv	privately owned
Inst	instrumentation; 2 2 2 2 – 4 2 3 1 tp pc hp str = 2 flutes, 2 oboes, 2 clarinets, 2 bassoons, 4 horns, 2 trumpets, 3 trombones, 1 tuba, timpani, percussion, harp, strings	pub	published (by)
		p-v	piano-vocal score
		rcdr	recorder
		Rec	recorded
		rpt	repeat
		S	soprano
		sd	side drum, snare drum
kbd	keyboard	str	strings
Loc	location where written	sus	suspended
ms	manuscript location	Sym	Symphony
ms-c	manuscript copy location	T	tenor
mvt	movement	tamb	tambourine
nd	no date	tp	timpani
nos	numbers	tpt	trumpet
np	not performed (as of 2010)	tri	triangle
		Univ	University
ob	oboe	vc	violoncello
orch	Orchestra, orchestral (version)	vla	viola
		vln	violin
org	organ	w/	with
pg, pp	page, pages	xyl	xylophone

APPENDIX 2

SONG TEXTS AND POEMS

The Brides of Enderby

1

The wind's fingers are strong or gentle but never sure
How to untangle the problem of the latch or bolt on the door.
Fingers of time, or of air, rest heavily upon
Or coax new ciphers from old metal and flesh and stone.
Beating the mountain down, ruffling the hyacinth,
Baffled by locks and corners of love, the labyrinth.

2

You were there, and nothing was said,
For words toppled on the edge or hovered in air.
But I was suddenly aware, in the split instant,
Of the constant, in a sort of passionless frenzy.
The mad wings of motion a textbook law,
Trees, tables, the war, in a fixed relation,
(Moulded by you, Primum Mobile)
But that you were there really was all I knew.[1]

3

In this spinning room, reduced to a common noun,
    Swallowed by the giant stomach of Eve,
The pentecostal sperm came hissing down.

I was nowhere, for I was anyone –
    The grace and music easy to receive:
The patient engine of a stranger son.

His laughter was fermenting in the cell,
    The fish, the worm were chuckling to achieve
The rose of the disguise he wears so well.

And though, by dispensation of the dove,
    My flesh is pardoned of its flesh, they leave
The rankling of a wrong and useless love.[2]

4

Nymphs and satyrs, come away.
    Faunus, laughing from the hill,
Rips the blanket of the day
    From the paunched and evil Will.

Each projector rears its snout,
    Truffling the blackened scene,
Till the *Wille's* lights gush out
    Vorstellungen on a screen.

Gwen and Blanche are whitely white;
    All their trappings of the sport,
(Lax and scattered) In this light
    Merge and lock to smooth and taut.

See the rockets shoot afar.
    Ah, the screen was tautest then!
Tragic the parabola
    When the sticks reel down again![3]

5

She was all brittle crystal,
Her hands silver silk over steel.
Her hair harvested sheaves shed by summer,
Her grace the flash of the flesh of a river swimmer.
That was not Nature's good who nothing understands
Horrible now she should use to her own ends.

6

Useless to hope to hold off the unavoidable happening
With that frail barricade of week, day or hour which melts as it is made,
For time himself will bring you in his high-powered car, rushing on to it,
Whether you will or not.

So shake hands with the grim satisfactory argument,
The consolation of bone resigned to the event,
Making a friend of him,
He in an access of love renders his bare acres
Golden and wide enough!

And this last margin of leaving is sheltered from the rude
Contrary tugging of winds, for parting, a point in time,
Cannot have magnitude,
And cannot cast shadows about the final kiss
And final tight pressure of hands.[4]

The Pet Beast

I

Pasiphae would pacify a lust
   Grown beyond questioning.
In Daedalus she knew at length she must
   Deposit trust:
This was a thing she durst not tell the king.

A wooden cow, she ordered, queenly. *Why
   Not*, the pared artisan
Said inly, only bowing else. *It is my
   Part to comply.*
He gathered tools and plywood and began.

*Why not a maze made from a ball of string,
   Why not a clockwork bird,
Or birds wrought of stale breadcrumbs that can sing?
   Beyond questioning
A royal statue, statute, though absurd.*

Minos the cold judged cases in his dreams.
   Awake, lithe at his task,
The other whistled, sawing pliant beams.
   Law is what seems,
The craftsman's place to act and not to ask.

The queen was to be bedded and then shut in
   (This was the queen's idea)
A box she might confess unholy rut in.
   The artist cut in
A door there and a small foramen here.

The king snored, a treeload of raven-calls
   Cried fear. The painted cow
Was carried to the plain outside the walls.
   Mobled in shawls,
The queen trod after, shivering somewhat now.

She crouched darkling waiting emwombed in wood,
   Awake, asleep, adoze.
Moon rise on empty grass. She started, could
   Through the eyed hood
See pleniluned the distant dust that rose.

She rocked then on a sea whose spume was dust,
   The sea began to bleed,
Its waves were snorts and roars. The white beast's lust
   Rent in one thrust.
A womb grown sudden hands to grasp the seed.

Moonset. And from the ruin hoofed apart
    She wanly signalled *Come*
To slaves whom not that act but prescient art
    Hot as her heart
Had rendered cruelly and coldly dumb.

They bore her sleeping whither she must sleep
    Next to the snoring king.
Daedalus had seen all, Daedalus must keep
    Silence as deep
As dumbness. Daedalus had not seen a thing.

She was a queen of cautions. Covertly
    Has seized his only son
Who, walled beyond the feasibility
    Of recovery,
Would be a hostage till her time was done.

Or till no time. As human deeds were shut,
    Dried flowers, in books of law,
So human will and love and pain were but
    Raw stuff to cut
To the gods' templates. That's what men are for.

She had done the gods' will anyway. And now
    The royal days went on,
The king his cases, queen her casing how
    She, calving cow,
Would fare if he observed she was far gone.

Myopic Minos, though, in books his eyes,
    But dry each nether eye
After two daughters and no son. But wise
    To recognise
Signs, changes, moods. And always spies to spy.

After three moon-rolls she announced she would
    Spend winter in the south.
He nodded, nodded, said he understood.
    The cold here. Good.
The thing within shot acid to her mouth.

A Father's Death[5]

    Anciently the man who showed
    Hate to his father with the sword
    Was bundled in a dark sack
    With a screaming ape to claw his back
    And the squawking talk of a parrot to mock
    Time's terror of air's and light's lack
    Black

And the slimy litheness of a snake.
Then he was swirled into the sea.
But that was all balls and talk
Nowadays we have changed all that
Into a cleaner light to walk
And wipe that mire off on the mat.
So when I knew his end was near
My breath was freer
Aerating a shedding then
Of all the accidents of birth,
And I knew myself more of a man,
Peeling the last squamour of the old skin.

But never underestimate
The comic cunning of the dead.
The snake that slithers in at night
To occupy most of the bed
Has learnt to wear my father's head.
And one day in the filthy shop
Of ancient rubbish I wound up
A 1914 gramophone
To hear a parrot voice intone
Some nonsense about sun and air,
The two things that were lacking there.
Something is swinging when I fix
Eyes upon eyes in the bathroom glass.
A load of stupid monkey tricks.
Turns me to him as the months pass:
Hair, eyes, jowl, teeth.
I hear him mine the floor beneath
Muffled: You'll not be rid of me.
Each morning when you shave you'll see
What the blood purposed you to be.
Among the things that I bequeath
That safety razor. Stock up with
Blades, particularly the brand that bears
The name of a notable swordsmith.

1937

Notes

1 A slightly different version of the poem is found in IME (38).
2 IME (44–7).
3 The versions of this poem published in IME (82) and LW (265–6) differ slightly from each other and from the text in *The Brides of Enderby*. Shadwell's lyrics are:

> Nymphs and shepherds, come away.
> In the groves let's sport and play,
> For this is Flora's holy day,
> Sacred to ease and happy love,

> To dancing, to music and to poetry;
> Your flocks may now securely rove
> Whilst you express your jollity.
> Nymphs and shepherds, come away.

4 This is the version of the poem set in *The Brides of Enderby*; it differs in some details from the versions published in LW (321) and EO (219–22).
5 Abbreviated versions of this poem appear in EO (360) and *Revolutionary Sonnets* (13).

APPENDIX 3

PROLOGUE TO A CLOCKWORK ORANGE

The scene is the Garden of Eden. Alex is Adam, his eventual girl friend Marty is Eve. This, of course, is a dream that Alex is dreaming. Early morning, delicate greenish light, a tumult of birdsong. Alex and Marty wake in each other's arms. Alex yawns cavernously, then smacks his lips.

ALEX: Zavtrak.
MARTY: What's zavtrak?
ALEX: It's a word that just came. Like all words. It means the first thing you eat when you stop spatting.
MARTY: Spatting?
ALEX: This. *(He does an exaggerated and brutal mime of sleep.)*
MARTY: What you mean is breakfast.
ALEX: Zavtrak tastes better. Or will when I've had it.
MARTY *(rising)*: I'll pick you some fruit.
ALEX: Always fruit. We might as well be wasps. You can't do a hard day's lazing about on fruit.
A VOICE: Beware of the yellow apple.
ALEX: He's up early. He's not usually round till the whatyoucallit.
MARTY: The cool of the evening.

God appears. He has a strong look of the prison chaplain of a later scene. He is in spotless white and long-bearded. He sits on a tree stump.

ALEX: Bog.
GOD: What's that?
ALEX: Bog. You said I'd got to give names to everything. Ptitsa – the thing that flies. Devotchka – her. Yarblocko – the hard round thing that grows on trees and that I'm fed up of eating. Bog – you.
GOD: Beware of the yellow yarblocko.
ALEX: Now I pony. You never skaz about why beware. Why?
GOD: You must not know too much.
ALEX: Why not?
GOD: Because there's limits.
MARTY: *Are* limits.

GOD: I stand corrected.
MARTY: Sit you mean. *(She goes off with her basket.)*
GOD: Sometimes it repents me that I made the – what's the word?
ALEX: Devotchka. Cheena. Look, Bog – what veshch is this about knowing too much?
GOD: Free will has to have limits. Your will must not be as free as mine. You see that?
ALEX: I viddy real horrorshow. After all, you're like in charge.
GOD: We've just had trouble in heaven. One I trusted – the one I placed in charge of the light – made up his mind that he was as free as I am. Free as I am meant being me. You see that?
ALEX: I viddy.
GOD: He had to go. That means that I'm responsible for a moral duality. He versus me. He calls me evil, he calls himself good. The truth, of course, is the other way round.
ALEX: These two slovos I do not pony.
GOD: If by that you mean understand –
ALEX: I'm in charge of the slovos. That was made very clear. What thing he calls by name, that is its name. Eemya. Naz.
GOD: Do not seek to pony. That would mean disaster.
ALEX: Eat that yellow yarblocko and we'd pony those two slovos.
GOD: Good and evil.
ALEX: It's me that's supposed to be in charge of the slovos.
GOD: Not those two.
ALEX: And yet it's there to eat. Reach up my rooker, pull it down, munch munch. Too easy, isn't it?
GOD: It's a way of testing your capacity for obedience. You're free to obey and free to disobey. That's free will. That's choice.
ALEX: It's not enough.
GOD: I beg your pardon?
ALEX: I like the sound of that holy angel or saint or whatever he was. He took a chance.
GOD: The chance consequent on his disobedience. He's created an alternative world.
ALEX: Why didn't you stop him?
GOD: That's not in the rules.
ALEX: Bog's rules.
GOD: Once rules are made, they're not to be changed. I detest the arbitrary.
ALEX: Those bolshy big slovos pony I not. I'd like to viddy this bolshy disobedient cheloveck.
GOD *(shuddering)*: You'll meet him.
ALEX: What does it mean – that slovo – *good*, was it?
GOD: It means accepting the divine order. My order.
ALEX: And the other one?
GOD: Disorder. Disruption. The irrational bestowal of pain. The dissolution of creation into chaos.
ALEX: And you couldn't stop it?
GOD: I abide by my own rules. I gave my creation free will. I gave it the power of choice.

ALEX: The choice between those two things.
GOD: I didn't say that.
ALEX: I did. Words are for thinking with. I'm in charge of words. Slovos. *You* said so.
GOD: Eat that forbidden fruit and the birds will grow talons, the beasts will bite, the solitary snake will manufacture venom, you'll discover death and have to find your own means of opposing it. She will bring forth in pain. There will be a populated world beset by conflict. I must abide by my rules and watch in impotence chaos supervene on creation. Do not touch that fruit. *(He gets up.)*
ALEX: Take it away then.
GOD: No. Remember the rules.

He goes off. Alex shakes his head, bemused. A bird calls. Whistling, he imitates it. He does more: he creates a cantilena of his own. He is excited by his act of composition. Marty enters with a basket laden with fruit.

ALEX: Did you hear that? *(He whistles again)*
MARTY: Nice. But what's it for?
ALEX: It needs a slovo. Mouse sick. Moose sick. I call it music.
MARTY: But what's it for?
ALEX: It just is.
MARTY: Listen – I met this man –
ALEX: Man? You can't have. I'm the only one. So far.

He tries to embrace Marty, and this makes her spill some of her fruit. Then Alex is struck by a thought.

ALEX: You say a *man*?
MARTY: More of an angel really. He helped me pick this fruit.
ALEX: He helped you to pick *that one*?

He means the large yellow one, orange really, that he picks up from the ground. He holds it gingerly to his ear.

ALEX: There's a noise inside. Like ticking. Ticking. I just made up that slovo. We'd better see what's inside. *(He pauses.)* It was only eating he said, wasn't it? No harm in looking. We viddy it every day.
MARTY: It smells all right.

Alex breaks the rind and juice spatters on to his hand. He licks it.

MARTY: Now you've eaten it.
ALEX: I don't call that eating. Taste.

She tastes. The music that Alex whistled is now heard on an orchestra. It is the theme of the last movement of Beethoven's Ninth Symphony. The light subtly changes. A man enters who is identical with the Ministry of the Interior of a later scene. He is smartly dressed in a suit of snakeskin.

MINISTER: Wasn't so difficult, was it? The world hasn't. changed. The old thunderer hasn't unleashed his lightning. He *wanted* you to do it.
ALEX: Wanted?
MINISTER: Of course. Why did he leave it hanging there?
MARTY: The world *has* changed. It's cold. I need some –
ALEX: Platties? Clothes?
MINISTER: You'll find clothes available. When you wake up from this dream. We all need protection from the cold cold world and the cold cold eyes of strangers.
ALEX: What's strangers?
MINISTER: People we don't know. The world's already seething with them. You see them out there? That's just a small sample.
MARTY: I don't see anything.
MINISTER: But you imagine them. Imagine them first, then create them. That's your job.
MARTY: I feel a terrible – I don't know the word.
MINISTER: Pain. Agony. Birth throes. You'd better go off and lie down. The pain will go. *(She painfully leaves.)*
MINISTER: Now things are going to be interesting. Who wants heaven? Who wants the Garden of Eden? See the world to come. Men and women exhibiting the most incredible kinds of ingenuity, the delicious fruits of disobedience. And they have to be ruled, of course. They have to be told how to be good. You too, my little friend.
ALEX: I know all about it. I'm *not* your little friend. I don't have to be told. We have to have the two veshches or there wouldn't be anything to choose. It's the choosing that counts.
MINISTER: I'll choose for you. That's my privilege.
ALEX: I'll choose for myself. That's mine.
MINISTER: You'll choose wrong.
ALEX: Who knows what wrong is? Only Bog has the secret.
MINISTER: You mean the old one? He's dead. I threw him out.
ALEX: That's why it's cold.

The lights dim. A wind drowns the music. The Minister laughs and goes off. Alex tries to warm himself. He huddles on the ground. He wakes to the music of the Prelude. It was all a dream. Naked, he is speedily dressed by his three friends or droogs. The play begins.

BIBLIOGRAPHY

I. WRITINGS BY ANTHONY BURGESS
BOOKS

Listed chronologically according to year written [in brackets when it precedes the year of first publication]. All other lists are alphabetical.

A Vision of Battlements. Illustrated by Edward Pagram. London: Heinemann, 1965; New York: Norton, 1966. [1951–1952]

The Eve of Saint Venus. Illustrated by Edward Pagram. London: Sidgwick and Jackson, 1964; New York: Ballantine, 1971. [1953]

The Worm and the Ring. London: Heinemann, 1961. Withdrawn and published 1970 in a revised edition. [1953]

Time for a Tiger. London: Heinemann, 1956.

The Enemy in the Blanket. London: Heinemann, 1958. [1957]

English Literature: A Survey for Students. London: Longmans, Green, 1958. Originally published under the name John Burgess Wilson. [1957]

Beds in the East. London: Heinemann, 1959. [1958]

Devil of a State. London: Heinemann, 1961; New York: Norton, 1962. [1958]

The Right to an Answer. London: Heinemann, 1960; New York: Norton, 1961. [1959]

The Doctor is Sick. London: Heinemann, 1960; New York: Norton, 1960. [1959]

One Hand Clapping. London: Peter Davies, 1961; New York: Knopf, 1972. Originally published under the name Joseph Kell. [1960]

Inside Mr Enderby. London: Heinemann, 1963. Originally published under the name Joseph Kell. [1960]

A Clockwork Orange. London: Heinemann, 1962; New York: Norton, 1963. [1960–61]

The Wanting Seed. London: Heinemann, 1962; New York: Norton, 1963. [1961]

Honey for the Bears. London: Heinemann, 1963; New York: Norton, 1964. [1962]

The Novel To-day. London: Longmans, Green & Co. for the British Council and the National Book League, 1963.

Nothing Like the Sun: A Story of Shakespeare's Love-Life. London: Heinemann, 1964; New York: Norton, 1964. [1963]

Language Made Plain. London: English Universities Press, 1964; New York: Crowell, 1965. [1963]

Here Comes Everybody: An introduction to James Joyce for the ordinary reader. London: Faber & Faber, 1965. [Introduction: "Chiswick, August 1964"]
Re Joyce. New York: Norton, 1965. (US edition of *Here Comes Everybody*)
Tremor of Intent. London: Heinemann, 1966; New York: Norton, 1966. [1965]
Coaching Days of England. London: Paul Elek, 1966; New York: Time-Life Books, 1966.
The Novel Now: A Student's Guide to Contemporary Fiction. London: Faber & Faber, 1967.
The Novel Now: A Guide to Contemporary Fiction. New York: Norton, 1967. (US edition)
The Age of the Grand Tour. London: Paul Elek, 1967; New York: Crown, 1967.
Enderby Outside. London: Heinemann, 1968. [1967]
Urgent Copy: Literary Studies. London: Jonathan Cape, 1968; New York: Norton, 1968.
Shakespeare. London: Jonathan Cape, 1970; New York: Knopf, 1970. [ca. 1969]
MF. London: Jonathan Cape, 1970; New York: Knopf, 1971. ["Deyá, Malta, Rome, 1969–70"]
Joysprick: An Introduction to the Language of James Joyce. London: André Deutsch, 1973; New York: Harcourt Brace Jovanovich, 1975. [Preface: "Bracciano, Rome. September 1971"]
Napoleon Symphony. London: Jonathan Cape, 1974; New York: Knopf, 1974. ["I and III, Rome, 1972; II and IV, Rome, 1973"]
The Clockwork Testament, or Enderby's End. Illustrated by the Quays. London: Hart-Davis, MacGibbon, 1974; New York: Knopf, 1975. ["Rome, July 1973"]
Beard's Roman Women. Photographs by David Robinson. London: Hutchinson, 1976; New York: McGraw-Hill, 1976. ["Montalbuccio–Monte Carlo–Eze–Callian, Summer 1975"]
Moses: A Narrative. London: Dempsey and Squires, 1976; New York: Stonehill, 1976.
A Long Trip to Teatime. Illustrated by Fulvio Testa. London: Dempsey & Squires, 1976; New York: Stonehill, 1976.
New York. Amsterdam: Time-Life, 1976.
ABBA ABBA. London: Faber & Faber, 1977; Boston: Little, Brown, 1977.
A Christmas Recipe. Illustrated by Joe Tilson. Verona, Italy: Plain Wrapper Press, 1977.
Will and Testament: a fragment of biography. Illustrated by Joe Tilson. Verona, Italy: Plain Wrapper Press, 1977.
Ernest Hemingway and his world. London: Thames and Hudson, 1978; New York: Scribner's, 1978. [Foreword: "2 July 1977, Monaco"]
1985. London: Hutchinson, 1978; Boston: Little, Brown, 1978.
The Pianoplayers. London: Hutchinson, 1986; New York: Arbor House, 1986. [1978]
Man of Nazareth. New York: McGraw-Hill, 1979; London: Magnum, 1980.
The Land Where the Ice Cream Grows. Story and illustrations by Fulvio Testa. London: Benn, 1979; Garden City, NY: Doubleday, 1979.
They Wrote in English. Two volumes. Milan: Tramontana, 1979.
Earthly Powers. London: Hutchinson, 1980; New York: Simon and Schuster, 1980.
Blooms of Dublin. London: Hutchinson, 1986. [1971/1980–1981; A Prefatory Word: "Monaco, December 13, 1985"]

On Going to Bed. London: Deutsch, 1982; New York: Abbeville Press, 1982.
This Man and Music. London: Hutchinson, 1982; New York: McGraw-Hill, 1983.
The End of the World News: An Entertainment. London: Hutchinson, 1982; New York: McGraw-Hill, 1983.
Enderby's Dark Lady or *No End to Enderby*. London: Hutchinson, 1984; New York: McGraw-Hill, 1984. [A Prefatory Note: "Lugano, November 1983"]
Ninety-Nine Novels: The Best in English Since 1939. London: Allison & Busby, 1984; New York: Summit Books, 1984.
The Kingdom of the Wicked. London: Hutchinson, 1985; New York, Arbor House, 1985.
Flame Into Being: The Life and Work of D. H. Lawrence. London: Heinemann, 1985; New York: Arbor House, 1985.
Homage to Qwert Yuiop: Selected Journalism 1978–1985. London: Hutchinson, 1986.
But Do Blondes Prefer Gentlemen?: Homage to Qwert Yuiop and Other Writings. New York: McGraw-Hill, 1986. (US edition)
Little Wilson and Big God: Being the First Part of the Confessions of Anthony Burgess by London: Heinemann, 1987. [Preface: "Principauté de Monaco. 1986"]
Little Wilson and Big God: Being the First Part of the Autobiography. New York: Weidenfeld & Nicolson, 1987. (US edition)
Anthony Burgess: Childhood. London: Penguin, 1996. (Extract from *Little Wilson and Big God*)
Any Old Iron. London: Hutchinson, 1989; New York: Random House, 1989. ["Lugano, July 1987"]
The Devil's Mode and Other Stories. London: Hutchinson, 1989.
The Devil's Mode: Stories by Anthony Burgess. New York: Random House, 1989. (US edition)
You've Had Your Time: Being the Second Part of the Confessions of Anthony Burgess. London: Heinemann, 1990.
You've Had Your Time: The Second Part of the Confessions. New York: Grove Weidenfeld, 1991. (US edition)
Mozart and the Wolf Gang. London: Hutchinson, 1991.
On Mozart: A Paean for Wolfgang, Being a celestial colloquy, an opera libretto, a film script, a schizophrenic dialogue, a bewildered rumination, a Stendhalian transcription, and a heartfelt homage upon the bicentenary of the death of Wolfgang Amadeus Mozart. New York: Ticknor & Fields, 1991. (US edition of *Mozart and the Wolf Gang*)
A Mouthful of Air: Language and languages, especially English. London: Hutchinson, 1992.
A Mouthful of Air: Language, Languages . . . Especially English. New York: William Morrow, 1993. (US edition)
Revolutionary Sonnets and other poems. Edited by Kevin Jackson. Manchester: Carcanet, 2002. [1934–1992]
One Man's Chorus: The Uncollected Writings. Selected with an introduction by Ben Forkner. New York: Carroll & Graf, 1998. [1978–1992]
A Dead Man in Deptford. London: Hutchinson, 1993; New York: Carroll & Graf, 1995.
Byrne: A Novel. London: Hutchinson, 1995; New York: Carroll & Graf, 1997. [1993]

COMBINED PUBLICATIONS

A Clockwork Orange and *Honey for the Bears*. New York: Modern Library, 1968.

Enderby [comprising *Inside Mr Enderby* and *Enderby Outside* referred to as Book One and Book Two, respectively]. New York: Norton, 1968.

Five Novels by Anthony Burgess: The Wanting Seed, Honey for the Bears, Nothing Like the Sun, The Right to an Answer, A Clockwork Orange. Mass market paperback, slipcase edition. New York: Ballantine, 1965.

Future Imperfect [comprising *The Wanting Seed* and *1985*]. London: Vintage, 1994.

The Complete Enderby [comprising *Inside Mr Enderby, Enderby Outside, The Clockwork Testament*, and *Enderby's Dark Lady*]. New York: Carroll & Graf, 1996.

The Long Day Wanes: A Malayan Trilogy [comprising *Time for a Tiger, The Enemy in the Blanket*, and *Beds in the East*]. New York: Norton, 1965.

The Malayan Trilogy [comprising *Time for a Tiger, The Enemy in the Blanket*, and *Beds in the East*]. London: Pan Books, 1964.

TRANSLATIONS, ADAPTATIONS, AND LIBRETTI

Belli, Giuseppe Gioachino. "Five Sonnets" translated from the Roman dialect. *Malahat Review* (44), Oct 1977, 17–21.

Berlioz, Hector. *L'enfance du Christ*. Singing translation (1966) for BBC-2 production conducted by Colin Davis, Christmas 1966; subtitles (1984) for broadcast by Thames Television (sung in French), Easter 1985.

Bizet, Georges, Henri Meilhac, and Ludovic Halévy. *Carmen: An Opera in Four Acts*. London: Hutchinson, 1986.

Burgess, Anthony. *A Clockwork Orange: A Play with Music*. London: Hutchinson, 1987; London: Methuen, 1998. [A Prefatory Word: "Lugano, July 1986"]

Burgess, Anthony. *A Clockwork Orange 2004*. London: Arrow, 1990.

Burgess, Anthony. *1789: An Opera Libretto*. Original libretto set to music by Lorenzo Ferrero as a marionette opera titled *Le Bleu-Blanc-Rouge et le Noir*. [Prem 12 Nov 1989]

Griboyedov, Alexander Sergeyevich. *Chatsky (The Importance of Being Stupid): A verse comedy in four acts*. Rhymed translation, 1992. [Prem 11 March 1993, London, Almeida Theatre Company]

Hopkins, G. M. *St Winefred's Well*. Unfinished play by Hopkins adapted & completed by AB, who also provided incidental music (played by solo flute). [Broadcast prem: 23 Dec 1989, BBC]

Joyce, James. *A Shorter Finnegans Wake*. London: Faber & Faber, 1966; New York: Viking, 1967 [Foreword: "London, 1965"].

Joyce, James. *Ulysses* adapted as *Blooms of Dublin*. London: Hutchinson, 1986. [Prem 1 Feb 1982, radio production by the BBC and Radio Telefís Éireann]

Pelegri, Jean. *The Olive-Trees of Justice* [*Les Oliviers de la Justice* translated by "Anthony Burgess and Lynne Wilson"]. London: Sidgwick and Jackson, 1962.

Rostand, Edmond. *Cyrano*. Lyrics by AB, music by Michael Lewis. Libretto Vocal Book and Piano Conductor Score published by Music Theatre International (New York, 1973). [Prem 13 May 1973, Palace Theatre, New York]

Rostand, Edmond. *Cyrano de Bergerac.* New York: Knopf, 1971. [Preface: "Princeton, N.J., December 31, 1970"]
Saint Pierre, Michel de. *The New Aristocrats [Les Nouveaux Aristocrates* (1960) translated by "Anthony and Llewela Burgess"]. London: Golancz, 1962; Boston: Houghton Mifflin, 1963.
Servin, Jean. *The Man Who Robbed Poor Boxes [Deo Gratias* translated by Anthony Burgess]. London: Golancz, 1965.
Shakespeare, William. *The MND Show: A Madrigal Comedy Celebration in E major*, for chamber singers, large choir, and instrumental ensemble. Based on *A Midsummer Night's Dream.* Text by AB, music by Stanley Silverman. Written 1971. [Prem 16 May 1973, Whitney Museum, New York]
Sophocles. *Oedipus the King* (Minnesota Drama Editions, No. 8). Minneapolis: University of Minnesota Press in Association with the Guthrie Theater, 1972. [Prem 24 Oct 1972, Tyrone Guthrie Theatre, Minneapolis, MN]
Sophocles. *King Oedipus, for Speaker, Chorus, and Orchestra.* Text by AB, music by Stanley Silverman. [Prem 16 May 1973, Whitney Museum, New York]
Strauss, Richard, and Hugo von Hofmannsthal. *Der Rosenkavalier: Comedy for Music in Three Acts.* Boston: Little, Brown, 1982. "The Cavalier of the Rose" (story adaptation), 21–68.
Weber, Carl Maria von, and James Robinson Planché. *Oberon Old & New: Burgess's new opera together with Planché's original text.* London: Hutchinson, 1985. [1983]

ON MUSIC

"A Conductor With a Talent for Resurrection" (profile of Roger Norrington). *The New York Times*, 8 Sept 1991, Section 2, 33.
"A Few Words About a Guitar Concerto". Undated typescript [1987].
"A mystery and its monument". Review of *The New Grove Dictionary of Music and Musicians. Times Literary Supplement*, 20 Feb 1981, 184.
"A Tale of Three Cities" (review of three recordings by Riccardo Muti ca. 1983).
"An Evening with Anthony Burgess and his Music". Program note for concert of Aïghetta Quartet at The Princess Grace Irish Library, 18 Jan 1989.
"Artist's Life". Typescript © 1983.
"Barbara Hendricks Sings Spirituals with Dmitri Alexeev" (review ca. 1983).
"Bernard Haitink Conducts Opera" (review ca. 1983).
"Blest Pair of Siren?" Essay for the Proms, 1988.
"Britten War Requiem" (review ca. 1983).
"Delius – A Life in Letters 1862–1908". Review for *The Guardian*, 25 Nov 1983. Published in French in *Harmonie Panorama Music*, No. 39, Feb 1984.
"Elgarité = Vulgarité?" 16 Oct 1984. Published in *Harmonie Panorama* © 1984.
"Food and Music". Published in *Cuisine* Magazine © 1983.
"Gentlemen v. Players". Review of *The English Musical Renaissance 1860–1940* by Robert Stradling and Meirion Hughes. *Observer*, 1 Aug 1993, 52.
"Haitink Conducts Elgar" (review ca. 1983).
"Handel, not Händel – A Tricentennial Tribute". Typescript © 1984 sent to *Die Welt*, 17 Dec 1984.
"How I Wrote My Third Symphony". *The New York Times*, 28 Dec 1975, Section 2 (Arts and Leisure), 1, 19.

"John Sebastian – A Personal Reminiscence". Typescript © 1988.
"Mozart and the Wolf Gang". *Wilson Quarterly* (16:1), Winter 1992, 110–20.
"Music and Literature". *Wilson Quarterly* (7:5), Winter 1983, 86–97. [Reprint of Chapter 5, "Meaning Means Language", from *This Man and Music*.]
"Musicalising *Ulysses*". Typescript sent 6 Feb 1982 to *Corriere della Sera* and other European publications for publication.
"Not Only Carmen". *The Observer*, 28 Dec 1986. Pub. as "A Librettist's Lament", *The New York Times*, 21 Dec 1986, H21–2. Typescript dated Nov 1986.
"*Opera and Ideas – From Mozart to Strauss* by Paul Robinson." © 1985. Review "Sent to Atlantic Monthly. Published?"
"Previn with the Philadelphia" (review ca. 1983).
"Richard Wagner". *The Lamp*, 1983.
"Shakespeare in Music". Review in *Musical Times* (105), Dec 1964, 901–2.
"Shaw as Musician". *Corriere della Sera*, 7 June 1981.
"Startalk" (about *The Planets*). Typescript dated 3 May 1982, for *Harmonie*.
"Symphony in C". Program note for concert of University Symphony Orchestra, University of Iowa School of Music, 22 Oct 1975.
"The Aïghetta Quartet". Liner notes for *Oeuvres pour Quatuor de Guitares* (REM N° 11032), 1987.
"The Arts". *Listener* (72:1855), 15 Oct 1964, 9.
"The Guitar and I". *Classical Guitar* (1:3), Jan–Feb 1983, 23 [© 1982].
"The Making of a Writer". *The New York Times Book Review*, 1982.
"The Music of Exile". Script for BBC television program on Bohuslav Martin , 1967.
"The New Grove". Review of *The New Grove Dictionary of Music and Musicians*, typescript dated Feb 1981.
"The Ninth". For BBC Radio Three, to be read prior to broadcast of Beethoven's Ninth performed by BBC Scottish Symphony Orchestra, 14 Dec 1990.
"The Ruination of Music". *Corriere della Sera*, 11 Feb 1981.
"The Twenty-four-string Guitar". Typescript published as "The Twenty-Four String Guitar" in *Classical Guitar* (6:9), May 1988, 48.
"The vocation of a virtuoso" (review of *Unfinished Journey* by Yehudi Menuhin). *TLS*, 8 Apr 1977, 419.
"The Writer and Music". *Listener* (67:1727), 3 May 1962, 761–2 (pub. within article titled "Did You Hear That?").
"Unravelling Ravel". Typescript dated 14 Jan 1987 with note, "Sent direct to *Corriere della Sera*".

SHORTER WRITINGS: FICTION

"A Benignant Growth". *Transatlantic Review* (32), Summer 1969, 10–15.
"A Fable for Social Scientists: In Which Our Leading Practitioner of the Trade is Quickly and Painlessly Skinned." *Horizon* (15:1), Winter 1973, 12–15.
"An American Organ". *Mad River Review* (1), Winter 1964–65, 33–9. Reprinted in *Sixty-Five Great Tales Of Horror*, Mary Danby, ed. London: Octopus Books, 1982.
"It is the Miller's Daughter: A Novel in Progress". *Transatlantic Review* (24), Spring 1967, 5–15.

"Muse: A Sort of SF Story". *Hudson Review* (21), Spring 1968, 109–126. Reprinted as "The Muse" in *The World Treasury of Science Fiction*, David G. Hartwell, ed. Boston: Little Brown, 1989.
"Precognition", in *The Terminal Man* by Michael Crichton. New York: Knopf, 1972.
"Somebody's Got to Pay the Rent". *Partison Review* (35), Winter 1968, 67–74.

SHORTER WRITINGS: NON-FICTION. *AUTOBIOGRAPHICAL SKETCHES, CHAPTERS, CONTRIBUTIONS, ESSAYS, JOURNALISM, AND TRANSCRIPTS*

Art and Literature: An International Review. Lausanne: Société Anonyme d'Editions Littéraires et Artistiques, 1964.
Becket, Samuel. *Waiting for Godot.* London: National Theatre, 1987. Theatre programme containing two-page essay.
"Burgess on Kubrick on 'Clockwork'." *Library Journal* (98:9), 1 May 1973, 1506–8.
Cassis, A. F., ed. *Graham Greene: Man of Paradox.* Chicago: Loyola University Press, 1994. "God and Literature and So Forth...", 317–25. (extracted from original item published, with same title, in *Observer*, 16 Mar 1980, 33, 35).
Cina. Milano: Mondadori, 1982. *"Presentazione."*
"Clockwork Marmalade". *Listener* (87:2238), 17 Feb 1972, 197–9.
Crystal, David, ed. *Eric Partridge In His Own Words.* London: André Deutsch, 1980, and New York: Macmillan, 1980. "Partridge in a Word Tree", 26–30. [This essay differs from the one with the identical title published in *But Do Blondes Prefer Gentlemen?*, 148–151, which originated in 1977 as a review of Partridge's *A Dictionary of Catch Phrases*.]
"Death Sentences". *Wilson Quarterly* (15:2), Spring 1991, 117–23.
Gaines, James R., ed. *The Lives of the Piano.* New York: Holt, Rinehart and Winston, 1981. Chapter I: "The Well-Tempered Revolution: A Consideration of the Piano's Social and Intellectual History", 3–39.
Hockney, David, illustrator. *Hockney's Alphabet.* New York: Random House, 1991.
"If Oedipus had read his Lévi-Strauss". *Washington Post Book World*, 26 Nov 1967, 6. (Reprinted in *Urgent Copy*, 258–61).
Imhof, Rudiger, ed. *Alive-Alive-O: Flann O'Brien's* At Swim-Two-Birds. Dublin: Wolfhound Press/Totowa, NJ: Barnes & Noble Books, 1985.
"Is America Falling Apart?", 424–30 (orig. pub. in *The New York Times Magazine*, 7 Nov 1971). Reprinted in *The Norton Reader: An Anthology of Expository Prose*, 3rd edition. Arthur M. Eastman, ed. New York: Norton, 1973.
Marqusee, Michael. *Venice: An Illustrated Anthology.* London: Conran Octopus, 1988.
McCormack, Thomas, ed. *Afterwords: Novelists on Their Novels.* New York: Harper & Row, 1969. Essay on *Nothing Like the Sun*.
Mitchell, James, ed. *The God I Want.* London: Constable & Co., 1967; New York: Bobbs-Merrill, 1967, 57–70.
Obscenity and the Arts. Valletta: Malta Library Association, 1973. Text of speech given before the library assocation.

"Poetry for a Tiny Room". *Yorkshire Post*, 16 May 1963, 4.
Schiff, James A., ed. *Critical Essays on Reynolds Price*. New York: G. K. Hall and London: Prentice Hall International, 1998. "Good Books", 88–9 (orig. pub. as review of *A Palpable God* in *The New York Times Magazine*, 12 Mar 1978, 14, 22).
Spain: The Best Travel Writing from the New York Times. New York: Abbeville Press, 2001.
"Summond [sic] by bell". Review of *Collected Poems 1937–66* by Martin Bell. *Spectator*, 11 May 1967.
"The Dictionary Makers". *Wilson Quarterly* (17:3), Summer 1993, 104–10.
"The Genesis of 'Earthly Powers'". *Washington Post Book World*, 23 Nov 1980, 1–2, 13.
"The Large World of Lawrence". Typescript © 1990.
"The Novel in 2000 A.D.". *The New York Times Book Review*, 29 Mar 1970, 19.
"Thoughts of a belated father". *Spectator*, 6 Sept 1968, 322.
"You've Had Your Time: Being the Beginning of an Autobiography". *Malahat Review* (44), Oct 1977, 10–16.

SHORTER WRITINGS: NON-FICTION. *FOREWORDS, INTRODUCTIONS, AND PREFACES*

Angeli, Daniel, and Jean-Paul Dousset, photographers. *Private Pictures*. New York: Viking, 1980. Introduction.
Armstrong, Alison. *The Joyce of Cooking: Food and Drink from James Joyce's Dublin – An Irish Cookbook*. Barrytown, NY: Station Hill Press, 1986. Foreword.
Augustus Carp, Esq., by himself: being the autobiography of a really good man (written anonymously by Henry Howarth Bashford). London: Heinemann, 1966. Introduction, xii-xiv.
Ballard, J. G. *The Best Short Stories of J. G. Ballard*. New York: Picador, 2001. Introduction.
Barber, David W. *Bach, Beethoven and the Boys: Music History As It Ought To Be Taught*. Toronto: Sound And Vision, 1996 (10th-Anniversary Edition). Preface ["Monte Carlo, December 7, 1985."]
Bates, H. E. *A Month by the Lake & Other Stories*. New York: New Directions, 1987. Introduction, vii–x.
Bowen, Elizabeth, et al. *The Heritage of British Literature*. London: Thames and Hudson, 1983. Afterword, 218–234.
Cato, Bob, and Greg Vitiello. *Joyce Images*. New York: Norton, 1994. Introduction, 7–15.
Chesterton, Gilbert Keith. *Autobiography*. London: Hutchinson, 1969. Introduction.
Coleridge, Samuel Taylor. *The Rime of the Ancient Mariner*. Milan, Italy: International Book Society, 1966. Introduction.
Collier, John. *The John Collier Reader*. New York: Knopf, 1972. Introduction, xi–xv.
Defoe, Daniel. *A Journal of the Plague Year*. London: Penguin, 1966. Introduction, 6–18.

Desani, G.V. *All About H. Hatterr.* New York: Farrar, Straus and Giroux, 1970. Introduction, 7–11.
Doyle, Arthur Conan. The White Company. London: Murray, 1975. Introduction.
Fleming, Ian. *James Bond: Dr No.* [New York]: Coronet, 1988. Preface.
Fleming, Ian. *James Bond: The Spy Who Loved Me.* New York: Coronet, 1962. Preface.
Fleming, Ian. *James Bond: You Only Live Twice.* [New York]: General Paperbacks, 1988. Preface.
Forkner, Ben, ed. *Modern Irish Short Stories.* New York: Viking, 1980. Preface, 15–19 ["Monaco, May 1979"]
Fossati, Gildo. *China: The Monuments of Civilisation.* London: New English Library, 1983. Foreword.
Hildebrandt, Dieter. *Pianoforte: A Social History of the Piano.* Translated by Harriet Goodman. New York: George Braziller, 1988. Introduction, v–ix.
Jerrold, Douglas. *Mrs. Caudle's Curtain Lectures.* London: Harvill Press, 1974. Foreword, 11–15.
Lawrence, D. H. *D. H. Lawrence and Italy: Twilight in Italy, Sea and Sardinia, Etruscan Places.* New York: Viking, 1972. Introduction, vii--xiii. ["Tarquinia, July 29, 1971"]
MacShane, Frank, and Lori M. Carlson, eds. *Return Trip Tango and Other Stories from Abroad.* New York: Columbia University Press, 1992. "Introduction: A Celebration of Translation", xvii--xxii.
Maugham, Somerset. *Maugham's Malaysian Stories.* Singapore/Hong Kong: Heinemann Educational Books, 1969.
Miller, Henry. *The Time of the Assassins: A Study of Rimbaud.* London & Melbourne: Quartet Books, 1984. Introduction.
Modern Masters from the Thyssen-Bornemisza Collection. Royal Academy of Arts, London 1984. Lugano: Thyssen-Bornemisza Collection; Milan: Electa International; London: Weidenfeld & Nicolson, 1984. Catalogue with introduction by Burgess titled "The Thyssen-Bornemisza Collection of Modern Masters: A Personal View", 13–18.
Mozart, Wolfgang Amadeus and Lorenzo da Ponte. *Don Giovanni* and *Idomeneo* (Universe Opera Guides). New York: Universe Books, 1971. Introduction, 7–22.
Nash, Ogden. *Poems of Ogden Nash.* London: Andre Deutsch, 1983. Introduction.
O'Brien, Flann. *At Swim-Two-Birds.* London and New York: Granada, 1982. Prefatory Word.
Peake, Mervyn. *The Gormenghast Novels: Titus Groan, Gormenghast, Titus Alone.* Woodstock, NY: Overlook Press, 1992. Introduction.
Peake, Mervyn. *The Gormenghast Trilogy: Titus Groan, Gormenghast, Titus Alone.* London: Penguin, 1970.
Peake, Mervyn. *Titus Alone.* Woodstock, NY: Overlook Press, 1992. Introduction.
Peake, Mervyn. *Titus Groan.* London: Eyre and Spottiswood, 1968. Introduction.
Petrocchi, Giorgio, and Maria Corti, eds. *Leggere* I promessi sposi. Bresso (MI): Tramontana, 1980. Introduction (in Italian).
Sandulescu, Constantin-George, and Clive Hart, eds. *Assessing the 1984* Ulysses. Totowa, NJ: Barnes & Noble Books, 1986. Foreword.
Schulberg, Budd. *The Disenchanted.* London: Allison & Busby, 1983. Introduction.

Selby, Herbert, Jr. *Last Exit to Brooklyn* [2nd, post-trial edition]. London: Calder & Boyars, 1968. Introduction, xiii-xvii.

Vidal, Gore. *Creation: A Novel*. New York: Vintage Books USA, 2002. Foreword.

Walter, Marc, artistic direction. *The Book of Tea*. Paris/New York: Flammarion, 1992. Translated by Deke Dusinberre. Preface.

Warner, Rex. *The Aerodrome: A Love Story*. Oxford: Oxford University Press, 1982. Introduction.

II. WRITINGS ABOUT ANTHONY BURGESS

BOOKS, DISSERTATIONS, AND COLLECTED STUDIES

Aggeler, Geoffrey, ed. *Critical Essays on Anthony Burgess*. Boston: G.K. Hall & Co., 1986.

Aggeler, Geoffrey. *Anthony Burgess: The Artist as Novelist*. Tuscaloosa: University of Alabama Press, 1979.

Biswell, Andrew. *The Real Life of Anthony Burgess*. London: Picador, 2005.

Bloom, Harold, ed. *Anthony Burgess*. New York: Chelsea House, 1987.

Boytinck, Paul. *Anthony Burgess: An Annotated Bibliography and Reference Guide*. New York: Garland, 1985.

Brewer, Jeutonne. *Anthony Burgess: A Bibliography*. Metuchen: Scarecrow Press, 1980.

Coale, Samuel. *Anthony Burgess*. New York: Frederick Ungar, 1981.

de la Fuente, Susan. *Musical Form in the Works of Anthony Burgess; Napoleon Symphony – Literary Landmark?* Unpublished masters thesis submitted 10 Apr 1979, Queens College / City University of New York.

De Vitis, A.A. *Anthony Burgess*. New York: Twayne, 1972.

Dix, Carol M. *Anthony Burgess*. Edited by Ian Scott-Kilvert. Harlow: Longman Group, 1971.

Farkas, Á. I. *Will's Son and Jake's Peer: Anthony Burgess's Joycean Negotiations*. Budapest: Akadémiai Kiadó, 2002.

Ghosh-Schellhorn, Martina. *Anthony Burgess: A Study in Character*. Frankfurt am Main: Peter Lang, 1986.

Ingersoll, Earl G., and Mary C. Ingersoll, ed. *Conversations with Anthony Burgess*. Jackson: University Press of Mississippi, 2008.

Jeannin, Marc, ed. *Anthony Burgess: Music in Literature and Literature in Music*. Newcastle upon Tyne: Cambridge Scholars Publishing, 2009.

Lewis, Roger. *Anthony Burgess*. London: Faber & Faber, 2002.

Mathews, Richard. *The Clockwork Universe of Anthony Burgess*. San Bernardino: Borgo Press, 1978.

Morris, Robert K. *The Consolations of Ambiguity: An Essay on the Novels of Anthony Burgess*. Columbia: University of Missouri Press, 1971.

Roughley, Alan R., ed. *Anthony Burgess and Modernity*. Manchester and New York: Manchester University Press, 2008.

Shockley, Alan Frederick. *Music in the Words: Musical Form and Counterpoint in the Twentieth-Century Novel*. Aldershot, Hampshire and Burlington, VT: Ashgate, 2009.

Stinson, John J. *Anthony Burgess Revisited*. Boston: Twayne, 1991.
Vernadakis, Emmanuel, and Graham Woodroffe, eds. *Portraits of the Artist in A Clockwork Orange*. Angers: Presses de l'Université d'Angers, 2003.
Wolf, Werner. *The Musicalization of Fiction: A Study in the Theory and History of Intermediality*. Amsterdam and Atlanta, GA: Rodopi, 1999.
Woodroffe, Graham, ed. *Anthony Burgess, Autobiographer*. Angers: Presses de l'Université d'Angers, 2006.

ARTICLES, ESSAYS, AND REVIEWS

Aggeler, Geoffrey. "Enderby Immolatus: Burgess' *The Clockwork Testament*". *Malahat Review* (44), Oct 1977, 22–46. [Interview with Geoffrey Aggeler, 16 Sept 1972]
Amis, Martin. *The War Against Cliché: Essays and Reviews, 1971–2000*. London: Jonathan Cape, 2001. "Anthony Burgess: Jack Be Quick", 113–27. (Reviews of *ABBA ABBA, 1985, Earthly Powers*, and *Little Wilson and Big God*, orig. pub. 1977–87)
Amis, Martin. *Visiting Mrs. Nabokov and Other Excursions*. New York: Harmony, 1993. "Anthony Burgess", 241–5. (Originally published in the *Observer*, 1980)
Anonymous. "A Novel Picture". *The Economist* (237:6634), 17 Oct 1970, 60–1.
Anonymous. "The Ultimate Beatnik". *Time* (81:7), 15 Feb 1963, 103.
Anonymous. Review of *Re Joyce*. *Choice* (3:5–6), July-Aug 1966, 408.
Aprahamian, Felix. "Drive-in Carmen". *Sunday Times*, 30 Nov 1986.
Aprahamian, Felix. "Mr Burgess's solution". *The Sunday Times*, 27 Oct 1985.
Barnes, Clive. "Langham Revitalizes the Guthrie Theatre". *The New York Times*, 20 Sept 1971, 31.
Barnes, Clive. "Plummer Triumphs in Musical 'Cyrano'". *The New York Times*, 14 May 1973, 37.
Benedict, Helen. "Shakespeare meets Cervantes" (review of *The Devil's Mode*). *The New York Times Book Review*, 10 Dec 1989, sect. 7, 38.
Bly, James I. "Sonata Form in *Tremor of Intent*". *Modern Fiction Studies* (27:3) Autumn 1981, 489–504. (Reprinted in *Critical Essays on Anthony Burgess*, edited by Geoffrey Aggeler, 158–72.)
Bones, Mark. "Burgess Praised". *American Recorder* (42:4), Sept 2001, 36–7.
Bosakowski, Philip. "Sound character evident in Burgess' 'Symphony in C'." *Daily Iowan* (Iowa City, Iowa), 23 Oct 1975, 3.
Bringardner, John. "Play fails to move like 'Clockwork'". *Daily Texan*, 4 May 2000.
Bunting, Charles T. "An Interview in New York with Anthony Burgess". *Studies in the Novel* (Denton, Tex.: North Texas State University, 1973), 504–29.
Burke, Tom. "Malcolm McDowell: The Liberals, They Hate 'Clockwork'". *The New York Times*, 30 Jan 1972, D13.
Butler, Francelia. Review of *Shakespeare* in *Library Journal* (95:20), 15 Nov 1970, 3909.
Clements, Andrew. "L'Enfance du Christ/ITV". *Financial Times*, 2 Jan 1986.
Clurman, Harold. "Theatre." *Nation* (216:23), 4 June 1973, 731 [Boytinck (214), 32].
Coale, Samuel. "An Interview with Anthony Burgess". *Modern Fiction Studies* (27:3), Autumn 1981, 429–52. [abridged from interview in Monaco, 7 and 11 July 1978].

Coale, Samuel. "Criticism of Anthony Burgess: A Selected Checklist". *Modern Fiction Studies* (27:3), Autumn 1981, 533–6.
Coale, Samuel. "The Ludic Loves of Anthony Burgess". *Modern Fiction Studies* (27:3), Autumn 1981, 453–63.
Coale, Samuel. Unpublished transcript of interview with Anthony Burgess, Monaco, 7 and 11 July 1978.
Cook, Bruce. "Here's Mr. Burgess, Full of Swagger and Guilt". *National Observer*, 27 Apr 1970.
Cornfield, Susie. "Shipwrecked with Ulysses". *Sunday Times,* 7 Feb 1982, 41.
Craft, Robert. *Small Craft Advisories: Critical Articles 1984–1988*. New York: Thames and Hudson, 1989. Includes "Burgess and Music", 237–8 (revised version of "Composition", review of *This Man and Music* pub. in *New York Review of Books* (30:20), 22 Dec 1983, and "A Flood in a Time of Drought", 232–6 (review of *Homage to Qwert Yuiop*).
Crist, Judith. "A Feast, and About Time". *New York* (4:5), 20/27 Dec 1971, 90 [Boytinck (132), 18–19].
Cullinan, John. "The Art of Fiction XLVIII: Anthony Burgess". *Paris Review* (56), Spring 1973, 118–63. Reprinted in *Writers at Work: The Paris Review Interviews: Fourth Series*, ed. by George Plimpton (London: Secker & Warburg, 1976), 323–58.
Daiches, David. Review of *Moses: A Narrative*. *Times Literary Supplement*, 21 Jan 1977, 50.
Donadio, Stephen. "*MF:* Anthony Burgess's Oedipus Rex". *The New York Times Book Review*, 4 Apr 1971, BR4.
Drapeau, George. "Unlikely baroque setting for Burgess poem" (review of *The Brides of Enderby*). *Gannett Westchester Newspapers*, 16 Oct 1978, B5.
Ferris, Paul. "Musical Blooms". *Observer*, 2 Feb 1982.
Finch, Hilary. "Enter dirty Carmen making wolves' eyes" (unidentified newspaper clipping, ca. Nov 1986).
Fuller, Edmund. "Shakespeare, in Lively Fiction and Arguable Fact". *Wall Street Journal*, 20 Jan 1971, 14.
Gale, William K. "SF-GT's *Clockwork* hints at what might be". *Providence Journal*, 8 Sept 2001, D3.
Gaskell, John. "Bizet as Burgess". *Sunday Telegraph*, 30 Nov 1986.
Gioia, Dana. "Deathbed Confessions" (review of *Byrne*). *The New York Times*, 30 Nov 1997.
Gioia, Dana. *Barrier of a Common Language: An American Looks at Contemporary British Poetry*. Ann Arbor: University of Michigan Press, 2003. "The Novelist as Poet (Anthony Burgess)", 90–6.
Goodman, Peter. "MUSIC REVIEW/T. S. Eliot to music". Unidentified New York-area newspaper, 2 Oct 1982.
Gottfried, Martin. "A Musical 'Cyrano'." *Women's Wear Daily*, 14 May 1973 [Boytinck (218), 33].
Greenfield, Edward. "Queen of the Gas Guzzlers". *Guardian*, 29 Nov 1986.
Griffiths, Eric. "A radiant Carmen in a pink Cadillac". *Independent,* 29 Nov 1986.
Griffiths, Paul. "A Carmen of cheap thrills". *The Times*, 29 Nov 1986.
Griffiths, Paul. "Misplaced urge to be earthbound". *The Times*, 25 Oct 1985.
Gussow, Mel. "To Plummer, Cyrano Is an Old Friend". *The New York Times*, 17 May 1973, 52.

Hartill, Rosemary. *Writers Revealed: Eight Contemporary Novelists Talk About Faith, Religion and God*. New York: Peter Bedrick, 1989. "Anthony Burgess: Unearthly Powers", 11–24.
Hayes, Malcolm. "Old cars for new 'Carmen'". *Sunday Telegraph*, 30 Nov 1986.
Heyworth, Peter. "Burgess gives Weber a nudge and a wink". *Observer*, 28 Oct 1985.
Hicks, Jim. "Eclectic author of his own five-foot shelf". *Life* (65:17), 25 Oct 1968, 87–97.
Huelbes, Elvira. "Appreciation: Anthony Burgess – The last words". *Guardian*, 26 Nov 1993, section 2, 7.
Irwin, Michael. "Tuckland, Their Tuckland" (review of *1985*). *Times Literary Supplement*, 6 Oct 1978, 1109.
Jacobs, Arthur. "'Oberon' at Glasgow". *Musical Times*, 25 Oct 1985.
Josselson, Diana. "Shorter Reviews". *Kenyon Review* (25:3), Summer 1963, 559–60.
K[alem], T. E. "Coolheaded Gascon." *Time* (v. 101), 28 May 1973, 55 [Boytinck (220), 33].
Kael, Pauline. "*A Clockwork Orange*: Stanley Strangelove". *New Yorker* (47:46), 1 Jan 1972, 50–3 (reprinted in *Stanley Kubrick's A Clockwork Orange*, 134–9).
Karpf, Anne. "Singing Bloom". *Listener*, 11 Feb 1982, 26.
Keller, Hans. "Phoneydom". *Listener*, 11 Feb 1982, 26–7.
Kennedy, Michael. "Climaxes and cold porridge". *Sunday Telegraph*, 1 Jan 1993.
Kenyon, Nicholas. "Chaotic, crashing Carmen". *Observer*, 30 Nov 1986.
Kermode, Frank. "Maggots, modesty, and Mozart" (review of TMM). *Guardian*, 16 Sept 1982.
Larner, Gerald. "A tale puckish to the core". *Glasgow Herald*, 25 Oct 1985.
Larner, Gerald. "Operation Oberon". *Guardian*, 23 Oct 1985.
Lodge, David. *The Art of Fiction: Illustrated from Classic and Modern Texts*. New York: Viking, 1993. "Ideas (Anthony Burgess)", 197–200.
Loppert, Max. "A rubbish-dump Carmen". *Financial Times*, 29 Nov 1986.
Loppert, Max. "Oberon/Theatre Royal, Glasgow". *Financial Times*, 25 Oct 1985.
M., M. "*Une création mondiale pour le bimillénaire: 'La sinfonietta pour Strasbourg' d'Anthony Burgess*". (clipping from unidentified Strasbourg-area newspaper, ca. 26 Nov 1988)
Mahon, Derek. *Journalism: Selected Prose 1970–1995*. Edited by Terence Brown. Loughcrew: Gallery Press, 1996. "Rome and Music: Anthony Burgess", 211–15. (orig. pub. in *Vogue*, 1975).
Malko, George. "Anthony Burgess" [interview]. *Penthouse* (3:10), June 1972, 82, 84, 115–16, 118.
Maslin, Janet. "'Quest for Fire,' A Prehistoric Odyssey". *The New York Times*, 12 Feb 1982, C4.
Maslon, Laurence. "The Winner By a Nose". Program note for the compact disk reissue of the original cast recording of *Cyrano*, Decca Broadway B0004083-02 © 2005.
Matthew-Walker, Robert. "Berlioz on Thames", *Music & Musicians*, London [ca. Dec 1985 / Jan 1986].
McDowell, Edwin. "Publishing: 'Clockwork Orange' Regains Chapter 21". *The New York Times*, 31 Dec 1986, C16.
McLellan, Joseph. "Laurentian Players". *Washington Post*, 2 Dec 1978, C4.

Mewshaw, Michael. "Do I Owe You Something?", *Granta* (75), Autumn 2001, 29–40.
Milnes, Rodney. "Carmen. English National Opera at the London Coliseum, November 27". *Opera* [ca. Dec 1986], 100–4.
Morrison, Richard. "Heralding a new age of music-theatre". *The Times*, 12 Dec 1985.
Morton, Brian. "L'Enfance du Christ. By Hector Berlioz". *Times Educational Supplement*, 10 Jan 1986.
Morton, Brian. "Burgess, Anthony" in *Contemporary Composers*. Brian Morton and Pamela Collins, eds. Chicago & London: St. James Press, 1992, 138–9.
Müller-Muth, Anja. "A Playful Comment on Word and Music Relations: Anthony Burgess's *Mozart and the Wolf Gang*", in Walter Bernhart, Steven Paul Scher, and Werner Wolf, eds., *Word and Music Studies: Defining the Field – Proceedings of the First International Conference on Word and Music Studies at Graz, 1997.* Amsterdam: Rodopi, 1999.
Noon, William T. Review of *Re Joyce*. *James Joyce Quarterly* (3:3), Spring 1966, 215–19.
Palumbo, Ronald J. "Names and Games in *Tremor of Intent*". *English Language Notes* (18:1), Sept 1980, 48–51.
Paterson, Scott. "Anthony Burgess: The Man and His Recorder Music". *American Recorder* (41:4), Sept 2000, 11–17.
Phillips, Paul. "Symphonic Shakespeare". *Anthony Burgess Newsletter*, Issue 2, Feb 2000, 48–59.
Phillips, Paul. "The Music of Anthony Burgess". *Anthony Burgess Newsletter*, Issue 1, July 1999, 11–18.
Phillips, Paul. "Burgess, Anthony" in *The New Grove Dictionary of Music and Musicians,* 2nd edition, Stanley Sadie, ed. London: Macmillan, 2001. vol. 4, 614–15.
"Playboy Interview: Anthony Burgess – candid conversation". *Playboy* (21:9), Sept 1974, 69–86.
Porter, Andrew. "Carmen: English National Opera at the London Coliseum, January 13". *Opera*, Mar 1993.
Ricks, Christopher. "Horror Show". *The New York Review of Books* (18:6), 6 Apr 1972, 28–9 [Boytinck (152), 22].
Robinson, Robert. "On Being a Lancashire Catholic". *Listener* (96:2477), 30 Sept 1976, 397, 399.
Rockwell, John. "Chamber: Laurentians". *The New York Times*, 2 Oct 1982.
Rodriguez, Bill. "Works-in-progress". *Providence Phoenix*, 14 Sept 2001, 1, 16.
Rozett, Martha Tuck. *Constructing a World: Shakespeare's England and the New Historical Fiction.* Albany: State University of New York Press, 2003. "Historical Novelists at Work: George Carrett and Anthony Burgess", 49–82.
Schaeffer, Susan Fromberg. "Beware of Justice, Truth and Beauty". *The New York Times Book Review*, 26 Feb 1989, sect. 7, 12.
Solway, Diane. "1990: Previews From 36 Creative Artists". *The New York Times,* 31 Dec 1989.
Swaim, Don. Anthony Burgess interview on *Book Beat,* 19 Sept 1985 (http://wiredforbooks.org/swaim/AnthonyBurgess.ram).
T. J. Medrek. "Chamber concert of composer's works runs like 'Clockwork'". *Boston Herald*, 25 Apr 2000, 53.

Tilton, John W. *Cosmic Satire in the Contemporary Novel*. Lewisburg: Bucknell University Press, 1977. "*A Clockwork Orange*: Awareness is All", 21–42.
Tovey, Roberta. "Two Children's Books for Adults". *New Republic* (176:22), 28 May 1977, 41.
Usden, Arline. "Opera: Carmen". *The Lady*, 26 Jan–1 Feb 1993.
Vick, Graham. "A fantasy opera . . ." Program book essay, Scottish Opera production of *Oberon*, [23] October 1985.
Vidal, Gore. *At Home: Essays 1982–1988*. New York: Random House, 1988. "Why I Am Eight Years Younger than Anthony Burgess", 231–40. Orig. pub. in *The New York Review of Books* (34:8), 7 May 1987.
Vidal, Gore. *The Last Empire: Essays 1992–2000*. New York: Doubleday, 2001. "Anthony Burgess", 122–4. Reprint of "Not so poor Burgess", *Observer*, 28 Nov 1993.
Wade, David. "Bloomsday to music". *The Times*, 6 Feb 1982.
Webb, W. L. "Musical Joyce". *Guardian*, 2 Feb 1982.
White, Terence de Vere. "Batting for England" (review of *Flame Into Being*). *Irish Times*, 31 Aug 1985.
Wood, Michael. "The Ladies Vanish". *The New York Review of Books* (23:15), 30 Sept 1976, 40–2. Review of *Moses: A Narrative* and *Beard's Roman Women*.

NEWSLETTERS AND PERIODICALS

Anthony Burgess Newsletter. Anthony Burgess Society. Issues: 1 (July 1999), 2 (Feb 2000), 3 (Dec 2000), 4 (Aug 2001), 5 (Oct 2002), 6 (Dec 2003), 7 (Dec 2004)
End of the World Newsletter. The International Anthony Burgess Foundation. Issues: (1:1) Spring 2005, (1:2) Dec 2005, (2) Nov 2006, (3) July–Aug 2009
Modern Fiction Studies; Special Issue: Anthony Burgess. (27:3) Autumn 1981. West Lafayette, Ind.: Purdue University. A.A. DeVitis, guest co-editor, with critical writings by A.A. DeVitis, Samuel Coale, Timothy R. Lucas, Philip E. Ray, James I. Bly, John J. Stinson, and Geoffrey Aggeler.

OBITUARIES

"Anthony Burgess, 76, Dies; Man of Letters and Music" by Herbert Mitgang. *The New York Times*, 26 Nov 1993, B23.
"Anthony Burgess" by Roger Lewis. *Independent*, 26 Nov 1993, 16.
"Anthony Burgess", anon. *Daily Telegraph*, 26 Nov 1993, 25.
"Anthony Burgess", anon. *The Times*, 26 Nov 1993, 23.
"Not so poor Burgess" by Gore Vidal, Michael Ratcliffe, and others. *Observer*, 28 Nov 1993. (Gore Vidal's tribute reprinted as "Anthony Burgess" in *The Last Empire: Essays 1992–2000*.)

WORKS BASED ON MATERIAL BY, OR DEDICATED TO, ANTHONY BURGESS

Boyd, William. *An Airful of Burgess*. "Masque" for radio produced by Dave Batchelor. Prem 21 Aug 1994, BBC Radio Scotland.

Clark, S. M. *ABBA ABBA In Memoriam Anthony Burgess*. Chamber work in four mvts for fl, ob, cl, bass cl, vln, vla, and pf, composed 1994–95. Last movement based on a theme from AB's Third Symphony. Prem 26 Aug 1994, Boston Chamber Ensemble, cond S. M. Clark, Cambridge, Massachusetts.

Gold, Jerome. *The Prisoner's Son: Homage to Anthony Burgess*. Seattle: Black Heron Press, 1996.

Kubrick, Stanley. *Stanley Kubrick's* A Clockwork Orange: *Based on the novel by Anthony Burgess*. New York: Ballantine Books, 1972.

Phillips, Paul. *Three Burgess Lyrics*. Work in three mvts for SATB chorus, solo-vln, and pf. Settings of three poems from *Byrne*: " 'Prudence, prudence,' the pigeons call"; "Bells clanged white Sunday in, a dressing-gowned day"; "I have raised and poised a fiddle". Prem 30 Oct 1999, Marsh Chapel Choir, cond Julian Wachner, Boston, Massachusetts.

Phillips, Paul. *A/B: A 90th Birthday Celebration of Anthony Burgess in Words and Music*. Work in nine mvts for actor, string quartet, harmonica, piano, percussion). Prem 13 Oct 2007, Aurea, cond Paul Phillips, Providence, RI.

INTERNET SOURCES

http://classicsnetwork.com/essays/An_Interview_with_Roger_Lewis/837 (transcript from BWP agency, Holland)

http://www.classicthemes.com/50sTVThemes/themePages/dragnet.html

http://www.entretemps.asso.fr/Hopkins/FallenRainAutograph.html

DISCOGRAPHY

MUSIC AND/OR LYRICS

Anthony Burgess, Biographer. Graham Woodroffe, ed. Angers: Presses de l'Université d'Angers, 2006. One compact disc included. *The Brides of Enderby*. Songs texts recited, tracks 1–6; performance of composition, tracks 7–12. Peter Hudson (narr), Armelle Orieux (sop), Ynes Muller (fl), Frédéric Potet (ob), Cécile Grizard (vc), Maureen Turquet (pf).

Burgess: Musique d'un écrivain anglais sur la Riviera. Aïghetta Quartett. *l'empreinte digitale*. ED 13049 (1996; recorded March and May 1995). *Quatuor No. 1, Quatuor N° 2*, and *Quatuor N° 3*. One compact disc (41'33).

Cyrano. Original Cast Recording. New York: A&M Records, 1973. Two longplaying records. Reissued in 2005, Decca Broadway B0004083–02. 32 songs. One compact disc (70'53).

Oeuvres pour Quatuor de Guitares. Aïghetta Quartett. REM Éditions. REM11032 (May 1987). *Quatuor en Hommage à Maurice Ravel [Quatuor (N° 1) pour Guitares]*. Disk also contains works by Johann Sebastian Bach (*Concerto en La Mineur/transcription en Si Mineur*) [based on the Concerto in B minor for Four Violins by Antonio Vivaldi], Ferdinand Carulli (*Quatuor en Do Majeur, Op. 21*), Antonio Ruiz Pipo (*Cuatro Para Cuatro*), and Robert Delanoff (*Ein Türkishes Volkslied*). One LP.

Oeuvres pour Quatuor de Guitares. Aïghetta Quartett. REM Éditions. REM311111 (November 1989). *Quatuor No. 2*. Disk also contains works by Robert Delanoff (*Tango sentimental; Ein Türkishes Volkslied*) and Federico Moreno Torroba (*Ràfagas*). One compact disc.

Portraits of the Artist in A Clockwork Orange. Emmanuel Vernadakis and Graham Woodroffe, eds. Angers: Presses de l'Université d'Angers, 2003. One compact disc included. *A Clockwork Orange: A Play with Music* (6 tracks); Bradley Naylor, Spyridon Antonopoulos, Stephen Schwartz, Paul Scharf (voice), Paul Phillips (pf). *A Clockwork Hour* (recorded live 7 Dec 2001 (2 tracks): Prelude from *A Clockwork Orange: A Play with Music,* and selections from AB's private musical library; Eleven Preludes and a Fugue from the *Bad-Tempered Electronic Keyboard,* Tango for Pianoforte, two of *Master Coale's Pieces,* Finale from *A Clockwork Orange,* and Sonata No. 3 for Great Bass Recorder (20 tracks); Thomas Dubos (bsn), Maureen Turquet (pf).

SPOKEN LANGUAGE RECORDINGS

LP recordings:

A Clockwork Orange. Caedmon TC 1417 (1973)

A Clockwork Orange / Inside Mr Enderby. Spoken Arts SA 1120 (1974)

Eve of Saint Venus / Nothing Like the Sun. Caedmon TC 1442 (1974)

Cassette tape recordings:

A Clockwork Orange. Caedmon Audio, CPN 1417 (1973). One cassette, circa 60'00.

Enderby / A Clockwork Orange. March 1966 at the Poetry Center of the 92nd Street Y, New York. Introduced by John Simon. Audio-Forum Sound Seminars. Jeffrey Norton Publishers Tape Library: 23246. One cassette.

Graham Greene. BBC Cassettes, ECN 129. One cassette.

1980 Edinburgh Festival: Use and Abuse of English; Anthony Burgess on Writing and the English Language. Interview by Frank Delaney on 27 August 1980. BBC Cassettes, ECN 162. One cassette.

Compact disk recordings:

A Clockwork Orange (unabridged). Performed by Tom Hollander on 6 CDs; Burgess performs excerpts from *A Clockwork Orange* on CD 7. Caedmon, 2007.

FILMOGRAPHY

A.D. (1985). Television mini-series. Studio: Proctor & Gamble Productions, Inc.; Exec. producers: Jack Wishard, George Jensen; Prod: Vincenzo Labella; Dir: Stuart Cooper; Script: Anthony Burgess, Vincenzo Labella; Music: Lalo Shifrin. First television broadcast: 31 Mar–4 Apr 1985; VHS release date: 1992; DVD release date: 1 Mar 2002. Running time: 12 hours in orig. five-part miniseries; 9 hours in video "Collector's Edition".

Anthony Burgess with A. S. Byatt (1989). "Writers Talk: Ideas of Our Time". Studio: ICA Video in conjunction with Trilion. Dir: Fenella Greenfield; Music, Conor Kelley, Sam Park. VHS: Roland Collections/ICA Video. Running time: 56 minutes.

Anthony Burgess' Rome (1978). Canadian television production. Studio: John McGreevy Productions/Nielsen-Ferns Ltd.; Prod. and dir: John McGreevy; Script and narr: Anthony Burgess; VHS: Learning Corporation of America. Running time: 50 minutes.

The Burgess Variations: *Theme and Thirty Variations on the Life and Works of Anthony Burgess*. (1999). Studio: BBC television. Prod: David Thompson; Script and narr: Kevin Jackson. Burgess; First television broadcast: 26 Dec 1999. Running time: ca. 120 minutes.

A Clockwork Orange (1971). Based on the novel by Anthony Burgess. Studio: Warner Bros.; Exec. producers: Max L. Raab, Si Litvinoff; Prod., dir., screenplay: Stanley Kubrick; Music: W. Carlos. Theatrical release date: 20 Dec 1971; VHS release date: 29 June 1999; DVD release date: 12 June 2001. Running time: 137 minutes.

Gli Occhi di New York (*The Eyes of New York*; 1976). Script and musical score by Burgess. Italian film commissioned by Mondadori for the emerging home videocassette market but never released.

Grace Under Pressure (1978). Television documentary on Ernest Hemingway. Studio: London Weekend Television; Prod. and dir: Tony Cash; Script and narr: Anthony Burgess. VHS: Films for the Humanities, 1978. Running time: 55 minutes.

Great Writers: Anthony Burgess (1997). Dir: Elisa Mantin. France 3/ADR Productions/BBC. Kultur DVD. Running time: 45 minutes.

Jesus of Nazareth (1977). Television mini-series. Studio: Lionsgate/Fox; Exec. producers: Bernard J. Kingham, Sir Lew Grade; Prod: Vincenzo Labella; Dir: Franco Zeffirelli; Script: Anthony Burgess, Suso Cecchi d'Amico, Franco Zeffirelli; Music:

Maurice Jarre. Theatrical release date: 3 Apr 1977; VHS release date: 1992; DVD release date: 1 Mar 2002. Running time: 382 minutes.

Moses (1975). Cinematic version of *Moses the Lawgiver*. Studio: RAI/ITC Ltd.; Exec. producer: Sir Lew Grade; Prod: Vincenzo Labella; Dir: Gianfranco De Bosio; Script: Anthony Burgess, Vittorio Bonicelli, Gianfranco De Bosio; Music: Ennio Morricone. VHS release date: 1992. Running time: 141 minutes.

Moses the Lawgiver (1975). Television mini-series. Studio: RAI/ITC Ltd.; Exec. producer: Sir Lew Grade; Prod: Vincenzo Labella; Dir: Gianfranco De Bosio; Script: Anthony Burgess, Vittorio Bonicelli, Gianfranco De Bosio; Music: Ennio Morricone. First television broadcast: 1975. Running time: 6 hours.

The Music of Exile (1967). Television documentary on Czech composer Bohuslav Martinů. Studio: BBC; Script and narr: Anthony Burgess. First television broadcast: 1967. Running time: ca. 60 minutes.

Quest for Fire (1981). Motion picture based on the novel by J. H. Rosny, Sr. Studio: 20th Century-Fox.; Prod: John Kemeny, Denis Heroux; Dir: Jean-Jacques Annaud; Screenplay: Gerard Brach; Special languages creator: Anthony Burgess; Body language and gestures creator: Desmond Morris; Music: Philippe Sarde. Theatrical release date: 16 Dec 1981 (France), 12 Feb 1982 (USA). VHS: CBS/Fox Video, release date: 1984; DVD: 20th Century Fox Home Entertainment, release date: 4 Mar 2003. Running time: 100 minutes.

The Rage of Lawrence (1985). "Profile of a Writer. Volume 5: Anthony Burgess on D. H. Lawrence". Studio: London Weekend Television co-production with RM Arts; Prod. and dir: Jill Freeman; Script and narr: Anthony Burgess; Readings by Ian McKellen. First television broadcast: 1985; VHS: Home Vision. Running time: 55 minutes.

Silence, Exile and Cunning (1965). Television documentary on James Joyce. Studio: BBC; Dir: Christopher Burstall; Script and narr: Anthony Burgess. First television broadcast: 1965; videocassette: 1971, distr. by Time-Life Films. Black and white. Running time: 42 minutes.

ACKNOWLEDGMENTS

This book would not have been possible without the cooperation of the late Liana Burgess, whose generosity in allowing me access to her late husband's works and papers is gratefully acknowledged. Additionally, I wish to thank the Harry Ransom Humanities Research Center at the University of Texas-Austin; Anthony Burgess Center at the Université d'Angers; International Anthony Burgess Foundation in Withington; the Brown University Libraries, including the John Hay Library, Orwig Music Library, and Rockefeller Library; Cranston (Rhode Island) Public Library; Providence Public Library; and the libraries of McMaster University, Royal Academy of Music, University of Tulsa, and Washington University. Brown University has generously funded my research, and I am deeply grateful to its students, faculty, librarians, and administrative staff for their sustained cooperation and support. Additional funding has come from the Brown University Creative Arts Council, Rhode Island Committee for the Humanities, and Rhode Island State Council on the Arts. Other organizations that have assisted this book's development include the American Musicological Society, Mount Holyoke College, Sandra Feinstein-Gamm Theatre, and the Yehudi Menuhin School. For their performances of Burgess's music, I wish to thank pianists Gary Steigerwalt, Dana Muller, and Maureen Turquet; vocalists Kathryne Jennings, Michelle French, James Kleyla, Rockland Osgood, Bradley Naylor, Spyridon Antonopoulos, Stephen Schwartz, and Paul Scharf; bassoonists Jeffrey Lyman (University of Michigan) and Thomas Dubos; the musicians of the Aighetta Quartet (Alexandre Del Fa, Philippe Loli, Pascal Rabatti, François Szönyi), Boston Conservatory Chamber Players (Marianne Gedigian, Laura Ahlbeck, Stuart Dunkel, Andrew Mark, artistic director Michael Lewin), McGill University Chamber Singers and Opera Chorus (Julian Wachner, director), and the members of the Brown University Orchestra and the Pioneer Valley Symphony.

Many individuals have generously provided information, materials, assistance, and opportunities that have enriched this book. They include, in alphabetical order, Kathryn Adamson (Royal Academy of Music), the late Larry Adler, Geoffrey Aggeler, Stephen Banfield (University of Bristol),

Dave Batchelor (BBC Scotland), Susanne Baumgartner, Nuria Belastegui (International Anthony Burgess Foundation), Deborah Berlin, Elisa Birdseye, Andrew Biswell (Manchester Metropolitan University), Ruth and the late Arnold Black, Howard Booth (University of Manchester), William Boyd, Paul Boytinck, Martha Caplin, Wendy Carlos, John Cassini (Université d'Angers), Len Cariou, David Chinitz (Loyola University Chicago), S. M. Clark, Samuel Coale (Wheaton College), John F. Cory, John and Ruth Covelli, Michael Coyle (Colgate University), Tess Crebbin, Margaret Cushing, Chris Dale (BBC Scottish Symphony Orchestra), Loriana De Crescenzo, Mireille Deveze, James Dixon, James Duda, Harold Farberman, Kim Field, Ben Forkner (Université d'Angers), David Fuqua, William Gale, Kathleen Garay (McMaster University), Leslie Gardner, Nigel Gore, Sigmund Groven, Jonathan Haskell (l'Orchestre de la Suisse Romande), Zeke Hecker, Dell Anne Hollingsworth (Harry Ransom Humanities Research Center), Randall Hooper (Tennessee Tech University), Kevin Jackson, Lisa Jones (Harry Ransom Humanities Research Center), Erica Jong, David King (University of Salford), Ronald M. Krentzman, George Lawson, James LeGrand, Michael J. Lewis, Philippe Loli, Merrily Lustig, the late Dame Moura Lympany, the late Mark P. Malkovich III (Newport Music Festival), Elizabeth McCreath (Royal Scottish National Orchestra), Patrick McDonagh (International Anthony Burgess Foundation), Melissa Meell, Gerard Menuhin, Jeremy Menuhin, Valérie Neveu (Université d'Angers), Richard Nutting, Gabriele Pantucci, my parents Vivian and Daniel Phillips, Philip Pierce, Nancy Protzman (Sarah Lawrence College), Bernard Rands, Esther Nettles Rauch, Mark J. Rawlinson (University of Leicester), Anthony Rhys-Jones, Frances Richard (ASCAP), Deborah Rogers, Shelley Roth, Alan Roughley (International Anthony Burgess Foundation), Jay Rozen, Ariel Rudiakov, the late Michael Rudiakov, Myra Teicher Russel, the late Stanley Sadie, Michael Schmidt (Carcanet Press), Stanley Silverman, James Sparling, Thomas F. Staley (Harry Ransom Humanities Research Center), the late Eric Swenson (W. W. Norton), Ward Swingle, François Szönyi, David Thompson (BBC London), Maureen Turquet, Emmanuel Vernadakis (Université d'Angers), Lory Wallfisch (Smith College), Ronald P. Weiss, Ann Williams (Clwyd Theatr Cymru), and Graham Woodroffe (Université d'Angers). The many faculty, students and staff of Brown University who provided support for this book deserve their own honor roll and include Stacy Ackerman, Jessica Ashooh, James Baker, Arlene Cole, Rosemary Cullen, Sheila Hogg, Nancy Jakubowski, David Josephson, Catherine Knapp, Selma Moss-Ward, Kathleen Nelson, Marc Perlman, Philip Pierce, Edwin Quist, Mary Rego, Gerald Shapiro, Charles Sherba, Consuelo Sherba, Rose Subotnik, Carol Tatian, Jeff Titon, Andrew Tobolowsky, Jennifer Vieira, Don Wilmeth, Todd Winkler, William F. Wyatt, and all of the members of the Creative Arts Council. To all these individuals, and anyone else who assisted with this undertaking whose name has been inadvertently omitted, I owe an enormous debt of gratitude.

Many thanks are due to all those who read the manuscript and offered advice and corrections along the way. A great effort has been made to eliminate all errors from the book, but for any that remain, I bear sole responsibility.

Finally, I offer my deepest gratitude to the three girls in my life – Kathryne, Joanna, and Alanna – for their extraordinary patience and forbearance during the 'Burgess' years at the Phillips household in Rhode Island.

MUSIC INDEX

ARRANGEMENTS

"An Afternoon on the Phone" (simplified version of Debussy's *Prélude à "l'après-midi d'un faune"*), 38 (**Ex. 04.01**), 46n
"An Apple for the Teacher" (regimental victory march), 42
Bach's Fugue in C minor from Book I of *The Well-Tempered Clavier*, 37
"The Ballad of Persse O'Reilly" (for guitar quartet), 4, 329
Ballet Egyptien, 37
"The Darktown Strutters' Ball" (pseudo-symphonic arrangement), 37
"The Folks Who Live on the Hill", 37
"Greensleeves" (for guitar), 322
"I Know Why", 37
"If We Never Meet Again", 37
"The Irish Washerwoman" (for guitar quartet), 4, 329
"The Lark in the Clear Air" (for guitar quartet), 4, 329
"Let's Have Another One", 37
"Let the Bulgine Run", 15
"Macushla", 38
"Mercury" from *The Planets* (for guitar quartet), 4, 297, 329, 330n
Oberon Overture (for guitar quartet), 4, 297, 329
"On the Track", 37
"Song of India" (*Chanson Hindoue* by Rimsky-Korsakov), 37
"Stardust", 37
"Thanks for the Memory", 37

COMPOSITIONS

Albumblatt for small orchestra, 18
Allegretto for oboe and piano, 332
"Allegro Risoluto", 361n
Andante for flute or recorder trio, 339, 340 (**Ex. 30.08**)
"Anthem for Doomed Youth" (Owen), 41, 189, 190 (**Ex. 17.08**)
The Bad-Tempered Electronic Keyboard, 4, 203–6 (incl. **Exx. 18.04–18.05**), 212n, 244, 293, 300n
bagatelle for John Covelli, 208
bagatelle for piano, 51
"Ball Tic Bass", 39
Barcarolle, 256
bassoon concerto, 125, 141n, 331, 332 (**Ex. 30.01**)
Bergamasque for oboe and piano, 333, 343
Bethlehem Palmtrees, 4, 152
"Birthday Greeting" (for guitar and piano), 322
"Black-out Blues", 30
"blues in waltz time", 37
The Brides of Enderby, xvii, 4, 43, 44, 104, 214–5, 217, 218–22 (incl. **Exx. 19.01–19.02**), 233, 284, 335, 380, 381
Brief Suite in A, 207
cabaret songs, 30
"Cabbage Face", 28
Carol Settings for Flute and Strings, 51
cello concerto, 41, 42, 254, 256
cello sonata, 42, 125, 254

Chaika, 99
Christmas carol for Diana Gillon, 99
clarinet concerto, 331
"Complaint, complaint I heard upon a day" (Pound), 23, 158n
Concertino per Corno Inglese ed Orchestra, 3, 334 (**Ex. 30.04**), 335, 339, 343, 344n, 378
Concertino for Harmonica and String Orchestra, 318, 321n
Concertino for piano and orchestra, *see Rome in the Rain*
Concerto for flute and strings, 105n, 125
Concerto for piano and percussion, 125
Concerto for Pianoforte and Orchestra, 3, 98, 99, 156, 199–202 (incl. **Exx. 18.01–18.03**), 207, 212n, 231, 236n, 255, 256, 336, 346, 381
Concerto for Violin and Orchestra, 3, 254, 256–8 (incl. **Exx. 23.01–23.05**), 323, 324, 326
Concerto Grosso pour Quatuor de Guitares en La mineure, 4, 230, 319, 327–9 (incl. **Ex. 29.08**)
Concerto per Chitarra ed Orchestra en Mi minore, 4, 293, 326–7 (incl. **Exx. 29.06–29.07**), 328, 329, 330n, 337
Dead March for Orchestra, 18, 382
Due Pezzetti "for flute or recorder & piano", 336
"Ecce Puer", 280 (**Ex. 24.07**); *see also* Joyce songs
"Everyone suddenly burst out singing" (Sassoon), 40
Fanfare for Three Trumpets, 289
Fantasia for two recorders and piano, 99, 335
Faunal Noon, 4, 315, 382
Festal Suite for Brass, 4, 290n, 293, 350
Feuerwerk, 208
"Fingers Off" or "The One-armed Fiddler's Waltz", 210–11 (**Ex. 18.07**)
Fugue and Impromptu for guitar, 322

Gibraltar, 41
A Glasgow Overture, 4, 316, 345, 346 (**Ex. 31.01**), 378
Guitar Quartets, 4, 5, 383; *see Quatuors pour Guitares*
Guitar Sonata in E, 322
"Happy Birthday!" for treble recorder and piano, 335–6
Hispanics for violin and piano, 40, 254
Homage to Hans Keller (unfinished quartet for bass tubas), 277, 278 (**Ex. 24.05**), 332
"Ic eom of Irelonde", 27
In Dulci Jubilo, 209
In memoriam Princess Grace, 4, 154, 254, 259–61 (incl. **Ex. 23.08**), 346, 379, 381
"In pious times, ere priestcraft did begin" (Dryden), 19
"Interlude for Small Organ", 72
In Time of Plague, 4, 203, 250–1, 253n, 378
"Inversnaid" (Hopkins), 50, 288–9
Ipswich (prelude and fugue) for organ, 40
"I sing of a maiden", 50
Joyce songs, 4, 154, 279, 280, 332
Kalau Tuan Mudek Ka-Ulu (Five Malay Pantuns for soprano and native instruments), 65
"Lines for an Old Man" (Eliot), 27
A Little Concerto for Oboe and Orchestra, 3, 333, 334 (**Ex. 30.03**), 343
little concerto for piano duet and percussion, 50
Ludus Polytonalis, 335
Malay pantun for Cathy Berberian, 65, 67n
Man Who Has Come Through, 4, 283–4, 285 (**Ex. 25.01**), 290n, 293, 346, 348, 378
A Manchester Overture, 4, 247, 333, 358 (**Exx. 32.03–32.04**), 361n, 381, 382
Marche pour une Révolution 1789–1989, 4, 352, 361n, 382
Mass in G, 50
Master Coale's Pieces, 202, 212n, 379

Meditations and Fugues, 4, 247, 350–2 (incl. **Ex. 31.06**)
Middeloceann, 63
Minuet in E minor for guitar, 322
Mr Burgess's Almanack, 4, 156, 327, 336, 346, 347 (**Ex. 31.02**), 369, 378, 381, 382, 384n
Mr W.S. ballet suite, 4, 5, 25 (**Ex. 03.01**), 111, 112, 116, 207, 247–50 (incl. **Exx. 22.01–22.02**), 251, 253n, 322, 331, 333, 337, 349, 350, 352, 358, 378, 381, 383, 384n
"Muchísimas Gracias", 41
Music for Hiroshima, 254
Nelson: suite for piano (one eye, one arm, one arse), 40
Nine Miniatures, 207, 208 (**Ex. 18.06**)
"La niña del bello rostro" (Lorca), 41
Nocturne and Chorale for four bassoons, 331–2
Nocturne for oboe, 332
Nocturne for oboe and piano, 15, 16 (**Ex. 02.01**), 333, 343
"Nu we sculan herian" (Caedmon's Hymn) for male voices, 27
"Ode: celebration for the Malay College for boys' voices and piano", 65
Orchestral Overture, 51
organ pieces, 51
"The Oxen" (Hardy), 4, 289, 290 (**Ex. 25.04**)
"*Pando:* march for a P&O orchestra", 68
Partita de Noël for String Orchestra, 51, 61n, 254, 265, 281n
"Passacaglia and Bagatelle for piano", 72
Passacaglia for Orchestra, 54, 61n, 105n
Petite Symphonie pour Strasbourg, 4, 247, 348–50 (incl. **Exx. 31.04–31.05**), 351
Pezzetto per Chitarra, 322
Piano Quintet, 51
piano sonatas, 40, 50, 51, 125
piano sonatinas, 27, 50, 51
Pieces for Harmonica, 4, 318–19, 329

La pioggia nel pineto (D'Annunzio), 4, 348 (**Ex. 31.03**), 369
polytonal suite for recorders, 50
"A Poor Man Can't Be Free" (Song for George Mikes), 294
prelude and fugue for the Holy Name organist, 18
Prelude and Fugue in D minor in the style of Bach, 18
Preludes, 99–102 (incl. **Exx. 10.02–10.07**), 105n, 199–201, 208
Preludio e Fuga per flauto, violino, chitarra e pianoforte, 323
Presto in Martin Bell's "Senilio's Broadcast Script: Riposte to Peter Porter", 98 (**Ex. 10.01**), 99, 208
Quartet for Flute, Oboe, 'Cello and Piano, 4, 329, 335 (**Ex. 30.05**), 383
Quartet for Oboe, Violin, Viola & Cello, 4, 333 (**Ex. 30.02**), 334, 343
Quartet Giovanni Guglielmi (1917–1945), 4, 233–4 (incl. **Exx. 20.04–20.05**)
Quatuor (N° 1) pour Guitares, 4, 293, 323–5 (incl. **Exx. 29.01–29.02**), 329, 331, 346
Quatuor N° 2 pour Guitares, 4, 325 (**Exx. 29.03–29.04**), 353
Quatuor N° 3 pour Guitares, 4, 257, 326 (**Ex. 29.05**)
Rhapsody for Bass Tuba & Orchestra, 332
Rhapsody for Oboe and Piano, 293, 332, 379
realizations of Purcell songs, 50
Romanza, 4, 316, 317 (**Ex. 28.01**), 318 (**Ex. 28.02**), 345
Rome in the Rain, 4, 26, 209, 229–31 (incl. **Exx. 20.01–20.02**), 236n, 319, 329, 330n
Sanctus, 50
Schnee in Savosa, 208
A Scottish Rhapsody for the 17th birthday of Andrew, 203, 342
Sinfonia No. 1 (1935), 25, 26 (**Exx. 03.02–03.03**), 230
Sinfonia (No. 2 – 1944), 358

Sinfonietta (abandoned), 50, 51
Sinfonietta (for jazz combo), 37
Sinfonietta for Liana, 4, 353 (**Ex. 31.07**), 371
Sonata 1 (St. John's) for recorder and piano, 4, 339, 371 (**Ex. 33.01**), 372
Sonata 2 for recorder and piano, 4, 339
Sonata 3 for recorder and keyboard, 4, 339
Sonata for Violin, Great Bass Recorder, and Piano, 4, 338
Sonata in C for great bass recorder, 4, 336
Sonata No. 2 for G.B.R. (great bass recorder), 4, 336, 337 (**Ex. 30.06**), 343
Sonata No. 3 for Great Bass Recorder or Bassoon and Piano, 4, 336, 344n
Sonata No. 4 for Great Bass Recorder and Pianoforte, 4, 327, 336–7, 338 (**Ex. 30.07**), 339
Sonate pour flûte à bec alto, 4, 336
Sonatina for Harmonica and Guitar, 4, 230, 318, 319 (**Ex. 28.03**), 320, 330n
Sonatina for Recorder, 4, 329, 336, 343
Sonatina in E minor for harmonica and guitar, 4, 315
Sonatina in G Major for Anne Field, 51, 52 (**Ex. 05.01**)
Song for Saint Cecilia's Day, 4, 229, 231, 232 (**Ex. 20.03**), 236n, 381
Song of a Northern City, 40, 74, 382
Song of the South Downs, 74, 75 (**Ex. 08.01**)
Song to a poem by Lance Godwin, 27
Spring Rondel, 50, 56, 57 (**Ex. 05.04**), 62n
Spring Songs for soprano and orchestra, 50, 56
Still to be neat (Jonson), 251
String Quartet in G major, 27, 254
string quartet (ca. 1972), 254
String Quartet (1980), 4, 254, 259–61 (incl. **Exx. 23.06–23.07**), 378, 379

"Strings", 279 (**Ex. 24.06**), 280; *see also* Joyce songs
Study for Cor Anglais or Oboe, 4, 333
"Suite for miniature organ", 72
Suite for oboe, 332
"Suite for small orchestra of Indians, Chinese and Malays", 65
Sweeney Agonistes (Eliot), song settings, 23, 51
Symphony in A minor, 41
Symphony No. 1 in E major, 24, 25 (**Ex. 03.01**), 49, 125, 250, 358
Symphony No. 2, "Malayan Symphony" or "Sinfoni Melayu" or "Sinfoni Merdeka", 66, 67n, 125
Symphony No. 3 in C, xviii, 3, 5, 25, 58, 66, 67n, 108, 125, 152, 185–95 (incl. **Exx. 17.01–17.07, 17.09–17.11**), 196n, 199, 201, 214, 255, 256, 263n, 292, 293, 300n, 319, 323, 331, 336, 349, 381, 383
Symphony [1984], 283
Tango for Pianoforte, 31n, 203, 212n, 379
Terrible Crystal, 289
"These things shall be" (celebration for Bedwellty Grammar School), 50
"This was real" (group of stage songs), 50
Three Little Pieces for Wind Quintet or Recorder Quintet, 336
Three Shakespeare Songs, 4, 50, 108, 109 (**Ex. 11.01**), 113n
Trio for flute, oboe and bassoon, 18
Trois Morceaux Irlandais, 117, 329
Trotsky's in New York!, see under STAGE WORKS WITH MUSIC
Twelve-tone polyrhythmics for piano, 99
twelve-tone studies for piano, 27
The Waste Land (Eliot), 4, 214–8, 222–6 (incl. **Exx. 19.03–19.05**), 233, 283, 381
Weep You No More, 250–1
"Who'll March with Essex?", 250
Wiegenlied, 51, 52, 53 (**Ex. 05.02**)

Music Index 441

The Wreck of the Deutschland, 4, 154, 288, 289 (**Ex. 25.03**)
"Ye Banks and Braes" fugue, 203
The Young Fiddler's Tunebook, 211
"Zodiac" Variations, 51, 382

FILM, TELEVISION, AND RADIO PROJECTS WITH MUSIC

A.D. (*Anno Domini*), 155–7 (inc. **Exx. 15.02–15.04**), 336, 346
Beard's Roman Women, 229
A Clockwork Orange, see under Kubrick, Stanley
Enderby film, 125, 141n
Gli Occhi di New York (*The Eyes of New York*), 4, 214, 237–8, 255
Moses the Lawgiver, 151–2, 319, 336
The Music of Exile (on Martinů), 103, 105n
St Winefred's Well (Hopkins), 289
Shakespeare da Noi (Shakespeare Among Us), 247, 250
Will (also called *The Bawdy Bard* and *Will!*), 110, 111, 112, 141n, 247, 250, 251, 265, 366

STAGE WORKS WITH MUSIC

The Adding Machine (Rice), incidental music, 50, 51
The Ascent of F6 (Auden-Isherwood), 28;
  incidental music, 50
Blooms of Dublin, xv, xvii, 4, 26, 154, 230, 246n, 256, 257, 264–80 (incl. **Exx. 24.01–24.04**), 280n, 281n, 282n, 288, 326, 346, 371, 378
Carmen, see under TEXTS FOR MUSIC
A Clockwork Orange: a play with music, xvii, 4, 43, 146, 166, 235, 302–11 (incl. **Exx. 27.01–27.06**), 313n, 369, 381
A Clockwork Orange: Prologue, 302, 311–13
A Clockwork Orange 2004, see under TEXTS FOR MUSIC
Copernicus opera, 27, 29
Cyrano, see under LYRICS
Cyrano de Bergerac (adaptation for the Guthrie Theatre), 126, 129–31 (incl. **Ex. 13.05**), 134, 141, 141n, 144, 332, 358
Doctor Faustus opera, 27
The Entertainer (Osborne), 234–5
The Eve of Saint Venus (opera), 54–5, 57–8, 62n
Freud opera, 369, 373n
Hassan (Flecker), incidental music, 28, 40
Hospital Blues, 39
Houdini musical, 132
A Midsummer Night's Dream (Shakespeare), incidental music, 51
Mr W.S. ballet suite, *see under* COMPOSITIONS
Murder in the Cathedral (Eliot), incidental music, 50
Oberon, see under TEXTS FOR MUSIC
Sweeney Agonistes (Eliot), incidental music, 51
Tobias and the Angel (Bridie), incidental music, 42
Trotsky's in New York!, 4, 238–40, 241–4 (**Ex. 21.01**), 246n, 379
The Waste Land (Eliot), musical score, 28
Winterset (Anderson), incidental music, 42

LITERATURE INDEX

FILM AND TELEVISION SCRIPTS

Anthony Burgess's Rome, 103, 154, 232, 236n
Attila the Hun miniseries, 155, 355
Byron/Shelley/Wollstonecraft television film, 110
Celebration (AB's return to Manchester), 103, 154
The Crystal Cave (about Merlin), 237
Cyrus, 154, 237
Grace Under Pressure, 103, 262, 373n
Jesus of Nazareth, 153, 157
Lynx (originally *Puma*), 245
Michelangelo biography, 103, 237
Onassis, Aristotle, biography, 237
Quest for Fire, 132, 154
The Rage of Lawrence, 103, 286, 291n
Silence, Exile and Cunning, 100, 115
The Spy Who Loved Me, 186
Stilwell, General, "Vinegar Joe", biography, 237
Writers and Places: "A Kind of Failure", 345

TEXTS FOR MUSIC: LIBRETTOS, LYRICS, STAGE ADAPTATIONS

1789: An Opera Libretto (for *Le Bleu-Blanc-Rouge et le Noir*), 352, 382
The Brides of Enderby, see under COMPOSITIONS
Carmen, 113n, 166, 298–300, 301n
Chatsky (The Importance of Being Stupid). Translation of *Gore ot uma* (*Woe from Wit*) by Griboyedov, 371
A Clockwork Orange: a play with music, see under STAGE WORKS WITH MUSIC
A Clockwork Orange 2004, 311
Cyrano (music by Michael Lewis), xvii, 3, 132–41 (incl. **Ex. 13.06**), 142n, 208, 237, 251–2, 342
Cyrano de Bergerac, see under STAGE WORKS WITH MUSIC
L'Enfance du Christ (Berlioz), 103–4, 298
The Eve of Saint Venus, see under STAGE WORKS WITH MUSIC
King Oedipus, for Speaker, Chorus, and Orchestra (music by Stanley Silverman), 132
Lord, I Was Afraid (Nigel Balchin), 50
The Midsummer Night's Dream Show: A Madrigal Comedy Celebration in E major (music by Stanley Silverman), 132
Mozart et son Wolf Gang: opéra en trois actes, 381
Oberon (Weber) 166, 295–7, 300, 301n, 329
Oedipus the King (music by Stanley Silverman), 126, 131, 142n, 234
Trotsky's in New York!, see under STAGE WORKS WITH MUSIC

WRITINGS

99 Novels, 262, 263n
"1889 and the Devil's Mode", 352

Literature Index

1985, 35, 261, 262, 262n, 263n
ABBA ABBA, 228, 232–3, 236n, 377
The Age of the Grand Tour, 109
"An American Organ", 209
Any Old Iron, 35, 166, 322, 355, 361n
"Artist's Life", 154–5
Beard's Roman Women, 116, 141n, 228–30, 231, 236n, 322
Beds in the East, 63, 65–6, 67n, 68, 71, 81, 128, 331, 343n, 367
But Do Blondes Prefer Gentlemen?, see *Homage to QWERT YUIOP*
Byrne, 61n, 166, 331, 343n, 371, 378, 382, 383, 384n
Carmen: An Opera in Four Acts, 301n
A Christmas Recipe, 253n
"Clockwork Marmalade", 92n, 93n
A Clockwork Orange, xvii, 4, 5, 11, 43, 75, 77, 80, 81–92, 92n, 93n, 94n, 95, 103, 143–4, 288, 302, 311
"A Clockwork Orange Resucked", 92
The Clockwork Testament, 61n, 147–8, 150n, 252, 286, 362n, 365, 372n, 377, 384n
Coaching Days of England, 109–10, 113n
Cyrano de Bergerac, see listing under STAGE WORKS WITH MUSIC
D. H. Lawrence in Italy (introduction), 286, 291n
A Dead Man in Deptford, 252–3, 253n, 370, 378, 381
Devil of a State, 69–71, 72n, 76, 296
The Devil's Mode, 166, 252, 258, 352, 353n, 354n, 361n
The Doctor is Sick, 72n, 75–6, 78n, 236n, 313n, 322
Don Giovanni and *Idomeneo* by W. A. Mozart (introduction), 293, 300n, 343n
Earthly Powers, xvii, 11, 35, 94n, 150n, 166, 251, 262, 264–6, 281n, 313n, 317, 382
Eliot Memorial Lectures, 31n, 250, 287, 292, 332, 345, 346
Enderby Outside, 104, 104n, 106n, 382

Enderby's Dark Lady, 111, 134, 166, 247, 250, 251, 253n
The End of the World News, 154, 209, 239, 240–6, 246n, 251, 293, 359
"The Endless Voyager", 354n
The Enemy in the Blanket, 63, 65, 67n, 70
English Literature: A Survey for Students, 22n, 69, 72n, 261
Ernest Hemingway and his world, 35, 262, 263n
The Eve of Saint Venus (novella), 5–7, 62n, 75, 77
"A Few Words About a Guitar Concerto by Anthony Burgess", 326–7, 330n
Flame Into Being, 284, 291n
Future Imperfect (foreword), 92n
"Girl", 44, 47n, 220, 227n
"The Great Christmas Train Mystery", 74
"Grief", 27
"The Guitar and I", 315, 320n, 322, 329, 330n
Here Comes Everybody, see *Re Joyce*
Homage to QWERT YUIOP (*But Do Blondes Prefer Gentlemen?*), 62n, 365–6, 372n, 373n, 378, 384n
Honey for the Bears, 95–7, 105n, 116
"How I Wrote My Third Symphony", 67n, 196n
Hun, 355, 361n
Inside Mr Enderby, xvii, 23, 47n, 75, 76–7, 78, 79n, 99, 104, 227n, 252, 294, 301n, 378, 382
I Trust and Love You, 77
"I Wish My Wife Was Dead", 213n
"John Sebastian – A Personal Reminiscence", 315–6, 320n
"Journal of the Plague Year (1951)", 51, 382
Joyce Images (introduction), 378
Joysprick, 115–6, 118 (**Ex. 12.02**), 122n, 281n, 330n
The Kingdom of the Wicked, 156, 157 (**Ex. 15.05**), 158n
The Land Where the Ice Cream Grows, 235

Language Made Plain, 117, 119, 122n, 154, 239, 370, 382
"The Large World of Lawrence", 286
Little Wilson and Big God, 9, 13, 19n, 20n, 21n, 22n, 31n, 35, 42, 45, 46n, 47n, 48n, 61n, 62n, 67n, 72n, 73n, 78n, 263n, 293, 354n, 361n, 366–7, 369, 373n, 378
The Lives of the Piano ("The Well-Tempered Revolution"), 198–9, 212n
The Long Day Wanes, see *The Malayan Trilogy*
A Long Trip to Teatime, 235, 236n
"A Meeting at Valladolid", 252
The Malayan Trilogy (*The Long Day Wanes*), 63–4, 70, 120, 367
Man of Nazareth, 153–4, 157n
MF, 11, 116, 126–31 (incl. **Exx. 13.01–13.04**), 141n, 144, 229, 282n, 292
Moses: A Narrative, 105n, 151, 152 (**Ex. 15.01**)
"The Most Beautified", 354n, 382
A Mouthful of Air, 239, 370, 373n, 382
Mozart and the Wolf Gang (*On Mozart*), 83, 93n, 166, 166n, 261, 293, 300n, 332, 358–61 (incl. **Exx. 32.05–32.06**), 378, 380, 381
"Murder to Music", 258
"The Muse: A Sort of SF Story", 251
"Musicalising *Ulysses*", 278–9, 280n, 282n
"A mystery and its monument", 384n
Napoleon Symphony, 4, 35, 107, 133, 148, 159–66 (incl. **Exx. 16.01–16.06**), 167n, 185, 196n, 292
New York, 237, 246n
"The Ninth", 93n
"Not Only Carmen", 157, 158n
Nothing Like the Sun, 5, 107–8, 110, 113n, 192, 247, 378, 382
The Novel Now (*The Novel Today*), 85, 119–21, 122n, 262
The Novel To-day, 119, 122n, 262
"Nymphs and Satyrs", 227n, 261
Oberon Old and New, 297, 301n

Oedipus the King, see listing under STAGE WORKS WITH MUSIC
Oeuvres pour Quatuor de Guitares liner notes, 324, 329, 330n
One Hand Clapping, 75, 77–8, 79n
One Man's Chorus, 62n, 94n, 141n, 158n, 379
On Going to Bed, 154, 158n
On Mozart, see *Mozart and the Wolf Gang*
"A Pair of Gloves", 213n
Pianoforte: A Social History of the Piano (introduction), 198–9, 212n
The Pianoplayers, 105n, 116, 166, 209–12 (incl. **Ex. 18.07**), 213n, 299, 322
"Poetry for a Tiny Room", 79n
Ransom Memorial Lectures, 332
Re Joyce (*Here Comes Everybody*), 103, 115–16, 121n, 280n
Revolutionary Sonnets, 47n, 227n
The Right to an Answer, 71, 73n, 74, 322
Der Rosenkavalier story adaptation, 154, 294, 301n
Sealed With a Loving Kiss, 77
Shakespeare (biography), 111–12, 113n, 196n, 251
"Shakespeare in Music", 108, 113n
A Shorter Finnegans Wake, 117, 122n
"Summoned by bell", 105n
"Symphony in C" program note, 66, 67n, 196n, 197n
They Wrote in English, 261
This Man and Music, 13, 18, 19n, 20n, 21n, 22n, 25, 31n, 42, 44, 46n, 47n, 48n, 50–1, 62n, 99, 105n, 108, 141n, 152, 154, 157n, 166, 166n, 167n, 196n, 197n, 209, 211, 222, 226n, 227n, 231, 236n, 250, 253n, 277, 281n, 287 (**Ex. 25.02**), 290n, 291n, 292–3, 300n, 320n, 323, 332, 343n, 366, 377, 380, 382
"Thoughts of a belated father", 331, 341, 343n, 344n

Literature Index

"The Thyssen-Bornemisza Collection of Modern Masters: A Personal View", 20n
Time for a Tiger, 3, 63, 66
Tremor of Intent, 11, 95, 103, 121, 122n, 127
"The Twenty-four-string Guitar", 324–5, 329, 330n
"Under the Bam: Thoughts on Words and Music", 346
Urgent Copy, 121, 122n, 141n, 365
A Vision of Battlements, 35, 42–6, 47n, 48n, 50, 58, 61n, 64, 227n, 322, 330n, 382
The Wanting Seed, 35, 80–1, 92n, 314, 320n
Who's Who entry, 366
Will and Testament, 251
The Worm and the Ring, 58–60, 61n, 62n, 75, 77, 116, 354n, 382
"The Writer and Music", 93n
You've Had Your Time, xviii, 20n, 31n, 47n, 73n, 78n, 79n, 92n, 104n, 105n, 106n, 113n, 121n, 122n, 125, 134, 141n, 142n, 149n, 150n, 157n, 158n, 166n, 167n, 196n, 197n, 213n, 218, 236n, 238, 243, 246n, 253n, 263n, 281n, 282n, 291n, 301n, 313n, 320n, 321n, 330n, 344n, 350, 353n, 354n, 361n, 366, 369–70, 372n, 373n
"You've Had Your Time: Being the Beginning of an Autobiography" (*Malahat Review*), 19n–20n

GENERAL INDEX

Academy of St Martin in the Fields, 316
Addinsell, Richard, *Warsaw Concerto*, 38, 39, 74, 119
Adelaide Arts Festival, 144
Adler, Larry, 314, 316, 317–18;
   It Ain't Necessarily So, 320, 321n
Adler, Raffael, 218
Aggeler, Geoffrey, 165, 264, 281n, 373n;
   Anthony Burgess: The Artist as Novelist, 167n;
   Critical Essays on Anthony Burgess, 106n
Aïghetta Quartet, 297, 322, 323, 326, 328, 329;
   Oeuvres pour Quatuor de Guitares, 326, 330n;
   Musique d'un écrivain anglais sure la Riviera, 326, 330n, 379
Albert Hall, 368
Alexander, Czar, 163
Alford, Kenneth, *Colonel Bogey March*, 357
Almeida Theatre, 371
AMAS Six O'Clock Musical Theatre Lab, 246n
American Recorder, 344n
Amis, Kingsley, 119;
   Take a Girl Like You, 119
Amis, Martin, 366;
   Visiting Mrs. Nabokov and Other Excursions, 372n
Annaud, Jean-Jacques, 154
Ansermet, Ernest, 16, 117

Antheil, George, 266
Anthony Burgess and Modernity, 93n
Anthony Burgess Centre, 379
Anthony Burgess Newsletter, 379
Anthony Burgess Society (*Les Amis d'Anthony Burgess*), 379
anti-Semitism, 29, 267, 269, 271–2, 359
Aphrodite, 162
Aprahamian, Felix, 301n
Ardwick Empire, 9
Arlen, Harold, 27
Armstrong, Louis, 37
Arnell, Richard, 199
Arnold, Denis, 92n
Arnold, Malcolm, 314, 343n;
   Fantasy for Brass Band, 351, 354n
Astaire, Fred, 317
Auden, W. H., 104, 119;
   The Age of Anxiety, 198;
   New Year Letter, 43;
   The Poet's Tongue, 226n
Augustine, Saint, 366
Austen, Jane, 98, 159, 165
Austin, William W., 352, 354n

Bach, Johann Sebastian, 18, 78, 120, 131, 203, 204, 207, 213n, 233, 244, 326, 334;
   "Air on the G string" (from Orchestral Suite No. 3), 208;
   Brandenburg Concerto No. 2, 318;
   Brandenburg Concerto No. 6, 84;
   Cantata No. 140, *Wachet auf, ruft uns die Stimme*, 84, 305;

Goldberg Variations, 117;
Passacaglia and Fugue in C minor
   (do minore) for Organ, 153;
The Well-Tempered Clavier, 37, 198,
   212n
Bailey, Andrew, 149n
Baker, Josephine, 255, 372
*Baker's Biographical Dictionary of
   Musicians, see* Slonimsky,
   Nicolas
Balchin, Nigel, *Lord, I Was Afraid,* 50
Banbury Grammar School, 58, 60
Banbury Guardian, 61n
Bancroft, Anne, 153
Bannister, Roger, 72, 73n, 76
Barber, David W., *Bach, Beethoven and
   the Boys: Music History As It
   Ought To Be Taught,* 212n
Barbican Virtuosi, 378
Barbirolli, John, 117
Barclay, William, *Jesus of Nazareth*,
   153, 157
Barnes, Clive, 130, 135, 141n, 142n
Bartók, Bela, 64, 277;
   Concerto for Orchestra, 25, 240,
      257, 338, 339, 347;
   Contrasts, 338;
   Dance Suite, 339;
   Sonata for Solo Violin, 255;
   Violin Concerto, 255
Basie, Count, 38, 39
BBC (British Broadcasting Company),
   4, 31n, 54, 71, 88, 115, 212,
   216, 218, 238, 240, 242, 246n,
   250, 252, 254, 264, 266, 275,
   289, 358;
An Airful of Burgess, 335, 378;
*The Burgess Variations: Theme and
   Thirty Variations on the Life
   and Works of Anthony Burgess*,
   379–80, 381, 384n;
Desert Island Discs, 117, 122n, 145;
Face to Face, 328;
Oscar Peterson Invites, 4–5, 6n, 88,
   93n, 316;
Tonight, 143
BBC Radio Scotland, 378
BBC Radio 2, 103, 298
BBC Radio 3, 93n, 275

BBC Scottish Symphony Orchestra,
   93n, 335, 378
BBC Symphony Orchestra, 16
The Beatles, 95, 104
Beckett, Samuel, 120
Beethoven, Ludwig van, 5, 15, 25, 64,
   78, 85–7, 93n, 144, 150n, 166,
   195, 245, 247, 265, 285, 286,
   345, 355, 365;
piano sonatas, 16, 17, 24, 286;
Piano Sonata No. 8, "Pathétique",
   304, 305 (**Ex. 27.02**);
string quartets, 45;
Symphony No. 1, 13;
Symphony No. 3 (*Eroica*), 4, 28, 90,
   148, 159–66, 185, 292;
Symphony No. 5, 21n, 86, 87, 90,
   145, 292, 306;
Symphony No. 6 ("Pastoral"),
   306;Symphony No. 7, 304;
Symphony No. 9 ("Ode to Joy"),
   46, 83, 84, 86–8, 92n, 144–5,
   148, 188, 303, 304, 305, 306,
   307, 308 (**Ex. 27.04**), 310,
   313;
Violin Concerto, 86, 145, 254,
   262n
Bell, Martin, 157n, 208, 300n;
Collected Poems 1937–1966: "Pets",
   105n;
"Senilio's Broadcast Script: Riposte
   to Peter Porter", 98–9, 105n
Belli, Giuseppe Gioacchino, 228,
   232–3, 377
Belmont, Georges, 153
Bender, Philippe, 328, 352
Benedict, Helen, 354n
Benjamin, Arthur, 314
Bennett, Richard Rodney, 320n
Beowulf, 28
Berberian, Cathy, 65, 384n
Berg, Alban, 208;
   Sieben Frühe Lieder, 284;
   Violin Concerto, 201, 255, 330n
Berger, Jean, 314
Bergeron, Katherine, 246n
Berghaus, Ruth, 246n
Bergman, Ingrid, 318
Berio, Luciano, 297

Berkeley, Lennox, 343n
Berlin, Irving, 266
Berlin Philharmonic, 117
Berlioz, Hector, 18, 329, 359;
L'Enfance du Christ, 103–4, 298;
Harold in Italy, 199;
"Queen Mab" Scherzo, 108;
Symphonie Fantastique, 13, 365, 384n
Bernstein, Leonard, 83, 93n, 335;
The Age of Anxiety, 198;
West Side Story, 240
Berthoux, André-Michel, 323, 326
Best, Pete, 104
Bethan Green Hospital, 341
The Bible, 151, 251, 273, 284, 311
Billingsley, Michael, *Gli Occhi di New York*, 237–8, 246n
Birmingham Festival of Music, 350
Birtwistle, Harrison, *Salford Toccata*, 351
Biscardi, Chester, 217
Biswell, Andrew, "Editing and publishing *A Clockwork Orange*", 94n, 313n;
The Real Life of Anthony Burgess, 20n, 31n, 61n, 72n, 73n, 78n, 94n, 149n, 150n, 213n, 301n, 380
bitonality, *see* polytonality
Bizet, Georges, *Carmen*, 18, 76, 113n, 130, 296, 298
Bliss, Arthur, 359
Blitzstein, Marc, *The Cradle Will Rock*, 239
Bly, James, 103, 106n
Boccherini, Luigi, 11,
The Bohemian Girl (Michael William Balfe), 267
Bohlman, Philip V., 246n
Bolcom, William, 212n;
Violin Concerto in D, 201
Bonaparte, Napoleon, *see* Napoleon Bonaparte
Bond, James, *see* Fleming, Ian
Boorman, John, 143
Boston Symphony, 383
Boulez, Pierre, 255
Boult, Adrian. 16

Bowles, Paul, 4, 6, 368;
Paul Bowles on Music, 373n;
The Sheltering Sky, 369
Boyd, William, 384n;
Homage to AB, 378
Boytinck, Paul, *Anthony Burgess: An Annotated Bibliography and Reference Guide*, 94n, 113n, 149n, 150n
Bragg, Melvyn, 291n
Brahms, Johannes, 64, 286;
Symphony No. 2, 19;
Symphony No. 3, 292;
Symphony No. 4, 19, 153, 256;
Violin Concerto, 254
Brecht, Bertolt, 30,
Bridson, Douglas Geoffrey, 28, 216
Britten, Benjamin, 58, 119, 191, 199;
Les Illuminations, 87;
Phantasy Quartet, 343n;
The Young Person's Guide to the Orchestra, 357
Bromley, Ann, aunt, 10
Bromley, Betty, cousin, 10
Bromley, Elsie, cousin, 10, 20n
Brown, Nacio Herb, 302
Brown University Orchestra, xvii, xviii
Brownwell, Sonia, 42
Bruch, Max, Violin Concerto No. 1 in G minor, 256
Bruno, Giordano, 247
Bull, John, 17, 111
Bullitt, W. C., 245
Bulwer-Lytton, Edward, 165
Bunting, Charles T., *Studies in the Novel*: "An Interview in New York with Anthony Burgess", 166n
Burgess, Anthony, born John Burgess Wilson
 Adderbury Drama Group, 51
 alcohol consumption, 42, 75, 188, 345, 366
 archives, 379–80
 artistic talent, 12, 14, 21n
 and astrology, 10
 as autobiographer, 9, 19n–20n, 44–5, 46, 47n, 66, 293, 366–7
 Bedford Dormobile, 126, 231, 342

General Index

birth, 10
and Catholicism, 10–11, 17, 30, 50, 368
children, attitude toward, 341
composer, ambition to be a, 12, 14, 15, 21n, 30, 35, 54, 55
composer, on being considered a musician and, 3, 5, 18, 45, 121, 125, 130, 186, 228–9, 247, 255, 351, 368–9
composer and arranger, activity as, 3–4, 5–6, 15, 18–19, 23–5, 27–8, 30, 36, 37–9, 40, 41–2, 45–6, 50–1, 54, 55, 63, 65–6, 68, 72, 74–5, 98–100, 105n, 108, 110, 111, 116–17, 125, 127–9, 130–1, 145–6, 151–3, 154, 155–6, 165–6, 185–6, 195, 198, 199, 202, 203, 204, 207, 208–9, 211, 212n-213n, 214–17, 229, 231, 233–5, 236n, 237–9, 255–6, 259, 264, 266, 280, 281n, 283, 288–90, 294, 297, 302–3, 315, 316, 318, 320, 322–3, 325–7, 329, 331–9, 341, 343, 345–6, 348–9, 350–3, 358, 369, 371, 372
on composing, 49, 55–6, 58, 154, 186, 212n–213n, 320, 372
conferences and symposia about, 379–81
as critic, 78, 79n, 99, 121, 255
on critics, 92, 255, 277, 298
daltonism of, 12, 14, 20n, 354n, 355
education at St. Edmund's RC Elementary, 11
education at Bishop Bilsborrow Memorial Elementary School, 12
education at Xaverian College, 13–14, 17–19, 21n, 23, 27
education at University of Manchester, 27–30, 300n, 381–2
employment, efforts at seeking, 23
as essayist, 121, 365–6, 370
eschatology, view of, 30
exile, 103, 114

and fatherhood, 59, 126, 339, 341–3
final decline, death, 337–8, 372, 377
guitar playing, 323
health, illness, 72, 75, 345, 350
honorary doctorate from the University of Manchester, 154
The Jaypees, 36–9
as journalist, 121
and love, 341, 343
lectures, 133
marriage to Liliana Macellari, 126, 341
marriage to Llewela Jones, 39, 46n
memorial celebrations, concerts, 261, 378–9
military service, 30, 35–46
on money, taxation, 5, 55–6, 112, 130, 144, 255, 283
on music academics, 44–5, 50
musical education, 12–19, 20n, 21n, 22n, 24, 27, 36, 50
name, pseudonyms, 20n, 63, 67n, 71, 78
obituaries, 122n
organ playing, 133
piano playing, 11, 13, 14, 15–16, 28–9, 36, 37, 38, 39, 40, 45, 50, 68, 74, 246n, 286, 316, 317
prolificacy, 155, 186, 361, 366
and Protestants, 10, 17
work on *Cyrano*, 132–141
rock music, antipathy toward, 104, 277
royalty income, 147
sexual activity, love affairs, 17, 21n, 29, 30, 39, 41, 49–50, 125–6
synesthesia, 12, 298
on taxation, 255
as teacher, 39–40, 41 49–51, 60–1, 63, 66–7, 68–9, 133
television, attitute toward, 254–5
theatre, activity in, 28, 50, 51
theft of manuscript in Bracciano, 115
violin playing, 12, 13, 256
vocabulary, 293
on writing, 58, 121, 186
Yorkshire Post incident, 78, 79n

– GEOGRAPHICAL LOCATIONS AND RESIDENCES:

Australia, 144
Bamber Bridge, 50, 154
Banbury (Adderbury), 50–60, 61n
Birmingham, 290n
Boston, 132, 135, 342
Bracciano, 115, 151, 342
Brinsford Lodge, 49–50
Broadway, 132, 133, 134, 135, 136, 141, 237, 342
Brunei, 68–72
Canada (Toronto), 105n, 135, 185, 342
Chiswick (24 Glebe Street), 98, 110, 125
Dublin, 114, 115, 266, 275–6
England, 36–40, 71, 149n
Etchingham ("Applegarth"), 77, 98, 105n, 262n, 263n, 300n
France (Callian de Var, Paris), 126, 150n, 20, 288, 368
Geneva, 346
Gibraltar, 35, 40–6, 92n, 256, 324, 355
Hollywood, 110, 111
Hove, 74–7
Israel, 151
Italy, 126, 147, 150n, 151
Leningrad, 82, 95
London, 111–12, 150n, 275, 317, 373n
Lugano (Savosa), 5, 150n, 208, 325, 351, 354n, 358
Malaya (Malaysia), 60–1, 63–7, 67n, 120, 154, 345
Malta (Lija), 59, 126, 151, 342, 373n
Manchester (and environs), xv, 9–16, 23, 28154, 233, 352, 356, 358
Minneapolis, 133, 134, 135, 342
Monaco (Monte Carlo), xviii, 5, 58, 105n, 150n, 155, 199, 201, 202, 203, 208, 231, 255–7, 258, 259, 261, 283, 288, 318, 324, 326, 342, 345, 348, 372, 381
Morocco, 98, 104, 369

New York, 132, 133, 134, 135, 146, 237, 350, 354n, 366, 368–9
Nottingham (Eastwood), 283, 286
Rome (Trastevere), 115, 131, 133, 151, 154, 185, 209, 228, 233, 247, 264, 315, 342
Scotland (Edinburgh, Eskbank, Glasgow, Inverness), 9, 10, 30, 35, 36, 345–6
Siena (Montalbuccio), 185, 231
Spain, 342
Strasbourg, 348, 352
Washington, D.C., 332

– INTERVIEWS AND PROFILES:

"Anthony Burgess" (M. Amis), *The Observer*, 366
"Anthony Burgess" (Malko), *Penthouse*, 3, 146, 150n, 366
"Anthony Burgess: Pushing On" (Clemons), *The New York Times,* 3, 6n
"Appreciation: Anthony Burgess – The last words" (Huelbes), *The Guardian,* 372, 373n
"The Art of Fiction XLVIII: Anthony Burgess" (Cullinan), *The Paris Review,* 331, 343n, 366
BBC radio (Januszczak), 246n
The Burgess Variations: Theme and Thirty Variations on the Life and Works of Anthony Burgess (Jackson/Thompson), BBC television, 379–80, 381, 384n
"Eclectic author of his own five-foot shelf" (Hicks), *Life,* 3, 42, 125, 141n, 331
"Great Writers: Anthony Burgess" (Elisa Mantin, director), 78, 79n
"An Interview in New York with Anthony Burgess" (Bunting), *Studies in the Novel,* 160, 166n
"An Interview with Anthony Burgess" (Coale), *Modern Fiction Studies,* 126, 141n, 213n, 366
Oscar Peterson Invites, 4–5, 6n, 88, 93n, 302, 316

"Playboy Interview: Anthony Burgess – candid conversation", *Playboy,* 3, 366
"Why I Am Eight Years Younger than Anthony Burgess" (Vidal), *The New York Review of Books,* 367–8, 373n

– THEMES AND STYLISTIC TRAITS:

adultery, promiscuity, wife-swapping, 44, 59, 60, 65, 71, 76, 97, 272, 273
alcoholism and substance abuse, 75–6
arithmology, 89, 90, 91, 94n, 222, 347
autobiographical representation in AB's fiction, 43–4, 58, 59–60, 64, 65, 66, 71, 75–6, 104, 106n, 209, 213n, 228–9, 233, 252–3, 265, 355, 367, 382
class conflict, 65
colonialism, 63, 66, 70, 120
Catholic-Protestant conflict, 54, 95, 103
Catholicism, 11, 59, 219, 236n, 261, 382
death, 147, 148, 250, 271, 274, 377
decadence of British society, 71, 81
disdain for music professors, 27, 44–5
doppelgänger, 44, 229
dystopia, 80–1, 82
Eastern and Western cultures, conflicts and commonality between, 63–4, 66, 71, 226, 261, 296, 345
Elizabethan language, 107
dictionary and encyclopedia usage ("aleatory means"), 107, 235
eschatology, 103
espionage, 95, 103
fatherhood, 59

free will, freedom of choice, 80, 82, 83, 85, 88, 89, 95, 97, 127, 147, 302–3, 305, 307, 311, 312
good and evil, 81–2, 84, 85, 95, 146, 265, 302, 311, 313, 380
homosexuality, 44, 56, 80, 97, 264, 370
humor, 154, 276
illness, medical treatment, 75–6, 382
incest-riddle nexus, 126–9
Islam, 70, 261, 295
Israel, Israelis, Jews, 50, 74, 355, 359
Italian unmusicality, 229, 265
Joyce's influence, 114–17, 119, 235, 267
leitmotif, motivic technique, 90, 91, 94n, 116, 119, 127–9
love, 218, 219, 271–2
lyrics inserted into books, 251–2, 253n, 265
Manichaeanism, 11, 95, 103
Mozart's music as symbol of divinity, 245, 293–4, 359
Muse, artistic inspiration, 104, 221
music in relation to literature, musicalization of fiction, 5, 6, 27, 49, 58, 69, 84, 85, 107, 108, 115–17, 119, 120, 127–9, 130, 159, 209, 228–9, 244–5, 262, 287, 292, 359, 377
musical allusion, imagery, metaphor, parody, symbolism, 5, 27, 30, 45, 63–4, 65, 70, 71, 76, 77, 81, 83–7, 96–7, 104, 105n, 107–8, 112, 115, 116, 117, 119, 120, 121, 127–9, 148, 151, 154, 160, 193–4, 219, 222, 225, 231, 233, 250, 265–7, 272, 285, 312, 331, 348, 350, 377, 383–4
musical notation inserted into books, 60, 115, 116, 117, 127–9, 152, 156–7, 235
musical structure applied to literature, 4, 5, 64, 83, 88–91, 103, 106n, 107, 120, 148, 150n, 159–66, 185, 244, 359–61

musical themes derived from words, names, numbers, solfege, 28, 30, 119, 128–9, 155, 156, 161–6, 167n, 185, 190–3, 208–9, 229, 234, 235, 236n, 265, 349, 377
mythology, 159, 161–2, 165, 219, 284, 293
Nadsat, artificial languages, 82, 84, 128, 132, 143, 144, 147, 154, 302, 304, 311-2
opera, 54–5, 57–9, 60, 69–70, 75–6, 84, 130, 164, 192, 209, 293, 303, 304, 365
Pavlovian conditioning, 81
Pelagianism versus Augustinianism, 80–1, 148, 265
plagiarism, 77, 104
puns, wordplay, 127, 231, 235, 242, 297, 383
sex, 81, 85, 86, 88, 89, 95, 97, 104, 147, 209, 218, 270, 272, 273, 274, 355, 360, 382
structuralism, Lévi-Strauss, 126–7
synesthesia, 45, 71, 85, 298, 331
Tudor notation, 128, 141n, 229
violence, 81, 82, 83, 84, 86, 87, 88, 89, 90, 91

Burgess, Liana, formally Liliana Macellari Wilson, second wife, xviii, 4, 59, 125, 141n, 166n, 208, 212n, 217, 256, 280n, 290n, 353, 372, 378–81;
as agent, 122n;
first husband, 253n;
guitar playing, 322, 323, 330n;
marriage to AB, 126, 341;
as mother, 341;
reaction to *A Clockwork Orange* film, 146;
representation in AB's fiction, 228, 233;
as translator, 154, 278
Burgess, Lynne, formally Llewela Isherwood Jones Wilson and generally known as Lynne Wilson, first wife, 3, 29, 31n, 63, 97, 104, 209, 366, 367;
adultery and sexual behavior, 30, 40, 43, 49;
alcohol consumption, 40, 43, 95, 110;
assault and injury, 42, 47n, 82, 83, 92n;
death, 110;
Duke of Edinburgh incident, 71–2;
marriage to AB, 39, 46n;
miscarriage, 42, 59;
representation in AB's fiction and poetry, 44, 59, 82–3, 220, 356;
suicide attempt, 98;
unmusicality and dislike of AB's music, 30, 54, 353, 368
Burgess, Sally, 300
Burke, Tom, 150n
Burns, Robert, 342
Burroughs, William, 98
Burstall, Christopher, 115
Burton, Humphrey, 275
Burton, Robert, *The Anatomy of Melancholy,* 23, 54
Bustin, Gwen, 60
Byrd, William, 17, 111
Byron, Lord, 198;
Childe Harold, 199;
Don Juan, 382

Caldwell, John, 253n
Callas, Maria, 78
Calvino, Italo, 121
Cambridge University, 78, 125, 286
Camelot (film), 110;
(musical), 136
Campbell, Joseph, *A Skeleton Key to Finnegans Wake,* 117
Canada, 105n, 135
Cantor, Eddie, 317
Caplin, Martha, 259, 358;
see also Primavera Quartet
Cappella Nova, 378
Carasso, Jean-Pierre, 352
Caravaggio, Michelangelo Merisi da, 294
Cariou, Len, 130
Carlos, Wendy, music for *A Clockwork Orange,* 144–5, 149n, 308;
Switched-On Bach, 144;
Timesteps, 144
Carmichael, Hoagy, 27

General Index

Carroll, Lewis, 154;
  Through the Looking-Glass, 235
Carulli, Ferdinando, 326
Caruso, Enrico, 10
Caruthers, Susan, 150n
Cassis, A. F., *Graham Greene: Man of Paradox,* 301n
Cato, Bob, 378
Catullus, 43
Cecchi d'Amico, Suso, 153
Center Stage, 278
Centre Pompidou, 352
Cervantes, Miguel de, *Don Quixote,* 252, 324, 330n
Chabrier, Emmanuel, 266
Chabrier, Hortense, 154
Chailly, Luciano, 315
Chaminade, Cécile, 372
Champion, Harry, born William Henry Crump, 355
Chaplin, Charlie, 266
Charlemagne, 296
Charles d'Orléans, "*Le temps a laissé son manteau*", 56, 62n
Charley's Aunt (Brandon Thomas), 60
Chattaway, Thurland, "Red Wing", 227n
Chicago, 240
Choice, 113n
Christie, Agatha, 120
Christie, Gilbert, 70
Christmas carols, 51, 99;
  Adeste fideles, 60;
  in *Will,* 110;
  "Good King Wenceslas", 207;
  "The First Noel", 207;
  "God Rest Ye Merry Gentlemen", 207
Choerilos of Samos, 84
Chopin, Frédéric, 348
Christ, Jesus, 155, 164–5, 377
Church of Santa Cecilia, 133
City College of New York, 133, 135, 237
City of Birmingham Symphony Orchestra, 350
Clark, S. M., 332, 381
Clarke, Arthur C., 120
Classical Guitar, 320n, 330n

Clemons, Walter, 6n
Cleopatra, 162
Clwyd Theatr Cymru, 301n
Coale, Samuel, 64, 107, 201, 209, 212n, 213n;
  Anthony Burgess, 67n, 113n;
  "An Interview with Anthony Burgess", 126, 141n
Cocteau, Jean, 60
Collins, Charles, 361n
Columbia University, 237
Conan Doyle, Sir Arthur, "The Adventure of the Red-Headed League", 263n
conductors, 3, 16, 27, 86, 103–4, 111, 160, 167n, 185, 283, 365
Connolly, Cyril, *The Unquiet Grave,* 43
Conrad, Joseph, *Chance,* 369
Conrad, William, 110, 111, 127, 251
Contemporary Composers, 42, 46n, 99, 105n, 209, 250, 330n, 380
Cook, Bruce, 62n
Cooke, Nicholas, 92n
Copland, Aaron, 368, 383
Corriere della Sera, 280n
Cornfield, Susie, 282n
counterpoint, polyphony, 19, 56, 58, 84, 110, 120, 145, 146, 151, 165, 186, 187, 188–9, 192, 199, 201, 203, 207, 219, 221, 222, 231, 233, 234, 244, 250, 267, 269–70, 273, 274, 284, 286, 288, 293, 307, 332, 333, 335, 339, 378, 382
Covelli, John, 133–5, 141, 208, 213n, 252
Covent Garden, 76, 78, 378
Cowell, Henry, 315
Cox, C. B., *T. S. Eliot The Waste Land: A Casebook,* 227n
Cox, John, 295, 297, 301n
Craft, Robert, 293, 366;
  Small Craft Advisories, 300n, 372n
Crebbin, Tess, xvii
Crispin, Edmund, *see* Montgomery, Bruce
Crist, Judith, 146, 149n, 150n
Crosby, Bing, 37, 42, 316

Cross, Lowell, 197n
Crump, Norman, 42, 47n
Cullinan, John, 343n
Cyrano de Bergerac (historical figure), 130
Czerny, Carl, 15

Dalton, John, 12
D'Annunzio, Gabriele, *La pioggia nel pineto*, 348
Daniels, Phil, 311
Daniels, Ron, 311
Dankworth, John, 108
Da Ponte, Lorenzo, 359
Davies, Robertson, 105n
Davis, Colin, 103–4, 298
Dean, Winton, *Essays on Opera*, 301n
Deane, Basil, 83, 92n
Debussy, Claude, 17, 24, 62n, 149n, 208, 266, 277, 284;
  Danses sacrée et profane, 228;
  "*Fêtes*" from *Trois Nocturnes*, 117;
  Feux d'artifice, 208;
  Ibéria, 16;
  La cathédrale engloutie, 46;
  La fille aux cheveux de lin, 99;
  La Mer, 21n, 156;
  Prélude à "l'après-midi d'un faune", 14, 15, 21n, 35, 55, 85, 86, 110, 331, 352;
  String Quartet in G minor, 84;
  Syrinx, 290n
de Bussy, Louis Philibert le Cosquino, 84
DeCarlo, Charles, 215, 218, 226n
de Falla, Manuel, 64
Defoe, Daniel, *A Journal of the Plague Year*, 51, 61n
De Laurentiis, Dino, 143
Del Fa, Alexandre, 323
Delanoff, Robert, 326
Delius, Frederick, 17, 24, 154, 199, 277, 285, 369, 383;
  Piano Concerto, 365
Deller, Alfred, 117
Dello Joio, Norman, 315
Denza, Luigi, 114, 121n
deVaron, Lorna Cooke, 132
Deveze, Mireille, xviii

Diamond, David, 21n
Dickens, Charles, 165;
  A Christmas Carol, 69
Dixon, James, 3, 185, 186, 195, 197n
Dr Allen G.P., 28
Donizetti, Gaetano, *L'Elisir d'Amore*, 70;
  Lucia di Lammermoor, 68, 70;
  Don Pasquale, 70
Doughty, Charles, *Arabia Deserta*, 23
Dowland, John, 17, 111, 251, 327, 329
Dragnet, 304 (**Ex. 27.01**), 313n
Driver, Minnie, 371
Dryden, John, *Absalom and Achitophel*, 19;
  A Song for Saint Cecilia's Day, 1687, 229
Dubos, Thomas, 344n
Duke of Edinburgh, 71
Dunne, Bernard, 18–19, 22n
Dvorak, Antonin, 103;
  Humoresque, 370;
  Symphony No. 9, "From the New World", 239
Dwyer, Agnes, *see* Tollitt, Agnes Dwyer
Dwyer, George Patrick, Archbishop of Birmingham, 18
Dwyer, Madge, stepsister, 10

The Economist, 6n, 112, 113n
The Edge, born David Howell Evans, 311
Edinburgh Festival, 297, 345
Einstein, Albert, 78, 245
Elgar, Edward, 60, 62n, 64, 66, 145, 154, 266, 277, 351, 365, 369–70, 383–4, 384n;
  Cockaigne, Overture, 357;
  Falstaff, 108;
  Pomp and Circumstance, 156, 235, 252;
  Symphony No. 1, 24, 117;
  Symphony No. 2, 29;
  Violin Concerto, 254
Eliot, George, born Mary Anne Evans, *Middlemarch*, 265
Eliot, T. S., 23, 165, 217, 265, 380;
  "Five-finger exercises", 51;

General Index 455

Four Quartets, 43, 51;
  Murder in the Cathedral, 29;
  "Preludes", 51;
  Sweeney Agonistes, 23, 50;
  The Waste Land, 28, 51, 56, 62n, 132, 214, 215, 216, 219, 222–6, 227n, 236n, 339, 344n
Eliot, Valerie, 217, 218
Elizabeth I, Queen, 112
Elkind, Rachel, 144
Ellington, Duke, 108;
  "Mood Indigo", 352
Ellmann, Richard, 115, 276;
  James Joyce, 121n
English National Opera, 298, 299, 300
Essex, Earl of, 252

Faber & Faber, 216, 217, 218
Fabulous and Ridiculous Theatre, 311
Farkas, Ákos I., *Will's Son and Jake's Peer*, 380
Feldman, Morton, 195
Fenice, La, 297, 329
Ferrero, Lorenzo, 352
Ferris, Paul, 281n
Fiddler on the Roof, 266
Fiennes, Judith, 226n
Finzi, Gerald, 383–4
Firbank, Ronald, 120
Firth, Colin, 371
Fitton, Mary, 112, 113n
Flecker, James Elroy, *Hassan*, 28, 40
Fleming, Ian, 103, 370
Florilegus, 54
Florio, John, 193, 196n
Forbes, Elliot, *Thayer's Life of Beethoven*, 93n
Ford, Ford Madox, 77, 265
Forkner, Ben, 141n, 379
Forman, Edward, 93n–94n
Fortune, Nigel, 92n
Franck, César, 290n
Freeman, Jill, 291n
Freud, Sigmund, 244–5, 284
Fromm Music Foundation, 132
Fryer, Jonathan, 373n
Fucik, Julius, "The Entry of the Gladiators", 70
The Fugitive, 316

fugue, fugato, fughetto, 14, 18, 40, 45, 65, 88, 120, 164, 190, 198, 203, 204, 207, 208, 209, 212n, 213n, 231, 234, 238, 249, 259, 260, 267, 284, 323, 324, 325, 327, 329, 335, 336, 348, 350, 352, 358
Fumed Oak (Noël Coward), 28

Gabrieli, Giovanni, 192
Gagnon, Roland, 132
Gaines, James R., *The Lives of the Piano*, 212n
The Gallic Wars (Julius Caesar), 18
Galuppi, Baldassare, 65
Gant, Roland, 58, 63
Garrett, John, *The Poet's Tongue*, 226n
Gaskell, John, 301n
Gengaro, Christine Lee, 93n
Gentlemen's Concert Hall, 9, 20n
Gershwin, George, 17, 317, 359
Gershwin, Ira, 317
Gibbons, Carroll, 17
Gibbons, Orlando, 17
Gifford, Don, *Ulysses Annotated*, 281n
Gibson, Alexander, 345, 346
Gilbert, Stuart, 115
Gilbert and Sullivan, 259, 276, 294;
  The Mikado, 43, 47n;
  see also Sullivan, Arthur
Gill, Brendan, 217
Gioia, Dana, 382;
  "Deathbed Confessions", 384n
Gluck, Christoph Willibald, 359, 379
Gobbi, Tito, 78
The God I Want, 361n
Godwin, Lance, 27
Goethe, Johann Wolfgang von, 368
The Golden Eagle, 10, 11
Golding, William, 341
Goldoni, Carlo, 10
Goodman, Benny, 38, 317
Goossens, Marie, 358
Goossens, Sidonie, 16, 17, 358
Gounod, Charles, 18
Grade, Sir Lew, 151, 152, 153
Granta, 344n
The Grateful Dead, 110
The Great White Hope, 141n

Great Writers: Anthony Burgess, 79n
Greene, Graham, 58, 66, 294, 301n;
The Heart of the Matter, 69
Gregorian chant, 10, 116
Gregson, Richard, 132–5, 252
Griboyedov, Aleksandr Sergeyevich, 371
Griepenkerl, Wolfgang, *Das Musikfest*, 92n, 93n
Grimes, Frank, 276
Grove, George, *Beethoven and his Nine Symphonies*, 93n, 163, 167n
The [New] Grove Dictionary of Music and Musicians, 21n, 277, 316, 365, 380, 384n
The New Grove Dictionary of Opera, 380
Groven, Sigmund, 320n
The Guardian, 293, 300n, 301n, 372, 373n
Guitar Hero II: Legends of Rock, 310
Gunsmoke, 316
Gurney, Ivor, 251, 253n
Guthrie Theatre, 129, 131, 132, 134, 141, 252, 358

Hába, Alois, 288
Hallé Orchestra, 14, 16, 24, 28, 227n, 355, 365
Halliday, Roy, 341
Handel, Georg Frideric, 15, 84, 86, 310;
Judas Maccabaeus, 235;
Messiah, 383
Handy, W. C., 266
Hardy, Thomas, 165;
"The Oxen", 289
Harrison, George, 316
Harry Ransom Humanities Research Center, 4, 212n, 318, 332, 379
Hart, Lorenz, 112, 317–18
Harty, Hamilton, 227n
Haskell, Jonathan, 346
Hathaway, Anne, 249
Haydn, Franz Joseph, "Clock" Symphony, 233;
Creation, 19;
"Surprise" Symphony, 233

Hebald, Milton, 151
Hecht, Paul, 130
Heffernan, Michael, 276
Heifetz, Jascha, 316
Heinemann, 47n, 58, 60, 70, 78, 91, 95
Hemans, Felicia Dorothea, 19
Hemingway, Ernest, 103, 120, 265;
A Farewell to Arms, 262
Hemmings, David, 143
Henry, Prince of Wales, son of James I of England and VI of Scotland, 196n
Herrmann, Irene, 373n
Hess, Myra, 10
Hibbard, G. R., 253n
Hicks, Jim, 141n
Hildebrant, Dieter, *Pianoforte: A Social History of the Piano*, 212n
Hill, Rodney, *The Encyclopedia of Stanley Kubrick*, 149n
Hinchliffe, Arnold P., *T. S. Eliot The Waste Land: A Casebook*, 227n
Hindemith, Paul, 25, 203, 233, 245, 335, 349;
Philharmonic Concerto, 16, 21n
Hines, Earl, 335
Hitler, Adolf, 30, 245, 382
Hoiby, Lee, *Trois Poèmes de Rimbaud*, 61n
Hofmannsthal, Hugo von, 294
Holland, Peter, 196n
Holst, Gustav, 266, 369, 383–4;
The Planets, 24, 51, 154, 156, 297, 329, 330n, 345
Homer, *The Odyssey*, 43
Honegger, Arthur, 16
Hopkins, Gerard Manley, 23, 30, 233, 259, 283, 286–8, 292, 380;
"Fallen Rain", 288, 289, 291n;
Inversnaid, 288–9;
St Winefred's Well, 289;
"The Windhover", 165, 287 (**Ex. 25.02**);
The Wreck of the Deutschland, 148, 165, 288
Horowitz, Vladimir, 365
The House with the Twisty Windows (Mary Parkington), 28

General Index 457

Housman, A. E., "Epitaph on an Army of Mercenaries", 234;
A Shropshire Lad, 293
Hovhaness, Alan, 315
Howells, Herbert, 50
Hutchinson, 261, 297
The Hudson Review, 251, 253n
Huelbes, Elvira, 373n
Hughes, David, *The Complete Kubrick,* 149n, 150n
Hussey, Olivia, 153
Hutchinson, Judson Joseph, "The Pauper's Funeral", 227n
Huxley, Aldous, *Antic Hay,* 285;
Brave New World, 82;
Point Counter Point, 120, 285

I Fagiolini, 378
Ingelow, Jean, "The High Tide on the Coast of Lincolnshire", 218, 226n
International Anthony Burgess Foundation, 380
Iranian Revolution (1979), 295, 296
Ireland, John, 199
Isaacs, Jeremy, 328, 379
Isherwood, Christopher, 368
Ives, Charles, 199, 245
Izambard, George, 61n

Jackson, Kevin, 379, 384n
Jacob, Gordon, 314, 315, 343n
Jagger, Mick, 143, 149n
Jahn, Friedrich Ludwig, 83
James, Henry, 77, 165, 359
Januszczak, Waldemar, 246n
Jarre, Maurice, 153
The Jaypees, 36–9, 40, 41, 76, 209;
 Paul A. Anderson, 37;
 William Brian, 37, 38, 41;
 N. Clafton, 37, 46n;
 Douglas L. Close, 37;
 William T. Elliott, 36, 37, 38;
 Sybil Elliott, 37;
 Babs Evelyn, 37, 46n;
 Pat Glover, 37;
 K. F. "Bob" Morgan (the Great Romano), 37, 39, 40;
 Edward (Ted) Norman, 37, 38;
 Richard Nutting, 37, 38, 46n;
 Tommy Smith, 37, 38;
 Jack Varney, 37, 38;
 Harry Walkling, 37, 41;
 Stanley L. Williams, 37;
 F. Edward (Ted) Wright, 37, 38;
 V. J. Willis, 37
jazz, blues, gospel, rock, popular music, 16–17, 27, 37, 38, 39, 40, 64, 66, 67n, 68, 99, 103, 104, 111, 119, 132, 134, 148, 186, 198, 199, 201, 211, 215, 216, 222, 224, 225, 230, 240, 266–7, 277, 292, 303, 304, 317, 335, 336
Jennings, Elizabeth, 113n
Jennings, Kathryne, 381
John XXIII, Pope, born Angelo Giuseppe Roncalli, 264
John Henry Faulk Living Theatre, 311
Johnson, Ben, 253n
Jones, Hazel, *see* Looker, Hazel
Jones, James Earl, 141n, 153
Jones, Llewela Isherwood, *see* Burgess, Lynne
Jones, Peter Cynfryn, 335, 378
Jonson, Ben, "Still to be neat", 251
Josselson, Diana, 94n
Joyce, James, xv, 30, 100, 112, 114, 119, 121, 122n, 147, 154, 159, 235, 265, 267, 287, 292, 346, 380, 384n;
 musical talent, 114–15;
 Chamber Music, 280;
 Finnegans Wake (*Work in Progress*), 23, 43, 115, 116, 117, 118 (**Ex. 12.01**), 122n, 127, 265, 329, 381;
 A Portrait of the Artist as a Young Man, 23, 121n, 150n;
 Ulysses, xv, 23, 43, 77, 85, 103, 114, 115, 116, 227n, 262, 264–7, 269–74, 276–9, 281n
Joyce, John, 114, 115
Joyce, Nora Barnacle, 115, 121n

Kael, Pauline, 146, 150n
Kafka, Franz, "A Hunger Artist", 209

Karolyi, Otto, *Modern British Music*, 373n
Karpf, Anne, 281n
Keats, John, 228, 232–3, 245, 377;
    Endymion, 233
Kell, Joseph, pseudonym of Anthony Burgess, 78
Keller, Hans, 276–7, 282n
Kelly, Grace, Princess Grace of Monaco, 254, 256, 259, 346
Kent, Jonathan, 371
Kenyon, Nicholas, 301n
Kenyon College, 332
Kenyon Review, 91, 94n
Kermode, Frank, 293, 300n
Kern, Jerome, 266
Khachaturian, Aram, "Sabre Dance" from *Gayane*, 96
Khomeini, Ayatollah Ruhollah, 295, 296
Khrennikov, Tikhon, 96
Kidd, Michael, 135, 141
King, David, 354
Kipling, Rudyard, 77
Kleinsinger, George, 315
Kodály, Zoltan, 64, 105n
Kol Nidrei, 274
Konya, Sandor, 117
Korngold, Erich Wolfgang, 151
Koussevitzky, Serge, 383
Khrushchev, Nikita, 95, 96, 99, 105n
Kravchencko, Alla, 283
Kubelik, Rafaël, 256
Kubrick, Stanley, 82, 89, 141, 143–7, 148–9, 149n, 150n, 159, 166n, 302–3, 307;
    2001: A Space Odyssey, 143, 145;
    Barry Lyndon, 148;
    A Clockwork Orange, 3, 4, 82, 144–9, 149n, 150n, 237, 308;
    Dr. Strangelove, 143;
    Eyes Wide Shut, 149;
    Lolita, 144;
    Napoleon film, 143, 148;
    Stanley Kubrick's A Clockwork Orange (book), 147

Labella, Vincenzo, 151, 153, 155, 156–7, 158n, 229, 233, 237

The Lady, 301n
The Lady Vanishes, 29
Lambert, Constant, *Music Ho!: A Study of Music in Decline*, 367, 369–70;
    The Rio Grande, 17, 21n, 117, 230, 357, 373n
Lancaster, Burt, 151
Lang, Fritz, 209
Langham, Michael, 129–133, 135, 141
Lansky, Paul, 384n
Lantz, Robby, 132
Larisch, Marie, 222;
    My Past, 227n
Larkin, Philip, 95
Larner, Gerald, 301n
Laurentian Chamber Players, 215, 217;
    Gerardo Levy (flute), 214;
    Ronald Roseman (oboe), 214;
    Catherine Rowe (soprano), 214;
    Michael Rudiakov (cello), see Rudiakov, Michael;
    Joel Spiegelman (keyboard), 214
Lawrence, D. H., 103, 120, 134, 283, 286, 346;
    Aaron's Rod, 286;
    Lady Chatterley's Lover, 95, 285, 291n;
    Mr. Noon, 286;
    The Trespasser, 286;
    Women in Love, 285
Lawrence, Frieda, 284
Lawrence of Arabia, 110
Laxness, Halldor, 120–1
Lee, Harper, 120
Lehar, Franz, *The Merry Widow*, 77
Leipzig Conservatory, 316
Leipzig Gewandaus Orchestra, 167n
Lennon, John, 104
Leoncavallo, Ruggero, *I Pagliacci*, 209
Lessing, Doris, *The Golden Notebook*, 120
Lévi-Strauss, Claude, 126–7, 131, 245;
    The Scope of Anthropology, 126, 141n
Levin, Harry, 115
Levy, David Benjamin, *Beethoven: The Ninth Symphony*, 93n
Lewin, Frank, 315

General Index 459

Lewis, Michael J., 132–5, 137–41, 252
Lewis, Roger, *Anthony Burgess,* 47n, 48n, 341, 344n, 380, 384n
Lewis, Wyndham, 265, 367
Liber Usualis, 116
Library of Congress, 215
Library Journal, 147, 149n
Lipman, Samuel, 212n
The Listener, 92n, 93n, 113n, 236n, 254, 262n, 277, 281n, 282n
Liszt, Franz, 17
Little Nellie Kelly (George M. Cohan), 11
Litvinoff, Si, 143, 144, 146, 147
Lloyd Webber, Andrew, *Cats,* 218
LoBrutto, Vincent, *Stanley Kubrick: A Biography,* 149n, 150n
Lodge, David, 81, 92n
Loesser, Frank, *The Most Happy Fella,* 240
Loli, Philippe, 323, 326, 327, 330n
London Coliseum, 299
London Weekend Television, 262
Looker, Ceridwen, niece, 52
Looker, Hazel, sister-in-law, 52, 54, 61n, 66
Looker, William, brother-in-law, 52
Loos, Anita, *Gentlemen Prefer Blondes,* 372n
Lowry, Malcolm, 119
Ludwig II, King of Bavaria, 222, 227n
Lustig, Merrily, xviii
Lympany, Moura, 199, 212n

Macellari, Paola-Andrea, *see* Wilson, Andrew Burgess
Macellari, Liliana, *see* Burgess, Liana
Maclaren-Ross, Julian, 40
The Madwoman of Chaillot, 132
Mahler, Gustav, 284, 285, 295; *Kindertotenlieder,* 219
Malcolm, George, 117
Malko, George, 150n
Man in the Moon Theatre, 278
Man of La Mancha, 132, 136
Manchester Central Library, 15
The Manchester Guardian, 12
Manchester School Children's Choir, 227n

Mandelstam, Osip, 96
Mangan, Timothy, 373n
Mankiewicz, Joseph, 111
Mann, Elizabeth, 370
Mann, Thomas, 245; *Doktor Faustus,* 85, 93n, 192, 370
Mantuan, *see* Spagnuoli, Baptista
Marlowe, Christopher, 252–3, 381; *Doctor Faustus,* 18, 27, 30, 50, 108
Marouani, Gilbert, 156–7
Marquez, Gabriel Garcia, 121
Marriner, Neville, 316
Martha (Flotow), 267
Martinů, Bohuslav, 103
Marx Brothers, 70, 72n
Mascagni, Pietro, 266
Maslon, Laurence, 142n
Mason, Douglas, 29
Mason, James, 153
Masur, Kurt, 167n
Mathis, Johnny, 304
Maugham, W. Somerset, 264
McCarthy, Joseph, 318
McCarthy, Mary, 300n
McCormack, John, 115
McCoy, Horace, *They Shoot Horses, Don't They?,* 209
McCracken, Stella, 335
McCunn, Hamish, 383
MacDiarmid, Hugh, 342
McDougal, Stuart Y., *Stanley Kubrick's A Clockwork Orange,* 149n
McDowell, Edwin, 94n
McDowell, Malcolm, 144, 145, 149n, 150n
Meldrum, William P., 42, 47n
Mendelssohn, Felix, 87, 355, 359; music for *A Midsummer Night's Dream,* 13, 21n, 132; Symphony No. 5 ("Reformation"), 29; Violin Concerto, 39
Menotti, Gian-Carlo, 5, 6, 57; *The Medium,* 271
Menuhin, Diana, 254, 262n, 263n
Menuhin, Yehudi, 42, 254, 256–8, 263n; *Unfinished Journey,* 255, 262n
Merimée, Prosper, 18, 299

Metropolis, 209
Metropolitan Opera, 294, 297
Mewshaw, Michael, "Do I Owe You Something?", 344n
Michelangelo, 103,
Middleton, Stanley, *Harris's Requiem*, 119
Midnight Cowboy, 316
Mikes, George, 294, 301n
Mikhashoff, Yvar, born Ronald Mackay, 31n, 203, 212n, 250
Milhaud, Darius, 314, 324
Miller, Glenn, 37, 38
Miller, Henry, 121
Mills, Kerry, "Red Wing", 227n
Milton, John, 69;
   At a Solemn Music, 292
Les Misérables, 136
Mitchell, Kirk, *A.D. Anno Domini*, 157
Mitgang, Herbert, xix–n
modal harmony, 15, 52, 130, 151, 155, 186, 189, 250, 284, 327, 331, 338, 339, 345, 349, 352, 358
Modern Fiction Studies, 106n, 126, 141n, 213n, 366
The Monkey's Paw (W. W. Jacobs), 28
Montaigne, Michel de, *Essais*, 196n
Monteverdi, Claudio, 365
Montgomery, Bruce, also known as Edmund Crispin, 4, 6, 57, 62n, 368–9
Monty Python, 3023
Moody, James, 315
Morley, Thomas, 17
Morricone, Ennio, 152
Morris, Desmond, 154
Morris, George L. K., 227n
Mostel, Zero, 266
Mozart, Leopold, 355, 359
Mozart, Wolfgang Amadeus, 64, 87, 150n, 159, 286, 293, 300n, 352, 355, 359;
   Don Giovanni, 121, 228, 270, 293–4;
   Eine kleine Nachtmusik, 245;
   "Hunt" Quartet (K. 458), 359;
   Idomeneo, 293–4;
   Oboe Quartet, 343n;
   Symphony No. 38 ("Prague"), 84, 87;
   Symphony No. 40 in G minor, 84, 87, 359–61 (incl. **Exx. 32.05–32.06**);
   Symphony No. 41 ("Jupiter"), 84, 245–6, 359;
El Mundo, 372
Murger, Henri, also known as Henry Murger or Mürger, 18
The Music Man (Meredith Willson), 74
The Musical Times, 108, 113n
Das Musikfest (Wolfgang Griepenkerl), 92–3n
Mussorgsky, Modeste, 97;
   Night on Bald Mountain, 239
My Fair Lady, 146, 267, 279, 294

Nabarro, Malcolm, 283
Nabokov, Vladimir, 119;
   Lolita, 144, 242;
   Pale Fire, 242
Napoleon Bonaparte, 199
Nash, Ogden, 54
Nashe, Thomas, *Summers Last Will and Testament*, 250, 251, 382
National Observer, 62n
National Opera Orchestra of Monte Carlo, 256
Nazis, Third Reich, 29, 30, 83, 148, 245, 261, 316, 382
NBC Symphony, 160
Nelson, Chris, 149n
Nettl, Bruno, 245, 246n
New England Conservatory, 132
The New Everyman Dictionary of Music, 380
New York City Opera, 133
The New York Herald Tribune, 369
New York Magazine, 149n
The New York Review of Books, 150n, 367, 373n
The New York Times, 67n, 94n, 130, 135, 141n, 142n, 150n, 188, 354n, 361n, 372, 384n
The New Yorker, 150n
Newman, Ernest, 11, 286
Nicholl, Charles, *The Reckoning*, 252

Nicholson, Jack, 143
Nin, Anaïs, 121
Nixon, Richard, 141n
Nobel Prize, 294
Noel, Thomas, "The Pauper's Funeral", 227n
Norman, Marc, 111
Norton, W. W., 91, 92, 146, 373n
Nottingham University, 284
Novello, Ivor, 266

Oath of Strasbourg, 348
The Observer, 157, 158n, 281n, 294, 299, 301n, 320, 366, 378, 384n
O'Brien, Flann, 120, 154
O'Casey, Sean, *Juno and the Paycock,* 51
"Ode to Joy", *see* Beethoven, Ludwig van
Oedipus Tyrannus (Sophocles), 131
Oliver, 136
Olivier, Laurence, 153
Oper Frankfurt, 246n
Orchestra of Monte Carlo, 199
Orchestre de la Suisse Romande, 117, 346
Orchestre Régional de Cannes Provence-Alpes-Côte d'Azur, 328, 352
Orff, Carl, 87
Oriana Concert Orchestra, 117
Orpheus, 231
Orwell, George, 40, 42, 80, 103, 262; *Animal Farm,* 43; *Nineteen Eighty-Four,* 82, 261
Osborne, John, *The Entertainer,* 234–5
Oxford University, 78, 286

Pagram, Edward, 55
Palace Theater, 237
Palmer, Peter, 283, 290n
Pantucci, Gabriele, 218
The Paris Review, 331, 343n
Parnell, Charles Stewart, 271
Parry, Hubert, 251;
    Blest Pair of Sirens, 357;
    Jerusalem, 357
Parker, Norman, 41, 45, 46, 47n

Parkinson-Bailey, John J., *Manchester: An Architectural History,* 20n
passacaglia, chaconne, 45, 72, 105n, 130–1, 153, 155, 203, 238, 256, 257, 260, 324, 325, 333, 334, 336
Paterson, Scott, 344n
Patterson, Frank, 276
Patterson, Paul, 315
Payne, Jack, 17
Pembroke, 3rd Earl of, William Herbert, 112, 113n
Penthouse, 146, 150n
Perle, George, 384n
*Pervigilium Veneri*s, 54, 55, 56, 62n
Peterson, Oscar, 4, 5, 88, 302, 316, 335
Petrarch, 233
Philharmonia Orchestra, 117
Phillips, Gene D., *The Encyclopedia of Stanley Kubrick,* 149n
Phillips, Paul, 381
Pierné, Gabriel, 315
Pindard, Mavis, 226n
Pinter, Harold, 302
Plain Wrapper Press, 253n
Planché, James Robertson, 295, 296, 297
Plautus, 84
Plaza Hotel, 366
Plummer, Christopher, xvii, 132, 135–6, 142n, 143, 153, 252
Plutarch, *Parallel Lives,* 293
Poe, Edgar Allan, *The Fall of the House of Usher,* 111
Pollack, Sydney, 209
Pollinger, Laurence, 290n
polytonality, 25, 50, 99, 233, 319, 324, 327, 329, 358
Pope, Alexander, 198
Porter, Peter, 105n
Poulenc, Francis, 65, 324
Pound, Ezra, *Cantos* 23, 152, 158n
Pountney, David, 298, 299
Portraits of the Artist in A Clockwork Orange (E. Vernadakis, G. Woodroffe, ed.), 94n
Powell, Anthony, *A Dance to the Music of Time,* 119, 120;
    The Kindly Ones, 119

Powell, Robert, 153
Pritchett, V. S., 300n
Primavera Quartet, 259–60, 358;
   see also Caplin, Martha
Princess Grace, see Kelly, Grace
Princess Grace Irish Library, 379
Princeton University, 237
Prokofiev, Sergei, 96, 359;
   The Love for Three Oranges, 273
Puccini, Giacomo, 286;
   La Bohème, 11, 18, 70, 266–7, 300n;
   La Fanciulla del West, 244;
   Madama Butterfly, 11, 239;
   Turandot, 238
Purcell, Henry, 130, 286, 324, 325;
   Music for the Funeral of Queen Mary, 145, 308;
   "Nymphs and Shepherds" from *The Libertine,* 219, 227n;
   "Rejoice in the Lord Alway", 117
Pushkin, Alexander, 119;
   The Little House at Colonna, 97

Quayle, Anthony, 151
Quilter, Roger, 108, 251, 253n
Quinet, Edgar, 92n

Raab, Max L., 143, 144, 146, 147
Rabatti, Pascal, 326
Rabinowitz, Peter J., 149n,
Rachmaninoff, Sergei, 74
Radio Suisse Romande, 346
Radio Telefis Eireann, 264
Raleigh, Sir Walter, 252
Rainier III, Prince of Monaco, 256
Rand, Lydia, 61n
Rands, Bernard, 297–8, 301n
Raphael, Frederic, 149
Ratcliffe, Michael, 378, 384n
Ravel, Maurice, 17, 100, 324, 346, 379;
   Bolero, 16, 21n, 318;
   Piano Concerto in G major, 200
Rawhide, 316
Rawsthorne, Alan, 199
Reger, Max, 284
Reilly, Tommy, 314–16, 318, 320
Renoir, Pierre-Auguste, 10

Rich, Adrienne, 148
Richardson, Ralph, 153
Richter, Hans, 365
Ricks, Christopher, 150n
Rimbaud, Arthur, 87;
   "Le coeur supplicié", 52, 61n
Rimsky-Korsakov, Nikolai, 145;
   Chanson Hindoue, 37
Robert Lantz Agency, 226n
Robinson, David, 228
Robinson, Henry Morton, 115, 117
Robinson, Robert, 236n
rock and roll, see jazz, blues, gospel, rock, popular music
Rockettes, 135
Rockhurst College, 289
Rogers, Deborah, 146
Rolling Stone, 149n
The Rolling Stones, 143
Roman, George, 301n
Le Roman d'un tricheur, 29
rondo, 25, 88, 230, 257, 325, 335
Rorem, Ned, 212n
Rossini, Gioacchino, 149n, 266, 359;
   Il Barbiere di Siviglia, 69;
   William Tell Overture, 145
Rostand, Edmond, *Cyrano de Bergerac,* 135–6, 219
Rósza, Miklós, 151, 313n
Roughley, Alan, 380
Rouse, Christopher, 201
Rousseau, Jean-Jacques, 366
Roy, Harry, 68
Royal Academy of Music, 50, 258
Royal College of Music, 44, 45, 50
Royal Scottish National Orchestra, 345, 346
Royal Shakespeare Company, 276, 311
Rozen, Jay, 332, 343n
Rubbra, Edmund, 383–4
Rubinstein, Arthur, 365
Rudiakov, Michael, 214–8, 226n
Ruiz-Pipó, Antonio, 326
Russel, Myra Teicher, 280, 282n
Russell, Bertrand, 78
Rutledge, AnnaCatherine, 311

Sacks, Oliver, *Musicophilia,* 203, 212n

Saga Music Publishing, 212n, 253n, 333, 336, 343n, 344n, 354n, 381
St Cecilia, 229
St James's Hall, 258, 263n
St Nicholas, 265
St Paul's Church, 378
Saint-Säens, Camille, 62n;
　Samson et Dalila, 352
Salford College of Technology, 350, 354n
Salieri, Antonio, 286
Sarah Lawrence College, 214, 215, 217
Sarasate, Pablo de, 258, 263n
Satie, Erik, 207;
　Vexations, 208
Scarlatti, Domenico, 65
Schaeffer, Susan Fromberg, 361n
Schifrin, Lalo, 156–7, 158n
Schiller, Friedrich von, "Ode to Joy", 83, 86, 92n, 93n;
　see also Beethoven, Symphony No. 9
Schirra, Walter M. (Wally), 141n
Schnabel, Artur, 365
Schnitzler, Arthur, 149;
　Traumnovelle, 148
Schoenberg, Arnold, 16, 77, 87, 208, 222, 245, 259, 277, 282n, 284, 327, 359, 369;
　Pierrot Lunaire, 15, 18, 361
Schubert, Franz, 108, 261, 286;
　"Trout" Quintet, 19
Schumann, Robert, 15, 222
Schumann, Walter, 313n
Schwarz, Robert L., *Broken Images: A Study of* The Waste Land, 227n
Scott, Cyril, 199, 314
Scott, Sir Walter, 154, 165
Scottish National Orchestra, *see* Royal Scottish National Orchestra
Scottish Opera, 299
Scriabin, Alexander, 40, 290n
Sebastian, John, 314–6, 318, 319, 320, 323, 380
Sebastian, John B., 316
Sebastian String Quartet, 117

Seiber, Mátyás, 282n;
　Ulysses, 277
Seidman, Robert J., *Ulysses Annotated*, 281n
Senator, Ronald, 246n
Seneca, 43
The Serpent, 27, 44, 227n
Sessions, John, 378
Shadwell, Thomas, *The Libertine*, 227n
Shakespeare, Hamnet, 249
Shakespeare, William, xv, xvii, 110–12, 114, 166, 190, 193, 195, 244–5, 247, 251, 252, 327, 337, 338, 345, 361;
　Antony and Cleopatra, 108, 223–4;
　As You Like It, 108;
　Falstaff (character), 250;
　Hamlet, 28, 42, 50, 116, 244, 250;
　Henry V, 250;
　King Lear, 119, 190, 196n, 250;
　Love's Labour's Lost, 108, 119, 185, 186, 190–5, 196n, 253n;
　Macbeth, 112, 329;
　Romeo and Juliet, 108, 112, 248;
　sonnets 107, 108, 138;
　Timon of Athens, 108;
　A Midsummer Night's Dream, 51, 295, 297
Shakespeare in Love, 111
Shaw, Artie, 38
Shaw, George Bernard, 62n, 259, 365, 384n;
　The Perfect Wagnerite, 59;
　Pygmalion, 279
Shelley, Percy Bysshe, 110
Sheppard, A. E., 361n
Sheppard, John, 56
Sher, Antony, 378
Shostakovich, Dmitri, 64, 96, 167n, 189, 190, 233, 259, 277;
　24 Preludes and Fugues, 207, 212n;
　Katerina Ismaylova (revision of *Lady Macbeth of the Mtsensk District*), 96;
　Novorossiyshiye kurantï, 97;
　Symphony No. 7, 239;
　Symphony No. 8, 97
ShowWorld, 311

Sibelius, Jean, 64, 77, 105n;
  Symphony No. 2, 333;
  Symphony No. 5, 97, 358;
  Symphony No. 7, 120, 186
Silverman, Stanley, 130–2, 134, 238, 254, 259, 341, 344n, 380
Simon, Roger Hendricks, 246n
Sinatra, Frank, 138, 228
Singapore, 70
Skalkottas, Nikos, 277, 282n
Skinner, B. F., *Beyond Freedom and Dignity*, 148
Slonimsky, Nicolas, *Baker's Biographical Dictionary of Musicians,* 195, 197n
Smetana, Bedrich, 70
Smith, Penny, 378
Smithson, Harriet, 365
sonata form, 4, 5, 25, 83, 88–91, 103, 159, 161, 186, 187, 188, 199–200, 319, 323, 328, 333, 336, 345, 349, 358, 359–60, 367, 381
songs, anthems, madrigals:
  "Any Old Iron", 234, 355, 356 (**Ex. 32.01**), 357 (**Ex. 32.02**), 361n;
  "The Ballad of Persse O'Reilly", 116–17, 118 (**Exx. 12.01–12.02**);
  "Beer Barrel Polka" ("Roll Out the Barrel"), 378;
  "The Brides of Enderby", 218;
  "Browning", 249 (**Ex. 22.03**);
  "Bye Bye, Blackbird", 11;
  "The Carman's Whistle", 111;
  "Finnegan's Ball", 11;
  "God Save the Queen", 73n, 208, 235;
  "The Golden Vanity", 15;
  "Hail Brittania", 235;
  "Here's Another One Off to America", 11;
  "I'm Going Back to Imazaz (Imazaz the pub next door)", 11;
  "*Integer vitae*", 60;
  "I Wore a Tunic", 266;
  "It Ain't Gonna Rain No More", 11;
  "I've Gotta Be Me", 138;
  "John Come Kiss Me Now", 111;
  "Johnny Pedlar", 41;
  "Let the Bulgine Run", 15;
  "Let the Great Big World Keep Turning", 225;
  "Little Harry Hughes", 116;
  "London Bridge is falling down", 226;
  "A Long Farewell", 115;
  "Love's Old Sweet Song", 267, 269, 281n, 286;
  "Ma, He's Making Eyes At Me", 11;
  "Me and Jane in a Plane", 11;
  "O western wind", 56;
  "The Pauper's Funeral", 225, 227n;
  "Red Wing", 216, 225, 227n, 266;
  "Sarawaki", 68;
  "That Shakespearian Rag", 224;
  "The Silver Swan", 108;
  "Singin' in the Rain", 145, 150n, 303, 307;
  "Song of the Volga Boatmen", 239;
  "Swanee River", 370;
  "Yes, We Have No Bananas", 11;
  "Yours", 41;
  "John Come Kiss Me Now", 111;
  "The Carman's Whistle", 111
Sotheby, William, 295
Sotheby's, 346, 354n
The Sound of Music, 135
Sousa, John Philip, 15
Southern, Terry, 143
Southampton, Henry Wriothesley, 3rd Earl of, 196n, 247, 249
Southwest Texas State University, 332
Sovern, Joseph, 233
Spagnuoli, Baptista, known as Mantuan, 193, 196n
Speculum Musicae, 132
Speculum Voci, 132
The Spectator, 99, 105n, 341, 343n
Spender, Stephen, 368
Spengler, Oswald, 219
Spenser, Edmund, 13
Spivakowsky, Michael, 315
Squires, Michael, 291n
Stalin, Josef, 96
Steiger, Rod, 143, 153
Steigerwalt, Gary, 381

Stein, Gertrude, 368
Stendhal, 352, 358, 359
Steptoe, Roger, 332
Stevens, Harry, 41, 47n
Stewart, Mary, *The Crystal Cave,* 237
Stinson, John J., *Anthony Burgess Revisited,* 213n, 236n
Stock, Noel, *The Life of Ezra Pound,* 158n
Stoppard, Tom, 111
Strasbourg Conservatory, 348
Strasbourg Oath, 348, 349, 354n
Strauss, Johann, 245;
    Artist's Life, 127;
    The Blue Danube, 120;
    Morning Papers, 127;
    Vienna Blood, 127
Strauss, Richard, 17, 284;
    Also Sprach Zarathustra, 120;
    Don Quixote, 119;
    Metamorphosen, 149;
    Der Rosenkavalier, 294;
    Till Eulenspiegel, 120, 267
Stravinsky, Igor, 17, 25, 60, 207, 215, 266–7, 277, 284, 318, 331, 365;
    Chanson Russe, 316;
    The Firebird, 219, 383;
    L'Histoire du Soldat, 331;
    Mavra, 97;
    Movements, 222;
    Petrouchka, 189, 358;
    Ragtime, 222;
    The Rake's Progress, 352;
    Le Sacre du Printemps (The Rite of Spring), 15, 16, 18, 24, 28, 189, 214, 216, 222, 223, 267, 350, 361;
    Three Easy Pieces, 208;
    Variations: Aldous Huxley in memoriam, 222
Streisand, Barbra, 152
Strick, Joseph, 281n
Stumpf, Thomas, 47n
Sullivan, Arthur, 365;
    The Prodigal Son, 114–15
Sunday Telegraph, 301n
Sunday Times, 276, 282n, 299, 301n
SUNY-Buffalo, 195, 203

Susato, Tylman, 130
Sutton, Terry, 78
Swaim, Don, , 281n
Swallow, Norman, 158n, 300n
Sweeney Todd, 136
Swenson, Eric, 91, 94n, 146, 372n, 373n
Swift, Jonathan, 80
Swingle Singers, 132, 142n
Swingle, Ward, 142n
Székely, Zoltan, 255
Szönyi, François, 323

Tannen, Holly, 61n
Tavener, Alan, 378
Taverner, John, 56
Taylor, A. J. P., 300n
Tchaikovsky, Piotr Ilyich, 119;
    1812 Overture, 239;
    Nutcracker, 18;
    Romeo and Juliet, 239;
    Symphony No. 5, 11, 13, 14;
    Symphony No. 6 (*Pathétique*), 97, 239
Tcherepnin, Alexander, 315
Teatro Comunale "Giuseppe Verdi", 278
Tennyson, Alfred Lord, 165
Terry, Fred, 361n
Testa, Fulvio, 235
Thames Television, 298
Thayer, Alexander, *Life of Beethoven,* 93n
theme and variations, 19, 64, 107, 165
They Shoot Horses, Don't They? (Pollack), 209
Thomas, Ben, 41
Thomas, Dylan, 40
Thompson, David, 379
Tilson, Joe, 251, 253n
Time, 91, 94n
The Times, 122n, 276, 281n, 289–90
The Times Literary Supplement, 255, 263n, 380, 384n
Tindall, William York, *A Reader's Guide to James Joyce,* 281n
The Tinted Venus (F. J. Anstey), 61n
Tippett, Michael, *A Child of Our Time,* 288

'Tis Pity She's a Whore (Ford), 77
Toch, Ernst, 318
Tolkien, J. R. R., 120
Tollitt, Agnes Dwyer, stepsister, 10, 13, 28
Tollitt, Jack, 13, 28
Tolstoy, Leo, *Anna Karenina,* 97
Tommy, 150n
Topol, 266
Torroba, Federico Moreno, 326
Toscanini, Arturo, 160, 365
Die Toten Hosen, 310
Townshend, Pete, and The Who, 150n
Tri-City Symphony, 195
Trotsky, Leon, born Lev Davidovich Bronstein, 238
Tsuchigane, Sonya, 311
Turbervile, George, 193, 196n
Turner, John Mallord William (J. M. W.), 370
Turquet, Maureen, 344n
twelve-tone music, 77, 96, 98, 99, 190, 201, 207, 266, 280, 330n, 332, 334, 335
The Twilight Zone, 251
Tydeman, John, 266, 378
Tye, Christopher, 56
Tyrone Guthrie Theatre, *see* Guthrie Theatre
Tytell, John, *Ezra Pound: The Solitary Volcano,* 158n

U2, 311
Ulysses (film by Joseph Strick), 276, 281n
Ulysses in Nighttown, 266
University College Salford, *see* Salford College of Technology
University of Amsterdam, 84
University of Angers, 331;
 Anthony Burgess Centre, 379
University of Birmingham, 350
University of Iowa, 3, 185, 195, 196n, 197n, 209
University of Malta, 151
University of Manchester, 27–30, 54, 154, 216
University of North Carolina, 56

University of Salford, *see* Salford College of Technology
University of Texas, 379
USA Today, 92n
Usden, Arline, 301n
Ustinov, Peter, 153

van Dieren, Bernard, 62n, 383
van Gogh, Vincent, 297
Vaughan Williams, Ralph, 24, 25, 186, 193, 194, 245, 277, 314, 318, 329, 332;
 Flos Campi, 357;
 arr. of "The Golden Vanity", 15;
 On Wenlock Edge, 117;
 A Sea Symphony, 245, 246n, 288, 357;
 Sinfonia Antartica, 119;
 Suite of Six Short Pieces for Piano (1920), 52, 53 (**Ex. 05.03**);
 Toward the Unknown Region, 357
Vega, Lope de, *Los Pastores de Belen,* 152
Venuti, Joe, 201
Verdi, Giuseppe, 229, 286;
 Rigoletto, 128;
 La Traviata, 295, 300n;
 Il Trovatore ("Anvil Chorus"), 70
Verlaine, Paul, *"Parsifal",* 225
Vidal, Gore, 367–8, 384n;
 At Home: Essays 1982–1988, 373n
Vidal, Paul, 352
Villa-Lobos, Heitor, 315
Village Voice, The, 150n
Vinyl, 143
Virgil, *The Aeneid,* 43, 44, 77
Vitiello, Greg, 378
Vivaldi, Antonio, 336

Wade, David, 276, 281n
Wagner, Richard, 5, 6, 15, 17, 44, 154, 198, 215, 222, 286, 359, 365, 379;
 Die Meistersinger, 14, 117, 162;
 Parsifal, 28, 60, 62n, 216, 225, 226, 245, 246n;
 Rienzi, 14;
 Der Ring des Nibelungen, 28, 58–60, 70, 76, 116, 225–6;

Tannhäuser, 22n, 223–4;
Tristan und Isolde, 28, 40, 76, 216, 222, 239, 267, 293;
leitmotives, 116, 127
Wain, John, *Strike the Father Dead*, 119
Walsh, John, 378
Walton, William, 155, 329, 369;
Belshazzar's Feast, 357;
Portsmouth Point Overture, 357;
Symphony No. 1, 24, 117, 188, 358
Warburton, William, 196n
war: Persian Gulf War (1991), 359;
World War I, 10, 190, 227n, 266, 290, 314;
World War II, 30, 35–46, 47n, 190, 355
Warhol, Andy, 143
Warlock, Peter, born Philip Heseltine, 62n, 108, 285, 290n, 331
Warner, Rex, *The Aerodrome*, 43, 154
Warner Brothers, 110, 111, 146, 147
Warrack, John, 301n
Washington Opera, 297
Washington Post, 281n
Washington University, 78n
Watergate hearings, 136
Waterhouse, Michael, 298, 301n
Waterloo, 143
Watt, Alan, 328
Waugh, Auberon, 378
Waugh, Evelyn, *Brideshead Revisited*, 43
WBAI, 246n
Weaver, Jack W., 122n
Weber, Carl Maria von, *Oberon*, 294–5, 329
Webern, Anton von, 208
Weelkes, Thomas, 17, 111
Weill, Kurt, 240, 365;
Der Dreigroschenoper, 30;
One Touch of Venus, 54, 61n;
Lady in the Dark, 239–40
Weingartner, Felix, 295
Weller, Sheila, 150n
Welles, Orson, 132
West, Kevin, 290n
Wheaton College, 201
When Worlds Collide, 245
Whettam, Graham, 315

Whitman, Walt, 105n, 245
Whitney Museum, 132
Wieland, Christoph Martin, *Oberon*, 295
Wignesan, M. T., 67n, 373n
Wilbye, John, 111
Wilde, Oscar, *The Importance of Being Earnest*, 45
Wilder, Victor, 93n
Wilkinson, Jimmy, 41
Williams, Eddie, 49
Williams, (Major) Herbert, 43, 49
Williams, Margaret, 29
Williams, Miller, *Sonnets of Giuseppe Belli*, 236n
Williams, Stephen, 283
Williamson, Malcolm, 199
Wilson, Andrew Burgess, born Paolo-Andrea Macellari, son, 59, 125, 331, 332, 335, 339–43, 381
Wilson, D. K., 350–1, 354n
Wilson, Elizabeth Burgess, mother, 9, 19n, 20n, 29, 209
Wilson, John Burgess, *see* Burgess, Anthony
Wilson, Joseph, father, 9–10, 11, 12, 13, 14, 20n, 21n, 23, 24, 28, 29, 199, 209, 213n
Wilson, Liliana Macellari, *see* Burgess, Liana
Wilson, Llewela Isherwood Jones, *see* Burgess, Lynne
Wilson, Margaret (Maggie) Byrne Dwyer, stepmother, 10, 11, 12, 13, 23, 28, 30
Wilson, Muriel Burgess, sister, 10, 209
The Wizard of Oz, 76
Wollstonecraft, Mary, 110
Woodrow Wilson Institute, 332
Woods, John E., 93n
Wordsworth, William, 165

Yeats, William Butler, 281, 370
Yorkshire Post, 78, 79n, 99
Young, Alexander, 117

Zamyatin, Yevgeny, *We*, 261
Zappone, Bernardino, 233, 236n
Zeffirelli, Franco, 153

EU authorised representative for GPSR:
Easy Access System Europe, Mustamäe tee 50,
10621 Tallinn, Estonia
gpsr.requests@easproject.com

www.ingramcontent.com/pod-product-compliance
Ingram Content Group UK Ltd.
Pitfield, Milton Keynes, MK11 3LW, UK
UKHW021839210426
5322IPUK00021B/368